ALSO BY SUSANNE DUNLAP

Émilie's Voice

Liszt's Kiss

The Musician's Daughter

Anastasia's Secret

In the Shadow of the Lamp

The Académie

To Tara

Listen to the Wind

The Orphans of Tolosa
Book I

1234-1243

Thanks for your willingness + patience!

Susanne Dunlap

BELLASTORIA PRESS

Bellastoria Press
P.O. Box 60341
Longmeadow, MA 01106
bellastoriapress.com

Cover designed by Christopher W. Gortner.

First Edition

ISBN-13: 978-1942209584

Dedication

To Arlie Parrish Sears
1955-2019

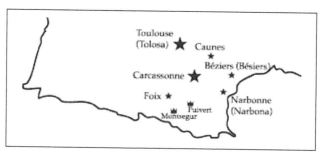

CHAPTER 1

Azalaïs watched a fat brown spider climb over a stone right in front of her nose and carry on toward a leaf just beyond it. She hated spiders, but she forced herself not to move so much as an eyelash. It would ruin everything. She had been lying flat on her stomach with one ear pressed to the ground in the spot Azemar told her about for what seemed a very long time. If she moved, she'd have to start all over again.

Half a league west, he had said, *by the side of the road that leads from Pamiers to Foix.* She went over and over his instructions: *You have to be patient. Let the shadows grow for at least a thumb's length before you give up.* Azemar, who was no better than she was except that he was a boy, told her he could lie still enough to hear a worm crawling just in that place, and she was determined to prove that she could too.

So far, she hadn't heard anything other than the everyday sounds of the forest—a handful of crows squabbling over some carrion just beyond the crest of the hill, the chucking of squirrels chasing each other up and down a tree. She wished they would all be quiet.

Then at long last her ear picked up something, a rumbling, deep in the earth. At first it was very faint. But as she listened, it grew.

1

And grew, and grew. *That's definitely not a worm,* she thought. But it certainly wasn't a normal forest sound either, and it was coming toward her fast from the northwest.

Azalaïs flattened herself even harder against the forest floor so she would remain concealed when whatever it was passed by. When the noise was so loud she thought that at any moment it would crush her, she peeked up through her lashes.

Three men on horseback trotted straight toward her. A knight in chain mail with a white cross on his surcotte led them. The second rider wore a leather tunic and had a longbow across his back, and the third wore only a short, green tunic and soft shoes with pointed toes. The knight's shield flapped in time with the horse's gait. All three of the men stared straight ahead.

When they were at their closest, Azalaïs could have stretched out her arm and touched a horse's leg. She squeezed her eyes shut to protect them from the dirt and flying bits of earth and debris struck up by the hooves. A stone hit her head and she bit her tongue to keep from crying out.

Soon the sound faded, and Azalaïs knew the riders were well past and hadn't noticed her, so she opened her eyes again.

That's when she saw it.

Right in front of her—in the middle of the highway, lying as if carefully placed so that she should discover it upon opening her eyes—lay a small, cylindrical object with a cord tied around it. Azalaïs darted forward and scooped it off the ground.

It wasn't like anything she had ever seen or held; not hard or solid, but pleasingly crisp, like an autumn leaf not yet dry enough to crumble, and it gave when she pinched it. One of the riders must have dropped it. She most certainly would have seen something so unusual if it had been there before.

Azalaïs tucked her treasure away in the secret pouch inside her tunic and scampered off into the woods to return to the encampment where she, Azemar, and a dozen other children lived, under the hostile eyes of domna Catelot and her brothers. *Wait until I tell Azemar!* This was even better than hearing a worm. He'd have to wait, though. She didn't want to give up her secret too quickly and spoil the fun of having one.

The next day, leaving the younger children to forage for mushrooms, Azalaïs and Azemar ran off into the woods to a stream they knew of where they could fill buckets with fresh water for the camp. There was a stream closer by, but they had long ago decided that this one—well out of sight and hearing of the Catelots—was enchanted, and the water that ran through it held miraculous powers.

The September rain soaked through their already threadbare tunics, but it didn't bother them as they sat on the bank in their special place, tossing sticks into the rushing water and watching them race downstream.

"You think you can keep a secret from me, but you can't." Azemar yawned and stretched his arms out, peeking out of the corner of his eye to see Azalaïs's reaction.

"What secret are you talking about?" Azalaïs examined a crack in her fingernail. How could he know she was keeping something from him?

"The one you've been hiding from me since yesterday, and which I will discover as soon as we return."

Azalaïs laughed. "You think I'm stupid enough to leave it—" Before she could move a muscle, Azemar's hand tightened around her wrist.

"So, you found something. I thought so. What is it? A precious stone? If you give it to me now, I won't torture you."

"You can't frighten me! I'm faster than you!" As she felt Azemar's muscles tense for action, Azalaïs wriggled her hand out of his grip and leapt up to run.

3

But Azemar's reflexes had been baptized at the altar of survival. He grabbed her ankle and she fell face down onto the soggy forest floor, tasting dirt and animal dung. Azemar sat on her behind, taking hold of her hand and pushing it up against her back until she screamed for mercy.

"All right! You win! I'll show it to you."

"You'll GIVE it to me!"

"NO!" Azemar pushed her hand up more. She yelped again, then wilted. "All right. Stop."

Azemar let go of Azalaïs's wrist and she slowly, painfully restored her arm to a normal position. He always pushed her as far as he could without doing her any serious damage. "You'll have to get off me if you want to see what I found."

Azemar raised himself up so she could turn over, then inched back and grasped her knees, pressing them to the ground.

"You're still hurting me!" she said.

"Give it to me and I'll stop!" He shifted more of his weight onto her knees.

Azemar didn't used to be so strong. She hated the idea of giving in to him, but with a choice between that and pain, she had no other option. She reached into her pocket and held up the scroll, just out of Azemar's reach. "I found it. I get to see what it is first."

"I'll cut the cord with my teeth for you," Azemar said.

"No! I want to be able to put it back exactly the same." Her small fingers soon picked the tight knot apart. She put the cord back into her pocket. The scroll kept wanting to curl up again, so she had to hold the corners in place with her fingers.

Azalaïs didn't know what she expected to find. It couldn't have held anything valuable, she knew that. Still, somehow she hoped for more than just lines in black scratched across in regular patterns, from the top to the bottom.

She tossed the disappointing treasure to Azemar and flopped back to lie on the ground. The rain had eased, and the fine mist it left behind felt soft on her face.

Azemar released her knees.

"What do you suppose it is?"

"I don't know. I don't care."

He turned the scroll this way and that, smelled it, tested it with his teeth. "It's made from an animal. And these lines…I know!" Azemar's eyes lit up. "It's magic! It's a talisman!"

"What magic could there be in a piece of animal skin with black lines on it?"

"It's a spell. This is writing. I've seen it before, but I can't remember where. It says something. We can pretend it says whatever we like and make it our charm." Azemar jumped up and skipped around her, randomly picking up stones and hurling them into the forest.

Creating stories they could act out with the other children, all orphans from Tolosa, transported them into a magical world where everything was possible, everyone was kind, and no one ever went hungry. This mysterious scroll was as good as a toy to them and might as well take its place in their imaginary kingdom.

Azalaïs picked it up from the ground where Azemar dropped it. She had to admit, there was something about it, appearing as it did out of nowhere. Perhaps it really was magic.

She stood and stretched her arms above her head, the scroll in her hand, and skipped along with Azemar. "And it came to ME, so if you take it from me, you might be CURSED!"

Azemar stopped skipping. "The others can be wood sprites, and you and I are the king and queen of the forest."

"Spirit of the forest, awake and hear me!" Azalaïs lifted the scroll to the sky.

All at once the clouds, so thick and dark all day, parted,

and a shaft of sunlight pierced through, turning the drops that clung to the leaves and twigs into sparkling crystals.

The hole in the clouds soon sealed itself up again, and big raindrops pelted them anew. Azemar and Azalaïs looked at each other, their eyes wide.

"What took you so long?" 'Na Catelot, the matriarch of the clan of thieves they'd been traveling with as long as Azalaïs could remember, cuffed each of them on the ear when she took their buckets of water. The men had caught a small fish and what nourishment it contained was being stretched to feed the entire group.

Rainy weather left everyone disgruntled. Better to stay out of sight as much as possible or risk a beating for no good reason. When the young ones spied Azalaïs and Azemar, they hurried to greet them and hid behind them as they waited for their only meal of the day.

By sundown the rain had stopped, promising fine weather the next day. Azemar and Azalaïs beckoned the children to a far corner of the camp to tell them about their discovery and weave their tale of magic and sorcery. With enough imagination, the scroll with its mysterious writing could keep them entertained for weeks. The young ones gazed at Azalaïs with awe for finding such a promising treasure.

Day by day, Azalaïs and Azemar's story became more and more elaborate and inventive. They played at knights and damsels and evil monks and heretics. They wove a story of kings and princes and beggars and thieves, enriching it with whatever scraps of memory and knowledge they could stitch together into a comforting blanket of fantasy to mask the hardships of their miserable lives.

A full moon passed after the children began occupying their days with their new game when fever broke out in the camp. The youngest and weakest child was first to perish, and after that, 'na Catelot herself. The old woman had never been a source of warmth and comfort, but she had kept the baser instincts of her brothers at bay.

Since her death and that of another child and soon after that one of the brothers, the remaining children took to spending more and more time away from the encampment. The men stopped pretending to feed them, and were as likely as not to lash out and beat someone just for looking at them.

One morning, as Azemar led the diminished band in a game that was part entertainment, part foraging for food, he heard a strange sound coming from the direction of the encampment and grabbed Azalaïs by the arm as she ran past.

"What?"

He put his finger to his lips. He heard voices. Angry ones. "It's Gascon and Hugos. Roger said they'd made threats."

"That's nothing new."

"Shh! Listen!"

The younger children were still running and laughing, too busy playing to notice anything unusual.

"Everyone, silence!" Azemar roared.

They all stopped what they were doing in mid gesture.

Curses and shouts of *"Fatilhièrs!* Sorcerers!" and "You can't hide from us!" grew more and more distinct.

Azemar sprang into action, taking the young ones two at a time by the arms and shoving them into the forest in different directions. "Run, all of you, and hide. Don't let anyone find you, hear?" Fear gave everyone wings and in an instant they had all disappeared into the underbrush.

Only Azalaïs and Azemar remained.

"What is it?" Azalaïs looked back and forth from Azemar to the sound of the approaching men.

"They want to get rid of us."

"Why?"

"They think it's our fault, the fever."

"Let's go together," said Azalaïs. She didn't remember life before Azemar.

"Better not," he said, poised on the balls of his feet, ready to spring away. "I'll meet you later," he said.

"Where? In Foix?"

"No, too close. Bésiers!"

"Where's Bésiers?"

"East!" Azemar leapt forward, kissed Azalaïs on the cheek, and tore off into the dense woods, looking back at her one last time as he fled. "Run!" he yelled.

At that moment Gascon broke from the forest into the clearing.

"Stop, you witch!"

Azalaïs sprinted away in the opposite direction from Azemar. She knew the contours of the forest floor as well as any animal, and in only a few moments the men's shouts had faded into the distance. *Just keep running,* she told herself, but when she could no longer hear any voices at all she glanced over her shoulder.

That was all it took. A fleeting lapse of concentration. She caught her foot on a protruding tree root and fell, twisting her ankle. She tried to get up and keep running, but the pain shot into her leg and she fell again. The voices approached, growing louder and louder.

All she could do was lie there, helpless, waiting to be caught. *I'm going to die.*

Fear was no stranger to Azalaïs. It had been her companion every day as long as she could remember. But this was different, this was a certainty, and she had no escape from it.

Azalaïs did something she'd never done before, at least not as long as she could remember. She started to cry. Not silent tears, but dry, wrenching sobs that startled the birds, made the deer look up in alarm, and would soon tell the murderous Gascon exactly where to find her.

In the woods nearby, an odd sound made *fraire* Goncort pause from his daily foraging for plants to take back to his hut and record in his herbarium. He heard a cry that wasn't like any animal he knew to roam these woods—woods that were as familiar to him as the psalms.

He moved toward the sound, and as he drew nearer his ears picked up another disturbance, deeper in the forest. Angry men's voices, and they weren't very far off, cursing and railing, shouting "Witch!" and "Sorcerer!"

"Dear, dear," he said, and continued toward what was clearly a cry of distress, and in another few paces, his toes came in contact with its source.

A child! No children ever wandered there. The nearest village was many leagues away. Dirty, bedraggled, eyes red, nose running, and an ankle that had swelled up like a melon, the pathetic little mite at his feet had obviously been running from someone, no doubt the angry men whose voices he could hear.

"What's all this?" He placed his basket on the ground and felt the wounded ankle. The child stopped weeping and shrank away from him, its eyes dancing with terror.

"I won't hurt you. Let me take you where I can tend to your injury," he said, and then added, after a glance in the direction from which the sound of voices was now accompanied by the sight of approaching men, "You will be safer under my roof than out here all alone. There are wolves, you know, and they are as hungry as the people. Come, lift your arms."

The child whimpered, but didn't struggle against him as he easily hoisted it up over one shoulder. *A lamb weighs more than this* he thought. Fraire Goncort picked up his basket with his free hand and hurried away, praying that the following men would not choose to take the same treacherous route as he did up the side of the hill toward the abbey of Bolbona.

CHAPTER 2

At first, Azalaïs didn't find it at all difficult to be a boy. As far as she could tell, there was no difference in it except that she had to try to piss standing up in case anyone happened upon her while she was out in the woods. She was used to being treated just like Azemar anyway.

"You see, I cannot keep you here if they know you are a girl. We're a very strict order."

Azalaïs mostly just listened to what the monk said, somewhat awed and suspicious of his gentleness toward her. She would have agreed to anything to be able to stay right there, warm and dry. He had even allowed her to keep the scroll that was the source of all the trouble she had fled from.

"What shall we call you?" fraire Goncort asked one evening before she ventured outside to test her ankle.

"Azemar." It was the only name she could think of. She wished fraire Goncort had found him, too.

It took only a week for her ankle to be well enough to walk with a slight limp, two until she could put all her weight on it and scamper through the forest as she used to.

After a month, she understood that if she could make herself useful, she would be able to remain under the protection of the gentle hermit for much longer. All she had to do was keep to the boundaries of the patch of forest he called his anchor. He promised she would be safe there.

Safe. Azalaïs didn't know what it was to feel safe. Not since the day when her mother had sent her out with the other children, saying, "Go, they are coming for us. 'Na Catelot has promised to look after you." Azemar, who was also being sent away, took hold of her hand when they climbed into the cart that bore them out of Tolosa.

After that, only Azemar cared for her, and his care was fickle at best.

It didn't take long for Azalaïs to notice that the monk's eyesight was failing fast. He never asked for help, thinking he could simply carry on as he always had. But he fell once or twice when they were out in the forest, and often bumped into the table in the hut. "Let me help you," Azalaïs said. "Just show me."

With some reluctance, fraire Goncort agreed. He started training her to do almost everything the monks up at the abbey expected him to do. He taught her how to gather the herbs and plants he used to make medicines and poultices and instructed her about their proportions and preparation. He taught her all the healing arts he knew and made sure she understood the liturgy so she could stand and kneel and recite whatever was required. And he explained how their days and nights followed the rhythm of the canonical hours to mark the passage of time and the time for prayers—Matins, Lauds, Prime, Terce, Sext, None, Vespers, and Compline.

And Azalaïs listened and learned, out of both curiosity and a sense of wonder that fate had placed her there where the Catelots couldn't find her. It was a pleasant existence, but she knew it couldn't last forever.

She had been with fraire Goncort close to a year when the monk's eyes became too dim to read and write. He did his best as long as he could, but Azalaïs could see by the way he peered so closely at the parchments on his table that soon he would not be able to see at all.

"I wish I could help you more," she said one morning when a heavy rain made their usual jaunt through the forest impossible.

Fraire Goncort stood with his hands before the fire, nodding slowly. "Perhaps you can…I shall give you a very precious gift, Azemar."

"A gift?"

"You shall learn to read and write, so that you can act as *servus a manu*," he said.

"What does that mean?"

"You'll find out when I have taught you enough Latin."

To read and write. Only nobles and monks and priests could read and write. And Latin—that was the language spoken by educated men. But from the beginning, fraire Goncort showed himself willing to teach her anything she was willing to learn.

Of course, this learning how to read and write in Latin and her everyday tongue had special significance for her: She yearned to read the script on her scroll. Fraire Goncort had put it out of sight a long time ago, but Azalaïs knew where it was and wondered about it often. After watching the monk fill sheets of parchment with lines that looked very like the ones on the scrap she and Azemar and the others had played with, she knew that the scroll was filled with letters and words and that it carried some message.

"The abbot has asked me to make a record of all the medicines, the herbs I use here. I could never do it myself now. So you see, Azemar, perhaps God sent you to me."

They began their lessons that very day. Azalaïs's hand cramped with the effort of holding the stylus in just the right way to make the letters on the wax tablet. The sky was dark by the time they finished.

"Tomorrow we'll work more," fraire Goncort said.

And they did, and the day after that, and after that as well. The monk smoothed the wax each morning, and Azalaïs filled it with the Latin or Occitan words he dictated to her, hour after hour.

After several months, the day came when fraire Goncort decided she was ready to use a quill and ink and write on parchment.

"Today we start something new. You have learned much. But unlike the tablet, we cannot easily erase your work in ink each day, so it has to be very good." He didn't tell her—perhaps deliberately—that with care she could scrape the ink off the unyielding surface of the parchment and start anew.

Azalaïs took the quill and stroked the feather. "A crow."

"You must hold the quill at exactly the right angle," he said. "Each stroke is like a breath. Down, up. In, out."

Her hand was used to the sturdy stylus, and Azalaïs gripped the quill so hard that it splintered. She glanced up in alarm. The anchorite had never yet thrashed her as 'na Catelot would have done for the slightest mistake. But she had been careful not to disobey him. Holy men were to be feared. Even Gascon used to quake when monks or priests were nearby.

"Never mind, we'll make another one."

Azalaïs let out the breath she'd been holding. "When will I be able to read my scroll?" she asked.

He smiled and patted her head. "You're not ready for that quite yet."

As the days shortened, they spent fewer and fewer of the precious sunlight hours on letters. Most of the time she and fraire Goncort wandered through the confines of his anchor, the patch of forest against the boundary of the abbey gardens he had vowed to God never to leave, gathering flowers, seeds and vegetation.

"You see these little blossoms?" he said one day as they crept through the woods, their basket already heavy with specimens.

"They don't look like flowers," Azalaïs said, taking a closer look.

"Flowers are not always pretty. These, however, are very useful, and they only appear in the autumn. It is amaranth. A good herb for the use of the entire order, which has taken a vow of chastity."

Azalaïs looked up at the monk from where she crouched close to the ground. "What is chastity?"

"Chastity, my child, is one of the virtues, and some say the greatest of them."

Azalaïs was about to press him on that point, but fraire Goncort put his finger to his lips. She hadn't heard anything, but the weaker his eyesight became, the more sensitive his ears. After a moment or two, she too heard the sound that had made him stop in his tracks, the faintest peeping, very soft and intermittent. Quietly and with great care, they moved toward it.

After about ten paces, fraire Goncort stopped and cocked his head, then crouched low and parted the leaves on the forest floor.

There, with one wing slightly askew, lay a baby owl, a *cavèc*.

"Now, little fellow, don't be frightened." Fraire Goncort's soothing voice had its usual effect, and the creature stayed still while he lifted it.

Azalaïs expected that she would carry the basket of plants and flowers they had gathered while the monk tended to the needs of this tiny, broken bird. But he held it out to her.

"I think you should practice some of the healing arts I have been teaching you."

Azalaïs's eyes widened. "What if it dies?"

"The Lord will decide what is to become of this poor thing. We are His instruments."

The baby cavèc was as light as a lock of hair and its feathers unimaginably soft. Azalaïs could feel the tremble of its heartbeat.

"Cup your hands around it like a nest," said fraire Goncort, and he showed her how to hold the cavèc securely without hurting it.

Azalaïs thought they would never arrive back at the hut. With each step, she was certain she would hurt the creature, or the relentless wind would pick it up and hurl it away, and because she was so careful it took twice as long as usual to cover the distance.

Despite her worries, she brought the owlet safely into the hut. They spent the rest of the day dressing its broken wing and making a nest of cloth near the fire where it would stay warm.

On fine nights, fraire Goncort sometimes taught Azalaïs outdoors. Their necks stiffened looking up at the stars, Azalaïs peering at the sky, fraire Goncort pointing from some distant memory. She soon learned to arrange them in patterns with names and learned how to tell the time of year, and to discern what direction it was to Lyon, to Paris, and to Aragon.

"Which way is Bésiers?"

"Why do you want to know? Is that the city you came from?"

Azalaïs shrugged. She didn't want to tell him that Azemar had called out, *meet me in Bésiers!* as they each ran in opposite directions to escape the Catelots.

"Ah, well. It does not matter. Not to me. But when you leave my care you must promise me never to act as if you don't know where you came from, or who your people are."

"Why?" Of all the dangers Azalaïs knew she might face beyond the safety of fraire Goncort's isolated domain, not knowing where she came from ranked lower than most.

"It's hard to explain, and better you don't know."

She was not satisfied with his answer and decided to ask him again later. "Why can't I just pluck a star from the heavens and put it in my pocket?" Azalaïs reached up and traced a constellation with her finger.

"Good evening, Fraire."

The voice, coming out of nowhere, startled them both.

"Who goes there?" asked fraire Goncort.

From the scrub below emerged a monk in a black mantle. "It's fraire Martin," Azalaïs murmured. Fraire Goncort did not like to expose the weakness of his eyes to visitors, afraid that they would either hurt him or make him abandon his hut in the forest and live in the monastery. The Dominican fraire Martin was often a guest at the abbey of Bolbona, stopping among the quiet Cistercians on his travels through the region. He was French, fraire Goncort told her.

"Greetings! Well met! What brings you out so late at night?"

"I might ask you the same," fraire Martin said, bowing from the waist.

As he righted himself, he kept his eyes on Azalaïs. She shrank back toward fraire Goncort.

"However, I came to ask if I might borrow your little helper, young Azemar here."

"I keep him very busy," said fraire Goncort. "I depend upon his aid for my work, and the hours of daylight are now very short."

A smile tugged at the corners of fraire Martin's mouth.

"Yet you seem to accomplish much without any daylight at all!"

"Fraire Goncort was teaching me to read the stars," said Azalaïs, interposing herself between them, her hackles raised. "And I'd rather not leave him."

Fraire Martin put his hand on Azalaïs's shoulder. His grip was strong. Almost as strong as Gascon's had been. "The choice, lad, is not yours to make. And the order has been tolerant to allow you to remain in the anchor, which is supposed to be occupied by fraire Goncort alone. We are all servants of God here."

Without letting go, the Dominican addressed fraire Goncort. "When the time comes that I need him, he shall be taken. I could use a companion on my journeys to seek out those who endanger their souls and the souls of others with heresy."

At that he relaxed his grip on Azalaïs's shoulder, but instead of taking his hand away immediately, he let it drop so that his fingers dragged down the length of her torso. Azalaïs flinched and shivered. He turned and without another word vanished into the night's obscurity as swiftly as he had appeared.

"What did he mean?" Azalaïs asked.

Fraire Goncort waited several moments before finally responding, "I find that I do not wish to tell you."

Azalaïs drummed her fingers on the table and watched fraire Goncort with his nose almost touching the sheet of parchment she had helped him fill with Latin words. Two years had passed, and she was now so proficient in writing and reading that she had taken on almost all the scribing work. "Fraire Goncort," she said, "I'd like to read my scroll now."

The winter rain had turned the hillside into a slippery mess. The weather reminded her of that day she and Azemar had first peered at the mysterious bit of parchment. She wished Azemar could be there now to see her read it. She would have enjoyed being able to do something that he could not.

The monk rose and reached up to the high shelf where he'd put the scrap of parchment years before. He opened the pot and pulled it out, handing it to Azalaïs with a courtly bow.

As Azalaïs undid the cord and flattened the scroll against the table, she imagined Azemar's face across from hers, squinting down at the marks on the parchment. His features were so familiar—more familiar to her than her own. She closed her eyes and imagined his curling lashes, his lips parted in concentration, and the unruly brown hair that kept him looking like a little boy even though he was several years older than she, old enough to be a man, he claimed. What did he look like now?

The only time Azalaïs ever saw what she herself looked like was on those few occasions when a pool of water was still enough for her to get a single reflected image, not one shattered into fragments by a wayward breeze. She wondered if she would ever see Azemar's face again. They had parted so long ago. Where had he gone? Did he ever wonder about her? As her mind followed those wayward paths she had the sensation that she was sitting atop a tall tree completely alone, exposed to the weather and to the hungry birds of prey. Azemar was far in the distance, his back toward her, becoming smaller and smaller as he walked away from her. Her eyes began to sting. She blinked hard.

"Come now, the poetry's not that bad!" fraire Goncort said. He leaned toward her across the table.

She did not look up. If she stared into those kindly, cloudy eyes, Azalaïs knew she would weep, and she didn't want to show that weakness. Instead, she focused hard on the scrawl that covered the parchment, bringing it into clarity by force of will and slowly, syllable by syllable, making out the words.

19

"It's about love, and singing. I still don't understand it," Azalaïs said, "Why does it talk of singing?"

Fraire Goncort sighed. "In our land there are nobles who entertain themselves by writing poems to one another, and then singing them aloud to their company, or having someone else sing them."

"How do they do it?" Azalaïs had only ever heard the chanting of the monks, or simple songs and rhythmic music for dancing with tambourines and whistles.

To her surprise, fraire Goncort closed his eyes, folded his hands over his paunch, and began to sing in his reedy voice.

> *Amics, tan ai d'ira e de feunia*
> *quar no vos vey, que quan ieu cug chantar,*
> *planh e sospir, per qu'ieu non puesc so far*
> *ab mas coblas que.l cors complir volria.*

"It's beautiful," Azalaïs said when the wandering, plaintive melody ended.

"Beautiful, yes, but much occupied with matters that are not of a spiritual nature. These songs are about earthly, not heavenly love."

Fraire Goncort took the scroll away from Azalaïs, rolled it up and tied it, and replaced it in the pot on the high shelf—a shelf now easily within her reach, which made her smile. They extinguished their daily candle—the one luxury fraire Goncort allowed himself during the winter months—and retired for the night.

But the words on the parchment kept dancing through Azalaïs's head to the tune the anchorite had sung, and she had visions of fine ladies and knights in golden castles. The poem had opened something up for her, the knowledge that—safe and comfortable though she was with fraire Goncort—

a whole different world lay outside the walls of the abaïa and the anchor.

She did not belong among the monks. Soon enough she would be forced to leave. But now, instead of dreading that moment, she began to think of it as the start of an adventure. She would go to Bésiers to find Azemar, if he could be found.

A world waited for her outside the confines of fraire Goncort's anchor, and her feet itched to discover it for herself.

CHAPTER 3

Three or four times at least since the day Azemar fled the Catelot's encampment he had been certain he would die.

Once he came upon a wild boar who charged him.

Another time he fell when he was scrambling over sharp boulders.

The third time, he trespassed on some land belonging to the count of Tolosa and caught a rabbit. The count's hunter had his bow drawn and aimed directly at Azemar, thinking he might be a wild boar fleeing through the underbrush.

The man would have been within his rights to kill him anyway, but God had lately spared his own son, and so the gamekeeper thought it was a sign that he should do the same for another boy. He let Azemar keep the rabbit, and pointed him toward a village where he might find shelter.

Azemar had been following the Hers River, which wound its way through the foothills of the Pirenèus in the Ariège. Years of subsisting in the forest had made him strong and resourceful, and for a while he had been able to scratch a meager existence out of the bounty of wild things—chestnuts, berries, small fish caught with the aid of a stick he had sharpened with a knife stolen from a sleeping drunk on his first night of running.

But soon he could not forage enough to satisfy his constant hunger, and when he passed a farm one day, he decided to exchange the labor of his back for food and a place to sleep.

Although it slowed his progress toward Bésiers, Azemar found it hard to resist the claims of his belly. The more accustomed he became to having enough to eat, the less inclined he was to roam. He was not able to stay long in any one place, though. Farming rarely produced enough extra to feed a mouth that was not part of the *ostal* to begin with.

For two years, Azemar roamed in this manner, learning all that the farmers could teach him about raising the crops of the region. He endured long days in wheat and barley fields, and his skin became brown in the hot sun when he picked vegetables and fruit.

To his knowledge of the forest he added the secrets of coaxing nourishment out of stony land. But most important of all was working in the vineyards. No other task gave him so much satisfaction. Each time he found himself in another vineyard, he learned a different facet of this complex, delicate process.

One farmer taught him how to tie up the vines so that the grapes would not trail on the ground and be eaten by insects.

And after that, another showed him how to tell when the fruit was at its perfect ripeness to harvest for wine, and which kinds of grapes made the best wine that would fetch a higher price in the faraway markets.

When he arrived at a vineyard in time for the pruning, they showed him how to cut back all the new growth until the fields looked as if someone had stuck misshapen black sticks in them, and it was impossible to imagine that anything had ever grown there.

It always struck Azemar as miraculous that come spring, the vineyards would be lush and green again.

Before long, his knowledge of the grapes gained Azemar access to the process of making the wine, crushing the ripe fruit, fermenting and aging the juice, and then storing it in barrels for the lords of the land who drank it or sold it to pay for their costly lives.

Two more entire cycles of growing passed, and Azemar had taken barely ten leagues out of his intended journey. Why go to Bésiers? he thought, after a time. He found out that the city was many leagues away. It was entirely possible—in fact, likely—that Azalaïs herself would not have managed to get there. Thinking back, he wasn't entirely certain what had made him say Bésiers, except that it was the only other city beside To-losa that came to mind, and he knew that going back to Tolosa was not possible.

Azemar didn't like to think what might have happened to Azalaïs. She was small for her age, and younger than he. But she was smart, too. Azemar clung to the belief that, just as he had, she would be able to use her wits to survive.

One day, having grown tired of the grumbling peasants who worked a vineyard where he had helped with the harvest and who had made it clear that his presence during the inclement winter months had been most unwelcome, Azemar packed up his meager belongings, secured his bag containing a few copper coins, and set out on the road again. He walked for a whole day, covering about six leagues, until he came upon a clearing, a patch of ground of about three or four *sesteradas* that had obviously been a vineyard at one time, but was now overgrown with weeds. Because it was early spring, the weeds had not yet covered the soil with their greenery and here and there he could see the remnants of a vine struggling to poke up through the tangle.

In the midst of this sad spectacle stood an old man, facing away from Azemar and looking up to the sky, his left arm out-stretched and his right arm dangling at his side.

"Please God," he said aloud, "give me the strength to continue, to make my vineyards bear fruit once again. And I beg your forgiveness for . . . for. . ." His voice faltered and he let his left arm fall, knelt down and kissed the barren earth. His shoulders shook. The man was crying.

Azemar continued forward cautiously, taking care not to make any noise. When he was close enough so that the man would hear his voice, he cleared his throat and said, "*Perdon,* but what are you doing?"

The man stood up and whirled around so fast he almost fell over backwards.

When Azemar rushed forward to steady him, he held out his arm with his palm toward him. "This is my property!"

Azemar stopped where he was. "I only wanted to help you."

"You must be a stranger in this place," the man said.

Azemar noticed that in all this time, the man's right arm had remained motionless.

"Who are you, and why have you come here?" The man's eyes darted about, as if he were trying to make sure Azemar was alone without making it obvious.

"I am Azemar of Tolosa, and I am on my way to Bésiers."

The old man's expression changed, and he looked at Azemar more closely. "The road to Bésiers is some way to the south. Why have you strayed from it?" He backed away a step or two.

"I have been working as I go." Azemar cast a critical eye over the latent vineyard. "It'll take an awful lot of work to get these vines to bear fruit."

The old man, whose stance had been tense and cautious to that point, let his shoulders drop. He looked small and weak, and Azemar now noticed a scar tracing a jagged path from his receding hairline down one side of his face to his chin. "Yes, that is my predicament. They have given me back my land, and it is useless."

"Your land? Is this vineyard yours?" Azemar's eyes wid-

Listen to the Wind

ened. Although the peasant farmers he had helped rented land that they cared for during their entire lives, it always belonged to someone else, a knight or the Church, and they paid hefty tithes for the privilege of working it.

"Such as it is. This vineyard, and another fifty sesteradas, some in vines, some in grain. Or it used to be, before . . ." He stopped speaking and simply shook his head, as if trying to clear it of some unpleasant memory.

"Where are the peasants? Don't you have tenants?" Azemar asked. He put his pack and hoe down on the ground.

"They have all gone to work on other estates. They were scared away, you see."

"Scared?"

After a pause, the man said, "You seem to be a strong lad. Perhaps you would like to work for me for a while?"

Azemar thought for a moment. What might frighten peasants away from a potentially fruitful vineyard? It would have to be something very dire. Yet this man did not look as though he could do anyone any harm. Azemar's last job was only a day's walk behind him. This landowner clearly needed help, and might be willing to pay well for it. What did it matter, after all, that he delayed his journey for another season?

"That depends," said Azemar. "I have learned a lot, and can help with the harvesting and wine making too."

"It may be more than a year before we can speak of wine making."

The two of them faced each other in silence until they were startled by a dove flying out of a furrow in the ground nearby. The bird glided above their heads, circled and flew off toward the sunset.

"It is a sign," said the man. "Come with me to my ostal and let us discuss what we shall do with my sorry fields and vineyards."

He gestured with his good arm toward a path that wound

26

away around a hillock. It would soon be twilight, and Azemar decided there would be no harm in listening to what the fellow had to say. A warm fire and a straw pallet were ample compensation for a few hours of tedious tales. And besides: he was curious.

Much to Azemar's surprise, the man did not lead him to a thatched hut, but to a fine house with fortifications and a roof made of wood. One part of the roof looked as if it had been crushed by a heavy object, like a tree limb, except that there were no trees near enough. But despite that, quite a large part of the dwelling was still habitable.

They entered a courtyard protected by a portcullis, crossed this and went into the residence through a tall, wooden door.

"Young man," said the fellow, noting Azemar's astonishment, "here is a lesson for you: never judge people solely on appearance. As you see, I am—or was—a *gentilòme*. Allow me to introduce myself. I am Corneil de Montpezat, baron of this estate, vassal of the Count of Tolosa and the King of Aragon."

Azemar did not know what to say, having never exchanged words with a noble in his life before. He followed the baron into his home, where an elderly servant greeted them.

"Dorde!" said the baron, "I may have found someone foolish enough to help me in the vineyards. Bring us some wine, and two bowls of your excellent stew."

He winked at Azemar to bring him into the joke, but Azemar had an uncomfortable feeling that foolish might well be the correct way to describe the undertaking he appeared on the verge of accepting. He could have bid his adieus then, taken the road and slept under the stars, but in March the nights were still frigid, and he already felt warmer, thanks to the large fire that heated a room Azemar judged large enough to house three families.

The intermittent presence of fraire Martin was the only shadow that extended over Azalaïs's life with fraire Goncort, which continued for two more years. To Azalaïs's dismay, the Dominican's travels brought him more and more frequently to the abaïa. In recent months, he had spent increasingly long periods in fraire Goncort's hut, talking to him about theology.

If Azalaïs was present, his eyes never left her. Fraire Goncort's vision had deteriorated to the point that he would not have been able to tell whether his visitor was looking at him or his young assistant, and Azalaïs could not bring herself to mention fraire Martin's uncomfortable gaze. She knew that fraire Goncort was none too pleased to have his peace disturbed by the Dominican, but his vows to God decreed that he must extend hospitality to any who sought him out.

"I intend to spend the paschal season here at Bolbona," fraire Martin said on a visit one warm March afternoon. He directed his comment at his host, but Azalaïs knew that his gaze was fixed on her.

"I had heard of an important council at Carcassonne," fraire Goncort said. "I assumed you would be going there since your work is so vital to the Church."

"You do my humble efforts too much honor. But I find I cannot refuse the request of the abbot here, who desires my presence at that time."

Azalaïs's ears always burned at the sound of fraire Martin's nasal, quiet voice with its trace of an accent. She hoped they were not bright red, and concentrated on her task of adding the names of several different kinds of mushrooms to fraire Goncort's large book.

The dried remains of assorted funghi they had gathered in the autumn littered the table. She knew which ones were harmless and delicious, which ones possessed healing powers, and which ones could kill a grown man with a single taste. Out of the corner of her eye, she saw fraire Martin lift a beaker of wine to his lips and sip at it, sucking a little air through a gap in his teeth at the same time. In her imagination she saw his face contort in the throes of agony—all it would take would be just a few morsels of a death cap in his drink. Azalaïs did not like to watch creatures suffer, but the idea of fraire Martin writhing in pain was curiously appealing.

"I hope you will ensure that young Azemar is present at all the observances during this holy time," fraire Martin continued.

"Azemar is not called to the monastic life, and so is only as observant as a good Catholic must be. At this time of year, we have much to do in the forest."

The two men dropped the subject of attendance at services and spoke of other things until the Vesper bells summoned fraire Martin up to the abbey. When he left, Azalaïs swore the hut felt cooler and smelled fresher. "I don't like him," she said to fraire Goncort.

"I know, child," he answered, "but he is a dangerous man to cross. We will ensure that he has no cause to complain of you to the abbot."

Despite fraire Goncort's effort to spare Azalaïs from contact with fraire Martin as much as possible, he had to accede to the wishes of the abbot, who requested the aid of "Azemar's" boyish voice in the Easter week celebrations, beginning with Palm Sunday.

The wind that day was fierce. It sent great puffs of clouds scudding across the sky and tore bits off them as they went. At first the clouds were bright white, revealing intermittent patches of vibrant blue. Gradually they darkened and piled up on each other to the point that the cloud cover varied between dark gray and lighter gray, with only an occasional, slanting shaft of sunlight piercing through a momentary gap.

Fraire Goncort rested his left hand on Azalaïs's shoulder

29

and with his right hand used a long stick to help him over the stony ground that led to the chapel of the abaïa. The clang of bells now rose, now faded on the wind as they made the climb.

In contrast to the joy with which fraire Goncort greeted the beginning of this holy week, Azalaïs's spirits were oppressed. She and fraire Goncort had been speaking of the fact that she must leave his protection. Despite his bad eyesight, even he could detect that soon it would no longer be possible to disguise her sex from the insular world of the abbey and its ecclesiastical visitors.

The interior of the chapel blazed with hundreds of long tapers, and the scent of spring flowers mingled with incense. Azalaïs's apprehensions melted away in the presence of so much beauty and the devout men and boys whose eyes shone with religious fervor. She felt the magic of the Mass seep into her as it never had before and sang out to God with abandon and joy.

At the end of the service, Azalaïs waited her turn to file out with the conversants once the monks had left through the door that led into the cloisters.

To her dismay, she saw the abbot take fraire Goncort's arm and lead him off where she could not follow. Doubtless he wished to discuss some theological matter, and Azalaïs would have to wait alone outside until fraire Goncort emerged so that she could help him down the hillside.

The clouds had evened out to a thin, flat shield against the brilliant sun. Up here, where the trees were short and the light bounced off white boulders, even on days where the sun never showed its face the glare could be blinding. Azalaïs closed her eyes against the sudden brightness and sat on a rock near the path.

All the lay brothers had filed off to the dormitory to rest on the Sabbath. They looked exhausted, Azalaïs thought. It was planting season, and no one ceased his labors until every task was accomplished. Azalaïs was so absorbed in her own thoughts that she did not hear fraire Martin approach.

"You have grown much these past years."

The monk's familiar and unwelcome voice startled Azalaïs. She recovered her wits quickly. "So I am told."

"We have had little opportunity to speak together alone. There are some things I would like to ask you," he said, placing his body so that Azalaïs would have to push past him to walk away. "Do you know your catechism? Will you remain in the anchor with your benefactor? Or might you join the devout here at the abbey and spend your days in prayer and work on the land? Or perhaps one day you will become a Dominican, like myself, and help us spread the word of God to this benighted land."

With each question fraire Martin moved closer. Azalaïs leaned back against the rocks.

"We could use a strong, healthy lad like you to help us," the monk continued.

"Fraire Goncort still needs me to read and write for him," Azalaïs said. "His eyes are failing."

All at once the monk took a step toward Azalaïs and grabbed her arm. "Perhaps that is why he does not see what a pretty boy you have become."

Azalaïs was not certain what fraire Martin planned to do to her, but she knew that if he touched her in one particular place her secret would be discovered. As his hands began to explore down her arms and then her torso, she struggled against him. His touch nauseated her, and she twisted and fought to escape his hands. But he was surprisingly strong.

Fraire Martin stood very close to her, pressing himself up against her body. She could smell his breath, feel his heart beating fast and his hands beginning to tremble. She knew she had to do something.

Just before he reached the place between her legs where

her lack of manhood would be all too obvious, Azalaïs closed her eyes, said a silent prayer for forgiveness, and brought her knee up sharply, landing a solid blow in his crotch.

At first, fraire Martin simply froze. Then his face wrinkled into a mask of agony and he doubled over, letting go of Azalaïs.

For only a moment, her instincts to come to the aid of a creature in pain almost overcame her revulsion to the monk, and Azalaïs took a few steps toward the abbey to fetch fraire Goncort. But then she realized that if she did that, she would have to explain how the Dominican happened to have been injured in such a way. She knew that not only would she be punished—probably beaten—if her deed became known, but that she would also very likely have to leave fraire Goncort immediately. He would never want to harbor someone who was capable of harming another soul.

Seeing no alternative, Azalaïs ran as fast as she could down the treacherous path back to fraire Goncort's hut. As she crashed and slid over the shrubby scree, she heard behind her a howl that sounded like a massive, wounded animal.

She wondered what fraire Martin would say to the other monks about how he hurt himself. For a short while, it would not be easy for him to speak. As for herself—even in the very depths of her conscience she wasn't the least sorry about what she had done.

CHAPTER 4

Some fifty leagues away from the Abbey of Bolbona, in the fortified city of Caunes, a young woman a few years older than Azalaïs and many stations above her in rank paced back and forth across her chamber in the *castel* where she lived. Her name was domna Jordane de la Moux d'Aniort, and she was the only surviving child of the principal landowner in the Minervois region.

Jordane was accustomed to having things her own way, and she was not pleased with what her father had just told her. "How can you treat with those who killed your sons?"

Her long, auburn hair streamed out in undulating wings behind her and glinted in the morning sun as she passed back and forth in front of the window in the solar. Every once in a while she paused and gazed out over the vineyards toward the *Montanha Negre*, whose forested slopes created a brooding eminence that bordered her father's fertile lands to the north.

The baron d'Aniort sat on a stool by the fireplace in his daughter's room. He crossed his arms over his broad chest and pushed his lips out. "I have my reasons. When the time comes, you'll do as I say. Besides, you were too young to understand then."

"But I'm old enough to understand now!" Jordane

marched up to the baron and bent over at the waist, leaning at him like a mistress scolding her maid.

Her father reached out with one strong hand, wrapped his fingers around her upper arm and pulled her off balance, so that if he had let go she would have fallen on the floor. "This is no business of yours. What's done is done, and I shall protect the honor and patrimony of my family."

"What's left of it!"

Before she even knew what happened, the baron lashed out with his free hand and slapped her hard on the cheek. He pushed her away from him. She did not cover the red mark his blow made on her white skin.

"Stay out of matters that do not concern you." The baron stood. Beneath his surcotte he wore a chain-mail hauberk, ready for his journey to lead his knights to join the French king's forces at Albi. He picked up his coif and helm from the floor and tucked them under his arm.

Jordane took a deep breath, determined not to let her father's anger silence her. "Since when do matters that could affect my own marriage not concern me?"

The baron's nostrils flared and the muscles in his face twitched. But he said nothing, spun on his heel, and walked out of the room without saying goodbye to his daughter.

As soon as her father left, Jordane collapsed onto the bench seat built into the wall by the window and hid her face in her hands.

Ever since the death of her mother the previous year, her father had been pursuing a course of appeasement with the French—who had for a long time been trying to get him to cement his allegiance to King Louis IX, now that the viscounty of Trencavel was entirely under French control. They wanted desperately to be able to claim that the baron d'Aniort owed fealty to France. His domain sat strategically between Carcassonne and Minerve, bordering on the Narbonès at its eastern marches—a prize catch for the French king.

Jordane's family had belonged to the region for as long as anyone could remember. The blood of her ancestors flowed in the wine that Jordane drank every day. The mere mention of Simon de Montfort's name affected her as if she herself had been there to witness his cruelty. The ambitious French knight had been crushed in the end, but the scars from that time were still visible in the faces of people who feared a repeat of the massacres at Minerve, Lavaur, and Bésiers, when thousands were put to the torch as heretics or slaughtered in the streets.

There were men and women still alive who remembered the stench of burning flesh and the screams of the victims.

The Aniort brothers died at the ages of twenty-five and twenty-three, in 1229 when Jordane was only ten years old. It was the year the second crusade against the heretics finally came to an end. Jordane remembered hiding beneath the table in the great hall after the food had been cleared away. Her nurse searched for her in vain while she listened to the men talk about *paratge*, about preserving their heritage against the northern usurpers.

Every night for an entire week, just before her brothers disappeared to fight for the last time, a traveling musician sang a song of battles against the French, of the count of Tolosa and his valiant knights. Jordane still remembered snatches of it. She hoarded them in her heart, thinking of them before she fell asleep at night and when she awoke in the morning; during her progresses through the small *castrum* where she was its most eminent female inhabitant; on her occasional forays into the countryside with a train of *damozels* and servants for a pleasure picnic.

The names of men who had fought and died had a music all their own. William Unauld, Senher Gerald, good Senher Hugh, Senher Almavis, Senher William Arnold, brave Senher

Hugh of La Mota, swift Senher Hugh of Pontos. When she recited them to herself now she added two that were close to her heart: Roger and Alfons d'Aniort.

A few moments after her father's footsteps faded away, the light patter of Johana's leather-slippered feet approached.

Johana had been her friend and companion since childhood. The daughter of a distant, less affluent relation, she had been orphaned during the crusade and brought to Caunes by the *barona* Esclarmonde, Jordane's mother. The barona raised both girls as if they were her own.

Jordane hadn't thought much about the difference in their stations until her mother died. The very next day her father would no longer allow Johana to sit next to her at the high table, and insisted the poor relation vacate her own chamber for an anteroom off Jordane's. Jordane vowed that one day she would make it up to Johana.

"Ma Domna!" Johana cried when she entered the room to prepare her mistress for dinner and saw Jordane's red cheek.

"It's nothing. Why must he be as he is!"

"Come, let me dress your hair."

Johana opened the oak armoire that occupied one wall of the room and took out an ivory comb, a hairbrush made with the bristles of a wild boar, and a round, polished silver mirror with a handle. She gave the mirror to Jordane, then sat behind her on the window seat and brushed the unruly, russet mane that spilled over domna Jordane's shoulders and all the way down her back. Every once in a while, she stopped and combed out a louse, crushing it between her fingernails.

"Do you think Raimon will come tonight?" Jordane asked.

"He should not come at all, Domna, you know that."

"With my father gone for months, what does it matter?" Jordane noted with relief that her cheek had already become less red.

"You rely too much on the loyalty of the servants. What would you do if one of them betrayed you to your father?"

"What? You think a peasant would run all the way to Albi to tell him that I'm flirting with the noblest man in the Minervois? Unless you think one of them has learned how to write, and would steal parchment, pen and ink to send a dispatch."

Jordane knew she was being unfair to tease Johana, but in truth she felt sorely tested. Raimon de Berenger, nephew and namesake of the count of Provence, was a knight whose feats of valor against the French were the stuff of legend. At one time, her father looked upon him as a son to replace his own lost boys. He had told Jordane that when Raimon's thirteen-year-old cousin Marguerite de Provence married Louis IX he assumed the young firebrand would see which side of the fence to come down upon.

Instead, the knight openly defied his family and became a rebel.

Jordane had shut herself in her room for days when her father told her that Raimon was too dangerous a guest for the Aniort household, whose loyalty was suspect at best, and she must sever all ties with him. If Raimon had not lost all his lands and become a *faidit* he would have been an excellent match for her, except that she had been promised to a prince from Aragon when she was born.

At least, she thought, this promise ought to prevent her being sold off in marriage to a French nobleman.

"When you are married then you can toy with senher Raimon all you wish. Until that time it is best to avoid scandal."

"Oh, who cares about scandal! I shall do as I please."

"You can't do anything until you are dressed, ma Domna," Johana said.

Jordane smiled. "We used to be just Johana and Jordane, like sisters."

"Those days have ended." Johana looked down at the brush and pulled a few long, coppery hairs out of it.

Jordane turned around again to let her damozel finish her hair. She angled herself so that she could see out the window, beyond the city walls. Raimon had said that he would write to her when her father was gone.

She wondered how long it would be until Claris, the musician, delivered a note in Raimon's handwriting as he had so often before. They were always a little smudged, as if Raimon didn't have time to wait for the ink to dry, or lacked a pouch of sand to scatter over it before he rolled it into a neat package and tied it with a silk cord.

The last time they had spoken she knew he was trying to raise an army to rise up against the French. She wished him success, but at the same time hoped his efforts would not keep him from her.

"Will the joglars come tonight?" she asked, her mind leaping from an image of Raimon seated at the high table for dinner to the delights of conversation and flirtation after the meal was over.

"They always come if they are within five leagues of Caunes. They know you will reward them handsomely."

"I hope they are near. I feel like dancing."

"If not, you can sing instead. I heard you practicing a new melody yesterday."

"Yes, it's nearly finished. I just cannot get the cadence right. I don't want it to be something expected. Perhaps I could change modes, right at the end." Jordane stood up. The fine comb was still stuck in her hair, but Johana knew better than to call her friend back from musing on her latest project.

At her mother's insistence, Jordane's education had been the same as her brothers'. It embraced the quadrivium: Arithmetic, geometry, astronomy, and music. The barona hired a monk from a local abbey to supplement her own teaching, and permitted her daughter to sit with Claris, a fine musician who taught her how to read the notes on a page and write down the ones she sang.

The barona Esclarmonde not only saw to her children's education, she also brought a library with her as part of her dowry. Twenty volumes—riches beyond imagining. But no book could have taught Jordane the way to sing as she did, bending the pitches even within a mode to tease the ear, to emphasize words so they would mean something beyond the surface. This Jordane learned through the exercise of her own acute senses, by listening to the traveling musicians, by listening to the music of the words themselves.

There were always guests at Caunes, and many of them came just to hear the domna Jordane sing a *canso* of her own composing. She possessed a distinctive, husky voice, deep for a woman's but sweet nonetheless, and had mastered the citole. Her own instrument was beautifully carved. Her father had brought her an ivory plectrum from the Holy Land years ago. Just lately, she decided to learn the vielle also. Claris was a patient teacher.

Once she had bound Jordane's unruly hair into one thick plait, Johana helped her mistress put on a clean, linen under-tunic and a rich, purple *blial*, which she tied under her bosom with a length of gold braid. It was spring and the mornings were still cool, so she added a sleeveless surcotte of green velvet. Finally, a white linen veil held in place by a *crespine* added a touch of modesty to her mistress's sumptuously maned head.

"It is a beautiful day for our picnic, don't you agree?" Jordane said.

"A beautiful day, so long as Ma Domna does not get into any mischief while we are out."

Jordane's golden laugh echoed off the stone walls. "Why,

I have no ability to forbid free men from roaming the country-side, and if one of them happens upon our revels, so be it."

Jordane had told Raimon in her previous letter that they were planning the outing for that day, the day her father was to leave again. She told him the precise route she intended to take, and hoped that he would interpret her specificity in the way she intended. They would make it a trip of a few days' duration, stopping at an inn for the night.

It was there that she hoped Raimon would find her. However much she wished he would dare to come to sit at their table, Jordane knew that it would be a foolish step to take. As Johana said, the servants could not be trusted. If he did not hear about it right away, her father would certainly know at some time in the future that she had flouted his authority. Encountering the knight outside the city walls was the best she could hope for.

"Come, let us break our fast." domna Jordane took Johana's hand. Johana gently but firmly pulled it out of her grasp.

"It is enough that I know you love me," she said.

The two ladies walked through to the main room of the solar where the other members of domna Jordane's entourage were doubtless already gathered, hungrily waiting for the mistress of the ostal, the noble house of Aniort, to join them so that they could eat.

CHAPTER 5

By the next morning, fraire Goncort had arranged for Azalaïs to leave. For her own safety, he said, as he tearfully gave her everything she needed to set her on her way.

She did her best to be strong, not to weep like a girl at parting with this dear friend who had given her so much. She smiled at him until she turned away, only then letting tears blur her vision. As long as she was in the anchor, she hardly needed to see to find her way.

But after only an hour's brisk walk Azalaïs's strides took her to the limits of the part of the woods that she frequently traversed with fraire Goncort. It surprised her that the distance was so small. Yet when she thought about it, whenever the two of them were out together they meandered and trod slowly and carefully, always looking for treasures hidden in the underbrush that they could collect, and so it took much more time to go anywhere.

She paused at the edge of the stream through which she would have to wade to begin her journey in earnest and sank to her knees. She knew she should utter one of the many Latin prayers she had learned, because Latin was the language God understood, according to the abbot.

But Azalaïs wanted to say something particular to him,

about fraire Goncort, and she did not know the right Latin words. She was still amazed that fraire Goncort had not chastised her severely for what had happened. Instead, he gave her beautiful clothes befitting a young man of good family, and a pouch of money—alms, he said, meant for the poor, but by his reckoning she needed them as much as any poor soul—to see her to Bésiers.

Once there, she was supposed to find a Senher le Martellier, an old friend of his, who would apprentice her until such time as it was expedient for her to transform herself back into a girl. Fraire Goncort had given her a sealed letter that she was to place in his hands when she arrived.

Azalaïs did her best to dry her tears. Much as she did not want to leave fraire Goncort, she knew that her action had only hastened something that was inevitable.

"I beg you, God," Azalaïs's prayer began, "Tend to fraire Goncort. Send him someone else to be his eyes. And please don't let him be punished because of what I did. I could never—"

A rush of wings and a "*grrrk*" interrupted Azalaïs. She looked up in surprise as her cavèc, the owl she and fraire Goncort had saved several years before, landed on her clasped hands. She had named the owl Savïesa, Wisdom, because of its knowing look, which it displayed now by circling its head and lowering one eyelid at her, as if to say, *you thought you could leave without me?*

Azalaïs sighed. "I wish you'd stayed with fraire Goncort. But maybe you'll get tired of me and go home. Come, we'd best be on our way."

From then on, the owl remained with Azalaïs, sometimes flying off ahead to perch on a branch and survey the forest before diving to retrieve some prey. At other times, Savïesa sat on her forearm, which she protected with a kerchief meant for cleaning her face, and nodded off to the steady rhythm of her strides. He often disappeared for hours at a time, but always returned in the end.

Azalaïs was just as happy to have some company when she broke from the forest into the scrubby hills patched with vineyards and groves and could see groupings of huts in the distance. She had spent so much of her life fleeing from such signs of civilization that she trembled at the thought of walking past them, of being in full view of peasants tending the vines with their spring growth and trying to grow vegetables or wheat in the resistant soil. She felt her face grow hot as women stared at her from cottage doorways, bowls of slops in their hands ready to toss out to a pig rooting around in its pen.

Fraire Goncort told her that she must be careful to avoid any roads the knights had taken. Although the crusade against the heretics had ended some years ago, knights eager to serve their quarantine—their forty days of service—still rode in bands through the countryside. They were not always careful to distinguish between the infidels and any honest strangers who happened to cross their paths, and thought nothing of claiming payment in the form of livestock and innocent virgins as they passed.

The evidence of their lawlessness was clear: Azalaïs saw shells of cottages that had been put to the torch and overgrown kitchen gardens whose owners had met their dooms at the hands of these marauders. She felt her pockets for the herbs she had brought with her to help protect her in the wide world, a mixture of pine bark and cloves to cure the ague and a small vial of salve to rub on wounds. She had taken them from fraire Goncort's store, knowing he would not mind. Although what help these paltry remedies might be in the face of a sword wound, she did not know.

Over the next few weeks, Azalaïs spent nights in the relative comfort of kitchen lean-tos, sharing meals with the peasants and bond servants who worked the land, and sometimes the local worthies who owned property in their own right. They looked at her with curiosity and were a little frightened of Savïeza, but were happy enough to take her *deniers* in exchange for their meager hospitality. Usually they gave her a pallet among the animals. Azalaïs was accustomed to the smells and welcomed the warmth provided by goats and sheep.

She slept with her money pouch beneath her head. Although she had little knowledge of these things, unused as she was to using currency for anything, fraire Goncort had cautioned her to offer only a few deniers for a meal and a place to sleep. Azalaïs did not at first realize that the pouch she carried contained three livres, a more than handsome enough sum to buy an apprenticeship and some new clothes when she reached Bésiers. Most inhabitants of the countryside would never see so much money in their lives. If anyone suspected she had it, she would be a certain target for robbers.

As Azalaïs made her way northward and eastward, the groupings of cottages and villages became more frequent, the hills smoothed out to gentle undulations and the mountains receded gradually into the distance. Vineyards covered more and more of the open fields, and Savïeza disappeared for longer and longer times, sometimes flying off at sunset and only joining her as day broke and she prepared to continue her journey.

Azalaïs was eager to reach her destination and begin her new life, yet each morning she awoke with an increasing sensation of dread. The back of her neck prickled in the way that it used to when fraire Martin stared at her.

More than once as she took her way she would whirl around suddenly, so vivid was her impression of being followed, thinking she might catch whoever it was off-guard. But she saw nothing.

At the beginning of the third week of her walk, her new clothing dirty and smelling and her leather shoes almost worn through, Azalaïs counted her money. She had used close to half a livre to buy food and shelter on the way, and to give a few sous to the beggars who besieged her at almost every small village.

And then, on Sunday she had gone to Mass in a *gleisa* in a village and put three sous into the box as an offering. She was relieved that her journey had so far been safe and uneventful. Far in the distance she could see the jagged outline of a cathedral rising above city walls. It was not Bésiers, but the peasants told her that Bésiers was only five days' walk from that city, called Narbona.

What Azalaïs could not have known was that despite her efforts to conceal the amount of money she carried with her she had unwittingly left evidence of her comparative wealth all along the road as she went. She ceased to wonder at how welcoming the villagers were, nor at the fact that each time she stopped, the price for a meal and some rough shelter increased just slightly. She had no previous experience with which to compare this one, and was not aware that news of her progress could fly faster than she could walk.

One morning, Azalaïs awakened with a dull ache in her belly and assumed that her host had given her yesterday's meat to eat. The pain increased steadily, and before she had walked half a league, she was in agony. It was all she could do to put one foot ahead of another on the path. Nausea gripped her, and she looked for a copse of trees or a stand of box with some shelter so that she could spill her guts unseen.

She felt too unwell to pay attention to that prickling feeling that had made her suspect she was being followed, and headed toward a stream that wound through a stand of oak trees, desperate for a drink. Just as she reached the bank, a sharp pain doubled her over, and she rammed her fist into her stomach in an effort to stop it. It was then that she felt the warmth of liquid oozing from between her legs.

I've soiled my hose, she thought, and lifted her tunic to determine the extent of the damage.

When she saw the deep, red blood stain spreading rapidly down her inner thighs, her head became light and the world began to spin around her. She closed her eyes and concentrated on breathing slowly, as fraire Goncort had taught her once when he had to remove a large splinter from the bottom of her foot.

Before long the pain eased and the danger of fainting passed. Azalaïs rushed to the stream, tore off her tunic so it would not become wet, waded into the water and sat down, rubbing away the stain. No sooner did she wash it away than the red spot flowered out again, and she realized that blood now seeped continually from between her legs.

It must be my courses, she thought, with a mixture of distress and wonder. She had known this would happen someday soon, but it still took her by surprise.

Her legs and arms dripped with water, and the cloth of her shirt, braies and hose hung heavy on her slight frame as she climbed the stream's bank. Azalaïs pulled some large oak leaves from the low-hanging branches and placed them on top of each other to form a sort of barrier. Then she looked around her to make sure she was alone, and stuffed them into her braies in an attempt to stop the ruin of her clothing. By then she felt better than she had that morning.

Having at least temporarily arrested the damage, Azalaïs returned to where she had left her tunic. Her money pouch still hung around her waist, but it had become wet as well, and the coins it held were clearly outlined. Worse, its weight made it dangle too low to be covered entirely by her tunic, which reached only to the middle of her thighs. Azalaïs knotted the cord to tuck it up so that it would be out of sight by the time she reached the highway.

Before she finished rearranging her clothes, Azalaïs had that odd feeling again that someone was watching her. She stopped and stood very still, listening as fraire Goncort had taught her.

Nothing.

She trod toe before heel as fraire Goncort had taught her, just as she had when trying not to injure so much as an insect, or when creeping up on some poor, wounded animal. Every once in a while she thought she heard something. But as soon as she stopped to listen, the silence closed behind her like a curtain.

By now Azalaïs was certain she was being followed, and that someone had witnessed all of her actions at the stream. She perspired despite the coolness of the early morning and the gentle wash of rain. All she could think of was that day she had tried so hard to forget, when Gascon had pursued her through the forest.

She was bigger and stronger now, but she began to tremble, and her heart beat so hard she felt as if it would burst out of her chest. As soon as she was in sight of the road, Azalaïs thought, she would be able to run, and then she might find a hut to give her shelter.

Azalaïs deliberately slackened her pace, hoping to catch whoever was behind her off-guard when she broke into a run. After a few more minutes of quiet progress, she could see the edge of the copse and the road just beyond it. In the open, she would be safer.

Across the vineyard was a stone hut and workers tending the vines. She could run to them for protection. Now is the moment, she thought. She gathered her strength, hoarding it in the balls of her feet, her calves, her thighs, ready to sprint away from harm.

Now!

She launched herself forward toward the road.

She easily outran the person who—as she suspected—followed behind her.

But she had no chance to escape from the one who dropped off the low-hanging branch of a chestnut tree right in front of her face.

Before Azalaïs knew what was happening, one of the men had pinned her arms behind her, and the other grabbed the money pouch that hung from her waist and wrenched it off, snapping the leather cord.

She opened her mouth to scream, but her cry was stopped by a dirty rag, pressed onto her tongue and then tied around her head with another rag. Azalaïs gagged. The two men laughed. One, she noted, wore a torn monk's cassock, and the other looked as though he had just come in from tilling the fields.

They must have noticed her inquisitive eyes, because in the next moment the one who was dressed like a peasant drew his hand back and hit her with all his might across her face. Azalaïs fell backward, and the world went black.

"He's only a boy! Whoever would have done such a thing to him?"

Azalaïs heard the words before she opened her eyes. The world spun around her, and she rolled onto her side and vomited into the dirt. She noted vaguely that someone must have removed the gag, although she could feel the abrasions from it on her cheeks.

"Oh you poor thing! . . Johana, help him. And then, if he is well enough, bring him to my wagon."

Azalaïs's eyes gradually cleared and the landscape steadied itself. She looked up to see who it was who had spoken so kindly. It was a lady's voice, very sweet and melodious. Not like the voices of the peasants Azalaïs had met on the road.

But no one was there by the time she could make her eyes focus, so she closed them again and started to weep, barely registering the intense pain in her head before falling unconscious once more.

The next time she awoke, she felt that she was in motion—or rather, that everything around her was in motion. She rocked violently from side to side, and it made her head ache terribly, so she opened her eyes slowly. At first she thought she might be in a coffin on her way to be buried.

But Azalaïs soon realized no coffin would be so large, and she was not bound in a winding sheet. Nor would a coffin be so ornate on the inside, where no one could see. Beautiful blue cloth stretched above her head and around her on a frame, and the low wooden sides were painted gold.

Azalaïs thought her head rested on a cushion, but when she shifted her eyes, she saw that it lay in the lap of a fine lady wearing a purple gown, with a headdress that hid all of her hair. Gauzy veils draped over her shoulders. Her eyes were a golden brown, and she smiled down at Azalaïs.

"You poor lad. You have been through quite an ordeal. We'll take you somewhere so that you can rest and heal. Then perhaps we may speak of what is to become of you."

Azalaïs recognized the voice. It was the same one she had heard when she emerged from being unconscious that first time. This fine lady had seen her vomit. Now Azalaïs wanted to disappear, to turn the time back and be on the road once again. And then, she thought of the merchant she was supposed to serve, and her hopes of finding Azemar. She tried to sit up. "I must get to Bésiers! I am expected there."

"When you are better we can talk," the lady said, "and see if we cannot put you back on your course. But perhaps we might persuade you to alter it, and stay with us."

"I beg your pardon, Domna," Azalaïs said, digging out

from her memory a time when she and Azemar had watched the progress of knights and ladies through the woods, and heard them addressing one another in so strange a fashion, "but who are you?"

The lady laughed. "You see, Johana, I thought he must be a foreigner!"

Azalaïs looked over and saw another lady, a little less elegantly dressed, with a close cap on her head and her yellow hair in a thick braid that lay over her shoulder like a snake. "Young man, you are lying in the lap of Domna Jordane of Aniort. Her family owns all the land in this area, and a good deal in other places too. She is a fine lady, destined to marry a prince."

Azalaïs tried again to sit up, now deeply ashamed of being in so helpless and embarrassing a position in front of a noblewoman.

"Shhh! Do not trouble yourself! When we reach the city, I shall see to it that your wounds are dressed. And then perhaps there may be some other way we can help you, as apparently the cord for your money pouch has been cut. Did you have a large fortune?" The lady sounded kind, but Azalaïs could hear the slightest note of amusement in her voice.

"It was enough to purchase—" Azalaïs realized that this domna—quite understandably—thought she was a boy. She did not want to have to explain everything right away. "To purchase my apprenticeship to a man of business," she answered.

She closed her eyes again. The two ladies switched from speaking Lemozin to Latin, doubtless, thought Azalaïs, because they assumed she would not understand. But fraire Goncort had been careful not only to teach her the liturgy, but many other words as well.

"Did you see the blood on his legs? Do you suppose his attackers mutilated him?" Johana said.

Domna Jordane sighed. "I cannot imagine. If they did,

then he will find it very difficult out in the world. His clothes are fine—although rather dirty—he must not be friendless."

"I have heard that men who have been so injured as boys make marvelous companions. The husbands feel that their wives are safe, and they are allowed to go anywhere, like a pet dog!"

Azalaïs did not like the tone of the laughter she heard the two ladies share.

"Well, let's see if he is capable of more than adorning our court with a pretty face. There is something about him that intrigues me, I must admit."

Azalaïs felt Domna Jordane's fingers as light as a breeze push some hair away from her forehead. This contact made the skin on the back of her neck rise in little bumps, as it had when she thought she was being followed. Her instinct turned out to be right that time. Was this the same? Was it a danger signal, this sensation?

Whatever she thought, Azalaïs was too weak to act on her vague notion that she should flee, and so kept her eyes closed. The ladies turned their talk to other things, and since Azalaïs did not know the people they referred to, or understand what *targas* or *trobadors* were, she eventually fell asleep once more, lulled by the steady rocking of the wagon.

"We have nearly arrived, young fellow." Domna Jordane shook Azalaïs awake.

She sat up slowly, at first a little lightheaded, but the spinning world gradually came to rest. The lady called Johana lifted one of the flaps and secured it. They had just passed through the gates of a city, and Azalaïs could see from the wagon a great many people rushing about their business—more people than she had ever seen in one place before, including the abbey.

There were men in long tunics, brows furrowed and heads nodding, deep in serious conversation. Fine ladies in tunics and

blials in more colors than she thought cloth could hold prome-
naded with their chins lifted, their servants going first to catch
any slops that were tossed out of upper windows. And there
were so many houses—made of stone and pressed up against
the narrow road, some even with glazed windows.

Their pace slowed to a crawl, waiting for the way to clear
in front of them and create enough room for oxen and a wagon
to pass. The wagon rocked violently when a page jumped down
from where he had been clinging to its side and ran forward.

"Make way for Domna Jordane!" the boy yelled.

To Azalaïs's surprise, people bowed politely as they went
by, most of them fixing her with openly curious stares. She was
glad to be awake for such a dramatic entrance.

"Are we in Bésiers?" Azalaïs asked, having no idea how
fast a wagon might go, and thinking she could have been asleep
for a very long time.

"No," Johana said, "we're in Caunes."

Azalaïs had never heard of Caunes. And even if she had,
it was not Bésiers.

Before too long the wagon pulled into a courtyard and the
driver dismounted and let down the side, ready to help them
out. It was time, Azalaïs thought, to separate herself from the
ladies.

"I thank you most kindly for helping me," Azalaïs said,
"but I think I must leave you and continue to Bésiers to find
Senher le Martellier. I am to be his apprentice."

Johana and Domna Jordane exchanged amused looks
again.

"I would be delighted to help you along your way, but
first allow me to furnish you with some new clothes, and have
an apothecary tend to your wound. I am afraid you may find it
rather difficult to walk all the way to Bésiers at the moment."

Azalaïs had no idea what Domna Jordane meant. She had
no pain and no wound that she could recall, except for the blow

that had given her a dull ache in her head. There was most certainly nothing wrong with her legs!

She looked down at them, and all at once understood why the ladies were so concerned about her, and what they must have meant when she overheard them talking before. Her inner thighs were caked with dried blood. If she had been a boy, she would certainly have lost her manhood with a wound that bled in such a way. To reveal that she was not only intact, but not truly wounded, would give her away instantly. Azalaïs needed time to think.

As the ladies gathered themselves to descend from their conveyance, she decided that she must pretend for a while, perhaps until everyone had gone to sleep so that she could steal away unnoticed.

Azalaïs leaned back against the seat of the wagon. Domna Jordane placed her hand upon her knee.

"Do not fear, young man. You shall be handsomely treated."

CHAPTER 6

The Baron de Montpezat's vineyards flourished, and during the second season they cleared more land, nursed more cuttings, and planted more vines. Azemar supervised the building of a large press and negotiated with the local cooper—a strong man who reminded him a little too much of Gascon Catelot—to make barrels out of the finest oak so the wine made from grapes that had grown on what was left of the older vines would mature properly and be ready to sell in a matter of months.

After two more fine summers, the new vines had begun to bear, and the estate was selling its young wine to cities as far away as Narbona, Perpignan, and Carcassonne.

In the evenings, when the work in the vineyards was done, Montpezat sat patiently with Azemar and taught him his letters, in Occitan, Latin, and French as well. He did not give Azemar the choice of refusing: with his bad right arm, he needed someone to take care of important communications and write contracts to sell his wine.

"You hold the quill so," he said, putting his weathered left hand over Azemar's to show him how to make the elegant strokes. Azemar concentrated so hard that he bit his lip, and a drop of blood stained the parchment.

"We won't waste it!" Montpezat said. "Dip your quill in it, and we'll write your name."

Slowly, carefully, but all on his own, Azemar traced over in his own blood the outline Montpezat had scratched with a pin.

"You have taken an important step," said the baron. "You are now master of your own name. Now you can sign contracts."

Although Azemar was a good student and soon learned the skills necessary to be Montpezat's true right hand, there was another skill, besides reading and writing, that occupied Azemar's fantasies as he worked in the field and before he fell asleep at night.

As the baron's establishment grew and prospered, it had gradually taken on the characteristics of a small court. This included hiring a musician—a *joglar*—to sing and entertain Montpezat and his guests, to play the vielle and the citole for dancing.

Azemar found himself enchanted by the beautiful songs. Some of them were about love. Others told long tales of brave endeavors, of fighting against the French and the wicked Simon de Montfort. He longed to be able to sing and play himself, and stayed to listen after the other members of the household had drifted off to their chambers or alcoves to sleep, until the musician, Fontredil, grew tired and started to yawn.

One evening, after a leisurely dinner followed by music and dancing, when the tables had been cleared away and the guests from the village were settled on the cots Dorde set up in the great hall, he summoned the courage to talk to Montpezat about it.

"How did Fontredil learn to play the citole so sweetly?"

"No doubt his father or another musician taught him."

"Do you think he would teach me?" Azemar blushed as he asked, although he did not know why.

Montpezat paused before they parted at the top of the stairs to go to their sleeping chambers and looked back at Azemar over his shoulder. "So, you are interested in playing and singing?"

"I – I don't know. But I'd like to learn how it's done."

Those were the only words they ever spoke about the matter. The very next day, the baron called for Fontredil, and Azemar began his lessons.

That year would be their first truly bountiful harvest, and quiet joy about that fact suffused the atmosphere all the long days of hard work in the fields and vineyards. The weather had been perfect, and the vines were heavy with beautiful clumps of ripe fruit, dark and glossy in the sun. Azemar stopped now and again to wipe the sweat off his brow as he bent down to cut off clusters of the purple jewels with his knife and place them in the basket at his feet.

It was hot still in the autumn, and that day there had been little breeze to relieve the sun's strength. He wondered how it was that the baron, who was not a young man, could work so tirelessly beside the peasants in the oppressive heat.

Just as they were about to stop their work for the day, a disturbance from the direction of the woods that edged the vineyard caught everyone's attention. One by one the peasants stood up from their tasks as a stranger stumbled past them, his clothes tattered and his face dirty and bloodied. He made his way along a furrow between rows of vines, but his uncertain progress caused him now and then to fall toward one of the precious plants. When he did so, a laborer would rush over to steady him, and then carefully inspect the vine to ascertain whether there was any damage.

Azemar and the baron stood transfixed watching the stranger's erratic progress in their direction. When he was close enough so that they could make out his features, the baron threw down his knife and rushed forward.

"Roger!" he yelled, throwing his arm around the fellow. "Azemar, help me."

Azemar sheathed his knife and ran to join Montpezat.

"I've come . . . warn you . . ."

The man's words sounded as dry and faint as the look in his eyes.

"Don't try to talk now. Come in and rest."

Azemar and the baron supported the man called Roger and together they walked to the castel. As soon as they stepped past the gate, Montpezat yelled to his house servants to bring water and bandages, bread and wine.

It was dark before Roger was able to talk to them coherently. He looked much better once he had been cleaned up, and the food and wine brought some color to his face which had been deathly pale beneath the dirt and crusted blood. He had a gash at his hairline, but it was not deep. He told them that he had been hit by a piece of debris that flew through the air when a boulder launched from a *trabuca* hit the ramparts of the castel he had been helping to defend.

"Our fortifications were not strong enough to withstand them. We had only a handful of Catalonian mercenaries to their five thousand knights. We lasted no more than a few days," he said.

"How many are left?" the baron asked.

"Most of us," answered Roger. "We surrendered before the losses were too heavy. But the terms were very harsh. I am afraid that some have been forced to tell secrets that have put many others in danger. Including you."

"What danger? Why?" Azemar asked, looking back and forth from the baron to his guest.

"There is no time to explain," Montpezat said to Azemar.

Then turning back to Roger he asked, "Which direction are the knights heading?"

"I am afraid," Roger said, lowering his eyes, "they are no more than a day's ride from your vineyards."

The baron asked Azemar to wait for him in the great hall before retiring for the night. "I have something I must talk to my friend about, and it is not for your ears," he said.

Azemar did as he was told, although he desperately wanted to stay and listen. He passed through into the hall at the center of the dwelling, the coolest place in the castel. The fire in the hearth was small, since there was not yet much need for heating, and only one torch pierced the gloom. Deep shadows obscured the corners of the room.

It was so quiet that Azemar kept thinking he could hear faint whispering coming from the places he could not see. He realized that it was probably only the wind, which had picked up after sunset and swept in violent bursts around the stones of the castel. Or perhaps it was the mice that waited until after dark to feast upon crumbs that were too small for the dogs to lick up. But he could not shake off the feeling that someone was watching him.

It seemed an eternity before the baron's candle lit the arched entrance to the hall. "I am sorry to have made you wait so long, but we have important work to do." Montpezat beckoned Azemar to a seat at the long table. "If we do not do precisely the right thing, all we have worked for here will be destroyed." The baron looked down at his left hand, clenched in a fist in front of him on the old oak surface. When he raised his eyes again, a fire burned deep inside them. "You must go and hide."

"Why?" Azemar asked.

"It is the northern knights. They are trying to rid our region of heretics at last."

Azemar had only a vague understanding of what was meant by the word 'heretic.' He knew it encompassed those who did not strictly adhere to the beliefs sanctified by the Church in Rome. "But I am no heretic!" he cried.

"I shall take care of making things ready here," continued Montpezat, ignoring him.

"What do you mean, making things ready?" Azemar asked.

The baron sighed deeply and put his hand on Azemar's arm. "I am determined not to lose everything for a third time. I shall open the castel to these unwanted 'guests,' let them look around and find nothing. I shall feed them and give them wine. But you must stay away until I send someone for you."

"Why? I have done nothing, and I believe in the teachings of the Church. I am not a heretic," he repeated.

"Yes, but you are a stranger, with no clear background or ancestry. This places you under suspicion by default. It is best, *mon filh*."

Montpezat stood, and at the same moment, Dorde entered the hall with a blanket rolled up under one arm, and a pack of provisions for Azemar under the other. Together they walked into the courtyard at the front of the castel.

"Follow that star over the first hill, and you will find a larger, rocky pog behind it. To the south from where you emerge, you will see a small grove of olive trees. Behind these is the entrance to the cave. You will find firewood and torches there, and unless the animals have gotten them, some salted meats. There is a skin of wine and some bread in your pack. Do not come down until I send Dorde to fetch you."

The baron said all this hurriedly, looking around him as if he expected at any moment that someone would jump out from behind a wall.

"You will come for me soon?" Azemar asked.

"As soon as it is safe for you to return," Montpezat answered. "Now go!"

Azemar's eyes soon became accustomed to the dark. There was no moon, but he knew the terrain well. The cave was about two hours' walk away from the castel. The opening was just as the baron had described it.

The moonlight spilling into the cave made it light enough for him to see a flint and a small pile of firewood that waited for just such a use. When the dry kindling caught and flames flickered to life, Azemar saw that the cave was larger than he thought it would be judging by its opening, and that there were one or two stout wooden boxes placed on clefts in the walls. The first room led to others through irregular, arched passageways, as though nature had created its own castel embedded deep within the mountain, with strange formations of rock hanging from the ceiling like unlit lanterns.

Azemar unrolled his blanket by the feeble light of the small fire. *At least it isn't winter,* he thought. Somewhere in the obscure heights of the cavern he could hear the squeaking and clicking of bats.

It amazed Azemar that he trusted the baron so completely that without question he did as the old man said. And although he was hidden from a threat he did not understand in a place that should have been frightening, he felt peculiarly at peace. Azemar closed his eyes and did not open them until broad daylight filtered into the cave the next morning.

Once he awakened, Azemar did not know what to do with himself. Without the press of unending chores to give a shape to his day he began to brood. What was happening down below, while he was up there hidden away? He paced around the cave, went exploring in some of the other rooms off the one he sat in, and when he tired of this, came back. *What is there, truly, to keep me here?* Azemar asked himself. It would take only an hour to return to the castel in the daylight. What if the baron needed him? Surely he could keep himself hidden and watch?

Before he could let his promise to the baron interfere with his decision, Azemar ran off across the countryside, taking care to keep well hidden as he went. This made his route a little longer, but he still arrived within sight of the castel in just over an hour.

He did not know quite what he expected to see, but the complete absence of people toiling in the vineyards took him by surprise. Then he remembered that it was Sunday, and although on most Sundays there were about half the number of peasants still working, because of the threat of the knights coming this way, the baron must have insisted that everyone go to Mass in the nearby village.

Azemar moved closer to the gates of the castel. All was quiet. He crept along the wall to the opening that led into a courtyard. As he drew closer, he heard voices speaking French. One of them he did not recognize, but the other belonged to a peasant who had come to work only a few months ago.

"I swear to you he was here! The son of a *bona domna*. His name is Azemar."

At the servant's words, Azemar gasped.

"What was that?" said the stranger.

Azemar crept quickly and silently along the wall and slipped around the corner. He heard the heavy footsteps and clanking of a man in armor followed by the lighter ones of the peasant walk out of the courtyard to where he had been standing a few moments before.

"Everyone is gone to Mass. It was nothing, perhaps the wind," the peasant suggested.

"Like your information, I'd wager!"

"You'll see! The baron is up to his old tricks, harboring heretics. I'll deliver him to the bishop by myself, and then I alone shall reap the benefits."

61

Azemar heard the sound of flesh hitting flesh, followed by a yelp of pain from the peasant. "You make one move without me," growled the stranger, "and I will turn you over to the inquisitors myself."

"On what grounds?"

"I don't need grounds, only suspicion. After all, you are working in the vineyards of a suspected protector of heretics!"

The heavy footsteps strode quickly in Azemar's direction. *If I am caught,* he thought, *the baron will suffer.*

Azemar scrambled to find hand- and footholds in the stones of the wall, and climbed to the top, which was more than a man's height over the stranger's head. The wall was thick, so once he was up, Azemar was quite secure. His heart banged inside his chest. He was certain that the knight and the servant would be able to hear it, or at least hear his breathing.

But they were too involved in their own dispute to raise their eyes, and continued on to where the knight's charger stood pawing the ground, tethered to a tree.

As they wandered farther away, Azemar carefully lowered himself down on the other side of the wall and crept back to the entrance of the courtyard. Without waiting to see what happened next, he ran for the cover of the woods, and found his way back to the cave.

CHAPTER 7

Toward sunset, Dorde came to let Azemar know that it was safe for him to return. He gathered up his few items, taking care to erase all evidence that he had been in the cave and to hide the entrance with sticks and brush, then followed the servant through the woods and across the fields back to the castel.

Azemar desperately wanted to have a moment with Montpezat alone, but he could not break through the air of celebration that buoyed everyone's spirits, now that the menace of the marauding knights was gone. The long table in the hall was heavy with fruits and meats, and the baron served one of his best wines to everyone, even the most menial scullery maid, a half-witted girl he employed more out of pity than necessity.

A few of the peasants formed into a band, using sticks to beat the time and create a tuneless sort of music, then Fontredil took up his rebec and joined them to play a sprightly *tresca*.

The peasant Azemar had seen that morning was not in the crowd. Azemar tried to get Montpezat's attention to tell him that all was not well, but the baron's relief that the knights had left his vineyards intact and accepted his assurance that he did not harbor heretics had intoxicated him with joy even before he tasted his cup of wine.

It wasn't until the next morning that Azemar was able to

steal a moment with his benefactor while they walked to the farthest vineyard on Montpezat's estate.

"How much do you know about all these peasants who work for you?" Azemar asked him.

"I know what I need to know. They want work, they do their jobs for me, I reward them."

Azemar did not know how to broach the subject with Montpezat without telling him that he was wrong, that his judgment at least in one instance had been faulty. "But supposing," he said, "there was one among them who harbored ill will toward you. How would you know?"

Montpezat stopped and took hold of Azemar's arm. "Is there something you want to tell me?"

They had arrived at a hillock that furnished a commanding view over the baron's now fruitful domain. Azemar related the story of his visit to the castel and the conversation he overheard, all the while keeping his eyes trained on a point far away on the horizon, beyond which he believed lay the Mediterranean Sea. When he finished speaking, he turned back to the baron, who stroked his chin and looked down at the ground.

"So, they will not leave me in peace." He gave a half-hearted laugh. "No, I suppose I don't deserve that."

Montpezat absently rubbed the top of his bad arm. He generally did that when something annoyed him, when—Azemar suspected—he wished he had the use of that arm to protect himself, or mete out punishment. It was usually best just to leave him alone until the mood passed over. Although his sword arm and writing hand were no longer at his service, the baron had not lost command of his tongue, and it could cut cruelly.

Knowing all this, Azemar risked Montpezat's displeasure by pursuing the matter further. "What did the peasant mean by 'bona domna?'" he asked. "And if my mother were one of those, why would that matter?"

The anger in Montpezat's eyes when he turned them in his direction was so intense that Azemar took a step backwards. "Why do you ask such questions?"

Azemar knew he had been impertinent to press his inquiries on this man who had done him so much kindness. Yet if he did not seize this opportunity, he might not have another chance to ask Montpezat such direct questions. "Does it concern me? Or my family?" Azemar's voice rose in spite of himself. He had long had the feeling that the baron knew something that had to do with him and yet refused to tell him. Sometimes, when he lay sleepless, he imagined that perhaps Montpezat even knew where he had come from and was acquainted with his mother and father. But in the bright light of day, such fantasies soon faded.

"It has to do with us all," Montpezat replied, and his shoulders sagged as if Azemar had just given him an enormous sack of grain to carry. He turned away and walked slowly toward the castel.

The next day, the baron summoned Azemar to his privy chamber, the room where he had spent hours teaching Azemar to read and write, and shut the door behind them.

"I have a task for you that will take you away from here," Montpezat said without looking at him.

"A task? How away?"

"There is a merchant in the city of Narbona who I suspect has been cheating me. He claims that he can get no more than fifty deniers for a barrel of wine, where everywhere else I sell my wine for sixty-five."

The baron motioned Azemar to his writing table and dictated a letter to him, to a man named Corbiu. It said nothing of the discrepancy in the price of the wine, Azemar noticed. It simply stated that Montpezat wished the merchant to take Azemar into his household, and said that Azemar was possessed of his own means and would use them to acquire the knowledge and skills of a gentleman—perhaps even a knight, if he were so inclined. Once he finished reading, Azemar turned his puzzled gaze on the baron.

"You wonder how you have been transformed into a gentilòme so swiftly?"

"Yes," answered Azemar. "Only more than that I wonder why you do not say when I shall return here to the castel."

Monpezat's expression, which had until now given away very little, softened slightly. "You are not to return. At least, not for a while."

Azemar had not expected that answer. In the past, when he left a place of employment, it was because the harvest was finished, or he had grown tired of the region or the people, or he began to feel guilty that he was not trying harder to reach Bésiers so that he could find Azalaïs. This departure from Montpezat, though, was not of his making and he could not make sense of it. "Have I, are you—"

"No, I am not dissatisfied with you Azemar. Far from it."

Azemar waited for the baron to continue, but he did not.

"Do not look so downcast!" Montpezat chided him. "I offer you an opportunity that most young men would grasp with two hands." He raised his one good fist to the ceiling. "You will like Narbona. It is a large city, with public baths and learned men. And it is by the sea."

"But how will you manage?" Azemar said. He did not mean to stare at the baron's bad arm, but he did so before he could look away.

"You think you are the only young fellow who knows how to read and write?" Montpezat shook his head. "No, you did not mean that." He clapped his hand on Azemar's shoulder. "I ask you to trust me. I have a task for you. Part of it is to take custody of a package whose contents you will not disclose to menher Corbiu, nor to anyone else."

Azemar's head spun with the effort to take in all that the baron told him. "When will I leave?"

"Next week."

There was no time to let the immediacy of the impending change sink in, because for the next hour, they discussed the details of Azemar's coming journey.

The baron had planned everything out with great care. Azemar was to ride a horse—which would mean that he would cover several times as much ground in a day as he could on foot—and would carry concealed on his person a sack of money that was enough to get by, but not enough to attract the kind of notice that would make him a likely target for robbers.

Once in Narbona, he was to apply to a Jewish banker in the archbishop's ghetto who would know who he was and furnish him with whatever funds he required.

"After that, you must make what you can of yourself. Perhaps you will find a wife."

The week passed quickly. Azemar helped with the harvest as usual, and gave instructions about managing the financial side of the estate to a peasant named Rimbalt who had been to school and was capable of taking on this more responsible role.

There was much to arrange, but some part of Azemar had been preparing for this departure for several months. Since the previous winter, he had begun to have disturbing dreams. The face of someone he thought was his mother floated in the sky next to the moon and her mouth moved, as if she were trying to tell him something. The face would grow larger and closer, until it became the face of Azalaïs, only it looked different because she was older.

This specter of Azalaïs would run away from him, turn and beckon him urgently, and when he tried to follow, he would discover that he was draped with iron chains, and that these were fastened to heavy iron weights that dragged upon him.

Each step required a monumental effort. He could not keep up with Azalaïs, and watched her figure grow smaller and smaller, until she disappeared entirely, and he would cry out in despair. His cry would wake him up.

The night before he was to leave, a tempest rolled across the garriga on its way from the mountains to the sea. The wind screamed around the stone walls of the castel and threw open shutters, sending them banging against the walls. Lightning rained down on the earth creating an unnatural, false daylight, and the constant rumble of thunder was only broken by even more deafening claps.

Azemar rose to fasten his own shutters closed and then ran throughout the castel with the servants looking for places where the wind had blown water in through cracks, working as fast as possible to board them up and stem the damage.

One huge, whirlwind gust shook the doors of the great hall so violently, that they bulged inward against the wooden brace that was lowered each night to bar the door against intruders. Azemar ran forward to examine the bolts that held those brackets to the timbers of the door, and as he did so the cover of the peephole, a square cut at exactly a man's eye level, flew off its much smaller hinges and bounced across the stone floor of the hall.

At that very moment, an animal cry cut through the roar of the storm. It came from the courtyard. Azemar put his hand before his eyes to shield them from the stinging rain, driven in sideways sheets directly through the peephole, and peered out.

A rare instant of total darkness at first made it impossible to see anything at all. But soon lightning flashes lit the night again, and Azemar gasped when he saw the baron, kneeling in the center of the courtyard, his back toward the door. He rocked back and forth, his good arm clutched across his belly as though he had terrible pain. Every so often, he threw his head back and let the rain pour into his mouth.

Azemar yelled through the opening, "Baros! Come out of the storm! You will be killed!" but the wind threw his voice back in his face. He thought about opening the doors and running out himself to drag the baron inside, but that would expose the hall to damage, and besides, lifting the bar required the strength of two men.

Instead, Azemar took a seat on one of the benches along the wall and waited there, to see which would end first: the baron's vigil or the storm itself.

He must have fallen asleep for a while. The baron's hand on his shoulder shook him awake. The storm had ended.

"Come with me."

Azemar rubbed the sleep out of his face and followed Montpezat into his privy chamber. He noticed then that the old man's clothes were completely dry, and a wayward curl in his gray hair gave the only indication that he had been soaked through not long ago.

"I told you that I would give you something to carry with you to Narbona," the baron said. "But that was only part of the truth. It is a package that you will take to Narbona, yes, but it will remain with you after that. I cannot yet tell you what you will do with it in the end, because I do not know for certain myself."

Montpezat opened the cabinet that held his store of parchment, ink and documents. He took everything out of it and reached deep inside. Azemar heard the muffled scraping of a rusty bolt against its sheath, as though the back of the cupboard concealed another hiding place. When the baron pulled his hand out, it contained a leather bag with something heavy inside it. He put this on the table, then reached in again and this time drew out a small book bound in leather.

He handed each of them to Azemar. The bag contained

something round and hard. Azemar was desperate to open it and see what it was, but Montpezat was speaking to him.

"These two objects are my joy, and my shame. Unfortunately I cannot give you one without the other. You must keep them safe always, and let no one know you have them—until the moment when it is necessary for you to use them because your life hangs in the balance."

My life? Azemar thought. Perhaps the baron had been struck by lightning that night, and had gone mad. Azemar started to untie the laces that held the bag shut.

"Go ahead. I see you are curious. The book you do not open, but the bag, with its heavy contents, you cannot resist." Montpezat sighed.

Azemar upended the pouch. A glassy, red stone tumbled out of it into his palm. It was exactly the right size to fit in the hollow in his hand created by the joints of his fingers. The flickering flame of the candle on the table reflected in it so that it seemed as though a fire burned in its heart, a fire in the shape of a white cross with arms of equal lengths. On the outside, the stone was polished to a surface so smooth that Azemar could not help rubbing his fingers over it.

"It is indeed beautiful. But its true worth has nothing to do with its appearance. I was given it by someone who trusted me when I journeyed to Tolosa years ago."

Azemar tore his eyes away from the blood-red stone and searched Montpezat's face for something—even he was not certain what.

"Yes, I found myself in Tolosa, at the end. Many heretics had fled the city. My sympathies were with them. Or at least, against the French trying to impose their dominion over a way of life that had suited us very well for a long time. A lady, the wife of a merchant who was a good man in all ways, gave this to me. She thought that it would be safe in my keeping, since she did not know what would become of herself, her husband and her young son."

"What happened to them?" Azemar's mouth had become dry. He noticed only then that it hung open as he listened to the old man.

"I cannot tell you. Many, I believe, fled to the safety of Montsegur and have lived there ever since that time."

"Is that the story of the stone?"

"What? No." Montpezat put the parchment and ink pots back in the open cabinet as he spoke. "The lady—I cannot now recall her name, I met her only once before she fled—told me that the stone was a precious symbol, that it was part of a vast treasure that had been amassed by the heretics and then dispersed among them for safe keeping. One day, she said, the treasure would be reassembled at Montsegur. She made me promise to find a way to get the stone back there. I know now that I shall never see that place. That is why I give it to you."

"But I am going east," Azemar said.

"For a while," the baron said as he latched the cabinet closed again.

"Might there not be some danger in carrying this piece of the heretic treasure?"

Montpezat gazed thoughtfully at the ceiling. "Danger. There is always danger. Now we should both sleep. You begin your journey tomorrow."

"Wait!" Azemar said, "I mean, *perdon*."

The baron stopped and fixed him with a steady stare.

"The book. What is it?"

"Read it sometime. You'll see."

With that the old man strode off, his good arm swinging in rhythm to his steps.

Azemar waited until he could no longer hear the soft padding of Montpezat's slippered feet and then climbed the stone steps to his own room, the leather pouch in one hand and the small book in the other. Montpezat had given him two precious gifts to take on his journey. Yet were they gifts? If all was as the baron suggested, then these things were not truly the old man's to give away, nor were they necessarily destined to bring him good fortune.

Azemar had been at Montpezat far longer than he had stayed anywhere—except in the forest wandering with the Catelots in what seemed now the distant past. In his time with the baron he had been treated well, had learned to read and write in two languages, and learned to understand spoken French. Now, it seemed that he was also possessed of wealth he never imagined. Yet that night he felt as bewildered as ever. All the knowledge he had gained by working at the castel was not enough to unravel the mystery of the baron himself. Why would he part with such precious possessions? Why risk his good name by sending a young man he knew almost nothing about to the household of a trusted associate?

Azemar did not for a moment believe the story about the price of the wine. Montpezat had often enough claimed to have little interest in the commercial aspects of his vineyards.

The storm had cooled and freshened the air. Azemar left his shutters open so the breeze would blow across his face, carrying the rich, decaying scent of autumn soil to his nostrils. The faintly acrid tang of fish told him that the wind had changed direction and now blew in from the south, from across the sea, which he had never seen, but knew lay only a few leagues hence. In the morning he would make his final preparations and leave the castel.

He tried to stay awake to think about all that had happened recently, about the events that had led the baron to send him away so suddenly, yet with so much munificence. In the end he could not keep his eyes from closing, and slept until the dawn cast a rosy glow across his pillow.

Once he had tucked the stone and the book safely away deep inside his satchel, Azemar took a final look around his small chamber with its wooden floor, its bed with a straw mattress and warm blankets, the table that held a pitcher of water, and the carved wooden chest that for the last three years had filled up with his clothes and belongings. It was empty now, and everything he needed was either in the satchel, or carefully rolled up in a pack that would fit behind the saddle of a horse—his horse, a gift from Montpezat. Never in his life before had Azemar been sorry to leave a place.

He could see through the window of his chamber that the day would be fine, despite the fact that a mist still hung over the ground. The storm had ushered in the threat of winter, and although the sun would soon warm the surface of the earth, it was no longer intense enough to bake away the water that had drenched the fields the night before.

Thank God the harvest was complete, Azemar thought. Otherwise they would sink into the mud as they gathered the fruit—if the pelting rain had not smashed the ripe globes in their clumps, that is. As it was, the vineyards were in a state of graceful decline, denuded of their fruit, waiting for their yearly pruning—a task Azemar enjoyed and was sorry to miss. In a cleft between two steep, rocky hills lay the distant, snow-capped heights of the mountains. The world, Azemar thought, was almost unbearably beautiful.

But it was time for him to begin his journey. Without looking behind him, Azemar walked through the door of his chamber and descended to the great hall. He expected that Montpezat would be there to see him off while everyone else went about his business, either in the castel or out in the fields. But to his surprise, all the servants and several of the peasants stood in a cluster, their caps in their hands, with the baron himself in their midst.

"We have a gift for you, Azemar," the baron said, and then

gestured to Fontredil, who left the hall for a moment. When he returned, he carried an object that was wrapped in cloths.

Azemar knew what was in the parcel even before he removed its covering. It was a beautiful, new citole. "Did you make this, Fontredil?" Azemar asked.

The musician smiled.

"I shall think of you whenever I play it, and will sing songs of the glory of Montpezat."

Fontredil bowed his head. Then one by one, the servants and peasants walked up to Azemar and bowed to him, saying "God bless you," or "the saints go with you." Each one left the hall after saying his farewells, until finally only the baron and Dorde remained. Azemar did not know what to say, and so he bowed to his patron. Then before he lost heart, he walked out to the courtyard, mounted his horse and rode through the castel gates.

CHAPTER 8

For several days after she first arrived in Caunes, Azalaïs walked with a slight waddle and winced every once in a while for effect. Fortunately, the apothecary they had sent to attend to her was too squeamish to ask to inspect her wound, and merely gave her a poultice and some rags done up so that she could wear them beneath her hose.

The first night, she had thought about running away. It would have been relatively easy to do: no one guarded her especially, assuming that she would be too unfit to try to leave. In any case, Azalaïs noticed that the watchman who was supposed to exercise vigilant guard over the quarters of domna Jordane and her damozels nodded off sometime after the compline bell had rung, and did not awaken until matins tolled at dawn.

But Azalaïs remained nonetheless, in part because she did not know what she would do if she left, and in part because she had never slept on such a thick straw mattress, nor had fine sheets draped over her.

Soon they gave her an alcove of her own near the ladies' solar. Although she could not sleep among them, her presumed injury rendered her harmless in their eyes and they did not fear the proximity of the boy called Azemar.

Staying at the castel built into the city walls of Caunes

had many advantages. Aside from never having to worry about food, clothing, or shelter, Azalaïs was able to watch what fine ladies did, see how they dressed, and become acquainted with the way they spoke. When the time came that she would be able to assume her true identity, she wanted the transformation to be instantaneous, so that anyone who saw her would not suspect that she had passed so many years of her life as a boy.

More than anyone else she encountered, domna Jordane continued to fascinate Azalaïs. While her ladies sewed and gossiped, domna Jordane was often to be found reading from books. The books were smaller than those fraire Goncort had in his hut, and many of them had magnificent pictures drawn on their pages with inks of vibrant red and blue—even gold.

But that was not ink, Johana explained to Azalaïs. It was a sheet of real gold as fine as angel's wings that skilled artisans rubbed onto the parchment. Azalaïs longed to see what domna Jordane was reading, but something stopped her from confessing that she knew her letters.

"Can you not sing, or play the citole?" domna Jordane asked one day when everyone languished in the hall, its wooden shutters closed against the intense, summer heat.

Azalaïs could not refuse to answer her, and did not want to lie. "I can sing, but all I know are the chants I was taught in the abbey."

"How dull." Domna Jordane gave Azalaïs a vicious pinch on the ear for giving her an answer she did not like. "But if you can sing at all, you must learn some more entertaining songs. At least we know your voice will not break!"

Domna Jordane's pointed jest made all her ladies titter. Johana was the only one who did not join in the teasing, and shot her mistress a look that would have shamed anyone else, but that domna Jordane simply shrugged off. "The next time the joglars come, we'll ask them to teach you a few tunes."

Azalaïs did not need the joglars to learn the tunes domna

Jordane spoke of. She simply listened to her mistress sing in the evenings while either domna Jordane or Johana played the citole.

Domna Jordane's husky voice brought the words of the poetry to life. The Lemozin tongue had never sounded so beautiful to Azalaïs, not since the time when fraire Goncort sang what was written on her scroll, which she had brought with her and kept hidden beneath her pallet in her alcove.

Some of domna Jordane's songs spoke of love. Sometimes she sang back and forth with a visiting nobleman, arguing some fine point of *cavalerie* using words laden with double meanings. Domna Jordane was so good at extemporizing that visitors came from many leagues away just to hear her.

But there were other songs, long ones, that barely mentioned love. These were obscure and subtle, and Azalaïs yearned to know what they meant. What were *bons oms* and *bonas domnas*, and what were the battles and sieges they witnessed? Whenever domna Jordane sang them, several of the ladies and gentlemen present exchanged watchful glances. Azalaïs wanted to understand, but kept her questions to herself, choosing simply to wait and see what happened.

After a few weeks, Azalaïs stopped asking when it would be time for her to leave. She began to doubt that there was any real reason for her to journey to Bésiers. Five years had passed since she and Azemar had parted, and who was to say that Azemar would still be waiting for her there?

With regard to fraire Goncort, Azalaïs's conscience was less at ease. He had given her a great deal of money, which she had lost through no fault of her own. And he would certainly not approve of this luxurious life.

But that, too, had not been her fault. Gradually, Azalaïs let the idea of continuing her journey slip from her mind. Within three months, she was as much a part of domna Jordane's court as any of that lady's intimates.

During that first summer, Azalaïs was amused to discover that, with the exception of domna Jordane herself, who had the duties of managing the establishment, and Johana, who appeared to be in charge of the domestic realms of food and laundry, the ladies passed entire days doing almost nothing. The only activity they indulged in was sewing. They did not make clothing, or anything useful, but worked elaborate designs upon fine linen from the Low Countries in silk thread that had come from Arabia.

To make the time pass, they gossiped about the townspeople, about politics, and marriages and alliances that were changing the landscape of the Minervois day by day.

"If we have one more baron come down from the north and marry a lady from one of our families, soon we will simply be part of France!" domna Jordane exclaimed after listening to a letter one of her damozels read aloud.

Azalaïs was fascinated by this letter, not because of what it contained, but because of the material it was made of. It was not parchment or vellum. It did not crack when it was folded, and could be creased as well. Its shape was a more perfect square than a sheet of parchment, whose dimensions were often determined by the natural outlines of a goatskin, and whose irregularities and mottled color were also unavoidable.

"Haven't you ever seen paper?" Domna Jordane's eyes were sharp. She never let the opportunity to tease someone slip by.

Azalaïs blushed.

"Let the lad have a closer look," the lady commanded, and they passed the letter to Azalaïs.

"How is it made?" Azalaïs asked.

"With linen, pressed very hard," Johana answered.

Azalaïs liked its feeling, but the ink soaked into the surface and the letters were not as elegant and clearly defined as they would have been on parchment. On the back were some strange characters she did not recognize. But she could not ask about them without revealing that she could read, and so she said nothing.

"They make it in the east. It's of inferior quality," domna Jordane said. "I doubt it will continue to be used."

With that, the subject of paper was dropped, and the ladies all attended to their work, calling "Azemar" to come and help them adjust their frames, or pick up a needle that had fallen on the floor.

By far the most frequent topic on those long days of languid conversation centered on knights and lords who had vowed to enslave themselves to domna Jordane—but only after she was safely married to the count from Aragon with whom her father was still negotiating. Apparently this marriage would achieve the object of combining their rich lands into one very powerful dominion.

"You are fortunate, Domna, that the Aniort properties have not been cut into little pieces," said one of the older attendants, a woman who by her headdress appeared to be a widow.

"I see nothing to celebrate in the demise of my brothers," domna Jordane retorted.

"No, but that is not the only reason your family still enjoys its wealth when so many others find themselves stripped of all their possessions."

Domna Jordane's eyes flashed bright and she drew herself up tall to face the lady who spoke those words, a young *donzel* called Katarin who had only recently joined the court. "It was my father's sensible and sound policies that preserved us."

"What some call 'sensible and sound' others might call disloyal." Domna Katarin stood and with a swish of her silk skirts left the room.

Domna Jordane frowned. Everyone else pretended to be deeply absorbed in sewing.

Azalaïs made her way nonchalantly to Johana, who remained seated, alternately looking down at her fancy work and up at her mistress. "Johana," she whispered, "What did domna Katarin mean?"

"Ma domna had two brothers who fought against the French in the last crusade. They were not heretics, but heresy was only one of the reasons King Louis IX's knights were sent to wage war on us.

"The baron d'Aniort, domna Jordane's father, made peace with the king when his sons were killed, choosing to accept peace and protection at any cost. That was more than ten years ago, when she was just a little girl, but Domna Jordane has always hated him for it."

"So," whispered Azalaïs with one eye on domna Jordane, who looked more and more angry, "domna Katarin's words were hurtful to ma domna."

"Yes, but she bides her time. If the negotiations go well, ma domna will marry into the royal family of Aragon, and her father's ties with him will be secure, thus protecting the estate from the French. Domna Katarin's father was imprisoned at Carcassonne—a baron named Montpezat gave his name under torture, along with many others, so they say—and all his lands were divided up among French knights. That is why she is here. She has nothing that would tempt a suitor."

"When shall the baron d'Aniort return? And what happened to domna Jordane's mother?"

"You ask too many questions!" hissed Johana.

Life in the Castel de Caunes followed its own, unvarying pattern of eating and sleeping and praying. Azalaïs grew and the flesh on her bones filled out with the bounty and ease of her new existence. Almost every dinner time, meats and bread, fruits and vegetables of every sort overflowed the tables in the great hall. Every evening was just as wondrous as Azalaïs's first meal in the castel, when she had recognized the rich smell emanating from the kitchens as cooking meat—even though she could not remember the last time she had eaten anything other than vegetables, bread, and fish. Yet somehow the aroma of a roasting haunch of venison reminded her of a time before memory, of a place lost to her imagination through years spent foraging and stealing, and the gentler times in the care of the good fraire Goncort.

She took her place at a table with the servants and waited for the procession to start. Roasted capons, stuffed partridges, meat pies filled with spices and dates, encased in a crust that fell apart on her tongue; whole suckling pigs bathed in a fragrant sauce; more bread than any kitchen she'd ever seen could possibly bake in hot, crusty loaves still steaming from the oven.

But most of all, the thing she could hardly believe, was that the salt was passed not just to the high table, but to every table in order of rank. By the time it reached theirs, the lowliest of all, only a few grains remained. But it was enough to make the flavors of the rich foods burst open on her tongue.

They washed it all down with young wines from the Aniort vineyards all around the city. There was enough not only to feed domna Jordane and her ladies, but also to nourish the scores of servants who performed a multitude of tasks in the fortified castel.

At first Azalaïs found it difficult to distinguish them one from another. In the kitchens were cooks, kitchen maids, spit turners, slaughterers, and a horde of menials who did everything from sweeping the floors to bringing wood to keep the ovens lit. The mangers at street level were home at some times of the year to goatherds, shepherds, and young girls who tended the poultry.

The huntsmen who lived in huts beyond the city walls

brought game for the table. The herald's bright fanfare divided the day into prayer times and mealtimes. Lineners, washerwomen, seamstresses—these all lived in their own part of the castel as well, and would sit down at the bare wood of the low table once the white linen cloths they had selected, cleaned, and mended were spread over the tables where the gentry were to sit.

Two stewards had the task of managing all the staff. There was one for the castel, and one for the lands outside the city walls, where peasants and laborers also depended on the Aniort estate for their existence.

Some servants only appeared at mealtimes. Ewers brought pitchers of water and bowls so everyone could wash his hands before dinner. The cup bearer filled the glasses of those who sat at the high table, and the wine steward selected the vintages for each meal.

Others attended to the ladies only. Three guards took it in turns to prevent any unwanted entry to the women's quarters. Attendants stood with linen towels at the ready for them when they emerged from their daily bath in the courtyard fountain. And there were the lackeys who ran errands and did odd jobs for them—Azalaïs was one of these. Even the lowest menials of all, the creatures who emptied the chamber pots, were given a seat at one of the low tables.

At the end of the evening meal, Azalaïs always felt drowsy and did not much care that her life had taken such a strange turn. It was a remarkable thing, to go to sleep with her belly full, not aching for something more and growling and keeping her awake, as it had even when fraire Goncort was taking such solicitous care of her.

Yet the ladies themselves seemed not to notice the bounty that surrounded them. They moved through their lives as though being waited upon was as natural as using the latrines after breakfast.

Dinner was the central event of every day, the one at which all the efforts of all the servants drew together to create a moment of unity that cut across barriers of rank or station, yet still preserved them in a play of ceremony.

Domna Jordane and her ladies sat at the high table interspersed with important guests from the city and beyond. The domna herself was placed in the middle of this table that sat upon a dais so that it rose above the level of the others, and everyone else was positioned nearer or farther away from her according to rank.

This domna who had taken her into her household was certainly beautiful, but gazes of admiration from men young and old glanced off her luminous exterior like arrows off a stone wall. She was always polite to every guest, man or woman, noble or *borge*, well-favored or plain. Yet she held herself apart from them, protected and remote. Her eyes remained distant, and her hands clenched and unclenched her napkin, as if whatever control she exercised over her face, her true feelings demanded to be shown by some other part of her body.

Azalaïs watched all this, taking it into her heart and turning it over and over.

CHAPTER 9

As a result of the baron's planning, Azemar arrived in Narbona in a few days with no mishaps along the way. He had been told of a secret knock he must use in order to gain admittance to the *Josiu's* home, where he would be able to replenish his supply of money, much of which he had expended on lodging and food along the way.

The man's name was Solomon, and he lived in a tall, narrow house built into the wall of the city. It looked so much as if it were part of the house next door that Azemar almost walked right past it.

"Tomorrow," said Solomon, "You will visit menher Corbiu. He will take you in, saying that you are his nephew. Once you are of his household, come to me only when you need money, and under cover of darkness. Otherwise we must have no contact whatsoever." The Jew gave Azemar the name of an inn where he could stay for the night.

As he rode through the crowded streets of Narbona, Azemar tried to comprehend all the changes that had been wrought in his life so recently. Seated atop a fine palfrey with his pouch full of money and bearing a letter of introduction from a nobleman, the world lay at his feet. Everywhere he had stopped on the way people treated him with respect, called him "Menher" and gave him the best seat at the table and the choicest bits of meat. While the baron had been fair to him—more than fair, teaching him for all those hours to learn his letters and arithmetic—the gulf between them had always existed. Now, without the old man there to serve as a contrast, Azemar felt the full effect of the superiority he had acquired by being the favored dependent of a baron.

"Ooh! Look at that one! Fresh from the country I'd wager."

The coarse comment provoked raucous laughter. Azemar looked to see where it came from, and blushed to the roots of his hair when his eye fell upon the exposed breast of a whore, standing in the doorway of a brothel with a crowd of her cohorts behind her. He continued riding, hoping that the inn he was going to would be in a different part of town.

As he proceeded, the foot traffic became denser and his progress slowed. He had never seen so many people of different stations and conditions so close together before in his life. Fine ladies paraded by in silks and jewels and beggars with hardly a scrap of clothing held out their bowls at their feet. Men wearing long robes and carrying books hastened among them, some focused straight ahead, others casting sidelong glances at the ladies, the whores, or both.

Azemar passed by the cathedral, which was only partly completed, and then the public baths. The inn was on the western edge of the town, near Corbiu's house, Solomon had said.

Despite his exhaustion from a full day's riding, Azemar's eyes would not shut as he lay on the pallet in the men's sleeping room of the inn, surrounded by other travelers. It seemed curiously broken into pieces, this world he had discovered since the time he ran from the Catelots. In his present state, between homes, between lives, he looked from the outside at everyone and everything and tried to make sense of it.

He had thought he understood the place of the farm,

Montpezat's and the peasants' threads of the tapestry that made up the Midi, having spent the last several years intimately connected with it, yet as it receded from him, he wondered if his vision was entirely accurate.

He had only a faint knowledge of the world complete in itself for the monks, priests, and bishops of the Church, and the elusive heretics who caused them so much trouble. Although he had touched it in a fashion, he suspected from all he'd heard and seen that most wealthy nobles had their own manner of existing, quite unlike Montpezat's.

The merchants like Corbiu formed yet another slice of the Midi, one that he would soon inhabit, although as yet he knew little more than how it bore upon the world of farming. He had an image of commerce as a fearsome engine, hurtling goods from one end of the world to the other, across stormy seas and over hostile lands.

And what of the knights and crusaders? There was hardly a life in the region that had not been scarred by events no one dared speak of, and that Azemar could only guess at from Fontredil's songs, and from obscure comments made by Montpezat.

The bolts and pegs that attached all these worlds to one another and prevented them from rolling apart were the bond servants, peasants, artisans, and laborers—the class through which Azemar passed on his way to becoming a gentilòme .

"Do it again, pretty," muttered a voice from the other side of the dark room. Someone was dreaming.

There, thought Azemar, was the most mysterious of all lives: the one inside one's mind and heart. Each person carried a world within him, too. He knew that he would have to search in himself for guidance through everything that lay ahead. Azemar hoped that he was strong enough for the task.

The next morning, Azemar followed Solomon's instructions and found the house of the merchant quite easily. It was large, with a stable at street level and glass panes in the windows in the three floors up above. Clearly the man prospered.

Azemar slid off his horse and approached a groom digging stones out of a horse's hoof. He drew a deep breath before he spoke.

"Menher Corbiu expects me. I am Azemar. The baron de Montpezat sent me."

The servant did not let go of the horse's hoof, but craned his head around on his neck and stared at Azemar. After contemplating him for a moment, he turned back and continued his task.

"*Perdon*, but I am here to see Menher Corbiu," Azemar repeated.

Very slowly, the servant placed the horse's hoof down on the ground, wiped his hands off on his leather apron, and stood. "Why, Menher, do you tell me this?"

"Is this not Corbiu's house?" he asked.

"*Oc*, it is," he said. "But if you just go up those steps there's a door you can knock on, and they'll let you in."

He said nothing more, but turned and sat down again to continue his task.

Azemar's face reddened. How foolish and raw he must seem even to the servants in this city! He climbed the stone steps and pounded his fist on the door. After a moment or two it creaked open. There stood an old lady, Azemar guessed by her clothing another servant, who said nothing, but opened the door wider so that he could enter.

"But my horse," Azemar said.

"Raolf!" yelled the woman, startling Azemar. In a moment, a stable boy appeared at the bottom of the steps. "Get 'is horse," she instructed him. The lad obeyed her without a word. Azemar entered the house.

Menher Corbiu, a man in his middle years, not tall but square-shouldered and proud, met Azemar in the entryway before leading him to a room at the back of the dwelling. Corbiu took the parchment Azemar gave him and read it in silence while Azemar shifted from foot to foot. When he finished, he cast it aside on a table nearby.

"Follow me," said the merchant.

He led Azemar to the top of his large house, up three flights of wooden stairs. "This is the only spare chamber I have at present," he said, opening a low door. "I shall have it more properly furnished in due course."

Azemar put his pack in the room. It's a storeroom, he thought, surveying the dark space, which had only a tiny window to let in the daylight.

"Now come with me."

Corbiu led Azemar back to the main floor of the house. This fine city dwelling was quite different from the baron's castel. It was smaller, but more comfortable. Although there was no need of them yet, Azemar could see that the fireplaces might actually heat the rooms, whose ceilings were much lower than those in the castel.

There was a room for eating and a room for receiving guests. The merchant had beautiful wool hangings on his walls, which gave the spaces an even greater feeling of warmth and comfort. Azemar saw from the window in the dining hall that the kitchens were situated across a courtyard, connected by a covered walkway a safe distance from the back of the house.

"Today is the ladies' bath day," Corbiu said to Azemar, sitting across from him at the large table in the dining room, "and so my wife and daughters are not here at present. We may speak candidly."

Corbiu's eyes became hard and his expression serious. "I welcome you into my home because I owe a debt beyond imagining to your patron. I shall see that you are trained in the ways of commerce and the ways of war, and ensure that you are well connected, perhaps procure for you a post in the viscount's household, or help you secure some other position of importance.

"What you make of your opportunity is in your hands. When you are not in my house, I expect you to conduct yourself with propriety and decency. While you are under my roof, your behavior must be exemplary. Above all, you must stay away from my daughters."

It took Azemar a moment to understand Corbiu's words. It had never occurred to him that this could be the reason for the merchant's cold reception of him. "Menher! I assure you—"

"Whether or not that was your design, I must tell you that I have already chosen their husbands, and our position in the city depends upon concluding these marital alliances successfully."

Azemar stood up from the table. "I came here only because the baron asked me to. I had no idea that you have daughters, or indeed anything at all about you beside the fact that I am to claim you as my uncle."

"I have offended you," Corbiu said. "Please, sit down. I only wanted to make my position quite clear before there was any chance for misunderstanding."

They continued talking for a while. Corbiu offered to have two new suits of clothes made for Azemar, in the fashion popular in the cities now. "I saw that you brought with you a citole," he said.

Azemar, thinking that Corbiu wanted to take advantage of his ability to play and sing in order to entertain his family, replied, "Yes, Menher. I would be happy to help your family pass the evening hours pleasantly by—"

"I forbid you to play it, or to sing, in this house."

Azemar was taken aback by Corbiu's response, but went on to enumerate the other skills he had learned at the baron's castel. "I can be helpful to you. I'm accustomed to working," said Azemar. "The baron taught me to read and write."

Just as Corbiu began to explain his business as a merchant of wine and silk, a commotion erupted toward the front of the house. The door opened and shut, and the excited chatter of young female voices echoed throughout the dwelling.

"But Mamà!" said a girl with a whine in her voice, "I wanted the red velvet!"

"Red is no color for a virgin, and it's too costly," came the sharp reply.

What sounded like a crowd of people approached the room rapidly.

"Is he in there?" the woman asked, and did not wait for an answer, but burst through the door and went directly to Corbiu to kiss him on both cheeks. She had in her train three young girls, the oldest of whom looked to be about fifteen, a year or two younger than Azemar, and all three were close enough in age to be rivals.

They were pretty and lively, and at first Azemar's eyes were so surprised by such a spectacle of exuberant femininity that he could barely distinguish one from the other. They rushed up to their father and clustered around him, all speaking at once, until he cast his eyes in Azemar's direction and the chatter stopped instantly.

The eldest girl blushed, the next younger girl bit her lip, and the youngest stifled a giggle. Domna Corbiu approached Azemar and gave him her hand to kiss. He bowed over it politely.

"This is Azemar de Tolosa, the son of a distant cousin. He has come to the Narbonès to learn a trade." Corbiu made the introductions, and Azemar noticed that instead of saying this in his calculating, critical air, he gave the impression that his nebot's arrival was both welcome and expected.

"My wife—your *Tanta* Corbiu—our daughters, your cosins: Elionor, Estacada, and Trescalana." Each girl curtsied at the mention of her name. The eldest daughter, Elionor, blushed still more deeply.

The introductions silenced everyone. Azemar decided perhaps he should be the one to say something. "It is very kind of you to give me shelter."

This brought forth another giggle from Trescalana. 'Na Corbiu frowned at her and pinched the girl's arm.

"I need some time with my nephew, *familha*. We'll meet again at dinner."

The female Corbius filed out obediently.

As soon as the ladies left, Corbiu reverted to his stern tone. Azemar wondered why this wealthy, confident merchant was so frightened of him.

"We must walk out into the city and I shall introduce you as we go. Once everyone sees you with me, and understands that you are now part of my family, you will be treated with great respect. Do not abuse it! It is my reputation—and my money—that will procure for my daughters advantageous alliances."

They strolled through the streets of Narbona which, in the glory of a late autumn morning, appeared more beautiful than they had the evening before. It was a fine city whose proximity to deep lagoons fed by the sea and the River Aude had made it a prosperous port for longer than anyone could remember.

It was not yet midday, and the air was fresh with a breeze that blew in off the sea. It seemed as if the entire city was out to enjoy the weather and greet their friends and neighbors. Many people bowed and curtsied to Corbiu. Clearly Azemar's "uncle" did not exaggerate his position in Narbona.

Yet the sheer quantity of people and their closeness to him made Azemar uneasy. City life would not be like farming, he could see. There everyone joined to achieve the same result: a good harvest, whether it was wheat, apples, or grapes. Here, Azemar thought he would never be able to learn the intricacies of people's livelihoods and ranks. He hoped that his new bene-factor would not find him dull and slow.

CHAPTER 10

When the courier came with a letter from her father, Jordane had just finished dressing and was on her way to the courtyard.

"Ma Domna, the baron said I was to make certain you read it right away, and to wait for your answer."

"Go to the kitchens and take some refreshment. I will read this and call for you when I am finished."

The courier bowed and made his way down the stairs and across the courtyard to the lean-tos from which the smell of cooking emanated. Jordane retraced her steps, started toward the solar, then thought better of it and turned toward the circular donjon. The ladies never went there, and she wanted to read her letter in private, give herself time to react to it on her own before everyone knew her business.

The circular room at the top of the donjon had once been occupied by a sentry at all times, day and night, in the time of the crusades against the heretics. Jordane and her family were not heretics, but they had many respected friends who were, and had given them shelter when the knights passed through. This made them fair prey. Now that her mother Domna Esclarmonde d'Aniort was dead and her father an ally of the French, they need no more fear attack or siege, and so the watchtower was generally empty.

Jordane unrolled the scroll and read. She was more curious than anxious. She had never received a letter from her
father before.

Filha,

*The matter we spoke of when I was last in Caunes has
become urgent. I found it necessary to confer with
Senher d'Arblay, the king's emissary and the man you
so rudely turned away from our castel last year when he
arrived in my absence. Let me tell you that your actions
have made such conferences as I have had with him very
awkward, since he is not a forgiving man.*

*As to forgiving, you must count yourself fortunate
that your refusal to send for a physician because he was
French, when his ministrations might have saved your
mother's life, did not result in my immediately sending
you into seclusion. Instead, I have taken it upon myself
to improve your fortunes through matrimony. I hope to
have some definite word to bring to you when I return
to Caunes.*

*I send this word ahead that you may prepare yourself to
be obedient and put yourself in the right frame of mind
for an honorable marriage.*

Aniort

She hadn't really expected endearments or apologies. Her
father had always been a remote figure, softened only by her
mother's intercession. Still, his reminder about the matter of
the physician was cruel. Jordane had agonized over it. It was
Domna Esclarmonde herself who vowed never to let a French

apothecary near her. But she was in her grave, and could not come to Jordane's defense any longer.

And now, the baron was going to torment her by allying her to someone approved by the King of France. *But I am to marry the Aragonese count,* Jordane thought, reading the letter through again, not willing to understand what her father was telling her, that new negotiations were taking place. If he was speaking with d'Arblay, then the match would certainly be one favorable to the French. *Ma Maire,* Jordane thought, *don't let him do it. I would rather die than disgrace your memory by marrying a French noble!*

Jordane rolled up the parchment again. The courier awaited her response. What response could she give? To hurl angry words at her father would possibly bring him back to Caunes, or cause him to send a detachment of guards to watch over her. There was nothing to do for the moment but pretend to be the dutiful daughter.

She took a circuitous route back to her bedchamber so that she did not have to pass through the solar and answer the questions of her ladies, who by now must have heard that a courier had come—such event was unusual enough to be talked of for days. Quickly, Jordane scratched a note to her father.

I am your obedient servant,

Jordane

She could not bring herself to say more, only hoping that those few words would be adequate to give her more time to decide what she would do.

By the time she reached the solar, Jordane was ready with a story to tell the ladies concerning what her father wrote with such urgency.

"He writes to me to say that he has hopes that I will be

married in the spring, and to bid me begin preparations." No need to tell them who she was supposed to marry. The general expressions of delight assured her that her evasion was success-ful. Only Johana did not join in the rejoicing. Later she would tell Johana all.

CHAPTER 11

Jordane's message from her father had arrived two years after Azalaïs joined the small court at Caunes. Azalaïs had grown taller, and found it increasingly necessary to bind her breasts tightly to her chest in order to remain in her masculine disguise. No one troubled much about her, though, as long as she did as she was told and entertained them. She only wished she could bathe properly, especially when she had her courses.

On one occasion, Johana came upon her rinsing the blood out of her braies. For a moment Azalaïs thought her secret would be discovered and she would be sent away. But the damozel simply assumed that her old wound had opened again, and gave her the recipe for a healing salve.

Azalaïs would never have known that anything could disrupt the tranquility of this small world if it weren't for a series of events that began on a day that started out much like any other. It was a market day, and the weather was fine enough—not too hot or windy—so that the ladies gathered themselves and a small army of guards and servants for a parade out through the castel yard to the town. Everyone they passed doffed their hats and bowed, but none of the noble train seemed to notice how their progress interrupted the daily activities in the castrum.

With their livres and silver marks the ladies strolled

through the market and purchased lengths of silk and velvet from the east, perfumed oils, saffron and golden trinkets, and returned to the castel, the lackeys following behind laden with their purchases.

All domna Jordane herself ever bought, though, was ink, quills, and parchment. Azalaïs suspected that it was Johana who saw to her mistress's wardrobe and jewels so that she would be fittingly attired and adorned.

The entire entourage had just rounded the corner to the town square when a disturbance broke out in a butcher's stall.

"Shoo! Ye beast, off of there!" The butcher's wife waved a long stick above a rack of skinned rabbits. Azalaïs could not see what provoked her strange antics, but everyone around the poor lady was laughing and shrieking.

Azalaïs approached to get a closer look. At first she thought her eyes and ears deceived her. But then she heard a shrill cry like the one Savïeza used to make when he spotted a mouse in the corner of fraire Goncort's hut, followed by the wing whir and the "*grrrk*" that had once been such a commonplace in her life. *It couldn't be,* she thought. She had long since resigned herself to the belief that Savïeza had either been killed, or simply made his home in the wild somewhere when he could no longer find her after her attack in the forest.

When she saw that one of the owl's wings was slightly bent, she no longer doubted it was her cavèc. She held her fist aloft, clucked and trilled. The owl stopped his flapping and swiveled his head around, then dove down and lit upon her hand. At first, Domna Jordane, Johana and the rest of the ladies shrank back in alarm.

"He won't hurt you," Azalaïs said. "His name is Savïeza."

A crowd gathered around them, keeping a respectful distance. "Is he a sorcerer?" a voice asked.

Azalaïs laughed. "No! I saved him when he was an owlet and had a broken wing. Now, well, it seems that he finds me wherever I go."

"Owls are bad omens," an old lady in the crowd said. No one paid her any heed.

"My," said Domna Jordane, "you are an extraordinary one, Azemar."

As they turned to wend their way back to the castel Azalaïs noticed a man standing a little behind the crowd, gazing at all of them with a peculiar expression. He was dressed like a peasant, but something fierce and proud in his face made Azalaïs suspect that, like herself, he was not as he seemed.

"Come along! We shall be late for the games," Johana said, drawing Azalaïs's attention back to the ladies.

Azalaïs stole a glance at Domna Jordane, who had fallen silent. Her cheeks, normally an even, rosy hue, were blotched bright pink. When Azalaïs looked back to see if the fellow was still there, he had vanished into the crowd. A chill ran down the back of her neck. There was a secret here, she was certain.

This odd moment brought to mind others that she had overlooked because they were too small to amount to much. But now with the addition of this one, they began to link together. Lately domna Jordane had been receiving letters that she kept private rather than read them aloud to her ladies, hand over to Claris the trobador to sing, or sing them herself to his accompaniment on the vielle, and she had been more than usually distant at dinner.

Her donzellas, too, had exchanged more than the normal number of meaningful glances when she snapped at some seemingly innocent comment. Azalaïs hoped she would find an opportunity later, when everyone was silly with wine, to ask Johana about it.

Before that time, though, they were going to watch two cockerels fight in a pit until one of them was dead. It was a brutal, bloody spectacle, and no matter how many times in the last two years Azalaïs had been forced to observe it she could never accustom herself to it. The ladies made wagers with one another to predict the winner.

Azalaïs had been even more horrified when Johana told her that in the north, when the men were not away on a crusade, there would be elaborate tournaments where knights fought instead of cockerels. Usually these were jousts or *targas a plaser* and the men were not killed, she said, but there was blood enough to satisfy thrill-seeking ladies. Once in a great while, two men had such a bitter rivalry that they would fight *a l.otrança*, to the death. But such entertainments were not common in the south, and in any case had been banned by the pope.

Savïeza provided a wonderful excuse for her to return to the castel without them, though. "He'll spoil the fight," she said, knowing that her fierce little owl would see in the distracted cockerels an easy dinner.

That evening of Savïeza's arrival, Azalaïs noticed that domna Jordane was unusually pensive and quiet. To suit her mood, Claris sang some common popular songs full of love and longing, which Azalaïs had heard before. She could have been mistaken, but it appeared to Azalaïs as though the castellane of Caunes might cry at any moment. She wondered if domna Jordane's odd frame of mind had anything to do with the man she had noticed in the marketplace earlier that day.

After about five songs, the musician handed his citole to domna Jordane. She shook her head, but the ladies all clamored for her to play and sing.

Domna Jordane, usually so eager to show off her skill, took the instrument reluctantly. At first she simply stroked her long fingers across the strings, not picking out any tune. Then she took the plectrum in her right hand and started up a song with her earthy voice, a song that was like no other that Azalaïs had ever heard. Its melody roamed around and teased, and domna Jordane's voice rose and dipped beguilingly, sometimes bending notes with such subtlety that one could hardly tell she was doing it. Her song spoke of a love that could not be. When she finished, the ladies all sighed at once.

Domna Jordane said nothing, rose, and signaled to Johana that it was time to retire for the night.

When she looked back on those days later, after events that changed her entire view of the world, Azalaïs realized that it was at that moment, when Savïeza returned, that her life took a turn from which it never recovered. The cavèc may not have been the cause of the alterations to come, but he was forever associated with them in her mind.

It all began the next day, when the ladies gathered to eat their morning meal.

"I expect we'll finally have news of the wars in the holy land when the baron d'Aniort returns," said a damozel named Jehanne as she sipped her tisane.

Her words went unchallenged in the early morning silence of the solar, where everyone waited for domna Jordane's arrival.

To Azalaïs's surprise, no one commented further on the remarkable fact that the baron d'Aniort would at last come back to Caunes, a man whose name was never mentioned without some undercurrent of fear or anger.

Azalaïs could not help but wonder why. She knew of his policy of cooperation with the French, but even with a limited grasp of the complexities of the situation, Azalaïs could easily understand how a noble who valued his domain might feel constrained to do just as the baron had done. She wanted to ask Johana if there were some other reason for the dismay she read on everyone's faces, but Johana would not meet her eyes.

When domna Jordane entered the solar a short while later, her red, swollen eyes announced that she had been crying.

Everyone pretended not to notice. No one mentioned the baron d'Aniort's name again that day.

Despite the pall that had settled over the household, Azalaïs burned with curiosity to see the liege lord of the region, the highest ranking noble since the fall of the Viscount of Trencavel, whom no one would even describe to her when she asked. She positioned herself where she would be able to get a good look at him when he strode into the great hall to greet his assembled household shortly before dinner that very night.

She did not know exactly what she expected, but certainly not a short, stocky knight with a sunburnt face and black hair. Domna Jordane was taller than her father by nearly a hand's breadth.

"*Bon vespre*, Paire," domna Jordane said as she knelt down on one knee and waited for his benediction.

"*Filha*," he said, and touched her head as quickly as he could. This show of affection, no doubt designed for the benefit of the spectators, had the effect instead of bringing the cool relationship between father and daughter into stark relief.

The baron's presence made everyone nervous. There was none of the usual lighthearted gossip among the servants, and Azalaïs suspected there would be no dancing after the banquet either. Perhaps it was because the knight almost never smiled. Even the guests from the city, who had all arrived dressed in their most opulent finery, were silenced by Aniort's distracted air. The supper, which should have continued well past curfew, broke up early. Azalaïs wasn't really surprised when the baron left again the next day.

CHAPTER 12

Seeing her father always made Jordane feel as though a cold hand had wrapped itself around her heart and squeezed it hard. This visit, his first in three years, had been even more troubling than most. Following his disturbing letter, he had arrived to tell her that he had ended the negotiations with Aragon for her marriage settlement. He said that another suitor had been found but that until those negotiations were complete, he did not want to tell her who it was. She no longer feared, but was certain that the one fate she most dreaded would come to pass.

"Johana, I cannot let him use me as a pawn in his game with the French."

Jordane sat in front of a mirror of hammered and polished silver that had been fixed to the wall of her bedchamber. Johana stood behind her, taking off her mistress's crespine and unwinding the ribbons from her hair. Their eyes met reflected in the mirror.

"Ma Domna, I am afraid your father can do as he pleases. You are his heiress, but you are also his property." Johana's soft, brown eyes gazed steadily at Jordane's reflection.

"Why can't I just stay here? The estate needs a strong hand to manage it. I have made it more prosperous in these last years than ever it was under my father's care. He was never here. He has always been too occupied with fighting to tend to planting and reaping."

"Perhaps he fears other influences, perhaps he fears that your heart may rule over your head and you will do something foolish."

Jordane looked away from Johana's gentle scrutiny. Raimon was back. She had seen him in the marketplace, and although she had tried not to let on, she could never hide anything from this friend who had known her since childhood.

"Oh, I doubt—he—thinks at all about the state of my heart. His letter was full of mysterious hints about a conspiracy, about heretics banding together against the inquisitors."

"Hush!" Johana said. "That is dangerous talk."

"We are safe here, surely."

"In these times, no one is truly safe," Johana said as she finished taking apart Jordane's headdress and helped her out of her surcotte, unbuckled her jeweled belt, and slipped her silk blial up over her head. While her damozel folded her clothes and put them in the armoire, Jordane untied her linen shift and let it fall around her ankles. Standing there in the midst of her dimly lit room, naked and vulnerable, Jordane shivered.

"Is Ma Domna cold?" Johana asked. "Would you like to wear a night shift?"

"No, not cold," Jordane answered. She climbed in between the soft, linen sheets on her bed and pulled the fur blanket over her. Its weight comforted her. If she were soon to be married, she would sleep in this room no longer. "I hope the man I marry is handsome," she said through a yawn. "At least he could do that for me. And rather he be French than one of our own traitors."

"Good night," Johana said.

The damozel took the candle from the table with her when she lifted the tapestry that hid her own alcove. For a short while, Jordane could see a thin band of light around the edges of the heavy cloth. After a moment she heard the sizzle of Johana's damp fingers pinching the wick, and complete darkness descended.

Jordane lay awake for a long time that night. It had been so easy to let her imagination and her wishes take control of her vision of the future when her father was not there to remind her what it really held for her. Now, the fate she had resigned herself to, that she had persuaded herself would be tolerable but not enjoyable, faded away, and in doing so left a cold, hard inevitability.

At first, she thought only of how she might persuade herself to bear it. But the more she thought, the more she tossed and turned, the more the idea of sharing a marriage bed with the enemies who had killed her brothers and made her mother's life a misery became intolerable. "No," she whispered to her empty room. "I cannot do it. I shall never, ever, betray my paratge, no matter what I have to do to avoid it. This I owe to the memory of my mother at least."

But how could she avoid her fate? To run away—when she was so well known and celebrated throughout the Midi—would not be possible. Her father would send his knights after her, and no one who valued his life would consent to hide her. She cursed her striking beauty. The dark red hair that had inspired so many poetic images and flights of enthusiasm in song would mark her wherever she went, and there were not many women who were as tall as she—as tall as most men and taller than some.

"Please, God, help me find a way to escape." Jordane clasped her hands together and prayed, more fervently than she ever did at morning services.

When she awoke the next day, Azalaïs came to a decision that she knew was long overdue. It was time for her to reveal something of her past to her benefactress and ask for release from her service. The rumors and whispered hints of change had begun to frighten her, and Savïeza's return served as a poignant reminder that her time at Caunes had been nothing more than a pause on her way to Bésiers to find Azemar—if he was to be found—and take fraire Goncort's letter—which, like her scroll of poetry, had been preserved from theft by having been kept close to her body beneath her tunic—to senher le Martellier.

Immediately following morning prayers, when the ladies scattered to use the latrines and otherwise attend to their personal needs, she would approach domna Jordane. Something told Azalaïs that she must leave with her mistress's blessing rather than run away at night, and possibly be accused of stealing so that a *bayle* might find her and put her in chains.

Azalaïs stood and blocked domna Jordane's way before she reached the solar. "I humbly beg your pardon, my lady." She accompanied her words with a low bow. During her time at Caunes she had become very familiar with the courtly behavior expected of gentilòmes.

Domna Jordane turned to face her. "Yes, Azemar?"

"I think I must not stay here forever, ma Domna. I am meant to be apprenticed to a man of business. Fraire Goncort, the anchorite who cared for me, gave me this letter for him." Azalaïs retrieved the parchment scroll from her pocket.

"A letter?" Domna Jordane said. "Let me see it." She held out her hand.

Azalaïs paused. All at once she wished she had not mentioned the letter. Azalaïs had been reluctant to break the seal, placed there by fraire Goncort himself, and so had never read it. Who was to say what the anchorite had written about her? But she did not know how she could refuse to reveal it now. Indeed, no one ever refused to do anything for domna Jordane, and so she gave her the scroll.

As Domna Jordane read, her expression changed from amusement, to puzzlement, to something between the two. "It seems, Azemar, that we have underestimated you."

Azalaïs looked down at the floor in confusion.

"Why did you not tell us that you were a learned lad? That you know your letters and much beside? I have need of someone like you who could help me with some special tasks. Tasks that I would rather my ladies did not know about."

"But Domna Jordane," Azalaïs said, "Senher le Martellier expects me."

Domna Jordane smiled a slow, knowing smile. "Yes, but this gentilòme is in Bésiers, no? and I believe that, at present, you have no means with which to travel. In fact, since I discovered you on the road and friendless, you are by rights my vassal, and cannot choose simply to leave."

Azalaïs did not expect domna Jordane to invoke the rules of vassalage for someone as lowly as herself. It was unnecessary, and a bit cruel.

"Of course," Domna Jordane said, "if you would rather be set out on the street like a beggar, I will not stop you going. It would be a foolish choice, though. I know of this merchant whom you seek. He would not think of taking in so much as a bond servant that I told him could not be trusted. He has harbored Jews, and I could report him to the inquisitors."

Domna Jordane was dressed in a yellow gown. A string of amber beads joined together by links of golden chain circled her neck. A similar circlet ringed her head, and her auburn hair flowed down her back and over her shoulders. The morning sun found its way into the chamber, and one beam illuminated Domna Jordane so that she looked almost as though she were on fire. "This fraire Goncort who took care of you says that he found you injured in the woods. Like your cavèc, no? What were you doing in the woods, Azemar?" she asked.

Azalaïs swallowed hard. She did not know what to say. "I was running away."

"From what? Or whom?"

"From some men who wanted to kill me."

Domna Jordane smiled again. "When you were nothing but a little child? It seems, young fellow, that you attract such unwanted attention. You were fortunate to be found by this anchorite. But why is it you are alone? There are only a few ways to have lost both your parents and become separated from all your family, without even a grandmother or distant cousin to take you in. Perhaps those to whom you belonged, too, were fearful of having you in their midst. Perhaps you are a heretic, and have endangered us all by being here."

Azalaïs remained silent. She had no idea why she had been sent away. "I don't know anything about my past," she answered, then whispered, "I am not a heretic."

"How old were you when you lived in the woods?"

Domna Jordane walked closer to Azalaïs, who backed away slowly. "I don't know," she said, painfully aware that this was not the right answer.

Domna Jordane lifted her hand and touched Azalaïs's chin. "Such a pretty face. Do not be afraid. I will tell no one your secret. All I ask is your loyalty. Your loyalty, and one or two small favors." She dropped her hand to her side and turned her back, speaking now toward the empty room. "And once you have done these things for me, I shall reward you handsomely."

"I don't understand," Azalaïs said, as much to herself as to Domna Jordane, who whirled around to face her once more.

"You really are naïve! Still, I know I can trust you now. I can keep your secret, and you will keep mine. Tomorrow, meet me here after dinner, and I will explain."

At that Domna Jordane held out her hand, palm down, to Azalaïs. She took Domna Jordane's fingers lightly and bowed down to brush them with her lips. But as she straightened up to leave, the lady who it seemed now held absolute power over her life gripped Azalaïs's hand in both of hers.

"Promise me you will not fail! You, who will never be a man, cannot possibly understand the strength of true passion." Before Azalaïs could say anything more, Domna Jordane pressed a hard, moist kiss upon her lips, and then pushed her away. Azalaïs put her hand to her mouth and ran from the room, almost crashing into Johana as she went.

CHAPTER 13

Something happened, something of immense importance in the lives of Domna Jordane and all her attendants that prevented her from keeping the appointment she had made with the eunuch Azemar. Early the next morning, a herald arrived while the ladies still yawned over morning prayers at Prime in the tiny chapel. The steward summoned domna Jordane from there to greet him in the great hall.

"You had best tell me quickly," Jordane said, her hands clenched so tightly that her fingernails dug into her palms.

The herald, a man named Sevis who had been a member of the household as long as Jordane could remember, had come from her father. "I bring you tidings that should give you joy," he began, although the fearful expression in his eyes belied his words. "Your marriage has at last been contracted."

She knew she would not be marrying the count from Aragon. Yet it is done so quickly, she thought. Another marriage must already have been arranged at the time of his visit, and he had been too cowardly to tell her in person.

". . . and so I bid you prepare for the proxy, who will arrive in a fortnight's time from Narbona. Once you are married, you will travel there with your servants and your dowry."

Jordane's ears pricked up at the mention of Narbona. "I'm

sorry, Sevis, I thought I heard you say Narbona."

"Yes, Ma Domna," he answered with a slight bow.

She drew herself up. "Narbona?"

Sevis coughed politely. "As I said, your esteemed father, the baron d'Aniort, has successfully concluded a marriage contract with the baron de Belascon, who has extensive lands in the viscounty of Narbona."

"Belascon? You said Belascon?" Jordane chewed on the side of her finger and her eyebrows drew together in an anxious frown. "Is he not a traitor? Did he not capitulate before the end of the last crusade?"

The herald looked down at his feet. His face flushed.

"And does this baron, this traitorous baron, know who I am? How comes he to desire my hand?"

"He has heard of your beauty and wit, Ma Domna, and was pleased with the dowry your father offered. And there is more news, Ma Domna."

"What news? What has happened, Sevis?"

The poor herald looked as though he might cry. "There has been murder. Terrible, brutal murder." He paused to gain control of his voice. "Arnaud and St. Thibery, the inquisitors. And all their retinue."

Jordane felt the bottom of her stomach drop down to her loins. Surely the rebels cannot have been so foolish as to provoke the Church in so public a manner? "Are you certain?"

"Yes, I am certain, Ma Domna." Sevis let tears wash down his cheeks, making no attempt to brush them away.

"Who?"

"Not all are known. Some were a party from Montsegur. They say Berenger was among them."

She did not want to believe it, but Jordane suspected that Raimon at least knew about this, and it was not impossible, as Sevis said, that he could have taken part in the action himself. She had not seen him or heard of him since that day in the mar-

ket the week before, until she received a note from him the previous evening, asking her to meet him outside the city walls.

"Leave me," she commanded, "and request the damozel
Johana to attend me in my bedchamber."

She heard the herald's rapid footsteps fade away behind
her. *I shall not weep,* she thought, *I will not let him make me weep.*

Jordane hurried through the solar, not stopping to answer the questions of the ladies gathered there. Johana already
awaited her in her bedchamber.

"What is it? What has happened?" Johana reached out to
stroke Jordane's cheek, but Jordane turned away.

"Only that my father has insulted me by choosing the one
husband whom I cannot—I will not marry! And those fools—"

The strain was too much, and despite her wish to remain
strong, Jordane doubled over in harsh, wrenching sobs.

Johana sat next to her and stroked her hair. After a time,
Jordane calmed herself enough to speak and told Johana the
entire story.

"Perhaps it will not be such an ordeal to marry this nobleman. They say the baron de Belascon has a magnificent domain," Johana said.

"Nothing, nothing can atone for his treachery. Was it not
he who gave his own first wife to the inquisitors?"

Johana shook her head. "But after what has happened you
must marry him. Don't you see? It is the only way your father
can be sure they will not think he or his kin had any responsibility for the. . ."

"The massacre? So you heard." Secrets were not easy to
keep in that region.

Johana did not reply, but continued what she had been
saying. "Besides, you will be mistress of a great estate, greater
even than your father's."

Jordane did not know how to convey to her damozel, her
oldest friend, the revulsion she felt at the idea of marrying Be-

lascon. In her heart, she knew she did not want to marry anyone except Raimon, but would have quelled her desire for the sake of a favorable alliance and their autonomy from the French. Now, circumstances had placed her in an impossible situation.

Raimon had asked to meet her. Perhaps he intended to tell her of his bloody escapades. Only now, with her betrothal announced, she would be watched too closely to be able to escape, even for a few hours.

If only, she thought, she could get away, foil her father's plan to cement their alliance with the French and separate her forever from Raimon. If only . . .

For most of the day after the betrothal was announced, the castellane and her donzel Johana stayed closeted with the herald, and everyone else tried pretend everything was normal. But despite Jordane's efforts, whispers and conjecture flew throughout the household.

By the time Jordane entered the great hall where residents and guests were assembled for dinner, excitement about the news was at fever pitch. Domna Jordane walked calmly to her place at the center of the high table. The herald followed her and stood behind her. She gestured for all to be seated. Once everyone settled, domna Jordane raised her hand to stop the chatter. "I have received word from the baron d'Aniort that we are to prepare for a wedding," she said.

Azalaïs could feel the excitement ripple through the room.

"Who is to be married?" asked one of the young girls, daughter of a wealthy merchant in the city. Her father hushed her loudly, and everyone else tittered.

"The house of Aniort is to be allied to that of Belascon of Narbona." When Domna Jordane made her announcement, her voice had an unmistakably sharp edge.

A hush descended on the assembled company. The herald looked down at his feet. It was unlike domna Jordane to be so openly testy. Her face was dark, and her forehead wrinkled up in a frown she tried hard not to allow to extend to her mouth.

Johana stepped forward and took her mistress's hand. "This is a great day for the family of Aniort, and for the Minervois. We must all rejoice. We will now owe fealty to our brethren in the north, and be loyal subjects of King Louis IX."

The stunned silence dissolved into murmurs, which grew in volume until one man, the most senior councilor of the city, stood and raised his hand to quiet the guests. "The councilors of Caunes join in the felicitations so warmly expressed by the damozel Johana," he said. "We look forward to learning how this will affect our trade routes and local customs."

For a moment it appeared as though domna Jordane would say something, but she was silenced by a look from Johana. Instead she sat down at her place, signaling that the banquet should begin.

"Why is this bad news?" Azalaïs whispered to Johana as she went to her seat at one of the lower tables.

"Don't ask questions!" she snapped.

Azalaïs glanced at domna Jordane from time to time throughout the elaborate meal. The lady hardly touched any food, and stood to retire before the sweets had been served. She walked past Azalaïs instead of going directly across the hall, and whispered as she passed, "I require your assistance, Azemar."

Azalaïs stood and hurried after her, feeling all eyes upon her.

Once they left the great hall, domna Jordane broke into a run. Azalaïs could hardly keep up with her mistress, who dashed through corridors, past anterooms and cabinets Azalaïs had never had reason to enter, and then climbed a narrow, spiral staircase that led to a room high up in the donjon.

The breeze entered through eight slits just wide enough for an archer to shoot through that were evenly spaced around the entire circumference. No stools, cushions or hangings softened the harsh emptiness of the small stronghold, and the rafters of the ceiling were joined in obscurity some twenty feet above their heads. Azalaïs stood still in the center of the inhospitable space and watched Domna Jordane walk in swift circles around her, one hand reaching out to touch the damp stone, breathing deeply and flaring her nostrils like a horse that had been running hard for hours.

"Ma Domna," said Azalaïs, "what troubles you?"

Domna Jordane stopped in mid stride and fixed her wild eyes upon Azalaïs. "You ask what has happened? Well might you! Those foolish, brutal idiots! Arnaut and St. Thibéry have been killed, and I am to be the forfeit." Then she muttered under her breath, "He did not think of that, I wager."

Azalaïs wrinkled her brow.

"Oh Azemar, truly! You cannot be unaware who they are?" Domna Jordane commenced her furious pacing once more, her fists clenched as though she wanted to hit someone. "They are inquisitors. The Pope's emissaries. They are charged with eradicating the heresy. Finding heretics, finding our region infested with them, only strengthens Louis's claim of dominion."

Azalaïs's look of incomprehension was replaced by one of shock. First, that holy men could be murdered, then that this event could in any way affect domna Jordane. "Where did this happen?" she asked, thinking perhaps it was right there in Caunes, and that was why Domna Jordane was involved.

"To the west, in Garóna, at Avinhonet."

Azalaïs had never heard of those places, but she nodded, not wanting to seem yet more ill informed.

"Now all who confess loyalty to Rome have justification for their aggression against us. King Louis will have no more difficulty recruiting crusaders to his cause. We may as well hand him the Tolosan, the Narbonès, the Minervois on a golden platter. Then the Counties of Tolosa and Bésiers, and the vassals of the King of Aragon will owe fealty instead to the northern criminals!"

Before Azalaïs could ask her what it all meant, Domna Jordane sank to the floor and sat with her knees pulled up and her face buried between them so that she looked for all the world like a quivering, sobbing, lump of silk-covered flesh and bones.

"What shall I do? What shall I do?" she cried and rocked back and forth on her heels. Azalaïs was afraid she would harm herself when she grasped fistfuls of her red hair and pulled until it started to come out at the roots.

"Don't you want to be married, Domna Jordane?" Azalaïs asked.

The lady lifted her face from her knees. Her eyes were swollen, and her nose streamed. She took a square of linen out of her pocket and wiped her face. "Do you know what it is to be married, my knight without a spear?"

Azalaïs chose not to understand her meaning. "Marriage is a woman's duty, and I think most ladies survive it."

"Yes, they survive. But how will I survive? I, who have such a secret! I want to tell you, Azemar. . . You say you spent your youth near Bolbona. That is in the Razès, the heart of the country where they say the heretics hide. Have you never seen these heretics? It is said that they gather in the woods in the dead of night to perform their rituals."

Azalaïs knelt down on the floor. "The heretics are evil. The Pope says so. God has ordained that they be destroyed."

"It matters not what the Pope says. In two weeks I shall be barona Jordane de Belascon. Will you stay with me? . . No! I need you to take a message." Domna Jordane stood up and began her frantic pacing once again.

Azalaïs was too confused to think what she should do next, and so she stayed where she was and let her eyes follow domna

Jordane as the lady measured the small space of the chamber over and over again. Just as she had worked up the courage to say something to her mistress, domna Jordane stopped again and stared straight at Azalaïs. "Go to my chamber. Here."

She gave Azalaïs a small gold key.

"This will open a cabinet next to my bed. You'll find a scroll of parchment in there, and a pot of ink and a quill. Bring them here. But do not let anyone see that you do it!"

She took hold of Azalaïs by the elbow and propelled her out of the door so that she stumbled on the stone steps. It took Azalaïs a moment to regain her balance, but she didn't dare pause. There was no telling what her mistress was capable of.

Azalaïs flew past the entrance to the hall, where joglars still entertained the company with their ribald songs. Even the dogs that normally lurked in the passageways waiting for scraps had deserted their haunts. Shouts of "Health to Domna Jordane! *Viu* the Baron de Belascon!" echoed after Azalaïs as she sped through the vacant corridors.

Once the glow of torches and candles in the hall were behind her, Azalaïs found herself in the dark hallways that led to the solar and the ladies' quarters. Later, when everyone stumbled to bed, servants would go ahead of them and put the oil lamps in their niches and what was left of the torches in their wooden holders. Fortunately, the moon had risen and cast enough milky light through the narrow windows so that Azalaïs could find her way.

A fresh breeze blew in and brought with it the sweet scent of olive groves and vineyards in flower. Doubtless Savïeza had flown off to hunt. At that moment, Azalaïs wished it were as easy for her to escape. She had a bad feeling—that familiar, prickly sensation on the back of her neck—about domna Jordane's distraught mood and desperate instructions.

She soon located the items domna Jordane requested and returned to find her mistress still in the donjon, still pacing back and forth, wringing her hands. Jordane stopped as soon as she saw Azalaïs, grabbed the parchment and spread it out on the floor, opening the pot of ink and scratching out a message so fast Azalaïs wondered if anyone would be able to read it. When she was done, she blew on the parchment to dry the ink, rolled it up and tied it with a ribbon from her hair.

"I want you to take this to the olive grove outside the city gate, after curfew. There you will see a young man waiting for it. He will not be expecting you, he will be expecting me. This message will explain everything to him."

Domna Jordane told her that, by the western gate, there was a way to get over the wall easily. One need only make sure the sentry was asleep before attempting it. Azalaïs was about to protest, but Domna Jordane rushed away, slamming the door behind her.

Azalaïs sank to the floor. Steal out of the castel after curfew? That was against the law. Yet if domna Jordane had been expecting to meet someone after curfew that evening she had no doubt done so before.

It was too late to join the festivities in the great hall, and so Azalaïs went to her own cubby near the ladies' wing. She lay down on her straw mattress and worried. What would happen if she were caught?

There was no chance of sleep for her that night, at least not before she accomplished the errand for her mistress. Awake and fretful, Azalaïs waited until only the sound of distant breathing and dogs barking broke the stillness of the night, then rose and crept down the stairs and on through the hall to the kitchens, which were separated from the main building and open at the back to the city street.

The curfew bell had rung so no one was abroad. Azalaïs knew how to move silently, but her stomach growled for lack of food. Domna Jordane had taken her away from the banquet before she had eaten her fill. She thought perhaps she would try to find a crust of bread on her way back through later—assuming she had not been taken away to prison.

Azalaïs did not like it, not one little bit, this added complication to her already precarious circumstances. Still, there was nothing she could do but obey her mistress.

CHAPTER 14

Long before Azalaïs was born, Caunes had been besieged for a few days until the heretics who lived there either gave up or fled to Minerve. More recently, many of those who tended the surrounding vineyards had hastened inside its walls when the knights marched through on their way to attack one of the other cities, where heretics still hid.

In recent years, the general population of Caunes followed the example of the castrum's most noble family and was careful to declare itself loyal to the Church of Rome and to support the efforts of the inquisitors, promising to root out any heretics in the city and deal harshly with those who protected them. They burned one poor old, half-witted woman on a pyre to prove the point.

Azalaïs had learned all of this from the servants and retainers in the household who, seeing in the mutilated young lad a weak dependent like themselves, did not hesitate to tell her everything she wanted to know—and more.

She found out that Bésiers, the city Azemar had named as their meeting point, had been virtually destroyed long ago, with many thousands slaughtered—men, women, children, heretics, and faithful alike. The city never quite recovered.

Azalaïs wondered what it was that had prompted Azemar to name Bésiers as their place of rendezvous. He must not have been aware of its bloody history.

Azalaïs's years of practice with fraire Goncort in creeping silently through the darkened woods served her well that night. She found the place her mistress had told her about where she could leave the city without detection. The soldier whose task it was to guard this door was—as domna Jordane had predicted—fast asleep. Azalaïs's sharp eyes spotted the hand- and footholds in the stone, placed to make it easy to climb up and over to the other side, and she scampered across with the agility of a squirrel. Straight ahead, the grove of olive trees where domna Jordane told her to wait was a patch of darkness in the moonlight. She felt her pocket for the scroll. It was still there.

Having arrived a little ahead of time and found herself alone in the grove, Azalaïs rested her back against a tree, closed her eyes, and sighed. Surely this was not the life she was meant to lead. Disguised as a boy, answerable to the whim of a willful noblewoman, at the beck and call of damozels with nothing better to do than stitch elaborate designs on squares of linen—Damozels who not only thought she was a boy, but who considered her even less than one for being devoid of that essential masculine equipment.

She was not a boy. She was a woman, desperate to wear women's clothes, to learn all those womanly arts fraire Goncort had hinted at and that she had observed so closely over her years in the castel. But she'd seen enough to know that she would not want to live in a castel, where women did nothing useful, only waited for others to decide their fates in marriages or the convent. No, that life was not for Azalaïs. She pictured herself the mistress of a farmer's ostal, spinning wool and raising children and goats, occupied all day and finally sleeping when her limbs were tired of work.

Perhaps, thought Azalaïs, domna Jordane's marriage would give her the opportunity to slip away unnoticed amid all the celebrations, with only her wits to protect her and Savïeza for company. Alone, she hoped she could evade the marauding crusaders until she found somewhere else to live and thrive.

It must have been the rich, spring air, or perhaps the full moon that was now sinking toward the horizon like a slice of a ripe orange—or maybe the wind, that constant companion that rattled the branches and whooshed across the garriga through the new leaves—but Azalaïs did not hear the man approach her from behind. Before she could move a muscle, he had one hand over her mouth, and the other across her breasts.

"Don't move, Jordane. How daring of you, to dress like a boy! And how clever."

The voice was smooth and soft. The man used his lips to play gently with Azalaïs's earlobe and blew soft kisses into her ear between each word. Then he kissed down her neck, still holding her tight, but the hand on her breast searched for her nipple beneath her linen tunic. Azalaïs's knees threatened not to support her. A peculiar sensation tickled her loins. She tried to turn around to alert the stranger to his mistake, but he would not let her.

"No! You are my captive. By the laws of war I can do with you whatever I wish, or demand a valuable ransom!"

At that, the stranger whirled her around and before Azalaïs had time to say a word, had covered her mouth with his and thrust his tongue inside of it. Azalaïs pushed away from him with all her might. He finally released her, and she tumbled backward upon the ground.

"I beg you, sir, you are mistaken!" Azalaïs whispered hoarsely.

"What's this?" the gentilòme said. "Not my lady, it would seem . . . but a girl nonetheless, dressed as a boy. . . Let me look at you." He crouched down by Azalaïs and lifted her chin. "No indeed. Not ma domna d'Aniort. But you'd be a pretty thing if you wore a blial and hadn't chopped your hair off. Tell me, why are you here?"

Azalaïs handed him the letter. "Domna Jordane bade me give you this. She cannot come to meet you this evening."

"Why didn't you say before?" The stranger sounded irritated.

"I tried, but you would not let me speak." Azalaïs was glad it was dark, so that this man, who seemed quite handsome and whose face was a little familiar even in the dim light, could not see her blush.

He chuckled softly. "Yes, you are right. I stole a sweet kiss from you. Was it your first?"

"I'm to wait for some word from you, after you read this letter." Azalaïs thanked God they were in shadow and he could not see her flaming cheeks.

The gentilòme continued to glance at Azalaïs every now and again as he slowly unrolled the parchment from domna Jordane. "Do you know what this says?" he asked her. "No, it is not likely that you can read."

He held the letter so that the light from the setting moon illuminated it. As he read, his face darkened, he frowned, and when he looked up again, all trace of amusement had fled his eyes.

Azalaïs waited a moment or two, then cleared her throat. "What message shall I give to domna Jordane?"

The man crumpled up the parchment, oblivious to the waste, and paced away from Azalaïs. She stood, brushing the dirt off her tunic and hose and straightening her hood, which had twisted around in her struggle to break free of his embrace. By the time she'd done so, the man turned and strode back toward her so fast she thought he would walk right into her. She shrank back, but he reached out and caught her around the waist, pulling her to him again.

"First, a question. Does domna Jordane know you are not a boy?"

"No, Senher!"

"Why are you dressed thus?" He tightened his grip, his fingers digging into her side.

"I- I'm trying to get to Bésiers, to find my friend. I cannot travel as a lady alone."

"Very well. I won't ask you more, now. But here is the message you can give to ma domna Jordane. Mind you deliver it exactly as I convey it to you."

At that, the stranger put his other arm around her and once more covered her mouth with his, this time more gently. Azalaïs's resistance crumbled and she allowed him, now, to explore the inside of her mouth with his tongue, sending waves of that peculiar feeling into her stomach and beyond. When the kiss ended, he held her away from him.

"Mind you, do it exactly as I did, young—what is your name? I mean your real name, not the one you have taken to carry out this absurd charade."

"Azalaïs." Azalaïs could barely speak, and her name stuck in her mouth.

"So, little Azalaïs, off you go. We may not meet again, but you will soon understand more than you probably wish to."

"And your name, Senher?" She had an overwhelming desire to know the name of this man who had kissed her so passionately and with such guile.

The gentilòme chuckled. "Ask your mistress."

In an instant, the stranger was gone, running soundlessly through the shadows to return to wherever he had come from.

A breeze caressed Azalaïs's face and she trembled. There was no sense hurrying back

CHAPTER 15

"Well, was there a message or not!" Domna Jordane's voice rose.

But how to answer her? Not as the man had instructed her last night. There was only one other solution, one Azalaïs dreaded, but circumstances had combined to give her no other choice. It was as if allowing herself so much as to think about shedding her disguise had destined her to do it.

"He gave me no spoken message," she said, her mind racing to find the right words.

"So he wrote it down. Where is it?"

Azalaïs swallowed. "It was not written, either."

"Don't toy with me, you wretch!" Domna Jordane struck Azalaïs across the face with all her might, and sent her flying to the ground.

It was too much. Tears of frustration, futility, and a sense of the injustice of her position washed down Azalaïs's face.

"Stop weeping like a little girl. Be a man! You must be old enough, even without a man's voice."

Domna Jordane's skirts swished against the stone floor as she marched back and forth across the little space.

"That's just it, Ma Domna," Azalaïs choked out between her sobs. "I'm not a boy! I'm Azalaïs! A girl. And your friend found me out, and bid me tell you."

Jordane stopped her pacing. Azalaïs braced herself for another blow. But after a while, when nothing happened, she lifted her eyes.

To her surprise, domna Jordane simply stared out of one of the arrow slits. "A girl. All this time. So, you fooled us all. What did you think to achieve by that?"

"I wanted nothing, Ma Domna, I took no joy in deceiving you. I only wished to continue my journey to Bésiers. But you were so generous, I could not bring myself to leave you."

All the stress of her exhausting and eventful journey, the difficulty of maintaining her disguise at such close quarters, and the disturbing events of the night before shredded what was left of Azalaïs's dignity. She put her head in her hands and wept so many tears she thought she would dry up like the countryside in summer.

After a time, she felt a hand on her shoulder and Jordane's spice-laden scent near her face. The lady—the same one who had cuffed her so brutally—took hold of her arm and helped her to her feet.

"Come, young Azalaïs. Let us put this behind us and start again. I think, perhaps, I may need you to perform a service for me for which you would gain rich rewards."

Domna Jordane held her at arm's length and looked straight into her eyes. "Just as I thought. You are about my size. . . Yes." She paused for a long time, examining Azalaïs top to bottom. "Turn around." When Azalaïs faced her again, she said, "You say you want to go to Bésiers?"

Azalaïs nodded. But there was a look in Domna Jordane's eyes that she did not trust.

"I may not get you all the way to Bésiers, but at least to Narbona, which is closer to that city than we are here in Caunes. Come, walk with me, and I shall tell you my idea."

It was May, and already the days were hot long before they were half over. Everyone looked forward to the June rains as respite before the blazing summer. Azalaïs wondered how she would bear the months of July and August swathed in a long, lady's under tunic covered with a blial that was tied with a cord below her breasts. Her breasts, now accentuated instead of hidden.

Only two weeks had passed, and she was now fully a woman—at least, for several hours each day. It was too sudden. But in shedding one disguise, she would adopt another.

In secret, with only domna Jordane and Johana present, Azalaïs had tried on the luxurious clothes she would wear in her coming role. The blial was made of fine silk that flowed like butterfly wings as she walked, but there was so much material that it constricted her movements and lay in folds around her when she sat. Long-toed shoes threatened to trip her at every step. Johana and domna Jordane laughed at her unmercifully every time she did. It was unkind, but Azalaïs knew they did it because they, too, were anxious.

She had been given no opportunity to refuse to cooperate with domna Jordane. Of course she had wished to become a woman. But this was not the time or the place she had imagined it would happen. This way was dangerous. Being one person of no significance pretending to be another of equal obscurity was one matter. Passing as one of the most celebrated ladies of the Minervois and beyond was something else altogether.

Domna Jordane and Johana had drilled her in all the habits and gestures of a well-born lady in the privacy of domna Jordane's bedchamber after curfew and before dawn. Sometimes Azalaïs believed she would be able to do as they instructed: move with grace and stillness, every gesture calculated to set off her beauty—something she still was not quite willing to own.

Most of the time, though, her heart fluttered with fear, certain that the deception would be obvious instantly to anyone, more obvious than her disguise as a boy had been for all the past years.

Despite the assurances and cajoling of domna Jordane and Johana, Azalaïs could not imagine that she would successfully take the place of her mistress in the proxy wedding—which would occur that very day.

"Now remember: you are the only surviving offspring of the house of Aniort. You are to marry the Baron of Belascon, and the match is approved by Louis IX, king of France. Your name is Jordane de la Moux d'Aniort." Domna Jordane kept repeating the details of her life to Azalaïs.

"What shall I say when they discover I am not who I claim to be?" asked Azalaïs for the tenth time that morning.

Domna Jordane ignored her question, as she had done every time before. "You will be showered with costly gifts, and fêted and celebrated. This is the wedding the French have been waiting for, bringing together one of the greatest houses of the Minervois with one that is closely connected to the house of Capet, in France. You will be a distant relative of the king of France himself."

Azalaïs still did not entirely understand why domna Jordane refused to go through with the marriage herself. Surely her passion for an obscure lover could not be enough of an excuse to defy her father, who, according to Johana, had spent months negotiating, deciding which properties were to remain under whose control and how big a dowry domna Jordane should have. He had done all this in secret. Domna Jordane had no idea anything had changed concerning her intended suitor until her father's visit, when he told her she would not marry the count from Aragon.

And besides, the marriage originally planned would also not have been with the man Azalaïs had met outside the city walls. The fellow who had kissed her was no count, she was certain. His local accent was enough to give him away, if his lack of manners hadn't already indicated that he could not be so well born.

Johana explained as much as she could about what would happen during the impending marriage and what her life would be like while she bathed Azalaïs in a large wooden tub draped with linen and filled with hot, scented water. Domna Jordane remained in the room, adding any details that Johana left out.

"What will you do, my Lady, while I am in your place?" Azalaïs asked domna Jordane.

"That, wench, is no concern of yours! The less you know, the safer we'll all be." domna Jordane exchanged a look with Johana that surely meant something, and sent a chill right into Azalaïs's bones.

"Will Johana come with me, or stay with you?"

"I'm to go with you, Domna," Johana said, mockingly adopting the mode of address she would have to use in order to carry off the deception.

At least that would be something. She would not be entirely alone.

Johana helped Azalaïs out of the tub. Before she could wrap her in a long, linen towel, Domna Jordane stepped up to Azalaïs and took her by the shoulders, pinning her to her spot with the gaze of her deep, golden eyes.

"Don't worry. The baron has no idea what I look like, and will be quite happy with you, I'm sure." She glanced up and down Azalaïs's naked body. "By the time my father finds out, it will be too embarrassing for him to acknowledge that we have played this trick. He sent word that he would not be at the wedding, and is unlikely to visit Narbona before winter, and by then you might be carrying an heir to this dreadful travesty of an alliance."

An heir, and all that such a thing entailed. Azalaïs's dread grew with every new realization. She had no doubt that this deception would be far more dangerous than her last. Before, it was only she herself who stood to gain or lose by her lies. Now, many powerful people might be harmed by them.

In her guise as Azemar, she had come to a vague sense of where she belonged in the world, what station could be hers. She had learned how to serve, how to fit in, how to be invisible. She could hide her true self easily, because she was never on display, never at the center of anything, only looking in from the outside.

Now, Azalaïs tried to imagine herself in a position where her every gesture, every word would be watched and weighed. She perspired and shivered at the same time. Her treachery was certain to be discovered, and if it was, she could face punishment of unimaginable harshness.

Very little about this "favor" she had been forced to do for domna Jordane gave her any peace. Her one comfort was that at least she would be in the Narbonès, near to the city of Narbona itself, which was closer to Bésiers. Perhaps once she was there, she might somehow be able to make inquiries about Azemar. She would have servants of her own, and means at her disposal. She might as well, Azalaïs thought, take advantage of her position of influence while it lasted.

It seemed a lifetime ago that she and Azemar had run from Gascon. Although she would never want to face the terrors of that wandering life again, Azalaïs often thought fondly of the time just after they ran away, of fraire Goncort's simple, quiet existence, absorbed with trying to help all living things. It was so different from the world that was about to engulf Azalaïs, where nothing was as it appeared, where if someone helped you, it was only to further a cause of her own.

An hour before the wedding, after Johana had artfully woven Jordane's shorn hair into Azalaïs's duller light brown locks so the color would not appear too different from what the baron might expect, she draped thick, white veils over Azalaïs's head so that no one would be able to see her face clearly. Only then did Jordane appear wearing the boy's clothing Azalaïs had given her.

The fit was perfect. It surprised Azalaïs how like a boy that lady appeared simply by wearing different clothes, and she understood how people who had seen her never looked past the surface, accepting what was before their eyes without question. The heiress of Caunes, hair cut short, could easily pass as a young man not yet old enough to grow a beard.

The agents of the baron were due to arrive at any time. After the proxy marriage, Azalaïs would be made to wear an iron chastity belt until she was safely ensconced in the castel near Narbona, under the protection of her husband's guards.

"There is one thing you must teach yourself how to do, for there is no time for me to instruct you now," Domna Jordane said to Azalaïs. "You know that if I possess any talent or renown, it is for writing songs. You have often enough heard me sing and play. Here are some verses I have written in the past, and a book that tells a little about how to write the tunes and the words. Study them, and try to do the same. If you do not, our deception will be suspected all the sooner. As long as you write something each month, you will be doing as I have done."

At that, domna Jordane gave Azalaïs a small book, beautifully bound in leather and gilt, together with a scroll of several uncut sheets of parchment—more than Azalaïs had ever seen in her life—and a fine quill and a pot of ink colored with woad. Perhaps, she thought, gently stroking her fingers over the parchment, there would be compensations she had not yet imagined in pretending to be domna Jordane.

At first Jordane felt unclothed wearing only a short tunic and hose. She cried when Johana cut her hair—her beautiful hair—as short as a boy's, then plaited it and fixed it to the much duller ends of Azalaïs's hair.

Yet by denying her beauty, she had secured her freedom. That was worth all the admiration in the world. And without making such a dramatic change, she saw no other way to avoid this marriage. That young girl, who had so successfully played the part of a boy, had given her the idea. And she was pretty, too, and tall. If someone of low birth with few talents could carry off such a role, then so could she.

Jordane planned to disappear quietly from the castel while everyone attended the marriage ceremony. Best to get away before she could have a change of heart.

Everything had happened so fast, she had not had any opportunity to tell Raimon about her scheme. She could hardly steal out to see him, and writing to him about it would have been too dangerous. There was no guaranteeing that she would even be able to find the knight, whose involvement in the murders at Avinhonet had driven him into hiding.

That, thought Jordane, was unfortunate—even shameful. The messenger had described the scene to her. The unarmed priests, their heads nearly severed, the floor awash in blood. And had it achieved their ends? Perhaps it frightened the clergy. But it would only make France more aggressive against them all—and now, justifiably so. Jordane suspected from hints Raimon had dropped in his previous letter that he would flee south to Tolosa or Perpignan, ultimately to the mountains and to the kingdom of Aragon beyond.

Jordane had never been as far away as that, nor had she traveled anywhere without an entourage of damozels and servants, and whenever she journeyed beyond the walls of Caunes, at least several archers and occasionally a knight accompanied her. She felt curiously invisible walking through the streets alone. Having been accustomed to drawing all eyes to her wherever she went, she found it both freeing and mortifying to be able to pass through a crowd and not attract the slightest notice.

The worst part about running away like this was having to leave her citole, her vielle and all her books behind. She hoped that Azalaïs would appreciate them, and do justice to the reputation of the heiress of Caunes. She herself must take care, she realized, not to yield to the temptation to sing, at least not until she was many leagues away.

Jordane took a position at the back of the crowd of common folk who lived within the city walls, gathered to watch their liege lady emerge from the chapel and climb into the waiting wagon. Outside of the city the rest of the caravan was at the ready with all the items specified in the dowry. Its wagons, donkeys, and oxen stretched nearly a league along the road.

"It won't be the same without her. The baron is not so generous to the merchants, and imports many of his goods from the north," said an old man in a long tunic standing right in front of her to a similarly clad man to his right.

"No, but the damozels who will stay behind, they will still need silks and jewels," the other answered.

"You think they will remain without domna Jordane to protect them? No, nothing has been right since the barona died."

They were right. Nothing had been the same since her mother's death. Her father might bring French ladies and their knights to Caunes, and who would know what their tastes might be? Jordane shook her head to rid herself of the image of a French woman taking her place as castellane, perhaps marrying her own father and becoming a new barona d'Aniort. She would prefer it if he took in one of the prostitutes who lived in a house on the edge of the city.

An expectant hush descended on the waiting citizenry. Jordane could feel everyone lean forward en masse, craning to get a look at the lady who was now barona de Belascon emerging from the proxy wedding in the church.

The herald stepped out first and put his hunting horn to his lips. Three harsh blasts announced the emergence of the bride and the baron's representative.

Jordane had left before the proxy arrived, and now stifled a laugh when she saw Azalaïs standing next to a wizened old man with a long, gray beard. It was an insult, calculated to put domna Jordane d'Aniort in her place, no doubt.

Azalaïs walked tall, though, just as they had taught her. Johana was right behind the "couple," eyes fixed to the ground in front of her. The sight of her closest friend brought a surge of doubt to Jordane's heart. She blinked away impending tears. *I am free, I am free,* she repeated to herself. And although no one knew it, her father's attempt to bring the most spirited noblewoman of the Minervois to heel had failed.

It might be months—or even years—before anyone discovered how thoroughly he had been out maneuvered.

CHAPTER 16

"Keep your hair covered for as long as possible," Jordane had said. Then, just before Johana lowered the veils over Azalaïs's face, Jordane took her hands. "I shall never forget that you have done this for me," and kissed her forehead.

The baron had sent his elderly tutor to be his representative, and the man had almost no teeth and smelled of rotting vegetables.

Azalaïs remained swathed in veils through the entire proxy wedding. She was doubly glad no one could see her. Not only was there little chance she would be recognized, but the tears that streamed down her cheeks and made her nose run would remain hidden from view.

Now she sat in a wagon opposite Johana, wearing the chastity belt that three servants had to watch her put on, still veiled out of modesty, Johana told them. The key was with the old tutor, who had ridden on ahead to prepare the baron's castel in the Narbonès for the bride's arrival.

The wagon had a frame and covering similar to the one that had brought Azalaïs to Caunes three years before, only it was even more beautiful. Silk tapestries hung on the inside, and the wooden seats were covered with cushions stuffed with feathers.

Only one thing comforted Azalaïs in her bizarre reversal of fortune. Just as she was about to climb into the conveyance that would take her and Johana the ten leagues to her new home, she heard Savïeza's gentle *grrrk*, and her lovely little cavèc landed on her outstretched hand. Before anyone noticed him Azalaïs climbed into her seat. Now Savïeza sat quietly sleeping by her side.

The journey was slow, mainly because they were accompanied by an army of pack animals with all the various items specified in domna Jordane's dowry, and three shepherds drove the herd of livestock that was included in the settlement. There were linens and vats of olive oil, silver bowls and tankards, lengths of lace and silk, two or three handsomely carved chests filled with other household items, and much more.

Azalaïs wished she were seated upon a horse rather than riding in the wagon, which jolted and lurched with each tree root or rut in the road. The chastity belt soon rubbed bloody sores on her belly and inner thighs. Even walking the distance from Caunes to Narbona would have been preferable to the uncomfortable wagon.

From just before the wedding until well along the journey, Johana did not look at Azalaïs, but kept her eyes down, watching herself thread and unthread her fingers together as though she were deciding how best to arrange them. Her eyelashes glittered, and every once in a while a tear dropped onto her gown. Johana had been with domna Jordane all her life. This separation would be difficult for both of them.

Azalaïs did not comment on Johana's silence, but let her nurse her private grief, instead going over and over in her mind the details of her new background and other facts that had been crammed into her head in the last two weeks.

The caravan had to stop for the night at an inn near Lézinhan. Johana helped Azalaïs secure her veils before descending from the wagon. They were too close to Caunes still to trust that she would not be recognized.

It was here, at this halfway point, that the drover and servants from Caunes would be replaced with some from Belascon who were already awaiting their arrival. Johana saw to it that the Caunes servants were rewarded for their pains while Azalaïs lay down on the bed she would share with Johana that night.

Despite her fatigue, Azalaïs could not sleep. Now that the formalities of the "wedding" were over, the extent of the differences between the life she used to lead and the one that had been forced upon her by domna Jordane were all too apparent, and fulfilled her worst fears. In her wakefulness she heard every creak of wood and snore in the inn around her while her mind raced trying to think of a way out of this impossible situation.

Before they set out the next morning, Johana helped Azalaïs put some soft linen pads between her skin and the places where the chastity belt had rubbed and she felt much more comfortable. Despite her fears about the night she must soon spend with her new husband, Azalaïs was eager to get the thing off.

"How much longer?" she asked.

"We'll arrive at the Castel de Belascon before supper."

"Where exactly is it?"

"Half a league outside Narbona, near the abaïa de Fontfred."

Near an abbey, Azalaïs thought. Well, that was at least something to comfort her.

The second day's journey was longer, and complicated by the fact that before they reached the castel, they had to ford the River Orbieu, which was full of spring rain and deeper than usual. They stopped for a long while on one bank while the servants tried to decide the best way to get everyone safely across. Azalaïs hooked up her veils and looked out. The oxen waded through the rising torrent quite easily, but one of the carts tipped far enough over to send a vat of olive oil bobbing off downstream. Two peasants nearly drowned trying to catch it and bring it back to shore.

"Shouldn't they just let it go?" Azalaïs asked.

"You're very free with your husband's property," Johana said, "and your servants' hides. They will be soundly beaten if one morsel of your dowry does not arrive intact."

Azalaïs was about to respond when the wagon lurched into motion. It was their turn to cross the river.

The roiling water rose right up to the bottom of the wagon and seeped through the boards beneath their feet. Any higher, and its strong current could sweep them away. Johana's knuckles were white as she gripped the edge of her seat.

Azalaïs was about to utter a word of reassurance, when something jolted the wagon and it tipped sideways.

"We're going to die!" screamed Johana and grasped Azalaïs's hands, a look of animal fear in her eyes.

But the burly drover waded up and lifted the other side of the wagon. "Wheel just hit a stone, Domnas. Not to worry." he said.

Soon they reached the safety of the opposite bank. Johana released Azalaïs's hands and smiled.

"Look," Johana said, lifting the curtain over the window next to her to reveal a vista up a hill with a road winding toward the castel. "It is a very fine dwelling, with a moat all around."

"Are we near already?" Much as she was desperate to remove the uncomfortable chastity belt, Azalaïs wished there were a few days yet of their journey. She was not prepared to parade her new self in front of others. At least, she thought, they would be strangers, and unfamiliar with domna Jordane's character at that.

But no matter how Johana exclaimed about the obvious superiority of the castel de Belascon compared to the castel at

Caunes, she would not look toward it. Instead, Azalaïs kept her eyes focused out over the countryside that spread itself around them. The air was so clear that she could see the Montanha Negre in the distance to the north.

As long as she gazed across the wild moorland and the cultivated fields, she could still feel like Azalaïs, the girl whose greatest familiarity was with the creatures and vegetation, not the politics and struggles of the great families of the Midi. She could imagine herself back in fraire Goncort's anchor, or even back with the scruffy children who ran half wild themselves as they wandered with the Catelots through the foothills of the Pirenèus.

Azalaïs wondered once more what had happened to Azemar since the day they parted when they were both children. Now, thought Azalaïs, he would never find her. How would he expect that the barona Jordane de Belascon was really his long-ago friend? It had been too many years, and she had been through too many changes to imagine that he might recognize her if they ever met.

Azalaïs's thoughts came to an abrupt halt when the caravan stopped to wait for the drawbridge to descend over the moat. She took a deep breath and sat up as straight as the chastity belt would allow her as the train of carts lurched into the castel compound.

They descended from their wagon in the middle of the courtyard, the household servants assembled in rows to greet the new barona. Azalaïs tried her best to stand tall and act as though she were entering a position to which she was born. Savïeza sat obediently on her gloved fist and provided a welcome distraction, drawing away some of the curious stares. Azalaïs smiled and nodded to the curtsying and bowing servants. At the door to the living quarters in the castel, the seneschal waited to greet her.

"Barona," he said, bending down on one knee and bowing his head, "I am Senher Hilaire Milos. I run the estate. If there is anything you require—anything at all—you need only ask." He stood and peered at Savïeza. "*Athena noctua*, if I am not mistaken? An unusual companion."

Azalaïs thanked him without explaining, and proceeded into the great hall, where a group of elegantly dressed ladies stood or perched on stools talking to each other. They all rose to their feet at Azalaïs's entrance—everyone except for one person, that is.

A much older woman dressed in a black blial with a gold belt and a white close cap covering all her hair remained seated in the midst of the others.

"Johana!" Azalaïs whispered. "I don't know what to say! Can't you tell them I have to rest after my journey?"

"You don't have to bear it for long. They'll expect you to go and refresh yourself. You still smell like a pigsty, after all," Johana whispered back.

Azalaïs knew that Johana would never have said such a thing to the real domna Jordane. But she could do no more than look at the damozel and stifle a laugh.

Johana smiled for the first time since the wedding ceremony.

The ladies curtsied and introduced themselves to Azalaïs one after another. Azalaïs continued to be grateful for Savïeza, who deflected their natural curiosity and provided welcome distraction.

After the last lady paid her respects, Azalaïs saw that the older woman at the back had not moved from her seat. She whispered to Johana, "What does she expect of me?"

"You must go to her," Johana replied.

Azalaïs walked forward.

Milos followed her and spoke first. "May I present the Domna Ermengarde, dowager barona of Belascon, your husband's mother."

The old lady grimaced as she rose with the help of a servant. Although Azalaïs had not been taught how to greet someone of such advanced age—well over fifty, she thought—she instinctively bent down on one knee and bowed her head, holding the arm upon which Savïeza perched out to the side.

"Your father has written to me to acquaint me with your character," domna Ermengarde said. She shifted her gaze to Savïeza. "Owls are omens of evil."

The old barona's voice silenced the whispers and titters that had begun to circulate among the ladies.

"I beg your pardon, Domna, but he will not harm anyone."

As if to prove her wrong, Savïeza flapped his wings and with an angry squawk, flew up in the air toward the dowager, missing her headdress by a thumb's width before circling around above the ladies and coming to rest on the carved head of one of the gryphons that decorated the vaults in the huge hall.

The woman's stony reserve shattered for a moment, and her eyes widened as they followed Savïeza's flight. As soon as it was clear that the owl would not attack anyone, she turned her angry gaze upon Azalaïs. "I beg you would attend me in the solar after you have bathed." She took a scented handkerchief out of her pocket and pressed it to her nose, turned her back and walked away, leaning her slender frame heavily on a carved walking stick.

Even without knowing the finer points of protocol, Azalaïs realized she had been insulted. The shocked expressions of the ladies who remained with her in the hall would have told her that, if nothing else. She drew herself up and smiled. "My journey has fatigued me. I beg your pardon, but I must refresh myself."

Johana whispered into her ear, "You must invite them to stay for supper."

"I would be honored if you would all join me—us—at our table this night."

A murmur of acceptance passed through the crowd. Azalaïs's heart was in her mouth as she turned to go. This was not a good beginning. She was so distracted thinking about her disastrous introduction to her *belamaire* that she started walking without thinking where she was going. She heard the steward clearing his throat and calling out, "Ma Domna!" too late to avoid going through a door that led to a small privy chamber rather than in the direction of what she later discovered were her own apartments. Two men who were seated at a table there looked up from their conversation in surprise when she entered. One was a rugged, older man wearing chains of office and a velvet surcotte trimmed with miniver. The other appeared to be a huntsman.

"Oh! I'm terribly sorry! I didn't know. I . . ." Azalaïs's voice shook and she was certain she blushed. She nodded and left as quickly as she could. As the door closed behind her she heard the men's laughter.

"Johana!" she whispered, "Get me out of here! I don't know where to go!" Azalaïs was close to tears. She could sense all the ladies trying not to laugh at her. Savïeza came down from the gryphon's head and alit on her shoulder, digging his talons through the fine cloth of her wedding garb.

Johana took her hand and squeezed it. "It's this way," she said, steering her to where Milos awaited them, looking apologetic and a little fearful. Azalaïs smiled at him and relief flooded his eyes.

The seneschal led them up a long flight of stone steps to the floor above. Azalaïs's solar was large, with several antechambers and even a bathing room and latrine. Rainwater kept in a cistern high up in the donjon flowed through a small aqueduct to fill the hand basin and stone tub. Johana showed her that one need only turn an iron spigot to control it. Even if this source of water dried up in the heat of summer, this was luxury far beyond that of the castel at Caunes.

The servants had already brought the chest that contained Azalaïs's gowns, as well as a casket of jewels that domna Jordane had been forced to relinquish when she set aside her identity. The principal chamber was dominated by a bed of carved wood with curtains to draw around it. One of the doors off it led to a smaller room where Johana was to stay.

"Johana, I must bathe. Can't I remove this horrible thing?" Azalaïs asked, taking hold of the iron straps of the chastity belt through her silk skirts.

"I'll see what I can do," said Johana.

Once she was alone in the quiet of her own chamber, Azalaïs walked to the window and opened it, placing Savïeza on the sill. His little head swiveled from side-to-side, almost as if he were examining his new home. "You'd better not upset people here, little cavèc," she said, stroking the feathers on his head.

After a moment, Savïeza flew off out the open window and went hunting. Azalaïs leaned on the windowsill and listened. The weather was fine. The glazed casement had been opened wide to let in the air that had been sweetened by the fertile countryside. The landscape here rolled a little more gently than it did in Caunes, but it looked much the same. She could see vineyards stretching out in patches, broken up by woods and fields of wheat with forests darkening wide spaces between them.

As she waited for Johana, bells that were not very far away tolled for vespers. Azalaïs leaned a little way out to see if she could find their source, but she could see nothing. Then she remembered that the castel was close to an abbey, the Abaïa de Fontfred. It comforted her to think of the monks there, Cistercians like those at Bolbona.

Soon Johana returned with the little gold key in her hand.

143

"God bless you!" Azalaïs said, and they set about unfastening the chastity belt and putting salve on the wounds it had given her. Johana filled the tub with cool water and scented it with rose essence.

Azalaïs closed her eyes and let her damozel bathe her while she thought about how she might smooth over the awkwardness with her belamaire. She could see that dealing with her new relative would be even trickier than navigating the rough seas that domna Jordane used to create around her. Azalaïs couldn't decide which she dreaded more: meeting the baron, or encountering domna Ermengarde again.

"There will be a banquet this evening. Over a hundred guests, mostly the wealthy folk from the city of Narbona."

So soon, Azalaïs thought, not at all confident that she could play the fine lady well enough to fool a hundred guests.

Sensing her unease, Johana helped Azalaïs into a shimmering silk blial the color of ripe strawberries, trimmed with deepest blue velvet wound with gold braid, and said, "You won't be expected to be perfect. You're a stranger, after all, and you don't know their ways."

"How did you find out about the banquet?" Johana had only left her for a few moments, Azalaïs thought to make use of the latrine.

"I went to the kitchens to tell them what delicacies you prefer to eat."

"Oh? And what delicacies are they?"

She cast a mischievous look at Azalaïs in the mirror. "Frog's legs, fish eyes, and breast of owl."

"Don't tease me!" Azalaïs laughed. "And what do they say about the baron?"

"They say he is very rich."

Azalaïs knew that already. She didn't like the fact that Johana told her nothing more. "How will I explain my short hair, which he may discover . . . later?" She feared Johana's artful arrangement would not withstand greedy hands.

"Tell him you were considering devoting your life to God if you were not able to wed him. Or that you caught it in a bramble and had to be cut free."

More lies, thought Azalaïs. "And the dowager? What shall I do about her?"

Johana stopped her work and turned Azalaïs's face toward her. "You must not, under any circumstances, let that woman suspect you are not who you claim to be. You would put domna Jordane in grave danger—and both of us as well. Domna Jordane is known to be willful and charming. It is essential that you act that part and assert your desires over those of an aging belamaire."

For a moment, Azalaïs thought Johana was cruel to frighten her when she was already so nervous. But in her heart she knew that really, Johana had done her a kindness. Lives were at stake, including her own. Aside from the political implications of domna Jordane's treachery, the humiliation of knowing he had been tricked could well provoke some violent retribution on the part of the baron de Belascon.

"Don't worry," Johana said, touching Azalaïs's chin lightly with her fingers. "You are beautiful and clever. The baron will soon discover the compensations of your bed. And it won't hurt nearly as much as wearing that chastity belt."

I, beautiful? Yes, she knew she had grown and her face had taken on a pleasing symmetry, but her eyes were too big—so the mirror in domna Jordane's chamber had told her.

She took hold of Johana's hand. "Promise me you won't abandon me. I have a powerful feeling I'll need friends here."

"I promise," Johana said, and kissed Azalaïs on both cheeks.

When Azalaïs entered the great hall followed by Johana, the

hunts-marshal played a fanfare on a curved ram's horn. The scraping of stools and benches on the stone floor as the assembled guests rose from their seats to greet her was deafening. Azalaïs saw the man she had accidentally walked in on earlier that day. He stood at the center of the head table, which was raised above the floor on a wooden platform just as the high table was at Caunes. The man wore the same clothes he had on before.

To her horror, on his left sat the dowager, whose steely eyes bore down on her. The gentilòme did not remain at his place, but walked around the table and down into the hall until he was directly in front of her. Then with even, formal steps he advanced toward her. When he was about a man's height away, he bowed gallantly.

"It's the baron," whispered Johana.

Azalaïs looked swiftly around in alarm, then checked herself and knelt on one knee before him. "*Baros*," she said.

"I bid you welcome, Barona," he answered, and then held his hand out for her and led her to a stool next to him at the high table, on his right hand. Johana sat a little farther down, in between two of the ladies who had greeted Azalaïs earlier that day.

Azalaïs tried to examine Belascon without making it obvious she was doing it. So this was the man she had married. He must be at least thirty! His face was craggy, and a scar ran from one corner of his eye all the way down his cheek. The baron's face, although not unattractive with its coal-black eyes and strong features, was one of those that relaxed naturally into a frown, so that he always looked as if he were displeased. Added to that, every time she looked in his direction she met the eyes of his mother.

"Fill the Barona's glass!" commanded Belascon. From nowhere a cup bearer came forward with a jug of wine and poured the red liquid into the vessel that sat before her at her place. It

146

was made of real glass, not pottery. And the charger in front of her was silver, as was the knife that lay next to it.

Azalaïs knew she should say something, but at that moment she was entirely incapable of speech. Another fanfare from the hunts-marshal saved her the effort. It signaled the beginning of a parade of servants bearing platters that overflowed with meats and dainties—more food than Azalaïs had ever seen in her life.

The sight and smell of boar's heads and ham hocks, meat pies and dressed fowl, olives and casseroles released the assembled company from the respectful silence they had maintained from the moment Azalaïs walked into the room, and a roar of voices and laughter commenced. The baron was soon deep in conversation with a man sitting next to his mother, and Azalaïs found herself alone in a sea of people she did not know.

Without looking at her, the baron sliced pieces of meat off the joint in front of her and placed them on her trencher, but she could hardly touch the food. She spent most of her time staring at a spot in the middle of the table between a suckling pig and a roasted peacock, one of the few remaining places where the fine, linen cloth showed through. She knew she should try to be witty and engaging, to fulfill the role domna Jordane would have, but confusion infected her tongue and her limbs, and they would not obey her commands. It was clear to Azalaïs that although everyone conversed loudly and seemed to be paying her no heed whatever, she was on display.

The cup bearer returned again and again to fill her glass. The journey had exhausted Azalaïs, and she was so bemused by the spectacle that without thinking she drank cup after cup of unwatered wine, and did not touch the meat. Before long her head began to feel odd, and the room started to spin around. The last thing she saw before the world went black around her was Johana rising from her seat with a look of concern on her face.

Azalaïs awoke from her drunken swoon and found herself tucked into the white linen sheets on the great bed in her room. Johana pressed a cloth soaked in vinegar water to her head. She smiled at Azalaïs. "You certainly got their attention, Barona!"

The cool cloth brought on a wave of intense nausea. Azalaïs leaned over the edge of the bed. Johana had anticipated this possibility, and put a basin beneath Azalaïs's mouth just in time to catch her vomit.

"Here," Johana whispered, "Chew these mint leaves."

Azalaïs felt much better once she had emptied the wine from her stomach.

"She awake?" came a deep, gruff voice from the other end of the room.

Johana stood and curtsied. "Yes, Baros."

"Leave us," he barked.

Johana cast one last glance at Azalaïs, then retired to her own chamber and closed the door behind her.

Azalaïs sat up. She must have embarrassed her husband, and now he had seen her vomit. "Baros, I am so sorry," she swung her feet to the floor and tried to stand. Her knees gave out beneath her and she sat down again.

The baron strode across the room toward her. His face looked so stern, Azalaïs shrank back in alarm.

"You're afraid of me? Ha!" his laugh held a trace of bitterness. Perhaps he was angry, but he did not strike her as Azalaïs feared he might. Instead, he put his strong, rough arm around her waist and hoisted her to her feet, continuing to hold her close to his body. "You're a pretty thing. They didn't lie."

Before Azalaïs could draw her breath, the baron brought his mouth to hers in a savage kiss. She could feel teeth against teeth, his thick tongue tasting of meat fat and wine invading her mouth. She wanted to retch again, and struggled against him.

"You won't win that battle, Domna!" he said, then he scooped her up and flung her down upon the bed.

Before Azalaïs could utter a word, the baron had pinned her down with his knee and pulled up her night shift. The look in his eyes was not human. He reached into his hose and pulled something out. Azalaïs saw it quickly before he began fighting to jam whatever it was inside of her. He rubbed against the sores from the chastity belt, and she cried out in pain. But that was nothing to the pain deep inside her when he managed to pierce her maidenhead.

After a few agonizing thrusts, the baron shuddered, his eyes rolling back into his head, and then he fell down on top of Azalaïs and lay still, breathing hard.

Azalaïs wept openly. After a short time, the baron pushed himself off her and stood, rearranging his clothing. He paused before he left, as if he wanted to say something to her. His face had reddened and he opened and closed his mouth, then said "Your lady will help you clean up."

He strode to Johana's door and pounded on it. "Your mistress wants you!" he yelled, before walking out the door without another glance at Azalaïs.

CHAPTER 17

The winter had passed pleasantly for Azemar in the Corbiu household. His patron soon trusted that he brought with him no intentions of marrying into the family, and took pleasure in teaching Azemar the ways of commerce.

The two men were about to begin going over the daily accounts when the Corbiu daughters burst into their father's study.

"What was she like? What dress did she wear?" Elionor asked. She blushed, as she always did when she spoke in Azemar's presence.

"Is she in love with the baron?" Tresca could always be relied upon to speak out boldly.

"Ha!" Corbiu waved his daughters away. "She looked pale and sickly like a sacrificial lamb. Everyone said she was pretty, though, and the silks she wore must have been imported."

They continued to ask him specific questions but nothing he said could satiate their curiosity about the new barona who had arrived just the day before. Corbiu and his wife had attended the banquet along with the other important citizens of Narbona.

"Why don't you ask your mother?" he said. "She will return soon enough from her visiting."

He shooed the three girls out of the study. "My daughters think only of the fine ladies who will come into town and have entertainments for all the people," he said, "and in truth, their patronage will do much to enhance our business here."

He rose and closed the door of his office securely, then returned to speak with his voice lowered. "But there are reasons why this alliance is not to be celebrated."

Azemar put down his quill. "Menher Corbiu, what do you mean?"

The merchant stood and walked to the window that opened out over the street and closed the shutters. This precaution seemed excessive to Azemar; the noise below would surely drown out anything they might say within the four walls of the house.

"Did you hear about Arnaud and St. Thibéry?" Corbiu said in a low voice as he returned to his seat opposite Azemar at the work table.

"No," Azemar answered. "Who are they?"

"Inquisitors. Or they were, in any case. A month or so ago they were murdered by knights said to have come from Montsegur."

Azemar hardly breathed as he listened to the rest of Corbiu's story. It was the first time his benefactor had ever spoken to him of such things.

"The inquisitors are instruments of the French, although they pretend to be emissaries of the Pope. They look for heretics, but terror makes innocent people implicate their neighbors. And then they make them swear allegiance to the Church and to the king of France all at once. Out of fear many nobles have opened their castles to the inquisitors and sworn fealty to Louis IX."

"What does the baron's marriage have to do with any of this?"

"Belascon allied himself to the French several years ago. He gave his own first wife over to the inquisitors, so they say, but I think it was the old lady who did it. She was furious that the barona could bear him no children, and wanted rid of her. The marriage was annulled. No one knows what became of the poor lady.

"Now the baron d'Aniort, from Caunes, to protect himself from the charge of harboring heretics, gave his daughter Jordane to Belascon. Their lands are therefore combined and the strength of the French is increased."

Azemar tried to fit what Corbiu told him into what he remembered from Montpezat. "And the baron de Montpezat? To whom does he owe fealty?"

"He is a vassal of the count of Tolosa, who in turn is a vassal of the king of Aragon. Count Raymond VII still fights against the French and there are those in the cities all over the region who are preparing to join him." Corbiu's voice grew quieter and he leaned closer to Azemar as he finished his sentence. "Azemar, this could be our last chance to preserve our own beliefs, our own language, our trade, poetry—everything."

"Why do you tell me this?" Azemar asked.

Corbiu leaned back. "Because I am no longer a young man and it would not do for me to fight. I have too much to lose, and I have my daughters to think about. Whatever happens I want them to find good husbands, here in Narbona, so that our family may remain strong. But I will not stand in the way of those who take up arms against the invaders and their traitorous friends on the soil of the Narbonès."

Corbiu's words burned into Azemar's heart, as if the merchant had found some deep secret there and carved it out with a knife. *I owe him everything. Including my life.*

They examined the books in silence for a while, but Azemar was not thinking about accounts.

In all the time Azemar had been in Narbona, the merchant had been careful not to talk to him about politics or religion, except in the most general way. The family attended mass at the cathedral once a month and said their daily prayers with devotion. Yet Corbiu made no effort to ensure that Azemar was schooled in the ways of the orthodox Church of Rome. The only politics they discussed were local: Azemar accompanied Corbiu when he went to his council meetings, and his patron would tell him about the general dissatisfaction with the tithes everyone had to pay to the Church and the rents that were due the Viscomtessa de Narbona and the baron de Belascon, who together owned most of the land in the region. Life in the city seemed so safe, so contained compared to the exposed, vulnerable estate at Montpezat.

"Supposing," Azemar said, interrupting Corbiu as he explained what trade routes currently carried cinnamon to the port of Narbona, "someone wanted to join with those who intended to fight against the French. How would he make it known that he was a friend?"

Corbiu said nothing, but pushed a scrap of parchment across the table to Azemar. "Now, my nebot, let us see how we might get a higher price for the new silks that have just come from Abyssinia."

He had returned to his normal tone of voice. Azemar tucked the parchment in his belt to look at later, when he was alone in his chamber.

Later that evening, after the family had said their prayers together and retired, and the curfew bell had long since rung and the sentries taken their places on the city's ramparts, Azemar kept his oil lamp alight so that he could read the note Corbiu had passed to him in such secrecy that morning.

In these days, you must not only learn the arts of peace, but of war. Attend menher de Tibout at his castel, three leagues west of Narbona, and north of the abaïa of Fontfred.

Azemar was not certain what it meant, but determined the very next day to ride his palfrey beyond the city walls and seek out this Tibout.

He set out as planned the next morning. Corbiu gave Azemar the excuse of an errand so that his wife would not be suspicious when he rode his horse out of the city.

It was easy enough to find Menher Tibout with Corbiu's directions. His was the only castel aside from the imposing fortress of Belascon, but his dwelling was modest by most standards and not much more grandly appointed than a prosperous peasant's house. It had ramparts and a donjon, the second floor of which was a great hall that was only a little larger than the reception room at the Corbiu home. Azemar waited there while a groom fetched his master.

"Welcome!" boomed a voice that preceded its owner into the hall. "So you wish to learn some tricks from me, I hear. What do you know how to do already?"

A grizzled fellow in a homespun tunic that dragged on the floor waddled bow-leggedly toward him, arms outstretched. A wide grin amplified the roundness of his face and revealed time-blackened teeth. Azemar shrank back a little, and Tibout stopped and bowed to him. "Corbiu told me that you are sent by Montpezat. A fine fellow, in his day."

Azemar was taken aback not only that Tibout had been acquainted with Montpezat, but that he had been told by Corbiu to expect him.

"Now, where shall we start?" The knight clapped his hands, and the groom reappeared laden with a mountain of chain mail. To Azemar's surprise, Tibout slipped his tunic over his head so that he stood there in only a short under-tunic and his hose. The groom gave him one of the lumps of chain mail, which he pulled on over his head as if it were as light as a shift.

"I should like to learn how to use a broadsword, and to ride with a lance," Azemar answered.

Tibout took another lump of chain mail from the groom and tossed it to Azemar. He caught it, but its weight took him by surprise and almost knocked him over. This provoked a hearty laugh from the old knight that echoed off the stone walls. "I can see we have some work to do!"

The groom helped Azemar don the hauberk and a coif so that he would be protected during his practice.

For the remainder of the morning, Tibout taught him the basic technique of using a broadsword in close combat.

"It's best to use the flat of the blade like a club to beat back your enemy," he said.

Azemar was strong, and could lift the bales of silk at the warehouses with little difficulty. But by the end of his lesson, his arms shook so that he could barely raise them.

"You'll need a hauberk that fits you, and a coif, your own sword and a shield. That will cost twenty livres."

"Twenty livres!" Azemar was horrified. That was enough money to maintain the entire Corbiu establishment for several months, and whole shipments of goods from the east arrived that would not fetch so much money.

"That's to start. If you want to learn to ride with a lance, there'll be your charger and at least three lances. But we'll get to that when we need to."

If Azemar had not been encouraged by Corbiu to acquire the skills of a knight, he would never consider spending so much money. "I'll have to visit the Jew, Solomon," he said to himself, forgetting that their association was meant to be secret.

But Tibout took it in stride. "No hurry. Why don't you come back next week? Give you time to raise the money and get your equipment."

Azemar was surprised to find not only that Corbiu barely flinched when he mentioned the sum he must pay for armor and weapons, but that funds in the amount of twenty livres—and much more, Solomon said—were apparently his to command, thanks to a note from the baron de Montpezat. Until then Azemar had earned his keep through the help he gave Corbiu with his business, and Corbiu himself always settled the account with the tailor who made the family's clothing, so Azemar had never before had need of his own financial resources and had no idea how extensive they were.

It took only a few days for the hauberk, coif, shield and sword to be made by a blacksmith in the city, a man with a face that was so accustomed to proximity to fire it was permanently flushed. He had measured Azemar carefully and tried to make him pay an additional five livres because he was quite tall. Azemar refused. Corbiu had taught him too well. The smith shrugged his shoulders and accepted the commission nonetheless, telling Azemar that his armor would be ready in a day or two. "I have to let the bishop know who I'm making this for."

"The bishop? Why?"

"Ordinance. In case we have to defend the city, they need to know who's got armor."

"Tibout didn't say anything about that," Azemar said.

"Tibout?"

"Yes, he's training—"

The blacksmith clamped one strong, sooty hand on Azemar's arm and with his other made a motion for him to be quiet. He drew him to a corner of the shop. "No need to say more. I can make an exception."

So, the smith knew as much as Corbiu, which was more

than Azemar did. Still, at least the bishop would not have to be informed that he was arming himself.

The blacksmith was true to his word, even asking only eighteen livres for the armor once it was completed. "It's not like you're some sly gentilòme who just wants to impress the donzellas."

Azemar wasn't certain exactly who the smith thought he was, but he accepted the lower price gladly.

Once he was equipped, Azemar returned to his instructor every day for several weeks, growing stronger, more adept and more sure. He soon mastered the broadsword and dagger, after which Tibout made him practice shooting a bow and arrow at targets in his small grounds.

Azemar enjoyed honing these skills, but he wanted more. He wanted to ride with a lance. The sword was only useful once a castel had been overtaken, and a longbow was for foot soldiers, not knights.

"You are not ready," Tibout said when Azemar expressed this desire.

"But I can ride well, and I'm strong!" Azemar protested.

"The skills you lack are not physical—although it is much more difficult than you probably believe. To use a lance requires strategy, and nerves that cannot be unsettled by distractions." The burly old knight put his heavy arm around Azemar's shoulders. "Besides, it is not really useful in war. Mostly now it's sieges and siege engines. Shooting with a bow and arrow is the best defense, and if you're attacking, all you need is a broadsword and dagger to finish off the job."

As Azemar came to know Tibout, he learned that the knight was a widower with five grown sons. Two were apprenticed to merchants in Narbona, one was in Montpellier learning to be a doctor, and two others had gone to Jerusalem on the crusade.

"Do none of your sons manage the land? The vineyards?" Azemar asked, thinking how pleased Montpezat would have been to have such a wealth of potential descendants at hand.

"I have no land. Just this castel, which they gave me back after I'd done my penance for harboring heretics," he said.

Azemar was sorry he'd asked, certain that he had offended his teacher.

"It makes no difference," Tibout said. "My boys will do well. I taught them to be smart, and virtuous. And with the sons of wealthy merchants to teach and keep me in wine and victuals, life's not so bad!" He clapped Azemar on the back so hard that he almost sent his pupil face down into the dusty courtyard.

Azemar looked forward to his lessons with Tibout. He liked to leave the city walls and be near the land again, and he felt himself growing stronger and more able to defend himself with each succeeding week. But there was something about Tibout's matter-of-fact attitude toward killing men that disturbed him. Although he knew that the techniques he was learning were precisely for that purpose, he did not like to imagine too vividly what would happen were he ever faced with such a task.

When he first came to Narbona, Azemar's interest in the vineyards would have made him highly aware of his surroundings, where the vines were in full flower and being tended by hundreds of peasants on a gorgeous, late spring afternoon. But that day, after his disappointing conversation with Tibout, he frowned as he rode his horse back toward the city of Narbona. He did not like being told that he was not yet ready to ride with a lance, and his mood soured his appreciation so that he did not notice the beauty of the countryside, or the way the sea scented the air in this part of the Narbonès.

Azemar was so absorbed in imaginary arguments with Tibout and with the vision of himself unseating every challenger in a *targa a plasers* that he took a wrong turn and went farther to the south than he intended.

He only realized his mistake when the sound of chanting floated to him on the breeze and disturbed his daydreams. The music ebbed and flowed with the wind, seeming at one moment to come from the south, and at the next from the east.

Azemar pulled his palfrey up and listened to the voices. Men's voices. They chanted the Requiem, the Mass for the dead.

The music grew louder, coming toward him from the east where he could see the thatched roofs of a small village, and beyond them the Abaïa de Fontfred atop its hill. Azemar looked around to see if there was a place he could hide so that he might observe the passing of what he assumed must be monks, very likely coming from the abbey. He knew nothing ill of these monks, but decided it would be better not to have to explain what he was doing there alone.

He found an outcropping of rock nearby, rode his horse around and tied it to an olive tree, then climbed up the rocky hillock and lay flat on a place between two boulders where he could see the dirt road below him.

In a short while, the front of a slow-moving procession of monks came into view. They were clad in the white robes of the Cistercians. Behind them was a small group of laymen, chains of office draped around their necks, and then a cluster of peasants. The monk who led carried a crucifix on a pole.

Several others in the middle of the group dragged a wooden cart, in which stood a naked woman—although she could hardly be said to stand. She was lashed to a stout pole, and her head hung down as though she could not lift it. Her arms and legs dangled as well, and her hands and feet were suspended at awkward angles at the ends of her limbs. She was so thin that her breasts sagged flat against her ribs, and her knees were the largest part of her legs. Azemar assumed she was dead. He could not imagine what accident had befallen her to break her so. But why was she not in a coffin?

To his surprise, the monks stopped just opposite where he was hiding and took the woman out of the cart on her pole. Azemar stifled a gasp when he saw her open her eyes and look around.

One of the official-looking men at the back stepped forward with another who carried a torch. Azemar thought it odd that he would do so in the middle of a fine, sunny day. The other men carried bundles of sticks and firewood. These they placed in a heap in the midst of a flat, grassy place. The monks propped up the pole with the woman fixed to it in the middle of the pile of sticks while the lay people circled around her. The peasants stood back a little, their eyes frightened and round.

The official gentleman cleared his throat and then addressed the small gathering. "Domna Peroleta, having been determined by the most holy Inquisition through her own confession to adhere to heretical beliefs and practices, and having refused to recant those beliefs, and being relaxed to the secular arm, is hereby condemned to death by burning."

After the speech, the man with the torch stepped up to the pile and lit the sticks.

At first Azemar refused to believe his eyes, or at least expected that at any moment someone would rush in and rescue the woman from this gruesome fate. Yet everyone stood quite still. One or two of the onlookers bit his lip, but no one so much as turned away. Azemar gripped the rock that hid him, for a moment wishing he had the courage to rush forward and rescue the woman himself. But she looked so near death already that he sensed his effort would be in vain.

The monks took up their chant again, and the woman opened her eyes wide. Azemar prepared himself for the sound of her screams as the flames licked her feet and made the skin of her ankles bubble up like pork rind.

But instead, an ecstatic smile spread across her features.

It was short lived. Before Azemar's eyes, the flames engulfed the broken woman, and her body gradually lost its shape.

After about an hour, all that was left on the ground was a smoldering pile of ashes. One or two of the peasants wept. Azemar hardly breathed as he watched the horrible spectacle.

Once the flames were spent, the entire group reformed and turned to wend its way back in the direction from which it had come. Azemar buried his face in his hands and listened to the chanting of the monks gradually fade into the distance.

All night after that, Azemar's dreams were disturbed by visions of the woman's naked body becoming a charred heap of ashes again and again. The next morning when he descended to pray with the family and break his fast, he found them all white-faced and trembling in the sitting room.

"He was my friend," Corbiu said, the fear in his eyes infecting the rest of the household. Even Trescalana did not have the heart to smile.

For a moment, Azemar thought they had heard about the horrible deed on the garriga. But then he realized Corbiu had said he. "What has happened?" Azemar asked.

"Jehan de Boncor has been taken by the inquisitors." Corbiu's voice was small and quiet.

"They say they are questioning all the merchants," domna Corbiu said, her eyes jumping from her husband to Azemar and back again.

"Not all," said Corbiu, leading his family to the hall where they ate their meals.

They sat in their accustomed places around the table, which was laden as usual with cold meats and bread. Corbiu stuck his knife into a slice of cured pork with more force than necessary. "They are not questioning all the merchants. Only those who have suspected connections with heretics."

Azemar glanced at his patron's grim face. he wondered if his own presence, because of his shadowy background, might put them all at risk. No one said anything to him, however, and the daughters and 'na Corbiu made an effort to go about their business as on any other day. But tension hung in the air, affecting even the servants, who dropped things and jumped at every little noise.

Fortunately, their fears for themselves proved unfounded, at least for the moment. No one knocked on the merchant's door in the middle of the night, although his old friend, an importer of gems from the east, was never seen again.

The previous day's scene on the garriga and the looming threat that disrupted the peace of the Corbiu ostal combined to crystallize in Azemar's mind a notion that had before then been vague and unfocused. This was a great evil, this terrible inquisition. Although he had never spoken of it to him, Azemar sensed that Montpezat had some close, personal experience somehow related to heresy and inquisitors. His fear of the knights, the fact that his land had once been taken from him, and other comments Montpezat had made combined to give him this impression.

Montpezat was a vassal of the Count of Tolosa. The inquisitors had been sent by the Pope, whose chief ally was the king of France. Azemar decided that it was time to find out what plans had been laid to rebel against those who used the pursuit of heresy to further the French cause. Something told him Tibout would have information, and he determined to ask him about it the very next day.

CHAPTER 18

At first, the sheer exhilaration of having no one watching her, no one telling her what to do or expecting her to play her role as castellane, kept Jordane flying on wings of joy. She had taken enough money with her to purchase a horse and all the necessary tack, and although she had never ridden alone before, she found it much easier to sit astride in the sturdy framework of a saddle than to perch like a lady on a pillion pad. It was not long before riding the gentle palfrey felt as natural as walking.

She was surprised at how little it cost to provision herself for several days' journey. Being alone, being one person, was a world away from having to organize a party of dozens for each sortie from the castel. For what she used to spend to provide victuals for a single picnic in the olive groves she could survive for weeks—possibly months. One might go to the ends of the earth so easily, she thought, as long as one had gold and a hearty constitution.

She escaped from the city just as she thought she might, during the excitement surrounding the exodus of the wedding caravan. It bothered her remarkably little to see a waif travel off with such riches—riches that were by right hers. What use was treasure if one could not be happy? If one were forced to submit to unwanted embraces and embrace unthinkable causes?

Jordane found it a little more challenging than she antic- ipated adjusting to being a man, however. The roughness and profanity of the lads she encountered at inns on her way south offended her. More than once she wished she could beg for a private room, rather than having to share a flea-infested pallet with three or four unwashed travelers who snored and told rib- ald stories before bed. But to exhibit such scruples could easily lead to suspicion. She was not dressed as a man of substance, and did not want to disclose her unusually ample resources.

Finding Raimon without asking dangerous questions was another matter altogether. She set out for the south based on vague knowledge from something he had said in their last di- rect communication, a note that Sevis had passed to her only two days before the wedding, that said he wanted to see her before he journeyed toward Aragon to go into hiding. She had sent word back that such a thing would not be possible, and asked him to tell her where he would go. She never received a reply.

Along the way, she had picked up hints that a group of unnamed participants in the murder of the inquisitors was traveling through the region, and followed the rumors as best she could. If it wasn't Raimon and his compatriots they spoke about, at least she might locate her lover through the others.

Jordane knew enough not to act aimless in her wander- ings. There was only so much time before she would be under suspicion for going from place to place without staying any- where, and without apparently having come from anywhere in particular.

"Where you from?"

The question, from a young boy sitting next to her, star- tled Jordane as she stared into the licking flames of a fire in the common room of a tavern. She had stopped for the night in Fabrezan, at an inn within the fortified town. "North," she answered. From his clothing Jordane guessed that the lad was the servant of someone else at the inn.

"Where you going?"

Jordane turned to face him. She hadn't spoken to anyone for about three days, and part of her wished she could let words come tumbling out of her mouth, ask about which way the rebels might have gone and share a few stories—or better yet, songs—with her fellow travelers. Better to say as little as possible. "South."

The boy gave a snort of derision. "Too high and mighty for me, eh? Well, if you knew who I served you'd change your mind, I can tell you."

"Forgive me. I am fatigued from sitting my horse for so many leagues. I would be glad of some conversation." If the boy was talkative, Jordane thought, she might learn something to guide her on her next day's travel.

"You're alone I see. It's not safe to be alone. We're going in your direction, a whole group of us. I could ask my master if you could accompany us some of the way."

"And who might your master be?" she asked, more just to keep the boy talking than out of any real wish to know.

"Oh, only a knight, as brave a knight as ever there was." He examined his fingernails as he spoke, as if he were giving her information that was common knowledge and she was a fool for not knowing it already.

Jordane realized that the lad's pride could easily lead him to give away important information to a stranger. Although she wished to have that information, if she were not herself but someone else, it could endanger those the boy traveled with. "Hadn't you better speak a little less freely?" She leaned toward him and lowered her voice, jerking her head toward the other men who had clustered in the kitchen of the inn to rest from their journeying and have a meal.

He laughed. "You're the only stranger here, my man. The rest of us know exactly where we stand."

"What if I were a spy? For the inquisitors?" Jordane could have laughed at the expression of alarm that instantly froze his face. "Don't worry, I'm not," she assured him, "but what makes you think I'd want to travel with you?"

The boy let out his breath in a low whistle of relief. "As I said. It's not safe to be on the roads alone, and I would think my master could use someone else with a horse who's not afraid of a little adventure."

"Picking up strays again, Guis?"

Jordane heard the deep voice behind her and felt a shock of recognition in the pit of her stomach. She hardly dared turn her head.

"This brave fellow here travels by himself, and I thought he might want some company part of the way," the boy answered, his face turning pink.

Before she lost heart, Jordane turned around on her stool, and prepared to face Raimon de Berenger, fabled knight, the man she had been seeking for three days, and the sole possessor of her heart. She hardly expected to come upon him so fortuitously, yet she had, after all, been following murmurs that seemed to point to him.

Years of hiding and disguising himself had taught the knight to control his reactions. But Jordane knew that in the slight raising of one eyebrow and the upward tilt of one corner of his mouth lay complete recognition, surprise, questions.

"He can come if he likes. I am Ucs de Montgard." He gave a small bow in her direction.

Jordane stood. "Jordas Gordos," she said, plucking a name from deep in her memory and hoping she would remember it herself in the future.

"And I'm Guis, squire to senher de Montgard."

Jordane realized now that the boy could not have seen

more than a dozen summers in his life. His mock courtly bow was awkward, and he was at least a head shorter than she was.

"Go and get us some wine, there's a good lad," Raimon said, tossing a copper coin into the air. Guis snatched it before it fell to the floor and scampered off to find the innkeeper.

"I don't know if you'll really want to stay with us. It's only fair to warn you that things might get a little difficult." Raimon sat on the stool that had been occupied by his young squire and indicated that Jordane should sit down again.

They faced each other in silence. Jordane could not take her eyes away from his. Raimon's were a dark, impenetrable brown, but when he smiled, a glint of fire came into them and burned into her soul. She wanted him to hold her, to feel his lips upon hers and the sensation of his fingers tracing the curve of her back, the indentation of her waist, the soft mounds of her breasts. But for the moment, she was not a woman. She was masquerading as a young man, and to act on her intense desire would appear unseemly, to say the least.

"Perhaps we may escort you to a place of safety, where your friends might find you."

"I have no friends, and do not wish to be found." Jordane stared him down.

"If you stay with us, you must be willing to take my command and throw your lot in with my men."

Jordane reached into the pocket of her surcotte and took out her leather money pouch. She dangled it in front of Raimon. "I am willing to do whatever is necessary. I have resources that may be useful."

He crossed his arms over his broad chest and cocked his head on one side. "If it's adventure you want, I can be certain you get it." He reached for the pouch. Jordane snatched it away.

"That treasure must be earned," she said, slowly placing the heavy leather bag in the pocket near her breast, letting her hand linger just slightly as she did so.

"Have you been near Caunes in the Minervois recently, Jordas?" Raimon pretended to make conversation, but Jordane could tell he was watching for her reaction.

"I came from that direction, yes."

"The rumor is that the domna Jordane wed the baron de Belascon, in the Narbonès."

"So I hear."

"The wedding took place, then?"

"It was a grand affair—although done by proxy, and without the presence of the baron d'Aniort—so I heard." Jordane could not explain more. She hoped Raimon would understand her meaning.

"Tomorrow we'll see how good you are with a sword," he said, abruptly closing the subject. "I'll introduce you to the others now."

He means me to stay, Jordane thought. She couldn't help smiling.

When Jordane awoke the next morning, an old man lay next to her near the fire, his foul breath poisoning the air she inhaled. She sat up quickly, in part to get away from the smell and distance herself from her pallet-mate, in part because she wanted to make sure of where she was.

At first, relief flooded over her to see that all was as she'd left it the night before. But soon anxiety and doubt crept in. She had found Raimon, and if her memory did not deceive her, he had implied that she would travel with him as a member of the rebel band. They spoke little, but once she had made it clear that she had no intention of returning to Caunes, he accepted her change of position without difficulty—almost with glee. A mischievous sparkle had leapt into his eye every time he said her name, as if to have that secret between them was a jolly game. Yet he had not greeted her with the ecstatic joy she pictured whenever she dreamed of their reunion.

Jordane rose quickly and splashed her face with water from the fountain outside. She sought out the stable lad and soon had her horse saddled and ready in front of the inn. Before long, all the other members of the rebel band gathered there.

Altogether they were ten: Raimon was the leader, there were two younger knights, three archers, Jordane, and three servants and squires—including the young Guis. After settling with the innkeeper they rode out and stopped in a sheltered copse of trees to talk about their plans.

"We know that the French and the clergy were unnerved by the action at Avinhonet," Raimon said. "Half their knights have returned to the north, not wanting to face such a fate themselves."

"I'd be glad to escort them beyond the Aveyron," said an older man in the group, one of the knights. A hearty, forced laugh broke the tension for a moment.

"We must take advantage of their weakness," Raimon continued. "We're expected at the castel of a faidit, in the Narbonès. I've heard rumors that some action might be attempted, and they're looking for willing men."

A murmur of acceptance passed among them.

"The meeting is set for a month hence. That gives us some time to sharpen our skills and pick up more men to fight. Plenty of sympathizers in the area to see that we're housed and fed in the meanwhile."

Jordane didn't know whether to feel terrified or elated. It appeared that she would truly have the opportunity to fight just as her brothers had, to defend their paratge, their way of life, from those who would assimilate them into France.

She tried to look serious and angry, but a smile threatened to spread across her face as she thought about her father. Not only had she disobeyed him by not marrying the baron of Belascon, but she had shed her identity and would soon actively

work for his enemies—possibly even meet him on the battlefield. It was exquisite.

The next time Azemar went to Tibout's for training, he told the
knight that he wanted to join whatever forces might be intending to fight against the French-sympathizing lords. Tibout's embrace nearly crushed him.

"There is a meeting here, soon. You must come. But we
have much work to do first!"

Azemar threw himself into training with new purpose.
Divorced from some vague sense that becoming a knight would
lead to his own glory, Azemar listened to everything Tibout
told him and did not argue with any of his commands. He took
pride in sending arrows flying toward the target painted on the
trunk of a beech tree and hitting it squarely in the middle. He
learned how to wield a pike and a mace like a common foot
soldier, and was glad of it.

A month later, Tibout took him aside and said, "Stay here
tonight. I'll send word to Corbiu not to expect you back until
tomorrow."

"Why? What is it?" Azemar asked.

"You'll find out soon enough."

Tibout was not a subtle man, and his sudden turn towards
the secretive disconcerted Azemar. His instructor did not say
anything more about it for the remainder of the day, maintaining complete silence toward Azemar as if he was afraid that if
he spoke at all he would say something unwise.

At twilight they sat down to a simple meal of roast mutton and bread. As they finished, Azemar heard bells tolling in
the distance. The monks at the abbey would be filing toward
the chapel now, he thought, remembering with a chill the procession of white monks he had seen on the garriga.

The house servant laid a fire in the fireplace and lit some oil lamps.

"Close the shutters!" snapped Tibout.

The weather was fine and soft. Closing the shutters would soon make it hot in the hall, but Tibout was acting so strangely that Azemar didn't dare say a word.

The two of them sat in silence in the stuffy chamber for what seemed a long time, until well after vespers, when the crunch of horses' hooves and hushed voices outside broke the stillness. Azemar glanced at Tibout, who put his finger to his lips.

The groom opened the door below and led about a dozen men up the stairs to the hall where Tibout and Azemar waited. Azemar recognized one or two as merchants who sat on the council in Narbona, friends of Corbiu. The rest were strangers. The chink of chain mail hauberks beneath their cloaks marked out some as knights. Others wore leather foot soldiers' tunics, and one or two were dressed like the common laborers they were, only they brought pickaxes and knives—whatever crude weapons they could find. The greetings were brief and names were not exchanged, and then everyone took seats on the benches at the long table.

At first they all sat in silence, as if they were waiting for someone else to start or for something to happen. The forced taciturnity and air of intense seriousness adopted by all the men, high or low, was so extreme that Azemar had to stifle nervous laughter.

A sharp knock at the door made everyone jump. Tibout nodded to the groom to open it.

Two more men walked in—at least, one was a man. The other, although tall, was clearly yet a boy. His face bore not a trace of whiskers and he was slender and delicately built.

"Welcome, Berenger," Tibout said, and ushered him to a

seat beside him at the head of the table. The lad sat a little way off on a stool.

Once they were settled, a dozen eager faces turned toward the stranger named Berenger. The attention appeared to agree with him, and his breast swelled with self-importance. "We must beat them on their own terms," he said, "with a bold attack. The castel can be taken if we act with haste." He punctuated his remark with a slap on his knee, then looked each man in the eye. "Are you with me?"

One of the men Azemar recognized from the council in Narbona rose. He pushed his chin out, placed his hands on his hips and said, "What can you know, Senher? You who were unable to prevent Aniort from betraying the cause. The only sensible course is to lay siege to the castel and force the baron to capitulate."

Azemar had seen this fellow, Gribon, adopt just such a stance in council meetings. Usually he brought up a point no one else wished to discuss, and prolonged a debate by forcing the other councilors to overcome his obscure objections before continuing to solve the problem at hand. Here he insisted on raising the issue of someone called Aniort, a name Azemar had heard from Corbiu but could not remember in what connection, but the matter at hand apparently had nothing to do with that fellow.

And besides, a siege was not the daring, hand-to-hand fighting Azemar had hoped for, and he waited anxiously for someone to contradict Gribon.

After a pause in which the only sound was of chairs and stools creaking as the men shifted in them, Berenger again spoke. "Aniort has betrayed our cause and become our enemy. Besides," he stole a glance at his young companion, who looked down at the slenderest pair of hands Azemar had ever seen on a boy, "our actions since then have made up for that."

"Murder is a dishonorable course." Another fellow, a drab, sad-faced peasant, stood when he spoke.

Tibout rose and put his hand on the speaker's shoulder. "Agree with it or not, 'tis done. Now we must take advantage of its effects and strike."

"How many are we?" asked an older man, a stranger to Azemar.

His question met with silence. Everyone looked toward Gribon, who was one of the wealthiest inhabitants of the city. He took a deep breath then expelled it. "I can raise a hundred foot soldiers from among my peasants".

Berenger said "I have fifty knights ready to ride if I say the word."

One after another, the men enumerated the forces they could muster. By the time they finished, their makeshift army totaled just over five-hundred men, of which only a hundred were knights.

"The king of France has many thousands, including mercenaries," Tibout said, giving voice to the pall of hopelessness that settled over the group.

Berenger stood. "Timing can be our ally."

Everyone waited for him to continue.

"The king is busy farther north and west. My sources tell me that the baron himself will ride out with his knights to join others at Bésiers tomorrow. He will leave behind only the castel guards. We could easily take it."

"So you are not speaking of a siege," said the peasant again. "You think five hundred men and a hundred horse enough to storm one of the most impregnable fortresses in the Narbonès?"

"If we do not act swiftly and bravely, the opportunity will pass. Who will join me?"

The blood in Azemar's veins boiled. Before he could think twice about it, he leapt to his feet and cried, "I will!"

His example jolted the others into action, and before long everyone had pledged support and men to the enterprise.

CHAPTER 19

After a month of having to submit to the baron's nightly assaults, Azalaïs was relieved to discover that he had been summoned to attend a council in Bésiers. Not only did she need a rest from his oppressive, brooding presence, but she felt as though she had ridden hundreds of leagues astride a horse without resting, and there were bruises on her arms and neck where he gripped her in the throes of his self-absorbed passion.

Married life was in most ways much less pleasant than being an insignificant attachment to a wealthy household whom nobody much heeded and who could come and go more or less at will.

"When I return, I expect to be greeted with the news that you will present me with an heir before the year is out," Belascon said to Azalaïs in the courtyard with a glance at his mother, who nodded approvingly.

The courtyard was thronged with servants and retainers assembled to see him depart for the north with thirty knights.

"I leave behind the guards, who will protect you from harm," he said, "and my mother, whose interests are as deeply interwoven with my fortunes as any other person's could be."

He bowed to Azalaïs, mounted his horse and rode away at the head of his small army. Just before he left the gate, he looked back. Azalaïs lifted her hand to wave. He nodded almost imperceptibly.

The moment the baron left the castel grounds, Azalaïs felt the dowager barona's grip on her arm.

"I would like to have a word with you," she said.

Not since her days in the Catelot encampment had Azalaïs been treated so roughly by a woman. The barona, an heiress in her own right as Ermengarde of Perigord, was small of stature but surprisingly strong, despite her lame leg. Her fingernails dug into Azalaïs's arm as she pulled her toward the anteroom where she had first seen the baron and not known who he was. Ermengarde thrust Azalaïs toward a stool, then whirled around and closed the door.

For an awful moment, Azalaïs was afraid her belamaire had discovered her secret and would have her whipped—or worse. She prepared herself to be completely undone, feeling almost relieved at the prospect of not having to pretend any more.

But it was not to be. "I am glad you are come to relieve me of some of the duties of castellane, which at my advanced age I begin to find somewhat onerous." The barona's tone was so angry that at first Azalaïs didn't realize she wasn't scolding her.

Azalaïs tried to answer with respect and deference. "Of course, Domna, it would please me to help—"

"But I must warn you of certain facts," the dowager interrupted, clearly bent on her own purpose and not expecting Azalaïs to comment. Azalaïs pressed her lips closed and folded her hands in her lap. "The first of these facts is that, as my son said, you must produce an heir to the Belascon estate within a year or you shall be divorced. I would see to it that you were able to retire to a religious house of women, if it comes to that, with an adequate annuity.

"Secondly, you must not expect to enjoy any of the power that might normally be attendant upon your status. My son and

I control the fortunes of this domain, and decisions that affect it materially are to be left to us. There are matters that do not concern you, and in which I will not brook interference."

Azalaïs had no clear idea of what domna Ermengarde was talking about, but even so, the old lady's way of saying it made Azalaïs's back stiffen with resistance. The dowager clung so fiercely to her position in the household that Azalaïs suspected more was at stake than simply the management of a large estate, although she could not imagine what that would be.

"Lastly—but by no means least importantly—I shall make it my special task to ensure that you do nothing that could in any way stain the honor of this ostal. And if you do, you will find that my wrath has power beyond even that of my son. I can arrange things so that you would wish that your eyes never opened to the light of dawn."

As she spoke, the old lady stepped nearer to Azalaïs until she was close enough to touch her. Azalaïs found herself at eye level with the gem-encrusted gold cross the Barona wore on a ribbon around her neck. She looked up into her belamaire's eyes. They were the blue of deep mountain ice, set in pale skin fissured with a network of fine lines stretched over the framework of her face. The lines had been etched by frowning and anger rather than by joy and laughter. For a moment, Azalaïs saw the old lady's visage as a map of her entire life, as if she had cast invisible nets to snare anyone who interfered with her purpose.

After a moment during which neither of them moved a muscle, the dowager turned and hobbled out of the antechamber, leaving Azalaïs alone on her stool.

Belascon's departure ushered in a substantial change in the way Azalaïs spent her days. From her conversation with her belamaire, she thought she would find herself unoccupied most of the time, like the ladies in the court at Caunes. But instead she had so much to do during most days that she and her belamaire hardly saw each other until the entire establishment met in the great hall at dinnertime.

Each morning Azalaïs received a stream of people from all parts of the estate. She presided over peasants' disputes concerning their rented *jornals*, the fields they tilled, each of which was the size that enabled a single man to plow it in a normal day. She helped them make decisions about planting, listened to their excuses for not paying rent on time, and permitted them to name their newborn daughters after her in honor of her marriage.

Then there were the gentry from Narbona and the surrounding suburbs and countryside. Day after day more of them came to pay their respects, and she found that everyone expected an invitation to dinner and to be entertained afterwards by joglars. But unlike domna Jordane's small court at Caunes, none of them stayed more than a night, and she had only distant, polite conversations with them.

In all that time, no female relative or dependent appeared, no aspiring ladies eager to attach themselves to a wealthy court.

"Shouldn't I have some of my own donzellas, such as those who lived at Caunes with domna Jordane?" Azalaïs asked Johana as they bathed together in the stone tub in the alcove off the solar. "There must be distant cousins who are poor, or whose mothers want to put them in the way of meeting wealthy knights."

"What, you do not find my company stimulating enough?" Johana replied, flicking water at Azalaïs.

"Of course I don't mean that! But isn't it odd?"

Johana gazed down into the water. "Yes, it's odd. They would have to be invited, of course. And with only the baron and his mother to do the inviting—well, it would be strange of him, and it seems as if she has no desire for anyone else."

"She barely tolerates me. I'm a little frightened of her. No, I'm very frightened of her."

"She has a fierce demeanor, that is true. But you are really mistress here. You could turn her out if you wished."

Azalaïs laughed at the thought that she—so recently a lowly servant—would ever dare such a thing. "Perhaps, then, she is frightened of me, and that is why she is so angry all the time."

Something had been troubling Azalaïs more than anything else since she had arrived at the castel de Belascon. She wanted to know something, but was afraid to inquire herself. Johana, on the other hand, had already become very thick with the servants. "Johana, do you think you could ask some of the older staff about the first barona? And I don't mean Ermengarde. What happened to the baron's first wife? Why does no one speak of her?"

"I'll do my best," she answered as she climbed out of the tub to fetch them both linen towels.

One morning when Azalaïs was on her way to discuss the slaughter of an ox that was too old to be serviceable in the fields, she noticed a young page lying in a corner of the kitchen looking very unwell. She laid her hand on his cheek and knew that he had a fever. Azalaïs instructed the cook to make a tisane with chamomile and ginger to give him, and told her to let him bathe in the cool water of the courtyard fountain, then be allowed to sleep undisturbed near the kitchen fire.

Her instructions were followed, and the page improved quickly. The news soon spread that the young barona knew about the healing arts. Soon Azalaïs found she had to set aside one hour each morning to attend to the complaints of the various household and farm servants, as well as the peasants from the surrounding villages who brought her their ailing babies and animals.

The page she nursed through his ague, a lad named Alix, became her helper. She sent him out on the garriga to look for the various flowers, leaves, seeds and funghi she needed to make her medicines, salves and poultices. She amused herself by teaching him about the plants and their qualities, an activity that comforted her, reminding her as it did of her own apprenticeship at fraire Goncort's side.

Azalaïs would have enjoyed playing the role of mentor even more if she could also have spent her days wandering the countryside alone to collect the ingredients. But the one time she tried to leave the castel gates unescorted her belamaire rushed out to stop her.

"What can you be thinking!" the old lady hissed. "A barona does not venture outside of her castel without her guards. There are thieves and rebels about. My son will be most displeased when he hears of it."

Azalaïs felt the eyes of all the nearby servants staring at her, judging the way she cowered before the dowager. "But surely, Domna Ermengarde, if I remain within sight of the castel walls no harm will befall me . . . I only wanted to collect some seeds."

"Indeed! There are others who can perform this task for you."

She whirled away, but not without a fierce glance at the guard who stood by the open portcullis.

Azalaïs scraped what was left of her dignity off the courtyard dirt and returned to the solar. It seemed that, for the moment at least, she must content herself with whatever glimpses of life found their way to her enclosure in the castel.

Most of the people she met were wealthy merchants' wives and daughters. They always brought gifts, and dropped veiled hints that her patronage would be most welcome.

"How can I purchase silks and trinkets and help bring prosperity to Narbona if we never venture into the city?" she asked one morning as Johana brushed out her hair before reattaching the auburn plait.

"Have you told anyone that you want to make such an outing?" Johana asked.

"N-no. I didn't dare."

"Some lady you are! If you wish it, I shall see what I can do."

Azalaïs was not entirely surprised when the old barona greeted Johana's suggestion with disdain.

"The Barona de Belascon does not wander through the market like a servant. I shall send for the finest cloth sellers and tailors who will bring their wares to you. You need only choose what you want."

"How will I pay for these purchases? I have no money of my own here." Frustration bubbled up out of Azalaïs and spilled into her words.

This only stiffened domna Ermengarde's resolve. "My son will settle with the merchants. You may choose two or three new tunics and blials to be made from the silks and linens our merchants show you."

No more was said about it as they sat in silence over their needlework in the solar.

When at last the dowager left them alone, Azalaïs said,

"Why is she afraid to let me out of the castel?"

"I have discovered something that may explain it. I cannot tell you in here." Johana took Azalaïs's arm and led her out to the castel yard.

It was late afternoon, and the slanting rays of the sun lit up the surrounding walls with a warm glow, yet did not penetrate to the ground. It gave the sensation of light without warmth, and Azalaïs shivered.

"Apparently the first barona used to go into Narbona frequently, and was a great favorite with the townspeople. She was generous in her alms giving, and always engaged the local artisans for any work to be done in the castel.

"But she also had a secret. The rumors were that she would meet a lover in the city. This is only conjecture, mind you . . ." Johana steered Azalaïs away from the kitchens, where dozens of servants were busy preparing the evening meal and might overhear their conversation. "They say the maid who helped her was found with her throat cut. She had been tossed among the pigs in the manger. And the lover was taken by the inquisitors."

"What about the barona?" Azalaïs's mouth felt as dry as the walls of the castel itself.

"The baron divorced her and sent her to a religious house of women in the north."

That would not be too terrible a fate, Azalaïs thought. But the previous barona had been a true noblewoman, and her kin would not have taken kindly to her murder. No one would regret Azalaïs's disappearance.

"Come, let me help you prepare for dinner."

Johana's light touch called Azalaïs out of her brooding. She wished she could cling to her donzella for comfort, but such displays of emotion would not be seemly in a high-born castellane—even less in a barona.

Knowing the history of her predecessor helped Azalaïs comprehend why, when men from the city came to visit, worthy gentilòmes wearing chains of office and other badges, they were ushered into the baron's cabinet to meet with the dowager barona instead of with her, which would have been customary.

Occasionally Azalaïs met them if they stayed to dinner, but they remained distant and reserved with her, as if they had been warned against showing too marked a regard.

After a few weeks, Azalaïs came to accept the situation as an unchanging condition of the place, and tried to put all thoughts of disappointment or concern out of her mind.

Instead, she bent her energies toward doing those things well that had fallen to her lot. Daily her renown as a healer grew, and her hour of tending to the medical needs of the estate gradually became two.

Azalaïs was on her way to prepare a salve that would relieve the pressure of a particularly nasty boil on the nose of one of the ladies who was a regular guest at the castel when the dowager Ermengarde limped out of the baron's office and called out to her.

"I have heard reports, that you are a healer."

She never called her by name, Azalaïs noted, as if acknowledging that someone other than herself held the title of barona would sap her of some power. "I know how to make medicines from the plants, that is all," Azalaïs said, sensing an impending rebuke.

"For the moment, it serves my purpose to have the peasants and laborers believe that you have some special ability. But this knowledge is sacrilege. I will not hesitate to use it against you if necessary."

The dowager's face betrayed no emotion. It reminded Azalaïs of a lizard's: still for long stretches of time, but at any moment a thin, sticky tongue might whip out and ensnare a fly.

"Against me?" Azalaïs said, weary of the constant strain between them. "Why should we be at odds? The prosperity of this house is now my concern as well as yours." Azalaïs's stomach churned. She knew that her words would provoke domna Ermengarde, but the real Jordane de la Moux d'Aniort would not have submitted to the old woman's dominance, of that she was certain. Besides, what had she done to deserve such treatment?

Ermengarde closed her translucent eyelids and took a deep breath. When she opened them, her impassive expression had changed to that steely anger Azalaïs had first encountered upon her arrival. "You have but one concern in this family, however you choose to occupy your days. That concern is to get an heir."

I can hardly do this while the baron is away in Bésiers, Azalaïs thought. She had just had her courses, but Johana counseled her to conceal her bleeding from everyone, pointing out that keeping that knowledge to herself might prove useful in the future. Nonetheless, Azalaïs feared that her belamaire would have her own ways of knowing the most intimate details of her daughter-in-law's life.

About three weeks after the baron had left for Bésiers, Ermengarde sent a note to Azalaïs demanding that she meet with Milos to count the linens in order to make sure none had disappeared since her arrival. Azalaïs considered not doing as her belamaire commanded. It was a pointed insult, and it would take her away from her usual tasks, keeping her out of sight in an airless cabinet for several hours.

She decided to acquiesce this time, however, especially since the baron was not in residence, and joined the seneschal in a small room with no windows, situated so that Azalaïs could hear but not see the comings and goings of anyone who penetrated farther than the main gate to the yard.

The room was hot and stuffy. "May we not leave the door open so that we can get some fresh air?" Azalaïs asked.

Milos looked up from unlocking the great coffers that held the linens, startled. "Leave the door open? That would not be wise, Barona."

"Why not? We'll sweat all over the linens the women have spent so much time cleaning and pressing."

"Well, uh . . ."

An odd thing to hesitate about, Azalaïs thought. It was not such an unreasonable request.

"Well, it wouldn't do to let the servants see such wealth all spread out in this way."

Azalaïs liked Milos and did not want to distress him, and so she said nothing more about leaving the door open. But she began to notice that every time heavy footsteps crossed the hall, or a new voice hailed a greeting to the dowager, his eyes darted away from their task and toward the closed door. There seemed to be a great many men coming and going that day, more than usual.

Finally, when Milos's distraction made them have to re-start their counting for the third time, Azalaïs could stand the secrecy no longer. "What business is being transacted today without my knowledge?" she asked.

The seneschal's face reddened. "Business? I know of no business, Barona."

"Yes, you do. It is your place to know. I am not blind—or deaf. If there is a crisis, or some danger, I want to be informed, not kept out of sight like a child."

Azalaïs wondered if the activity had anything to do with the vague murmurings she had heard from the servants about unrest outside of the castel walls. Johana had told her that Er-mengarde had been meeting with the city councilors in her son's absence, although she could not discover whether this was anything out of the ordinary.

Before Milos could answer her, Dreu Barasc, the land steward, entered. "Barona," he said, removing his cap and bending down on one knee, "The new-born foal has broken a leg. I request your permission to kill it."

"A foal broken its leg? How can that be?" Azalaïs turned to Milos. "I must go. We can finish this ridiculous chore later."

For a foal that had only been born the day before to break a leg there must have been some neglect or abuse, unless the mother had rejected her babe, which hadn't seemed likely from what Azalaïs had seen the previous evening. Even if it had not been her duty to look after the valuable property of the ostal, the steward's message reminded her too much of her own Savïeza, asleep on his perch by her bed, and she could not ignore it.

The livestock were kept in a large wooden structure attached to the kitchens. At this time of year, a shepherd tended the goats and cattle in the grazing lands up where the ground was too rough to till, so only the pigs in their pen and the chickens shared the shed with the horses, which were too valuable to leave out in the open. Each one had its own stall, and they had roped off a special place for the mare to give birth. Azalaïs herself had assisted in the event the previous morning.

The palfrey stood with her baby, a wobbly, furry brown creature with enormous eyes and long, spindly legs. Azalaïs spoke softly to mother and foal when she entered their enclosure. After giving the mare a piece of an apple she had taken from the kitchen on her way through, she stroked the foal and ran her hands down each of its legs.

"This animal is sound," Azalaïs said, standing and putting her hands on her hips. "Why have you brought me here?"

Dreu approached her, casting his eyes around to make sure no one else could hear them. "Barona, I have heard things from Narbona. You know that the citizens are angry about the baron and his alliance with the French, and ever since those murders—" He paused and looked around furtively again. "Those murders have stirred everyone up."

"What are you saying?"

"I have heard," he whispered, "that there will be an attack upon the castel tomorrow."

An attack? Was this why all the men were coming and going to visit her belamaire? "Why? Who?" Azalaïs asked.

"There are knights and foot soldiers."

"Knights? What knights?"

"I can say no more. I wanted to warn you. You are in great danger!"

The fellow backed away.

"But what shall I do?" Azalaïs absently stroked the foal's back, and the mare nudged her hand away.

"You must leave the castel. I will help you!" But he ran out of the shed before she could ask him anything more.

Leave the castel? Azalaïs wandered back across the yard and through the hall in the direction of the solar. Even if she wanted to, what would she say to Ermengarde? Dreu had said the castel would be attacked. Was it the truth? Azalaïs had overheard enough of the whispers about how everyone hated the French, and domna Jordane herself had told her about the murder of the inquisitors by the knights from Montsegur—a place about which wild speculation circulated. One of the visiting noblewomen had called it the devil's haven. Others, mainly the peasants who worked around the castel, uttered its name with reverence as if speaking of a holy place.

Yet this had nothing to do with her. Perhaps it would have had something to do with domna Jordane, though. And if she were not to give away her deception, she should try to think just as domna Jordane would have, to behave the same way. Or at least, behave as domna Jordane would have if she had truly embraced her position as barona de Belascon.

An attack on the castel. Why?

By now Azalaïs had reached the solar with its cushioned seats, and her coffers and wardrobes full of beautiful clothing and jewels. She did not feel as if any of those things were truly hers. It was in the evening, wearing finery and sitting at the high table in the hall, that she was the most certain that someone would stand up and point a finger at her, denouncing her for a fraud. She cringed under her belamaire's searing gaze and knew that the suspicious lady counted every bauble, every silk ribbon her daughter-in-law wore, and watched for the slightest stumble in propriety.

Why should it matter to me, Azalaïs thought, *if this domain to which I have no real ties were attacked and overcome by those an-*

tagonistic to the French? Yet like it or not, Azalaïs did have ties. She and the baron were bound by law. However much she did not desire this position into which she had been placed, it was her life now. She must do something with this knowledge that had been thrust upon her. If only she could ask someone what.

Azalaïs wandered to the open window. From her vantage point above the steward's office she could see out over the garriga all the way to the snowy peaks of the distant Pirenèus. It was a busy time of year. The peasants labored in the wheat fields and toiled in the vineyards. Such peaceful pursuits drew everyone together to ensure harvests that would see the population through the winter.

Who would want to attack the castel just now? Azalaïs had already come to know many of the tenants by name as they had presented themselves to her in her role as healer and arbiter of disputes. Could it be those people, who came before her with respect but without humility, who were now plotting to overthrow the baron and terrorize her—the young barona? Or was it the merchants from the city whom she was barely acquainted with, and who thought nothing of sharing the bounty of her munificent table?

Perhaps if she had been in these circumstances domna Jordane would decide to gather her personal possessions and run away in the middle of the night, leaving her crotchety belamaire with the guards and the peasants to do what they could against those knights and foot soldiers the land steward mentioned. Perhaps she should do the same.

Yet where would she go? If she simply ran off, they would hunt for her. She might be severely punished if they found her. And supposing she managed to get away. How would she live?

Azalaïs decided in that moment that she had no choice. She would have to stay at the castel. She would not give her taciturn husband a reason to blame her for his destruction. She must go to Ermengarde and find out what the old lady knew. Perhaps even ask for her help.

She must behave like a castellane. When—or if—the attack came, however small their forces, they would be ready.

First, Azalaïs thought, *I have to send a message to Belascon.* She sliced a bit of parchment from the larger roll and scratched an explicit plea for her husband's immediate return.

But as she started toward the door to seek out Milos to find a courier, she stopped. It would be too easy for someone to intercept such a note and ensure that it did not reach Belascon. She threw the parchment in the fire.

She watched the discarded message curl and bubble, and smiled. Of course. She would do what she suspected domna Jordane might have done if she had made the choice to remain. With resolve, Azalaïs sliced off another piece of parchment and wrote.

> *The fragile walls of my heart*
> *Are in danger of falling apart*
> *Without your firm hand*
> *To make sure they stand.*
>
> *I beg you return to our home*
> *I cannot make my stand alone*
> *Without your strong arm*
> *To work its great charm.*

Her own guile made her laugh. No one would question a young wife's impulse to send an amorous canso to her absent husband. She hoped that Belascon had enough intelligence and subtlety to understand the message.

Belascon in Béziers. Azalaïs sighed. Perhaps Azemar had reached that city and waited for her in vain to join him there. Chances were small that he actually survived to this day, but it was not impossible. After all, she, little Azalaïs, had managed it.

She shook her head and rolled the canso up into a small scroll, sealing it with wax before going in search of the seneschal. He would know how to prepare for the danger they all faced, and would send for Marcu to take the letter to the baron.

On her way, Azalaïs passed Johana carrying her basket of sewing in the direction of the solar.

"Johana, come with me," Azalaïs commanded.

"Yes, Ma Domna."

Azalaïs didn't have time to notice Johana's surprise at her tone of command.

Milos had remained in the linen cabinet awaiting her return so they could continue their inventory of linens. "This task will wait for another day," Azalaïs said, "I wish you to send for Marcu to take a message to the baron at Bésiers, and then we must go speak to ma domna Ermengarde."

The seneschal clapped his hands and two house servants appeared. "Put these away, he said. "And send Marcu to me."

The three of them strode to the baron's privy chamber and stopped when they reached the door. Azalaïs raised her fist to knock, but halted her hand before her knuckles touched the wood and glanced at Johana, who raised an eyebrow. With a deep breath, Azalaïs grasped the iron handle and pushed the door open without knocking.

Domna Ermengarde sat alone at the table with a sheet of parchment in front of her. As soon as she saw who entered, she rolled the parchment up. "Have you finished already?"

"I have more important matters than linens to discuss with you," Azalaïs said. "I have been made aware of a certain danger that affects us all." Azalaïs motioned Johana and Milos to sit at the table then closed the door.

The old barona's face darkened, but before she could speak, Azalaïs said, "I have been informed that there is a plot to attack the castel tomorrow."

Azalaïs didn't know how she expected her belamaire to

respond, but certainly not with an unsurprised, impatient sigh. "There will be no attack. I, too, heard the rumors and archbishop Amiel assures me that they are untrue." She waved the parchment in Azalaïs's direction.

So, Azalaïs thought, you were worried enough to send word to the archbishop of Narbona. Something told her that this moment would be important, that she must make a stand now or accept a position of perpetual subservience to this lady who ruled over the baron's domain in his name. She knew that she might be horribly mistaken, or had quite possibly been deliberately misled. *So be it,* she thought.

Azalaïs stood and folded her arms across her breast. "I have not had the benefit of speaking to the officials of the region, yet my information comes from a trusted source. I, for one, would not wish to provoke the baron's wrath by not acting on the suspicion that his domain has been threatened while it is weak." Azalaïs stared down her mother-in-law's piercing gaze without flinching.

Ermengarde pressed her lips together just a little harder, and then, at long last, turn her eyes away.

Now what? Azalaïs thought. She looked to Milos.

He cleared his throat. "As you mentioned to me earlier, Barona, you wish me to examine what defenses we possess and do our best to make certain they are in place."

Azalaïs flashed him a grateful smile.

"You mean to squander my son's resources to ready the castel for an attack that will not occur?" the old lady hissed, still not looking at Azalaïs.

"Milos? Our defenses?" Azalaïs said.

"There are twenty archers skilled enough to repel attackers for a time. The moat, although not very full with water at present, is wide and difficult to cross without leaving oneself exposed. The peasants are good with knives, and a few are strong enough to use broadswords."

"And that, Barona, is why we must trust the archbishop, who tells me that even if there had been a plan, it has now been averted."

"And how, pray, could a priest who hides away in his luxurious palace know of such matters?" Azalaïs repeated something she had overheard one of the servants say about Amiel's reluctance to involve himself in politics of any kind. Domna Ermengarde turned away from her again, indicating to Azalaïs that she had inadvertently struck some truth.

Yet there remained the difficulty of what to do. Azalaïs knew nothing about warfare or defense, having acquired only the most rudimentary knowledge from listening to countless conversations at dinners at Caunes and at Belascon. But she had no need of extensive knowledge to glean from the seneschal's description that they were not at all well defended. "Have we no knights to call upon?" she asked.

"The baron took them all to Bésiers."

"There are other ways to defend ourselves," Johana said.

Three pairs of eyes turned to the damozel, who had remained silent until that moment.

"Have the kitchens prepare as many vats of boiling water as possible," she said, "to pour onto the men when they try to breach the walls. And make piles of rocks and stones to throw down on their heads."

"And if they have siege engines?" It was Milos.

"I doubt they will. They would have to have been planning this for a long time."

"This is absurd!" Domna Ermengarde's commanding voice silenced them. She addressed Azalaïs directly. "The baron will punish you severely on his return. And at one word from me, no one will heed your command." She pushed down against the table and stood.

Azalaïs's face flushed. What Ermengarde said could well be true. But it was too late to back down now. "What must we do," she said to Milos, "to alert the peasants to the threat?"

"I suggest, Domna, that we—you address them in the yard, and ask for their help in repelling the attackers."

Azalaïs nodded to him. "I pray you assemble the household and all those you can from the fields."

Milos looked back and forth between the two women, then whirled around and strode off to do as Azalaïs said.

Azalaïs, Johana, and Ermengarde remained in the chamber. Already sounds of loud voices and running came to them as the servants and peasants rushed to the castel yard. "If we are seen to disagree about this, the household will be in turmoil," Azalaïs said. "If no one comes, then all the better. But I would not like my husband to return to an ostal in chaos whatever transpires."

Ermengarde's face twitched with anger. Azalaïs had no doubt that if she could have sent daggers flying from her cold eyes she would have. "You . . . you . . . The name of Aniort is not so fine, nor to be trusted. But my son would have the wife reputed to be the most beautiful. It is as I suspected. I will not forget this," she said, then left Azalaïs and Johana in possession of the baron's privy chamber.

"This is not a good beginning," Johana said.

"What do you think domna Jordane would have done?"

Johana shook her head. "I cannot say. Shall I speak to the kitchen servants about the boiling water?"

"First, I would like you to take a cup of chamomile tea to my belamaire, and put this in it." Azalaïs gave Johana a vial that contained a liquid she had distilled from some dried mushrooms. It was a sleeping potion, which she had in her pocket to give to a servant who was plagued with terrible nightmares. "Two drops of this will send her into a nice, long sleep."

Johana smiled at Azalaïs. "The baron is luckier than he knows."

Azalaïs had a foreboding that she had not made the right

decision. She doubted her ability to command respect, had no knowledge of warfare, and did not know whether she would have the wits or the strength to fight.

At that moment, she wished with all her heart that Azemar could be there to help her.

CHAPTER 20

Before dawn the next morning Azalaïs, Johana and all her motley defending army crowded into the chapel. Domna Ermengarde did not appear, but everyone was too anxious to notice her absence.

The chapel had been designed originally to hold only the family and guests for morning prayers and vespers. It could barely accommodate the fifty or sixty peasants armed with a scattering of longbows, knives, clubs and other crude weapons, who had gathered, white-faced, to prepare to fight for the new barona.

The guards remained posted on the ramparts. The kitchen fires had been kept going all night. As soon as one of the menials had drawn water from the well in the courtyard, another servant took it in a bucket to the kitchen and poured it into cauldrons to boil. A fug of steam hung over everything, and the early summer heat oppressed and deadened the atmosphere.

A monk from the abbey droned Latin words that Azalaïs did not attend to. Doubts and fears assailed her. A war raged in her own head and its principal victim was her peace of mind. In addition to their lack of men, Azalaïs discovered that the castel was not well stocked with arms, and those they had looked old and in disrepair. The baron had taken the best equipment along with the best men to Bésiers. Clearly he felt secure enough that the castel would not be attacked. Each of the archers had only a quiver-full of arrows to use—hardly enough to last a single onslaught, and if the attackers were numerous enough to come in waves, they would be undone.

As soon as they had received the benediction everyone emptied out of the chapel and into the castel yard. Not only men but also women came to swell the ranks. On the advice of Milos, Azalaïs had sent all the children out to the surrounding countryside for safety or to relatives if they had any in the villages nearby.

As Milos helped her climb upon a barrel upended so that she could be seen by all, he murmured, "I know we are ill equipped, but we have some excellent archers among us, and many brave souls. Courage."

She squeezed his hand in thanks before letting it go and raising her arms above her head. He remained close to her, ready to remind her what she should say. "*Amics*," she said, stilling the incipient tremor in her voice, "Friends, soon the baron de Belascon will return with his knights to defend the castel. All we must do today is ensure that no one passes beyond the ramparts. Do not let your arrows fly unless you have a good chance of hitting someone squarely. We cannot afford to run out of them too soon."

She continued to recite the words Milos had made her memorize the night before. The seneschal proved a useful resource, and once he had decided to take Azalaïs's part against her belamaire, he guided her in all aspects of the preparations, down to telling her which peasants should carry which weapons. Azalaïs wondered how such a kind, capable man came to be at the castel de Belascon. Whatever his history, she was thankful.

In one corner of the yard, some young servants had stacked boulders and rocks to use as missiles. Two of the guards had already started bringing some of these up to the ramparts so they would be near at hand if they became necessary. The cook and a stout peasant woman carried the first of the cauldrons to its position by the portcullis, and there were five more waiting to be placed in strategic locations.

Although it was still dark, they had not lit any torches, hoping to make their attackers—if they came—believe they were all still sleeping and had remained ignorant of the plot.

Before long the yard came into view as dawn crept onward. When Azalaïs climbed up to the ramparts she could see the eastern sky beginning to glow. The abbey, silhouetted against it, took on more definition.

"Barona?"

The voice startled her, but it was only Milos. He had a broadsword in one hand and a longbow and quiver of arrows in the other.

"You, too, must carry a weapon, even if you do not use it. It is my hope that the rebels will not attack, or will back down when they see that we are ready for them. Which would you prefer?"

Azalaïs looked at her two choices blankly. It had not occurred to her that she might be in physical danger. She had focused only on the safety of the castel and its inhabitants—and on enforcing her will over that of the dowager.

All at once, Savïeza flew up over the edge of the ramparts, "*grrrk'd*" and settled on the stone wall by Milos's right hand, the hand that held the broadsword. A dead mouse hung from the cavèc's curved beak.

"I'll have the sword," Azalaïs said. "I would not know how to use a bow and arrow, and at least I can thrash around with a sword." That was one thing fraire Goncort had not taught her, Azalaïs thought: how to kill.

Milos nodded and held out the iron sword with its wooden grip. The blade was flat, but it had a slight ridge down the

LiSTEn to tHE Wino

middle. Both edges had been honed to razor sharpness. Azalaïs took the grip with one hand. It was too heavy for her to hold.

"Use two hands, Ma Domna," Milos said, "Keep your elbows slightly bent and hold it out in front of you if you are charged." He demonstrated the stance.

Azalaïs did as he showed her and practiced walking up and down with the sword in front of her. Her arms ached just from holding it for a few moments, but there was something reassuring about it. Although her belamaire would doubtless be quite pleased if she lost her life in battle, Azalaïs had no intention of dying just yet.

"Barona!" The sentry standing next to them pointed out toward the west.

At first Azalaïs saw nothing. But after a short while, she noticed movement on the crest of a nearby hill, and after that what looked like a swarm of ants flowed downward from it to the plain. Soon she could see that in the front were foot soldiers, and at the back, mounted knights.

Her heart beat fast. She said a quick prayer then turned to the sentry. "Remember we have little with which to defend ourselves. Wait until you have a clear shot."

"Perhaps Ma Domna should go inside the keep," Milos said, his brow creased with worry at the size of the army.

Azalaïs turned to him in astonishment. "What? How can I? I have asked the servants to risk their lives so I must do the same."

Milos shook his head, but did not press her further.

Azalaïs called out to the waiting peasants. "They are coming!"

Her words sent them into frantic activity. In the process, one of the boiling cauldrons was upset and a young lad badly scalded. Azalaïs clambered down the ladder as fast as she could with the broadsword in tow and hurried to give instructions for the fellow's care. "Cold water, and then a salve of mint and camphor."

The sentries ran back and forth on the ramparts in disorganized haste. "Where is Johana?" Azalaïs asked an archer who rushed past her. He shrugged his shoulders.

"Someone must guard the animals," she said, suddenly recalling Milos's instructions and grasping the shirt of a servant rushing past her to the pile of boulders. She pushed him in the direction of the shed. They had brought in as much of the livestock as they could the night before. The sheep baahed nervously, and once in a while a donkey brayed.

Azalaïs stopped and gazed at the faces around her, now clearly illuminated in light that heralded a beautiful day. Fear distorted their expressions, and these people she had come to know in recent weeks looked like strangers.

The door of the hall opened. Johana emerged wearing a padded leather cuirass over her blial. She carried another in one hand, and a knife in the other. "Ma Domna," she said, "Please wear this."

"Where did you get these?" Azalaïs whispered.

"One of the servants told me of a store room with extra armor. This was all there was." She helped Azalaïs into the heavy vest. It weighed on her slender shoulders and made her feel less nimble. But she knew that Johana was right. She must try to protect herself.

At last some sort of order prevailed as everyone found a place to position him or herself to await the attack. Azalaïs clambered back up to the ramparts so she could see. No one said a word.

As the army approached, Azalaïs could make out the faces of the archers in the foreground, and see the well-armored knights in the rear, waiting to ride in once the walls had been breached. *How dare they!* she thought. No doubt they knew the baron was not there and chose to attack a castel full of women and servants.

Anger sharpened her resolve.

One of the knights rode through the foot soldiers and took up a position at the front. He removed his helmet with a flourish and called out, "Castel de Belascon! I bring you greetings, and beg you would lower your drawbridge that we may refresh ourselves at your hearth."

The sentry nearest the portcullis looked over at Azalaïs with a question in his eyes. Azalaïs sought Milos among those gathered near the portcullis, and called to him, "Milos, what do we say?"

Milos instructed the sentry, "Say that the household is still asleep, and we have not accommodation for so many."

The sentry did as he was told.

Even from that distance, Azalaïs could see the look of mock surprise on the leader's face. "I beg you spare the castel and its inhabitants and allow us to enter peacefully," he said.

Azalaïs's blood rose into her face. "Tell them," she said to the sentry without asking Milos first, "That your mistress does not give you leave to open the drawbridge."

No sooner had the sentry uttered the words than an arrow sang through the air, sailing over the sentry's head and landing in the middle of the yard. Fortunately no one was hurt, but it acted as a clarion call, and a great roar rose up from the massed battalion below.

Heat coursed through Azalaïs's veins and into her arms and hands, now gripping the hilt of the broadsword. Her eyes darted over the scene. Everyone looked to Milos for guidance, and he showed himself to be quite adept at marshaling their meager forces. His sharp eyes and ears followed the movements of the foot soldiers and knights outside.

"I am hit!" screamed a sentry, who stumbled down a ladder into the yard, clutching at the arrow that stuck out of his shoulder.

Azalaïs threw down her broadsword and rushed to him. *Let Milos manage the battle,* she thought. *I shall tend to the wounded.*

There were three now, and Azalaïs tore linen strips off her tunic to stanch the bleeding. Arrows clattered to the ground around her.

"I beg you, Ma Domna! Retire!" Milos shouted.

Azalaïs was too focused on her task to hear him.

The strong, well-fortified castel was their best ally against the attackers' superior forces. Yet arrows continued to rain down injury and death upon the servants, and Azalaïs could not attend to them all.

"Ma Domna! I cannot hold them back!"

The cry came from a lad of no more than thirteen years who stood alone on a side wall, hurling rocks down on the heads of archers who were trying to scale it.

Azalaïs climbed back up to the ramparts, ran around the perimeter, and joined him. Soon her hands bled from lifting the rocks and pitching them over the side wall. She could not look as she did it, saying a silent prayer every time that her missiles would only push the soldiers back, not actually harm them.

Her broadsword lay on the ground at her feet as the pile grew smaller and smaller. At one point she felt the wind of an arrow whistle past her ear. One thumbnail closer and it would have gone through her eye.

When there were only half a dozen boulders left, Azalaïs lifted the broadsword and stood with it as Milos had showed her. A knight's helm rose above the ramparts, and the poor boy whose hands were rubbed raw from lifting rocks shrank back in alarm, coming perilously close to falling into the yard fifteen feet below.

The sight of the chain-mail-covered knight with his hammered iron helm and nose guard transfixed Azalaïs. She stood immobile with the broadsword thrust out before her and watched him climb slowly over the wall to stand in front of her. To her amazement, rather than rush at her, the knight lifted off his helm.

Azemar had felt a surge of power through his body when at last Raimon gave the signal to charge. Terror and exhilaration urged him on. His *destrier*—an old war horse borrowed from Tibout— instantly snapped to attention, pasting his ears back and lifting his knees like a yearling.

In one place as they crossed the moat the water reached Azemar's knees, but the animal, excited by the metallic scent of blood, pressed forward until Azemar could get a foothold on the wall where archers had already suspended a rope ladder.

When he saw that the defender in this vulnerable place was no more than a young boy with no armor and only stones for weapons, Azemar began to lose some of his lust for action. It would be no victory to overcome such a foe.

The archers and other foot soldiers kept the fellow busy, managing to dodge the rocks he and someone hidden beyond the wall threw with increasingly exhausted arms. Azemar reached the top of the wall and climbed over to stand on the ramparts. The lad backed away, fear dancing in his eyes.

He turned to see how he might locate the seneschal, or whoever had been left to defend the castel in the baron's absence, and froze. Before him on the ramparts, her face and hands bloodied and her tunic torn, stood a lady.

Her expression of grim determination struck something inside him. She held an old broadsword trembling out in front of her. Her breathing was labored and her mouth hung open.

The lady had obviously been working and fighting as hard as her vassals and servants.

There was no doubt in Azemar's mind that he stood face-to-face with the barona de Belascon.

Something about her struck a familiar note, and he thought probably Corbiu's description of her had been better than he remembered. He would not fight against a lady. He removed his helm.

At the sight of his face, the barona lowered her sword. Her expression changed. Rather than fear or defeat, her face betrayed surprise.

"Azemar?" the lady said, as if she could not believe it herself, "It couldn't be."

How could she know my name? Before he could think of anything to say in answer, a call came from his comrades below.

"We are done for! It is the baron de Belascon, returned from Bésiers!"

At that, Azemar nodded to the barona, rammed his helm back over his head, and scampered down the wall as fast as his armor would allow.

The horse wheeled in circles in the shallow, weedy water, nickering and whinnying. Azemar launched himself into the saddle and spurred the charger back across the moat, intending to turn and fight the baron's knights. But the small army that had ridden out with such confidence that morning had already scattered in all directions. Azemar found himself in the midst of well-armed soldiers he did not know.

He galloped away, not caring what direction he went, only hoping to put as much distance as possible between himself and these knights who would kill him as soon as look at him.

CHAPTER 21

In the course of training with Raimon and his men, Jordane had discovered to her amazement that she was an excellent marks-woman. She earned everyone's respect with her ability to aim an arrow true and hit the heart of her target. She had even sent the arrow flying that finished the kill of a wild boar, which they slaughtered and roasted to share with the villagers in Boutenac.

The morning of the attack on the castel, the name of which no one had uttered for fear of being overheard, Jordane sat her horse with pride and eagerness swelling her heart. The tense excitement in the air brought color to everyone's cheeks. The horses pranced and snorted, the more high-strung ones rearing up and pawing the air restlessly.

"We'll wait in formation just over the ridge. At sunrise, we ride forward."

Raimon's tone of command and grim face made Jordane ache with love. That, she thought, was what her brothers would have been like had they lived. It was how she wished her father would be. Fighting for the right side instead of the wrong one.

Jordane shook her head. Why was she ruining the moment by thinking of her father? Best to concentrate on Raimon's commands. His voice continued to ring out over the assembled force. It was powerful, confident, positive. Just like everything about Raimon. The harsh voice cutting through the early morning silence sounded the way his muscles felt. She could not help imagining his arms encircling her with strength.

They had lain together only once, in a stolen moment after a banquet at Caunes. He caught hold of her on her way to the solar and took her into an alcove lined with tapestries. It was furtive and quick, and she was still not certain of what had really happened between them. Again she shook her head to chase away her thoughts, this time because they were too pleasurable.

From her right came hooves galloping toward her. "Berenger sent for you." It was the man who led the archers. He delivered his brief message and then wheeled his horse around and galloped back to his position.

Jordane turned and cantered toward the row of knights, trembling to approach so near to Raimon at the moment of battle.

Before she was quite at his side, Raimon yelled out, "You must deliver a message for me." He beckoned her to come closer, yet his expression was not welcoming. This man in armor seated atop a jittery horse had transformed into a stranger.

"A message?" she asked, "But we will soon fight."

"The first rule of battle is never to question your commander!"

She caught her breath at his sharp tone, stifling a prick of tears behind her eyes. *No, not now,* she thought. It doesn't matter. And besides, she was being given a special task, to deliver a communication that—she reminded herself—was important enough to warrant pulling her out of battle formation.

Raimon freed his fingers from one chain mail glove and reached into his surcotte. But instead of a parchment scroll, the hand he withdrew held a small knife.

Before Jordane knew what was happening he sliced

through her reins and the strap that attached her quiver of arrows to her saddle. The arrows spilled on the ground. Her horse trampled them in confusion and broke several of the shafts.

"Forward!"

Raimon's harsh voice sent a jolt of pain into her ears and set the entire, makeshift army into motion—all except Jordane. She was stuck, unable to control her horse and without arrows to shoot. In a matter of moments the dust the pounding chargers kicked up in their wake obscured the knights. She blamed that same dust for the tears that washed it off her face in streaks.

When she recovered herself a little Jordane reasoned that Raimon was trying to protect her. He must have wanted her out of harm's way. But why couldn't he simply have said something to her at a quiet moment? Found some reason to take her aside? The old knight's ostal had nooks and crannies enough, and they had stayed there nearly a month. Or perhaps he thought she would interfere with the attack in some way?

Jordane slid off her confused palfrey and did her best to knot the reins together so that she could regain a measure of control over the animal. She picked up what was left of the arrows and stuck them in her belt. It was a little difficult to mount without spearing her own leg, but she managed it.

In the distance she could hear the shrill whinny of frightened horses and the occasional shouts and screams of men and women. The rebels had engaged the enemy.

In her sudden aimlessness, Jordane began to wonder which castel it was that Raimon and the rebels now attacked. She did not know the countryside well, but she knew that they were in the region of Narbona. From her vantage point she could see the roof of an abbey sticking up above the treetops on a distant hill. What abbey was near Narbona? She had known once, and had a vague feeling of unease about it. Perhaps her mother had mentioned it. It began with an "F". Font-something. Fontfred! Yes. An abbey of the white monks. They were feared, but not as much as the black monks, the Dominicans. And the castel?

No, she thought. *It could not be.* And yet, what other noble house was there so near Narbona and an abbey?

The more she thought about it, the more likely it seemed. She knew of no other fortresses belonging to French allies that would be similarly situated. Azalaïs and Johana might be under attack at this very moment. Her heart pounded. They must surely have escaped, or else were safe in the donjon where an arrow could not reach them.

And yet, what if they weren't?

If Raimon did not want her there in the heat of battle, at least she could ride around the castel and see if her friends needed help. They were not French allies. In fact they had most materially helped to foil the true alliance of the house of Aniort with the house of Belascon—although they didn't really know how thoroughly yet.

"*Vai!*" she cried to her horse, whose ready response took her a little by surprise. *He's just as eager to see battle as I am*, she thought. She took a path around to the north, skirting the route she knew from their discussions that Raimon had taken with the knights, archers and foot soldiers. Once she rounded the hills that had shielded them from view by the sentries at the castel, the entire scene spread out at her feet.

The large, well-fortified compound with high ramparts punctuated by occasional battlements ringed a small plateau upon which sat the donjon and the residence. From the sparse arrangement of archers and others on the fortifications, it was obvious the castel had few resources with which to fight. Still, with the wide moat and only three arrows in her quiver, entering the castel grounds would not be possible.

From where she was, it looked as though Raimon's forces had not yet managed to breach the ramparts either, and that the meager defending castel guard was holding its own.

She watched three volleys of arrows sail over the walls

and heard the screams that followed moments later when some of them hit home. Odd how they looked so beautiful, that the smooth action of the archers drawing back the gut strings on their long, tensed bows created a shape that was as perfectly proportioned and balanced as that of a fine musical instrument. And the satisfying whip of the strings as they released the slender arrows into the blue morning sky had its own music, too. Then that arcing flight, like dozens of thin birds diving for prey, traced lines in the air so prettily that it was difficult to imagine that at their ends lay death.

Jordane remembered the look in the boar's eyes when her own arrow had found its home in the beast's neck, hitting the point that would cause blood to pulse out to the beat of the creature's heart. She had been close enough to see the life fade, to see the wounds the boar spears had made and read the feral questions in its heart: *Why me? Why now?* It had been a vigorous animal, they told her. Perhaps it had sired a brood. Something about it, as she thought now, reminded her of Raimon. Pride, perhaps. Anger and arrogance, more like.

Raimon was below her somewhere in that indistinguishable mass of fighting men, charging and thrashing just like the boar. He had armor and weapons, but so had the wild animal who could not escape her arrow.

Jordane dug her heels into her palfrey's flank and sent the two of them hurtling down the hillside toward the castel. She didn't care anymore if Raimon was angry at her for disobeying him by following the army when he clearly intended her to stay behind. She wanted to be the one whose arrow would protect him. Nothing else seemed important now.

About half way to where Raimon's forces were fighting, Jordane sensed something amiss. At first she thought the wind had come up as it often did, fierce and relentless off the garriga, or that the ground was preparing to heave and shift as it did from time to time in an earthquake.

She pulled her horse up and listened. What had started as a distant roar became thunderous, and it was behind her and closing fast.

She turned to face away from the castel. *My God!* It was another army, thousands of men and hundreds of horse, flowing like a swarm of bees over the garriga in their direction.

She wheeled her horse around and galloped toward her compatriots. "Beware!" she screamed, but her voice was not strong enough to carry over the shouts of battle and the noise of the shrill cries of horses and men sloshing through the shallow, murky waters of the moat. Ahead of her she spotted an archer she knew by name. "Simo!" she screamed, over and over until her voice was hoarse.

At last he heard.

"Simo, look!" She pointed at the army, now closing so that the fastest riders could be distinguished as individuals, streaming out ahead of the mass.

Simo stood, dropped his bow, turned toward his comrades and cupped his hands around his mouth. "We are undone!" The others turned and saw the approach of the horses, and in only a moment the rebel forces had retreated from the castel walls and begun to scatter over the countryside.

Where was Raimon? Jordane had not seen him. She trotted along the edge of the moat, recognizing none of the fighters except for one young knight named Azemar—who looked as though he had seen a ghost—and turned her horse to head over the hills to the south.

But as she galloped away a strange sound cleft the general roar like an evil whisper in her ear. She rode on without heeding it, thinking only that she must find Raimon and help him flee. Yet the rebels had scattered in a hundred different directions and she hardly knew which way to go.

As she rode, the reins became heavy and required more

effort than she could muster to hold onto. She entered a forested area, thinking she was simply exhausted and might find a stream where she could drink and decide what to do next.

It was then that she looked down and saw the arrow sticking out of her thigh. All she remembered when she thought back to that moment later was how fast the ground approached her face.

A searing pain in her leg woke Jordane some time later, at first obliterating any other sensations. She gritted her teeth and opened her eyes. "Where am I?"

She tried to sit up and figure out where she was when a strong, rough hand pressed her shoulder back down onto a wool-covered straw pallet.

"You're in no shape to run *ma chère*."

Jordane turned her head. A peasant woman in a homespun tunic with a rope tied around her waist sat on a stool next to her, knees spread apart with a basin nested between them, plucking the feathers off a chicken. By her feet was another earthenware basin containing water of a pale pink hue, the color of the early morning sky. The woman put the plucked chicken and its basin on the floor and retrieved the other one, reached into it and swished it around. She pulled out a cloth, which she wrung, then lifted the blanket that covered Jordane and pressed it on her thigh.

"Argghh!" Jordane's yell made a sheep, the only other occupant of the hut, bleat in fear.

"I've put on a poultice that should help with the pain. But you can't stay here long. They're pulling apart every hideaway in the area for rebels." She cackled. "You've got a good enough disguise to put on, though. One God himself gave you. What's a fine lady doing being shot at by the French?"

Of course the woman had taken off Jordane's clothes to tend her wound. Her hand went to where her pouch of coins would have been.

"Ye're probably looking for this," the crone said, and fished out from between her own large breasts Jordane's leather money pouch.

"That money is mine! It's all I have." Jordane closed her eyes after the effort of snapping at the woman.

"Huh! Not much gratitude for someone who saved your life. The French went around slicing the heads off the wounded."

A wave of nausea passed over her. *Please God,* she thought, *preserve Raimon.* It must have been dangerous for this woman to take her in. What were a few coins, after all? "I'm sorry. I don't know what I'm saying. I'm very grateful, and I can reward you amply, but I need means to continue on my way."

The peasant tossed the heavy bag onto Jordane's pallet. "Gold's not much good to me anyway. They'd soon haul me off to prison thinking I'd stolen it if I tried to buy anything. Now your horse. There's another matter."

Jordane was in no position to bargain. But without her horse, how would she continue? How would she find Raimon again?

Her eyes took in the squalor of the old lady's hut. Its only furnishings were the pallet upon which she lay, two stools, a rough plank table, and a manger with hay for whatever livestock the woman possessed. From the clucking sounds that filtered into the small enclosure, Jordane judged that beside the one now destined for a pot there must be other chickens in a coop attached to the outside of the hut. Where would the old woman keep a horse? If she left it outside, someone would steal it from her. "What good would a horse do you?"

The woman shrugged. "I'd trade it. For a few more sheep, maybe a goat or two and some measures of grain."

"Is my wound deep?"

"Deep enough to keep you here for a week, I'd say. But if

the French come looking, I'll have to turn you out."

"Very well," Jordane said, closing her eyes once more. "The horse is yours. But I'll need you to get me some clothes, lady's clothes, with some of my gold."

"That won't be difficult. I know the cook up at the castel."

"What is the castel called?" Jordane asked.

"Belascon."

Nausea threatened to overcome Jordane. She fought it down and asked, "And the barona?"

"Word is that she fought right beside her servants."

"Is she . . ."

"She's fine, they say. Only a few servants were killed. It's always the lowly that suffer. Belascon returned just in time to scare the rebels off."

Jordane let herself sink into sleep again, praying that what the old lady said was true, that both Azalaïs and Johana were unharmed. She did not care, for the moment, about her horse or her treasure. She was alive, her friends were safe, and all wanted to so was heal so that she could continue her search for Raimon.

CHAPTER 22

Corbiu did not ask Azemar where he had been when he returned later that day, dirty and sweating and with a gash on his chin where his helm had caught it in his haste to divest himself of his incriminating armor. All he said was, "Come to the office when you are finished bathing."

The kitchen maid, Petra, took him at his word when he said he had had a particularly strenuous lesson with Tibout and wished to bathe alone. They pulled the wooden tub out of its corner where it had been used as a storage bin for cured joints of meat, draped linen cloths over it, then filled it with hot water and rosemary boughs.

Azemar took off all his clothes and lowered his aching body into the steaming liquid. Once Petra finished washing him vigorously with a rough cloth, she left him to soak while she went on preparing turnips for the evening meal.

Aside from wanting to clean away all traces of the blood that had splattered him when one of the foot soldiers next to him had been hit by an arrow, Azemar needed time to think. The barona—who, to his knowledge, he had never before met— knew his name. How could that be? He had not yet attended a banquet at the castel, and had never been in Caunes, the city of her birth. And yet her face looked so familiar. Perhaps it reminded him of someone. A face in his dream. His mother? No, he did not really remember her. And her looks were quite different from those of the Corbiu daughters.

Azemar bolted upright and splashed most of the water out of the tub. *Azalaïs*. The barona reminded him in some fashion of his childhood friend, whom he had not seen for so many years. Surely, he thought, it was simply a resemblance. And yet she had called him by his name. No, it was impossible.

Yet she had the same fierce, challenging eyes. Just as in the days when he used to torment her and rouse her to a fury so that her face would turn red and her eyes glitter with tears. Then, he thought with shame, he would laugh at her for being so weak.

So much time had gone by—nine long years. Surely it could not be Azalaïs. And more, how was it possible that the humble orphan would now be the barona de Belascon? No, Azemar thought again, he must be mistaken.

But she had called him by name. He could not account for that simple fact. Azemar sat back against the wet linen and gazed at the wooden boards that covered the kitchen lean-to. If he had gone through so many changes and ended up here in Narbona, a young man of means and with the protection of a wealthy merchant, then was it not equally possible that similar events had befallen Azalaïs? Still, the barona's given name was not Azalaïs. It was Jordane, and she was the heiress of Aniort, one of the wealthiest families in the Minervois. Azalaïs had come from Tolosa, just as he had.

The water cooled. Azemar stood and climbed out of the tub, reaching for the linen towel that Petra had left nearby for his use. Once he had covered his nakedness, he climbed the wooden stairs at the back of the house up to the third floor, hoping to avoid the Corbiu daughters on his way. Tresca always tried to steal his wrap when he finished his bath, and Elionor blushed whenever she saw him.

Azemar managed to reach his chamber undetected and put on a clean tunic and hose and fastened on a fine leather belt before returning downstairs to find Corbiu. He wondered if the merchant had already heard that the attempt on the castel had failed. Anyone who was caught would most certainly be tortured until he gave the names of all those who took part in the attack, and if that came to pass, Azemar would be in grave danger. This could also put Corbiu at risk. One traitor—like one heretic—infected the entire ostal.

This thought disturbed him, but not nearly as much as the idea that Azalaïs and the barona de Belascon might possibly be one and the same person.

"Azemar, see what has come in on the latest ship from Abyssinia," Corbiu said, pointing to a large parchment scroll weighted down at the corners, drawing him into the office and closing the door behind them.

When they were alone, he spoke. "I know everything. We will simply wait and see."

Belascon's knights made quick work of killing and dispersing the attackers. Azalaïs was too exhausted to do anything but stand in a corner of the yard, leaning on her broadsword like a cane. She heard the drawbridge's familiar groan and squeak as the guards lowered it into place so that the baron could ride triumphant into the castel compound.

Domna Ermengarde emerged from the hall with her hands clasped before her. "God be praised that you have delivered us from harm!" she exclaimed.

Milos approached the baron and knelt down before him. A groom helped Belascon dismount. Azalaïs was too far away to hear what Milos said to her husband, but after a moment the baron turned his face toward her. From across the yard she could feel his examining eyes and was ashamed of how she must look.

He would doubtless be angry with her for her boldness and lack of decorum, and at the first opportunity, no doubt his mother would regale him with stories of her willfulness. Azalaïs began rehearsing her supplication for mercy as he strode toward her, his face set in a dark scowl. When he was about three steps away, she knelt down on the ground and bowed her head, waiting for a blow.

Instead, he grasped her arm and set her on her feet.

"*Mollier,*" he said, an unexpected softness in his voice, "you have indeed proven yourself worthy of the name Belascon."

Then to her immense surprise, he knelt down in front of her and bowed his own head before her. All the weary servants and archers in the yard murmured their approval.

The baron rose, offered her his arm, and led her into the hall. As they passed by domna Ermengarde Azalaïs could not resist glancing in her direction. The old lady's face was a mask. Not a hint of emotion played upon it.

After they passed into the hall the baron lifted her hand off his arm and brought it to his lips. "I am weary, Barona," he said, "and I must confer with Milos. Let your donzella attend to you, and then we shall feast in the hall. Invite the good Marcu, who delivered your message to me, to sit with us at the high table."

Azalaïs bowed to her husband and then climbed the stairs to the solar. Out of the corner of her eye just as she turned she saw domna Ermengarde lead the baron into his privy chamber. She wondered how her belamaire would twist things around when she talked to her son, but was too tired to do anything to prevent it.

By the time she arrived in the solar, Johana was already waiting for her beside the stone tub, which had been draped with silk and filled with fragrant, hot water. Azalaïs had never been so happy to remove her clothes and bathe. Johana rubbed her down and washed her hair, now grown to below her shoulders and curling softly. All the stress of the day melted away, and she was about to fall asleep under the relaxing ministrations of her companion, when Johana whispered in her ear. "Ermengarde saw you with the knight."

"The knight?"

"The handsome one who breached the ramparts, who took off his helm."

Azalaïs's heart started to flutter in her breast. "I thought my belamaire was asleep. Did she see the knight's face?"

"I don't know. Why would that matter? And why did you not run him through with your broadsword, or call for help?" Johana took Azalaïs's face in her hands and forced her to look directly in her eyes. "What do you know of this knight?"

"I—I don't know anything. He took me by surprise, that was all." Azalaïs lied not because she did not trust Johana. She lied because she was terrified for all that she did not know, for all she suspected but was afraid to believe, and for what her belamaire might make of the strange occurrence.

Johana let go of Azalaïs's face and fetched the soft, linen towel that she had earlier placed over two stools in front of the fire. She wrapped her mistress up like a baby and cradled her on her lap, rubbing her back. When she was dry and warm, Azalaïs put on her velvet robe and let Johana comb her hair.

"You must dress and go down to the hall," Johana said. "Your husband has ridden with his guards half the night and fought valiantly against the traitorous army."

"Johana, supposing they capture the men who did this. What will they do to them?"

"They will treat them as outlaws. They will be locked away or killed."

Azalaïs's eyes threatened to close all through the impromptu banquet in the great hall, attended by all the dependents of the domain who had fought so hard on behalf of the absent baron. She did her best to raise her cup with the rest of them as toast followed toast. So many brave deeds were recounted that anyone who had not witnessed the battle would have thought the men had just returned from fighting the Saracens.

"I hear, Mollier, that you faced down not only the foot soldiers who tried to breach the walls, but a knight." The baron spoke so that only Azalaïs could hear.

She smiled at him. "It was fortunate for me that your return was so timely."

Azalaïs looked down. She could not face her husband's gaze. Something in it differed from the way he had looked at her before. Gone was the implacable hardness, the judgment that found her lacking. Seeing him like that disconcerted her. For the first time she noticed his brown eyes flecked with gold, and his hair curling in unruly twists that, although dark, revealed glints of bronze where the sun had touched it. But the set of his jaw, the downward turn of his mouth at the corners, remained to remind her how he had been before.

They had no music that night. Marcu sat at a place of honor at the high table for his role in the day's victory. Toasts were given, people cheered. But fatigue settled more and more heavily on Azalaïs's bones. It was all she could do to lift her fork and stab the pieces of meat her husband put on her trencher. Although everyone appeared grateful that disaster had been averted, Azalaïs wondered how many of their own retainers had secretly hoped that the rebels would overcome the castel.

"Ma Domna does not look pleased to have tasted the excitement of battle," said the baron.

"Ladies would prefer to taste the delights of the bed,"

one of his knights quipped, setting off uproarious laughter at the table.

"My bed is indeed uppermost in my mind," Azalaïs said, "but tonight, its delights for me are those that might be enjoyed by the most chaste of virgins. I speak of sleep and dreams."

"I was fortunate to have enjoyed an exceedingly restful sleep last night," said domna Ermengarde to the general company.

So, the old lady figured out that she had been drugged. "Did you take a sleeping draught? For I could well use one myself this night. I wish to sleep away tomorrow as well, that I may receive my evening guests in a manner befitting the occasion." Azalaïs had bested the dowager, and it gave her new-found courage. Who was her belamaire but a crippled old woman, after all?

Johana rose. "I shall now act the nursemaid to my mistress, and insist that she retire to those very delights this instant."

Azalaïs smiled her gratitude at Johana, but the baron frowned. Was he displeased?

"The barona deserves her rest," he said, rising from his seat and helping Azalaïs stand.

As she walked with Johana through the hall and up the steps toward the solar, everyone she passed bowed to her. Although she had been treated politely since her arrival by all except her belamaire, this was different. Now she knew the respect was sincere. Despite her fatigue, a thrill of pleasure welled up inside her.

Just as they were about to leave the banquet behind them, domna Ermengarde hurried toward them and they had to stop. "A blessing upon you, ma filha," she said aloud.

Azalaïs paused to let her belamaire place her hand upon her head and then kiss her on both cheeks. At the second kiss, domna Ermengarde whispered, "Don't think I am not aware of what you did." She stepped back from Azalaïs, a smile distorting her face.

The day after the battle, the baron de Belascon closeted himself in his privy chamber. A succession of advisors and councilors came and went from early in the morning until late in the afternoon. Azalaïs assumed that domna Ermengarde was there with him, and went about her business as she had become accustomed to in her husband's absence. Tending to those who had been wounded in the previous morning's fighting occupied most of her time.

Yet while she was busy, Azalaïs could not banish the image of the knight's face from her mind. It was so like Azemar's. She mused about possible explanations for the resemblance as she rubbed salve on wounds and splinted sprains.

She had just finished dressing the last wound when Johana approached from the direction of the great hall. "This is for you, Barona," the donzella said, handing Azalaïs a small scroll of parchment tied up with a red silk cord.

Azalaïs clutched her heart, and her hand shook. The scroll was identical to the one she had found on the high road so long ago, only it was new and unsullied by time and the ravages of travel and concealment.

"Ma Domna, this is no cause to upset yourself!" Johana said, leading Azalaïs to a stone bench. "Your name is already being celebrated throughout the Narbonès. I hear from the servants that you have been named the Warrior Barona. You will receive many of these from admirers." Johana changed her voice to a whisper. "It is likely only a canso. You remember, just like the ones domna Jordane used to receive. She told you how to write them. They are verses of praise. Or if it is a tenso, then it is a conversation between two people where the verses pile up as you write back and forth. And remember, whatever this is, you must answer it skillfully, or people will be suspicious! Domna Jordane was known throughout the Minervois for her poetry. After dinner, Marcu will sing it."

This bit of parchment indeed resembled many that had passed through domna Jordane's hands in the years Azalaïs was at Caunes. Yet she was still afraid. She opened the scroll and read the beautifully inked lines.

> *Domna, the sunshine in May*
> *On your features does play,*
> *As the flowers display,*
> *Their beautiful hues*
>
> *Tho my claim is not meet,*
> *I crouch by your feet*
> *Content and discreet*
> *To kiss but your shoes.*
>
> *I ask only the claim,*
> *As the breeze—just the same,*
> *To whisper your name*
> *And pay you love's dues*
>
> *A word from your pen,*
> *And I'll ne'er speak again,*
> *Oh answer me, then,*
> *Or my heart you will bruise.*

"It is not signed," Azalaïs said. "How can I answer it?"

Johana took the scroll from Azalaïs and turned it this way and that. "There is a cypher somewhere in it that will tell you the author's identity," she answered. "He says, 'his claim is not meet,' which means he is either less than or more than a gentilòme. My guess is more. . . Perhaps it is the Marqués d'Auras.

He could not take his eyes off you at dinner last week."

"Yes!" cried Azalaïs. "That would explain the reference to 'breeze,' *aura*."

"And when you answer him, you must show that you understood his meaning by playing the same games with the words."

Azalaïs was not at all certain that she would succeed. It seemed such a strange reversal to be an object of flattery after her recent warlike role.

Yet thinking of what she would write in response to the verse was a pleasant way to occupy her mind, to keep it from dwelling on the knight who so resembled a grown version of Azemar. She had already decided it must have been a trick of her overheated imagination. It would have been impossible for such a thing to happen. Azemar had gone to Bésiers, or he had died. On the other hand, she had neither gone to Bésiers nor died, and she was in such a strange situation.

Foolishness. It was easier just to tell herself it had not been Azemar.

Azalaïs took pains to avoid domna Ermengarde all that day. But the very idea of the woman who hated her so was a dark presence that accompanied her everywhere. When she walked across to the livestock sheds to visit the new foal, she felt her belamaire's eyes watching her from an upper window of the residence. But when she looked, no one was there.

Around every corner she turned when she went to fetch her basket of medicines for her daily patients she thought she caught sight of a wisp of black silk, following or anticipating her, but it was never more than a fleeting impression.

She would have to face domna Ermengarde soon enough at the great banquet that evening, to which all the important citizens of Narbona had been invited. At least in front of guests, the dowager must treat her well. Never since the days when fraire Martin would appear like an unwelcome, foul breeze had she felt so uneasy.

Azalaïs had finished her ministrations and wandered back toward the hall. Johana came from the kitchens and met her, taking her basket from her. "You are still tired, I see," she said, with a look that had so much kindness in it that Azalaïs wanted to cry.

"Yes, simply tired. I'd like to rest before this evening."

Before Johana could say anything more, one of the servants ran out from the entrance to the great hall, looking over her shoulder as if she were being chased by a *singlar*, a wild boar. "Barona! Donzella Johana!"

"What is it? Calm yourself!" Johana took the serving maid by the shoulders and steadied her.

"It's your father," she said, turning to Azalaïs. "He's here."

At first, the words did not make any sense to Azalaïs. Her father? She had no father.

Johana's expression brought Azalaïs suddenly to her senses. Their visitor was the baron d'Aniort, and he would expect to see not her, but his real daughter, domna Jordane. A cold hand gripped Azalaïs's heart.

"Thank you," Johana said, waving the serving girl away.

"What shall I do?" Azalaïs gasped as soon as the girl was out of earshot.

"Go to your room. I will greet him, and tell him that you are refreshing yourself after your morning walk."

Azalaïs rushed off to a side door that would let her into the castel without having to pass through the great hall, which was doubtless where the Baron d'Aniort awaited her. As she fled up the narrow back stairs, she could hear Johana's voice saying, "Baros! Why did you not tell us you were coming so that we could make preparations?"

Once in her room, Azalaïs could not sit still. Her day of reckoning had arrived. *The baron will know. And I will be killed.*

Could domna Ermengarde have had anything to do with this? If she had sent word to the baron, then she must have suspected something.

Whatever the case, there was nothing to be done. It seemed unfair to be punished so severely for events that were never in her own control. She did not choose to come under the influence of domna Jordane, nor had she asked to take her place.

Rapid, heavy footsteps and the squeak of thick leather approached. Two voices, one high and light, one deep and rough grew in volume.

"I beg you, Baros, she is still exhausted after her frightening adventure yesterday!"

"Nonsense! I want to see my daughter. My daughter who for once did my bidding!"

Azalaïs faced away from the door. She heard it open and usher in a scent of horses and dusty roads. Just before the baron reached her, she turned.

There in front of her was a man she had seen only once before, whose short stature, dark hair, and deep gray eyes bore so little resemblance to domna Jordane's lithe, striking beauty.

He had spread his arms wide to embrace Azalaïs but stopped in mid gesture. "Where is my daughter?" he said, his eyes flitting from Azalaïs to Johana and back again. "Where is the Barona?"

"I am the Barona," Azalaïs said, holding her hand out to the baron, willing it not to tremble.

"Baros, I tried to tell you . . ." Johana curtsied deeply and stayed down with her head bowed.

"What mischief have you all been up to!"

Azalaïs said nothing. What explanation could she possibly offer? She was merely a pawn in a chess game, like the ones the ladies used to play at Caunes, sacrificed for the sake of a knight, or a bishop.

At last Johana stood. "Do not be angry at this lady. She was forced to dissemble, for your daughter's sake."

The baron raised his hand as if to strike Johana, then thought better of it. Azalaïs bowed her head.

"Are you saying that my daughter did not marry Belascon?" The silence drilled painfully into Azalaïs's ears.

After what seemed an eternity, the baron spoke again. "How is it that Belascon has not discovered this deception?" Again receiving no answer to his question, Aniort walked to the window and looked out over the parched, summer countryside. His hands gripped the windowsill. Azalaïs felt her throat contract, as though those hands were wrapped around it.

"No one told him," Azalaïs said. "He did not know what domna Jordane looked like before he married her."

Aniort whirled around and faced Azalaïs and Johana, who had not moved from their places. "Someone will pay for this!"

"Do not judge your daughter too harshly, I beg you, baros." Johana took a step toward the baron. "She gave her heart to another."

"It was not hers to give!" he roared, and Azalaïs and Johana both shrank back. "This folly will reap punishment, I can tell you. There are places ladies can go where they disappear forever. I will not hesitate—"

"Baros!" Johana interrupted. "Only think. If you expose the substitution now, how will that dispose the baron de Belascon and his allies toward you?"

"Has this marriage been consummated?" The baron stared at Azalaïs.

She looked away. "Yes, Baros."

The baron's shoulders drooped and he let his head fall forward. "Does anyone else know of this?"

"No," Johana said.

"How shall I face the baron? How make him believe that this stranger is my daughter?"

"The baron is in council with his advisors. You can leave before he knows you are here," suggested Johana.

"He already knows," the baron said. "It was the lady Ermengarde who sent a messenger for me."

This was too much for Azalaïs to bear. Her knees gave way beneath her and she collapsed on the floor. *Only run me through with your sword,* she thought, *and I shall welcome death.*

Johana helped Azalaïs to her feet and supported her to her bed. The baron stood by and watched them, then turned and left.

That night the banquet was almost as magnificent as the wedding feast had been a few months earlier. The baron ordered his finest wine to be served, and twelve pigs were slaughtered so that there would be enough for half the city to eat.

Azalaïs had to sit between the baron d'Aniort and her husband. She could feel Aniort's angry tension and shrank from it, every so often bumping into her husband's arm.

Belascon reached his hand under the table and placed it on her knee whenever she touched him accidentally. Each time, he rested it higher up her leg until she could feel his fingers near her crotch. She was in agony, and kept her eyes glued to a spot in the middle of the table in front of her for most of the evening.

When the noise of conversation and revelry was at its highest pitch, and her husband was so drunk that he shouted ribald jokes from one end of the long table to the other, Azalaïs dared to lift her eyes. She scanned the guests, not certain exactly what she was looking for.

It came as no real surprise, however, when she saw Azemar—or at least, the knight who looked like Azemar—sitting next to the merchant Corbiu among the distinguished guests from the city. He stared in her direction.

Their eyes met for only an instant, and in that moment, she knew she had been right about the knight, and that he, too, recognized her for who she was. Nine years of growing and becoming adults melted away. All she saw was the boy who had protected her in the encampment, who had teased her without mercy, but who had shared her fantasies and dreams nonetheless.

Through the distorting lens of time her memory of those days acquired an idyllic sheen. Her present miseries seemed so much greater than anything she had suffered in the past that she longed to be a nomad once more, instead of being caught and caged in an existence that should never have been hers.

There was Azemar. Alive, strong. Yet she could not reach out to him without endangering them both. He was either very brave or foolhardy to attend this banquet. If Ermengarde had indeed seen him, she would not forget his face. *God preserve him,* Azalaïs thought. *Let him not be undone because of me.*

After the guests had eaten as much as they could of the baron's lavish feast, Marcu took up his citole and wandered among the tables, singing a long poem about the Warrior Barona and her feats of bravery. It was a very clever composition, and everyone admired him for it. Belascon gave him a velvet purse full of silver coins when he finished.

A little way down the head table sat the marques d'Aura. He beckoned Marcu and whispered in the musician's ear. Marcu wore a mischievous smile as he walked with a swagger to where Azalaïs sat and then stopped opposite her.

"Ma Domna la Barona," he said, sweeping a low bow, "It has come to my attention that you require my services to sing a verse, sent to you by one of your many humble servants today."

Fortunately, Johana had warned Azalaïs that she had better bring the canso with her, just in case someone called for it to be sung. She reached into her pocket and gave the parchment to Marcu, who read it through a few times. Each time his eyes traveled down the page his head nodded more and more rhythmically, until it was clear he had taken the measure of it and was ready with a tune.

Azalaïs's face grew warm as the suggestive poem became yet more florid with the addition of music. Marcu had a very expressive voice, and he bent the pitches and dwelled on certain words so that their meaning could not fail to be understood by anyone. Several times he was nearly drowned out by the laughter of the guests.

When he finished the song, Marcu bowed, then held the citole out toward Azalaïs.

"Oh! I—" She glanced around in confusion. Johana was seated too far away to be able to whisper advice in her ear. "Why don't you play that tune again, Marcu, and I will sing it with my own words."

Marcu nodded and plucked out an introduction. Azalaïs's mind was buzzing trying to recall the exact answer she had made up earlier in the day before the arrival of Aniort had chased any thought of it out of her head. Slowly, drawing out the time so that she could think as she went, she sang a short reply.

> *If a breeze lifts my skirt,*
> *Then I'm simply a flirt,*
> *And my husband I'd hurt,*
> *To discover my ruse.*
>
> *I beg my lord's leave*
> *To make him believe*
> *That I cried in my sleeve,*
> *At my noble abuse.*

Azalaïs looked at Johana when she finished. The donzella nodded her approval, and the applause and laughter that greeted her was genuine. She breathed deeply and sat down again, hoping no one would request another song from her.

Curfew rang at that moment, saving Azalaïs from the necessity to sing any more. Some of the more illustrious guests stayed in the castel, but many would ride out that night to Narbona with servants bearing torches to light the way. Azalaïs knew that the Corbiu family was not important enough to be invited as house guests. She longed to have an excuse to approach their table and speak with Azemar. But her belamaire never took her eyes off her.

As the festivities drew to a close, the baron leapt up on a dais at one end of the great hall and raised his hand high. The music stopped, and all talking ceased.

"Friends!" he roared, his voice a little soft at the edges from drinking so much wine, "I would like to commemorate my return and our deliverance from traitors with an event that pays tribute to our friends and allies to the north. I have received permission from the Pope's emissaries to have a celebration that will include some harmless show of the prowess of my loyal knights. Tomorrow, I shall send my man-at-arms to the baron de Vaucler. We shall have a small targa, three days hence, here, on the field near the castel. All are welcome, and those who wish to gain the favor of the barona should prepare to challenge myself and my knights on the lists."

A great roar went up from the assembled company. Azalaïs's heart leapt into her mouth. The ladies in domna Jordane's entourage used to speak of these contests of knightly skills, and Azalaïs knew that they were brutal and dangerous. She scanned the hall for Azemar and saw him near the door, preparing to leave. He gazed in her direction. When their eyes met again, he bowed his head to her. Azalaïs had to turn away to prevent her husband seeing her distress.

When she and Johana ascended the stairs to the solar, Azalaïs prayed that the baron would be too preoccupied with other matters to come to bed right away, and that she would be spared his attentions. She sat on a stool in front of a mirror while Johana brushed her hair, gazing through the polished silver beyond her reflection. She longed to be far away from there. Even Savïeza sensed something unpleasant in the atmosphere, and flew out of the window to hunt as soon as he awoke from his sleep.

The baron's heavy footsteps approached, but they were slow and unsteady. He was still drunk. Azalaïs looked beseechingly into Johana's eyes and grasped her wrist. "Do something!" she whispered.

The door flew open. Belascon entered, drawing himself up and concentrating on appearing to be in control. He almost managed it, except that he swayed forward and back on his heels. "Mollier!" he said, is if this explained what he was doing there.

"*Marit,*" replied Azalaïs, rising and then bending in a deep genuflexion before him. Johana did the same, but she stood again quickly and approached the baron.

"Senher le Baros," she said. "I beg you would not importune the barona this evening."

"Huh?" he said, a frown creasing his brow.

Johana leaned toward him and whispered something in his ear that Azalaïs could not hear.

He stood back from her, shocked, and tried to bring Azalaïs into focus in his bleary eyes. "Well, that's something," he said. He made his unsteady way to Azalaïs and lifted her chin. "You're a good mollier. Done your duty." Then he patted her on the head and turned to leave the two women to their nightly ablutions.

CHAPTER 23

The baron's impulsive gesture of hosting a tournament sent his establishment into frenzied preparations. No one believed for a moment that it would be anything other than a grand affair. The Pope's interdiction would mean little once the men in their armor had assembled on the field. Because many knights were still engaged in fighting around the region and in Jerusalem and would therefore be unlikely to take part, the baron took measures to limit the extent of the festivities. Instead of the usual three days of games, it would be only one.

"What will happen?" Azalaïs and Johana had come to the walled garden—the only place outside the castel fortifications she could go without causing alarm—to speak privately while they pulled up weeds and cut back straggling plants.

"I have never seen a tournament, but I have read of them. I believe that you must watch it all, sitting next to your husband when he is not jousting. Many knights will ask if they may wear your token. I suggest you bring extra handkerchiefs." Johana explained that they would use wooden lances with blunted tips so that no one would be seriously hurt. "Your husband will give gifts to the visiting musicians and acrobats, but you must also. You should ask him for some money so that you may do your duty as castellane."

The thought of asking the baron for anything filled Azalaïs with dread. She preferred not to speak to him unless it was absolutely necessary. She was relieved that the baron had continued to leave her alone at night, and yet puzzled. "What did you tell the baron the night of the banquet so he would leave me alone?"

"I told him you were with child," Johana said.

"What!" Azalaïs stood and threw her cutting knife into the ground, then yanked it out and started slashing at the roots of a garlic plant. "How could you tell such a lie? What will happen when I have my courses?"

"Well, you could be *encencha*, and if not, we'll just say you miscarried."

"Oh, Johana! News like that will travel like a summer fire. Do you suppose Belascon has informed the baron d'Aniort that he may soon have an heir?" Azalaïs stood and marched over to the rose bushes. She snapped the dead flower heads off with such fury that her fingers soon ran with blood from the thorns.

"If I were you I would not be angry," Johana said. "My lie could well save your precious hide."

Before Azalaïs could retort, she spied the baron d'Aniort approaching them from the direction of the castel. When he reached them, both ladies knelt down and then rose, and despite his scowl, he spoke words of affection to Azalaïs. "I bid you adieu, and good health, my daughter."

"You are leaving before the tournament?" Johana said.

"I am wanted in Carcassonne." He avoided looking directly at Azalaïs, but pressed a pouch of money into her hand as he gave her the requisite embrace.

His action took her by surprise.

By way of explanation, he said, "I understand from your *marit* that you will present him with an heir before the year is out. This will bring much honor to both houses."

The way he said honor stabbed at Azalaïs's heart. He had

232

made a decision not to expose the deception at the moment, but he was not going to leave the matter alone.

She wanted to tell him how sorry she was that she was not truly his daughter and explain how she had had no choice but to do as domna Jordane wished. Something told her that he would make a dangerous enemy. "Your gift is very generous," she said, and knelt down to kiss his hand. He pulled it away as quickly as possible. The baron only behaved as everyone expected him to: it would have been a great insult if he did not give her something to demonstrate his pleasure at her welcome news.

He kept his eyes averted as they walked together to the castel yard. Azalaïs and Johana stood at the head of the crowd of servants and guests assembled to see the baron and his archer ride out of the castel gates and over the drawbridge. When they were at last out of sight Johana said, "Come, Barona, do not weep. Your father will be safe, and your duty is here."

Until Johana spoke, Azalaïs was unaware that her cheeks were wet with tears. She could not explain why she would feel such great sadness at the departure of the one person who could destroy her with a word.

The servants wandered back to their tasks and she wiped her eyes on the sleeve of her blial. "Now at least I do not have to ask for money," she said with a rueful smile, giving the pouch to Johana.

Johana pulled apart the gathered opening and peered inside. "You cannot give away gold, Domna!" She held one of the coins up between the thumb and first finger of her right hand. "Your husband will give you smaller coins."

Azalaïs held out her hand, and Johana dropped the gold piece into it. Odd, she thought, having lived for several months in the midst of a household that was much larger and wealthier than the one at Caunes, she had not ever seen currency change hands. The seneschal and the steward took care of all accounts, paid for provisions and gave salaries to the servants high and low.

She handed the coin back to Johana. "See that the pouch is hidden." She spoke in Latin so that the servants busy in the hall would not understand.

But she had no time to instruct Johana further. She had to meet with the slaughterer to decide on the meats for the day of the tournament, and with the steward to confer about who was to stay in which rooms in the castel. She had barely finished these tasks when the baron's valet bade her attend her husband in his privy chamber.

Azalaïs couldn't imagine why he would send for her at such an odd time of day, when he was usually to be found hunting or settling disputes among the peasants who worked his vineyards. But she could not ignore his summons.

The baron was not alone in his chamber off the great hall, the same chamber Azalaïs had strayed into on her first day in the castel. He sat with his mother and, facing away from Azalaïs as she entered, a monk—not a Cistercian with white robes, but a Dominican, who still had on his black traveling robe. All three of them had cups of ale in front of them. Bread crumbs littered the table. They had just broken their fast.

"Barona," Belascon said. "We have a distinguished visitor, an acquaintance of my mother. I have asked him to remain here at the castel de Belascon so that you may be spiritually prepared for your confinement."

The monk who faced away from Azalaïs now stood and bowed to her. When he righted himself, it took all of Azalaïs's self-control to remain upright.

"This is fraire Martin, from the Dominican house in Tolosa," the baron said. "He has come for the council at Narbona."

Please, please don't remember me! Azalaïs's palms started to sweat and for a moment the room swam in front of her eyes. When he showed no immediate sign of recognition, she realized that he would hardly expect a noblewoman to be the young boy he had tried to molest.

Yet the sight of fraire Martin's drawn, stern face gave her a peculiarly mixed sensation of dread and longing. Life with fraire Goncort had been so much simpler. She wished she could ask fraire Martin whether the aging anchorite was still alive. But even if she had never rammed her knee between his legs it would be impossible to expose herself at this juncture. She curtsied, not meeting his eyes.

"I must ask you, Mollier, to answer me truthfully concerning a very important matter," Belascon said.

Ice spread out from Azalaïs's heart and course through her veins. This was the end, at last. Fraire Martin must have somehow discovered her secret. He was simply pretending not to know who she was. She stood very still.

"How did you come to know of the attack on the castel before it happened?"

Azalaïs's relief was so great that she had to suppress a smile. "It was Dreu Barasc who came to me," she said without hesitation. "He warned me, and told me to prepare."

The baron nodded. "Thank you, Mollier, you have proven yourself truly loyal."

"Will you join us later, for vespers, Barona?" fraire Martin said.

"Of course." *At least*, she thought, *I need not look at him when I am praying.*

"Leave us now, Mollier," the baron said.

Azalaïs curtsied to her husband and took care not to hurry away until after the door closed behind her.

Tibout's entire body expanded and then deflated with his profound sigh. "Three days is hardly enough time to learn how to ride with a lance. And where do you expect to find a full suit of mail that fits you? You cannot wear the armor you wore the other day, it is too damaged, and there is no time to have the chausses or a great helm with your own crest made. Besides, who will deign to ride against you, when you do not wear golden spurs? And what if . . ."

Tibout did not finish his thought, but Azemar knew he would have said, *what if you are recognized as one of the attackers of the castel?*

Azemar stood his ground. "Nonetheless, I must do it. And I have money to purchase my own armor and a horse. I must prove myself worthy of a certain . . . person."

Tibout's eyes darkened as he fixed them on his pupil. "A knight is a warrior. He must serve when called by his overlord, and fight to the death if necessary."

Azemar looked down at the ground. He realized that although he had joined a cause to which he felt drawn, he had no particular allegiance to his overlord, a man he had never laid eyes on and barely heard of.

"Some knights join the holy crusade to free Jerusalem from the Saracens. If you are called by religious zeal, you might choose to join the Templars. They are ordained like monks to uphold the word of the Church and are pledged to protect the weak, guarding the roads for pilgrims. But not all Templars are in the holy land."

Tibout led Azemar out of the hall as he spoke, motioning the groom to prepare the weapons. Then he spoke more quietly, his deep voice like stones tumbling down the hillside after a heavy rain. "There are some Templar houses here, in the Razès, in the Ariège, and near Perpignan. A peculiarity in the vows of these knights has caused them to be drawn into an unholy alliance with the heretics. The Templars in the mountains lend their swords to defend the good men and women, who have been hunted by Louis IX's knights. The Templars do not themselves believe in the errors of the heretics, but they accept their treasure in payment, as mercenaries."

Tibout spoke of good men and women: *bons oms* and *bonas domnas*. The last time Azemar had heard anyone referred to in that way was when he crept up on the peasant and the knight who threatened Montpezat. And yet the Templars were not fighting against them. How could that be?

"May I not present myself as an independent knight? All knights need not belong to some order or other, or serve a particular master."

"*Oc*," Tibout said, "That is strictly true, although few have followed that course. But once you take up the lance, you will have responsibilities. A merchant's life will no longer be possible for you. Order or no order, it will be your calling."

Azemar kept his eyes on the stony ground of the courtyard, noticing that the summer drought had already carved deep cracks in the packed dirt. He knew he faced a decision that would change his life—once again.

Yet this was truly the first time he had a choice whose outcome he understood. He could have chosen not to help Montpezat. He could have chosen to take the baron's money and ride away to Bésiers in hopes of finding Azalaïs there. He had not done so, and he had been rewarded by finding her anyway.

Or had he? Was it a reward or a punishment? But Tibout was waiting for an answer. Azemar had known what it would be from the beginning. "I understand all you say. I am ready."

After taking a deep breath and blowing it out through his lips like a horse, the old knight instructed the groom to bring out two wooden lances, two great helms and two pairs of chain mail leg armor. He also called for a cuirass—the newest form of armor, a padded leather garment for Azemar to wear over his hauberk for extra protection. The groom helped Azemar into the cuirass and saw that the *ventail* on his coif was securely fastened across his mouth. A roll of linen made a makeshift arming cap to support the helm. Finally, he lowered the heavy, flat-topped iron jousting helm over Azemar's head and fastened it down.

Before mounting his horse, Tibout showed Azemar how to couch the lance in the rest built into the cuirass. "Just being able to ride without falling off is enough to expect in only three days. You'll make a fool of yourself, or I'm a fine lady from Paris."

How difficult could it be? Azemar thought. He had gained a great deal of strength since he had been learning how to wield a broadsword, and now had the confidence of real battle experience—however brief.

The groom handed Azemar the lance. He watched as Tibout lifted his own lance with ease and settled it in the couch. Azemar tried to do the same, but the weight of the long, oak weapon made him lose his balance. The additional armor was too unwieldy to allow him to correct himself, and he fell with a clatter of his heaume onto the hard dirt in the stable yard.

Tibout let out a hearty laugh. "So, you thought it would be easy to hold a lance up while you're on a horse!"

Two grooms helped Azemar stand again and led him to the mounting block. He tried to ignore that the ill-fitting cuirass dug into his armpits, and the closed-in great helm restricted his vision and brought beads of sweat to his face that dripped into his eyes and mouth. He could only see what was directly in front of him through the narrow sights, and very soon the heat of his breathing made not only the helm but all his armor into an oven—despite the numerous breaths pierced through around his nose and mouth, and the joints that allowed him a small degree of movement. Instead of feeling invincible in the armor, Azemar felt completely vulnerable.

After three painful falls, each more embarrassing than the last, he managed to remain in the saddle while the horse walked around the yard. He even trotted a little with his lance held vertically, and pictured himself riding up to the reviewing stand and asking for Azalaïs's pledge. But the moment he tried to level the lance as if to charge, he fell off the horse once more.

"That is enough for today," Tibout said. "And you didn't even wear a surcotte!"

The groom unfastened the cuirass and helped a hot, bruised, humiliated Azemar out of it.

"You didn't do as badly as I thought you would," Tibout said. "Jaquin will fix everything so that it fits you better. We'll try again tomorrow."

Were it not for the image of the barona—who he now knew beyond certainty was Azalaïs herself—Azemar might have regretted his decision to start training on the lance so he could enter the tourney. When he mounted his own horse, every bone in his legs rubbed against the saddle, and the places that had been chafed by the cuirass and the helm gave him excruciating pain.

He gritted his teeth. In two days, unless he injured himself to such an extent that he could not ride, he would have to show his devotion to Azalaïs by risking his life. He had to find out what she had done in the last nine years. He burned to ask her forgiveness for not trying harder to find her before.

Patching his life together by connecting all the threads that had gone into making him who he was—that was his task, and Azalaïs held the key.

All through mealtimes and prayer times Azalaïs could feel fraire Martin staring at her. She wished she could retire to her bedchamber and remain there, but with her husband and all the guests present in the castel, she had to stay and submit to being feted and celebrated. More than once her cheeks grew hot and her heart pounded because she was certain the Dominican monk knew who she really was. But he said nothing—in fact, he addressed not a word to her.

Azalaïs was particularly worried about acquitting herself well at the tournament. Johana did her best to tell her everything that might happen and how she should behave, but if she made one tiny mistake in front of fraire Martin, any vague suspicions he might have could blossom into a deeper inquiry into her past.

Already pledges and tributes began to pour in from the surrounding estates, and the shields of twenty knights were displayed in the stable yard for all the ladies to see. Everyone wanted to wear Azalaïs's token. Instead of one or two *tensos* and *sirventes* to sing in the evenings on the nights before the contest, there were twenty. With so many, the poor citoler's voice gave out.

"Why doesn't the Barona sing for us again, as I heard she did so beautifully at the banquet the day before my arrival?"

Azalaïs did not have to look to know exactly where the request had come from. It was fraire Martin. If she sang, there was every possibility he would recognize her voice from the monastery. More than one monk had commented on it, and he had sometimes surprised her while she was singing when he came unannounced to fraire Goncort's hut.

"Come, Mollier! There is an answer. Your voice is pretty enough."

To her horror, at the baron's suggestion Marcu stood and approached her with the citole, holding it in front of him for her to take. She had managed to avoid having to display her ignorance of playing the other night, but it would be almost impossible to refuse to comply a second time.

"Your fame as a trobairitz is celebrated throughout the county," Marcu said. Azalaïs knew he meant to flatter her, but all she could manage in response was a weak smile.

"With your permission," Johana said. The donzella leapt from her seat and intercepted the trobador before he reached his mistress. "My domna prefers it when I play for her."

Azalaïs stifled her sigh of relief and flooded Johana with a grateful gaze. Her damozel picked out the beginning of a tune on the citole to give the form, and Azalaïs took the parchment from Marcu. The moment had arrived when she must sing before this monk who, if he knew who she was, could send her to her death.

Azalaïs decided only one tactic might save her. She must sing out confidently, with no fear. If her voice would give her away, singing quietly would not help, and if not, she needed to uphold domna Jordane's reputation as a trobairitz or risk discovery by not demonstrating enough skill and flair.

Something about pretending, about taking that leap, transformed Azalaïs's voice. It was hers, but in calling to mind domna Jordane's supreme artistry, she willed herself to expand and fill that other lady's personality. She wove the thread of melody around the complex form of the poem, leaning on some notes, altering her tone to emphasize others. It was almost as if she had always sung that way, or else had in that moment been enchanted by some good sprite who came to her rescue. She knew that fraire Martin would not recognize the young boy in the woman's voice. The thought made her smile for the first time since the battle.

The guests roared with pleasure at Azalaïs's performance. The baron was so pleased that he sent the seneschal off to retrieve one of the family treasures—a circlet of gold studded with garnets—which he presented to Azalaïs before the entire company. Azalaïs avoided fraire Martin's eyes, but she could feel him staring at her. He knows, he doesn't know, he suspects, but he's not certain, circled like a chant in her mind.

"The barona needs her rest," Johana said. All the gentlemen rose and bowed to her, and then Johana took Azalaïs by the arm and led her out of the hall to the solar.

When they were finally behind closed doors, Johana spoke. "The Virgin be praised! How did you do it? I knew you could sing, but if I closed my eyes I heard Jordane herself. But I shall have to teach you to play the citole, and quickly. Jordane was quite adept. Now that they have heard you, it will not be long before they insist that you accompany yourself." She said all this while helping Azalaïs remove her layers of sumptuous clothing. "Still, with such a voice, why did you look like a death mask when the monk asked you to sing in the first place?"

"It doesn't matter now," Azalaïs said. "I was tired, that was all."

After that, nothing Johana asked could make her explain any further.

CHAPTER 24

The morning of the joust, Johana woke Azalaïs before sunrise. The baron's heralds had ridden far to cry the tournament, and the castel burst at the seams with visitors from courts and estates from the Fenouillèdes, the Tolosan, the Carcassès—even from the Albigeois. Azalaïs would have to be attired in her very best clothes, and it would take Johana some time to dress her hair with the pearls and jewels she must thread through it.

"I shall have to use some henna root on your hair. Your new crespine will not cover it all. Everyone will want to see your jewels."

"Explain again how everything will go. I think I have it, and then I forget something."

"The joust itself won't start until noon," Johana said, "but there will be other contests first. And morning prayers will be especially long."

She threw open the shutters and let the fresh, pre-dawn air flood into the room. Azalaïs slipped her arms into her velvet robe—a material so miraculously soft that she found every excuse to ask for it whenever the *sartors* came to take her order for new clothing. She leaned her arms on the broad sill, drinking in the scent of salt from the nearby sea borne on a breeze through fields of young grain not yet ready to be harvested.

In a whir of wings, Savïeza flew in from his nightly hunt for mice and large insects and perched next to her. Azalaïs stroked his head with her finger.

And then, she froze. "Johana." Azalaïs turned slowly.

Something in her tone commanded her companion's attention. "What is it?"

"My cavèc must remain in this room today. No one must see him."

"What does it matter?" Johana asked. "Everyone knows of his existence, and the servants have become quite accustomed to him."

"Accustomed enough not to say anything to the visitors, I hope."

"I don't understand why you're making such a fuss about little Savïeza."

Azalaïs's heart had stopped beating for a moment when she realized what might happen if fraire Martin saw Savïeza. It would be too much of a coincidence for her to have a tame owl, especially one with a crooked wing. Owls did not normally live with people. They were not like hawks, or songbirds.

She wanted to explain everything to Johana, but she was afraid to give her so much knowledge. It was bad enough that she knew Azalaïs was not Jordane de Belascon. "Please don't ask. Let's just keep the shutters and the doors closed today."

Johana sighed and did as she was bid, then began to work her magic on Azalaïs's hair. Once she had fixed the false braid in a knot at the nape of her neck, she pulled the crespine made of silk netting with garnets and emeralds at each intersecting silk cord over the bundle of hair mixed in with rope. On the top of her head, Azalaïs wore the circlet her husband had given her the night before. Because the weather would be hot, she wore a white linen chemise and cotte of embroidered silk. A leather belt studded with jewels circled her waist, its long tongue hanging down to her knees.

By the time she appeared in the chapel, the baron already occupied a position at the front of the rows of benches and had his hands clasped in front of him. Surrounding him were all the visiting ladies and knights kneeling in silent prayer. Fraire Martin stood near the shrine to the Virgin, and upon catching sight of Azalaïs, he walked to the center and began to intone the prayers that marked the beginning of the day.

Everyone had risen early, and the sun still hung low in the eastern sky when the ladies went to the great hall to break their fast. The knights each took a hunk of freshly baked bread and some aged cheese, then hurried off in fierce silence to find their grooms and pages, who had spent the night polishing and oiling great helms and readying lances and swords for the games.

Azalaïs wandered among the ladies not really feeling as if she had anything to do with them. They all came from a world that was still as strange to her as it had been that day when she first met domna Jordane.

"There hasn't been a tournament since the old baron's day," said the barona de Fabliau to a lady whose name Azalaïs could not remember.

"I wonder that the baron dared to defy the Pope. He must be very well connected."

"They say he has been most helpful to the inquisitors."

Johana happened by and took Azalaïs's arm to draw her toward another group of ladies, whose conversation concerned the latest cargo of silks that had just been unloaded in Narbona's port.

"They have come directly from the Holy Land, on a Templar vessel, and I have been told that among them are several magnificent surcottes that were taken from the Saracens."

"Yes, I had heard that some of the Templars have been called back to these shores to help in the fight against heresy," said a particularly pinched looking lady with a large, wooden cross dangling from a cord around her neck.

"What are the Templars like?" Azalaïs asked, curious about this order of warrior monks who, because they spent most of their time in the east, were more often heard of than seen.

Her question set off a flurry of answers, each more outlandish than the rest.

"I was told they had dispensation from the church to eat the flesh of their heretical victims," said one.

"Nonsense!" broke in another lady, an elderly countess from the north. "If anything they are in league with the heretics, hired out to them to protect them in their disgusting, secret rituals."

Everyone started talking and arguing at once. Azalaïs had no idea that her simple question would provoke such violent disagreement.

The cacophony continued until the door of the solar opened to admit the dowager barona de Belascon. All the ladies stopped talking and curtsied to her as she made her stately way across the floor. She walked up to Azalaïs and stopped a short distance in front of her.

"What causes all this disturbance, Domna?"

Azalaïs flushed at the insolence of her address in front of all their noble guests. "We were merely discussing the Templars and the fine cloth that has newly arrived at port on one of their ships." She tried to suppress the bitter edge that often tinged her voice when she spoke to her belamaire. It would not do to start these vicious tongues wagging all over the Midi and France.

The twitch of a smile flitted across the barona's face. "You shall all have the opportunity of seeing these Templars for yourselves. Two of them will take part in the targa."

After delivering this astonishing news, the dowager turned and left. As soon as the door closed behind her, the excited chatter began again.

246

How could it be that I did not know of this? Azalaïs thought. It appeared that, despite her vivid demonstration of loyalty, the baron still did not confide in her. She had been pushed back into her place, a place she was more and more certain domna Jordane would never have consented to occupy. That lady had understood that the marriage had been solely a matter of property. Property that now attached itself to Azalaïs by proxy. The baron could not acquire this property without the lady, and into the bargain their blood should mix to create a human symbol of that combined domain. That was all. That domna Jordane would take such extreme measures to avoid that fate now ceased to puzzle her.

What else, Azalaïs wondered anew, occupied the baron in his privy chamber, talking for hours with his mother and the men who came from castra throughout the Narbonès and beyond? What did the link to the house of Aniort do for Belascon that he would consent to mix his bloodlines with theirs, to bed a girl he had never seen before his wedding day? And why would they play host to Templar knights?

Johana must help her find out. Azalaïs knew she could not make inquiries herself without coming under suspicion, especially since fraire Martin's arrival. The monk had been there all along among the ladies, nodding and exchanging pleasantries, but all the time Azalaïs knew he had one corner of his eye fixed upon her.

The Corbiu family was atwitter from the moment they awoke at dawn to make preparations to go and watch the tourney at the castel. Although they would not have seats on the reviewing scaffold, as respected members of the community they would be admitted to stand beneath awnings on the grass and watch the events from a distance.

"I've never been to a joust!" exclaimed Tresca for the hundredth time that morning.

"Nor have any of us," said Elionor, trying once more to make the girl stand still so that her plaits could be tidied.

In fact, the merchant and his wife had never seen such a thing either. In honor of the occasion, Corbiu had permitted all his female family members to purchase lengths of silk for new gowns, and given his wife a beautiful gold circlet worked like a garland of tiny flowers.

Corbiu had insisted that Azemar accompany them. At first, Azemar thought this would put an end to his plan to participate in the tournament. But after conferring with Tibout, they decided that the old knight would wait for him outside the castel grounds with the horse and Azemar's new armor. At the beginning of the games he would plead indisposition and excuse himself from the Corbiu family, then hurry to meet Tibout. He hoped that he would be able to ride in, request Azalaïs's token, joust, and acquit himself admirably without anyone— aside from Azalaïs—knowing who he was.

Once all members of the family were attired to the satisfaction of domna Corbiu, the ladies climbed into an open cart drawn by a gentle old workhorse. The groom, Vaquer, took his place with pride. Corbiu and Azemar mounted their palfreys and rode along beside the cart when there was room and ahead of it when the press of houses did not permit them to stay abreast.

By the time they reached the road to the castel, it was already jammed with carts and horses, people on foot, ladies in bright-colored silks, woolen tunics and cottes, and men and women both wearing blials over their tunics or kirtles, some bearing family coats of arms, others adorned with gold- and silver-studded belts. Blue, red, and yellow standards flew from the four corners of the carts, and the brown countryside stretching out on either side of the road intensified the brilliance of the parade. The sight awed Azemar, and the castel itself hadn't yet come into view.

It was slow going to reach the field, visible from several leagues away. The peaks of the tents all flew the baron's standard, a black ground with a red stripe. Lately they had added a quadrant with a gold fleur de lys. The standards flapped and the blare of hunting horns sailed out on the breeze.

With each fanfare, Estacada cried out with tears in her voice, "That must be the Barona arriving, and we have missed it!" or "The knights are surely parading now, and it will be over by the time we arrive!"

Domna Corbiu tried to comfort her daughter, observing that they would hardly start all the festivities before the townspeople were there to witness them. "After all," she said, "The baron wants to impress us as much as anyone. If we fear his might, then we will pay yet more dearly for protection."

Corbiu shot his wife a warning glance.

"Well, it's true. I think our filhas should be made aware of the way things are." She folded her arms across her ample bosom and settled her face into a pout.

Azemar, too, worried about not arriving in time to execute his plan. But to seem too anxious might cast suspicion upon him, and so he did his utmost to remain calm, to pretend to have no greater interest in the proceedings than any of the other family members.

At long last, they reached the scene of the tournament. On the side closest to the castel, in a field that had served as grazing land for the sheep over the growing season, workers had erected a wooden stand covered by a canopy of striped canvas. The two rows of chairs that would accommodate the ladies and the judges were empty. Azemar silently thanked the Lord for arranging things so perfectly.

The huntsmen heralded the arrival of each knight arrayed in armor, which were the fanfares they had heard from so far away. The Corbiu girls wept with joy that they had not missed any of the spectacle.

Already it was difficult to find a place to stand where the jousts would be visible, but Tresca managed to wiggle her way through the crowd and mark out a prime position for the rest of the family. Corbiu and Azemar dismounted and let one of the baron's grooms lead their horses away.

Azemar was too restless to remain with the merchant and his family. He excused himself as soon as he was able and wandered around in the crowd. He did not recognize many of the people; some looked foreign, with their fair hair and pale eyes. They must be from the north, he thought.

He considered leaving right then to meet Tibout, but with people still arriving in droves, he did not want to risk being seen, and so he simply melted into the throng, keeping his eyes focused on the reviewing stand.

After a time, a prolonged fanfare settled the crowd into a subdued buzz. Azemar had managed to wander near the reviewing stand and he had a clear view of the noblewomen and elder judges as they filed into their seats. Last of all was Azalaïs, who even from a distance, glowed. Azemar's heart beat harder, and he clenched his jaw.

Although he had had no opportunity to speak to her at the banquet, the guarded look in her eyes had told him that she was not only unhappy, but fearful. Had it been the attack, in which he had taken part without knowing whose life he would be putting at risk? Or was there some other cause for her fear? He longed to know what had led her to the Narbonès. If he could find a way to meet her secretly they might talk. First, it was essential that he prove to her his loyalty by competing for her favor.

Once he was certain that all the spectators fixed their attention on the stand and the parade of knights in the field, Azemar stole away.

CHAPTER 25

Azalaïs's nerves were as tightly strung as a citole. Johana sat next to her and patted her hand every now and again when she wasn't nudging her to tell her to stand, or to give one of the dozen handkerchiefs she had brought to each knight who trotted up to beg for her token. She tried to let the joglars and acrobats distract her, but she could not dismiss the dread that sat in the pit of her stomach. She had never seen knights ride with lances, but from Johana's description, she knew that despite the blunted lances, men could be killed, and only for sport.

A herald came forward to address the judges in the stand and the knights in the field, all of whom sat on their horses with their standards raised on the ends of their lances.

"High and powerful princes, lords, barons, knights and squires, each and every one of you, please raise your right hand on high, towards the saints, and all together, as you will in the future, promise and swear by the faith and promise of your body, and on your honor, that you will strike none of your company at this tourney knowingly with the point of your sword, or below the belt, and that no one will attack or draw on anyone unless it is permitted, and also that if by chance someone's helm falls off, no one will touch him until he has put it back on, and you agree that if you knowingly do otherwise you will lose your arms and horses, and be banished from the tourney; also to observe the orders of the judges in everything and everywhere as they order delinquents to be punished without argument; and also you swear and promise this by the faith and promise of your body and on your honor."

After the knights all murmured their gruff replies, the challengers presented themselves one at a time. Since there were no grievances, and the day's activities were a simple display of skill at arms, the vanquished did not have to suffer beatings at the hands of the victors.

Nonetheless, the brutality of the spectacle stabbed at Azalaïs's heart. Each time two snorting, prancing destriers faced each other from opposite ends of the jousting frame, their armored riders immobile with grim concentration, she gripped Johana's hand. The pounding hooves approaching at a slow, inevitable canter echoed the beats of her heart, thumping against her ribs until they seemed to stop altogether at the moment of impact. If a lance splintered, she shuddered as if it were her own arm bone that had broken.

The baron rode to the lance every other time. In between, other knights challenged each other, including the two Templars domna Ermengarde had promised.

After ten challenges, Belascon remained undefeated. He trotted up to the stand and removed his helm. His lip was bloodied from where he had bitten it, but his eyes flashed with excitement. Azalaïs recognized that look, and feared that Johana would not be able to prevent her husband from exerting his marital rights that night.

"I respectfully relinquish the field to other contestants. I have no need—"

A fanfare interrupted his courtly speech. One more knight rode onto the field accompanied by a page. His armor was plain. He wore no surcotte and his shield did not bear any markings nor his heaume any crest, and his horse was an old, scarred beast that had obviously seen battle.

The rider sat proudly as he approached the reviewing stand. When the stranger arrived in position, he did not uncover his head. Instead, the groom who ran along beside him spoke on his behalf.

"My master, who wishes to keep his identity concealed, begs the favor of Barona Jordane de Belascon."

"Ask him who he will challenge," whispered Johana.

"Against whom does this strange knight seek to prove his mettle?" she asked, her voice quaking.

"Against the Baron de Belascon."

A murmur of surprise went through the spectators, and the ladies in the stand all whispered into each other's ears.

"What shall I do, Johana?" Azalaïs murmured.

Before Johana could answer, the baron himself spoke. "So, Mollier, which of us will you allow to wear your token? Your marit, or this young boy who is not brave enough to show his face, but who dares to challenge the Baron de Belascon?"

Something in her husband's tone provoked Azalaïs to a small act of rebellion. She stood and approached the rail that separated the ladies from the field. "My marit, the baron, has proven himself already worthy of my esteem, and does not need my favor to prevail on the jousting field. I therefore grant my token to this stranger, that he may not come to serious harm at the hands of so formidable an opponent."

She held out a silk kerchief. The knight eased the fingers of one hand out of his leather glove and rode up to take it from her. He grasped her hand for a moment.

Azalaïs paled and steadied herself on the railing. *It's Azemar.* She did not have to see his face to know. As she turned to reclaim her seat she caught sight of the baron. A moment ago he had radiated magnanimity. Now, he was a thundercloud of rage. *What have I done?* But she knew. Her moment of pique had assured that her husband would ride against Azemar with murdering fury in his heart.

"Why did you do that?" Johana hissed, pinching her hard.

"I had to." What else could she say? She blinked back tears of frustration and confusion.

As Azemar and the baron rode to opposite ends of the field, the entire unruly crowd held its breath. What the incognito knight had done was highly irregular, and contravened the tournament code. The stranger had not presented his arms the day before so that they could be inspected by the ladies—a mark of the greatest disrespect.

Azalaïs thought she would die if her husband mortally wounded Azemar. Having just found him, she did not want to lose all hope of their being reunited in some way, however unlikely that might be.

The chief of the judges waited until the opponents had taken their positions on either side of the tilting frame, and then dropped his white kerchief on the ground. As soon as it hit, the horses began to move toward each other, gathering speed, but only breaking into a canter just before the moment of impact.

Azalaïs closed her eyes. When she opened them, she was relieved to see that both riders remained seated. The second pass began, and again Azalaïs found she could not keep her eyes open at the moment when the lances hit the shields.

"You must watch!" hissed Johana, pinching her again. "He will ask you about it later."

Azalaïs knew that Johana was trying to protect her, but at that moment she hated this companion who had been thrust upon her by circumstances. If Johana knew what it was she asked of her, perhaps she would feel sorry that she had been so cruel. Despite her anger, Azalaïs did as her damozel said, and forced herself to watch the two combatants meet on the third pass.

All her heart went out to Azemar and she prayed that he

would unseat the baron so that he could ride unharmed away from the field.

But it was not to be. The baron was too accomplished a tilter, and his arm had been strengthened by jealousy. His lance hit true on Azemar's plain, pointed shield, and lifted the young man off his saddle and onto the ground.

Azemar lay completely still. The baron dismounted and ran forward to him, drawing his broadsword as he went. At the same time, several grooms ran as fast as they could to intercept him. Death was the punishment for killing a downed, defenseless man at a tournament.

When Azalaïs realized her husband's intentions, she stood and screamed "Belascon!" at the top of her lungs.

It was at that moment that the grooms reached the baron and stayed his arm, which held the sword up high over the vulnerable point between Azemar's heaume and his hauberk. The sound of Azalaïs's scream shook Belascon out of his murderous frenzy, and he turned toward her. He stepped back and removed his helm.

The grooms sat Azemar up, helped him to his feet and led him off the field.

The baron strode toward the reviewing stand. When he reached the point directly in front of Azalaïs, he knelt on one knee. "Now will Ma Domna the Barona de Belascon acknowledge the victor?"

Azalaïs suppressed the urge to spit on her husband's uncovered head. Instead, she took the last of her handkerchiefs, and held it out to him. "To the victor," she said, unable to raise her voice above a whisper.

Azemar lost consciousness for the briefest second when he hit the ground. He woke up just in time to see Belascon's face above him with blood lust in his hard eyes, and saw the point of the broadsword aimed at his throat. If I am saved, Azemar prayed, I pledge myself hereafter to whatever task God sees fit to give me.

As if they had heard his silent vow, four grooms appeared and grasped the baron's arms. They drew him away from Azemar, and then helped him stand.

"That'll teach you to go after someone twice the man as you!" said one of them, but Azemar could feel the groom's hand shaking all the way through the chain-mail sleeve of his hauberk.

They led him to his horse, which had come to a halt away from the crowds and munched the dry grass as if nothing had happened. One of the grooms gave him a leg up. Azemar trotted out of the tournament grounds to find Tibout where he had left him, behind a stand of cypresses some distance away. He dismounted and shed his armor, then donned his silk tunic. Fortunately, he had no real wounds, but had only been winded by the fall. He had made a fool of himself, but an honorable fool, he thought. All his vague longings and uncertainties had been knocked out of him with his wind, and Azemar knew what he must do next.

"I'll return to Menher Corbiu. But I want to know what I must do to become a true knight, so that I may fulfill my destiny as a warrior."

Tibout clapped his beefy hand down on Azemar's shoulder. "You know not what you ask." Tibout took his hand away and nodded to him.

Azemar strode off to join the merchant and his family in the tournament grounds.

"Menher!" cried Tresca when she saw Azemar approaching. "You missed it! The most exciting thing. A challenger, no one knows who he was, but the baron thrashed him."

"He drew his sword against a defenseless man," Elionor said, her eyes showing evidence of recent tears.

"I heard the crowd roar, but I'm afraid I must have eaten something that did not sit well in my stomach." Azemar did his best to look sick. His face was still pale from the shock of the fall and from believing that the baron would kill him, so the Corbiu ménage accepted his excuse quite readily.

As the acrobats returned to entertain the guests with their antics, the judges declared the baron the winner of the tournament—despite his near disgrace—and the nobles left the reviewing stand to return to the great hall. All the wealthy merchants of Narbona had been invited to the feast. Tresca grasped Azemar's hand and pulled him in the direction of the Castel. "The Archbishop is here, they say," said Tresca to no one in particular.

Ahead of them, a stream of brightly clad domnas and gentilòmes strolled across the wide drawbridge and through the portcullis. Inside the ramparts the ground rose up. The residence and donjon of the castel sat on the crest of a hill, making them visible almost in their entirety despite the high, outer wall. Already torches blazed in the windows, and the stream of guests snaked up the path that curved around within the ramparts to make it a gentler ascent.

Azemar knew that if he remained with the Corbiu family and attended the banquet he would see Azalaïs. He knew that she had recognized him and witnessed his defeat. He had entered the baron's hall, eaten at his table, once since the attack without being recognized. He was afraid to tempt fate by accepting his hospitality a second time.

"I fear that I am not well," Azemar said to Corbiu. "I do not wish to disturb the enjoyment of my fellow guests, and beg your leave to return to Narbona," he said.

"Eh? Well, that's too bad. You'll miss quite a feast, and

there will be joglars and trobadors, I'm told," Corbiu said. "But do as you must."

His three daughters cast disappointed glances over their shoulders at Azemar as they followed their parents toward the castel.

Azemar did not hurry back to the city. The days were still long, and he knew he would arrive before the sun went down. Everyone within twenty leagues of the castel had been invited to the tournament and the feast, so there was no one on the road. He let the peace and solitude soothe him as he walked back to the city.

His palfrey needed no urging to walk in the direction of home, and Azemar took advantage of the opportunity to think about what he must do in the coming days. As yet, only Tibout knew that he had decided to become a true knight. Azemar felt in his heart that Montpezat would be pleased with his decision, if he knew of it.

Yet as Tibout stressed, to be a knight was to be a warrior, and the baron—despite his sometimes sharp words—was a man of peace. To Azemar's knowledge, there were no weapons at the castel de Montpezat, except for the bows and arrows they used to hunt singlars and other game.

This was just one of many questions that troubled Azemar, and that had as yet remained unanswered. Each day new ones came to confuse him all the more. *I must think about returning to Montpezat,* Azemar thought. The fact of his challenge to Belascon could hardly remain a secret for long. That and his participation in the attack made two reasons why his presence in the merchant's household might cause difficulties for the family. Leaving seemed the only honorable course to take.

Leaving, though, would mean parting from Azalaïs again, before he had a chance to find out more about what had happened to bring her to that exact place at that exact time.

Azemar's thoughts distracted him, and he arrived at the door of the Corbiu house without having noticed how he got there. He dismounted and led his horse into the stable.

"Raolf!" he called to rouse the stable boy who, with Petrona the kitchen maid, had been left behind. Nothing stirred. The pigs were penned in the corner and snuffling around in their straw. Perhaps Raolf had gone to the kitchens to flirt with Petrona.

Azemar tied his horse to a post and then returned to the street. The kitchens were at the back. They could be approached either by wooden steps from the other side of the house, or from a narrow alleyway that separated the Corbiu residence from their neighbor's.

The sky still had a trace of sunlight in its western corner, but the streets of the city grew dark. Only the Bishop's Tower was tall enough to be touched by a few golden rays. At that time of day, the shadows played tricks on the eyes, and were more difficult to navigate through than the black of night, when one could become accustomed to the dark, or when the moon sometimes cast its own, wan illumination over the landscape. Azemar felt his way down the sheltered, dusky alley. Ahead was the small wooden door that led into the courtyard and the kitchen.

Azemar stopped about a man's height away from the door. He heard something. Or had he? He stood still and listened. Perhaps he'd imagined it.

He took one step forward and stopped again. The door ahead opened. Two figures in dark tunics with hoods over their heads hurried out, disappearing around the corner before he had a chance to open his mouth and call out to ask who they were.

Normally only the servants used this door to bring in wood for the fires and provisions for the kitchens so that they wouldn't have to walk through the house. The men did not look like servants, at least, none that belonged in the Corbiu household.

Once the men were far enough away not to hear him, Azemar continued into the courtyard. "Raolf!" he called again. Again no answer. He went on to the kitchen and found Raolf over by the oven, splayed out with his mouth wide open and snoring loudly. An empty wineskin lay on the ground next to him. Azemar shook his shoulder until he woke.

"Who were those men?" Azemar asked.

"What men?" Raolf replied.

"I saw two men leave the yard through that door." He pointed. Raolf shrugged and yawned.

"Where is Petrona?"

"She was here, but she went in to bed," the groom said, stretching. "The others back too?" he asked.

"No, I returned early."

Clearly Raolf had seen nothing. Azemar took a lamp and lit it with a stick from the fire, then climbed the back stairs to enter the house.

The lamp did little to pierce the gloom inside, and as Azemar crept through the rooms, it came to him that never before had he been in this house alone. Only at that moment did he fully sense how it exuded the lives and personalities of Corbiu and his wife and daughters. He could smell domna Corbiu's light scent from the sachet of spices she always wore at her waist, and the sound of Elionor, Estacada, and Trescalana laughing seemed to have seeped into the stones. As he passed Corbiu's office, a faint, dusty smell of parchment scrolls and books wafted toward him. If he returned to Montpezat, he would leave all this behind.

He ascended the wooden stairs that joined the main floor to the floor above where the family bedchamber was located—containing two large, curtained beds, one for the merchant and his wife, the other shared by the three sisters. Except for the occasional creak of wood under his feet, all was quiet. Perhaps he had been mistaken. The men he saw could have come from behind the kitchens, taking a shorter route on their way to somewhere else. Nothing so far seemed to have been disturbed. All was neat and tidy as usual.

Azemar took the stairs to the top floor. This floor contained the house servants' room and his bedchamber—which had been rendered much more comfortable since he had arrived. His bed had a feather mattress, and a fine linen coverlet that Elionor had worked in silk with a pattern of rabbits. His clothing, citole, and few other possessions were hidden away in an oak armoire.

Relieved, Azemar unclenched his shoulders and shook his head to clear it. His harrowing experience at the tournament had no doubt made him skittish. He was about to drop into the wooden chair in the corner and take off his boots, when he realized that something about the room was not right. Once more on alert, he held up the oil lamp so that it shed the most possible light and circled, illuminating every corner of the room as he went.

It was the armoire. One of the doors hung slightly ajar. Azemar rushed over and threw it open.

At first, nothing appeared to have been disturbed. But he knew he had closed the door himself before leaving that morning. He had only one possession worth stealing. In a frenzy, he yanked his clothing out and threw it on the floor, looking for the bag Montpezat had given him.

It was gone. No one in the house would have known it was there. It had been so long since he had even thought about it, that Azemar wondered for a moment if it hadn't, in fact, vanished long before. But the evidence of recent tampering was too obvious.

They must truly have been thieves, Azemar thought. The

red stone would have been a temptation. He did not know what manner of gem it was, but its brilliance and mysterious heart of fire made him suspect that it was of great value. Yet how would common thieves have known to look for anything in a room that was likely to have been occupied by a servant, on the top-most floor of a merchant's house?

The faintest whimper coming from the room next door to his roused Azemar. He dashed across the landing and burst through the bedchamber shared by the cook, the housekeep-er—who had both been given leave to attend the joust with friends—and Petrona. The kitchen maid lay on one of the pal-lets on the floor, her hands bound behind her back and a rag tied to cover her mouth. He knelt by her side.

"What happened?" he asked as he undid the knots as quickly as his fingers could manage.

The girl—who was no older than Estacada—wept copi-ous tears as soon as she realized it was Azemar. "Oh Menher! Two men in black tunics—how they smelled, and I'll be for it if they broke any of domna Corbiu's good crockery." She paused to wipe her streaming nose on the sleeve of her tunic.

"What did they want?"

"I—I don't know. They asked where you stayed, and made me show them your room."

Why would they be interested in him? "Did they not ask you anything else?"

"Only whether you read to the family from any books."

"What did you tell them?"

"I said you and the *maistre* often had to do with books, but they was mostly full of figuring for the business. Did I tell them ought I shouldn't have?" The maid cowered at the trou-bled look in Azemar's eyes.

"No, no you did just right," he said. "Why don't you go and have a bit of wine to calm your nerves?"

Petrona hurried away as if she was afraid he would change

his mind. Once she had gone downstairs, Azemar returned to his own bedchamber.

He had not expected this. Why would anyone be interested in whether he read from books? He possessed only the one. It contained a few prayers and instructions, all written in Lemozin. Some of the instructions concerned what to do in the case of a legal dispute, others described the gestures and movements that were to accompany certain ceremonies, which resembled a church service but were not quite the same. There was no mention of the Eucharist, or of sacraments.

He had had his suspicions concerning the purpose of the tome, but he had never investigated it. In part, he simply put it out of mind as he was overtaken by the events of his life. In part, he truly did not want to confront its possible meaning.

Now, the book and the stone were gone. And the men who had stolen them must have come on purpose to find them, and therefore had some idea of what they were and consequently who he was, and who might have given those strange items to him. That would mean that both Montpezat and Corbiu could be in danger.

He had only one choice. He must leave immediately and return to Montpezat to warn the baron. He must depart from the house of the merchant before his presence exposed the family to danger. He feared that it might already be too late to protect the Corbiu ostal.

Azemar took an extra tunic, hose and braies from his armoire and rolled them up in a blanket from his bed, securing the neat package with a leather belt. Then he carefully wrapped his citole—which had lain unused atop his trunk ever since he came to Narbona—in the same oiled cloths that had protected it a year ago. The palfrey would not be too tired to start out that night. He would have to find Solomon the Josiu and get some money from him before he departed. After that he would stop at Tibout's for his hauberk, broadsword and shield. It was best to be prepared for anything.

Only one matter remained. Azalaïs must know that he recognized her, but that circumstances had prevented his trying to find a way to speak with her.

On his way out of the house, Azemar entered Corbiu's workroom where he knew he would find parchment and a quill. He wanted to assure his childhood friend that although his departure was unavoidable, he would return as soon as he could. But how to accomplish this without putting her in danger too? Giving him her token at the tournament had already, no doubt, provoked her husband's displeasure.

Azemar placed his blanket roll and the citole on the floor. The instrument gave a faint twang as he did so, and all at once he knew exactly how to get a message to Azalaïs. Everyone would expect the castellane to receive cansos from admirers looking to curry favor with her and her wealthy and influential husband. He could simply behave like one of the ambitious crowd and write her a verse that would tell her everything, and yet would tell everyone else nothing.

It was difficult to concentrate on using the correct form for the verses when he simply wanted to pour out his heart to Azalaïs. Beautiful lady, he began. *Bella domna.* It was a courtly convention. Every lady was beautiful.

Yet Azemar paused after writing those words and stood, staring at the tapestry behind Corbiu's desk. Azalaïs *was* beautiful. The scraped and scraggly little girl who had shared his hardships and adventures had grown into a woman with soft, gray eyes and lips that promised sweet kisses.

This was not exactly what Azemar had thought would happen. When he imagined them reunited, it was always to be friends and companions as they once were, like brother and sister. He did not expect that Azalaïs's slender body and easy grace would arouse feelings in him that, until now, he had reserved for his visits to the brothel—a weekly ritual Corbiu had insisted was necessary to stave off any potential mischief with his virtuous daughters.

Azemar shook his head and bent to his task once more. He banished the image of Azalaïs's face from his mind so that he could proceed with his verse, then rolled up the parchment and tucked it in his pocket as soon as he penned the last line. He knew it might smudge, but he had already spent too much time at the house. Before long the family would return, and he did not want to encounter them on his way out. The letter to Azalaïs would have to go from Tibout's, where he would stop before he left the region.

Azemar paused when he reached the cobbled street. He had not realized until that moment how fond he had grown of these people who had let him into their hearth knowing almost nothing about him, only trusting the words of an elderly baron who had in his turn taken him—a stray, with no home and no heritage—into his home.

Azemar had been sorry to leave Montpezat, but his time in Narbona had been full of gentle pleasures. Corbiu had taught him a great deal, and not all of it was about trading in silks and spices. This was the first time Azemar had ever been a member of an ostal, a true household with a mother and children, had not only watched from outside, but felt in his heart how a close-knit family drew together for nurture, safety, and love.

He would never forgive himself if somehow their kindness to him led to their downfall.

By now the moon had risen above the rooftops, and cast its own pale silver light over the honey-colored stone of the buildings. The wind had shifted. There would be rain. Azemar wondered how the vineyards fared at Montpezat, and how soon they would begin their harvest, and how big the previous year's harvest had been, and what sort of wine they had made from it.

He tried not to think about it, but knowing now that someone was looking for him, Azemar wondered, too, if the vineyards would be there at all.

CHAPTER 26

In vain Azalaïs looked for Azemar among the guests at the banquet. The Corbiu family was there in full strength, but the knight she now knew for certain as the boy she had parted from nine years ago was not with them. There were too many more important visitors for her to have an opportunity to speak with domna Corbiu, and so she was forced to endure the dinner and entertainment without knowing what had become of her friend.

The baron was occupied talking and laughing with the knights who sat at the head table. Azalaïs and domna Ermengarde were the only ladies among them. Johana had been relegated to a lower table, giving way to higher ranking nobles and their ladies.

Although she did not look at him, Azalaïs noticed that the baron downed cup after cup of wine. She could feel his anger cross the small space that separated them, so different from the other night, when he could not keep his hands away from her. She prayed that he would imbibe enough to pass out before he could storm into her bedchamber and demand his rights.

More than an hour after the banquet began, fraire Martin entered the great hall. Until that time, Azalaïs had not noticed his absence. Then, too, she realized that the Templar knights were not among the guests either.

The monk's presence cast a dark shadow over the evening. Every time Azalaïs looked up, he turned away, as though he'd been caught staring at her. Out of the corner of her eye she saw him ooze from table to table like spilled wine, stopping conversations, subduing laughter, and leaving a foul taste behind. When he at last made it to the high table, he remained near domna Ermengarde, his head bent to hers, whispering.

After the guests had eaten more than their fill, the musicians and jugglers and acrobats returned and so did the celebratory atmosphere—until, that is, one of them staged a parody of the baron's victory over the unknown young *cavalièr*.

The laughter in the hall quieted, replaced by shocked silence. Azalaïs cast an uneasy glance at the baron, whose face darkened despite his inebriation. The hapless joglar realized his mistake and froze with his mock sword-hand held high.

It was fraire Martin who broke the tension by leaving the table and walking up to the fellow. "He but reminds us of the lordly restraint shown by the baron de Belascon, when he could have held the unlawful challenger to account. I thank you, minstrel, for your lesson." He clapped the joglar on the back, and relieved chatter once more echoed off the vaults of the great hall.

The evening was unbearable. "Is it proper for me to leave now?" Azalaïs mouthed to Johana across the hall.

"Not until the baron leaves," she mouthed back.

It was only then that Azalaïs noticed how many of the guests looked tired and ready to depart after a long day of revelry, but nonetheless remained at the banquet. Until the festivities ceased, those who would stay the night could not take their places on the folding beds that the servants would set up in place of the tables in the hall.

But they did not have to wait much longer. After a short while the baron stood spoke out over everyone's heads. Fraire Martin placed himself next to and a little behind him.

"Thank you, my loyal friends and vassals. Those of you who depart tonight I bid safe passage back to your homes. My heralds will light the way with torches."

The baron stepped down from the table, the signal for all its other occupants to do the same. Having managed to remain outwardly calm so far, Azalaïs's entire body trembled as if she'd been left outside on a frigid night. She waited for her husband to reach her. He put out his arm, which she took, wondering if he could feel her shaking. She hoped the wine had dulled his senses.

When they reached the stone stairs that led to the solar, he stopped and bowed to her. "I have business to transact this evening." He stumbled as he turned to leave. Out of nowhere, fraire Martin appeared and steadied him.

Azalaïs said a silent prayer of thanksgiving, and took Johana's arm to ascend the stairs. The baron did not trouble her that night.

Johana retired to her antechamber and Azalaïs let her believe that she was on the way to sleep herself. But as soon as her companion closed the door, she rose from her bed and carried her candle to the writing table.

She took a sheet of parchment and began to compose a poem to Azemar. It was time to make sure he understood how things were. She must find a way to tell him what had happened to her.

> We should have met in Bésiers
> But I am here, and alone
> although you may think I toy with you.
> My journey has been long, and
> deception is my life.
> I love not, but I bear
> a burden that never should have

been mine to bear.
Please tell me if you recall
those times of childish joy,
or would you put them behind you
and leave me to my misery?

The thought of what might happen to Azemar if the baron discovered who he was terrified Azalaïs. Although she never saw his face, she had no doubt at all that it had been Azemar beneath that helm and chain mail. If she had any hesitation, his absence at the banquet was confirmation enough. She had managed to guess his identity, and if she could, then others would too. Azemar was in danger.

Flight was the only course open to Azalaïs now. Yet to flee on her own, without Azemar? The thought filled her with fear—and loneliness. To have found him again, and then to run away where he might not be able to find her.

No, her only hope was that they could escape together. She knew he was brave enough to do it, if he could. It didn't matter that the baron had unseated him at the tournament. But she needed to get a message to him to let him know that she was brave enough, too. Azemar would protect her with his life, of that she was certain now. He had done so when they were children, and he would again.

More than that, she would protect him too.

Azalaïs scattered sand over the parchment to dry the ink, rolled it up and tied a cord around it. She brought it to her bed and tucked it beneath her feather pillow, keeping her hand on it. The knowledge of that message comforted her. Tomorrow she would have to find someone to deliver it to the Corbiu house.

Marcu—that's who she would give it to. He had been the means of conveying other people's anonymous verses to her, and would think merely that she was writing a reply to one of those. He would not suspect that any real importance lay in the note she sent.

Azemar rode to Tibout's castel directly from Narbona. His arrival roused the groom, who rushed out to take his horse into the stable.

"I beg only a bed for the night, so that I may take my leave of Senher Tibout tomorrow," Azemar told him.

The groom insisted on waking the old knight to greet him—possibly because he was afraid to let Azemar in without his master's approval. Tibout came to the great hall in his night robes.

Azemar told him that thieves—or some other men of ill will—had ransacked his room at the Corbiu residence.

Tibout brought him into his privy chamber and called for wine. "You have not told me what they took from you," he said, once they were alone behind closed doors and had both drunk deeply of the ruby liquor.

Azemar hesitated. He did not want this worthy gentilòme to know anything that might endanger him. "It's best that I not say."

Tibout nodded. "I presume it was not just a sack of Moslem gold, or you might have gone to the authorities with a complaint."

"I must leave the Narbonès tonight. I have a message that I beg you—or someone you can trust—to deliver to the castel."

Azemar could feel the heat rise into his face and hoped the candlelight hid it from Tibout.

But the knight was too observant to miss it. He gave a derisive snort. "You young lads! Don't you know that love will get you in trouble? Families like Belascon's don't treat with love." He leaned across the table until he was nose-to-nose with Azemar. "Stay here for a day or two. Wait and see what happens. It may be that by running far away you put yourself in greater peril than by remaining close by. By running away you confirm their suspicions about you—and quite possibly lead them to Montpezat."

"What you say makes sense. But I still don't understand why they are watching me—whoever they are."

"Well, let me see: you arrive a wealthy gentleman from nowhere. You purchase armor and become trained as a knight. You challenge the liege lord of the region to a joust when you can barely sit a horse. I'd be curious!"

Azemar couldn't help smiling at Tibout's description. "Very well, I shall do as you suggest. With your kind permission I will wait two days before departing."

"Then we can see that you have everything you need for your own safety in your travels, and it will appear as if you planned the journey instead of fleeing in panic," Tibout said. "My servants are well trained to keep their counsel. You need only remain within my domain and you will be secure."

The two men finished their wine and a house servant showed Azemar to a small but comfortable chamber above the keep and below the watchtower, a room where, in an earlier day when the crusade was still being pursued with savagery, guards would have slept when they were not on duty above keeping watch against attack.

Azemar was glad of the opportunity to wait for a possible response to his verse from Azalaïs. One way or the other, he must know her wishes.

The following morning dawned gray and foggy. The wind had changed in the night, chasing the fine weather away, but bringing the promise of rain from the Montanha Negre to help nourish the vineyards that terraced the slopes of the Corbières. Azalaïs awoke with a heavy feeling in her heart.

The baron and his knights had departed again early that morning to join Arcis and the French at Bésiers. Azalaïs could not send for Marcu until the hour when such pastimes as music and poetry would be expected, and so she carried her message to Azemar concealed in her money pouch all day. She found it near impossible to concentrate on anything, and spent a long time working one tiny patch of her embroidery amid what remained of the visiting ladies in the solar.

"Good afternoon, Barona."

The voice behind Azalaïs's shoulder made her jump, and she pricked her finger. A drop of blood soaked into the fine, white linen ground of her handiwork. She looked up, and there stood fraire Martin, staring down at her in a way that reminded her of the horrible day at the abbey near Bolbona.

"I apologize, Barona!" he said, pulling his hood back from his head to reveal his tonsure. "It's simply that having heard your blessed news, I was eager to pray with you."

Azalaïs regained her composure with difficulty. "Thank you, fraire Martin." She bowed her head for his blessing, as did the other ladies. "Would you like to sit?" She gestured to a stool near the fireplace. The damp stone walls made the castel chilly despite the mildness of the day.

He walked to the stool, never removing his eyes from Azalaïs's face. "Your marit bid me tell you that he has been called away to join King Louis's forces with his own knights, and does not know when he shall return." The monk reached into his cassock and with a great flourish, took out a square of linen and held it out toward her.

At first, Azalaïs stared at the white cloth with no comprehension. After a moment she realized the monk expected her to break down in tears at the idea of parting from her husband at so critical a time, when she had just discovered she was expecting an heir or heiress to the Belascon estate.

She could not bear to touch something that belonged to fraire Martin, and so she stood, deciding on a different response. "My marit must serve as he is called by his station. It is not for me to keep him tied to the hearth like a woman."

"Well said, child." Fraire Martin then sank to his knees on the floor, and made a gesture that he expected Azalaïs to do the same.

She knelt before him and pressed her palms together, causing all the other ladies to creak to their knees as well.

In nomine Patris," the monk began, and then proceeded to repeat a prayer that lasted until Azalaïs thought her knees would make dents in the wooden floor.

When at long last fraire Martin finished his invocation, Azalaïs and the other ladies stood. The monk was old, however, and had difficulty rising to his feet. He held his hand out to Azalaïs for support. She could not refuse to take it, but his touch made her skin crawl. The last time his hand had made contact with her flesh, she knew that he had very unholy thoughts in his mind.

"Your marit feels that it is time you were made aware of the important work we are doing here for the future of the Church. A chair will wait for you in the courtyard tomorrow at the none bells."

There was simply no arguing with fraire Martin, and so Azalaïs bowed her head. "Tomorrow, then."

The monk let go of her hand and bowed to her, then left the solar as quietly as he had entered.

Azalaïs wished she would have an opportunity to add something to her verse for Azemar that would make him come and carry her away from the castel that very night. But with all the guests around and the constant scrutiny of the monk, she resigned herself to having to keep her appointment with fraire Martin the next day.

It was not until after dinner that she had an opportunity to speak to Marcu and give him her poem. "Please make certain this reaches Azemar, at the ostal of Corbiu the merchant," she whispered.

Marcu bowed and tucked the scroll in the pouch that hung from his belt. "Ma Domna," he said, "a messenger arrived earlier with something for you."

He passed a similar parchment scroll to Azalaïs, but before she could read it, both her belamaire and fraire Martin entered. She had to sit through a long evening of conversation and music before it was finally time to retire to her chamber.

After Johana had closed the door of her own cabinet, Azalaïs unrolled the scroll Marcu had given her, holding it close to her bedside candle so that she could read it.

As she knew in her heart all along, it had come from Azemar. She hesitated to read the words themselves, only looking at the letter as an object, a talisman, marveling at the confident hand that had scratched lines over one surface, at the fact that the rough boy she once knew could put words of his own down on parchment and send them to her.

The old image of him was fading from her memory and being replaced with that of the young cavalièr she had seen now on two occasions, but it was not altogether gone. And the terror of that day long ago in the forest would never leave her. If they had known then—but it was useless to think about it. They would probably have died anyway, if not at the will of Gascon, then by the icy hand of hunger or disease.

Azalaïs traced the lines with her finger as she read, imagining Azemar's hand holding the quill. She read so slowly that at first she did not connect anything into a coherent thought. Until she came upon the word *parte,* she assumed that the note

275

contained only some kind of acknowledgment that she was right, and that he knew her as well.

She read the letter again, quickly this time, to get its meaning whole and direct. Azemar was going away. They had just found each other against all odds and despite a great many changes that should have kept them apart for good, and now he would willingly depart from the region.

A great, howling emptiness opened in Azalaïs's heart. It was likely that he would never receive the note she had asked Marcu to deliver, at considerable risk to both of them, and would never know how desperately she wanted to go with him.

As if he knew that his mistress needed him, Savïeza did not fly off into the darkness to hunt that night. Instead he perched on the table by Azalaïs's bed, his eyes wide and staring at her. He flapped around the room once or twice in pursuit of mice, but otherwise remained in the same place, watching over Azalaïs as she cried herself to sleep.

CHAPTER 27

The following day, Johana helped Azalaïs prepare for her excursion with fraire Martin. The monk had left her a note that said he would meet her at the destination to which the porters had already been instructed to convey her in a litter.

"Where do you suppose he is taking me?" she asked Johana, although after getting Azemar's letter the night before, she had little interest. Yet she was not so caught up in her own disappointments that she didn't notice Johana's guarded and fearful expression, and a trickle of apprehensive seeped into her consciousness.

The donzel leaned into the chair, pretending to arrange Azalaïs's veils and clothing. "I have heard that you are to be conveyed to the abaïa," she said.

Having spent many hours in her disguise as a boy at the Cistercian abbey near Bolbona, Azalaïs was somewhat reassured by this information. The monks at Bolbona were quiet, gentle, and industrious. Because they belonged to the same order she had no reason to assume that those at Fontfred were any different. Perhaps fraire Martin simply wanted her to make a charitable donation to the abbey, to support their work with the poor.

"I wish you could come with me, Johana," Azalaïs said

as the donzel closed the door of the litter. Johana's quiet, wise company always consoled her. Johana did not answer, but simply squeezed Azalaïs's hand.

She braced herself against the jolt of being picked up off the ground and rocked back and forth until the bearers got their balance. At some other time, and for another purpose, Azalaïs might have been happy to be outside the boundaries of the castel grounds. She had only been once to Narbona itself, to the cathedral for Mass on Pentecost. It seemed a pleasant, busy city and she longed to wander unseen through its lanes. But her belamaire had seen to it that she was deposited directly at the west doors of the unfinished cathedral and accompanied at all times by guards.

That morning, instead of looking forward to going beyond the confines of her domain, she wished she could have stayed behind, and was grateful for the thick veils that covered her eyes, still red from crying the night before. She was glad that the blinds were drawn so that no passing peasant could see in and she could not see out.

The abbey of Fontfred sat atop a steep hill, surrounded on all sides by the garriga—the rough, scrubby moorland broken only by well-tended vineyards, grain fields and olive groves. Although Azalaïs could tell they traveled up an incline and felt sorry that the young pages had such a difficult task to perform in carrying her, by the time they set her chair on the ground again, she had no sense at all of where she was or how far she had traveled. Even knowing where she was going did not help, so that when a page opened unlatched the door and helped her climb out, the sight of the imposing abbey surprised her.

A raucous chorus of birdsong filled the air, and the scent of herbs was so strong she thought perhaps she had been brought in through the kitchen garden. A white-robed monk greeted her and put a finger to his lips, then led her in through a small door hidden by vines that grew from the ground and out of the cracks in the wall itself.

Once the door shut behind her, she found herself in a windowless corridor that excluded all sounds of the countryside. The cold, stone-bound air sent a shiver through her entire body. "I can't see!" Azalaïs said.

The monk turned to her and lifted two layers of her veils so that she could more easily watch her feet, then beckoned her to follow him down the long, increasingly dark corridor.

They eventually reached a spiral stairway only wide enough for a single person that led yet deeper into the ground. As she descended, Azalaïs could hear dripping water, its hollow echo growing louder the deeper they went. She told herself to breathe slowly. This was only a temporary state of affairs. She was the barona de Belascon and they would hardly leave her to rot in some underground prison. Especially not when the baron expected her to present him with an heir before two seasons passed.

When at last they reached the bottom of the stairs, the monk pulled her veils down again and led her on toward the open door of a chamber lit by the glow of torches. A low-pitched murmur of men's voices reached her ears.

Her guide motioned her to stop just outside the door, in a place where she could see into it but would not be visible to those inside the room.

A rough-hewn wooden chair stood directly in her line of sight. At the floor near it were leg irons and chains with iron cuffs dangling from its arms. A circular metal band with bolts on either side of it hung above the back of the chair.

A few moments later, a door opened from another side of the chamber, it sounded as if something was being dragged across the floor. A man's weak voice bleated out, "No! No!"

Two hooded monks put a thin, naked man into the chair. He shook violently as they fastened his arms and legs into the irons and lowered the band so that it fit around his forehead. When they moved away so that Azalaïs could see his face, she gasped.

"Senher Barasc, you have refused to reveal to us the names of the traitors who banded together to attack the castel de Belascon. You will be punished after death as you are being punished on earth."

Blood pulsed into Azalaïs's ears. Her mouth went as dry as the stone walls surrounding her. The voice belonged to fraire Martin.

A tear trickled down Barasc's ashen face. Two hooded men who were not wearing monks' cassocks stepped forward and twisted the bolts on either side of the band around his head. Azalaïs wanted to look away, but it was as if fraire Martin had cast a spell over her that compelled her to keep staring at the land steward's eyes, bulging and bewildered with pain. He uttered not a sound.

As the hooded men twisted and twisted, Dreu's eyes swelled and became shot with blood. He strained against the short chains that held his arms to the chair, his mouth twisted in a horrible grimace.

Crack! like a whip. At that moment, the two men unscrewed the contraption and lifted the band off Dreu's head. As soon as it was free of its constraint, his head lolled forward, now misshapen. Azalaïs turned away, lifted her veils, and vomited.

The monk who had been her guide rushed out from where he must have stood out of sight in the room, closing the door to the chamber behind him. He took her arm and led her back up the long stairs, down the dark corridor, and finally out to the sunlight.

Azalaïs breathed deeply for a few moments, struggling to still her trembling. The porters rushed over to help her back into the litter.

"The barona was much affected by religious fervor," the monk said to the porters by way of explanation for her distress.

The downhill journey went quickly. As soon as she was within the wall of the castel, Azalaïs threw off her veils and ran up to her chamber.

"What is it?" Johana had been arranging Azalaïs's gowns in the armoire but stopped as soon as she saw her mistress.

Azalaïs shook her head. "Not now. I'll tell you later."

It was not until late in the afternoon, after she had sipped the hot tisana that Johana instructed the kitchen how to prepare that Azalaïs could begin to tell her companion what had happened on her visit to the abbey.

"It's because of me. They only knew it was Dreu because I told them. Why, why did they do such a thing? Why could I not have predicted it, and thought not to mention his name?" Azalaïs asked, her tears flowing again as they strolled in the garden before dinner.

"I don't know," Johana answered. "But you say they asked him about the others who were involved in the plot, and that he did not tell them. Those others owe poor Dreu a debt indeed."

Azalaïs could not reveal her worst fears to Johana. If they could do such a thing to the man who had made it possible for her to defend the castel and send word to the baron, then what might they do to any of those who had actually taken part in the attack if they ever found them? She prayed that Dreu had not let any names escape his lips before she had seen him, although she could hardly blame him if he had.

And then, there was her other worry, the one that had not left her since the moment she traded places with Jordane. "What would happen to me if they ever found out who I really was?" she whispered.

"Don't speak of it!" Johana's voice was sharp. "We would

both be in great danger, as would domna Jordane and all of her family," she whispered.

They turned back to the castel and finished their walk in silence.

When Azalaïs retired to her chamber, she saw a small scroll of parchment on her table that had not been there before. "Marcu must have brought it," she said.

"Another admirer," Johana said, then excused herself to go and rest before dinner.

Yes, Azalaïs thought, I must be playing my role well to fool so many. With little interest she untied the cord that held the scroll closed and unrolled the dried skin.

> *The southwest corner of the orchard, after the compline bells. I'll wait until matins if necessary.*

That was the entire message. *Azemar!* She recognized his hand in an instant from the other note he had sent her. So he had not left the vicinity after all, and must somehow have received her verse.

Despite all that had happened that day, a flood of joy washed through Azalaïs's body. He would come and they would leave together before anything even more terrible could happen.

The prospect of stealing out to meet someone beyond the castel walls brought to mind the last time she had gone to meet someone secretly after curfew, in Caunes. The blood rushed through her veins to the pit of her stomach as she remembered the stranger's kiss. Surely there would be no kisses tonight, though, she thought. She and Azemar were childhood friends, nothing more. He wanted to see her to help get her out of her impossible predicament.

But there was no time to waste idly speculating about Azemar's motives. She must find a way to get out of the castel at night to keep her appointment with him. It would not be as easy as it was for her in Caunes, where she was nothing more than a valueless servant. Aside from the fact that here, the guards had been doubled since the attack, each night at curfew great iron chains pulled up the bridge over the moat, groaning and squealing like a wounded beast, and the bridge was not lowered until after dawn.

Yet there must be a way to get out. The servants, she'd heard, often slipped away to visit their sweethearts after their long day's chores were completed. She had even overheard her belamaire once complaining that someone was smuggling provisions out of the kitchen.

She might find this secret exit, but what if she were caught? How would she explain what she was doing? If they stopped her while she was inside the castel, she could say she had a sudden craving for some delicacy from the kitchens, and had lost her way in the dark. But once she strayed beyond the ramparts—that would be a different matter. She shuddered to imagine the dowager punishing her. Something told her the old lady would enjoy watching her suffer.

And of course, there was the matter of the moat. In the rainy season and in the wintertime the encircling barrier filled with water. At this time of year it was not deep, however, yet still treacherous to cross—as she'd witnessed when several of the attachers had become entangled in the weeds that choked it and—despite its shallowness—sank beneath its opaque surface and drowned. The servants spoke of seeing snakes there, too. There was even a legend about a great monster serpent, used to frighten children into obedience.

Yet if others managed to get across, there must be a way. Perhaps the small skiff that the peasants sometimes used to take diseased animals away from the rest of the livestock and to carry refuse out of the castel compound was left unsecured.

Even in the best of circumstances, it would not be easy.

At least, she thought, the baron had taken his knights with him again, leaving only a skeleton force of archers behind.

Later, when Johana awoke from her rest and came in to help her bedeck herself with silks and jewels for yet another fine banquet that evening, Azalaïs caught Johana's serene, friendly gaze in the mirror and held it. "I need to ask you an enormous favor."

"What is it?"

"I don't know . . . I need your help"

"For what?" Johana turned to fetch Azalaïs's casket of jewels from the table behind her.

"It's just that . . . Supposing I needed to get away from the castel at night. Do you think it would be possible?"

Johana stopped just before placing the casket on the dressing table, half bent over so that her face was quite close to Azalaïs's. "What can you be thinking of?" she whispered.

Azalaïs reached into her pocket and pulled out the scroll that had arrived earlier.

Johana's eyes widened as she read it. "Who did this come from?"

"I cannot tell you. I must meet him. You know that it is not my fault that I am here." She hoped that Johana would add the words, *you owe me this,* on her own.

Johana's shoulders drooped and she shook her head. "It will be very dangerous. After what you saw today, it's insane to try."

"But I must!" Azalaïs grabbed Johana's arms and swiveled on the stool so she could look directly into her eyes.

Johana sighed. "I think I can find out from Marcu how to leave the castel. I overheard him talking to one of the servants after the last banquet about some way to get out to visit a sick relation." She lifted the jeweled circlet out of the jewel cask and settled it on Azalaïs's head. "Besides, he's devoted to you. You can trust him."

At the mention of the trobador, Azalaïs had a pang of guilt. Her actions, if discovered, could set off a chain of retribution that would reach far into the castel hierarchy and beyond, to the city of Narbona itself. Yet she had no choice but to act. "Will you—please?"

Johana nodded, and neither of them spoke of the matter again until they had once more endured a public dinner and evening of song and dancing.

Just before the guests departed for the night, so that the monk and the dowager would be too occupied to notice, Johana whispered in Azalaïs's ear, "There is a tunnel, beneath the wall near the kitchen. The door is next to the ovens. The servants use it sometimes to go and hunt without anyone knowing. A *batèu* is tied up between the wall and the bank of the moat. You must row straight across, or the weeds can entangle the oars. The bank is steep, so be careful. Stay no longer than it takes for the moon to travel from one corner of the castel to the other."

Azalaïs tried to behave as usual as she prepared to retire for the night. She curtsied to her belamaire and suffered fraire Martin to place his hand on her head in benediction, strolled without hurrying toward the stairs, and bid her guests goodnight as if she really wished to prolong the evening instead of make the time until compline hasten by.

When at last she lay alone in the dark, her senses sharpened. Every tiny hair on her body could feel any slight movement in the air around her, and every time a sleeping guest rolled over on a cot in the hall, a shock went through her. She would need to have ears as sensitive as fraire Goncort's to escape the castel that night. The prospect was terrifying, yet the idea of being able to speak to Azemar again, to find out how he came to be in Narbona, gave her courage.

Although she had wondered from time to time as she studied with fraire Goncort and then while she was in the Aniort household whether Azemar had survived, she never seriously doubted that he had, and presumed he was somewhere in the world. She always believed in her heart that they would see each other again. Now that she knew her instincts had been correct, she had more questions. Perhaps that night they would at last be answered.

Azalaïs waited until she could not hear a soul stirring in the castel before sliding out of bed. She pulled a plain tunic over her head, tied a silk belt around her waist and crept barefoot to her door, with her skirt lifted so it would not swish against the wooden planks. The latch made a click that echoed in the silent castel, and the door creaked a little on its hinges. Azalaïs had never noticed those sounds before. Surely they were loud enough to awaken the entire household.

But nobody stirred at the noise, and once her eyes became accustomed to the dark, she swiftly found her way through the corridors and halls of the castel to the small side door that led from the kitchens, just as Johana had said. She grasped the latch, tried to lift it as quietly as possible, and then pushed against it.

It didn't give.

She pushed again, harder. Still no luck.

Locked. Of course. The seneschal saw that all the doors of the castel were locked after curfew. Although Azalaïs had felt like a prisoner since the moment she had been thrust into her borrowed identity, the hard reality of her incarceration broke over her at that moment, when all that stood between her and freedom was this wooden plank door.

She leaned her head against the frame of the door and struggled not to sob aloud. As if by squeezing herself against the rough oak she might wish herself on the other side, Azalaïs pressed her body against the door and reached her arms out, curling her fingers around the edges, feeling how the wood met the cool stones of the wall.

"Ouch!" she whispered, and stood back. She pricked her finger on a nail that jutted from a crevice between two stones.

Azalaïs took a closer look and saw that the mortar was loose there. More out of curiosity than anything else, Azalaïs began to wiggle the stone out of its place.

It took a few minutes, but the stone was small enough that she could manage it, and the hole it left was just at her eye level. She peered into the darkness, and thought she saw something there. Although she knew she risked finding a sleeping scorpion in such a dark, cool hiding place, Azalaïs reached her hand in and felt around.

Yes. A key. After she replaced the stone, she tried the key in the lock. It fit, but at first it did not turn. Grasping it with both her hands, she worked it slowly, listening for a sign that something was giving inside the door.

At last, a click, and the bolt eased out silently from the door frame. She touched the bolt's cavity, and could feel that it had been smeared with goose grease. Others had gone before her and had also not wanted to be heard leaving this way.

Azalaïs pulled the door shut behind her, taking care not to make a sound, and plunged herself into profound darkness. Keep going, she thought. Johana said the tunnel was short—only the depth of the thick castel walls—so she tamped down her rising panic and felt her way along. Already her nostrils flared at the brackish scent of the moat. After about twenty steps, she saw the outline of an opening and heard the gentle lapping of water stirred by the breeze.

There, as Johana had said, was a small boat pulled just far enough up the narrow bank that it wouldn't float away. Azalaïs had little experience with boats. She had never rowed in her life, although she'd seen vessels plying the rivers when she took her journey from Bolbona to Caunes, and knew that it was necessary to face backward and pull the oars toward her through the water.

Getting into the skiff was more difficult than she thought it would be, and panic rose in Azalaïs's throat when she realized how easily she could tip over in the water. Already her skirt was wet at the bottom from the muddy swill that had splashed into the boat as she climbed in.

She knelt in the middle, becoming even wetter in the process, dipped the oars and began pulling. Her arms—once quite strong from carrying firewood and bearing loads of brush back to fraire Goncort's hut—had become useless and ladylike. At first she cut a jagged path, but once the boat was underway, she straightened and picked up speed. It wasn't long before the boat bumped into the opposite bank.

Unlike a river, in the moat there was no shallowing by the shoreline, so although she had made it across, Azalaïs could not figure out how to step out of the skiff and drag it up on the dirt. If she did not secure the boat, it might drift away and she would be unable to return the way she came. *I've gone to all this trouble,* she thought, *risked so much, and perhaps I'll just have to row back and give up.* Tears pricked in the back of her eyes.

At that moment, she saw a figure emerge from the olive grove a short distance away. She held her breath. It had to be Azemar. Yet if it were not . . .

As the figure drew closer, it quickened its pace, first walking faster, then trotting, then running to the edge of the moat.

"Azalaïs!"

Before Azalaïs had a chance to utter a word, Azemar grasped her upper arm and helped her out of the boat with one hand and took hold of the gunwale with the other. Once she stood safely on firm ground, he dragged the boat out of the water.

Azalaïs gazed in wonder at Azemar as he scanned the castel and the surrounding countryside and drew her away from the moonlight reflecting off the surface of the moat. He had a sure grace, the confidence of a man who had made his way in the world. The mischievous boy was there, yet time and danger had honed and tempered him.

"It's safer in the shadows," he said, and they ran to the shelter of a chestnut tree.

Azalaïs wished they could stand in the strong sunlight so that she could really see her old friend. In the moon shadows he had an insubstantial quality that made her doubt his actual presence. "Is it really you?"

He did not answer, but fixed his eyes on hers. They were so deep, reflecting her back at herself and yet hinting at limitless horizons. She wanted to sink below that surface and seek inside them the times now past.

In those first moments, she and Azemar had gradually moved toward each other until they were touching. She did not register the transition from separateness to connection. All she knew was that they wrapped their arms around each other, and they kissed. Once they started, they could not stop. Eyes, cheeks, lips, necks. In between each kiss, Azalaïs smiled so hard that the tears she had been fighting to suppress squeezed out of her eyes and dampened her cheeks.

When they could bear to step a little away again, Azemar was the first to speak. "We must not stay so close to the castel." He took her hand and they ran through the olive grove to a larger copse of trees just beyond. Under cover of the rustling chestnut leaves, they embraced again, then sank down, still clinging to one another, and leaned against a tree trunk.

"How is it you are the Barona de Belascon? What happened to you after we parted?" Azemar whispered, wiping Azalaïs's eyes with a linen kerchief.

"I might ask you, too, how you come to be in the household of a prosperous merchant, and clearly a man of means yourself."

They lapsed easily into their old teasing ways, only now, they needed to touch each other, to be in constant physical contact. They sat pressed together, fingers interlaced, and talked. Soon each knew the other's story as if it were his own.

"Things just happened. I feel as if nothing is in my control, that everyone is using me in a game whose rules keep changing." Azalaïs nestled her head in the curve of Azemar's neck and let the silence envelop her.

"And yet," Azemar said, "Everything has led us back to each other."

"I'm afraid." Azalaïs pressed closer to him.

"Yes." The unasked question hovered between them.

"We have found each other, but we cannot be together. I am the Barona, and I am a prisoner." Azalaïs told Azemar about how she had found the key to let herself out of the castel. "Fraire Martin is watching me for any sign of what, I don't know. All I do know is that he would tell the old lady if he ever discovered that I stole out to meet you. And you know how she threatened me."

"What happened with this monk? You said you knew him from Bolbona."

"I—I'd rather not say. But it was because of him that I had to leave. No, I would have had to go eventually, but what happened with him made me go when I did."

"I see."

"And then, I must think about Johana and Marcu as well. I have endangered both of them through my actions tonight. No one would believe my donzella knew nothing about it. I tell her everything!"

They sat together in silence for a moment or two. A night bird broke the stillness and reminded them that time was passing.

Azemar resumed his tale. "It is clear that someone has marked me out, for what purpose it is impossible to say. I, too, cannot continue to endanger my friend by remaining under his protection. I must go from this place tomorrow. I do not wish to leave without you. But for now we must part."

Azalaïs looked up at the sky. The moon had almost

290

reached the opposite corner of the castel. It was time. Yet she felt a searing pain near her heart at the thought of letting go of Azemar, of leaving him and returning to her imprisonment in the castel. "Can we not go tonight? Now?" She pressed herself into his arms, shaking. He gently but firmly pushed her away.

"You have to return. There are matters I must attend to before I leave for good, and you can hardly take a long journey with only a tunic to protect you from the weather. In two months, it will be winter."

At that moment Azalaïs felt the dampness that had crept up her skirt, and she began to shiver. Azemar was right. She would need time to gather some of her things together, to plan how to hide and survive.

"Tomorrow, at the same hour. I'll bring a horse for you." Azemar punctuated each phrase with a gentle kiss.

They crept in silence back to the moat and Azemar launched the boat and helped her into it again. The other shore would be easier: the landing place was well-used.

As she rowed across the black water, Azalaïs felt sad and lost, and yet not without hope. She was no longer alone. Azemar would help her get out of the castel, away from the baron, his mother, and fraire Martin. They would be together again. Whatever happened after that, whatever trials they had to face, would be easy to bear.

With some difficulty, Azalaïs managed to climb out of the boat and drag it up the steep slope by the kitchen. She found the tunnel opening easily. The door at the other end was just as she had left it, and she locked it behind her and replaced the key where she'd found it. *Tomorrow*, she thought, *I shall leave this place forever.*

She crept through the sleeping household and crawled back into bed, unable to close her eyes and sleep before the sky grayed to dawn.

CHAPTER 28

Tibout had seen to it that Corbiu received Azemar's note telling the merchant that he would know where Azemar was—in case circumstances made it necessary to locate him. He did not think Corbiu would avail himself of the information so soon, and was surprised to receive a letter from the merchant while he was busy making sure the horse he had purchased from Tibout would do for Azalaïs.

> *I send you bad news. The baron de Montpezat is very ill. Wherever you are, you must go to him immediately. His seneschal wrote to say that he asks for you.*

Azemar stopped what he was doing and sank onto a stool. Could this be a trap? Or was it true that Montpezat needed him? He recognized Corbiu's writing. But he could have been coerced into composing the message. In any case, there was no easy way to know. It would mean postponing his plans with Azalaïs. If they went that night, together, they would easily be traced to Montpezat.

It took only a moment for Azemar to realize that he could not ignore this summons. Without Montpezat, he would never have found Azalaïs. He owed everything to that man.

Azemar tucked Corbiu's note into his money pouch and went inside Tibout's castel to write a verse for Azalaïs, to give her the message that their plans to escape must be postponed. He prayed that she would receive and understand it before risking her life by waiting in vain for him to come for her that night.

Azalaïs fidgeted while Johana helped her dress and arranged her hair. It was the morning of the day she would flee with Azemar, and she was too occupied with her own concerns to notice that Johana was unusually thoughtful and quiet. For a while the damozel said nothing, simply winding Azalaïs's plait—now almost as much her own as Jordane's hair—around her head so that she could cover it with a crespine. Several times during the process, Johana took a deep breath and opened her mouth as if she would speak, and then, thinking better of it, turned the gesture into a sigh.

"Johana, what is it?" Azalaïs asked, finally shaken from her own self-absorption by Johana's odd behavior.

"There is a young damozel here who would like permission to be one of your attendants," she said, not meeting Azalaïs's eyes.

A new member of her court. The timing was unfortunate, but perhaps the damozel's coming would take everyone's attention away from her own actions that day. "So, suddenly I'm respectable enough for a young lady to want to attach herself to me? Well, show her in. If she is of a good family and has a pleasant disposition it will be a blessing to have her here."

Azalaïs was surprised at how much she sounded like domna Jordane when she said that. She would be giving up her charade just at the moment when she began to feel capable of it. Or maybe she felt capable simply because she knew she would not have to carry on with it forever.

Johana curtsied to Azalaïs and then opened the door to the bedchamber to usher in a lithe young woman whose head was covered with veils, and who limped and leaned heavily on the donzella's arm.

"Good morning, Barona."

That voice. It was so familiar.

Azalaïs stood so fast she knocked her stool over, strode over to the damozel and lifted the veils that covered her face. "Domna Jordane!" she whispered. "What are you doing here?"

Jordane was very pale and her smile seemed forced. "I—I—"

Before she could answer, Jordane's eyelids fluttered shut and she fell to the ground. "Help me get her to my bed," Johana ordered.

Without pausing to notice how quickly Johana reverted to treating her as an inferior, Azalaïs lifted domna Jordane's feet while Johana hooked her arms beneath her armpits. Jordane was very thin, but still they struggled with her dead weight.

They laid her on Johana's narrow bed in the antechamber. "I'll get some vinegar water," Johana said, leaving Azalaïs by domna Jordane's side.

Jordane's tunic had become disarranged in the transfer from floor to bed, and one of her legs lay completely uncovered. Azalaïs immediately saw what had caused domna Jordane to faint. A small but deep, messy wound just above her knee was swollen and oozed yellow liquid. If Azalaïs had not been forced to attend to the injuries of the peasants during the attack she would not have been able to recognize it for what it was: clear evidence that an arrow had pierced the lady's flesh, and that the wound had not been cared for as it should have been.

She quickly pulled the tunic across to hide it from Johana, who returned with a wooden basin filled with cool water and vinegar and with a soft cloth in her hand.

"I'm afraid she needs a little more help than this," Azalaïs said in a quiet voice. "Stay here while I fetch a knife, a needle and thread, and some of the salve I prepared for Joris."

"The cooper? Who was so badly hurt in the fighting?" Johana's eyes opened wider and her voice rose.

"Sssh! Just stay with her."

Azalaïs ran to the door of the solar and took a calming breath before walking out. She did not want anyone to suspect she was in a hurry.

The needle and thread were simple enough to collect from the small chamber where Johana often spent the mornings doing needlework. It would be necessary to get a knife from the kitchens, and what was left of the salve Azalaïs hoped would still be in the pot on the shelf where she kept her medicines and herbs.

Reaching the kitchen necessitated passing through the hall and crossing in front of the door of the baron's privy chamber. Although her husband was still away, fraire Martin and domna Ermengarde made that room their regular haunt. Azalaïs was curious to know what they could be talking about for hours on end, but not curious enough for her to overcome her aversion to fraire Martin and actually seek them out.

She was about to go through the great doors from the hall into the yard when her belamaire's voice stopped her in her tracks.

"Barona Ma Filha," she said—ever since the day of the attack and her son's obvious gratitude to Azalaïs, domna Ermengarde had addressed her with forced affection—"Fraire Martin and I have need of some advice concerning the health of the monks at the abaïa. There has been an outbreak of fever there, and I know that you possess knowledge of medicines."

Azalaïs turned. Domna Ermengarde held out the hand that was not leaning on her walking stick toward the privy chamber, whose door stood open. Azalaïs had no choice but to enter.

The room was airless and hot. They had kept the shutters closed against the searing wind that raced across the landscape from the west. Fraire Martin had removed his black mantle and sat in just his sweat-stained white cassock. Beads of perspiration dotted his forehead.

"What manner of fever afflicts the monks at Fontfred?" Azalaïs asked, not wanting to waste any more time than necessary.

"I must confess that was not truly our reason for asking you to join us here," fraire Martin said. "You were so dutiful in telling us how you came to know of the attack, and there are now rumors which we would like you either to confirm or dispel."

Azalaïs's stomach churned. The image of poor Dreu Barasc rose before her. "I am not likely to send others to be tortured."

Domna Ermengarde exchanged a look with Fraire Martin. "What could you possibly mean?"

"I—" Azalaïs stopped herself. Could it be that Ermengarde did not know what she had seen at the abaïa? She stole a glance at fraire Martin. His features were perfectly composed, but there was something in the set of his mouth that warned Azalaïs to tread very carefully. "It's only that I have heard of such things happening to suspected heretics."

"We did not mention heresy." Domna Ermengarde's voice was ice.

"There has been a small misunderstanding, that is all," said fraire Martin, who rose and placed his hand on domna Ermengarde's bony shoulder. She stiffened her back as if his touch sent a shock through her. "We are simply trying to track down all those who took part in the attack, that they may be brought to justice by the bayle, and then tried in Narbona—as is the law."

"I know nothing more about them than I told you last week," Azalaïs said, hoping her assertive tone was not too emphatic.

"A pity." Fraire Martin released domna Ermengarde's shoulder from his grip and resumed his place at the table. "For we have heard rumors that several of the rebels are still hiding in the vicinity, either because their wounds prevent them from running away, or because their ties are too strong to sever so abruptly."

"I assure you, no news of these people has reached my ears."

"But what of the knight you saw? The one who removed his helm?" Domna Ermengarde slapped her hand on the surface of the table as she stood, making Azalaïs flinch.

"Ma Domna Belamaire, I was too preoccupied with preserving my domain to notice the appearance of a single knight."

"Thank you, filha," said fraire Martin, moving to place himself between domna Ermengarde and Azalaïs as if to prevent any further communication between them.

Azalaïs paused to still her heart after the door of the chamber closed behind her. Both Azemar and domna Jordane were in terrible danger. She now knew for certain what she had only suspected when she saw Jordane's wound: she must have taken part in the fighting, no doubt still disguised as a boy.

She hurried to the kitchen where she retrieved a knife and found the pot of salve, relieved to see that it still contained enough for her purposes, then returned to the solar without hurrying, trying to appear as if all was as it should be.

"Where have you been?" hissed Johana, her eyes red from weeping. "She is much worse."

"My belamaire delayed me." Azalaïs did not elaborate. There would be time to tell her later. Right now it was essential to see to domna Jordane. If she died there, in the castel, it would be very difficult to account for her presence in the most private apartment.

Domna Jordane was now in a state of delirium, whether from pain or fever Azalaïs could not tell. Her half-open eyes flicked back and forth, and sweat streamed down her face. Her fingers played nervously with the linen sheet.

"Wad up your handkerchief and let her bite on it. Stay by her head and mop her brow with the cool water. You may have to hold her down. If she can feel this she may struggle against me."

Azalaïs had never had to deal with a wound that festered so. The peasants she tended to after the attack either had superficial injuries or were in too dire a condition to be saved. She held the blade of the kitchen knife in the flame of the oil lamp, wiped the soot off on her tunic, clenched her teeth together, gripped the handle, and pierced the knife point through the skin of domna Jordane's thigh right next to the wound. Putrid-smelling, thick yellow and black liquid poured out of the incision. "Give me the water!" she commanded.

Domna Jordane did not make a sound, so Azalaïs assumed she had swooned. Johana's face was white, and she looked as if she, too, might faint at any moment. "Don't leave me!" Azalaïs said. "Look away. Think of something else."

She poured the vinegar water into domna Jordane's wound and washed it out until only blood oozed from the small opening. Then she threaded her needle, pulled the edges of skin closed over the gash, and sewed it shut. When she was finished, she smoothed the salve over the entire area, making sure to save enough to put on later.

"Will she be all right?" Johana said.

There were tears in the donzella's voice, but Azalaïs did not look up. "I don't know. I've done all I can. But that is the least of our problems right now."

Johana took the smelly, dirty sheet away. "I'd better find a way to burn this," she said, "or the laundress will be suspicious."

Azalaïs nodded. "We will have to lock her in here. It is essential that both of us go about our business as usual."

"What caused her wound?" Johana asked, taking hold of Azalaïs's arm and making her look into her eyes.

"Can you not guess?"

Comprehension dawned in Johana eyes.

"It's worse than that. Fraire Martin and domna Ermengarde are watching for strangers who might have been involved in recent events. I don't think they have any reason to suspect that one of them was a woman, however."

"My God why did she do it!" Johana buried her face in her hands. "Why was this all so important? Could she not simply have done as her father wished?"

"When did domna Jordane ever bow to anyone else's wishes, unless they accorded with her own?"

Azalaïs and Johana went down to the small, east-facing chamber off the hall where they sat most mornings. Once a servant had left them a collation of bread and cold meat, they deemed it safe enough to speak in whispers about their guest upstairs.

"Did she say anything while I was gone?" asked Azalaïs.

"She muttered something about hiding with a peasant woman in the forest, and about the French searching all the huts in the vicinity."

"We can keep her safe here for a very short time. If she becomes well enough to make a more public entrance I shall introduce her as a new donzella, a distant kinswoman on my father's side. What should her name be? I pray that the baron d'Aniort does not return." And once she herself had run away, who knew what would happen.

"She was foolish to do as she did. I told her she would

come to grief!" Johana spoke aloud, but not really to Azalaïs. "And now to arrive like this. She is tempting fate."

"Whether she should have come or not, she is here now." Azalaïs paused with her needle in the air. "First we must get new clothes for her, and make up some history, some explanation."

"I think she would want to be called Clara, after the young trobairitz who died just a few years ago," Johana answered. "She greatly admired her."

Azalaïs stayed in the small parlor and continued to work on her embroidery, a scene of a pleasure picnic with the castel in the background. Making the tiny stitches helped take her mind off the disturbing developments of the morning and the night's coming events.

Johana left to prepare the way for domna Jordane by pretending that Azalaïs had received a letter. Azalaïs was not at all certain the deception would work. Domna Jordane's beautiful face, although gaunt now, would soon regain its fairness, and her hair—now lackluster—would in very little time take on its remarkable, coppery sheen, if she survived her wound. Anyone who had heard her described might easily recognize her, and from there, the possibility of exposure was only a hair's breadth away.

Azalaïs's mind soon turned from domna Jordane to her own impending escape. It was too bad she would not be here to take care of the lady's wound and help her recover, but there was nothing she could do now. It was not so big, and the infection had not spread. Perhaps Johana would be able to manage, and all would be well.

She did not let herself dwell on what would happen to the two ladies after she vanished. Instead she tried to think only about the immediate future: how she should dress so that she would be adequately prepared to run away, whether she should bring money, or whether that would lay her open to the charge of thievery, since it was not truly hers. She still had the gold coins from the baron d'Aniort. She could not ask Johana's advice. No one must know.

As soon as she could do so without arousing comment, Azalaïs went to the solar to look in on domna Jordane. At least she could give her every chance of surviving by caring for her wound to the best of her abilities.

Azalaïs had never seen someone with so strong a will to survive as domna Jordane. By the time she and Johana went for their customary afternoon stroll along the paths near the castel, domna Jordane had sat up and taken some chamomile tea. She would have risen from bed, except that the pain of putting weight on her right leg was still too severe.

Azalaïs and Johana didn't speak of their guest until they reached the farthest point in the garden. "She said it was better a few days ago, but then she became ill. By tomorrow we must introduce her as a distant relation. The longer she remains hidden in your chamber the more likely someone will discover her."

"The servants told me that fraire Martin will be extending his stay. The abaïa has given him leave, on the grounds that you must be spiritually prepared for your impending confinement." Johana did not look at Azalaïs when she said it.

Of course. She was supposed to be pregnant. Another factor that would make her escape still more dangerous. She started when Johana gently touched her arm.

"Don't worry, Barona. Tomorrow we will sew some padding into your gowns."

Azalaïs tried to smile. "Yes, but when there is no baby, what then?"

"A first pregnancy rarely results in a baby," Johana said.

If she had been planning to stay, pretending to lose the infant when she next had her courses would have been the best idea. No doubt domna Ermengarde would insist on the most intimate inspection to verify that what she said was true.

Yet even if they managed to fool everyone, Azalaïs could not imagine how the baron would treat her if she remained at the castel and failed to present him with the heir he desired. Deceptions were piling up like the stones of the walls that enclosed her in the castel at night. If one of those stones were dislodged from the bottom, the entire edifice would crumble. Better to leave and face whatever consequences resulted.

When they returned to the solar to dress for dinner, to their surprise they found domna Jordane walking up and down, leaning against the wall or clutching the furniture for support. She looked very pale.

"Give me some rouge. Johana can arrange my hair so that it does not appear short. I must be seen at the banquet."

"But your leg," Azalaïs protested, "it is not nearly healed enough." At that moment, as if to give added weight to Azalaïs's entreaties to domna Jordane to stay hidden and rest a while longer, Savïeza let out a loud "grrk."

"Ha! You still keep that infernal bird?"

"He comforts me, but he frightens the servants. I keep him up here, out of sight, and I think almost everyone has forgotten he exists." By everyone, Azalaïs meant—hoped—Ermengarde.

Together Azalaïs and Johana helped "Clara" put on a gray tunic and green, sleeveless surcotte that belonged to Johana, after which the damozel went in search of a stout walking stick. To explain why she used it, they had decided to tell everyone that Clara had been crippled as a child, which was why, despite her beauty and education, she could not get a husband.

"I can arrive publicly, like an unexpected house guest." Jordane drew herself up tall and lifted her chin.

Even with a dire wound, she still exuded strength and purpose. It would have been so much better if she had married the baron, Azalaïs thought. Domna Ermengarde would not have been able to get the better of Jordane.

But there was no time to indulge speculation. Johana must spirit domna Jordane out of the castel the back way. After that, Jordane would come around the front and make it appear that she had come from the nearest inn. Jordane paused at the door. "Won't people wonder why I don't have a horse, or arrive in a litter?"

"Perhaps if you adopt a religious demeanor it would help. Like a pilgrim. You could be returning from visiting a holy relic to pray for your leg," Johana answered.

Azalaïs laughed out loud at the idea of domna Jordane as a holy woman.

"I'm delighted that I amuse you, Barona," Jordane said, although her face expressed anything but amusement.

Azalaïs quickly composed herself. "I'm sorry. It's just been such a strange, difficult time being here, and now this." She shook her head. "You'd best do as Johana says. I'll introduce you to domna Ermengarde at dinner as the lady Clara the Cripple, who has returned from a pilgrimage to Santiago, and tell her it is my wish that you remain here at the castel for as long as you like."

As she watched domna Jordane hobble off after Johana, Azalaïs had a bad feeling about the increasing complications of her life. All she wanted was for the events that were to come to have passed, and to be at Azemar's side, the two of them bound by their shared childhood and a simple desire to live out their lives far away from the intrigues of the castel de Belascon.

The company in the great hall that evening struggled to maintain the air of celebration required by the news of Azalaïs's pregnancy. Jordane's arrival furnished momentary relief from the subdued atmosphere now that the baron had gone. But the wine did not flow as freely, and the prayers went on too long.

Instead of the echo of men's laughter, ladies' titters and whispered conversations were the only sounds that broke the oppressive formality.

Fraire Martin was given the place of honor at Azalaïs's right side, domna Ermengarde sat on her left; the seneschal and a few local landowners occupied the seats near the head of the long table; and after them, Johana sat between two ladies from Narbona whose fathers were particular friends of the baron.

Domna Jordane sat among some less prosperous *borges* and the wealthier peasants who leased the baron's vineyards, while the house servants sat at the other long table. The menials served, and a cluster of beggars melted into the walls, waiting for their moment to pick up the crumbs from the floor. Altogether about thirty people dined in the great hall, with another thirty milling around the tables for one reason or another. A small gathering compared to the hundreds immediately after the tournament.

Azalaïs kept one eye on domna Jordane, who she could see was forcing herself to eat and drink heartily despite the fact that the pain in her leg probably made her feel quite ill. *Please don't call attention to yourself,* Azalaïs prayed, hoping Jordane would behave in an uncharacteristically demure fashion. But in her heart, she knew that Jordane—even if she wanted to—could not avoid notice. A life of privilege and her natural beauty gave her an air Azalaïs knew she herself would never be able to adopt.

"You say, Donzella Clara, that you are from Caunes? Why did you not accompany the Barona on her wedding journey?"

Azalaïs started. Domna Ermengarde had yelled her question across the eight or so guests who took precedence over the lady everyone assumed to be of approximately equal rank with Johana.

Unperturbed, Jordane replied, "I was away on a pilgrimage when that happy event occurred," and flashed her most ingratiating smile.

Azalaïs judged that the wine had helped Jordane overcome her pain, and recognized the mischievous glint in her eye that always signified trouble.

"Ah yes, I understand you were at Santiago. Is it not unbearably hot at this time of year? And did you encounter a priest by the name of Father Pedro?"

"Hot yes, but nonetheless salutary, although it did not entirely cure my affliction." Johana smiled and nodded at domna Ermengarde as though she had not really heard the question, then returned to flirting provocatively with the gentlemen on either side of her.

Jordane's feverish gaiety drew all eyes to her, including fraire Martin's. "Donzella Clara," he said, "I wonder that we did not have news that you were traveling here. The baron de Belascon, I am certain, would have sent guards to protect you on your way."

"I thank you, kind fraire, but I am not sufficiently high born to warrant such a courtesy. I traveled only with my old nursemaid, who has begged my leave to depart and return to her own family in Bésiers."

Azalaïs, who was so agitated she could hardly bear to touch her food, wondered how domna Jordane dared spin so elaborate a falsehood.

"Barona?"

Marcu had been standing beside Azalaïs for some time, clearing his throat politely and waiting for her to notice him. She turned at last. "What is it, Marcu?"

"It would be my honor to sing and play after dinner, to celebrate the arrival of the new donzella."

As he spoke, he placed his hand on the table. When he withdrew it, Azalaïs saw that he had nudged a small piece of parchment underneath her trencher. "Thank you, Marcu. Your songs do much to soothe us all, especially in this time of the baron's absence."

Azalaïs placed her napkin over the edge of the table and through it grasped the parchment to pull it out of its hiding place and keep it securely in her own hand. She was certain no one would notice, but when she cast her eyes around her they met those of domna Jordane, who gazed directly at her, a smile spreading over her face.

The rest of the meal passed without incident. Once the tables were cleared and moved so that everyone could gather around for singing and dancing, Marcu took up his usual place in the center and began with an alba full of hidden meanings that soon had everyone laughing until the tears came. He followed this with a rousing performance of a popular tresca, and Johana drew Azalaïs from her seat to join the ladies in a dance.

In the process, the napkin that Azalaïs had kept clutched in her hand as if she needed it to wipe her tears of laughter from her eyes fell to the floor, and with it the scrap of parchment from Marcu. Before she could stoop down to pick it up, domna Jordane hobbled over and scooped it up from her feet.

"Allow me to serve the Barona by holding her kerchief while she dances."

Domna Jordane's courteous gesture received polite applause, but Azalaïs could barely contain her anger and panic. What did she think she was doing? She had no doubt that Jordane had seen Marcu pass her something and saw where she had hidden it.

All the while they hopped and skipped with the steps of the tresca she tried to position herself so that she could watch to see if domna Jordane examined the note, which she herself had not yet had the opportunity to read.

The dance ended, and everyone sat down exhausted, prepared for Marcu to entertain them with a gentle canzon. The musician put down his tambourine and took up his vielle. But as he plucked the strings to tune it up, Domna Jordane again rose from her place—leaning more heavily on her stick now, Azalaïs observed—and made her way to him.

"Kind Marcu, do me the favor of allowing me to relieve your voice and your fingers." She held out her hands for the vielle, which he relinquished with some reluctance.

Domna Jordane settled herself on a silk cushion in the middle of the room, finished tuning the vielle, lifted it to her shoulder and took up the bow with her other hand. She began to sing a doleful canso with a popular air, but the words were of her own making, Azalaïs was certain. They told the story of a wandering trobador looking for the lady who was beautiful and good enough for him to worship.

Her strong, pure voice sobbed and twisted around the notes with skill and artistry that far surpassed that of Azalaïs, and even Marcu could not match her ability on the vielle. The way domna Jordane played it, the instrument sounded like a second human voice, blending and enlarging her own, with all the sweet melancholy of someone bemoaning a lost love. When she finished, the guests loudly clamored for more from the visiting donzella.

Marcu, Azalaïs noted, sat over to the side, his gaze fixed on Jordane. She could not say whether his expression was admiring or sad. She thought perhaps some combination of the two. He was a skillful trobador—skillful enough to know when he had been out-sung and outplayed.

"Perhaps the donzella Clara is fatigued," Azalaïs said. "Dear Marcu, why don't you favor us with another canzon?"

Her request snapped the trobador out of his daze, but Jordane's mood clung to the vielle even after she relinquished the instrument. Marcu's subsequent songs were more than usually full of loss and longing. The musician had a pleasant voice and knew how to wring expression from the notes, yet he could not match the beauty of domna Jordane's performance. Soon there was a general clamoring for "Clara" to perform again.

How well Azalaïs recalled the spell Jordane used to weave over the residents and guests at Caunes. No one who had ever heard her would be likely to forget the experience. Azalaïs prayed she would never have to sing in front of anyone who had. They would identify her immediately for a fraud.

Jordane yielded to the requests of the crowd and sang again, miraculously holding up despite her wound. Azalaïs tried to notice all the nuances of expression she used, thinking it might be possible to imitate some of them when next she was called upon to favor anyone with a song. Azalaïs liked to sing; she always had. But if everything went as planned that evening, she would only sing for Azemar in the days to come.

Domna Jordane proceeded to extemporize a few more verses designed to tease the gentlemen present by flattering their skill on the battlefield and in bed. After making every-one in the room blush, Jordane reached into a fold of her tunic and, with a great flourish, removed from it the very piece of parchment that Marcu had surreptitiously left on the table by Azalaïs's trencher. Darkness prickled in front of Azalaïs's eyes. She struggled to bring herself back to a state of equanimity and pretend she was not deeply alarmed.

"I find myself in a position to serve my noble patroness," domna Jordane said. She let her eyes wander over the entire company, briefly pausing at Azalaïs. "This opportunity delights me more than I can express. Earlier today, a little while after I ar-rived, someone dropped this tribute in the yard and I was there to rescue it from being trampled underfoot by a mule. Some unknown cavalièr who is too shy to sing for himself wishes to pay homage to the Barona. And so, I shall be his voice."

An approving murmur passed through the company at this skillful conceit. While it was unlikely that anyone would suspect anything other than the courtly convention of a distant admirer, Azalaïs knew without looking that fraire Martin's eyes burned into the back of her neck. She wanted to leap from her seat and snatch the parchment from domna Jordane, but she could do nothing. She simply had to sit where she was and smile, accept the compliments or ridicule that were to come. She imagined—hoped—that the message was from Azemar, perhaps with more details of their plans for escape that evening. By singing it aloud to the assembled company, domna Jordane would ruin everything, and she, Azalaïs, would be imprisoned at Belascon forever. Jordane could be cruel—of that she had had evidence enough in Caunes—but this was unwarranted. Perhaps the pain she suffered despite all outward appearances had made her cross. Or perhaps all that she had undergone since they parted ways months earlier had embittered her and marred her judgment.

But Azalaïs could tell by the expression on domna Jordane's face that she completely understood what she was doing, that far from succumbing to her own pain, she relished the moment, knowing that it would very likely inflict torment of a different sort on Azalaïs.

"It is a strange form, and so I shall change it just a little to make it fit my tune," she said, looking directly at Azalaïs. Then she began to sing, at first slowly and quietly. But as she warmed to her subject, her voice rang out with a kind of certainty that marked her as a true trobairitz.

> *Domna, I have found in you my home*
> *like a star that completes a pattern*
> *in the heavens,*
> *But like a star, you are distant and cold,*
> *And therefore I must leave you to roam*
> *And seek a lady to whom I owe my life.*

May your star guide another
to try his fortunes at your feet.
And may he rise in strength.
Let him kiss the hem of your gown,
for I shall never return
to claim the privilege for my own.

Azalaïs clapped politely along with her guests. They cast puzzled glances at her, as if they wondered who would dare to write so disrespectful a verse to such an illustrious castellane.

The words surprised Azalaïs as well, and it pained her to have to remain in the great hall for another hour while domna Jordane continued to sing and captivate the company. She tormented herself with wondering what the poem meant. If it had indeed been written by Azemar, what was he saying? That he would not come for her as he promised? She wanted to run weeping from the room. Johana had to nudge her twice to remind her to applaud at the end of songs.

At long last the guests departed, and after blessing the entire company fraire Martin retired to the apartment he had been given in the men's wing of the residence. Azalaïs struggled not to appear too eager to climb the stairs to her bedchamber on the floor above the hall, but once everyone except Johana was out of sight, she ran to her room, flung the door shut behind her, threw herself on her bed, and drenched the silk coverlet with her tears.

Azalaïs was crying too hard to notice that someone had entered the room. It wasn't until she saw the crumpled piece of parchment in front of her eyes, tossed there as if by accident, that she realized she was not alone. She looked up, her nose running and her eyes red.

"You always were faint of heart," said domna Jordane, wincing as she lowered herself to sit on the edge of Azalaïs's bed. "You'd better read it. Then you'll know what a kindness I did you, in exchange for your hospitality. And for healing my leg." She pulled her tunic up to show Azalaïs the wound. It lay flat against her thigh, clearly no longer a danger to her. Azalaïs herself was a little surprised that her treatment had worked so well and so quickly.

She took the parchment in her trembling hands. When she read the words that were actually there and saw how different they were from those that domna Jordane had sung, she shook her head. The message was indeed from Azemar, telling her that he had been called away for a reason he could not divulge, and it would prevent his coming for her that night, and perhaps ever.

It crossed Azalaïs's mind at that moment that she could fling open the shutters at her window and leap out of it to her death, saving everyone from the troubles to come and ending her own despair. But it was not in her nature to take such a step. "Why? Why did you do what you did this evening rather than simply let me keep this and read it alone?"

"It was that horrible monk, the inquisitor. And the dowager, who it is easy to see despises you. They saw Marcu give it to you. You would have been killed if they had found this, which they most certainly would have if I had not taken it away from you."

There it was again. Azalaïs felt the ground shift beneath her, just as she had when she was first in the service of domna Jordane. Now that things were the other way around, somehow their relationship was no different. How did this lady manage it, even when her circumstances were so reduced and bedeviled? It occurred to Azalaïs that it would have been better for domna Jordane if she had been a man. Then her scheming and manipulating might have been put to more constructive use.

But that did not alter the way things were at that moment. Domna Jordane spoke the truth, of that she was all too aware.

Johana gave up her own bed in her cabinet and slept on

a thin pallet on the floor. Azalaïs could tell by the expression in the donzella's eyes that she was deeply grateful to have domna Jordane returned to her. Although Johana had been helpful and kind to Azalaïs in the months since they left Caunes, there was something in her devotion to domna Jordane that went beyond mere affection, or even a sense of loyalty. If domna Jordane had had a sister, she could not have been more solicitous than Johana.

Azalaïs waited until the others were asleep before she allowed herself to cry her sorrow and disappointment into her pillow.

With his broadsword at his side and his citole wrapped in oiled cloths, Azemar departed from Tibout's household to ride back to Montpezat.

His path south took him between the castel de Belascon and the abaïa de Fontfred, where the white monks kept their silence and the Dominicans brought heretics to confess. The southern sky, normally the deepest azure at this time of year, was heavy with dark gray clouds. Wisps dangled from them like tendrils of hair blowing in the stiff wind. There would be a storm, and it would wash away the nourishment from the vineyards, parched by a long summer of unrelenting heat, and swell the rivers to flooding. Azemar's horse swiveled his ears nervously with each gust and started at the twigs and leaves that swept in crisp waves across his path.

As he rode by the castel, Azemar searched the high windows for a glimpse of a light, or anything to indicate movement or life, and that therefore might be Azalaïs.

But he saw nothing. It was late. Possibly she had already retired for the night. He hoped that his note had found its way to her, and that she would understand why he could not keep his promise to her to carry her away that very night. The idea that she might wait in vain for him in the grove was too painful to contemplate.

Before Azemar had put three leagues between himself and Narbona, great, hard drops of rain began to stain the dirt road. In minutes, the downpour was like a waterfall, and his saddle slipped on his horse's back.

But Azemar pressed on toward Montpezat, the knowledge that the baron, the man to whom he owed everything, might be dying at that instant acting like a long chain that pulled him onward. He urged his horse to a canter, determined to reach his destination before dawn.

CHAPTER 29

Her leg burned with pain and her fever rose and fell making her intermittently lightheaded, but Jordane was afraid enough for her life that she gritted her teeth and smiled and sang, night after night. In that household, with the menacing belamaire and the inquisitor seemingly around every corner, the merest suspicion that she had been with those who had taken part in the attack would result in a painful death—of that she was certain. And since Azalaïs and Johana were now complicit in her deception, all of them could lose their lives.

Jordane realized all this within an hour of gaining entrance to the castel.

But it wasn't until she saw the musician pass the note to Azalaïs and then read the note herself that Jordane could take the full measure of the risk they all faced. Before then, she'd thought that as long as Azalaïs played her role well, she and Johana would be safe. On the surface of it, the girl wasn't doing too bad a job in the position of castellane. She walked well, addressed the servants with condescension but not disdain, and discoursed intelligently at dinner.

This other matter, though—how could it be that in such a short time Azalaïs could have a lover? Until she produced an heir, any hint of scandal could ruin everything. If what the note said was true, at least it appeared she would not be running off anytime soon. That would give them all an opportunity to figure out a course of action, preferably something that would make it possible for her, once her "visit" came to its conclusion, to leave the vicinity without suspicion, perhaps even with Johana.

As a visiting donzella of uncertain rank and family, Jordane could stray into the kitchens and outbuildings and mingle among the peasants without seeming out of place. Her weeks of traveling and training with men of all conditions had taught her how to blend with the lower classes. Although she cared little about the petty concerns of the local blacksmith who had accidentally crushed a finger with his mallet, or the wet nurse who had so much milk she could suckle two infants at the same time, she nodded and creased her brow and murmured as though what she was hearing utterly fascinated her.

Within a few days she had gained the trust of all the household menials and could start her subtle questioning to see if anyone knew anything about Raimon or the other rebels.

One afternoon about a week after that first banquet, Jordane sipped ginger tea while she sat on a stool by the cook, who peeled turnips for dinner. Two young boys turned a spit with a whole sheep on it. The large woman stood every once in a while and brushed the mutton with rosemary boughs dipped in olive oil.

"I've conversed with the seneschal—Milos—and he seems to be a good man, upright I mean, and fair." Jordane paused to wait for the cook to resume her seat nearby. "But I am surprised that an establishment of this size does not have a land steward." Jordane knew her question would provoke some response. She had heard murmurs among the children about someone named Barasc who had vanished after the attack. She thought perhaps he had gone to join the rebels, and that someone might know which way he had set out.

The cook pulled her stool closer to Jordane's and leaned forward, saying in a ginger-scented whisper, "There was a land steward, only we daren't mention his name."

Jordane leaned closer to her. "Truly? Was he a thief?"

"Not a thief, but they took him up there—you know, to the abaïa." She nodded sagely, as if Jordane should understand what she meant.

"You mean he became a monk?"

"Sshhh!" said the cook. "He didn't go willingly, I can tell you. They thought he could tell them something about the attack on the castel."

After that, the cook refused to say another word. But Jordane did not give up. She was certain there were others among the servants who knew more than they would tell without some inducement. Fear of death—or torture—was a powerful disincentive to sharing secrets. She would keep an eye on everyone at dinner that night to see who looked uneasy, who looked dissatisfied. Then tomorrow, she thought as she crossed the yard and climbed the stone steps to the great hall, she would concoct some excuse to seek that person out and become his or her confidante.

"Domna Clara?" The timid voice broke through her concentration just as she had her foot on the bottom step to the hall.

"Marcu! What is it you want?"

The musician looked down at the ground and traced an arabesque in the dirt with his toe. "I wondered if—you are so fine a musician yourself—"

Poor fellow doesn't know what to say, she thought. "Perhaps you would like to sit with me sometime and discuss music, so that we may share our thoughts on the subject to our mutual benefit?"

Relief flooded his face. "Yes, Donzel, that would give me great pleasure."

"I have long wished to learn how to play the citole with

greater skill. I understand from the Barona that you are very adept at this instrument."

"Would you, I mean, I could spend some time with you now, if you wish," he said. His eager expression made Jordane suspect that increasing his musical knowledge was not his only motive in approaching her.

"Very well. There is a room off the hall where we can sit for a while before I must attend the barona and the donzella Johana."

Together they ascended the stairs and she led him into the cool, vaulted hall, now devoid of the magnificent tapestries that were brought out only for festive occasions and thus revealing the doors all around—doors that led to corridors and other smaller rooms.

The privy chamber where she had noted that domna Ermengarde hid herself away much of the day was at the opposite end from the stairs up to the solar and the women's apartments.

Since that first dinner, when she saw how the dowager behaved toward Azalaïs and the looks she exchanged with fraire Martin, Jordane had wanted to have an excuse for sitting in the room next to that chamber so that she might listen to the old barona's conversations with the unpleasant monk. But until Marcu approached her, she could find no reason to be in that small room with one tiny window rather than on the floor above in the large solar with its light airiness and sumptuous furnishings.

"Perhaps you would get your citole. I shall await you here." Jordane smiled at the musician. He ran off happily toward the men's wing.

The small cabinet—it could hardly be called a room—contained two stools. Jordane moved one so that she could sit against the wooden wall that separated her from the privy chamber. She stayed very quiet, not even moving, concentrating on listening for sounds from next door. Nothing. Probably the dowager and the monk were not in there. No matter. Once the habit of their lessons had been established, she could arrange to meet Marcu at any time in the future and not arouse suspicion.

The young musician returned quite out of breath, citole in one hand and vielle in the other. "I brought the vielle because I hoped you would help me with my technique. You played it so beautifully the other night."

His eyes brimmed with admiration. He pulled the other stool close to Jordane's, drawing as near as he could without actually touching thighs with her. When Jordane leaned away a little, he inched closer.

As I suspected, she thought. *He's in love with me.* Or at least, he thinks he is. She stole a glance at the young musician's feminine features, his long lashes and rosy cheeks. He had a highish voice for a man, but really he sang quite well.

Jordane doubted Marcu had much experience with love— aside from the courtly sort that he sang about almost every evening. This was an unexpected development, but she might be able to turn it to advantage. Instead of always leaning away, as they demonstrated tricks and shared subtleties with each other Jordane let Marcu brush against her from time to time. He trembled slightly, she noticed, just as she did whenever Raimon drew near to her.

"Let me see you play the vielle," Jordane said. Marcu lifted the instrument up to his shoulder and gripped the bow in his right hand, almost as tightly as making a fist. "Ah, I can help you play with much more ease. Let the instrument drop a little, to rest against your upper arm. And don't grasp the neck, just rest it in the 'V' of your thumb and forefinger. You must let the body of the vielle stay alive to the vibration of the strings. And the bow: you cannot make it stroke the strings gently if you clutch it like a whip!"

She worked with Marcu for a while until his nervousness at her touch began to disappear, and they were able to enter the world of pure music. Jordane herself almost forgot the reason she had brought him there in the sheer delight of concentrating on the sweet sounds they drew from the vielle, a finely wrought instrument that had clearly been made by a master craftsman.

"Who made this vielle?" Jordane asked.

Marcu's blush of pride gave her the answer.

"I would be honored to own such an instrument. Would you make one for me? I will gladly pay you."

Marcu opened his mouth to answer her question when Jordane heard the approach of the dowager, her walking stick tapping as she crossed the hall from the door that led to her apartment. Jordane put her finger to her lips and whispered into Marcu's ear, "Best not to arouse suspicion by letting anyone know we have spent so much time alone together."

Ermengarde entered the adjoining chamber, and moments later Jordane heard the slower footsteps of the monk approach and then enter as well. She tried to hear what they were saying, but their voices were too quiet. She could make out one or two words, though, and she thought she heard the old lady say 'Barona.'

"You had better creep away first," Jordane whispered to Marcu, deliberately letting her lips touch the musician's earlobe.

He stood and bowed to her. His face had turned a deep crimson. Without a word he slipped silently out of the alcove. Once she found herself alone in the cabinet, Jordane pressed her ear to the thin, wooden wall that separated her from the monk and the dowager.

"We shall . . . proceed with caution," Ermengarde said, words going in and out of listening range as if she was turning her head this way and that as she spoke, perhaps following the monk's pacing.

"I am certain I know this lady. She was in hiding close to Bolbona. The minx pretended to be a boy."

319

A moment of silence followed that shocking pronouncement. Jordane held her breath.

"I hardly know . . . believe it. If we act unwisely. . . destroy an important alliance. The baron d'Aniort will be humiliated. . . strike back."

"I bow to your greater wisdom in political matters, Domna, but what if this—lady—your son's barona—is a heretic?"

"She has been careful . . . observe the Catholic rites. Heresy would serve. . . a useful charge . . . no heir."

Jordane stepped back from the wall intending to steal away before domna Ermengarde and fraire Martin emerged from their conference, but her tunic caught the stool she had been sitting on and tipped it over.

The voices next door ceased abruptly. Any instant someone would come to investigate. In one swift move she opened the door of the little room, grasped her walking stick and held it out in front of her as though brandishing it to strike something.

She had barely taken up her position when fraire Martin appeared in the doorway of the cabinet. "Donzella Clara," he said, "What brings you from the ladies' wing at this hour of the day?"

"I followed a rat, chasing it away with my stick. The monster came in here and then disappeared. Must have gone down there." She pointed her stick toward a mouse hole at the juncture of the wooden wall and the floor.

"It appears your foe was a very small rat, Donzella," he said. Jordane did not like the smirk on his face.

"Well, he frightened us all, and since I had a stick, I went after him."

By that time, Domna Ermengarde had made her way to stand next to the monk. "Are you in some difficulty, Donzella?"

"No, I think now the rat is in some difficulty. He will not bother us again today!" She smiled and walked forward. They parted to let her pass. She did not think for a moment they believed her, though.

Jordane's ears rang with what she had overheard in the cabinet. If the two most dangerous members of the household knew Azalaïs's secret, there was no time to lose to save all three of them from bitter retribution. They must escape somehow, and soon. First she would find out if Azalaïs were truly with child. If not, it would only take a few weeks more to make her deception obvious to all but the least observant inhabitants of the castel. The dowager and the monk were clever and devious. Out-maneuvering them would not be easy.

For only a moment, Jordane wondered if it hadn't been a terrible error to send Azalaïs in her place as bride to the baron de Belascon. Had she been the barona, she might have worked from the inside, from a position of strength as the rightful heiress and equal in rank to Ermengarde.

But it was too late to do anything about it now. She could still salvage the situation and undermine the alliance her father's cowardice had forged. The difference was that she would have to depend on the cooperation—and strength of purpose—of others.

Raimon had disappeared. So be it. She would find him again, and together they would drive the northerners out of their dominions in the Midi. If she could but gather a little more information first, then she would be able to assist him in a way neither of them could have foreseen, with intelligence that would give him a valuable advantage.

Yes, it was just possible, Jordane thought, that she could fight more effectively from where she was. Fear did not enter her heart. She would risk everything she had, everything she was or could have been, to aid her lover and the rebels.

Risk it all, or die in the attempt. For Jordane, there was no middle ground.

CHAPTER 30

The rain slowed Azemar more than he had hoped. The road became muddy and his horse slipped and struggled. He had to proceed at a walking pace for much of the way, and did not arrive at Montpezat until dawn had already painted the undersides of the clouds pale rose.

As soon as he was in view of the castel, the seneschal, Rimbalt, ran out to meet him. The fellow looked as though he had not slept in many days. "You are come! Thank God. He is still with us."

So, Corbiu's note told the truth. No ambush awaited him. Azemar said a silent prayer, slid from his horse and tossed the reins to a stable boy who trotted forward at the sound of hooves, still rubbing the sleep from his eyes. Without removing his sword, Azemar ran into the building and dashed up the stone steps to Montpezat's chamber.

The room was awash in candle glow. Azemar had never seen so much light from little flames in one place before. Montpezat lay in his bed, propped up with cushions so that he was sitting close to upright, but it was clear that he no longer had any control over his body. He looked half out of life already. Blue veins showed through his translucent skin and his eyes moved restlessly as though looking for escape.

But it was the baron's left hand that struck Azemar most. That strong hand, his one tool for working alongside the peasants in the vineyard, was thin and shaky. Montpezat's fingers picked at the white linen cover. His right arm lay as it always had, useless and shriveled.

"Baros," said Rimbalt, approaching him and speaking quietly into his ear, "it is Azemar here to see you."

Azemar stood in the direct line of Montpezat's gaze. He blinked back tears as the expression in his friend's face changed from complete vagueness, to recognition, to something that intensified and softened to a look Azemar had never seen on his patron's face before. The baron lifted his left hand a few inches off the coverlet and curled a finger to beckon Azemar closer.

"My son," he whispered, with barely enough breath to make a sound, "I must tell you . . ."

Azemar took the baron's hand in his. His touch awoke something in Montpezat and the dying man clutched him and squeezed hard, lifting his head just slightly off the pillows in an effort to lean toward Azemar.

"It is likely that I know . . . your mother and father. I lied."

The baron lied? What was he saying? Azemar hadn't thought about his family in years. His life had gone on so far away from them, what little memory he'd had fading with every new experience. He had found Azalaïs, which was more than he thought he ever would accomplish. And now, so unexpectedly, here was Montpezat saying something about his mother and father. Know, thought Azemar, he said "know," not "knew."

"They may be alive still. At Montsegur, with the others."

"The others?" asked Azemar. But the baron sank back into his cushions. Azemar had been concentrating so hard on listening to Montpezat that he had not noticed someone enter the room and stand next to him.

"He is leaving us."

The woman's voice startled him and he stood, his hand flying instinctively to the hilt of his sword.

At first Azemar wasn't certain whether or not the creature who stood before him was human. Her thin frame was crowned with hair so white it appeared to shed its own light. Not even a wisp of gray threaded through it. If her skin had been any more translucent Azemar would have been able to see the bones of her skull, and her eyebrows and eyelashes were as white as her hair.

But her most extraordinary feature was her eyes. They burned like two red coals in the middle of her white face. What made her pallor appear even more striking was the fact that she wore a black tunic, tied at the waist with a simple rope.

Without saying a word to Azemar, she moved forward and placed her hands on Montpezat, one on his forehead, one on his arm. She recited the *pater noster* then said some words Azemar had never heard spoken in church before.

> *Gratia Domini nostri Jesu Christi sit cum Omnibus vobis. Benedicite, parcite nobis, amen. Fiat secundum verbum tuum. Pater et Filius et Spiritus sanctus parcat vobis omnia peccata vestra.*

Moments later, in a transition that was so gradual it seemed not to happen at all, the baron died.

A warm hand pressed Azemar's shoulder. Only then did he notice that, as the strange woman recited her prayer and the baron slipped away from life, he had knelt down by the bed and taken hold of Montpezat's lifeless hand.

Now, with the touch of the pale lady, the three of them were connected in a chain of life and death. At one end the baron lay inert, his body now a meaningless shell.

At the other end, the lady with the pale face and red eyes

was pure spirit, as if the translucent protection of her skin held not blood and bones, but a presence that went beyond life itself.

In the middle, Azemar was suddenly aware of his awkward state, full of needs and desires, caught between the nothingness of Montpezat's body and a higher state, a state that the lady standing next to him had apparently reached.

He stood and broke the chain, not able to sustain the intensity of the moment.

"We are sorry for your loss, and pray that you find peace in the baron's ascension to heaven."

The words were spoken by a different voice, another woman's. Azemar glanced around the room. He had thought that only the three of them were present at that final moment, but in the shadows he saw someone else. Another woman, also clad in black, but her hair was gray, and her eyes and skin were as one would expect of an old woman: time-wearied and sun-browned.

The pale woman spoke. "I am domna Blanca. Rimbalt sent for us to attend the baron's final hours. It was his wish." She reached her hand out toward the other woman without turning. "And this is domna Rixende."

At the sound of her name, domna Rixende stepped forward and took domna Blanca's arm. In contrast to the eerie blandness of her companion's face, domna Rixende's was full of warmth and life. Azemar unclenched his fists. He did not realize that he had balled them into hard knots of tension the moment he let go of the baron's lifeless hand.

"You have been traveling and should eat something," domna Rixende said. She turned domna Blanca around and led her to the doorway. *Of course,* Azemar thought, *the pale lady with the red eyes was blind.* He shivered.

A small supper of fish and salad had been prepared for them in the great hall. Everyone sat with Azemar: house servants, peasants from the vineyard whom Azemar knew from before, Rimbalt, Dorde, domna Blanca and domna Rixende. They ate in silence, although Dorde sniffed loudly every now and again, and did nothing to stem the flow of tears down his cheeks. Each of them looked at Azemar from time to time as if waiting for him to speak.

The setting seemed all wrong without the baron presiding, and Azemar expected that any moment Montpezat would walk through the door from his privy chamber and join them at supper.

Eventually the seneschal rose. He picked up a parchment scroll that he had placed on the floor by his feet while they ate, cleared his throat, and read aloud to the company.

> *I, Baron Corneil de Montpezat, knowing that I shall soon die with no blood heirs or relations to take over my land, wish to name Azemar of Tolosa as my heir, with sole control and power over my land, my treasure, and my heritage.*

Rimbalt looked up and stared straight at Azemar. "You are now the baron de Montpezat."

Azemar went cold. He knew the assembled servants all fixed him with stares of questioning wonder, but he could not meet their eyes.

"You must tell us your intentions," Rimbalt said, more quietly.

"I—I don't know. I did not expect . . ."

"We all want to know, will you stay here? Will things change or remain the same?"

Azemar could hardly comprehend this unforeseen change in his condition. He wanted time to consider it, but clearly that was something he did not have. He forced himself to confront the sad faces of the estate's dependents then let his gaze pass

326

over the stones of the walls, the rough wooden floor, the fire in the ancient hearth.

His heart ached with longing to remain in this place and among its people. Although his time as their compatriot had been only a few years, Montpezat had taught him so much, given him so much. If he could remain here, run the estate, tend the vineyards and continue Montpezat's way of life—then perhaps he could be content.

Yet beyond this estate lay forces in wait to destroy everything Montpezat believed in and worked for. And eastward, in the Narbonès, Azalaïs waited for him to take her away from an impossible existence.

However much he wished to, Azemar knew that at that moment, he could not simply retire to this beautiful ostal. The difficulty was in knowing exactly what he should do, where he should go next, where he and Azalaïs might find refuge once they were together again.

It must have been his lack of sleep, or the strange circumstances of the baron's death and the appearance of the two serene, black-robed women, but Azemar swore that he heard the baron's voice, speaking in a normal tone but very close to his ear. *I know your parents,* he said. *They are at Montsegur with the others.*

Azemar looked over his shoulder and then around at all the other people. None of them had noticed anything at all and continued to pick at their meals and sip their wine, sunk deep in their own thoughts.

All, that is, with the exception of domna Blanca. She had turned her face toward Azemar, and a calm smile spread across it. Her blind stare disturbed him, and so he rose from his stool to address the household.

"Friends," Azemar said.

A sigh of relief escaped from everyone at the table.

"We all mourn the baron, but his passing was good, and

blessed. I believe the best way to honor him is to continue the life he created here."

There was no mistaking the joy in everyone's face at his words.

"However," he continued, "it is not yet my time to remain among you. I shall leave you in the capable hands of Rimbalt, who has acted as seneschal here in recent years, but I must continue my life's journey. I promise I will return one day, either to live out my time in tranquility or to be buried next to my dearest friend . . ."

Azemar could say no more. He felt as if he had swallowed sand and could not breathe. He gulped for air, and this action released something in him, driving wrenching sobs out of his chest. He hid his face in his hands. One by one the peasants and servants left the table. By the time Azemar's tears were spent and he could once more raise his head, the only people who remained were domna Blanca, domna Rixende, Rimbalt, and himself.

He looked from the unseeing eyes of one to the imploring gazes of the others. "I shall stay to see him buried, and then I must leave."

Later that night, domna Blanca entered Azemar's chamber on the arm of Rixende. "Why do you carry a candle?" Azemar asked before he had a chance to remember his manners. But the pale lady did not seem to mind the question.

"I cannot see shapes, but I am able to discern light. And light is the essence of our belief, of the belief of many people. Yet we have found it necessary to take our light beneath the ground."

Domna Blanca reached her hand out and Azemar guided it to a little table. She set the candlestick down, then groped her way to Azemar's bed and sat on its edge.

"Your mother and father were followers of the light. For

many years, they were *credente*. In recent years, together, they became *boni omini*, They are now among the Perfect."

"You mean they are heretics?"

Domna Blanca smiled. "We are in the thrall of a corrupt Church, a Church that has strayed so far from the true ways of Christ that they live in luxury and indolence, and eat the flesh of animals."

"But, the Pope—he is the messenger of God!"

"This is what they would have us believe, so that the people are frightened and will pay their tithes to them. Their beliefs are flawed at their very foundation."

For the next hour, Domna Blanca explained the ways of the heretics to Azemar while Rixende sat quietly by her. She told him that they could trace their lineage back more than a thousand years to the time when Christ showed that the evil God who had created the material world, a world full of impurity and temptation, was balanced by a good God, who was not of the world, but was pure spirit.

The heretics believed there were two divine forces, not one. Nothing that took material form could be good. Man must struggle between the allure of the material world and the achievement of complete purity in the spiritual world. If he failed in one life, he returned again as another human being until he achieved this perfection and was able to lead the life of a good man, a *bon om*. Only then would he ascend to heaven.

"Why do you tell me these things?" Azemar asked. "Simply by knowing them I may be taken by the inquisitors, and then everything I know will put you at risk."

"We are not afraid. Our time is coming to an end. We are not allowed to fight, to shed any blood at all, and so we cannot challenge the Church on its own terms."

"My parents—I heard something . . ."

"They have been with us, in the south, in a community of heretics that has so far escaped capture by the crusaders. You were sent away with all the children when they were driven out of Tolosa."

Azemar tried hard to think back to his dim memories of that time. What domna Blanca told him made sense. He had never before been able to understand why his mother and father would have sent him from them to an uncertain future. Now he knew that they were trying to protect him. "Did the baron know who I was?"

"The roster of children who had been sent out into the world was written and carried by pairs of the Perfect, who passed the information from mouth to mouth among the credente. Everyone who heard it memorized the list so that if ever the records were lost, we would know our own. We were all pledged to keep you safe, and one day tell you of your heritage. We need you, all of you, to carry our secret, our treasure, into the future."

"Was the baron a Perfect?"

"When he died, he was. I administered the *Consolamentum* so that he could enter heaven and not be forced to lead another life here on earth." Domna Blanca stood. "He gave you two precious gifts to carry forth into the world. Keep these with you always. They will protect you and assure those of our faith that you do not mean us harm."

Azemar nodded. He was afraid to tell her that the two items she referred to, the stone and the book, had been stolen.

"Show them to no one, until you reach Montsegur. Now you must rest. There is much for you to accomplish." Domna Blanca walked without feeling her way to the table where she had placed her candle as if now, having once negotiated the room, she had no need of sight or guidance. Rixende emerged from the shadows again to take her arm.

When domna Blanca left him, Azemar paced back and forth. The stone, the red stone and the book, would identify him to those who knew about his family. And now, he no longer possessed them. Did those who stole them from his wardrobe understand what they were? How would he find them again? It was clear that he could not go on with his journey until he tracked down the thieves who had robbed him of what he now knew to be his only link with his past.

His journey. She had said, *until you reach Montsegur*. Azemar had not planned to go to Montsegur. He had only the vaguest idea of where the castel was. But if going there meant he had a chance to discover the secrets of his own past—and those must be the secrets of Azalaïs's past, too—then perhaps Montsegur should be their destination when he was finally able to free her from her captivity.

By the next morning, sleep had worked its healing power. Although he felt the loss of the old baron keenly, Azemar was also awake and full of purpose. All that he had learned and talked about the day before had crystallized to a single, urgent desire. More than ever, he knew he must rescue Azalaïs from her life at Belascon. Only once she was by his side would he continue on his journey, first to find the red stone and the book, then to go to Montsegur.

When he descended to the great hall, he asked Rimbalt to call the two heretic ladies to him. He intended to tell them about his plans.

"They are no longer here," the seneschal said. "They departed last night, while you were asleep."

Although he was at first surprised that they would have gone without taking their leave, on reflection Azemar realized that their secretive departure had been necessary. No one must know they had been there, or the baron's household might be marked as a place that harbored heretics.

The rain had stopped and the sky was once more brilliantly blue. The smell of wet earth and decaying leaves tugged against Azemar's resolve to return to Narbona, an overpowering reminder of his life tending the vineyards with the baron. As tempting as it was simply to hide himself away and get his hands into the earth again, he knew in his heart that such a future was not for him.

At least, not yet. Azemar was dizzy with the vista of his past and the possible future that had opened to his understanding within the span of a day. Now he knew why he and Azalaïs had a bond that went beyond that of childhood friendship. If he was the son of heretics, then Azalaïs must be the daughter of heretics.

Although he had not had the chance to ask domna Blanca if Azalaïs's family members had also fled to Montsegur, everything she said convinced him that the same motive for safety had thrown all the children together. The names. He should have asked domna Blanca to tell him, but he didn't think of it. Now they were gone, and it was too late.

These thoughts went through Azemar's head as they laid Montpezat to rest in the grave next to the late barona's. They marked it with a plain stone that had come from the vineyards, and said no words of liturgy over his remains. He had received a benediction in his chosen faith before he died.

The sun was high in the sky by the time Azemar had mounted his horse and was ready to return to the Narbonès.

"Will you not stay a few days to help us with the wine making?" Rimbalt asked as the servants finished loading his panniers with provisions.

"I cannot. There is someone very dear to me who does not know the danger she is in, and I must return to her. After that, I shall journey to the south."

The seneschal did not press Azemar to stay, but assured him that everyone on the estate would continue to work for the prosperity of all. Then he drew close to him, pretending to fix a strap on his saddle. "The Jew, Solomon, will give you money when you need it, but there are some jewels." Rimbalt glanced quickly over his shoulder then turned his attention back to his task. "Not many. The knights took most of them the second time the baron. . ." He stopped. "Only as many as would fit in a small coffer. I put them in a bag. It might help, for your lady."

Azemar could not imagine what he would do with jewels, but the seneschal's thoughtfulness threatened to make him weep again. He embraced a surprised Rimbalt, then clambered into the saddle.

As soon as the castel was out of sight, Azemar turned his thoughts to the future. He had only the time of the ride back to think of how he might save Azalaïs from her impossible position with the baron. He prayed that Belascon himself would remain with King Louis's knights long enough to make it possible to effect whatever scheme he thought of. It did not matter that Azalaïs had married another man. Her marriage was a Catholic ritual, and not honored by the heretics.

Azemar pulled his horse up. Did he consider himself a heretic? Just because his parents were Perfects did not mean he must adhere to the same beliefs. Domna Blanca had said that each individual must choose for himself, that there was no easy way to adopt their religion. One could not simply be born to it.

He clucked his horse to a walk and then a faster, but still gentle, traveling pace. More troubling than his own beliefs was the question of whether Azalaïs would welcome a transition from wealthy barona to poor, wandering nobody. She had told him that she had passed years in poverty and servitude, but that did not mean she would wish to return to such an existence.

He must convince Azalaïs that her destiny was with him, that their parents' shared beliefs drew them together in a bond that distance and time would never dissolve. With only a quill, ink and parchment to convey this vital message, he would have to choose his words with care. In his mind, Azemar began to compose a tenso.

After one night at an inn, Azemar arrived at Tibout's just before vespers the next day.

"What news?" the old knight asked, although he did not seem surprised when Azemar told him of the baron's death. Tibout rose and knelt down on one knee, bowing his head to Azemar when he finished his account of the burial. "As baron de Montpezat, you are now a great man, with many sesteradas of land, tenants who owe you fealty, and much wealth. But there is something you ought to know about the old baron." He rose and glanced around to make sure no one was near and then he spoke. "Montpezat was captured and imprisoned at Carcassonne for harboring heretics. Not once, but twice."

Azemar had heard Montpezat's name linked with the fearsome prison, but had never learned what happened and why. "Go on."

"The first time, he convinced them they had the wrong man and they let him go. The second time he was not so fortunate. A Dominican inquisitor from Tolosa would not relent with him until he had spoken the names of many of his friends."

At first, Azemar did not understand. Was Tibout implying that Montpezat had betrayed those he had sought to protect? "But . . ."

"The instruments of torture are not so easy to resist. He held out until they very nearly pulled off one of his arms."

Of course, thought Azemar. And that is why the baron would never tell him how he had come to be injured.

"So you see," continued Tibout, "it is only you, now. You must go forward and restore the honor to the Montpezat name."

How could he, a person of no background who had stumbled upon Montpezat by chance, accomplish such a thing? What must he do?

It was too much on top of everything else that had happened recently, and he could not think about it just yet. He had barely had time to grieve, or even to think what it meant to grieve. He would turn his mind to the problem once he and Azalaïs managed to flee from the Narbonès.

Without telling Tibout of his precise plans, Azemar continued to make preparations to take Azalaïs away. This time he would try a different tactic. He was fairly certain that no one at the castel knew him as anything other than the nephew of the good Corbiu, and he had not been there frequently enough for anyone to recognize him.

Sometimes bold actions were the best. If he were to ensure that circumstances were still favorable to Azalaïs's escape, he must go there himself. He did not want to send his tenso without knowing that it stood a chance of reaching her hands. Only after that would he be able to decide the best course of action in the coming days.

CHAPTER 31

Azalaïs, Johana, domna Jordane, domna Ermengarde and fraire Martin all sat together in the solar on an unseasonably hot, lazy afternoon two days later when a house servant told them that the baron de Montpezat had come to call. Fraire Martin had been reading St. Augustine aloud to the ladies, but at the visitor's name, his voice faltered, he became distracted and closed the heavy book.

Azalaïs held her breath. She thought instantly of Azemar. Why would the man she knew was her old friend's patron be in the Narbonès?

When Azemar himself entered and bowed gallantly to the company, Azalaïs's heart jumped. She fought to restrain herself from leaping up and embracing him. In a glance she took in everyone else's response to his arrival: Johana seemed a little frightened; fraire Martin expelled his breath as if he had been holding it until he saw Azemar; domna Jordane exchanged a glance with Azemar that carried some meaning, and clearly disconcerted him. In fact domna Jordane had acted very strangely in the past few days, as if she knew something important but didn't want to say what it was.

"Please, join us, Baros," said Azalaïs, looking her question at Azemar as she welcomed him to their company.

"I was passing through to pay a visit on an old friend and courtesy bid me call upon a liege lord of the Narbonès," he said, seating himself on the only available stool, which was between domna Jordane and fraire Martin. "I was not a baron until two days ago, when the baron de Montpezat, my benefactor, died. He made me his heir."

"I am sorry for your loss," domna Jordane said, the only one who was not stunned into silence at this news.

"Yes, yes, my condolences, *requiescat*," fraire Martin muttered.

"He was an old man, but vigorous. I do not know what caused him to decline so rapidly." Azemar directed his comment to Azalaïs.

"An old man, but a heretic." Domna Ermengarde's words burned through the delicate fabric of the conversation.

"That is a heavy accusation, Domna. I knew him only as a generous patron, a good farmer, and a devout Christian." Azemar looked directly into domna Ermengarde's eyes when he spoke.

"And now you are a man of position, Baros." Domna Jordane chimed in, attempting to steer them out of murky waters.

"Was it a good death?" Fraire Martin asked.

"He slipped peacefully away," answered Azemar.

"I mean, did he die in the grace of God?"

"Yes, most certainly. He was a very good man."

Azalaïs saw a flicker of something pass among Azemar, the monk and domna Ermengarde. She wished she could ask Azemar privately about what had happened on his trip. Although she had as yet had little opportunity to become acquainted with him as a grown man, compared to the brief time they had before he went away he had changed in some manner that she could not identify.

Perhaps it was his new position of power and influence.

"Would you stay and take dinner with us, Baros?" she asked. She found it difficult to keep the tremor out of her voice.

"Alas, I cannot. I came only to pay my respects. I shall continue my journey on the morrow. I do not know how long I shall be absent. I have many affairs to attend to."

"What affairs might these be? There is a pilgrimage setting out from the abaïa of Fontfred in the morning that might afford you company on your way," fraire Martin said.

"My business, Fraire, is too pressing to allow me to wend my way with a train of pilgrims."

"Perhaps instead of staying to dinner the baron would do us the honor of accompanying us on our walk in the grounds," Azalaïs said, setting aside her needlework and rising from her stool, eager to interrupt this line of questioning.

Everyone filed down the stairs, through the hall and outdoors toward the garden. To reach it they had to cross the drawbridge and pass into a walled enclosure that at least kept the wind out, if not always the animals.

The insects buzzed happily, and the birds sang in a desultory manner as if the heat sapped them of strength. The bright blue of the sky, which would soon enough be welcome in the cold, winter months, now tormented them with its unremitting glare.

Azalaïs strode ahead, putting some distance between herself and the others, and Azemar hurried to catch up to her. Johana was content to walk with domna Jordane a little behind them, but fraire Martin—whose joints were stiff and painful from walking many leagues during his days as a wandering monk—stayed with the infirm domna Ermengarde and fell farther and farther behind.

"We shall have to go back to them soon," Azalaïs said to Azemar. "Tell me quickly what you must."

"I leave tonight to seek my mother and father," he said.

Azalaïs turned to him, her eyes wide. "But how—Take me

with you!" she whispered, just before Johana and domna Jordane were close enough to hear.

There was no time to discuss matters further. Domna Ermengarde's call to them to wait could not be ignored. "Belamaire! I am sorry. We shall walk more slowly." Azalaïs led the group back to the old people.

"I have preparations to make, and must take my leave," Azemar said, bowing over Azalaïs's hand. She felt him press a very small piece of parchment into her palm before he walked toward the stables to fetch his horse.

He recognized the visiting noblewoman as Berenger's squire as soon as she spoke. With Azalaïs's story about her substitution for the willful noblewoman, everything fit together a little too well. How had the lady who had been introduced to him as damozel Clara, who had acted as Berenger's squire, and who had fought alongside them against the castel now be a welcome guest?

During the battle, Azemar had lost sight of the lad he now knew to be a woman, but they passed each other on the retreat, when the baron's knights and foot soldiers returned to rout them. Azemar saw him struck by an arrow and assumed at the time the wound had felled the squire.

Yet it seemed the arrow had not struck true, and the boy / woman had somehow managed to find aid. Very clever to hide in plain sight, he thought. Whoever she was, she was an accomplished actress. She had also recognized him, he was certain, and yet maintained her composure without effort.

But Azemar could waste no time worrying about this counterfeit squire. He had other matters to arrange. No doubt news of his visit to the castel would fly through the ranks of the servants and peasants at Belascon and soon find its way to Narbona. Before Corbiu heard about it another way, Azemar decided he must call on the merchant. He owed the family some explanation for recent events, and knew Corbiu would be able to apprise him of all that had happened since his departure.

And on his ride back from Montpezat, Azemar had decided what to do with some of the jewels Rimbalt had put in his saddle bag. He would repay an immeasurable debt in a manner the good merchant could not refuse.

It was market day in Narbona and the streets teemed with buyers and sellers. As he made his way through, Azemar picked up snatches of conversations he had had many times since he'd joined Corbiu's business enterprise. "I can do much better elsewhere." "I assure you, it's the finest to be had anywhere." "You'll never be offered such a bargain again." "My grandmother wouldn't pay so much!" Merchants and customers danced around each other with practiced subtlety until they hit upon the price that would be acceptable to those at both ends of the transaction.

Azemar paused to watch Corbiu standing stern-faced before an array of gaudy silks. A fellow in a strange, padded headdress smiled broadly, revealing a scattering of teeth in his sunbrowned face. From a distance, Azemar knew that the foreigner had mentioned a high price, which he reduced each time Corbiu shook his head. Finally, the merchant started to walk away.

The silks were beautiful. Corbiu wanted them, of that Azemar was certain. He also understood that his employer had become wealthy by pushing his negotiations to the point where he risked losing the deal altogether. "There will always be more goods to buy," he had said to Azemar time and time again.

This was one of those times, though, that his tactic worked. The eastern gentleman ran forward and touched Corbiu's sleeve, put his palms together and bowed over them. A broad smile lit the merchant's face, and he bowed in return. Azemar rode up to him just as the bargain was being concluded.

Corbiu greeted him with joy. "Come! My wife and daughters will be so happy that you have returned."

Azemar slid off his horse and walked next to Corbiu. He told him quietly about the baron's death. Corbiu stopped, put his hand to his forehead and closed his eyes. Tears gathered in their corners, but before they spilled out over his cheeks, the merchant rubbed them vigorously away. "Montpezat was the best of men. A true champion of our way of life. I have no doubt you will do honor to his memory."

Tresca was leaning out the window waving when they arrived at the house. A servant must have run ahead to warn them that he was coming.

Domna Corbiu and all three daughters ran out of the house and surrounded Azemar, all talking at once and asking questions.

"Why did you leave without saying goodbye?" Tresca was always the most blunt.

"That's none of our business," said the reserved Elionor, pulling her sister away.

Domna Corbiu knelt down and bowed her head to Azemar, gesturing to her daughters to do the same. "We were sorry that you had to depart in such haste. Now I realize what called you away. The baron was a good man."

Azemar wondered if domna Corbiu meant all she implied with the designation 'bon om'. "He was the best of men, and I do not deserve the honor he bestowed upon me in making me his heir."

A gasp escaped Estacada's lips before she could stifle it. So they didn't know that he was the new baron de Montpezat.

He must show that he was just the same, that nothing about their relationship had changed. "It warms my heart to be once again among the family I have come to regard as my own."

"You must be hungry. Come." Domna Corbiu took his

arm and led him to the table, which the cook had already laid with meats and cheese and wine. They all sat, chatting about what had happened in his absence, the daughters of merchants who had contracted to marry, a visit of a troupe of acrobats, the rain that had almost flooded the canals. But no one mentioned the theft on the night of the tournament.

Azemar finished his cup of wine and cleared his throat. "The night I left, when I returned early, I found the kitchen maid in some distress. Is she recovered?"

"We believe it must have been a cruel joke, perpetrated by my neighbor's *peon*, who it turns out wanted to ask young Petrona for her hand. She has now left our service, and has been taken into my neighbor's house."

"But Baros," Tresca said, "there were such doings the night of the tournament! Some knights came and searched through houses all around the *ciutat*—"

Domna Corbiu shushed Tresca with a look.

"What's this?" Azemar asked.

"It seems," Corbiu said, "that the tournament was simply a way to empty the city. They came just before we all returned from the banquet and searched houses of suspected heretics. Several men of my acquaintance were taken away, and have not been seen since."

Azemar looked down at his trencher and pretended to pick up a crumb to eat. Why had they not taken Corbiu, if they had searched his house and found Azemar's stone and the book? "This house was not searched, I hope?"

"We are not heretics here. What reason would they have had?"

Azemar nodded. But his heart was not easy. "I should have waited for you to return before I parted from your ostal. Your kindness to me did not deserve such discourteous treatment. And now, I am afraid that I cannot stay. Business matters take me south."

"But you've only just come back!" cried Tresca, running to him and plopping into his lap, her arms around his neck. She was only eleven and could claim the privileges of childhood for another year—but no longer.

Azemar gently loosened her grip. "I have an estate, and duties to perform. Perhaps you will all come to visit me some day."

Elionor blushed. She had really blossomed, Azemar thought, and would make a good wife sometime soon. But not for him.

"We understand," said Madame Corbiu.

"I will not return immediately to Montpezat, but must take an extended journey through the region. I require some help in provisioning myself for this sojourn."

Azemar's hosts were only too ready to oblige him. He realized that, now that he had a title and an estate, although he did not consider his prospects altered in any way, they might well harbor some hope that he would choose shy Elionor for his wife. "Menher Corbiu, I must speak with you privately."

Corbiu led the way to the office. Through the closed door, they could hear the girls' voices chattering, no doubt speculating about what Azemar would say to their father. It would disappoint them, Azemar knew.

"It grieves me that I must depart without having a chance to express my gratitude fully for all you have done for me," he began.

"Nonsense, I—"

"Whatever you say, express it I shall, but not with words."

Azemar reached into the folds of his tunic and drew out a leather bag that contained almost all of the jewels Rimbalt had hidden in his saddle bags. He upended it and spread its glittering contents over Corbiu's desk. Among them were three handsome rings.

"The sapphire I thought could be for Elionor, the emerald

343

for Estacada, and the ruby for Tresca. For their dowries." He knew that Corbiu would understand that this was his way of making it known that he had no intention of claiming any of them as his barona.

"Baros, this is too generous!" Corbiu lowered himself to kneel, but Azemar stopped him.

"It is no more than I owe you for your kindness to a stranger. I wish you and your family nothing but happiness and good fortune."

Tears fell from Corbiu's eyes. In those uncertain days, one was never sure whether goodbyes were for the time being or forever. And with what Azemar knew was ahead, he was certain that he would never see any of these kind, generous people again.

By the end of the day, Azemar had been furnished with everything he required, including two blanket rolls for sleeping on the ground, a skin of wine and a skin of water, and a dagger which fit into a sheath that was strapped to his calf and hidden by his high leather boots. He also had a pouch full of soldi that Corbiu had sent for from the Josiu.

Domna Corbiu gave him a little package of special treats from the kitchen, in addition to the well-stocked basket of provisions that the new kitchen maid had settled on the back of a donkey, which Azemar would see that Tibout returned to them after his departure.

"Why must you start out at night?" asked Tresca, as usual saying what everyone else dared not.

"Because I must," Azemar replied. He thought it best not to attempt an explanation. His plan was to return to Tibout for his armor to wear beneath his regular clothing, and transfer the provisions and extra bedding to the palfrey he had already bought from Tibout for Azalaïs to ride.

The family waved him off. The corners of Elionor's mouth

trembled with the effort of smiling. Estacada and Trescalana made no attempt to put on brave faces. Their sorrowful expressions struck Azemar to the core. Life was easier, Azemar thought, when survival had been his only concern. Now he would go through the days with the weight of remembered kindness and true affection on his heart.

If justice were truly to be done, Corbiu would live to see his daughters well married and have a brood of lively grandchildren climbing over his knees. But justice was a stranger to their world, ever since the troubles with the French had begun.

As soon as he left the gates of Narbona, worries beset Azemar about whether Azalaïs would understand the message he gave her earlier that day. He would wait for her after compline, just as he had the last time. If she did not come, he would wait another two nights, hiding somewhere nearby during the day. If at the end of three days she did not join him, he would assume it was either not her wish to journey with him, or she found it too difficult to get away, and he would be forced to continue without her.

Azemar shared a simple meal with Tibout in his small ostal. They said little to each other, but afterwards, Azemar pressed a pouch containing fifty livres into the old knight's hands.

"This is too generous, Baros," Tibout said. "I do not need such riches now."

"Then use the money to provision knights who want to fight for our cause," he said. Our cause. The words rang with noble sentiments. But they reeked of death.

As soon as the darkness was deep enough to hide him, Azemar mounted his horse, his citole strapped to his back, and grasped the rope that the groom had tied to the bridle of the other animal. From Tibout's expression, Azemar guessed that the knight had figured out that the second horse was not merely to transport provisions—especially since he had purchased a saddle for it, which would only be necessary if it was to be ridden. He was grateful that Tibout refrained from asking any questions, though. He would not be able to lie to the old knight, and to give him such knowledge would put them all at risk.

The day's heat had released its grip, and a fresh breeze blew from the direction of the sea. What had been a clear, blue sky now transformed to a moonless blanket of brilliant stars against a velvety black backdrop. The ride to Belascon was not long, and soon Azemar had hidden himself in the copse of trees where he would wait for Azalaïs.

A short while later the compline bells clanged in the distance. Azemar let the horses graze on the dried tufts of vegetation while he gazed toward the castel, searching—hoping—for Azalaïs's approach.

Ever since Belascon's departure the day after the tournament, fraire Martin had insisted on having private conversations with Azalaïs several times a day to quiz her on religious matters. In between he made her recite Latin prayers until their words became meaningless. Every once in a while he would ask some seemingly innocent question about how she had been raised.

That afternoon, after Azemar's departure, they sat in one of the small chambers near the great hall shortly before the evening meal—the same one in which Jordane met the musician for their "lessons," although Azalaïs did not know it.

"Were you taught the names of the flowers and herbs in the garriga?"

"Oh, yes!" said Azalaïs, "I mean, my tutor brought me specimens from the nearby forests to study."

"You read Latin and Lemozin, I see. Were you also taught French?"

Azalaïs was uncertain how to answer. She understood French a little, but did not read it. And she did not remember whether the same was true of domna Jordane. "We spoke it a bit. But I had no need for reading French, since everything my mother found it necessary to teach me was in Latin. Caunes is a small, provincial town. We had few French visitors, and those who came spoke Latin."

Azalaïs hoped her explanation would satisfy the monk, whose insistent interrogation pushed her closer and closer to revealing her days in Bolbona. She was afraid that at any moment she would say something that would give her away.

Their conversation was cut short by a disturbance in the castel yard. Shouts of, "Off! Away!" and banging on pots penetrated to the chamber.

"If you will excuse me, Fraire," Azalaïs said. She rushed out without waiting for his consent and was so relieved she felt like thanking the noisy servants for rescuing her.

"What is the trouble?" she asked. Immediately they stopped their shouting and beating and knelt on the ground.

The cook, a fat woman who obviously spent most of her time tasting the dishes she prepared, pointed up toward the roof of the chicken coop. There, to Azalaïs's horror, sat Savïeza, with a fine, young cockerel gripped in his sharp beak. His prey was twice his size, but the Minervan owl was a born hunter. He had snapped right through the cockerel's neck.

"Get the huntsman!" someone yelled.

"No!" shrieked Azalaïs. She took a towel that a stable boy had been flapping in the direction of the owl and wrapped it around her hand, then held her fist up high. "Savïeza!" she called, and made the clucking noises she had learned to imitate that brought him to her. The owl flapped his wings and tried to rise from the roof, but the cockerel was too heavy. He opened his beak and let his prey drop amid the chickens, making them squawk and screech in terror.

347

Everyone backed away when Savïeza alit on Azalaïs's raised fist.

"How did you get out here, you mischievous bird?" she murmured. She had been careful to keep him shut in her bed-chamber during the daytime, letting him out at night after the chickens were asleep in the coop. Now it would be necessary to take him through the castel. And even if she could manage this without being seen by fraire Martin, doubtless the owl's antics would be a lively topic of conversation at dinner. There was no hiding Savïeza now.

She held him around his feet so that he could not easily get away then strode through the hall and up the stairs to the women's quarters. Just as she was about to close the door be-hind her, she glanced across the large room to see fraire Martin standing in the open doorway of the privy chamber. He smiled.

Dinner that evening was sheer torment. Fraire Martin kept his eyes fixed upon Azalaïs, and it made her so nervous that she knocked over her goblet and splashed wine over everyone near her at the table. She no longer doubted that he knew she had some connection with his past, and feared that he had guessed the entire, complicated deception that had led her to this place.

All she wanted was to retire to the solar and bar the door until it was time for her to creep away and meet Azemar, but everyone clamored to hear the damozel Clara sing and play. Lately she and Marcu had begun acting out tensos, entertaining the household with their spirited sparring. That evening, the singing went on for hours. The members of the household and about twenty guests stayed in the great hall long after curfew had rung.

At long last, the servants took down the tables and un-folded the beds for the house guests. The residents and high-er-ranked servants disappeared to their quarters. Azalaïs entered her bedchamber off the solar as quickly as she could. Fraire Martin would not dare to follow her there.

With Johana and domna Jordane, she made an effort to pretend that it would be a night like any other and bid them *bon ser*, gave a loud yawn and slipped her tense, naked limbs between the sheets. *Once I run away*, she thought, *there will be no more soft beds for a long time—perhaps ever.* And her silk and velvet blials and tunics—she would have no more need of these.

Azalaïs had already decided that she could not take any of the jewels, or she would surely be accused of stealing. All she dared carry off with her was a few of the gold coins the baron d'Aniort had given her when he visited, and whose existence was known only to Johana.

Peace soon settled over the castel, except for the little night noises of rats scrambling about and floor timbers creaking. Savïeza had already flown away for his nightly hunt in the forests nearby. When she thought it was safe, Azalaïs crept from her bed, pulled on a homespun under-tunic, a linen blial and a plain woolen surcotte, and tied on her sturdiest leather shoes. She fastened her money pouch to her belt and then began the long walk to the door that would lead her to Azemar, and to freedom.

She passed domna Ermengarde's room without making a sound. Her light footsteps made little noise as she descended the staircase. All that remained was to cross the hall and descend to the kitchens, remove the stone where the key she had found before was hidden, and let herself out into the tunnel. Then, a short row to the other side of the moat, and she would say farewell to this castel forever.

Azalaïs thought she was safe when she reached the door. She pulled the stone out of its niche. Without looking, she put her hand in to find the key. But her fingers felt only stone dust.

"Looking for this?"

The quiet voice sent a chill down Azalaïs's back. She turned, not knowings what she expected, but it was not to see domna Jordane walking toward her with her hand extended, the key lying in her palm. Behind her, dressed for a journey, was Johana.

CHAPTER 32

The mournful call of the matins bell woke up the sleeping in-sects and night birds, and the moon commenced its climb over the horizon to the east, an orange disc filling a valley between two craggy hills. Azemar breathed a quiet sigh. He knew that his waiting was over for the night, one way or the other. Either Azalaïs would come to him soon, or something had prevented her, and she would not.

So far, there was no sound of oars dipping in the moat. It seemed that he would be forced to find a cave or some other place to hide with the horses until tomorrow night, when he would begin his vigil once more.

He had gathered the reins to mount when his ears picked up the faint plash of water. Azemar's heartbeat quickened. He left the horses tethered and rushed forward to cross the open ground to the moat.

The boat bumped into the bank. Azemar quickened his pace so he would be there to lift Azalaïs out of the skiff again. But before he reached the moat, someone's head appeared over its edge. Somehow she must have managed it alone.

Then another head appeared, and another.

He froze. Their plans had been discovered. But these were not guards coming to arrest him. From that distance he could see by their long tunics and slender forms that they were women. Could it be servants stealing out on some jaunt to meet their sweethearts? He put his hand on the hilt of his broadsword and watched as the group approached and gradually took on distinct features.

Azemar recognized them as they approached. Azalaïs first, followed by the damozels Clara and Johana. All three of them wore traveling clothes.

"There is no time to explain," whispered Azalaïs, who reached him first. "After we are away I will tell you all. You have to trust me."

Azemar led them to the trees where the horses waited, cursing whatever had happened to disarrange their plans. Azalaïs slung Azemar's citole over her shoulder and he lifted her to his horse, her long skirts wrapped around her legs so that she could sit astride behind him.

"Help us," Johana whispered. She climbed atop the smaller palfrey easily enough, but the other lady's injury made it difficult for her to follow.

"You'd better have a good reason for this," Azemar muttered to domna Clara as he lifted her onto the horse behind Johana.

Without a word, they walked off toward the south. As soon as they were far enough from the castel so that the sound of pounding hooves would not be heard, Azemar urged his horse to a canter and they continued at that pace on the dusty, pebble-spotted road until the sky turned ashen and the east was streaked with orange light.

"It's time to rest the horses," Azemar said, slowing his mount to a walk. Its breathing was loud, and foam had been flying from its mouth around the bit for some time. "We must find some water. After that, I want an explanation."

A little farther on Azemar stopped by a stream that fed the River Berre and they all dismounted. At this time of year the stream was more of a rivulet, but the horses could drink from it and munch on the few shoots of green grass by the bank.

"Now, talk." Azemar shifted his hard eyes back and forth from Clara to Johana.

Azalaïs placed herself between Azemar and the two women. "Let me explain. It's all so complicated, and I couldn't leave them behind." She took Azemar's hand and led him a little away from the others. "Clara is not what she seems."

"I realize that. I recognized her, although she has changed quite a bit since I saw her a few weeks ago."

"You saw her?"

"'She' was a 'he' at the time, squire to the knight who led the attack on the castel."

"It's even worse than that," Azalaïs said, leading Azemar yet further away from the others. "Remember I told you about domna Jordane, the lady whose place I have taken?" She glanced in the direction of their unexpected traveling companions.

"What are you saying?"

"Clara is the true domna Jordane d'Aniort."

This was more than a complication. Not only was he helping the barona de Belascon abscond, but in his company was another noblewoman who, if discovered, could bring catastrophe down on all their heads. Azemar ran his fingers through his hair, gripped a handful and pulled on it hard, as if doing so would rearrange the confused thoughts in his mind. "This is preposterous."

"Domna Jordane just wants to find Raimon de Berenger. She said that she will leave us as soon as we are far enough away from the castel, and Johana will go with her."

Worse and worse. "We must not have anything to do with Berenger if we are to survive long enough to reach our destination."

"But we cannot simply abandon them. Is there nowhere

it would be safe for us to part ways? Where they might stop a while until domna Jordane can make her inquiries?"

"If she can find Berenger she'll be doing better than all the inquisitors and knights in the Narbonès and the Tolosan." He looked back at the two women. They clung to each other, one a loyal servant, the other a wounded fugitive.

Azalaïs was right. They could not simply abandon them in the middle of nowhere. He thought for a moment. "There are caves," he said, "near Montpezat. The peasants on my estate will make sure they are fed. It's all I can do. When the servants at the castel de Belascon discover you are missing—I wager they must certainly have done so by now—they will send knights out to look for three ladies, and they may well assume that at least one person acted from the outside to help you. As long as we stay together, it will be an easy matter to find us."

"But if they are discovered . . ."

"We are all in danger. I do not know how much time we have, but you and I have important business to accomplish."

Azalaïs knew he was right. Danger surrounded them, even without the unexpected company of Jordane and Johana. The others would slow them down, and although she had felt Azemar's chain-mail hauberk beneath his woolen tunic when she wrapped her arms around him to ride, and saw that his broadsword hung by his saddle, one armed and armored man could do little to protect three vulnerable women.

Jordane bristled when Azemar told them what would happen. "A cave? I have certainly sacrificed much for my convictions."

"It is the only way," Azalaïs said. "Once we separate, we will all be safer."

"I think I know where Berenger will go—perhaps already has gone—but two ladies cannot travel there alone. You promised, Azalaïs!"

Promised what? She thought. "I said we would help you get away, that was all!" Azalaïs bit her tongue to keep from pointing out that this entire situation had been caused by Jordane the moment she had decided to send Azalaïs to marry Belascon in her place.

"This is no daring skirmish, domna Jordane," Azemar said. "Your lover will be tortured if he is caught, and the future of the region depends upon him and some others who are still working to keep the French at bay. It is all we can do for you. Either you follow us or stay here."

Jordane scowled. "Very well. We shall part at these caves you speak of. But my endeavor is also vital, and I cannot guarantee that I will not do whatever is necessary to see that I succeed."

Azalaïs well understood the implication that domna Jordane would betray them if it suited her own purposes. But they had no choice. They were easy targets if they all remained together.

The four fugitives rode in unbroken silence through the night and the next day. Azemar left the three ladies to wait for him with the second horse in the woods near the castel de Montpezat. By the time he entered the yard it was long past curfew, and although the portcullis was not lowered, Rimbalt had bolted the residence against intruders.

Azemar dismounted and pounded on the great wooden door with the side of his fist hoping to rouse the seneschal from his rest. At first the noise only sent some bats that were hiding in the crevices above the portal swooping out into the night. But Azemar continued to pound, and soon he saw the faintest glow of a candle seeping from between the door planks. As the light grew brighter, he heard footsteps, and then the rusty sound of the bolts being drawn.

At the sight of Azemar, Rimbalt's fearful expression relaxed into a smile. "Baros! Back so soon? We did not expect you."

"I had no way to send word and I am not here to stay. I need your help."

In as few words as possible, Azemar told Rimbalt about the two ladies who needed to be hidden in the caves for a time.

"I will arrange everything. But they cannot stay there forever." Rimbalt poured Azemar a flagon of new wine while two of the house servants who had been roused by the noise scurried around to find blankets and lamps and other provisions.

"Eventually they must leave and go far away. It is our only hope." Azemar drank down his wine and stood.

"Rest a while longer, Baros!" Rimbalt said.

"I cannot." Azemar had not told the seneschal that waiting outside with these two fleeing women was his childhood friend, whom he had thought he would never see again. He sought to protect both Azalaïs and Rimbalt by keeping this information to himself.

The seneschal accompanied Azemar out to the courtyard where his horse stood waiting, a basket laden with provisions already secured behind the saddle. "The peasants miss you. The vineyards miss you," he said. "An estate needs a master. And the other day there came a message for you." He reached into his tunic and withdrew a scroll of parchment, about the size to accommodate a canso.

Azemar was curious about who would write to him at Montpezat, hoping that it was not Tibout with terrible news about the state of things in Narbona. He did not know how to protect Corbiu and the rest of his family if somehow the connection between him and Azalaïs were established.

But he could not delay now. He took the message and tucked it away without reading it. Whatever it said would not change the fact that the two women must hide in the caves, and that he and Azalaïs must put as much distance as possible between themselves and Belascon.

Azalaïs, Johana, and domna Jordane waited where he had left them with the second horse, behind a grove of olive trees in the deep shadow of a limestone outcropping. It was the beginning of the path to the caves. "We will lead the horses. It is too difficult to ride."

No one said a word as they climbed up to the cavern entrance. Azemar thought of that other time when he had hidden in the cool vaults beneath the outcropping, soon afterwards to be sent to Narbona for his and Montpezat's protection. That was the first time he realized that his past could harbor secrets that put him—and all who knew him—at risk.

Without yet understanding everything—why the baron had named him is heir, why he had kept his knowledge of Azemar's parentage and the whereabouts of his mother and father for so long—knowing what he did now gave him a purpose. Between what Montpezat had gasped out with his last breath and what domna Blanca had told him afterwards, it was clear that he should head south and west toward Montsegur, that place that held the remnants of a faith gone into hiding. There he hoped to reconnect the broken threads of his life, perhaps of Azalaïs's life too.

But to what end? With Belascon's knights pursuing them, their chances of reaching their destination were slim. And once he and Azalaïs reached the fortress, what would happen next? Nowhere in the world would be safe for them ever again.

Once the ladies had dismounted and placed the provisions in the cave, Azemar said, "We must leave you here. My steward, Rimbalt, knows of you and will help you all that he can." He lifted Azalaïs onto the horse Jordane and Johana had been riding, then swung himself back up into the saddle of his own animal.

"What are you doing? Are you not leaving us a horse? You leave us here with no means of escape?" Jordane's voice rose.

This woman was accustomed to getting her way, no doubt about it, and didn't consider that the horse belonged to him. "I did not plan on your coming, and the faster we can travel the safer you will be, too."

Azalaïs leaned over and reached her hand out toward the others. "It is for the best." Johana came to her and grasped her outstretched hand, kissing it and leaning her cheek against it.

"You have done more than we ever had a right to expect," she said, silencing the protest that was about to explode from Jordane's lips. "I hope we meet again, but if we do not, know that you have a true friend in me."

"Come, Azalaïs. We must leave before it is too light."

Azalaïs squeezed Johana's hand. Jordane had turned her back. "Farewell," she whispered.

Azemar glanced back at her and nudged his horse with his spurs.

Without looking behind her, Azalaïs rode away from the women. There was no time to think of the past. From now on, she would have to look ahead, focusing on Azemar's strong back as he sat his horse, toward the prospect of finding out something about her past when they reached Montsegur, and toward . . . what? There was only one certainty in life. And Azalaïs was not yet ready to confront death.

She caught up to Azemar and extended her hand to him. He grasped it, and she pulled up on her reins, making both of them stop. They had reached the crest of a hill, and the forested countryside stretched away ahead of them toward the mountains. "Listen," Azalaïs said.

"To what?"

"Don't you hear it?"

Azemar listened. The horses took hollow breaths, steam

just starting to rise off their haunches. Somewhere a morning bird began to sing.

But there was another sound, a sound Azalaïs remembered from her very earliest life, a sound so constant all who lived on the garriga grew accustomed to it.

"It's the wind. It sings as it curls around the trees and the rocks. I used to think it sang for me," she said, wondering if Azemar would think her words strange.

"We should go," he said, but he made no move to urge his horse on, only gazed at her, with a look full of love and questions.

He hears it too, Azalaïs thought, although he didn't say. "Yes. We have a long way to go," she said.

They rode on toward the mountains, guided only by hope, facing together whatever the future would bring.

AUTHOR'S NOTE

I began work on this book in 2005, shortly after my first novel, *Émilie's Voice*, was published by Touchstone Books of Simon & Schuster. With a Yale PhD in music history under my belt, I longed to bring to life the many remarkable stories of music in eras gone by, particularly of women's place in shaping them.

One of the most fascinating stories to me was about the *trobairitz*, the women troubadours who flourished in Languedoc and other parts of southern France. More than singers and poets, these were accomplished, high-born women who brought the art of poetry and music to a pinnacle, writing verses with complex formal and metrical rules—much more sophisticated than the simple rhymes dotted throughout this book. (I apologize to those brilliant women for my poor efforts!)

This poetic and musical practice was at the very foundation of a rich culture, distinct from that of France.

The land that is now France was, at that time, divided into two or three large regions, each of which was subdivided at different times by ruling families. Lovers of history know that the region of Aquitaine changed hands back and forth between England and France in the middle ages.

The other autonomous region in what is now France was

361

the Langue d'Oc, a patchwork of counties and baronies with the Count of Toulouse (Tolosa) as overlord in the western part, and the Trencavel family in charge of the eastern part. These powerful families in turn owed fealty to other overlords in other parts of Europe—including England, Germany, and Aragon.

The name of the region has its origins in the language. It was the Langue d'Oc, literally, the language where they say "*Oc*" for "Yes." The language some still speak in the south of France is known as Occitan. The north, France, was the Langue d'Ouil, or the language where they say "*Oui*" for "Yes." The region at the time was commonly known as the Midi.

In many ways, Occitan is more akin to the Catalan language than to French. The foreign words I use in this text are, as much as possible, Old Occitan. Where I couldn't find an equivalent in the old language, I used modern Occitan.

The laws of this Langue d'Oc region, known as the Midi, were liberal and religiously tolerant—but not always by design. The Count of Toulouse was a loyal Catholic, but heresy was so prevalent among the population that eradicating it would have entailed massacring close to a third of the inhabitants of the region, and so he resisted calls from the Pope to do so.

Because of the laws of heredity, women had more financial and political rights than women did in other parts of Europe. Yet these same laws sowed the seeds of the region's downfall. There was no such thing as primogeniture. Properties could be inherited by a count's multiple children (male or female), thus either breaking up large lands into smaller parcels or leaving them to be managed by someone with no stake in them—and thereby weakening any defenses against aggressors.

In addition to its glorious cultural heritage, the Midi was rich in farmlands and vineyards and bounded by the natural barriers of the Pyrenees, the Alps, and the Mediterranean Sea, making it an attractive prize for the ambitious French. Although

Louis IX's predecessor King Philip was not eager to join a crusade when he was busy fending off aggression by the English—especially against a Christian land—the subsequent weakening paved the way for the French to annex the region and consolidate their power. In the process of dominating the Midi county by county and violently imposing the Catholic faith on its inhabitants, conquest by the French also tolled the death knell for the centuries-old culture.

The characters in this novel are all fictional, as are the events that directly concern them. Many of the places are real, and the larger historical context is accurate.

Azalaïs, Azemar, Jordane, Johana, Belascon, Berenger, fraire Martin, and the others continue their adventures in Part II of this trilogy, *The Spirit of Fire*. You'll find the first chapter at the end of this book.

ACKNOWLEDGMENTS

I owe many thanks to people who have believed in me over
the years, my dear partner, Charles, chief among them.
Charles never gave up on this project, even when I did.

I am especially grateful to the warm community of
historical novelists who support each
other in person and online, who are ready with advice and
encouragement, and ready to help pick up the
pieces through disappointments and
cheer each other on through triumphs.
Thank you all. You know who you are.

Special thanks go to generous and talented author of
historical novels everyone should read,
Christopher W. Gortner,
who designed the beautiful cover for this book.

Discussion Questions

1. Despite the brutality of their early lives and the perils they face in a hostile and unforgiving environment, the orphans Azalaïs and Azemar survive and flourish. What has fostered their resilience?

2. Each of the orphans finds a mentor who not only teaches them invaluable skills but also offers them the security and trust they need to develop more fully emotionally. Do you see similarities in the relationship between Azalaïs and her monk and between Azemar and the baron? What was significant about each relationship in leading the orphans to maturity?

3. *Listen to the Wind* is an adventure story in the tradition of epics told throughout history. Did the story resonate with you? Why do you think stories in this mold capture the imagination of listeners/readers, even in the 21st century?

4. Setting is often considered a "character" in story. Was the history of the Midi familiar to you? How important was the setting to your understanding of the lives of Azalaïs and Azemar? Could their story have taken place in another time, or was it unique to the Midi in the 13th century?

5. Which character did you find most compelling? Why?

6. Why do you think Azalaïs was able to disguise her gender for so long?

7. What do you think about the decision of the parents of Azalaïs and Azemar to send their children away and the

consequences of such an excruciating choice? Could you have done that?

8. What did you think was the most unexpected part of the story? What about it surprised you?

An Excerpt from

THE SPIRIT OF FIRE

The Orphans of Tolosa
Book II

1244

CHAPTER 1

"Well, they could have left us a horse, at least."

Jordane watched Azemar and Azalaïs ride off into the night, fuming that the two had left her and Johana in a cave with no means of transport. It would not take long for the Baron de Belascon's men to trace them so far, especially if they were able to tie Azemar's disappearance to theirs. The first place they would look would be Montpezat, the estate Azemar had inherited from the late baron, his benefactor.

"The floor is dry, and we have food and warm blankets. We can rest here while we decide what to do." Johana had already set about unrolling the blankets, trying to make their temporary quarters as comfortable as possible.

Jordane wrinkled her nose at the musty smell of the cave, now illuminated by the lamp that Johana had lit with a flint. The small pool of warm light revealed that this first chamber had been swept clean and its floor leveled. At the back, gaping holes suggested that the caves continued into the hillside. Jordane wondered if any animals lurked in their depths. Although she could not see into the obscurity above, she could hear the squeaking and clicking of bats in their thousands. "We cannot remain here forever." Jordane paced restlessly back and forth, chewing on the side of her index finger.

"Come, Ma Domna. We can do nothing tonight."

Jordane stopped her pacing and looked down at Johana, seated on one of the blankets. Her dear friend was tired. "It was unfair of me to involve you in this."

"You know I would never have let you take the risk alone. Besides, if both you and the Barona disappeared and I stayed behind, what do you think would have happened to me?"

"I don't just mean escaping. You should have stayed at Caunes. You would be safe there now if you had."

Johana sighed. "Without you, Caunes would have been unbearable. At least by traveling with Azalaïs I had a change of scene, and something to do."

"A great deal more to do than you bargained for, I think." Jordane crouched down and stroked her friend's cheek. "And there is more to come as well."

Johana looked away, pretending to smooth the blankets. "So, you think Raimon has gone to a fortress in the south?"

"Yes. I overheard some of the men talking about a castel that began with a p. Puivert, or Puylaurens perhaps. Either that, or he has chosen to hide among the French."

"You can't mean it, Ma Domna!" Johana's eyes widened in disbelief.

Jordane was too tired to explain. She kissed her friend lightly on both cheeks. "Good night," she said, and lay down on one of the unrolled blankets. Johana covered her, then stretched out herself.

The ground was harder even than the thin straw pallets Jordane had been forced to sleep on when she traveled with Raimon and his knights. Despite her exhaustion, she could not close her eyes. The wound in her leg had almost completely healed, yet that night it pulsed with a persistent ache, like someone jabbing a finger into her and saying, beware!

Soon Johana's breathing evened and slowed. Jordane was

glad her damozel could sleep. But her own mind raced with questions she could not answer. How would the two of them ever be able to travel without attracting notice? How would they explain who they were if someone found them? Perhaps they would be forced, after all, to remain in the cave for a while. Its entrance was well hidden, and it would be possible to gather their strength and plan. And if some of the peasants nearby would be willing to help them, then they could rejoin the rebels with renewed purpose and be ready to take their part.

Fleeing as they had was foolhardy. Staying would have been akin to signing their own orders for execution. Jordane had overheard enough of the dowager Barona de Belascon and the Dominican monk's conversations to know that the world would soon have collapsed around them there, and they might all have found themselves stretched upon racks at the Abbey of Fontfred.

Jordane stood, wrapped herself in the blanket and walked out into the warm night. The river made its silvery way around hills washed with pale moonlight, disappearing behind the castel and then reappearing to continue toward the sea. Here and there the scraggy black shapes of denuded vines marked out a vineyard, and down at the castel a curl of smoke rose from what must have been the kitchen fireplace. Soon the matins bells would toll in the nearby village, which Jordane assumed must be just out of sight over one of the hills.

How could it be, she wondered, that she—daughter of one of the most illustrious houses in the Minervois—could find herself hiding in a cave in the Corbières, dependent on the kindness and discretion of servants for her survival? This wasn't at all what she imagined would happen when she ran off in pursuit of Raimon.

Raimon. Where was he? Jordane understood that the knight would have been foolhardy to stay around Belascon long enough to see what had become of her. She had heard enough talk to know that the French would have given him no quarter if he had been caught. And yet—and yet. If were the one who had been injured, and she had had the opportunity to flee, she would have given her own life to save his rather than leave him to his fate.

That was different, though. She was a woman, not a brave knight who would drive the French out of the Midi, back to the other side of the Rhone in the east and into Aquitaine in the west. The others who could have led the scattered, beleaguered knights and foot soldiers to victory had died and so it was down to Raimon to save them all.

In the silence and solitude of her hillside perch, Jordane could feel her lover's presence as if he sat beside her, his face set in concentration as he honed his broadsword. The jingle of his armor, the leathery squeak of his cuirass, the smell of his hair. She could not banish him from her mind and it drove her wild with desire. She wanted to taste his lips again, feel his strong arms around her and his hairy chest against her soft breasts. She wanted his manhood, his passion, his love.

But more than that, Jordane wanted to fight beside him. She had proven she could do it. Her injury was only a temporary setback, and as soon as she was able she had marched boldly into the enemy camp to gather information. Now she was possessed of knowledge that she could use. She had not told Azalaïs, or even Jordane, the smallest part of what she overheard during her music lessons with the innocent Marcu.

Belascon was a pawn. It was the dowager Ermengarde who, with the monk, had masterminded an action that they intended to be the final stand against the heretics, and the death knell for the way of life that the nobles had enjoyed in this gentle land for time beyond memory. In retribution for the murders at Avinhonet, a large army would amass at Montsegur, a fortress set high on a pog in the hills below the Pirenèus where the heretics fled to practice their religion out of sight of the Church.

Jordane had overheard them say that when Belascon went to Bésiers it had all been decided. He had been well prepared by his mother to further the plan to march in the spring and then lay siege. Jordane's own father, the baron d'Aniort, would be among the besiegers. They intended that by summer, they would overcome the fortress and destroy it.

Someone must reach the community on the mountain-top and warn them so that they would be prepared to resist. Jordane was no heretic, but she was determined to defend her paratge. Her taste of action, of how it felt to be a man and to fight, had whetted her appetite. She had no desire to stay in a cave and hope to save her own skin. If Johana did not want to come, so be it. But inaction was not for her.

From her vantage point, Jordane could clearly see the lay-out of the castel de Montpezat. It was not large enough to warrant the digging of a moat, but fortified nonetheless with a high stone wall and a portcullis. She noted that this had not been lowered, as if the seneschal had no fear of intruders. At the far end of the courtyard, the residence and the donjon—both small-er than the castel at Caunes, and modest compared to Belas-con—pressed up against a wall that overlooked the river. Two other sides of the courtyard had wooden structures, one for the kitchens, and one that must house the livestock.

The livestock. Surely the seneschal had a horse? She and Johana could ride one horse.

Jordane was now wide awake. There was no time to waste in idle fancies and regrets. She whirled and swept into the cave. "Johana! Johana!"

The damozel sat up, but her eyes stared vacantly as if she could not figure out where she was. "What? Is it time to dress?"

"We are dressed. We are in a cave, remember?" Jordane shook her and patted her cheek.

"Oh, yes, yes."

"We shan't stay here. Will you come with me? I think I can

find us a horse."

Johana stood, now fully awake. "Where? What can you be thinking, Ma Domna?"

"He left us here. He owes us a horse."

Jordane quickly rolled up her blanket and started repacking the provisions. "We are not far. We can carry these down. You'll wait outside the walls and I'll go in and get the beast."

"How do you know they have one?"

"The seneschal must. How else would he oversee the estate?" Jordane saw the doubt in Johana's eyes. "We cannot stay here, don't you see? I know things, things that will help Raimon. If we do not find him, all will be lost." She stopped. "I mean, if I do not find him, all will be lost. You don't have to come. I will understand if you choose not to."

Johana shook her head and smiled at her sadly. "And what else would I do?"

Moments later, they began their careful descent. Jordane meant to steal the horse before matins and be on their way before the cook's boy rose to stoke the fire. She stopped from time to time to help Johana over a difficult place, but they clambered like children over rocks and through dense brush before finally reaching the edge of the wild growth and the beginning of the cultivated fields of Montpezat.

"You wait here. Two of us might be seen."

Jordane did not give Johana time to protest,but tossed her pack of provisions on the ground at the donzella's feet and struck out across the vineyard that separated them from the castel. So far, Jordane noted, no one stirred. It was that hour when even the night birds have gone to sleep, when, she suspected, terrible crimes might be committed with no other witness than the criminal's own heart.

I am a criminal. The realization brought Jordane up short, and she slowed her pace. Worse, she was about to commit a crime against someone who had helped her.

She shook her head and rubbed her eyes. Idle doubts had no place in her plans. Within sight of the entrance to the castel yard, she dashed forward the last distance and arrived undetected at the manger that housed the domain's more valuable livestock.

To her surprise, the door of the wooden building was not locked. She had half expected to find it necessary to climb in through a window. But the large door moved easily and quietly on its hinges, and soon she found herself inside the dark, animal-warmed space.

Two milk cows raised their sleepy heads as she approached, but did not low. Likewise, a few sheep of a sort she had never seen before simply followed her with their soft, innocent eyes as she crept toward the place where two horses were tethered, munching thoughtfully on hay they pulled out of a wooden cage attached to the wall.

"Easy there," she murmured, careful not to startle them by approaching from where they could not see her.

"I could get the bayle, and you'd be hung as a horse thief."

Jordane gasped and turned around in a circle, looking for the source of the voice. It was not until a man dressed in brown clothing with bits of straw stuck to him here and there stepped out of the shadows with a pitchfork pointed in her direction that she found it. "Forgive me, I was just . . ." the excuse died on her lips. She shrank back, looking for some way to flee, expecting at any moment that the man would call for help.

To her surprise, he lifted his fork up high, and with some satisfaction she thought when she remembered afterwards, flung it not toward her, but into a bale of straw.

"The baron said I was to let you take the horses if you decided you needed them."

Jordane's heart fluttered in her breast. When she calmed herself enough to understand what the fellow said, a wave of anger surged through her. If Azemar had been there she would gladly have wrapped her fingers around his throat and squeezed the life out of him. "And why didn't he just let us go last night?"

"He thought it better that you all not travel at the same time."

The man—groom, shepherd, steward, she did not know what—had already flung a heavy saddle on the back of the larger of the two animals. When he finished, he lifted another saddle off a rail and prepared to put it on the second horse.

"What are you doing?" Jordane asked.

"There are two of you, I was told."

Jordane's anger melted away like the snow that covered the Pirenèus in the spring. Azemar—and his servant, for the fellow could easily have chosen to disobey a master who had gone away for an unknown period of time—was willing to give up two valuable beasts, creatures needed to work on the estate, to draw the cart that would bring their wine to market, to let the land steward collect rents from the tenants. "I—I feel so ashamed. I was going to steal a horse. And truly, Menher—"

"Rimbalt. I am seneschal here."

"Menher Rimbalt, we need only one. Have you a pillion pad?" Jordane spoke quickly, before her conscience could quite overtake her.

Rimbalt shrugged. "If you wish."

She noticed that he accepted her suggestion without blinking an eye, but who could blame him? She did not begrudge him his parsimony.

Before long the horse was ready to bear its burdens. Rimbalt led it out to the courtyard and helped Jordane mount. He held onto the reins for a moment before letting her ride away. "My master, the baron. Do you think you will see him?"

"I don't know," answered Jordane, "But I may. I believe we seek the same outcome, and that may lead us to the same place."

Rimbalt nodded and relinquished the reins. Jordane urged the horse forward, left the castel yard and struck out across the vineyard to where Johana and the provisions waited.

"Ma Domna! I was beginning to worry."

"It turns out you needn't have," she answered. Jordane dismounted and explained what had happened while together they figured out how to arrange the blankets and panniers so that they could both fit on the horse.

The horse moved less willingly with its heavier load, but it was healthy and rested. "Where are we going?"

Johana's question seemed oddly incongruous. The moment she decided that they must leave, Jordane had worked out everything, perhaps not all the details, but at least in the main, and it appeared so self-evident to her that she did not know why she would have to explain it to anyone else. "To Puivert, naturally," she said.

"To Puivert? Why Puivert? What is there? I think it is rather far."

Despite Johana's justifiable irritation, Jordane knew they were on the right course. "Because it is a castel that is sympathetic to our cause, and where a trobairitz will be welcomed with open arms." If Raimon happened also have settled on that destination, he would be able to disguise himself and blend in with the usual assortment of guests who assembled at this wealthy estate in the heart of the most fertile farmlands of the Ariège. Even in Caunes they ate fruits from Puivert, and guests frequently told stories about lavish entertainments and contests among trobadors. It was a regular stop for any of the traveling musicians of lower birth who had to earn their way. Although the golden days of Peire Alvernha were no more, one of the Trencavels had wrested the castel back from the French a few years ago and reestablished its cultural reputation. It seemed the most likely of all the estates beginning with a "p." It would be the perfect setting to muster her strength and regain her foothold in the rebel cause.

Through her back she could feel the deep breath Johana drew into her chest and the long sigh that let it escape from her again. "I hope you will not place yourself in yet more danger," she said.

"Don't worry," Jordane replied, "We shall be among friends."

"If we ever get there," Johana said, and rested her forehead against the nape of Jordane's neck.

...To be continued

Go to OrphansOfTolosa.com for more information about the history and culture of 13th-century Langue d'Oc—and sign up for updates in your inbox on *The Spirit of Fire*.

CPSIA information can be obtained
at www.ICGtesting.com
Printed in the USA
FFHW021014040919
54765417-60443FF

More Advance Praise for *Invest in Yourself*:

"Marc Eisenson can find more ways to 'beat the bank' out of interest on your mortgage, credit card, or bank loan than anyone I know. Saving money can often build your wealth faster and safer than investing can. This book is essential reading."

—William E. Donoghue, publisher, *Donoghue's WealthLetter* and author of *The Millennium Advantage: 100% Income Tax-Free Wealthbuilding*

"At last a book that really helps you take control of your future. I know you will refer to this book over and over again and probably buy extra copies to share with your family and friends."

—Jim Jorgensen, author of *Money Lessons for a Lifetime* and syndicated radio host

"Over the years I have come to respect the authors for their sensible approach to finances. They speak my language and make learning this stuff really fun. . . . *Invest in Yourself* takes the otherwise fairly boring subject of personal finance and makes it exhilarating."

—Mary Hunt, editor and publisher, *Cheapskate Monthly* newsletter

"*Invest in Yourself* won't tell you how to make a lot of money, but it will explain how you can live better on less than you think while *saving* money. The payoff is substantial: reduced stress, more security, a happier family, and a richer enjoyment of life. When the authors tell you to *Invest in Yourself,* they want you to recognize that you can use your knowledge and abilities to make a better life—and do it on your own terms.

—Paul S. Havemann, vice president, HSH Associates

"This is the ultimate how to get a life book, it should be on every family bookshelf. It is an easy read to help you reshape your priorities and give you a new perspective on life."

—Linda Golodner, president of the National Consumer's League

"If you truly want to enjoy life's riches—financial security, family, peace of mind, and a job you love—follow the six secrets that Marc Eisenson, Gerri Detweiler, and Nancy Castleman share in *Invest in Yourself.* They make it easy."

—Dr. Susan Ginsberg, publisher and editor, *Work and Family Life* newsletter

INVEST IN YOUR-SELF

....

SIX SECRETS
TO A
RICH LIFE

....

MARC EISENSON
GERRI DETWEILER
NANCY CASTLEMAN

John Wiley & Sons, Inc.
New York • Chichester • Weinheim • Brisbane • Singapore • Toronto

GD: To my family—Kevin, Mom, Dad, Gail, Tony, and Gary

NC: For Len, Anita, Janet, Ben, and Rachel

ME: For Robin, Sharon, Adam, Sam, Alan and their families—too numerous to mention, too much loved to forget. With a special thank you to Nancy. In the beginning and in the end, this, too, is Nancy's book.

This book is printed on acid-free paper. ∞

Copyright © 1998 by Marc Eisenson, Gerri Detweiler, and Nancy Castleman.
All rights reserved.
Published by John Wiley & Sons, Inc.

Published simultaneously in Canada.

No part of this publication may be reproduced, stored in a retrieval system or transmitted in any form or by any means, electronic, mechanical, photocopying, recording, scanning or otherwise, except as permitted under Section 107 or 108 of the 1976 United States Copyright Act, without either the prior written permission of the Publisher, or authorization through payment of the appropriate per-copy fee to the Copyright Clearance Center, 222 Rosewood Drive, Danvers, MA 01923, (978) 750-8400, fax (978) 750-4744. Requests to the Publisher for permission should be addressed to the Permissions Department, John Wiley & Sons, Inc., 605 Third Avenue, New York, NY 10158-0012, (212) 850-6011, fax (212) 850-6008, E-Mail: PERMREQ @ WILEY.COM.

This publication is designed to provide accurate and authoritative information in regard to the subject matter covered. It is sold with the understanding that neither the publisher nor the authors are engaged in rendering professional services. If professional advice or other expert assistance is required, the services of a competent professional person should be sought.

Library of Congress Cataloging-in-Publication Data:
Eisenson, Marc. 1943–
     Invest in yourself : six secrets to a rich life / Marc
Eisenson, Gerri Detweiler, and Nancy Castleman.
          p.   cm.
     Includes bibliographical references and index.
     ISBN 0-471-24888-6 (hardcover : alk. paper)
     ISBN 0-471-39997-3 (paper : alk. paper)
     1. Finance, Personal.   2. Investments.   3. Life skills.
     I. Detweiler, Gerri, 1964– .   II. Castleman, Nancy, 1948– .   III. Title.
HG179.E397   1998
332.024—dc21   98-15212

Printed in the United States of America.

10 9 8 7 6 5 4 3 2

Contents

v

Acknowledgments

Our goal for *Invest in Yourself* is to motivate you to take charge of your life and make the most of your time, energy, and money.

While we can't promise you a fairy-tale future, we will offer lots of suggestions for how you can live the way you want, even if you have a pile of credit card bills, hefty mortgage payments, loans out on a clunker or two, a job you don't love, and a bad case of the "I'm tired of living payday to payday" blues. Whether we succeed or not is a judgment only you can make.

The success we have had up until now is thanks in large part to the hundreds of members of the Fourth Estate who have helped share our ideas with their readers, listeners, and viewers. So our first thank you is to each and every reporter, producer, editor, and on-air personality who has taken the time to understand our ideas, to ask us tough questions, and to help us get our message out.

One of those journalists, a well-respected personal finance writer and author, is Debra Wishik Englander. Now an editor at John Wiley & Sons, Inc., Debby is *the* reason a copy of *Invest in Yourself* is in your hands. She "saw" the book when it was just an idea, and helped us take it to what it is today.

Our wonderful agent, Alan Kellock, carefully and creatively wended his way between the rocks and hard places of three independent-thinking, skittish authors and the long established traditions of the publishing industry. He made it possible for us to sign on the dotted line.

While Debby and Alan created the opportunity for this book to happen, Linda Spiciarich and Marcy Ross were the ones who helped us bring it to life. We can't thank them enough for their dedication to our cause and for their hard work. To say their effort was way beyond the call of duty is truly an understatement.

We're delighted to have our book published by John Wiley & Sons, Inc., the nation's oldest independent and still family owned publishing company. We've found the Wiley team approach to publishing both unusual and refreshing, and want to say "Many thanks!" to the committed team of often unacknowledged graphic and cover designers, marketing people, publicists, sales staff, and wordsmiths who have worked with us on *Invest in Yourself*: Ruth Acosta, Amelia Blanquera, Doug Chilcott, Michael Detweiler, Lauren Fransen, Dean Karrel and his sales department, Peter Knapp, Ann McCarthy, Olga Moya, Joan O'Neil, Andrea Price, Ellen Silberman, Laurie Thompson, and Myles C. Thompson.

Special thanks also go to Christine H. Furry, Lisa Kochel, Beth Oberholtzer, and their teammates at North Market Street Graphics; Sherry Christie, Sharon and Alan De Michele, the reference librarians at the Brooklyn Public Library; and Bobbie Armstrong and Cherie Beam at the Red Hook Recycling Center.

Marc Eisenson, Gerri Detweiler, and Nancy Castleman

Introduction

There really are only two possibilities: You're living the life of your dreams, or you're not.

If you're not, perhaps we can help.

Chances are, even if you're handling your money fairly well, you think you don't have enough. You're not alone. Surveys show that nothing—including sexual fantasies—occupies more of our brain time than thoughts about the almighty dollar: how to earn, invest, borrow, and spend it.

Maybe you once thought everything would be okay if your paychecks were only larger. But every time you got a pay raise, you spent more, and the government took more. Soon you were right back where you started, living paycheck to paycheck, at dollar amounts and stress levels that kept getting higher and higher.

So maybe a raise won't buy you the life you want. Maybe gobs of cash is the answer. Publishers Clearing House amounts. Or maybe the answer is in working less and leading a simpler life. But then you fear you'd have to sacrifice too many of the creature comforts you've come to enjoy, and you'd fall behind on those bills.

Wouldn't it be great if you could just leave all your money worries and job stress behind? Well, you can! And you don't have to move into a cave to live a freer, happier, healthier life. Nor do you have to choose between your work, your pleasures, your friends, and your family.

All it really takes is the right investment portfolio. A portfolio not just of stocks and bonds, but one that includes investments in yourself and in your family. Like any good portfolio, the best investments you can make in yourself are diversified, flexible enough to change as you and your goals do, carefully managed, and geared to the long term.

1

To create the portfolio that's right for you, you've got to invest time and energy in figuring out what you *really* want—and what will get you there. While the good life is different for each of us, and one-size-fits-all formulas don't work, everyone, no matter how deep in debt, no matter how unhappy at home or at work, *can* change direction and make dreams come true, without being irresponsible or reckless. Sometimes all it takes is a bit of fine-tuning. At other times, major modifications may be in order.

Once we become adults, we often lose track of life's simple pleasures and of our own personal goals. We take a wrong turn or two, then spend a good part of our lives doing things we'd rather not—while not doing many of those things we'd enjoy. While we may obsess about how unhappy we are, we don't focus clearly on what we can do to change the situation: on how we can invest our time, energy, and yes, our money to consciously create the life we want.

Change is scary. It takes courage, and often arouses conflicts with the ones we love. That's probably why so many folks stay in the ruts they've dug, unhappily spending a good portion of their days wishing they could get out, but not being able to do anything constructive to make it happen.

Getting from where you are today to where you'd like to be is rarely a goal that can be achieved instantly, any more than you could expect to lose weight and improve muscle tone overnight, or succeed at a new business, sport, or hobby the first time out.

Deciding what you want, and then figuring out how to get there requires some planning, commitment, time, and knowledge. But the journey can be as satisfying as the destination—if you don't put yourself on a starvation diet to achieve your goals. (They never work, anyway.)

Perhaps you really can't stand your job, but you're working too many hours to look for a new one, and you need the money too much to quit. Or maybe you'd really like to start an exercise program so you'll have more energy, but you're too tired to get started.

To get what you want in life, you first have to make room. And that means letting go of the things you don't want, even though you may have invested a lot of time and money in them along the way. While this is often difficult, the benefits will make it well worth the effort.

You *can* change your life. We know, because we've changed our lives, and we've spent a combined 38 years helping others make smart choices about their finances and their futures.

We'll help you pull it all together—by keeping you focused on you, and on how your investments of time, money, and energy can best benefit you and your family. We'll ask you the key questions, and remind you of what your alternatives are for finding the answers that will work best—for you. But you're the boss. You get to make the final decisions.

Often, your best investment in yourself will be to do more research, so you can really figure out where you stand and what you want. We'll frequently refer you to our favorite books, Web sites, and other resources. But there are great resources right there in River City, where you live. Your friends, relatives, and clergy may be a lot more help than you realize. But you have to ask! Learning more about a subject is a great way to tune in to the pros and cons—for you—of a career or lifestyle change, for instance.

But if at the same time, you listen carefully to what's going on inside your mind, that great snowball effect will start to happen. As you learn more, you'll try more. Some of what you try will make you happier, and hopefully, wealthier. Soon you'll be motivated to push yourself even further to create the life you really want.

. . . .

WE'RE JUST THE MESSENGERS

In many ways, this is a personal book. It grew out of our lives and our work, which are inseparable. We try our best to intentionally do things for money that we would want to do anyway. Over the years, thousands of people like you have come to us for advice. What you'll read here is what we've gleaned from their experiences and from our own.

While our message is clear, "You *can* take control of your future," we hope you won't confuse the message with the messengers. Our goal is to inspire you to create the life *you* want to live. We'll tell you how we did it, and how others who succeeded did it as well, but you'll have to chart your own course.

We'd love to hear about where you've been, where you are now, and where you hope to be after you've put the ideas in *Invest in Yourself* to work. Write and let us know! For snail mail, it's Invest in Yourself, c/o Good Advice Press, P.O. Box 78, Elizaville, NY 12523. Our Web address is www.investinyourself.com. Feedback@investinyourself.com is our e-mail address.

. . . .

Your personal rut may be well worn or only recently started. Some ruts are deeper than others, and some could more accurately be described as trenches. But none are so deep that you can't get out.

We'll supply the ladder, and we'll even hold it for you. But you have to decide to climb it, and you have to choose where you'll be going next. Life, after all, is a series of choices.

Even the wealthiest people can't have or do everything they fantasize about—at least not all at the same time! But all of us can have most of our needs and reasonable desires met, most of the time.

SIX KEYS TO A HAPPIER, RICHER LIFESTYLE

Are you ready to live the life you crave, without feeling deprived, without making drastic changes, and without always having that black cloud of debt over your head? To pull it off, you'll need to develop a take-charge attitude, which is a surprisingly easy thing to do—if you embrace the six *Invest in Yourself* secrets that we're going to spell out. They can power up the rest of your days, leaving you happier, healthier, wiser, and richer in every sense of the word. We guarantee it!

I. Make Your Own Lifestyle Decisions

Money management is no longer just a matter of how you earn, invest, and spend your income—it's about how you choose to live your life. There's no "correct" way to go. We'll help you weigh the pros and cons, in terms of both the financial consequences and the way you feel about your alternatives. Then you'll decide what will work best for you and your family.

For example, say you've just had a baby. Congratulations! Now you find yourself thinking how nice it would be to only work part-time or to work from home. But you're used to a certain lifestyle, and you don't really want to change that. How can you pull it off, pay the bills, and not feel deprived?

Or perhaps your kids are approaching school age, and you're thinking about moving into a better school district, even though real estate is more expensive there. How can you swing it? Will it be worth the sacrifice?

Or maybe you're wondering if you'd be happier leaving the city for the country—or leaving the suburbs for the city. Perhaps you're wondering, "What can I do, right now, to enhance and simplify my life without making major changes?"

Before you can make positive lifestyle changes, you'll need to get clear on your priorities and your realistic options. You can do it! You're not a dummy or an idiot. You're not clueless, and you're not from Mars or Venus.

II. Put Your Family First

Back in 1984, when the late senator from Massachusetts, Paul Tsongas, was diagnosed with lymph cancer, he chose to give up his prestigious job in order to spend more time with his family. As a friend wisely told him, "Nobody, on his deathbed ever said, 'I wish I had spent more time at the office.' "

Sometimes we're so focused on what we should do to get ahead that we get our priorities screwed up, forgetting to put our time and energy into those people and things that matter most to us. You can earn all you need, meet all your financial obligations—even prosper—and still break free of workaholic addictions that keep you too busy to go to the little league games, to mend a fence or two, or to stop and smell the roses. (Be careful around those thorns!)

In short, the family that plays together, stays together and prospers, whether it's a family in the Ozzie and Harriet tradition or one of the many variations that now coexist.

III. Wherever You Work, Be in Business for Yourself

To succeed today, you need to nurture an entrepreneurial attitude, to be multiskilled, flexible, good at selling yourself, savvy about personal finance, clear on your priorities, and always prepared for the ax to fall or the bottom to drop out. Today's worker needs to be prepared to job-hop, on average, every four to seven years.

One way to protect your future is with a home business. Over 25 million people work from their homes and more are joining the movement every day.

Starting a very small business or two—*before* you need it—is a good, inexpensive way to get up, running, and experienced. We think of it as an "Ace in the Hole." You may like your Ace enough to leave the rat track, or you might work for a corporation until you retire. But either way, being prepared and willing to make the transition into a different company, a new line of work, or a business of your own will provide you with much more than a strong safety net.

IV. Make the Most of the Money You Bring Home

Believe it or not, it's worth the time and effort to pinch pennies. Small though they are, they quickly add up. Need dramatic proof? Put a penny in a big jar. Every day, add twice as many coins (the second day, two; the third day, four; the fourth day, eight; and so on). Soon you'll need a very big jar, because by the end of the month, you'll have more than $5 million—half a billion pennies. Now imagine what you could accomplish by pinching a few dollars here or there.

V. Turn Your Debts into Golden Investment Opportunities

Working as hard as they can to convince us that there are things we didn't have or need yesterday, but *must* have today, is a $186 billion a year advertising industry. Assisted by a multitrillion dollar banking system, they promise to put us in the driver's seat, on a fabulous vacation, or on a mall shopping spree, whether we can afford it or not, with one play now, pay later loan after another.

While few can buy a house without borrowing, by the time a typical $100,000, 30-year loan has been repaid, the homeowners will have mailed in 360 payments totaling a quarter of a million dollars or more!

There's a big difference between what bankers pay savers (some 3% to 5%) versus what lenders charge borrowers (up to 20%, sometimes more). Yet lots of folks (perhaps you?) keep thousands of dollars in various savings accounts while paying very high interest on their card balances. If you have a typical $3,500 credit card balance, and only send in the minimum payments, you'll end up repaying $11,162. (That's *not* a typo.) Investing just two bits, one little quarter a day, will save you up to $3,300 in interest. (Also not a typo.)

Every little bit extra you send in with each credit card, mortgage, car loan, or student loan payment will save you money—tax-free, risk-free, and absolutely guaranteed. For someone in the 28% tax bracket, who is carrying a balance on a typical credit card with a 17% interest rate, pre-paying is the same as earning 23.5% before taxes on a more conventional investment.

VI. Map Out Your Own Financial Future

Assuming your family always earns just the median income, you're still going to bring in over $2 million during the course of your working life. That's a lot of money to manage! This part of the book will help you take a fresh look at your investment alternatives, and make it easy for you to decide on the mix that makes sense for you.

And because more people would rather get a root canal than create a financial plan, we won't be assigning tedious homework, detailed budgets, or dogmatic lists of shoulds and should nots. Similarly, since few people are likely to stick to a path that leaves them feeling deprived or guilty, you won't be asked to give up the financial equivalent of the dieter's chocolate cake.

NO RULES!

Invest in Yourself is not intended to be a rule book. While we three authors share a take-charge philosophy, we don't agree on every detail, and we prefer different lifestyles.

For example, Marc and Nancy left the fast track years ago—Marc as a licensed Professional Engineer and Nancy as a grant maker and loan officer for a foundation in New York City. They've been championing the value of a debt-free, simple lifestyle off the proverbial dining room table since 1984—long before "downsizing debt," "voluntary simplicity," and "tightwaddery" were in vogue. They live simply in an old farmhouse, with cows as their nearest neighbors. If they never went to another meeting or into a city again, that'd be just fine by them. They'd rather be in their 10,000-square-foot organic garden.

Gerri, former executive director of Bankcard Holders of America and policy director at the National Council of Individual Investors, is an authority on the burgeoning credit industry. Her views are sought in the halls of Congress, in the headquarters of financial giants such as Master-Card and NationsBank, and by organized labor. She lives in a townhouse in a bustling suburb of Washington, D.C. Gerri also recently received a master's degree in Adult Education/Psychology with a focus on financial education and problem solving.

Gerri believes in the benefits of exercises, like keeping track of your expenses in a little notebook for a month or two. "It gives a clear picture of where the cash is leaking out of your wallet," she says.

Marc wouldn't dream of reading (much less writing) a book that required a reader to have a pen in hand. "Too much like being back in school," he says.

Nancy, as she often does, suggested a compromise. "Let's write an easy-to-follow, life-changing book," she said, "but offer voluntary exercises in sidebars for those people who would benefit from doing them."

Hence, the occasional "Gerri's Toolbox."

....

GERRI'S TOOLBOX: ONE A WEEK

As you read this book, you'll discover many high-leverage, low-pain, nitty-gritty suggestions for changing the ways you spend your money and your time. And our ideas and questions will spur plenty of your own.

While we can't tell you where you want to go, we can help you map the route. So keep a blank calendar beside you, and look for 52 things that you can do this year to invest in yourself. For example, you may decide to spend one evening this week at the library investigating career options. Who knows? That one evening may lead you to someplace where you'd be happier 9 to 5. (Or will it be 8:30 to 2?)

Or you may decide to try to cut back on your spending a bit, here or there, in some of the ways we recommend. *Just one small change a week will dramatically change your life.* Don't believe us? Try it for a year and prove us wrong.

· ·

We encourage you to set the bar high, no matter what you're aiming for in life. It may seem at times that we're advocating simple or frugal living, but we're not. We're advocating a self-designed life, where you invest your time and energy getting what you want and doing what you believe in—not wasting them on things you don't really want, but think you should have.

For some, that may mean a simple life. For others, it may mean a luxurious home in the Caribbean. Whatever. It's your choice. But to get where you want to go, you have to be clear about what you really want. To pull it off, you have to make honest choices based on the facts: both the financial facts and the way you feel.

MEET OPRAH, OR MAKE YOUR DREAMS COME TRUE

In her commencement speech to the 1997 graduating class of Wellesley College, Oprah Winfrey told the story of her "Wildest Dreams" show, where she asked women to share their wildest dreams so she could fulfill some of them. One woman got to ride a camel in Egypt. Another asked for and got a house. A third dreamer had her college debt paid off. Many other women had a simpler dream. They just wanted to meet Oprah.

Those women also got their wish, but were upset when they found out what Oprah had done for the others. As she said in her speech, ". . . some of them afterwards were crying to me, saying that 'we didn't know, we didn't know, and this is unfair!' and I said, 'That is the lesson: You needed to dream a bigger dream for yourself.' That is the lesson. Hold the biggest vision possible for your life and it can come true."

Come on. Let's get started.

MAKE YOUR OWN LIFESTYLE DECISIONS

SOMEWHERE ALONG THE WAY, YOU GOT LOCKED INTO LIVING AND financing a particular lifestyle. Maybe you thought it was because you wanted to create a stable, enriched home life for your family. Or maybe you thought it was because that's all you could afford. Or maybe you didn't think through your alternatives at all.

The number one, most important part of your *Invest in Yourself* portfolio is the knowledge that you have a right to make conscious choices about how you live the remainder of your life. You have alternatives about how you invest your time and energy, as well as where and how you bring up your children.

Your path in life shouldn't be set in stone. Nor should it be decided by whomever you call "boss," by Madison Avenue, by your spouse, your mother, or your father. You're a grown-up now. You get to call the shots.

CHAPTER 1

....

Charting a Course to the
Way of Life You Want

○ If you had your druthers, what would your life be like?

○ How to get clear on your priorities and your lifestyle options

○ Finding the balance between your money, time, and values

○ Looking at your situation objectively—financially and emotionally

○ How to take your dreams for a test-drive without chucking everything

○ The domino effect

Not everything that is faced can be changed,
but nothing can be changed until it is faced.

JAMES BALDWIN

....

IF YOU HAD YOUR DRUTHERS

If you had a magic wand and could go back 10 or 20 years, knowing what you know now, what would you have done differently? Having made those alternative decisions, what would your life be like now?

- Would you marry the same person?
- Would you spend more (or less) time with your children?
- Would you move to a new city, town, or country?

- Would you change jobs or careers—perhaps return to school or go into business for yourself?

It's your life. If the balance is wrong, if your debts are too high and your pleasures too few, perhaps you're stuck. There's security in routine, and change, especially dramatic change can be frightening.

Still, the world around us keeps changing and we keep growing older—and hopefully a bit wiser. The life you sought yesterday or 20 years ago may not be what you'd choose today. *Knowing what you'd choose today is what's important. You can't do much about decisions you made in the past. Let them go.*

If you're going along unconsciously, and things just seem to happen to you, it's time to take control of the process and to thoughtfully resolve the key issues of how you live your life. As difficult as that may sound, you're going to be buoyed along the way by the knowledge that the steps you do take will bring you closer and closer to happiness and contentment.

Rather than obsessing about an extreme solution—getting a divorce, quitting your job—begin by focusing on something you can do now that will improve your situation, something that might turn the negative into a positive. Begin to look at new career options. Talk to your spouse and perhaps with a counselor. Make a serious effort to return to those wondrous days of yesteryear.

If Only

Certain words and expressions in the English language have a tendency to eliminate all of life's gray areas. Yes, when we were toddlers, we may have had limited ability to make independent decisions—when to cross the street, for instance. Back then, our parents used clear, black-and-white statements to tell us how to behave. "You *should never* cross the street alone." But you're old enough now to cross safely by yourself, to make your own decisions.

If only, it's their fault, can't, won't are all good words to consider removing from your vocabulary. You don't have to, but they're excuse words. If you're in a situation at home or at work that is problematic for you, and you're not doing anything about it, you've got a loser in your portfolio.

This book is not about excuses, blame, or impossible dreams. It's about making the most of what you have, earn, save, and owe—and of your time and energy—so you'll have the most options for how you live your life. It's about making conscious decisions, based on both the facts and on how you feel about them.

The Choice Is Yours

The way we see it, wealth is simply having more than you need, and poverty is having less. Many folks with little money and few possessions are far wealthier and happier than high-income earners who are in hock up to their eyeballs and working at jobs they hate.

Money isn't the only resource you need for the good life. Since many of the things we enjoy also require the involvement of others, we need the support of friends and family. And, of course, we need and want to be in the best health that we can achieve. But to do those things that make us feel good about ourselves and our lives, we also need time. We need the time to do what we enjoy, and we need the freedom to take that time.

Like money, we have a limited amount of time to spend. But unlike money, we can't spend time we don't have. No bank is issuing a Master-Card where we can charge more time than we were originally allotted.

Money can be earned or borrowed. Time can only be spent. Good health and fortune might affect how we consume our time, but if we burn ourselves out, no bankruptcy court will let us clear the decks and restart the clock.

Name some things that you've always wanted to do, but haven't done.

1. _____

2. _____

3. _____

4. _____

Do you feel as though some of the best life has to offer has been passing you by? Who or what have you been blaming for keeping you from your goals? Why haven't you been able to live the life you want? Is it money? Is it the children? Is it a spouse? Is it a job? Is it a bad break? Is it "*them*"?

WHERE TO BEGIN

Not at the very beginning. It makes no difference where you were born or even why. What matters is where you are today, what excess baggage you're carrying, and whether your load can be lightened, redistributed, added to, or made a more enjoyable part of your life—either now, or with planning, sometime in the future.

With profound changes taking place all around us, virtually everyone needs to be prepared to make some lifestyle adjustments from time to time. But we're not identical. Our needs, interests, and dreams differ. There is no "correct" way to go. There are as many paths to follow as there are people to follow them. What can you do to take a little stroll down your next path today?

Making changes in your life doesn't have to mean making drastic changes. Very often, reasonable baby steps that are easily managed and won't drastically upset anyone's applecart (including your own), will take you a little closer to your goal.

Can you, maybe with the help of your mate or a good friend, come up with a few baby steps you could take to get a feel for what the change would be like? You could start by asking yourself if there's another way to go, different from *the way* you've perhaps taken as a given, that might get you closer to the life you want. Maybe you'd like to begin by reading about how other people have changed their lives.

....

GERRI'S TOOLBOX: WHAT'S STOPPING YOU?

At a creative problem-solving conference, Min Basadur, a management consultant, taught me a helpful way of looking at a roadblock. Min calls it the "Why—What's Stopping You Analysis."

First, identify something you really want in your life. Let's say it's more time with your children. Ask a complete question, "*Why would I want to* . . . spend more time with my children?" Then ask, "*What's stopping me from* . . . spending more time with my children?"

Next, give the answer in a simple, complete sentence. For example, "I have too many outside activities that don't include the kids."

Then restate the answer to create a new question: "*How might I* . . . cut back on outside activities?" Or "*How might I* . . . include my children in my outside activities?"

The advantage of looking at a problem in this way is that it gives you something concrete to work on. Rather than just feeling terrible because you don't have enough time, money, or whatever, you can look at your problem from a perspective that makes it manageable. Because you'll be asking and answering your own questions, you'll come up with solutions that appeal to you and that you'll be able to implement. If you still find yourself stuck while doing this exercise, ask a couple of friends to help you. They may offer a perspective that never occurred to you.

It may sound simple and obvious, but Min has used this technique to help companies develop best-selling products, as they make and save millions of dollars in the process. Why not give Min's idea a try?

. . . .

$$E = mc^2$$

Albert Einstein discovered that matter could be converted to energy and that energy could be converted into matter. When you work, you're trading your energy for matter we call *money*. When you spend that money, you're really spending the time you expended to earn it.

In this giant barter we call life, you have 168 hours every week to trade for whatever you'd like. Once those 168 hours have been spent, they're gone forever! While we all begin and end life in the same way, the middle is a blank slate. It's your turn to come to the board and write your life story. Editing as you go is strongly advised. Feel free to include what you want to happen in the next chapter of your life and to think about how you could make it work.

. . . .

MARC AND NANCY'S STORY

We're often asked how we've managed to support ourselves as consumer advocates all these years. The hardest part was deciding to try. Once we left the fast track, the transition was relatively easy. We're convinced that anyone with a good idea and a stick-to-it attitude can transition from (or for that matter, to) the fast track.

First, we chose to cut back voluntarily to a lifestyle that we knew we could support, no matter what happened to the economy. We don't need much money to support ourselves, and because we have no debts, we automatically save the fortune that almost everyone else wastes on interest. Every $1,000 we save means $1,400 or so (before taxes) we don't have to earn. Although we'll never be rich, we're financially free.

No debts, few desires, and lots of "spit and glue" add up to thousands of hours a year when we don't have to face a traffic jam, put on business suits, or leave home.

We rarely choose to enter a store other than the supermarket, and even there, because we grow much of our own food, our spending is modest. Pretty much everything else we buy is used, which means it's cheaper and probably better constructed.

Take clothing, for example. We'll do almost anything to avoid being "malled." Our wardrobes come from the Salvation Army, Goodwill, thrift shops, and garage sales. We also borrow, lend, and trade clothes. If you've seen Marc on TV, you've seen his friend Roger's suit. The silk ties that go with it cost 25 cents each at tag sales. Even daughter Robin's wedding gown was "pre-worn."

We build it, repair what we already own, scavenge—and if it ain't broke, we certainly don't fix or replace it. Our seven appliances are recycled and kept humming because Marc has been willing to teach himself a lot about washing machine cycles, dishwasher wiring, and the rubber bands that make clothes dryers spin and VCRs play. Over the years we've saved thousands of dollars in purchase costs, repairs, and service contracts, not only on our creature comforts, but also on our office equipment (primarily used, of course).

Here's the Kicker . . .

A house like ours, on hundreds of pristine acres not far off the beaten path, costs a fortune. To own such a home, we'd have to abandon our cause based on Marc's book, *The Banker's Secret* (which explains how to pre-pay on mortgages), give up our desktop publishing company, Good Advice Press, and get "real jobs" to earn big bucks. So we *rent.*

Sure, we chuckle about the irony of two long-term leasees teaching homeowners how to save thousands of dollars. But thanks to our wonderful landlords, Tom and Louise Odak, renting helps make it possible for us to do what we want to do and live where we want to live.

You don't have to cut expenses to the bone the way we have to attain financial independence and find meaningful employment. There are lots of ways to get there. All you have to do is figure out which one you want to try on for size next.

—MARC AND NANCY

. . . .

Cultivate a Simple Attitude

By slowing down, by simplifying, by breaking some of our consuming and spending habits, by teaching our kids simple pleasures, and by adopting simple pleasures ourselves, we can create a beautiful, happy, fulfilling life. And we won't have to work as hard as we have been to maintain it.

—ELAINE ST. JAMES, *Living the Simple Life*

If you *choose* to live more simply, if you cutback voluntarily, it doesn't feel like deprivation to be:

- Less focused on meaningless material possessions.

- More self-reliant.

- More family-oriented.

- Less career-oriented.

- More concerned about the environment.

- Carrying little or no debt.

- Working at something you enjoy, even if it pays less.

- Leading a slower-paced life.

- Leaning toward a healthier diet.

- A recycler, reuser, and repairer, rather than a replacer.

Do all practitioners of voluntary simplicity wear ragged clothes and live on mountaintops eating brown rice? Hardly. You'll find simple livers in penthouses as well as in country cottages.

As trends forecaster Gerald Celente explains in his book, *Trends 2000,* voluntary simplicity doesn't mean doing one specific thing differently. Instead, it's doing many little things, all in answer to these three main questions: "How much do I really need? How much do I really want? How much am I willing to do to get it?"

Simple living isn't necessarily easy living. In fact, often, it's much more physically demanding as well as emotionally challenging. It's not always easy to march to a different drummer. But consider the alternative:

> When we believe the advertiser's fiction that "you are what you consume," we begin a misdirected search for . . . the next thing that will make us happy: a new car, a new wardrobe, a new job, a new hairstyle, a new house, and so on. Instead of lasting satisfaction, we find only temporary gratification. After the initial gratification subsides, we must begin again—looking for the next thing that, this time, we hope will bring some measure of enduring satisfaction. Yet the search is both endless and hopeless.
>
> —DUANE ELGIN, *Voluntary Simplicity*

The real trick to simplifying your life is to do it slowly. There's no hurry. It's not like a furniture sale. Prices have not been marked down "for the next 12 hours only." You have plenty of time to choose areas where you can cut back a little—by being thrifty or creative. With just a bit more emphasis on your ingenuity, you'll find all sorts of clever ways to make your life simpler, more enjoyable, and easier on yourself and your family.

That in turn will open you up to all sorts of other lifestyle possibilities and career changes.

For leads on how to simplify your life in the cyber age,* go to:

The Simple Living Network: www.slnet.com

Millennium Institute:
    www.igc.apc.org/millennium/links/simplive.html

The Simple Living Journal: www.simpleliving.com

The Use Less Stuff Report:
    www.cygnus-group.com/ULS/About_ULS.html

Center for a New American Dream: www.newdream.org

THE BALANCING ACT

A little fantasy. A little reality. A dash of cash. A cache of skills. A bit of courage. A desire for change. And patience for the process. These ingredients, if mixed in the right proportions, will coalesce into a balanced life for you. No pain. Lots of gain. Unfortunately, much as we'd like to, we can't tell you what the exact proportions are or what the final result will be.

And there's another problem. Even when everything in your life seems to be in perfect balance, you can't slack off. The mix is unstable. Achieve one fantasy and another pops up. Look around, and the reality of your life has changed. Put some money aside and an unexpected expense knocks at your door. Become proficient at a job and all of a sudden, the need for it disappears.

Investing in yourself isn't a one-time thing, any more than investing in the stock market should be. Yes, some lucky or brilliant investors buy a stock when they're young, hold onto it for life, and keep getting richer and richer. And some people know early on exactly what they want to do with their lives and never have a moment's doubt that they're joyously living the life they set out to create.

For most of the rest of us, we need to adjust, fine-tune our life decisions, and set off in a new direction from time to time. Balance is the goal to aim for—balance between your money, time, and values.

---

* The World Wide Web is new, and we're all still finding our way around. Sites disappear, names change, new sites appear. You're bound to find that some of the virtual places we send you to have been swallowed by black holes. Sorry. Let us know about the ones you do find and the ones you don't find, the ones you like and the ones you don't like. As we hear about changes, we'll post them on our Web site, www.investinyourself.com.

Challenge Authority

As you carve out your route, you'll be resisting a lot of messages from well-meaning folks (many with something to sell), who will tell you how you should do a certain something. Here are some of the messages we fight every day:

- You must save a substantial amount of money so you'll have a secure retirement.
- A home of your own is your most important investment.
- The stock market is the best way to amass wealth.
- Small businesses usually fail, most often due to a lack of capital.

Throughout this book, we'll show you why questioning conventional wisdom may be the best thing you can do in shaping the life you want. Money alone, no matter how much you have, *won't* buy a satisfying retirement. Renting may make a lot more financial sense for you than owning. You can earn high, risk-free returns without buying a single share of stock. And, like the three of us, you *can* start a successful small business without a big bankroll.

Here's another example: Some "experts" will tell you that you'll need a mountain of money for your kids' college educations, and you better start saving—yesterday. But perhaps one parent would rather stay home to raise the kids, instead of taking a full-time job. In the long run, which is the better investment? Sacrificing some possible savings for college or sacrificing the time with your children when they're young? Some investments simply can't be measured in dollars and cents. It's your call.

So next time the experts tell you that you should do this or that, ask why. What will happen if you do it another way—*your* way?

More!

At some point we begin to think we'd like something more, and not just money. We start thinking we'd like more satisfying relationships, a more livable home, more relaxing vacations, more of a sense of community.

Although there's no *right* time to make major life changes, there are *wrong* times: in a fit of anger, right after the death of a spouse, or on an impulse.

Changes, except those triggered by catastrophes, rarely happen overnight. We go over them again and again in our minds before we can act. Don't beat yourself up about it.

Major changes take time. They deserve serious research and planning. Not only do we have to be personally prepared, but in fairness to the other key players in our lives, we want them to have a chance to prepare as well. That's why we usually give the boss two weeks' notice.

> "Some people plan meticulously for a two-week vacation . . . yet don't thoroughly educate themselves for making lifestyle decisions that affect their whole future."
>
> —MARILYN AND TOM ROSS, *Country Bound!*
> *Trade Your Business Suit Blues for Blue Jean Dreams*

Before making major life changes, procrastinate. Go shopping. Not mall shopping. Go to the library or go on-line, and try to focus on concrete next steps that you could take to learn more about the pros and cons of your options.

If you come up against a brick wall, either of your making or perhaps your spouse's, it sometimes helps to get logical. List the pros and cons of any lifestyle change you're considering. Be as objective and clearheaded as you can about the likely consequences for you and your family. It doesn't matter how many possible outcomes you consider.

What does matter is that you take the time to think through the alternatives and the effects that they're likely to have. What would the benefits (if any) be for you?

Once you've done that, it's time to switch gears. Go back and rate each one based on how good or how bad that outcome would make you feel. Then it's time to get some other input. While there is a lot to be said for getting expert help, no matter what lifestyle issue you're working on, most of us have free access to incredibly perceptive experts—our close friends and family members. Their perspective on the objective pros and cons, as well as on the emotional side can give you a whole new way to look at your options.

Don't overlook your local newspaper, the weeklies (*U.S. News & World Report, Newsweek, Time*), and monthly magazines. Many of their syndicated columnists and personal finance writers have devoted years to developing their expertise. Then they put in even more time to distill it all for you, analyzing the key money versus lifestyle debates.

Invest a Few Bucks for a Lot of Great Ideas

For other important viewpoints, spend a few bucks and a few minutes to get samples of our favorite newsletters:

Mary Hunt
The Cheapskate Monthly
P.O. Box 2135
Paramount, CA 90723-8135
562-630-8845
www.cheapskatemonthly.com

Edith Flowers Kilgo
Creative Downscaling
P.O. Box 1884
Jonesboro, GA 30237-1884
770-471-9048
www.mindspring.com/~kilgo/

Jim Jorgensen
It's Your Money
118 Camino Pablo
Orinda, CA 94563
800-558-4558
www.itsyourmoney.com

Larry Roth
Living Cheap News
7232 Belleview Avenue
Kansas City, MO 64114
816-523-3161

Marc Myers
Moneysworth
P.O. Box 53751
Boulder, CO 80322
800-816-4744

Robert E. Frank
No-Debt Living
P.O. Box 282
Veradale, WA 99037
509-927-1322
www.nodebtnews.com

Diane Rosener
A Penny Saved
P.O. Box 3471
Omaha, NE 68103-0471
402-556-5655

Austin Pryor
Sound Mind Investing
P.O. Box 22128
Louisville, KY 40252-0128
502-426-6284
www.soundmindinvesting.com

Humberto Cruz
Winning at the Savings Game
P.O. Box 4410
Chicago, IL 60680-4410
800-788-1225

Send them each $1 and a self-addressed stamped envelope (SASE). While you're at it, send a buck for a sample of Marc and Nancy's newsletter, too:

The Pocket Change Investor
P.O. Box 78
Elizaville, NY 12523
914-758-1400
www.goodadvicepress.com/pci.htm

DO OVER

You've had it. "I can't take one more day of this," you say to yourself as you stew yet again in a massive traffic jam. So where will you be tomorrow? Right. Stewing in another traffic tie-up. It's okay. You *can* break the pattern. But give it time. Stop being angry at the other drivers and start thinking of what you can do about it. What are your alternatives?

Can you leave for or from work earlier or later? Take the bus or train? Move to the city? Get a new job? Work at home? What alternative is most appealing? How can you give it a whirl?

You've had it. "I can't take another day of this," you say to yourself after one more fight. So where will you be next Tuesday? Right. Stewing from yet another stupid fight.

You can break the pattern, but give it time. (Unless it's a truly dangerous and abusive relationship—in which case, put down this book and get to a shelter right now.) Perhaps one day, one partner threatens to leave or actually does leave. Often, there's a reconciliation followed by a repeat of the pattern. The final split, if there is one, comes only after the yo-yo string finally breaks.

If that sounds like your home life, it'd be great if you and your partner could devise some rational ways to work out your differences. Maybe you can come to some new understandings. Perhaps it's time you finally agreed to get some counseling. Rarely is a bad relationship solely the other person's fault. It takes two to tango, two to bring a marriage to new heights, and two to break it apart.

Maybe you'll decide to go your separate ways. If you have children, the way you part and how you relate to each other after you do, will affect them for the rest of their lives. There are at least 50 ways to leave your lover, as Paul Simon has sung. It's well worth investing the time and energy to find one where your trials do not become your kids' tribulations.

> Fighting scares the children and makes them feel guilty. It also wastes time, money and resources that could have been spent more positively on your children.
> —VIOLET WOODHOUSE AND VICTORIA F. COLLINS, *Divorce and Money*

You may want to find someone in your community to help make this already stressful transition a little easier on you all. Your physician or minister, the school psychologist or guidance counselor, or your friends and relatives can help you find a therapist. Speaking of stressful situations, if alcoholism is tearing your family apart, read *The Goodness of Ordinary People* by Faith Middleton.

Testing the Waters

Marc remembers being on a Florida beach with his grandmother, some 50 years ago. He would run right into the waves, while Grandma would enter the water an inch at a time. She'd bend down to splash some water onto herself, first on one arm, then the other. Grandma was testing the waters, acclimating herself to the change in temperature. To Marc, it seemed to take her forever to do what he did in an instant, without a care in the world. (Marc's more like Grandma now, and his grandchildren will no doubt remember him in the same way that he remembers her!)

There's a lot to be said for testing the waters. Think of it as further research and insurance. Before diving in, know what you're apt to find, protect yourself as best you can from surprises, and make sure you have a way out.

Find a way to try on your dream life, to make sure it fits. To test the waters:

- Take a leave of absence.
- Try another job part-time, after hours, or on weekends.
- Volunteer.
- Vacation on your fantasy island . . . preferably not as a tourist.

If you're not ready to leave the drawing board yet, consider the following:

- Do some more research.
- Find or create a support group or study circle. (If you'd be interested in one in your area that meets to discuss voluntary simplicity, go to www.slnet.com.)
- Go for some counseling.

TAKING YOUR DREAMS FOR A TEST-DRIVE

Once you've dreamt up your fantasized life, don't jump ship to try it out. You may discover that you absolutely love it, or you may decide to head back to the drawing board. Writer Mary Rowland and her husband Robert toyed with the idea of escaping the city for the country, but they really weren't sure it would work for them, both professionally and personally, or for their two kids, Krista and Thomas.

So they tried it out, by spending six weeks at a friend's country home, where they confirmed that living outside the city would indeed be fine for all of them. They sold their co-op and now live in upstate New York's beautiful Hudson Valley.

Consultant and author Kent Brunette's dream car was a BMW, but he wasn't sure he wanted to commit to the payments. So for six months, he practiced paying for one—by making BMW-sized payments on the Jeep he was then driving. In the process of test-driving his fantasy, Kent confirmed that he could keep up with the higher BMW payments. As a bonus, he paid off his Jeep early, saving quite a bit on interest.

Compare Kent's approach with that of others who decide they must have the car of their dreams, and end up struggling with impossible monthly payments.

Brenda and Terry Chain saved enough money to leave their Alaska home in an RV for leisurely travel in search of their dream, which was owning and operating a small resort in the lower 48. Because they could afford to spend the time visiting a number of different places, they learned a lot along the way. When they discovered the Beachcomber Resort in Lake Ozark, Missouri, they knew they had a great deal, and went for it right away.

You don't want to buy the magic carpet without taking it for a flight. Find a way to take your fantasy out for a spin.

. . . .

GERRI'S STORY

I never set out to become a consumer advocate, but soon after college, I fell into a job with the nonprofit credit education organization, Bankcard Holders of America (BHA). Pretty soon, that's what I was! Within several years, I was executive director of the organization, a high-visibility position in that field.

The job was great in many ways, *forcing* me to develop skills I would never have thought myself capable of doing: public speaking, interviews on television and radio, writing a book. Although there were many benefits to working at BHA, as time went by, I started recognizing an independent streak in myself that just wouldn't let me fit into a regular job anymore.

Deciding to go out on my own was one of the toughest decisions I've ever made. In the small town where I grew up, my parents and my friends' parents worked in basically the same jobs all their lives, so I didn't really have any entrepreneurs as role models. I also worried about how I could survive without a regular paycheck, especially since I live in one of the country's most expensive areas.

One thing that helped immensely was paying off my debts. I racked up a nice chunk of credit card charges after college, and it took me a couple of disciplined years to pay off the seven or so cards that I had maxed out. But once I did, the strategies that I had used to pay off debt, plus tracking my spending and trying to make conscious choices before buying, helped me save money—so I was able to leave with a little safety net.

After BHA, I landed an assortment of writing and consulting jobs that have allowed me to continue to work from home. It hasn't always been easy. In truth, there have been some real rough spots. Some things I've tried have gone absolutely nowhere. But more important, there have also been some great times, times I've worked on a variety of fun and challenging projects, like the two autumn months I spent in the Hudson Valley collaborating with Marc and Nancy on a credit hotline, enjoying spectacular hikes on the weekends. Or the time I found myself in a recording studio taping spots for a radio show I was cohosting. Even though the day was long and exhausting, I kept smiling, thinking, "This is so much more fun than being in an office!"

I love how I work, and I love my commute (two flights of stairs). I get to collaborate with great people, and I can say, "Thanks, but no" to projects I don't want to undertake. I hope through this book, Marc, Nancy, and I will inspire you to find a way to do what you love. We believe you can!

· ·

What Do You Think Has Most Kept You from Changing Your Life?

- Fear of lost income?
- Dread of upheaval at home?
- Fear of change?

And what do you most want to change? Nancy knew it was time to change her life when she realized that she was spending many hours every single day thinking she had to leave New York City, even if it meant changing her great job. She just couldn't take the crime rate or the crowds any longer. What she really longed for was a nice, big garden.

How many hours a day do you focus in your mind's eye on changing your life? When you mentally play out the change, however you define it, what's the first obstacle you come across? For Nancy, back in 1980, it was the money. "How could I possibly support myself? Even though I made over $40,000 a year, had only my one mouth to feed, and had great benefits, I lived paycheck to paycheck. I was stuck. Then it finally dawned on me that since I was so dependent on that paycheck, I'd be most comfortable coming up with a way to change my life without giving up my income stream."

Once that lightbulb went off, Nancy quickly arranged to cut down on her hours at the office—to go into the city three or four days a week and work from home the rest of the time. Her plan was to gradually move her base of operations to upstate New York, where she would buy a house. Same job, different home address.

She made arrangements to crash three nights a week at a city friend's home, and started looking to buy a house upstate. Her hope was that she'd eventually find a way to make a living outside the city, but she realized that keeping her city job was a wonderful, albeit temporary, bridge.

"Once I found that bridge, I could begin to explore my alternatives, not just to think about them all day long. All of a sudden, things began to fall into place. I decided where I wanted to buy a house and began looking at properties. I had about given up, when someone said, 'I know the person who'll help you find a house.' That's when I met Marc, and the rest, as they say, is history."

How can you begin to explore your alternatives now? Are there any bridges you can build that will make it easier for you to move in the direction you want to head?

THE DOMINO EFFECT

When you begin to make changes in your situation, you build your courage for the next change or new experience. And so one change follows another. You hate your job, so you start a small home business of your own. Your business grows, so you feel you can leave your job. And you do—or at least you take some vacation days or a leave of absence to try it out.

You have more time for your business, so it continues to grow, and you also have more time for yourself and your children. You get to know them better, and you have more freshly cooked, healthful family dinners together, at home. You save money on day care and sitters, to say nothing of restaurants.

You need fewer work clothes, the dry cleaning bill evaporates, and you find that you need fewer things to console you for what your job was making you miss at home. In short, your expenses go down and your pleasures go up. Your job no longer binds you to where you've been living, and you begin to think about moving to a place where you've always wanted to live.

You develop new hobbies and interests. You're more alive. You watch less TV and do more in the community. Change, you begin to realize, is good.

But it's not always easy. There are ups and downs. The new business grows slower than you hoped, you feel lonely working at home, there's less money than you expected, and you're putting in longer hours.

What went wrong?

Maybe nothing. It's hard to change your life, especially when it's not your choice . . . a divorce, a layoff, a flood. But even when you've finally done what you've always wanted to do, there are bound to be bumps in the road.

And the process of beginning to change is a long and winding road. It's been on your mind for a long time, you've gone back and forth, you've had to make hard decisions, you may have to hurt someone you love.

A friend of Marc's used to say that waiting for something to happen would be a lot easier if only he knew exactly when that something would occur. So he'd set a date, not as a goal, but as a way of getting past the *when* and on to the "What can I do to make it happen?"

With determination, time, a good support network, and a belief in your right to be happy, you can and will break free. *You* get to decide when.

SECRET II

PUT YOUR FAMILY FIRST

ONLY YOU CAN DECIDE ON YOUR PRIORITIES, ALTHOUGH LOTS OF people and organizations will try to influence your decisions. Parents, teachers, children, charities, friends, churches, bosses, political parties, advertisers, strangers on the bus will all try to tell you what's best for you and yours. The advantage we have at the moment is your attention, and we suggest you direct it toward your family.

Whether you have a spouse, 2.2 children, a cat, and a dog—or whether you live by yourself, there are key people in your life. Whatever you call the people closest to you, you're part of a family. No matter who is elected the next president, no matter what new technology becomes available, no matter how much your boss depends on you, in the event of a personal crisis, you'll turn first to your family. Make sure you regard them as the resource they are for you. Their care and feeding come first.

It's our hope that you'll make good financial decisions that will enhance your life. But we believe and intend to convince you that much more important than your financial portfolio, is how you invest your time and energy on behalf of your family and your future.

We'll help you analyze your time and energy investments so you can objectively gauge the kinds of returns you're earning. If it's time to rebalance and dump some underperformers, we'll help you find a family-friendly way to do it.

Unlike financial matters, this is one job you can't turn over to some advisor. It's up to you to become a savvy life investor. If you don't put you and your family first, who will?

....

CHAPTER 2

···

Making the Most of Your Time

- ○ Investing your time, energy, and money for better returns
- ○ How to figure out what's really important
- ○ How to raise your quality-of-life quotient and bring your portfolio back into balance
- ○ Investing in futures—your family's

Treat each other like you are the most important people in the world—like each other's thoughts, and feelings, and well-being are more important to you than anyone else's. If you take care of each other in this way you will enjoy the great happiness and content-ment that a wonderful marriage can bring. And your family and friends will be gladdened and enriched by your happiness. I can't take credit for this wisdom. I learned it from the most wonderful woman in the world, my wife Beth (hey, we can all use some extra points at home).

DR. HOWARD EISENSON,
IN A WEDDING TOAST

···

Time is a concept invented by humans, the only creatures on earth who can live in the past, present, and future. For all other species, the future is meaningless, the past is quickly forgotten, and the present offers plenty of time to deal with basic needs (sustenance, shelter, sleep, and sex).

We *Homo sapiens* never have enough time for our chores and responsibilities, let alone our pleasures. Every year we buy umpteen time- and energy-saving devices that will supposedly free us up to accomplish yet more and more every day. Every year we have less time to do those things that matter most to us.

Between FedEx, faxes, and the freeways of cyberspace, we've managed to create instantaneous crises that require speed of light solutions. No longer do we have time to think, contemplate, innovate, or even procrastinate. We are always rushing, always running late.

From an *Invest in Yourself* perspective, making the most of your time isn't a matter of time management, or squeezing as many chores, meetings, and projects as possible into your day. That's not making the most of your time—it's making the least of it!

Making the most of your time means making choices, then working it out so you can do what you choose. Making the most of your time means doing nothing when nothing is what you want to do and staying up all night to work on a project, read a book, or dance until dawn, when that's what you choose.

There are lots of reasons we can't always do exactly as we please, including the need to earn a living, the desire to stay out of prison, and the hope of maintaining our key relationships. However, we can dramatically increase our life's options by decreasing our outside dependencies.

While there are numerous paths leading to personal freedom, our favorite is the path of most resistance—resistance to unnecessary expenditures of our three key assets: time, energy, and money. The more frugal you are with these assets—the less of them you commit to projects that have little personal meaning for you, the more you'll have for those that do and the better you'll feel about the quality of your life.

Thinking about your time and energy as investments, just like the money you have in the stock market or the bank, is a good way to become conscious of how these two assets are performing in your life portfolio. In the same way that a good Wall Street investment appreciates in value, you want your investments of time and energy to offer high yields. They should make you feel good—happy, satisfied, energized, or relaxed. If you're lucky, they may even help you make money.

But if it's Monday morning and you're tired of the grind, then your portfolio may be unbalanced. Is it full of too much work, too many chores at home, too hectic a schedule, too much guilt? Then stop making bad investments! It's that simple (and complicated).

To get more of what you want in life and less of what you don't, start by analyzing where you spend your time and energy each day. Ask yourself as you move through each activity, "What's my return on this investment?" If your answer is "nothing" or something negative, then you're best off either finding a way to improve your return or dumping that piece from your portfolio for another investment that's more in keeping with your life goals and your values.

You may not be able to do it overnight, but you *can* begin to change the mix. Start small. If your schedule is already jam-packed, don't try to force yourself to do an hour of yoga, every day. You'll just feel worse when you can't reach your goal. Instead, start by investing just 15 minutes of your time and energy today in something you really want to do, whether it's a hot bath or a quick cruise on-line to research some career options. Try to give yourself at least those 15 minutes every day.

As you begin to make decisions about your future, you might choose to cut your costs, cut your waste, or cut your work, but we hope you won't cut off your family or your pleasures in life. After all, there are some things in life that are well worth an investment of our time, energy, and assets, and some that just aren't. Taking the time to clarify your priorities is a great investment.

THE QUALITY-OF-LIFE SCALE

To paraphrase Supreme Court Justice Potter Stewart, we can't really define quality of life, but we'll know it if we live it.

Score those factors that contribute to how you feel about your quality of life. On a scale of 1 to 10, how would you rate the following:

- The quality of your relationships

    With your spouse   _____

    With your children   _____

    With your parents   _____

    With your boss   _____

    With colleagues   _____

    With your friends   _____

    With your God   _____

- The quality of your work life   _____

- The quality of your health   _____
- The quality of your shelter   _____
- The quality of your food   _____
- The quality of your leisure time   _____
- The quality of your exercise program _____
- The quality of your optimism   _____
- The quality of safety where you live _____

Add as many categories to the list as you want. Then look carefully at your responses. Decide where you need to invest more time and effort. The nice thing about this kind of test is that there's no passing score. Only you know how high you'd need to score to feel truly satisfied.

You know that you have a high quality of life (QL) if you feel good about who you are and what you're doing, and you enjoy your life enough to want to jump out of bed and start the day. (That's figurative. It's okay to want to start the day by spending a little extra time in bed.) So many of us expend so much of our energy on our work and our obligations, we leave little for ourselves or our families.

The Longer You Tread Water, the Longer You'll Get Nowhere

Even if you take absolutely no intentional actions to change your life, it *will* change. Time refuses to stand still. And as time moves on, we age with it, and our options change and often diminish. Therefore, the best time to begin fine-tuning your life is now—and the best place to start is with something *easy,* where a small change can make a big difference in the quality of your existence.

Let's choose something that we all have in common: eating. While this probably doesn't apply to you, let's assume that you don't always eat three delicious, well-balanced, home-cooked meals a day. And because of that, food on your QL scale scores only a 6 out of 10.

Building it up to 10 might be nearly impossible because of your job, dislike of cooking, small kitchen, lack of time, and the expense of organic produce. But you could easily punch it up to an 8 or even an 8½—more than a 40% improvement.

How? Don't stop for breakfast on the way to work. In the time it takes to make a cup of coffee, you can make fresh-from-scratch oatmeal. (By the way, it tastes better than the instant varieties, costs less, and doesn't contain any guar gum, caramel flavor, or other additives.) And if you buy organic oats at a health food store, there'll be no pesticides and you'll save money.

Or get everyone involved in meal preparation—even if it's just one night a week. How about a regular TGIF date for some homemade pizza or tacos? Olé! Let everyone choose their own toppings. No fights. Healthy, cheap, fun. QL up.

When cooking is feeling like a chore, focus on how you can turn it into a more pleasant activity:

- Find a cooking buddy. Get together for meal-making marathons. It's an easy way to stock a couple of freezers with some great dinners.

- Cook up a storm and share. The neighbor down the street makes great chicken soup, and your chili is mighty fine. Both are easy to make in large quantities. Cook up a double batch and split the spoils.

- Make Saturday or Sunday a cookathon where everyone in the family helps, and create a week's worth of meals in one fell swoop.

- Chop up a week's worth of vegetables at one time. You know it's a good idea to use lots of cut vegetables at every meal, but all that chopping takes time and makes a mess. Do it once, and your veggies for stir-fry, pizza, salads, and sticks for dips will stay nice and fresh if you wrap them in a damp towel before you put them in your refrigerator.

SOMETIMES IT PAYS TO INVEST MONEY

Being a Super Mom, Super Dad, Super Boss, Super Volunteer, or any other kind of superhero can be a tough act to keep up for any length of time. So drop the do-it-all mentality.

Something's wrong if you work all week to make enough money to hire someone to do the landscaping you enjoy, but just don't have the time to do. By the same token, if you work all week and really want to rest on your weekends, or climb Mount Washington, or whatever, then it's perfectly reasonable to buy some quality of life by bringing someone in to clean your house, rake your yard, paint the kitchen, go to the supermarket, or do your taxes.

I'll Wash Your Back if You'll Wash Mine

See if you can work out a trade. You can sew, babysit, or change the car's oil for a neighbor who would rather bake or weed. Or you can cook while your spouse (friend, mother, whoever) cleans.

Wouldn't it be nice if the senior citizens next door were willing to cook or make curtains or refinish a piece of furniture for you—while you raked their leaves, shoveled their snow, or trimmed their hedges? Why not suggest it? Not asking is an automatic no!

Love cooking? Help a friend! Maybe you could cook for a crony, in exchange for one of your hated chores.

Cleaning: Necessary Evil or Obsession?

It's in the eye of the duster. We all prefer to live in sanitary conditions, although our opinions may differ on what clean means. If you hate to do housework and your mate tunes it out, hire someone or barter it away. From our perspective, if you can afford the alternative, by all means, choose to avoid those repetitive chores that you'd really rather not do and that only cause conflict. But if you can turn a chore into a family game, you'll save money, get the job done, and probably have a few laughs along the way.

The average house can pretty well be done in about two hours with a team of two or three. Get *Speed Cleaning* by Jeff Campbell and read it with the family. Start holding a weekly cleaning contest to see how fast everyone can complete their part with an acceptable level of quality. Then celebrate with some inexpensive treat.

We want you to decide where you can best invest your time, energy, and money. You can spend your time doing the dreaded chore, you can spend your time making enough money to hire someone else to do it, or you can work out a trade. You decide.

But decide! There's no benefit in throwing away time and energy obsessing about something and bugging everyone else to spend their time and energy meeting your standards. Come up with a plan that works for everyone, where no one is investing more in the chores than their comfort level dictates.

CREATE YOUR FOUNDATION

Imagine a chaotic office where nothing's organized, everything takes twice as long to accomplish as it should because no one can find anything, and the equipment's always on the blink. What in your life is like that office? Is it clutter at home—stuff that takes time to clean, keep up, and insure (not to mention that you can't find when you need it)? What about all those little daily annoyances and irritations that make you wince, but that you never seem to get around to fixing?

Whenever you notice something in your environment that has been an irritant for more than a couple of days, find a way to eliminate it. Don't just put it on the "Honey, Do" list, and then nag until it gets done. Find a way to make it happen. Perhaps a trade will work: "Honey, if you fix the faucet this afternoon, I'll wash your car." You'll free up an unbelievable amount of energy and rest better at night.

....

GERRI'S TOOLBOX: LEARN TO SAY NO!

Start dropping activities that aren't benefiting your time and energy portfolio. Then don't take on any new activities unless you eliminate one that you enjoy less. Encourage other family members to do the same. If you find this tough, at least give yourself 24 hours to think over any request to participate in a new activity. That will give you the chance to step back and decide if you really want to get involved.

One trick is to block out key time slots on your calendar for yourself and your family weeks in advance. When everyone pulls out their schedules to plan the next meeting, you'll look at yours and say, "Sorry, I can't make it then." The meeting will probably be put off to a time when your calendar's empty. Put your foot down. The weekends *can* be family time. No exceptions.

It's often easier to say no when it comes to money than to value our precious energy or time enough to say, "Sorry, that's more than I want to spend." Remember, unlike money, time can't be accumulated to use later. Use it or lose it.

....

Money is something we choose to trade our life energy for. . . . Life energy is all we have. It is precious because it is limited and irretrievable and because our choices about how we use it express the meaning and purpose of our time here on earth.

—Joe Dominguez and Vicki Robin, *Your Money or Your Life*

In what direction would you like to head next? With time limited—29,220 days in an 80-year life span—investing your days, nights, and weekends in jobs, relationships, homes, communities, or careers that are no longer satisfying is a terrible waste of your most precious assets. It makes much more sense to build the kind of home life and career you want.

For example, if on the highway of life, your career lane were about to end, you'd have no choice but to look behind, in front, and to your side

for an opportunity to change to a different career lane. If you're not paying attention and your lane ends suddenly, slamming on the brakes and
swerving to the right could be dangerous! Unfortunately, speed often kills
in a far subtler way, depriving us of a lifetime we could have better used if
it weren't for the fact that we were always in such a rush.

When You're Feeling Important

Do you ever find yourself thinking, "I can't go to Johnny's school play,
because I'm the only one who can . . . ," or "If I take a mental health day,
the office will fall apart," or "The family won't be able to function," or
"Our team will lose"?

One of the wonderful things about the American system of government is that it proves, over and over again, that no one is indispensable.
Presidents, mayors, senators, representatives all come and go, but the
nation's business keeps getting done. (Whether you like the way it gets
done is another issue.)

Business is the same. A boss retires, an employee leaves. It makes little
difference.

It's True! Today Is the First Day
of the Rest of Your Life

Today, do something that you'd really enjoy. Begin to chip away at the old
routine. Stop making decisions by default, and start making conscious
choices. Begin the process of change.

But remember that change is rarely easy. And while it's smart to start
boosting your QL with easy changes, some things that will really improve
your life are tough. You may decide that to be truly happier, a move to
another part of the country is in order. It may be time to say good-bye to
your boss. Unhappy relationships may have to be cut.

Sometimes, the work that you do to *prepare* yourself to take action is
just as important as the actual change. Researching other locales, scouting
out the job market, reading books like *The 7 Habits of Highly Effective
People* by Stephen Covey, or going for some counseling sessions may give
you the information, insight, or courage you need to make a change and
create the life you want.

Symbols of Sanity

There are some time and energy investments that can symbolically, as
well as practically, raise your QL.

Turn off the tube. The average family watches about seven hours of television a day. Cut the family sitcom allowance gradually and fill the time in fun ways: Sing, play an instrument or a game, make believe, read, tell stories, bake, go to bed earlier. You'll be far more rested come morning, and with the late-night TV silenced, you'll probably find other ways to entertain yourselves.

> I talk to many parents who say the toughest thing they do is come home at night and put in some good, focused time with their children. The parents who do this will see their efforts pay off tremendously. But I see how hard it must be.
> —C. EVERETT KOOP, FORMER U.S. SURGEON GENERAL

Cut back and go the extra mile. Find ways that don't hurt for everyone in the family to scrimp on little things. For example, take one less taxi a week and walk instead. Between you, saving a dollar or two a day will be a piece of cake. Fifty dollars a month and you'll have a nice little vacation fund started. But don't put the money in the bank—send it in on your highest-interest credit card bill and earn upward of 20%.

On the subject of cutting back, are you still smoking? Even at a low cost of $2.50 a pack, one a day means more than $900 up in smoke, every year—until it kills you! If you manage to last another 40 years, that's $36,000 blown to the wind. You'd have to earn $50,000 before taxes to finance your habit, not including any new taxes on tobacco. Invest that $900 a year at 8%, and in 40 years, instead of risking lung cancer, you'll have put aside $261,826.

Lots of habits are expensive in more ways than one. Price them in terms of their real benefits to you and yours. Then decide whether they're worth the cost.

Get rid of the clutter!

> Unfortunately, for many of us, what we do best with our clutter is to fret about it and mull it over. . . . Get the areas of clutter that bother you under control and quit beating yourself up over the rest.
> —JEFF CAMPBELL, *Clutter Control*

Clean out your closets, basement, attic, and garage. Get rid of anything you haven't used in ages and are not holding onto for sentimental reasons. Give it to someone who might benefit from it, or have a yard sale. Much of what uselessly takes up space in your home and your life could improve the lives of others. It is far better to give than to store.

Stop all that junk mail. Who needs it? Our booklet, *Stop Junk Mail Forever,* tells you what to do to get off—and stay off—the direct marketing lists, without stopping the catalogs you enjoy. It will also help you nix the telemarketers, and squash the spam (junk e-mail). See page 328.

Burn calories instead of money. If not the most important thing we can do for our bodies, exercise is certainly high up there on the list. It can keep weight down, lower blood pressure, help stave off some cancers and osteoporosis, strengthen hearts and souls, ease depression, and help us sleep better at night.

Whether you get your aerobic workouts by jogging, walking, bicycling, or climbing a make-believe staircase at a health club, just do it! Start with a modest commitment (three times a week or 10 minutes twice a day) and find a way to stick with it. Your QL will rev up as you do!

Don't join a gym on our account. We'd rather see you park the car 10 blocks from the office and hoof it, or climb a few flights of stairs at lunch. When the time comes to cut the grass, try pushing one of those human-powered rotaries. They start every time, cost next to nothing to maintain, never run out of fuel, and seem to last forever. As you trim the lawn, you can listen to the birds, hold a conversation, and enjoy the smell of the fresh-cut grass instead of fuel fumes. And you can mow at the crack of dawn without jolting the neighbors out of their sleep. (For lots of other great tips to keep your family fit, go to www.shapeup.org.)

··

INVESTMENTS YOU WON'T REGRET

To limit your regrets, invest time and energy in the following ways, which we culled from Stephen M. Miller's excellent overview on the subject, "The Bright Side of Regrets" (*Woman's Day,* June 3, 1997):

1. Learn a skill or hobby.
2. Have kids and spend time with them.
3. Worry less about work.
4. Live a more healthy lifestyle.
5. Develop a deeper spiritual life.
6. Watch less TV.
7. Spend more time with friends and relatives.
8. Manage your money well.
9. Show compassion.

··

YOU CAN DO IT

Learning a new skill can be half the fun, as well as one of your best investments, saving you money while enhancing your life and self-esteem. For example, say you want to add a room to your house or finally build that deck, but you have no idea where to begin. Just because you can't tell a hammer from a saw is no reason to give up.

Hire a neighborhood jack-of-all-trades to work with you on the project. You'll learn by doing—from pouring the foundations to framing and insulating, right on through to putting on the final coat of paint.

When Marc's daughter, Sharon, needed a new roof on half of her house, she engineered it so that her brother, sister, husband, brother-in-law, a few friends—even her height-phobic father—were all up there working alongside a local roofer, ripping off the old tar paper and putting on the new roof. Sure, everyone worked up quite a sweat and an appetite, but they had a good time, too. Enough so that they all came back for the return engagement when the other half had to be reshingled.

While major projects will cut into your free time, if you tackle them this way, you'll save money, learn a thing or two, get some helpful experience, spend time with people you like, and improve your living space as well as your QL. You'll also increase your home's cash value. Now that's what we call investing in yourself!

....

YOU *CAN* DO IT YOURSELF!

If you dream of home improvement projects, but don't know where to start, pick up a copy of *A Consumer's Guide to Home Improvement, Renovation and Repair* by The Enterprise Foundation. It features alternatives by cost and complexity so you can decide how much to invest both effort-wise and dollarwise.

....

Pricing Your Baby's First Step

Were you at the office when your toddler took that first step? Were you putting the finishing touches on an underarm deodorant ad when Johnny graduated from nursery school? Did you postpone your honeymoon because you couldn't take time off from work? Was it really worth it?

No, you can't leave the office any old time you please . . . or can you? That's what this book is about, it's about living the life you want, *now,* not after you've first made money doing something you'd rather not be doing.

You've probably heard that it takes less time to do something right the first time than to do it over. This sentiment is especially true for raising children and maintaining a satisfying relationship. From our perspective, there's nothing more important.

Are you dragging yourself to a job or two you resent? For your sake? By mistake? Or for your family's sake, wondering how you'll ever be able to pay for college? Good question. If it's a burning one for you, fast-forward to Chapter 15 for some fear-calming advice on financing those four years. Just remember, once your offspring leave for college, chances are pretty good (although not guaranteed!) they'll be gone, and you'll wish that you had spent more time together when they were right there.

If you haven't already, now is the time for you and your family to discuss, openly, honestly, and in an unhurried atmosphere, what your priorities really are. Would you rather have more time together now, or more toys to console yourselves while you're apart?

It's not just about money. According to research by Arlie Russell Hochschild, in *The Time Bind,* many companies *are* offering family-friendly benefits, only to discover that parents aren't taking full advantage of the opportunity. Why?

- Home is where the stress is. For many families, home life has become frantic, whereas the workplace offers a relatively calm, supportive, adult environment.

- Men especially are afraid of being laid off or losing their career climbing momentum if they're seen as more family- and less work-oriented.

Whether you're male or female, you have a perfect right to your career, community involvement, and social engagements. But if you're a parent, your children have needs, too. It's a tough balancing act, but the consequences of not investing both quality *and* quantity time with your offspring could be quite serious. What's a parent to do?

One big change that may raise your family's quality of life significantly is for one parent to take care of the kids full-time. This usually means Mom (sometimes Dad, sometimes part-time for each) leaving or cutting back on an outside job for one as a homemaker. This is not an easy transition for many couples who are used to bringing home two paychecks and spending more than both of them combined!

The key to living on one income in a two-income world is to plan ahead. If, before you make the leap, you have learned how to live on less, paid off many of your debts, and started a side business for extra cash, the transition will be a lot easier.

To find out if it's feasible, practice living on one paycheck for a couple of months. Use the other check to pay off credit cards and bank some emergency cash that you *do not* touch during that time. If you can pull this off or come close, you'll be ahead of the game, because once you're working at home, your commuting, child care, and work-related expenses will drop. In fact, many families discover that the cost of that second job is so high that the loss in giving it up is surprisingly small. Two of our favorite books on this subject are *Miserly Moms* by Jonni McCoy, and *Shattering the Two-Income Myth* by Andy Dappen.

Planning's Value

In our survey of more than 600 working mothers who had decided to return home, almost 60 percent said they had made an impulsive, emotional decision to quit work. But nearly 92 percent said they wished they had planned the move better. Of those mothers who later had to go back to work, nearly 100 percent said it was due to the lack of planning before they quit.

—Larry Burkett, *Women Leaving the Workplace*

Conscious Deceleration

Another way to boost your QL is to change the mix of time that you devote to work versus family. Marc's daughter Robin decided that as much as she enjoyed her job, it was depriving her of time with her new son, Zachary, and her husband, Danny.

So she spoke to her supervisor at the international bank where she worked and negotiated a cut in pay for a cut in hours. By coming in a bit earlier and taking a shorter lunch break, Robin was able to do her job and still get home by 3 P.M. Because she was able to accomplish so much in the shorter time, Robin was soon back to earning what the full-time job had paid—and she had far more time and energy when she got home. Robin made the most of her time, as did her boss. Everybody came out ahead. The old maxim proved true: A project fills the time allotted for it.

There's nothing sacred about working 9 to 5. In numerous cases, it's been discovered that production does not go down when hours are cut—in fact, it often goes up!

Male or female, if your job offers flextime or family-friendly policies, think carefully about what kind of investment you want to make in your family versus your career, and then make a fully conscious decision. If the opportunities aren't there, propose something to the boss, like Robin did. (Not asking is an automatic no!) Your time is limited. Choose how you spend it.

It may make sense to look for work with a family-friendly company. Each year, firms are ranked on various criteria such as pay for women, flexible work schedules, and day care facilities. For a list of companies that make the grade, check out www.womweb.com/100intro.htm. If your company isn't on the list, you may want to use these findings to advocate change where you work.

. . . .

IN PRAISE OF THE ACADEMIC CALENDAR

"Summertime, and the living is easy." But not for working parents! School's out, and the kids are home. But even if that's when Mom and Dad take their vacation, most parents still have to work for most of the summer.

What to do with the kids? Where in the world can you afford to send them that would be a great, safe place for them to be for all the time that you really need them to be there? Nowhere!

Whatever arrangements parents pull together for their children's summer daytimes, it's almost always less than ideal—with 6- or 7-year-olds going to basically the same day care centers as toddlers, or 11- and 12-year-olds home alone more than anyone would like.

There are over 10 million latchkey kids in the United States. No matter how old they are when you leave them alone, you'll still worry, "What if something goes wrong?" To help your 8- to 14-year-olds cope, get *Disaster Blasters: A Kid's Guide to Being Home Alone* by Karin Kasdin and Laura Szabo-Cohen.

And then there are all the school holidays and snow days. Working parents have an awful juggling act, even if their kids never get strep throat. What's a parent to do? Focus on the job or the family? Our vote is always for the family.

Great. Where does that leave you? Is there a family-friendly alternative? There are many. The working women of the 1950s figured one out—*get a job that puts you on the school calendar.* Whether you teach, work in the cafeteria, or drive the bus, being on the same schedule as your children helps you avoid a multitude of day care problems, at least once the kids are school age.

You could take the summer off entirely or do something else during that period to earn money. Maybe you could get a job at a camp. You could work it out so your kids attend free, and you'd all have a great summer. If you have or will have children, it's really worth thinking about switching to a school-time, flexible, or home-based job.

....

Invest in Good Child Care

For many parents, especially single parents, financial demands or personal preferences mean that putting the kids in day care for at least part of the day is a must. Young children can benefit greatly from good day care programs, of which there are many. Unfortunately, researchers keep reporting that there's more bad day care than good.

With 70% of day care centers rated "barely adequate" by a multiuniversity study and 15% considered abysmal, working parents face a double whammy: They're often guilt-ridden about having to leave their children—and they're panicked about how to find a nurturing, stimulating environment that's convenient, safe, and affordable. As with the college search you'll be doing (amazingly soon), the search for quality day care is one of those things in life that, in our view, deserves a serious investment of your time and energy.

Whether your preference is for a larger, more structured child care center, a family day care provider, or in-home care, you have a choice. Obviously, personal referrals from people you trust are great. Maybe the organization where you work keeps a referral list of child care providers. (If it also offers a child care center, give your boss 10 points from us.) Or you can check with your county social service agency to see if there's a community agency referral service or guide.

The Childcare Aware Hotline, at 800-424-2246, can hook you up with a local referral source to licensed day care in your area. And there are some other good resources out there:

- National Association for the Education of Young Children (1509 16th Street NW, Washington, DC 20036-1426, 800-424-2460, www.naeyc.org), an accrediting organization for preschool/day care centers.

- National Association for Family Child Care (206 Sixth Avenue, Des Moines, IA 50309-4018, 800-359-3817, www.nafcc.org).

In all situations, ask for—and check—several references. Ask those references if the provider is flexible in terms of scheduling, how children are disciplined, and whether any problems came up in the relationship. Ask for advice on how to make things work out best with the provider, and consider these seven suggestions:

1. Think through your priorities and concerns.

2. Plan ahead—don't wait until the last minute. The best centers and providers have waiting lists. Call and make appointments to visit them now.

3. Personally interview the people who would be providing the care, and look over the setting to make sure there are no unsafe conditions.

4. Don't forget to check those references!

5. Start slowly—ease your child into the situation. Visit the facility together for an hour or so and see how it feels. Then send your child for a couple of hours and extend from there.

6. Drop in unexpectedly from time to time to see how things are working out.

7. Trust your gut. If something doesn't feel right, don't ignore it. There may be a plausible explanation—but don't talk yourself into accepting a situation that gives you pause, either at the get-go or over time.

We're a long way from having high-quality, affordable child care available to all, but if you're patient, know what you want, and invest the time, you're likely to find a decent alternative. Remember, finding the right caretaker to pinch-hit for you while you're at work is one of the best investments you'll ever make for you and your child.

More Ways to Improve Family Life

At No Extra Cost

- Take walks together.
- Have a cookout.
- Give each other backrubs.
- Give each other space to be alone or with individual friends.
- Talk . . . and listen to each other.
- Give each member of your family personal attention, one-on-one.

- Laugh . . . and shrug off the little things.
- Do your weekly shopping together in the evening rather than wasting time on the weekend.
- Play a game.
- Read a book together.
- Make time to have uninterrupted family meals—take the phone off the hook at dinnertime.
- Come home from work an hour early more often.
- Send the kids to grandma's for a sleep-over while you indulge in a candlelit evening at home. You'll have some quality time, grandma and the kids will have fun together, and you'll save money.
- Use up all your vacation time—even if you choose to spend it hanging out under the oak tree out back.
- Become a Big Brother or a Big Sister—and expand your family.
- Build a house with Habitat for Humanity, and extend your family to include someone in need. In the process, you'll learn some skills that'll help you around your house.

Low Cost

- Hire a baby-sitter, whether you want to go out and about—or up to take a nap.
- Find something you can all enjoy doing together in the great outdoors—skiing, shell collecting, hiking, sailing.
- Call just to say "I love you" or "hi"—even if it isn't during a discount calling time.
- Buy each other a little treat for no reason at all. Nothing expensive. Maybe something practical—a new kitchen utensil, a cute key ring that could be used for decades, a single flower, a favorite candy bar, a CD, whatever.
- Go out for pizza. There'll be no dishes, and it's cheap.
- Male or female, pamper yourself! Get your hair washed and cut, have a massage, do something personal. Such luxuries force you to focus on yourself and may remind you that you are important.
- Throw a party. Invite your favorite friends over for an activity (touch football, anyone?) or to chat while lounging on your porch. Throw a

cul-de-sac social or a potluck block party, and get to know your neighbors.

- Start a tiny vegetable patch and a compost pile. A few tomato plants, along with some basil, dill, mint, and arugula will convince you like nothing else can how delicious a simpler lifestyle can be.

- Organize a Halloween parade or a swim meet. Prizes for everyone! Make it an annual tradition.

- Take a class at a local college or grad school, or simply opt for continuing education courses. You could go for something down-to-earth—auto repair, plumbing, electrical, carpentry, or cooking, for example. Or maybe you'd like to try something different, either alone or with a friend or spouse—languages, ceramics, flower arranging. It really doesn't matter.

High Cost, but Might Be Well Worth It

- Take several short vacations a year together. Or if you prefer, a nice long one. Whether you choose to relax at a Club Med or to spend a weekend backpacking, getting away from your own surroundings helps to clear away those nagging thoughts about all the things that need to be done.

- Build an extra bedroom or playroom. Modernize the kitchen. Add a deck.

- Hire a helper (au pair, lawn mower, cleaning person—whatever you need).

- Join a gym. If doling out the cash is the only way you'll engage in some physical activity, then try it out with a trial membership. Now all you have to do is *go!*

- Buy a washer/dryer, dishwasher, microwave, or bread maker if it'll help you make more time for yourself.

- Take a leave of absence if you can, and spend it on your self-improvement goals.

- Move to a better school district, even if it means a pay cut or a bigger mortgage. The sacrifices might be worth the gain. But only you can decide.

- Send your children to private school . . . or home-school them.

INVEST IN YOUR LIFE

The United States was knee-deep in the war in Vietnam when President Nixon declared a second war—this time against an enemy that was killing hundreds of thousands of our young and old alike.

The war on cancer was neither funded nor pursued with the vigor or finances being aimed at what was then North Vietnam, but over the years, billions of dollars have been spent and some progress made.

We can't guarantee ourselves good health, no matter how much gold we've got stashed. But we can take control of our health to a much greater degree by taking some surprisingly easy and obvious steps: Exercise, reduce stress, eat healthier meals. These are investments that pay infinite returns in the QL department!

Investing in your health is no guarantee against illness, but it can help, and it can aid recovery if and when misfortune strikes. When Nancy, who has a family history of breast cancer, was diagnosed with it back in January of 1990, she and Marc took control of her treatment by investing the time and effort to research the latest findings, treatments, and trials. Then, working with her doctors, they fashioned a state-of-the-art treatment program that was years ahead of the medical mainstream. She remains cancer-free, able to do everything she wants to do.

You won't like it, but someday you or someone you love will get a diagnosis like Nancy's that will make your heart drop to your toes. Maybe you'll have a clear next step, coupled with top-notch medical care right from the start, but, to be sure, invest the time necessary to become a truly knowledgeable patient or advocate. It's not hard to do. It beats sitting home and waiting—feeling panicked, powerless, and overwhelmed. Studies show that people who are actively involved in their treatment live better—and longer.

How you go about it, of course, depends on the ailment. Although you might be plagued by a truly rare situation, chances are you'll have to deal with one or more of the biggies—cancer, heart disease, stroke. And although you may have a problem that needs immediate attention, there's usually plenty of time to do it right. When Nancy's cancer was first diagnosed, she wasn't sure whether she wanted a lumpectomy or a mastectomy, or who she wanted to perform the surgery. The first surgeon she saw wanted her to go for a mastectomy within the week. Nancy and Marc weren't sure and decided to spend that week doing research.

....

HELP IS THERE

> National Cancer Institute: www.nci.nih.gov (800-4-CANCER)
>
> American Cancer Society: www.cancer.org/frames.html
>   (800-ACS-2345)
>
> American Heart Association: www.amhrt.org
>   (800-AHA-USA1, for heart disease and strokes)
>
> American Lung Association: www.lungusa.org (800-LUNG-USA)
>
> American Diabetes Association: www.diabetes.org (800-DIABETES)
>
> AIDS Education Global Information System: www.aegis.com
>
> HIV/AIDS Treatment Information Service: www.hivatis.org
>   (800-HIV-0440)
>
> Arthritis Foundation: www.arthritis.org (800-283-7800)
>
> National Institute of Mental Health: www.nimh.nih.gov
>   (800-421-4211)
>
> National Institute of Neurological Disorders and Stroke:
>   www.ninds.nih.gov (301-496-5751)
>
> Alzheimer's Disease Education and Referral:
>   www.alzheimers.org/adear (800-438-4380)
>
> Alzheimer's Association: www.alz.org (800-272-3900)
>
> National Institutes of Health/Office of Alternative Medicine:
>   altmed.od.nih.gov (888-644-6226)
>
> Alternative Medicine Homepage: www.pitt.edu/~cbw/altm.html

Notes: For diseases or conditions not listed, go to www.healthfinder.gov for leads to both government and nonprofit agencies that can help.

To check out any doctor's background, go to the "Doctor Finder" at www.ama-assn.org.

....

When It Happens to You or Someone You Love

Make the calls, visit the Web sites, go to the library and skim a few books, and keep track of all your questions. Become familiar with how the disease works, what the standard treatments are, and what the current thinking seems to be on the subject.

Talk to some people who have already been through it. There are excellent support groups for pretty much every ailment, and they're easy to find through the organizations just mentioned or through the Self-Help Clearinghouse (973-625-3037 or www.cmhc.com/selfhelp).

Nancy learned that her greatest threat was not from the disease in her breast but its systemic nature. She decided on the most minor surgery (a lumpectomy) and the most aggressive chemotherapy. She also chose a surgeon closer to home who was known for performing lumpectomies with excellent results.

When you see the doctor in this kind of circumstance, don't go alone. Bring your list and someone who can help you decide what to do—your spouse, a grown child, or a sensible friend. Don't let the doctor or the office staff intimidate or rush you. Stay in your chair until your questions are answered. Yes, the doctor is busy, but when you're dealing with a serious decision about a serious disease, put yourself and your needs first.

Curing or treating a serious illness takes time and care. If one doctor doesn't have time for your reasonable questions, find another who does. If you'd be more comfortable learning more from just plain folk, ask your doctor to refer you to another patient or two who might help. (Nancy's surgeon and oncologist know they can give out her phone number.)

· ·

FEED YOUR SOUL: MARC'S REFLECTIONS FROM THE GARDEN

Our garden feeds us, body and soul. It provides great food and exercise, gives us a quiet reprieve from the stress of the workday, and offers a reminder of our place in nature's eternal cycles of birth, growth, death, and rebirth. When it comes to weight-lifting exercises, we prefer baskets of tomatoes, onions, and sugar snap peas to barbells. They're just as heavy, but they sure taste better. And gardening burns as many calories as brisk walking.

In nature, nothing goes to waste. Seeds sprout, grow, flower, reproduce, and die—giving back to the earth everything they previously borrowed. Nancy and I try to emulate nature's recycling program, and we hope you do likewise.

Plants take nothing personally. Although well equipped to deal with adversity, they never seek vengeance. They never whine, or feel sorry for themselves. Trim some lettuce plants to the ground, and they won't complain. They'll simply grow new leaves.

Nature is in no hurry for progress. Birds fly using pretty much the same equipment, and at the same speeds, as their forebears. Earthworms plow the soil as they have for eons. Peepers contentedly sing their same old songs. And the last thing raccoons want are faster cars on better roads.

Mother Nature's desire seems to be for balance, for the maintenance of life pretty much as it's always been.

They are neither friends nor enemies. Whatever apparent good or harm plants, insects, animals, and birds may do is inadvertent, natural, and necessary for their survival.

Except for our overfed cats, who occasionally kill a mouse only to abandon it, most of our garden's visitors and residents never harvest more than they can eat, nor do they crave possessions. Wouldn't it be great if we humans gave all we could and just took what we needed?

There are no guarantees. What worked so perfectly in one year's garden, can't be depended on to work again the next. But it might—which leads some gardeners to cling to ritualized behaviors, like planting certain crops by the full moon, others at the new moon, and peas on St. Patrick's Day. Truth be told, some years are better for some crops than for others, and half the fun of gardening (as well as living) is seeing how it'll all turn out this time.

There's no right way to garden. Pretty much every way works. Long rows, wide beds, raised beds, organic or inorganic fertilizers, heavy or light mulching—whatever we do, more often than not our plants grow.

How you or I choose to cultivate our own gardens is personal. Fortunately, there aren't a lot of laws decreeing the right way to grow tomatoes—because there isn't a right way. I don't mean to offend anyone, but I wish we could all let go of the feeling that we know exactly what's morally right or wrong for others to do, feel, or believe.

Ghettos are no good. Large tracts of a single crop, grown in the same place, year after year, begin to weaken and die. That's because ghetto-grown crops tend to deplete their own environment of the very nutrients they need to survive, and their predators can find them easily.

Mixed colonies, on the other hand, tend to thrive. It doesn't bother Nancy's purple basil one iota to live amidst green basil, next door to variously colored lettuces, or in the same neighborhood as cauliflower. Indeed, some gardeners swear that basil thrives at the feet of tomatoes. (I can surely testify to how well they get along in my mouth.)

Bugs get a bad rap. I know spiders and insects are strange-looking, but they don't deserve to be treated as if they were dangerous invaders from outer space. They've actually been keeping the earth habitable since time immemorial, taking care of a million chores around the garden, from pollinating crops to aerating the soil to feeding birds, each other . . . and maybe me.

There is a free lunch. Even in our well-maintained garden, a bountiful harvest of tasty, nutritious weeds, such as lamb's quarter, amaranth, and purslane, are usually ripe for the picking (even if Nancy never includes them when she's the one making salad).

My real favorites are the edible wild foods—daylily flowers, mulberries, cattails, blueberries, horseradish, asparagus, mint, watercress, mushrooms, and hickory nuts—that grow free and strong in our meadows, forests, and swamps.

They were thriving that warm summer morning 17 years ago when Nancy and I first met on a mountaintop. I took her on a wild-food walk, and she claims to have fallen in love with me during the first 10 minutes.

I've often wondered, was it my considerable charm and wit—or the wood sorrel I enticed her to eat along the way?

—MARC

··

CHAPTER 3

The Great Sneaker Debate

○ How to raise your kids well without spending a fortune

○ What you can do to help your kids become savvy shoppers instead of mindless mall walkers

○ Turn your little spenders into smart savers and investors

○ Allowance strategies for kids of all ages

It is possible to triumph over the tube. . . .

STEVE AND RUTH BENNETT,
365 TV-Free Activities You Can Do With Your Child

··

While it's true that multimillionaire basketball stars wear special high-tech sneakers, it is not true that special, high-tech sneakers will turn your child into a multimillionaire basketball star. What *is* true is that children:

- Are impressionable.
- Watch TV.
- See about 3,000 commercials a month.
- Are seduced by innumerable shows glamorizing possessions.
- Have friends with high-tech sneakers.
- Are easily swayed by peer pressure.
- Want to be liked.
- Represent a $500 billion market for retailers.
- Know how to make you feel guilty for "depriving them."

And deprive them you do—or at least you *think* you do. You work long hours, you don't and can't spend quantity time with them, so you try to substitute quality time. And even though you know you can't afford to buy them every single piece of trendy trash or designer clothing that they absolutely "must" have, you feel tempted to make up for the personal attention gap by buying them whatever they want. That's a bad move, and you know it.

AH, TO BE A CHILD AGAIN!

We've taken an informal survey and have discovered that few adults would choose to be children again. (Younger, yes. Back in school? A teenager? Thanks, no!) Rules, regulations, lack of a car and sleep, curfews, limited money to fund maximum desires, acne, overloaded backpacks, and homework, homework, homework are a modern teen's lot in life.

But kids do come and grow, with each milestone in age adding its own costs. Baby formula alone can run $1,000 that first year—unless your baby is "best fed by being breast fed." And diapers can deplete assets at the same rate as formula. In one end and out the other, all of the time draining your savings, to say nothing of the environment.

As they age, children continue to cost big-time. Whether it's day care or health care, supercolossal toys or boom boxes generating noise, nannies replacing moms or high school proms . . . the money goes as the child grows.

Where to draw the line? You have to decide. But given the high cost of raising a modern child, one of the very best financial investments you can make is to bring up your kids to have reasonable desires. Fad followers can drive you crazy and into the poorhouse, as they spend like crazy. Your challenge is to focus on your child's present and future financial welfare—without letting them spend the family onto public welfare.

After all, many children developed into fully functioning, loving, caring, and happy adults before: TV, Toys "Я" Us, the Gap, electronic games, tai chi classes, and $100,000 educations.

While music lessons, gymnastics, ballet, martial arts classes, college prep courses, state-of-the-art computers, specialized summer camps, journeys to far-off amusement parks, designer clothes, pierced body parts, and backyards filled with plastic pleasures all entertain, and can sometimes even educate our young, none were mentioned as inalienable rights in the Declaration of Independence.

Do you remember when children went outside to play, and running to catch falling leaves occupied entire afternoons? Leaves still fall and the outside is still there. Your challenge is to find the time and the ways to turn your kids on to such simple pleasures, and to nurture their enjoyment of those things money just can't buy. Everyone will benefit. So will your pocketbook.

NEVER UNDERESTIMATE THE POWER OF THE BOOB TUBE

You're in direct competition with the television industry, so it's in your interest to make it a point to watch TV with your children. Especially tune in to some of the thousands of commercials they see every year. Help them understand that products are heavily hyped and what they see is not what they'll get.

Here's a particularly effective technique: Compare something your child "had to have"—and got—with the commercial that was so bedazzling, be it a toy, snack food, cereal, makeup, sports gear, clothes, games, or computer equipment. Point out how the product fell way short of your kid's expectations. But try not to say, "I told you so!"

It's important that children learn from their spending mistakes, but as you know, they don't respond well when the message is pounded in. Tell them about a time or two when you made a dumb decision of your own. (Haven't we all?) They'll remember the lousy purchases, theirs and yours, and hopefully make better choices in the future.

While we wouldn't dictate what children can or can't purchase with their own money, you can easily pass along your ideas on what's worth buying. For example, let your kids know that you're happy to buy them a perfectly fine pair of sneakers for $20, but if they decide to upgrade to the $100 designer pair, it'll be with their own funds. Also, feel free to point out that they'd then have $80 less to spend on other things they'd really enjoy—now or in the future.

Will they feel deprived if they don't get every single thing they want? Here and there, for a little while. Eventually, kids need to learn that no one, no matter how wealthy, can do it all or have it all. Better they learn their spending priorities from you, than from the boob tube.

ALLOW YOUR KIDS TO BECOME GREAT MONEY MANAGERS

When was the last time you went shopping, picked something up on impulse, then as you waited at a cash register, money in hand, asked yourself, "Do I really need this?" Can't remember? Well, when was the last time you told a pleading child, "You don't need that," or "You just had a treat," or "That's a waste of money"?

Kids watch how we spend money on ourselves and compare that to how we allocate it to them. They recognize the arbitrariness of grown-ups' rules, and you can bet they resent the typical parental response, "It's my money."

Double standards are unfair and counterproductive. As part of the family, we think children are entitled to a fair portion of the family pie—in other words, an allowance. And within some limits (for example, no cigarettes), kids should be *allowed* to spend at least a portion of that money on what they want. That's why it's called an *allow*ance.

Done right, giving your children an allowance is one of the best investments you can make. It's among the most valuable tools in your arsenal to teach them smart money management techniques. They get to learn what things actually cost, how to make choices about spending *their* money, and when it pays to save for something they really want. No doubt along the way, they'll also have to endure more than a few painful but important lessons about the pros and cons of wasting money. Better it be on your nickel when they're young than when they're in college and $17,000 in debt on credit cards they couldn't manage. (We'll give you our pearls of wisdom on credit cards and college students in Chapter 15.)

While we don't think an allowance should be tied to a long list of responsibilities or paid out as a series of fees for each service your child performs, that doesn't mean that kids, like all household members, shouldn't have regular chores—or that you can't offer them ways to make extra cash by doing extra jobs. If your personal philosophy differs from ours, develop a clear, written set of tasks (with dollar amounts attached) that the kids are expected to do in exchange for their allowance.

Before you set an allowance, talk to your kids about what they need money for, and how much they need. Help them create a budget that will cover those things you think ought to be included, perhaps school lunches or some clothing.

Be clear on your expectations. Is it important to you that a portion be earmarked for savings or charitable giving? If so, say so up front. Will you provide matching funds up to a set amount if they bring in a deposit for the banking program at school?

If there isn't a savings program in your child's school, contact Save for America (4095 173rd Place SE, Bellevue, WA 98008, 425-746-0331, www.schoolsavings.com). This nonprofit organization has helped 6,000 elementary schools set up saving programs in conjunction with local banks. Colorful stickers, contests, and other incentives encourage and reward students for participating.

Or you could simply open a savings account in your child's name at the local bank and make a big deal out of going to the bank together every week and contributing to their account. In any event, a great time to help your children develop a savings plan is when there's something they "must" have that you won't buy, and they don't have enough to pay for it themselves. Explain how they can put aside a set amount of money every week, until there's enough in the till to buy what they want.

You want your youngsters to have an early victory—preferably within a few weeks—to see the great benefit to saving for something they want. That will up the odds that they'll be motivated to save again. Perhaps next time it will be for something that will take a little longer to finance, and may be a little more meaningful.

....

GIFT GIVING MADE CHEAPER

When Peter and Lucy Banks started tracking their own spending and creating a budget, they discovered that they were blowing a lot on gifts for their children's friends. It seemed like every time they turned around, there was another birthday party, and that meant another $15 or so for a gift.

They decided to do two things. The first was to put both their children, David and Alison, then ages 5 and 9, on a weekly allowance, which they believe was one of the best things they could have done. Then they set guidelines as to what that allowance would cover, and explained that each child could expect $5 per gift from their parents. If they wanted to give their friends gifts that were more expensive than that, they'd have to make up the difference.

"It's amazing," says Peter, "how the average price per gift dropped! Although it's hard to let your kids make dumb purchases, it's good to let them find out for themselves whether what they bought was worth the price." Peter explains, "I'd rather they learn now that a lot of what's for sale isn't a good value."

....

Once you've decided what—if anything—the allowance should cover, be sure that you've left enough to allow your kids to spend at least some of it however they wish. Pick an amount that won't leave your kids feeling as though they're struggling to make ends meet. It's bad enough if you have trouble getting from payday to payday. Don't let your offspring start off that way.

While the general rule of thumb is $1 for every year (e.g., $5 a week for a 5-year-old), that seems kind of steep to us, especially for the little ones. We know of one 13-year-old who gets $30 a week! Times have really changed.

- Base the amount you give on the custom in your community. You can ask other parents, at school, and at church.

- Be consistent and don't be late! You don't want your kids to get the idea that it's okay to pay bills late. Give them their allowance at the same time every week—preferably not right before the weekend, when the temptation to blow it all may be too great. Sunday night is often best, since it's just before kids begin the school week.

- Know your child. Some experts suggest starting an allowance at age 3. Sounds a wee bit young to us. Feel free to wait until first grade if your tyke just isn't ready for the responsibility before then.

- Short-circuit any money-handling problems you think your child is likely to have *before* they happen. Does your child need a wallet to carry to school and a secure spot (say a piggybank) for the reserve cash at home? We know one set of parents who waited months to start an allowance because they feared that their daughter didn't have a good spot to hold the money. When Nancy heard this, she offered a cute little basket with a tightly fitting cover that now holds that child's wealth securely. Problem solved, allowance initiated, money a lot less likely to get lost.

But whether given as a right, as payment for services rendered, or as a combination of both, whether a lot or a little, started early or late ... these days especially, parents have to do a lot more than dole out the dough. Invest as much of your time and energy as is required to make your children's early money experiences positive. You want to do everything you can to help them succeed as they learn the basics.

MOMMY, PLEEEEASE!

With the average child seeing 30,000 to 40,000 commercials a year, it's more important than ever to help kids learn how to distinguish needs from wants. But before you can help to do that, you must:

- Be able to distinguish your own wants from your genuine needs.

- Understand what a child your child's age can understand.

- Remember that satisfying some wants is important. Children cannot live on needs alone!

Unfortunately, far too many adults are themselves confused about needs and wants, and they set a bad money management example as a result. Youngsters who see their parents' impulse buying will have a hard time understanding why their wants can't also be immediately satisfied. And youngsters who often hear their parents fighting about money may end up with money problems later on.

I Want It, I Need It, I Must Have It!

When you go to the store, are you a smart shopper who uses a list, but also keeps a lookout for items on sale that your family regularly uses? Remember that long before they can communicate, your children are watching and learning. Just as little ones watch you in the kitchen and then want to cook, too, they watch how you shop and want to play "grown-up" and be just like you. If you simply "must have" everything you want right then and there, you'll have a tough time convincing your kids that designer clothes and sugarcoated cereal in the shape of cartoon characters don't qualify as "needs."

Money lessons, like all the rest of learning, depend on the age and development of the child. As your children grow older and begin to understand more, help them learn how to make more and more difficult distinctions. As every parent learns, flexibility is the key.

Babying Your Baby

From birth to about 18 months, most of a child's wants *are* needs. They need food, comfort (emotional and physical), and attention. Kids in this age range can watch a commercial dozens of times or see something at the supermarket and never ask for the item—unless they've been previously introduced to it. So if you don't want your young children to have or want chocolate éclairs, for example, don't give them any in the first place. After all, they'll learn about junk food and start badgering you to spring for it soon enough. Why start them early and set yourself up for a fight? There'll be plenty of time for those later!

. . . .

THIS . . . OR THAT

A typical mistake made by parents of young children is what we call the "free-association breakfast," although it can occur at any time of the day, and often does, around money issues. A free-association breakfast works something like this:

> PARENT: What would you like for breakfast, darling?
> CHILD: A chocolate doughnut.
> PARENT: No!
> CHILD: That's what I want. You asked me what I wanted!

You get the picture. Here's how to take a bit more control:

> PARENT: Darling, do you want oatmeal or Cream of Wheat for breakfast?
> CHILD: Oatmeal, with apples and cinnamon, please.

Much better. Open-ended questions allow for unexpected and unwelcome answers. Multiple choice is more likely to limit the responses to acceptable alternatives.

. . . .

That First Word Won't Be the Last

With speaking comes wanting—everything, immediately. And no one knows how to break down your resistance better than your children. They employ whining, crying, begging, and perhaps the worst, just being doggone cute! It's hard to say "No!" to a three-year-old who knows just how to say, "Pleeeease!"

From about 18 months to 7 years, your best line of defense will be an ability to distract, along with as much creativity as you can muster. Distraction is an underappreciated art form that works best when handled subtly.

This is the stage when kids are learning to want what others have, especially in the food and toy departments. Although you may never have bought chocolate-covered pretzels, it's likely that between TV, classmates, and the bus, your child has already seen and tasted them.

When you get to the store, the battle begins: "Pleeeease can I have chocolate-covered pretzels? Kia's mom buys them for her!!" Your child begins to throw what looks like the queen of all temper tantrums. What's a parent to do? You could try to reason, and explain that while

Kia's mom chooses to buy them for her, you don't think they're healthy, and anyway, they cost too much. But too often, that will be a wasted investment of your time and energy.

Sometimes, you really are better off compromising quickly. Maybe you could allow your daughter to choose her own snack from three or four items you preselect. Or let her buy the pretzels on her own, out of her allowance. Once you make that offer, she may decide she doesn't want them after all.

When reason alone just sets off more fireworks, speculating in "futures" often succeeds. Not the kind of futures you can buy through a commodities trader, but what you can offer for some day down the road. For example volunteer to get those chocolate-covered pretzels for your child's next birthday party or at some other distant time. Perhaps by then, they'll hold no more interest or have been forgotten. But if your child does remember, don't be surprised or renege. You want to be true to your word about money matters, so your child will be, too.

Distraction is often harder with toys. You can't easily replace lust for a Destructo car with an offer of lima beans for dinner! If your five-year-old wants a Destructo car, *she wants a Destructo car!* Don't berate yourself for saying no. It's okay. It doesn't mean you're a bad parent, no matter what your child says.

If "No!" doesn't work, if "Honey, we just can't afford it" doesn't work, offer to go garage or rummage sale hunting for Destructo. The next Saturday morning, go out with a certain dollar amount (say $2) in your child's pocket with the hope of finding a Destructo car. One of three things will happen. You'll find it and your child will scoop it up. Your child will see something else that she "must have" and spend her money on that instead. Or your child may decide that $2 in her pocket is way cooler than a Destructo car and hang onto the cash.

This is the age when children can understand the concept of wants versus needs and make it part of their daily life. You don't always have to say, "You don't need that. I know you want it, but we can't always get what we want, now can we?" But do often tactfully remind your children of the difference between wants and needs. That understanding can save your child and you a fortune, now and forever.

Unless you deny yourself life's every pleasure, it's okay to cave to your child's wants sometimes. It's not reasonable to always expect your child to be reasonable about money matters (or anything else). Just be sure you're choosing to do the caving and are not being coerced into it. A child doesn't have dictatorial powers unless you cede them.

. . . .

A SIMPLE WAY TO SOOTHE YOUR IMPULSIVE BEASTS

Marc and his three children developed a wish list, an often discussed (but never written) record of what they most wanted to have or do. They called it their "eventually list," and it helped them all to prioritize. Sooner or later, most everything on the list got covered . . . or lost its appeal.

Knowing that it would indeed happen "eventually," seemed to calm the need for instant gratification—most of the time. So next time your kids "must" have something, add it to their "eventually list" and help them save for it, a little at a time—just like you do, right? If they don't lose interest along the way, they'll really value the "prize," once they've saved enough to make it theirs.

. . . .

MONEY DOESN'T GROW ON TREES

Talk to your kids about how you earn, spend, and save your money. Even the little ones ought to know that the cash coming out of the ATM isn't magic money, that you work hard to earn every penny, nickel, and dime.

Ditto for checks. Double ditto for credit cards. We're particularly incensed by a preschooler "play store" that boasts "real shopping sounds" and drones out "credit approved," reinforcing the use of those plastic monsters at a way too tender age. Are they trying to create the financial equivalent of the late Joe Camel?

All those empty billboards remind us that it's time for a commercial break of our own: While you may not see him under the lights any time soon, Harry the Gorilla is going to help today's youngsters (in grades K–3) learn how to make smart choices about money. Remember, you met him here first.

The brainchild of Marc's son, Adam, an elementary school teacher, Harry's the lead character in *The Peanut Butter and Jelly Game* (which Marc and Nancy's Good Advice Press published). He's the perfect foil to help parents battle the "gimmes"—that affliction kids seem to develop immediately upon entering a store. You can buy the book (see page 328) and read it to them or simply tell them the story. To wit, Harry impulsively blows a week's grocery money on a bright, shiny new baseball mitt that he absolutely must have, never thinking twice about the consequences. It comes as a great surprise to Harry—but not to his level-headed best friend, Bradley the Porcupine—when the hungry gorilla discovers that he's run out of food.

Harry then tries to bum the ingredients for his favorite meal, a peanut butter and jelly sandwich, from his friends, who include Matilda, the hard-of-hearing hippo, and Gertrude, the absentminded scientist skunk. After numerous humorous encounters, Harry learns that with a little advance planning he can have the food he needs as well as the glove he wants.

As Harry copes with the consequences of his impulsive spending, kids learn valuable lessons about saving, sharing, and helping friends. And the colorful, very detailed, and amusing illustrations by Joe Walden, also a teacher, appeal to all ages.

OLDER, BUT NOT NECESSARILY WISER

By about age 8, children hit the milestone where popularity in school really matters, and name brands hold more and more clout. If you've shown that you don't succumb to labels and fads, you're likely to have less of a battle. But you'll have some friction over money, no doubt about it.

For example, even if—or maybe because—you delight in getting all your clothes at yard sales, your kids will want pricey brand-new duds from designer stores. A compromise here could certainly be in order! Sometimes, it makes sense to give in, before the tears and wars begin, and before you're labeled the meanest person in the whole wide world.

How's this for a plan? If you're going to do your back-to-school shopping late in August, announce your budget in early July. Then remove everything that no longer fits from your children's closets and drawers, and together make two lists—one for necessary clothing and another for luxuries. Go to the stores you can agree on and get an idea of how much those necessities are going to cost you. Any excess can go into the luxury fund. Then help your children earn money for any purchases over your budget. They'll have plenty of time over the summer to do it.

The Young Entrepreneur

Yard sales are great income producers for youngsters and provide invaluable financial educations. Your children can sell old toys, clothing that no longer fits, your castoffs, and maybe even some of their own baked goods. They'll not only earn money, but they'll get an understanding of depreciation, earnings, making change, advertising, customer satisfaction, and the need to invest time in order to earn money. Having a multifamily sale can make it "way cooler," and selling stuff at yard sales may just make your brood more willing to shop at them.

If a yard sale won't work, offer special jobs around the house. Maybe they can weed or water the garden, mow the lawn, wash the dishes or clothes, clean out the fridge, whatever. Or maybe your children can do chores at your office—filing, for example.

Young Capitalists

Enterprising youth will want to move on at some point to a part-time job or even to a business of their own. Here's a list of reasonable possibilities:

Setting up the good old-fashioned lemonade stand

Pet-walking, pet-sitting, pet-grooming

Plant-sitting

Painting (house, fence, railings, etc.)

Shopping for neighbors

Selling flowers or plants

Child care (mother's helper when young, baby-sitter when older)

Car washing

Putting on entertainment for kids' parties

Tutoring younger children

Giving lessons (music, computer, drawing, etc.)

Washing windows

Cleaning out garages and basements

Delivering newspapers

Making handicrafts

Stacking wood

Doing household chores for homebound seniors (emptying garbage, bringing in the mail)

Setting up a booth at a flea market (to sell baseball cards, Barbie dolls, or an eclectic collection of miscellaneous treasures)

Before you let your child undertake any of these jobs, explain what every entrepreneur must do: Assess the need for the product or service, decide how much to charge, and figure out how and where to market it.

If you need some ideas on how to get started, see Chapter 8, then head to the library together to do some research.

Start with a copy of *Better Than a Lemonade Stand: Small Business Ideas for Kids* by Daryl Bernstein. Or turn on the computer and go to www.littlejason.com/lemonade, an on-line version of a game where kids set up a stand and figure out costs and profit margins.

Investing the time *before* they get going will be well worth it. After all, you want them to succeed in their moneymaking ventures.

Who gets to decide what they do with their money? We say, when they've earned their own money, and it's an item that you're not morally opposed to, let them buy it. You've instilled your values by now, so let them make their own beds. (You wish!) But there's nothing wrong with again making your thoughts clear. Helping them make wise spending choices without hindering their learning from bad choices is your best shot.

. . . .

For an excellent collection of books, videos, and board games available to help you teach your kids about money, get the *Money-Book Store Catalog* from the National Center for Financial Education. It's on-line at www.ncfe.org, or send $2 to NCFE Catalog, P.O. Box 34070, San Diego, CA 92163-4070.

. . . .

ESPECIALLY FOR THE CHILD WHO HAS GREAT DESIRES—BUT NO INTEREST IN WORK

There'll be plenty of years when they have to work. So if your kids aren't interested in getting a head start on making money, focus on steering them in another important direction that will help them develop key values—spending less.

It's often overlooked, but children can easily come up with money without very much effort *by saving some of yours.* Let's say your kid saves $25 of your fall clothes budget by wearing hand-me-downs or yard sale finds. Let the money they save go into their luxury column. It'll cost you the same, and they'll have learned another valuable lesson about money: that if they cut back on spending in one area, they can get more of what they really want without having to make the sacrifices to earn more.

Start Them Socking It Away Early

Should you force you kids to save for college? If so, at what age? Compare the strategies of these parents: The first one tried to encourage his 13-year-old son to save for college, first by offering to match each dollar he contributed to a mutual fund. "The allure of instant gratification was too strong," says his father. "I then increased the offer to double it, then triple it, then five times. Finally, I offered to put in ten times the money he did."

Alas, this boy would rather have money for Nintendo, movies, and fancy sneakers. Dad is thinking about forcing him to save, but he'd rather get his son to save voluntarily. "He might be persuaded if I let him use the money for a car, but college is just too far away for him to consider."

Parent number 2 wasn't interested in incentives. He simply insisted that his 14-year-old make regular contributions to a mutual fund account. Since they opened the account right around the beginning of the rising stock market, this youngster has profited handsomely. Now in his twenties, he's already an experienced, eager investor.

As we pondered these two stories, we wondered what our lives would have been like if we had been forced to save. We'd have had yet more fights at home, but also a lot more money in the bank. After all, even young kids can become enthusiastic investors. What do *you* think?

Turning Your Spender into an Investor

When it comes to stocks, don't sell short your kids' ability to process all this information—or at least enough of it to understand what it means to own a piece of the company whose products they're using, eating, wearing, listening to or playing with.

—JANET BODNAR, *Dr. Tightwad's Money-Smart Kids*

Among the money lessons you share with your kids, help them learn how Wall Street works for long-term investors. Start by having them make a list of the companies whose products they and their friends enjoy, be it McDonald's or Nike. Explain that the stock market is risky and that investors need to do homework. Help them do some research over the Internet, starting with Edustock at tqd.advanced.org/3088 (note: no www. here). Or visit your local library, where *Value Line Investment Survey* will be a helpful resource. Then let them make their best educated guesses about which companies will grow the most.

When they've narrowed down the list to one or two choices, buy them a few shares. Some on-line brokerages charge nominal fees (for example, www.suretrade.com), or go to www.dripinvestor.com to see if you can purchase the stock directly from the company.

Or you can pretend, with a make-believe $1,000—or $10,000 if you'd like. Or you could do what Marc did, when his son Adam was playing stock market "pretend" for a high school class project, wishing he was Donald Trump. Adam liked the game a lot, and talked about how much money he could make if only he were "allowed" to really invest. And he talked about it, and he talked about it, and he talked about it.

Thinking it would be a great experience for Adam, Marc sent off a check for $1,000 to Adam, who lived with his mother at the time. It was no special occasion, just a good time to give his son an opportunity and to send him a note, which went something like this:

Dear Adam,

Here's $1,000. Happy Unbirthday! It's yours, no strings attached. You can use it to buy stocks, deposit it in the bank, put it under your mattress, invest it in baseball cards, do some of each—in other words, use it however you want.

Although I admit I'll be curious, you don't have to tell me what you use it for—or if you decide to invest it, how much you make or lose. And I'll try never to ask!

Good luck!

Luv ya!
Dad

Eventually, Adam did tell Marc what he had done with the grand old grand. Here's Adam's perspective, some 15 years later.

"I spoke to a stock broker," Adam recalls, "the one Mom uses, and I invested the entire $1,000 in a 'hot' penny stock.

"It went up and up and up. My instinct was to sell—but the broker said to wait. I listened to him and kept those shares. Then the company went belly-up, and the commission on selling the stock would have cost more than it was worth."

Did Adam learn anything?

"I learned that nothing's a sure thing. And it doesn't matter what you're worth on paper—the profit isn't real until it's in your pocket. My instinct was to sell, and I should have gone with my instinct."

Adam still dabbles in the stock market, where his investments have by and large done quite well. He doesn't want to be "The Donald" anymore—which is fortunate, because as a grade school teacher, limos aren't likely in his future, no matter how his portfolio does!

However you go about it, helping your kids become savvy about money is one of the best investments you can make in their futures—and in yours.

CHAPTER 4

Paradise Found

- Making sense of the buy versus rent debate
- Smart ways to cut home-buying costs dramatically
- How to search for greener pastures
- Homeowner's tax myths demystified

The rich and famous may be able to travel to and live just about anywhere they want. But for the rest of us, choosing an ideal location will be based on very mundane factors. . . .

WILLIAM SEAVEY, *Moving to Small Town America*

One of the best ways to dramatically improve your quality of life is to live someplace that you love. Investing the time to consciously choose where you want to put down roots, then, is smart. After all, it's one of the most important decisions you get to make in life—again and again.

And one of the most expensive. Each move and mortgage means thousands of dollars in fees and bank interest, to say nothing of family upheaval and a big change in the quality of our lives—not always for the better.

HOME SWEET HOME

Why do you live where you live now? Is it someplace you carefully chose, or did you just end up there? If it "just sorta happened," given your current circumstances and preferences, where do you really want to be living now?

69

This is a difficult question, one that takes a lot of careful soul-searching and planning. Even if your job is keeping you tied to one location, you probably still have choices. You might be able to choose between a house in the country with a long commute, a shorter commute from the suburbs, but with a lot less land for your dollar, or even a condo in the city within walking distance of the office.

If you're debt-free and have few ties to your present community, you may be able to move across the country, wherever your heart takes you. How do you make that decision? The first step is to really think about what's important to you:

- Cost of living
- Taxes
- Climate
- Schools
- Population
- Crime
- Recreation
- Work opportunities
- Where your friends and family live

You probably can't have it all—no place is perfect, but resources such as the *Places Rated Almanac* and *Retirement Places Rated,* both by David Savageau, can put a practical spin on your fantasies. *Money* magazine also rates places to live each year. Look at several issues for suggestions. Then, for those that pass your initial screening, ask the chambers of commerce to send you information. You won't get the skinny from them, but you will get lots of information about why you should move there. Go to www.virtualrelocation.com for dozens of links to helpful sites on pretty much any area you're considering.

Put the word out to everyone you can about locales that interest you. You'll be amazed at how many people will know someone living in that area who you can call. Subscribe to the local newspaper for awhile, or see if it has a web site. While you're on-line, chat with people who live there.

If you belong to a professional association, see if there is a local chapter or members nearby, then call, write, or e-mail. Tell them you're going to be visiting to check out the area, and ask for suggestions. They may even offer to take you on a guided tour! Visiting a church or synagogue in the area is another way to meet the natives.

Then plan your trip, or better yet, your trips. Make them as long as you can. A short visit may fool you with unusually nice weather and not enough reality. When you do visit, remember that you're on vacation. The new place will almost certainly seem more appealing than home. After all, you're not fighting traffic or running the kids to and from activities! So make it a little more realistic. Drive in rush-hour traffic (if there is any). Visit schools. Try local recreation facilities you'd be likely to use.

If you're in a position to take a leave of absence from your job while you try to find the next right spot to live, do it! Once you do figure out where you want to be, *rent for a while* until you're ready to make a commitment to a home and neighborhood.

Another option (a thrifty one at that) is to become a property caretaker in the area you're considering. You'll live rent free and sometimes earn a nice living, as well. For more info, go to www.angelfire.com/wa/caretaker or send an SASE for the "Report on Caretaking," to *The Caretaker Gazette*, P.O. Box 5887, Carefree, AZ 85377-5887.

If you're yearning for a move from the city or burbs to the country or a small town, check out *Moving to a Small Town* by Wanda Urbanska and Frank Levering, *How to Find Your Ideal Country Home: Ruralize Your Dreams* by Gene GeRue, *Finding & Buying Your Place in the Country* by Les and Carol Scher, *Country Bound! Trade Your Business Suit Blues for Blue Jean Dreams* by Marilyn and Tom Ross, and *Moving to Small Town America* by William Seavey. The Simple Living Network at www.slnet.com offers additional resources.

SHOULD YOU BUY?

Conventional wisdom says that owning a home is:

- A great investment.
- A fabulous tax shelter.
- The American Dream.

Owning a home may be the American Dream, but it can also turn out to be a nightmare. It's a great goal to strive for—when you can achieve it. But if you buy more house than you really can afford, and then lose your job or get divorced, your dream could easily evaporate, as it does for the estimated 500,000 families who lose their homes to bank foreclosure every year.

Even if the next house you pick is one you can afford to buy, whether it'll be a great investment will depend more on the state of the local economy when you sell than on anything else. You may or may not have a choice about when you sell, and you certainly won't have much control over the economy. If your next move has to occur during a buyer's market, will you be able and willing to hold out for a good price—or will you be forced to dump the house?

"Is a house a good investment?" The knee-jerk way of answering goes something like this: "I bought the house for $100,000 and sold it for $150,000, so I made a 50% profit." Unfortunately, that leaves out a lot of the crucial, often ignored costs of home ownership—for example, closing costs, private mortgage insurance, broker's and lawyer's fees when you buy and sell, real estate taxes, home insurance, maintenance, landscaping, and mortgage interest. The interest alone on your home could end up costing you twice as much as you paid for the place.

The tax shelter question is also muddy. Before you sign the papers, do a sample tax return and see what owning would save you, if anything. You may be surprised by how little tax benefit you'll get.

Even if you have substantial deductions to itemize, the tax benefits will not outweigh the costs. While you'll be able to deduct a percentage of what you pay in real estate taxes and mortgage interest, a 28% deduction on your federal income taxes would mean you'd still be out 72 cents on every dollar you fork over.

And because of the standard deduction we're all entitled to, the first $7,000 or so you shell out won't buy you and your spouse a nickel's worth of tax benefit. Since the standard deduction goes up every year, while mortgage interest goes down, itemizing will be of less and less value to you as time goes on. (While your real estate taxes will no doubt keep going up and up, we know you don't see that as a benefit of home ownership!)

But there are other costs you have to weigh as well. Your next home can be a great place to live—or a big mistake, not only financially, but personally. We know one family that moved into a development with their exuberant terrier, only to learn that the next-door neighbor absolutely refused to tolerate the pooch putting one paw over the property line. It made for a strained relationship, to say the least.

If they had taken the time to ring the bell of this potential neighbor, they surely would have looked elsewhere. So investing the time to make sure a particular house in a particular neighborhood is really the right next home for you and yours is well worth it. Along the way, you may find some welcome alternatives that would serve you better and be less expensive.

For example, if your current house is too small, it might cost less and be easier to renovate than to move. Get some construction estimates for that new bedroom, bathroom, or other space that you need.

EITHER A BORROWER OR A RENTER BE

Especially if you're moving to a new city or town, being a tenant for a year or more can help you avoid serious mistakes by giving you a chance to carefully check out the various neighborhoods and school districts.

While it's absolutely true that rent money, once spent, is gone forever, when you look carefully at the numbers, you may discover that renting "buys" you a house you could never afford to own and leaves you with more assets than if you bought.

Meet John and Mary Homeseeker. After scanning ads and touring with local brokers, they're considering buying a $125,000 house in a nearby development. They're also intrigued by a secluded mountaintop home, with scenic vistas, that they saw advertised for $950 a month.

Putting aside the lifestyle questions these two options raise—that only John and Mary can answer—which alternative makes the most financial sense? To find out, we crunched the numbers.

But first, we made some assumptions about the Homeseekers. By using appropriately selected assumptions, we could, of course, produce any result we want. (Anyone can—politicians and advertisers have been doing it for centuries!)

So don't conclude that our numbers for the Homeseekers prove that you should either buy or rent. Decide based on your own assumptions, feelings, dreams, plans for the future, willingness to take risks—and the financial calculations.

We assumed John and Mary could negotiate the $125,000 asking price down to $112,500 and that they have enough cash on hand to put down 10% ($11,250) and to cover an expected 5% worth of closing costs ($5,063 based on the $101,250 home loan they'd need). The Homeseekers will have to come up with a total of $16,313 at the closing. (That up-front cash is currently in a 90-day CD that earns 5%, or $68 a month.) (See Table 4.1.)

John and Mary checked at www.hsh.com for current mortgage rates, and discovered that they could borrow $101,250, at 8.5% for 30 years, which means their monthly mortgage payment would be $779. They'd have to pay property and school taxes, and their maintenance costs would be higher than if they rented. And because their down payment is only 10%, the bank will require private mortgage insurance (PMI). While there are a bunch of

Table 4.1 Buy or Rent: The Facts

	PURCHASE	RENTAL
Negotiated price	$112,500	$ 950
Down payment/security	11,250	1,900
Mortgage	101,250	None
Closing costs and points	5,063	None

PMI programs that protect lenders when borrowers can't come up with at least a 20% down payment, to keep our example as simple as possible, we're going to assume that the Homeseekers have to come up with a $45 premium every month until their equity in the house finally reaches 20%.

The Homeseekers have no other tax deductions, which means that if they buy, their tax breaks would be $98 a month—much less than they expected. How could that be?

Real Estate Tax Deductions Demystified

Mortgage interest and real estate taxes are worth far less on your 1040 tax form than you may realize. Whether you rent or buy, the IRS gives you a standard deduction. It's $7,100 in 1998 for married couples. (Two singles living together get a higher deduction, $4,250 each in 1998, or $8,500. The $1,400 difference is often referred to as "the marriage penalty.")

So for John and Mary Homeseeker, the first $7,100 they paid in mortgage interest and real estate taxes would bring them *absolutely no tax benefit*. Say they moved in on January 1 and didn't pre-pay on their mortgage. By year's end they'd pay $8,577 in interest and we'll assume $2,500 in property taxes, totaling $11,077.

Our tax system is so confusing, the Homeseekers may believe they'll save the full $11,077 in taxes. Or maybe they think that since they're in the 28% tax bracket, they could write off only 72%, $7,975—or only 28%, $3,102.

Actually, their tax benefit will be 28% of $3,977 ($11,077 minus the $7,100 standard deduction they'd get any way). They'll save $1,114 (28% of $3,977)—or $93 a month. That's barely 10 cents back for every $1.00 the Homeseekers will spend on interest and real estate taxes. What a deal. (See Table 4.2.)

John and Mary's monthly housing costs would be $187 less if they rented, than if they bought ($1,172 − $985). If John and Mary were to rent, and systematically invest the $187 a month difference it would grow to $18,761 (even at 5%), by the time they get the 7-year itch to move. This

TABLE 4.2 Buy or Rent: Monthly Costs

MONTHLY PAYMENT	BUY: $779	RENT: $950
Private mortgage insurance	+ 45	None
Taxes	+208	None
Maintenance	+100	+ 25
Insurance	+ 65	+ 10
Subtotal	1,197	985
Lost Investment Income	+ 68	None
Less Tax Savings	− 93	None
Monthly cost	**$1,172**	**$985**

doesn't include any earnings that would accrue on their $1,900 security deposit.

If, instead of going for the 5% return, the Homeseekers used that $187 a month to keep out of consumer debt or went for a higher-yielding investment, they'd fare even better.

But they expected the early rental advantage to be wiped out by equity gains and tax benefits over the seven years they anticipated living in the house.

Do we have a surprise for the Homeseekers! (See Table 4.3.)

As buyers, they'd spend $32,021 more over the seven years than they would as tenants ($114,761 − $82,740).

TABLE 4.3 Rent versus Buy Comparison at Seven Years

	PURCHASE	RENTAL
Total monthly costs	$ 98,448	$82,740
Plus cash up front	+16,313	+ 1,900
Amount invested	114,761	84,640
Less security refund	0	−1,900
Cash spent	$114,761	$82,740

Prophet, Prophet, Where's the Profit?

But how about all the money John and Mary would make as homeowners when they sell in seven years? Absent that crystal ball, Table 4.4 shows a few scenarios.

TABLE 4.4 **Apparent Homeowner's Profit at Seven Years**

	SELLING PRICE		
	$100,000	**$125,000**	**$150,000**
6% commission	$–6,000	$–7,500	$–9,000
Received at closing	94,000	117,500	141,000
Mortgage balance	–94,242	–94,242	–94,242
Cash after sale	($242)	$23,258	$46,758

If home values drop, the Homeseekers clearly would come out ahead as tenants. That's no surprise. But maybe home prices will go up over the next seven years. If they do, we're looking at some real profits for John and Mary, right? Not so fast! Take a look at Table 4.5.

TABLE 4.5 **Actual Homeowner's Profit at Seven Years**

	SELLING PRICE		
	$100,000	**$125,000**	**$150,000**
7-year home cost	$114,761	$114,761	$114,761
Less cash from sale	– (242)	–23,258	–46,758
Homeowner's cost	115,003	91,503	68,003
Renter's 7-year cost	–82,740	–82,740	–82,740
Apparent profit (loss)	(32,263)	(8,763)	14,737
Renter's earnings	–18,761	–18,761	–18,761
Real profit/loss	($51,024)	($27,524)	($4,024)

Bottom Line

Even if they could get $150,000 for the house, when you factor in the amount the Homeseekers could put aside as tenants, they'd still be out $4,024. But maybe they could get even more for the house. At $154,024 they'd break even, and anything above that would be a profit. Is it worth the risk? The effort? The paperwork?

Renters *can* end up wealthier than homeowners. And when home sales are slow, they can often find fabulous houses to rent—ones they could never afford to buy.

INVESTING IN THE DREAM

There's no law that says you must always do what's financially smart. Even if it might cost less to rent, you have the right to go for the Dream. There are lots of good reasons to own your house. Renters don't always come out ahead, and the right house can be a good investment. Owning a home gives you a place where you can pretty much do as you please, and one of the best benefits is the emotional comfort you might derive from a home that is *yours.*

If you do decide to buy your next home, you can make it a better financial investment by following these four simple rules.

1. Buy location—where lots of people want to be. But avoid the neighborhood's most expensive home, because improvements to it aren't likely to increase its market value.

2. Live in the house for a year before making major renovations. By then, you'll be so used to the little quirks that the changes you originally considered may seem less important and you'll be able to pocket the savings.

3. Don't go for the most expensive house the lender says you can afford. Why chain yourself to high monthly payments? If anything happens to your income stream, or if you have unexpectedly high expenses, your house will soon become your prison.

4. Pre-pay on your mortgage. After seven years of monthly payments, the Homeseekers would have paid the bank over $65,000 on their home loan, yet reduced the balance by only $7,000. (See Chapter 13.)

When You Think You're Ready to Find a House to Buy

Brace yourself. A laundry list of miscellaneous fees known as *closing costs* could immediately add 5% or more to your home's purchase price. What's worse, they won't buy you a nickel's worth of anything you'll ever get to enjoy. Ouch!

You'll pay for lawyers (yours and the bank's), engineering inspections as well as those for termites, water quality, and radon, a few months of up-front escrow payments to cover property taxes and homeowner's insurance premiums, application fees, appraisals, credit checks, title insurance, surveys, recording fees, and points.

Don't forget, if your down payment is less than 20%, you'll also shell out thousands of dollars over time to pay for private mortgage insurance (PMI), which protects the lender—not you!—in case you default.

With all these extra expenses, it's smart not to even look at homes that are out of your price range. Why fall in love with a dream that can only turn into a nightmare?

Instead, do something practical, like getting prequalified for a loan. It's helpful to know your borrowing capability *before* you fall in love with a house and feel pressured to make an offer. Before you seriously start shopping for a house, read "Buying the Right Mortgage—New or Refinanced" and "Seven Smart Steps to Cutting Closing Costs" in Chapter 13, to save thousands.

Speaking of "before," interview, negotiate fees with, and hire an attorney *before* you sign a binder. It's best to get advice before you make the mistakes.

You can't count on getting good advice from real estate salespeople and brokers. They generally work *for the sellers* (although some are now "buyer's" brokers). Seller's brokers are required to share anything useful you tell them with the sellers. In other words, when a seller's broker is showing you a house, don't think out loud such thoughts as, "I love this house and would be willing to go as high as $150,000, but let's start with an offer of $125,000."

Take the time to know the house and the neighborhood before you make an offer. Is there a nightclub on the next block? During the rainy season, will your living room be the perfect setting for the movie, *A River Runs Through It, Part 2?* Is there a homeowner's association that will be watching your every move?

Check the asking prices as well as the actual selling prices on similar homes in the neighborhood—before you begin negotiating the price. Many brokers will have a "comp" book that lists recent sales, giving both the asking and the final sale price. Table 4.6 shows you how to compare the two. Add up the columns, and then divide by the number of homes. If you find a 10% spread, for example, then offer even less. That way, you won't bear more than your fair share of the usual give and take.

For more good advice on home buying, we recommend *100 Questions Every First-Time Home Buyer Should Ask* by Ilyce R. Glink, *The Homebuyer's Survival Guide* by Kenneth W. Edwards, and *The Homebuyer's Kit* by Edith Lank. Keep your eyes out for current stories by these authors, as well as those by syndicated columnists Ellen James Martin, Pamela Reeves, and others.

TABLE 4.6 How Much Is that House Really Worth?

HOUSE NO.	ASKING PRICE	SELLING PRICE	% DISCOUNT
1	$100,000	$ 95,000	5%
2	97,500	92,000	6%
3	112,500	105,500	6%
4	109,900	97,500	11%
5	130,000	115,000	12%
6	126,500	110,000	13%
7	105,000	90,000	14%
Total/Average	$781,400	$705,000	10%

Cyberspace addresses that can help are www.realtor.com, www.ired.com, and www.inman.com.

Buyer Be Vigilant

Laura had lousy luck with her new house. A few years after moving in, a trench began to form along a back wall. Digging showed rotting wood where concrete blocks had been specified. Although the builder assured Laura that appropriate construction inspections had been made, the entire foundation had to be replaced. Then it turned out that the electrical system didn't meet code requirements, either, and it had to be upgraded. Final resolution is now in the courts.

To limit the likelihood that Laura's luck will be yours, watch what's going on during construction if you're buying a new house. Read the specifications, and insist on seeing building permits as well as certificates of compliance. When possible, be on-site during inspections and ask a lot of questions. And be sure to read *The Owner-Builder Book* by Mark and Elaine Smith. It'll save you a lot of money.

Before you buy any house, do some inspecting on your own. Using the photos, drawings, and checklists in *Your Home Inspection Guide*, by William L. Ventolo, you'll be able to find both obvious and hidden defects on your own.

And defects there will be, hidden by walls, floors, earth, shrubs, furniture, appliances, and snow—elements of a home's construction that can fail and may already have done so. Since you're not an experienced contractor, you'd never notice any of those problems. So before you agree to buy the castle, you decide to call in an inspector. Good move!

But you're new to town, so you ask the broker for a recommendation. Bad move! The last person you want to get advice from, when it comes to protecting your interests, is the seller's broker. Even if the broker's heart is in the right place, self-interest and the seller's best interest might mean you'd end up with the town's laziest inspector rather than the most thorough.

Get recommendations from your attorney, neighbors, disinterested brokers, contractors, or the local building inspector. Call a few inspectors and interview them—preferably in their office. What is their background, how long have they been doing inspections, how many have they done, could they give you the names of a few clients they inspected for a year ago? (That's long enough for most missed problems to have surfaced.) Call them up and get their feedback.

When the day comes, follow the inspector around and ask questions. Do your own thorough inspection both beforehand and at the same time. But be advised, the same potential defects that are hidden from your view will be just as hidden from the inspector's. And even inspectors who are members of the American Society of Home Inspectors (ASHI) will make only visual inspections, which are "not intended to be technically exhaustive." (Go to www.ashi.com or call 800-743-2744 for brochures on home inspections and referrals to members in your area.)

Our advice? Invest in your knowledge, as usual. While a pro can pick up things you might miss, if you're going to shell out the bucks to live in the house, you might as well understand how its various systems function. The more you know, the less you'll spend.

Down to Basics

The inspector will not check to make sure the building meets code or zoning requirements, will not look for ants, termites, or Mickey and his family. You won't find out from the inspector if the septic system is functioning properly, if the appliances work, if the hidden plumbing or electrical systems are in trouble, if the wall insulation is adequate, if hidden foundations are about to crumble. Unless you pay extra, you won't learn about radon or discover that the previous owner spilled a 55-gallon drum of poison in the cellar.

Although every other player in the home-buying game is licensed, few states license building inspectors. The only thing that may be keeping you from being an inspector yourself is business cards. While there are excellent people in the field, it's up to you to find one.

If you want to be extra prudent—and why shouldn't you be, you've got a lot at stake here—it's smart to call in plumbing, electrical, roofing, and general contractors. Most will look over the house for free, in the hope that you'll hire them to fix those things they'll carefully search to find, including code violations.

Specifically, ask for written disclosures from the broker and the seller. They're required to tell you of any problems that they know of with the house. If they don't, and you find out that they did know, you'll have some recourse.

Are we trying to scare you? You bet! Plug something into every outlet (the inspector will check a "representative number"), check every switch, light, faucet, drain, door, and room air conditioner. The inspector will tell you whether the heating system is working as of this minute, but not if it will adequately warm the living room. You better find out for yourself.

No matter who you hire to help you with the purchase of your home, you and your family are the ones who'll suffer if a mistake is made. It's well worth the investment of a chunk of your time to make sure your next home isn't a nightmare on Elm Street.

IS THERE A BROKER INSIDE YOU?

The opposite of buying is selling, and if you've done the first, you'll eventually do the second. Often, selling and buying happen at the same time, when you leave the home you now own for one you just bought. Like a buyer, a home seller needs to research the asking and selling prices of comparable homes before setting a price. You can certainly ask brokers for their opinions, but, as Marc's dad used to say, "Free advice is generally worth what you pay for it."

A professional appraisal will cost a few hundred dollars, but may help you sell faster and at a higher price. Of course, sitting in a broker's office and looking through comp books is a no-cost way to be your own appraiser. Your home will not sell for substantially more or less than others that are very similar.

A three-bedroom home may be worth less than a four-bedroom home, and a large lot may be worth more than a small one. In comparing, take these variations into account. But try to be objective and to find houses that are really comparable. Neither the lovely chartreuse you've painted the living room nor the walk-in closet you're so proud of having built will raise your home's value. But an additional bathroom might.

Having answered the big question about your home's market value, it's time for the next question, "Do I sell it myself or do I list it with a broker?"

There are two main advantages to selling it yourself:

- The commission you may save.
- The fact that brokers have hundreds of homes to sell and you have only one, which means you may put a lot more effort into making the sale.

The main disadvantage to selling on your own is that you'll have taken on a very intensive project. However, since this book is entitled *Invest in Yourself,* learning how to sell your home and then doing it could save you a substantial commission on this house and the next and the next.

While brokers will happily tell you what the standard commission is in the area, like most other home buying and selling costs, commissions are negotiable. Assuming you were to pay a 6% commission on a house that sold for $150,000, that would be $9,000. (*Note:* You probably won't save the full commission, because informed buyers will want to at least split the savings with you. If they can't also benefit, they'll figure that they might as well buy the house down the street and get whatever assistance they can from the broker.)

Even if you just save half the commission, $4,500, how much of your effort is that worth? And how many times will you move during your life? At $4,500 a pop, those savings can really add up. You can plow them into the next house you buy—and get a bigger house, more land, or a smaller mortgage. You could always use that money to pay off some more expensive debts, or you could sock it away in your college or retirement fund. Your choice. Any way, you win!

....

A SALES TECHNIQUE WE WISH WE HAD THOUGHT UP

The premise to *How to Sell Your Home in 5 Days* by Bill Effros is really quite simple. Rather than set a high price on your home and then wait (and wait and wait) while potential buyers wait (and wait and wait) for you to drop your price, you advertise a low price. A very low price.

Then you schedule an open house for a weekend and wait for the crowds to arrive. They will. After all, everyone loves a bargain. On Sunday night, you hold a phone auction. The high bidder gets to buy the house, and as the law of supply and demand says, and Bill has proven again and again, the final price will be the fair market value—well above your offering price, which will appear with the following three words in your classified ad: "or best offer."

Bill's method brings out everyone who's looking for your type of home. Unlike conventional sales methods, it brings them all out at the same time. Everybody wants what so many others want, and the magic takes place. There are steps you need to take before you place the ads (carefully explained in Bill's book), but your up-front effort should result in a fair price and quick sale.

· ·

Going to List with a Broker?

Be wary of brokers who assure you that your home is worth far more than what the comp book shows or than the quotes you got from the other brokers you interviewed. (You did interview more than one, didn't you?) In the end, the home won't sell for more than its fair market value. Putting too high a price on it will only slow down the sale—and perhaps cause you to become desperate enough to dramatically cut your price.

If you sign any agreement, make it for a short term, preferably for no more than 90 days. If it turns out your broker is more interested in getting listings than in selling or is asleep at the wheel, you want to be able to change horses. And if possible, sign an "Exclusive Agency" contract with the broker.

That gives you the right to sell the house on your own without paying a commission. An "Exclusive Right to Sell" contract means you pay a full commission even if your twin brother ultimately buys the house due solely to your brilliant sales pitch. (Won't he ever learn?)

One final condition: Insist that your home be immediately listed with the local Multiple Listing Service (MLS). The more brokers who know it's for sale, the better your chances of selling. The listing broker will have to split the commission should a different broker bring the buyer. That makes some brokers slow to add properties to the MLS, because they'd like to try for the whole commission. You can't blame them for trying—but you can stop them from delaying.

And you can help sell the house. First of all, clean it up! Buyers have an imagination and can see through some problems, but chipped paint, clutter, 2-foot-high grass, ripped carpeting, fist-sized holes in closet doors, dirty bathrooms, and smelly kitchens all point to haphazard care—and don't instill confidence.

If the roof leaks, either fix it or be honest about it from the beginning. Otherwise, you'll lose the sale before the closing and may have to start all over. You may even be sued later. It pays to be honest.

INSURING YOUR HOME

Fire, flood, earthquakes, hurricanes, falling trees, and broken water pipes are just a few of the villains that might damage or destroy your home and its contents. Then there are the thieves waiting for an opportunity to steal your valuables.

Whether you're an owner or a renter, you really need to take a deep breath and create a detailed, personal inventory of your possessions. It will help you figure out how much coverage you need. Then down the road, should you ever file a claim, you'll have the documentation at hand.

....

RENTER ALERT!

Your landlord's policy won't protect your possessions against loss or damage. And it won't protect you against personal liability if, say, your babysitter trips on the rug and sues you. The money-saving tips we offer here will also help you find the best deal on a renter's policy.

....

Comparison shop! The money you save will be your own. Policies are not identical. Costs, coverage, and conditions can vary, as can the financial stability of the insurer.

Basic policies don't cover earthquakes, floods, or nuclear attacks. If you live in a floodplain, call the National Flood Insurance Program (800-638-6620). It could happen to you! And if you live in California, you're going to need earthquake coverage. It's going to cost you a pretty penny, and the deductible will be high.

Knowledge is money in the bank, so don't wait until you're in a panic the day before a closing to call an insurance broker. Not only may you pay too much, you may find that you're not adequately covered when you do put in a claim.

Get quotes for the replacement value of your home and its contents, with both a $500 and a $1,000 deductible, as well as the more typical $250. The higher deductibles could shave 10% to 25% off your premium, year after year.

Check with the agent who wrote your car insurance. Are you eligible for a price reduction because you're a long-time customer bringing in more business? Similarly, ask other agents if you'd be eligible for a multiple-policy discount, if you let them write both your home and car insurance. You could save about 10%.

Put smoke alarms on every floor, and make sure the agent knows about them. In addition to maybe saving a life, they'll pay for themselves in a year or two with the 2% or so that they'll save you on premiums.

Ask if there are other safety features that could save you money on the policy—for example, burglar alarms. Was your home built with fire-resistant materials? Is yours a nonsmoking household? In other words, ask for all possible discounts . . . and then a few more. Another example: Insurance on a new house built with state-of-the-art construction should cost less. And some companies offer discounts to retirees.

You may want to pay more for extra "floater" coverage on valuables such as jewelry—if they're worth more than the standard policy limits. But if you normally keep some of your gems in a safe-deposit box, be sure to ask for a break on the cost of the floater.

The biggest favor you can do for yourself is to read *Smarter Insurance Solutions* by Janet Bamford before you take out a new policy or renew an existing one. Then, before you sign on the dotted line, take the policy home and compare what it says to what you thought you were getting . . . with Bamford's book by your side. By the way, her book also gives detailed advice for auto, life, health, disability, and long-term health care.

Second best: For a free copy of *Insurance for Your Household and Personal Possessions: Deciding How Much You Need,* call the National Insurance Consumer Helpline (800-942-4242).

. . . .

DO YOU NEED INSURANCE FOR YOUR KID'S STUFF AT COLLEGE?

Your policy will probably cover your children and their possessions while they're living in a dorm, and some policies will also cover a student who lives off campus during the school year but at home during the summer. It's a good idea to double-check. If your student has anything of value, once he or she has an apartment, it's time to get a renter's policy.

. . . .

Check the health of your insurance company. A trip to the library will get you the latest ratings. See *Best's Insurance Reports, Weiss Ratings Insurance Safety Directory,* or go to www.inswebpro.com/carriers/stdpoor.

CUTTING YOUR PROPERTY TAXES

You wouldn't dream of letting the IRS figure how much income tax you owe. . . . So why assume that your property tax bill is correct without giving it a once-over?

—ELIZABETH RAZZI, *Kiplinger's Personal Finance Magazine*

Tax assessors, being human and hassled, make mistakes. Doesn't everyone? But their mistakes can cost you money, year after year, for as long as you own your house. Therefore, making sure they are correct is an investment of your time that may cut your homeowning costs for years to come.

1. Visit the tax assessor's office and request a copy of your assessment.

2. Go over it in detail. Note any discrepancies—especially major ones: For example, it says you have three bathrooms, not two, or your house is listed as 3,500 square feet but it's closer to 2,500.

3. If you find mistakes, speak to the assessor and request that they be corrected. If there's a local grievance process to go through, ask for the procedure.

4. If there are no mistakes, or they are in your favor, you still want to make sure your assessment is no higher than those of comparable homes. Find a few through the comp book at a broker's office. You can double-check the assessment books and/or tax records to verify what they pay. If it's less than you do, you have a reason to appeal for a lower assessment. (It may pay to hire a professional appraiser.)

You Can Fight City Hall

"Nationwide, fewer than 2% of all property assessments are challenged. In the vast majority of cases, those who do appeal get their taxes cut. So it's well worth the effort," advises Steve Carlson,* author of *Your Low–Tax Dream House*, which includes descriptions of the property tax systems in every state, an excellent review of the assessment process, and ways to cut your real estate taxes.

Good luck!

---

* In addition to being an expert on property taxes, Steve puts out a wonderful catalog of books published by small presses on subjects ranging from abuse and recovery to spirituality and social issues. Visit www2.upperaccess.com or call 800-356-9315.

TABLE 5.1 How Far Will It Go?
(Monthly Withdrawals from Various Nest Eggs)

NEST EGG	YEARS	NET INTEREST RATE					
		2%	3%	4%	5%	6%	7%
$ 25,000	10	230	241	253	265	278	290
	20	126	139	152	165	179	194
	30	92	105	119	134	150	166
	40	76	90	104	121	138	155
$ 50,000	10	460	483	506	530	555	581
	20	253	277	303	330	358	388
	30	185	211	239	268	300	333
	40	151	179	209	241	275	311
$ 100,000	10	920	966	1,012	1,061	1,110	1,161
	20	506	555	606	660	716	775
	30	370	422	477	537	600	665
	40	303	358	418	482	550	621
$ 150,000	10	1,380	1,448	1,519	1,591	1,665	1,742
	20	759	832	909	990	1,075	1,163
	30	554	632	716	805	899	998
	40	454	537	627	723	825	932
$ 200,000	10	1,840	1,931	2,025	2,121	2,220	2,322
	20	1,012	1,109	1,212	1,320	1,433	1,551
	30	739	843	955	1,074	1,199	1,331
	40	606	716	836	964	1,100	1,243
$ 250,000	10	2,300	2,414	2,531	2,652	2,776	2,903
	20	1,265	1,387	1,515	1,650	1,791	1,938
	30	924	1,054	1,194	1,342	1,499	1,663
	40	757	895	1,045	1,206	1,376	1,554
$ 300,000	10	2,760	2,897	3,037	3,182	3,331	3,483
	20	1,518	1,664	1,818	1,980	2,149	2,326
	30	1,109	1,265	1,432	1,610	1,799	1,996
	40	908	1,074	1,254	1,447	1,651	1,864

CHAPTER 5

How Much Is Enough?

○ Why you don't have to be a millionaire to retire well

○ Overlooked investments that can make a stellar retirement portfolio

○ How to know when enough is enough

○ Wills, estate plans, insurance, and other dreaded details

. . . money can't buy the things that count most: good health, a close family, warm friendships and authentic interests. And all the fancy toys it can buy and exotic areas it can take you to are not likely to be an adequate substitute.

RALPH WARNER, *Get a Life: You Don't Need a Million to Retire Well*

There came a time when Marc's parents took a well-deserved fantasy vacation in the Philippines. They stayed with extremely wealthy friends, who threw gala banquets, chartered boat trips, assigned them personal maids—his mother even had a seamstress at her beck and call. "They treated me like a queen," Mom often recalled.

Like most vacations, that one drew too quickly to a close. It was not a happy departing. They were high over the Pacific, having left paradise for a return to their high-pressure business, when Dad turned to Mom and wondered, "How much do we need? When is enough enough?!"

It took a few months, but they found a buyer for the business, sold out, and retired. Enough was enough.

Marc was a bit younger, about 30, when he and his brother Sam followed their parent's lead and sold their construction business. While they had achieved a level of success they could be proud of, all the future held was making more money, building more shopping centers, and experiencing more stress. The brothers knew when enough was enough, and changed course. Sam retired to North Carolina a few years later, and Marc semiretired to a simpler and far more satisfying life as a consumer advocate—or as he likes to put it, "a non-consuming advocate."

QUESTION: How will you know when you've had enough—and have enough?

ANSWER: When you no longer enjoy your work, and you've reached the point where, having taken control of your finances and your life, you're living on less than you earn. Your time will truly be your own—if you plan it right.

YOU DON'T NEED TO BE OLD OR A MILLIONAIRE TO RETIRE

Between the stories you read, the experts you hear on radio or see on TV, and all of the ads from investment advisors, it's not surprising that retirement for many is feared rather than happily anticipated.

Relax. Get a grip. You're not going to spend the last 40 years or more of your life eating cat food. Chances are, you're already doing a lot more to save for retirement than you realize, and by the time you've finished *Invest in Yourself*, you'll be saving tens of thousands of dollars that most Americans waste on bank interest. You'll also be cutting your expenses, cultivating a simple lifestyle, and creating new sources of income.

Not to Worry

When people think about retiring, they usually start with the question, "Can we afford it?" By itself, money in the bank won't make for a wonderful retirement, but it can make things a lot easier. If you come away from this book with nothing else, we hope it'll be the realization that you *can* accumulate a lot more cash for your golden years than you ever thought possible—and that you'll need less than you expected.

For starters, even though you've almost certainly been paying into Social Security for years, your confidence in its future probably depends a lot on your age. Although you may not be able to collect benefits as soon as you'd like, chances are it *will* provide a base for your retirement. If

you've built up your nest egg and learned to live on less, th[...] est Social Security check will be quite helpful.

Contact the Social Security Administration (800-772-12[...] gov) to request your "Personal Earnings and Benefit Estima[...] Fill it out, return it, and in a month or so, you'll get an est[...] future benefits.

So, How Much Is Enough?

The short answer is, "No one knows for sure." But we've com[...] easy way for you to get a handle on how far beyond Social S[...] other assets might take you. Allow us to introduce you to Ta[...] supersimple approach to retirement math. Imagine for the m[...] you're about to retire a millionaire (hey, you never know), wh[...] ments will be earning 9%, while inflation chugs along at 3%.[...]

To make your calculations a lot easier, we're going to facto[...] tion, by using what we call the "Net Interest Rate"—which is[...] ence between what your money earns and inflation. You'll be a[...] at the future purchasing power of possible nest eggs in differe[...] ios, as if every buck will buy as much bread tomorrow or decad[...] future as it does the day you retire. In our example, the Net Int[...] equals 6%—your 9% earnings minus the 3% rate that inflation[...] averaging over the last 70 years.

Since we wish you only the best, let's assume you'll have 40 w[...] years, rocking on your porch. Now look down the nest egg co[...] Table 5.1 to $1 million. Find 40 years, and follow it over to the[...] umn. You'll discover that your monthly "allowance" will be[...] Because of how we designed the chart, assuming the Net Intere[...] averages out to be 6%, that $5,502 will have the same purchasing[...] in your fortieth year of retirement as it does in your first.

Keep in mind that once you get that last check (which may b[...] smaller than the others), your pot will be empty. Of course, that [...] after 40 years of living quite well, and along the way, you'll probabl[...] created new income streams.

FOCUS YOUR CRYSTAL BALL

Now it's time to ask yourself five key questions:

1. *How much will you need?* Most experts say you'll need about 70[...] whatever you're earning right before you retire. We hope you'll get by[...] less. But there'll be unexpected expenses and higher taxes. So think ab[...]

TABLE 5.1 (Continued)

NEST EGG	YEARS	NET INTEREST RATE					
		2%	3%	4%	5%	6%	7%
$ 350,000	10	3,220	3,380	3,544	3,712	3,886	4,064
	20	1,771	1,941	2,121	2,310	2,508	2,714
	30	1,294	1,476	1,671	1,879	2,098	2,329
	40	1,060	1,253	1,463	1,688	1,926	2,175
$ 400,000	10	3,681	3,862	4,050	4,243	4,441	4,644
	20	2,024	2,218	2,424	2,640	2,866	3,101
	30	1,478	1,686	1,910	2,147	2,398	2,661
	40	1,211	1,432	1,672	1,929	2,201	2,486
$ 450,000	10	4,141	4,345	4,556	4,773	4,996	5,225
	20	2,276	2,496	2,727	2,970	3,224	3,489
	30	1,663	1,897	2,148	2,416	2,698	2,994
	40	1,363	1,611	1,881	2,170	2,476	2,796
$ 500,000	10	4,601	4,828	5,062	5,303	5,551	5,805
	20	2,529	2,773	3,030	3,300	3,582	3,877
	30	1,848	2,108	2,387	2,684	2,998	3,327
	40	1,514	1,790	2,090	2,411	2,751	3,107
$ 750,000	10	6,901	7,242	7,593	7,955	8,327	8,708
	20	3,794	4,159	4,545	4,950	5,373	5,815
	30	2,772	3,162	3,581	4,026	4,497	4,990
	40	2,271	2,685	3,135	3,616	4,127	4,661
$1,000,000	10	9,201	9,656	10,125	10,607	11,102	11,611
	20	5,059	5,546	6,060	6,600	7,164	7,753
	30	3,696	4,216	4,774	5,368	5,996	6,653
	40	3,028	3,580	4,179	4,822	5,502	6,214

* Note: These numbers were calculated with *The Banker's Secret Software* (see page 327)

how much you need to live on now. (Omit major bills you'll have paid by the time you've retired, such as college tuition and mortgage payments.)

For example, let's consider the Goodlives, whose living expenses are modest. They expect to have a home business for many years to come (to supplement their income while it keeps their taxes low). They'd like to budget the equivalent of today's $3,500 a month for their retirement, or $42,000 a year, and expect that amount to cover taxes as well as living expenses.

The more you withdraw from your nest egg, the bigger your tax bite will be. Therefore, you may want to pad your living expenses by 25% or more to cover those pesky taxes, as you consider the next question.

2. *How long will you live?* Be sure to be optimistic in answering this one! It's much better to run out of breath with something still in the till than it is to run out of money while the old heart's still pumping. The Goodlives' goal is to fund a 30-year retirement. Et tu?

3. *How much interest will your money earn?* Since there's no sure way to predict the nation's future economic condition, be conservative. Let's assume the Goodlives' investments will earn 8%.

4. *How will inflation eat away at your purchasing power?* Inflation will weaken every dollar that you squirrel away, and then every dollar you withdraw. Assuming inflation will average 3%—that means the Goodlives' net interest rate is 5% (8% interest minus 3% inflation).

5. *How much will you be collecting from Social Security, and at what age will you begin?* Between them, the Goodlives expect to see about $2,000 a month, starting at age 65. That means they'll have to come up with about another $1,500 a month.

Now back to Table 5.1. Look down the 5% column until you find $1,500 (or more) opposite 30 years. You'll see that with a $300,000 nest egg, the Goodlives will be able to withdraw the future equivalent of today's $1,610 every month until they're 95 years old.

What if the Goodlives assets total only $125,000 by the time they retire? How much income would that give them a month, assuming a Net Interest Rate of 5% and 30 years of retired living? You won't find $125,000 on the chart. What can you do?

Since $25,000 plus $100,000 equals $125,000, look at the 5% column—again for 30 years. Add the $134 from the $25,000 nest egg to the $537 from the $100,000 one. They'd be able to withdraw $671 a month ($134 + $537). Because that amount of money won't cover their anticipated expenses, "Plan B" would have to go into effect.

The Goodlives could voluntarily live on even less, and/or gear up to earn more during their retirement years. Or they could put off retirement for awhile—to sock away some more and to increase their take from Social Security.

Now assume their Net Interest Rate turns out to be 6% and they anticipate needing their $125,000 to carry them for only 20 years. By then, a rich elderly aunt will have certainly met her maker, and they're her only living kin. After all, a whopping $8 trillion will be inherited from today's seniors. That $125,000 would yield $895 a month ($179 + $716) for the 20 years.

YOU BE THE BANKER

Now it's time for you to look at some alternative scenarios. For example, say you accumulate $200,000 and want it to last 30 years. How much would that yield if your Net Interest Rate is 4%? The answer is $955 a month.

Take another gander at the numbers we've been talking about: $955 a month for 30 years at 4%. Don't they sound just like mortgage numbers? That's exactly what they are! (And don't you wish you could get one at 4%?!)

Retirement math works just like a mortgage—except *you* get to be the bank. *You* collect the compound interest. For example, assume the Good-lives stash $300,000 and withdraw $1,610, twelve times a year for 30 years. That adds up to $579,600, or $279,600 more than they'd socked away. Ah, the power of compound interest. How nice to be the lucky beneficiary for a change!

To ponder nest eggs that don't appear on the chart, *The Banker's Secret Loan Software* will make it easy for you to ask as many what-if questions as you want about your future finances. (See page 327.)

Filling in the Gap

If your nest egg, combined with your Social Security or pension checks, isn't going to fund the kind of lifestyle you'd like in retirement, you have choices. One is to create a small, part-time business that will help you fill in the gap. Chapter 8 explains how to turn a hobby, passion, skill, or just an interest into cash.

Another option is to downsize your lifestyle. Learning to live comfortably on less can be rewarding in more ways than one. If you treat it as a challenge, you may tap some creative skills you didn't even know you had. And you'll feel a great deal more freedom as you discover that you *do* have options. Turn to Secret IV for lots of penny-pinching tips.

And of course, you can fill in that gap by tapping into your largest asset: your house. Hopefully, you'll have burned your mortgage long before you run for the 8:04 that last time, as we'll suggest in Chapter 13. It's one of the best moves you can make in planning for your retirement. Just think of all those years after you retire when you won't have to come up with the money to meet mortgage payments. At $734 a month on a typical $100,000, 30-year home loan—over $8,800 a year—it's a fool-proof way to cut your costs considerably.

The Younger You Are, the More You'll Need

Okay. So now you know how far you could get on your nest egg . . . *if* you were to retire today, or if you already have that nest egg invested to earn at least enough to cover inflation. But what if you're 10, 20, or even 50 years away from the mythical gold watch, and your money tree hasn't yet borne fruit? You'll need to put aside more than Table 5.1 shows. How much more? See Table 5.2.

Let's say that after you take into account Social Security, your 401(k), and the equity in your home, you'll still be $100,000 shy (in today's buying power) of what you want in your nest egg when you retire in 25 years. According to Table 5.2, you'll need to put aside another $209,378.

Table 5.3 will show you how much to squirrel away each month to meet your goal. Say you expect an annual return of 7.5% on your invest-

Table 5.2 The Future Value of Money
Based on 3% Annual Inflation

TODAY'S VALUE	YOU'LL NEED THIS MUCH IF YOU'RE RETIRING IN:						
	1 YEAR	3 YEARS	5 YEARS	10 YEARS	20 YEARS	25 YEARS	50 YEARS
$ 25,000	25,750	27,318	28,982	33,598	45,153	52,344	109,598
50,000	51,500	54,636	57,964	67,196	90,306	104,689	219,195
100,000	103,000	109,273	115,927	134,392	180,611	**209,378**	438,391
150,000	154,500	163,909	173,891	201,587	270,917	314,067	657,586
200,000	206,000	218,545	231,855	268,783	361,222	418,756	876,781
250,000	257,500	273,182	289,819	335,979	451,528	523,444	1,095,977
300,000	309,000	327,818	347,782	403,175	541,833	628,133	1,315,172
350,000	360,500	382,454	405,746	470,371	632,139	732,822	1,534,367
400,000	412,000	437,091	463,710	537,567	722,444	837,511	1,753,562
450,000	463,500	491,727	521,673	604,762	812,750	942,200	1,972,758
500,000	515,000	546,364	579,637	671,958	903,056	1,046,889	2,191,953
750,000	772,500	819,545	869,456	1,007,937	1,354,583	1,570,333	3,287,930
1,000,000	1,030,000	1,092,727	1,159,274	1,343,916	1,806,111	2,093,778	4,383,906

TABLE 5.3 **Monthly Deposit Needed to Create a $100,000 Nest Egg**

YEARS TO RETIREMENT	INTEREST RATE			
	5%	7.5%	10%	12.5%
1	$8,144	$8,051	$7,958	$7,867
3	2,580	2,486	2,393	2,304
5	1,470	1,379	1,291	1,208
10	644	562	488	422
20	243	181	132	94
25	168	**114**	75	49
50	37	15	6	2

ments, you'll need to put aside 2 × $114 every month for the next 25 years. You can do it!

Reverse Mortgages: How to Sell Your House and Keep It

If you're a homeowner who actually owns your home, you also have a nice piece of retirement income stashed in the roof over your head. You can sell, move into a less expensive house, and pocket the difference. Or once you and any co-borrowers have both turned 62, you can take out a reverse mortgage and stay right where you are.

Imagine going to a closing and instead of handing over checks, you get them. Talk about being the banker! And you don't have to sell your house to do it. Sort of. Here are the basic facts.

A reverse mortgage allows an older homeowner who owns a house free and clear (or close to it) to borrow against its equity. Just like a regular, old-fashioned mortgage, the loan gives the bank a lien on your home in exchange for money. You can get a lump sum up front, receive monthly payments for a fixed term or for as long as you live in your home, or take a line of credit to draw on when needed. You can also go for a combo package. *Example:* An 80-year-old homeowner who qualifies for a $125,000 loan could get a $10,000 line of credit and monthly payments of $489. For other scenarios, go to www.reverse.org.

The house doesn't have to be sold, and the loan proceeds don't have to be repaid—until the borrower no longer occupies the house—either because of a permanent move on this earthly plane, or on to another. If at that time the loan is for more than the sale price, the lender eats the loss. Anything left over, on the other hand, would go to the borrower's heirs.

There are so many conditions, costs, and what-ifs attached to these relatively recent creations that the Feds require lenders to send potential borrowers to a counseling session given by a government or nonprofit organization. You should be able to get a list of approved counseling agencies in your area from a lender, your local office for the aging, or the HUD Housing Counselor referral line at 800-569-4287.

If you're considering a reverse mortgage, you'd be very wise to have someone accompany you to the session (or for you to accompany your parent) where reverse mortgages will be explained and other alternatives explored. For example, some local governments offer low-cost, deferred-payment loans to help make home repairs and improvements for seniors. Property tax abatements may also be available. Perhaps the home can be sold to a child, niece, or on the open market with an option for a life tenancy.

While the counseling session can give a good basic understanding, the details and options are so complicated that most people will require far more information and perhaps expert help (say, from an accountant) to assess the alternatives. Before signing up for a reverse mortgage, it would be prudent to research other options.

It also pays to talk over the matter with the likely heirs. One set of siblings we know decided to each kick in a set amount (about $100 a month) to help Mom out. They concluded that would be easier—and cheaper—than going the reverse mortgage route.

Warning: Reverse mortgages carry very high up-front fees. If the loan is held for only a few years, its cost can be extremely high. And because the interest compounds in the bank's favor, the younger you are, the less you'll get. For example, HUD estimates that a 65-year-old can borrow up to 26% of a home's value, and a 75-year-old can borrow up to 39%, while an 85-year-old can get up to 56%.

But reverse mortgages may turn out to be a blessing for those whose home is their biggest, and perhaps only, significant asset, who need additional cash for living expenses, and who don't need to leave the home to heirs. For more information, go to www.aarp.org/hecc/home.html or write to AARP Home Equity Information Center, 601 E. Street, NW, Washington, DC 20049, and request a free copy of its *Home Equity Conversion Kit. Reverse Mortgages for Beginners* by Ken Scholen is also helpful.

IT'S NOT JUST ABOUT MONEY

Your retirement is going to be most enjoyable if you're in good health, stretching your mind and your horizons, spending time with people you care about, and doing things you enjoy.

If you're working long hours now trying to accumulate more "stuff" or more money at the expense of family, friendships, and your health, it's unlikely you'll be able to buy them back later on. So stop looking at preparing for a secure retirement as just stashing away as much money as possible. Diversify your retirement portfolio by building your investments now in people, your health, and all the other things that truly make up the good life.

Research has shown that both exercise and social contact contribute to longevity and can significantly improve your quality of life. And as with all investments, the sooner you begin, the more you'll be worth. So take a walk, or better yet, organize a walking club. Volunteer for causes for which you have a passion. Start a small business. Challenge yourself by learning something you've always been curious about, whether it's origami or flying down the slopes on a snowboard with the grandkids. Disconnect the tube and reconnect with those you've been too busy to spend time with.

Curl up with a copy of *Get a Life: You Don't Need a Million to Retire Well* by Ralph Warner, *Kiplinger's 12 Steps to a Worry-Free Retirement* by Daniel Kehrer, and *100 Best Retirement Businesses* by Lisa Angowski Rogak. Browse through some magazines geared to the over-50 crowd, like *Modern Maturity* and *New Choices*. And send self-addressed stamped envelopes for sample copies of these two newsletters: *Kiplinger's Retirement Report*, 1729 H Street, NW, Washington, DC 20006-3938; and *Spectrum Tidbits*, 43430 East Florida Avenue, Suite F-295, Hemet, CA 92544.

BEAT THE DEADLINE

Living is a rather unpredictable experience. We can work hard, raise a family, put aside some money, plan for the future—and still have the rug pulled out from under us.

Take Peg and John Willess, childhood sweethearts, who have been married for 14 years. At 35, Peg's a reporter for a great metropolitan daily, and at 37, John's a high school science teacher. They have two wonderful children, a springer spaniel, and the requisite middle-class mortgage, credit card bills, and a couple of aging cars.

Peg and John kept meaning to get together with a lawyer friend to sign wills. The subject came up just last night over dinner, during their monthly night out for a meal and a movie. Unfortunately, a drunk driver made it their last supper. John was killed instantly. Peg made it to the hospital, but never had a chance. No one could believe it, especially the kids.

It took two years to untangle the Willess's estate. There was far more grief than anyone needed or deserved. The kids ended up being separated for most of the next two years. Relatives who were once close are now bitter enemies. It was crazy—but crazy things happen under these circumstances.

Lawyers, court-appointed guardians, accountants, a judge—everyone got into the act, eating up much of what Peg and John had accumulated. The springer spaniel was taken in by a neighbor, but everyone else would have been much better off if Peg and John had just taken a few hours to plan their estate and put those plans into legalese.

The Willesses, as you've no doubt guessed, are fictitious. While they've never existed, their sad story is repeated every day. Our goal is to help you have many, satisfying "next" lives in this world, before you're recruited for the next. Knowing that you've planned for the end can ease your burden in the present. Hence the following suggestions for planning a fine finale—one in which all of your last wishes are honored. Taking control of your finances shouldn't end when you do. Here's what to do:

- First, cover the basics. Make sure your family will have enough ready cash available for at least a few months of living expenses.

- Get your papers in order. Sooner or later, somebody will have to do it. Make it easy on your family by taking care of it now. Search out all your important records. Put together a chart showing what you have and where everything can be found. (Yeah, it's boring. Do it anyway! It'd be so much harder for anyone else.)

- Make sure that your will, insurance policies, funeral preferences, and living will (if you want no heroics) can be easily located when needed. (They should *not* be in a safe-deposit box!)

- Then add up your assets and liabilities. Twice. Once for everything you currently own and owe. Then a second time to include any pension money or insurance proceeds that your family would receive upon your demise.

- *Important:* We know that this is not a light and lively subject, but dying may be the most expensive thing you ever do! It's well worth the time and money to make sure you make the most of what you've earned and own. While, like any good citizen, you and your heirs ought to pay your fair share, you surely don't want your family to pay a penny more in state or federal estate taxes than is required. Right?

- So do your homework. The more estate law basics you know, the more your heirs will receive. No, you don't have to enroll in Harvard Law School. But you do want to learn the current state of the estate statutes in your state. It's a task that can be done simply—if you're willing to invest the time.

Go to the library and look over the assortment of plan-your-estate-type books you find there. You want something that's current and that you'll actually read. We're partial to *Plan Your Estate* by Denis Clifford and Cora Jordan and *The Five-Minute Lawyer's Guide to Estate Planning* by Michael Allan Cane.

For a very complete treatment of probate, trusts, wills, insurance as an estate planning vehicle, and long-term-care insurance, go to CPA Michael Palermo's "Crash Course in Wills & Trusts" on the Net at www.mtpalermo. com.

Another easy way to learn about estate planning is to attend one or more of the free introductory seminars that lawyers offer quite regularly these days. Look for ads about them in the newspaper. While we don't recommend that you commit to working with that lawyer (at least until you've asked around and interviewed a few others), it's a cheap way to learn.

While every state makes—and changes—its own rules, there are some key questions that you'll want answered, wherever you live: Is yours a community property state? What will state taxes cost your estate, if anything? How much of your money are your spouse and children automatically entitled to inherit?

You also want to think about what will happen if you die first. Second? What if you go together? Do you need more insurance to pay off the house, cover college, pay for a funeral? You need to decide if your assets should be owned individually, jointly, or in trust. How large can an estate be in your state without going through probate (costly court rituals)?

Watch out! If your individual estate is likely to be over $625,000 (in 1998), there could be estate taxes of 37% to 55% due on the excess. (These limits will be bumped up to $650,000 in 1999, $675,000 in 2000, $700,000 in 2002, $850,000 in 2004, $950,000 in 2005, and $1 million in 2006.) If your estate is likely to exceed these limits, learn the rules about how you can cut taxes by:

- Giving some money away while you're among the living.
- Paying a child's or grandchild's college and/or medical expenses.
- Setting up an irrevocable trust. (Revocable trusts are to avoid probate, not to save on taxes.)

Warning: If you're married and rich when you die, you can pass on an unlimited amount to your spouse, and no estate taxes will be due. However, when he or she goes, anything over the limit at that time will be taxed. For a couple to avoid taxes on a large estate, the first to die has to have left the limit to others or set up a trust. It's complicated. We hope you'll have enough money to worry about it!

....

IS A REVOCABLE TRUST FOR YOU?

After 18 years in court, Marilyn Monroe's heirs received a bit over $100,000, while $1.5 million was devoured by *probate*, the arcane process of deciding, through the courts, who inherits what.

Say your lawyer charges 2.5% for handling the estate. Assuming you've had a 40-year career, 2.5% of what you've accumulated represents the rewards of a whole year's worth of your working life.

Don't want to spend a year working to pay for some lawyer? If you'd rather see more of the fruit of your labor go to your family, consider a *revocable* (or *living*) *trust.* Here are the pros and cons.

Trust Advantages

- Avoids probate, saves time, money, and hassle. A trust is especially useful if you have property in more than one state.
- The courts won't freeze your assets for months, maybe years.
- You retain complete control of your property while you're alive.
- Your trust can be changed or terminated at any time.
- You can structure your trust to allow for uninterrupted business or asset management during illness or incapacity.
- Your privacy will be protected. The bequests in trusts aren't public record, while the probate process is. (That's why everyone knows the details of Marilyn's estate problems.)

Trust Disadvantages

- Setting up a trust can be expensive and complicated.
- Your estate could still end up in probate if you fail to register a pricey asset or two in the trust's name.

Trust Misconceptions

- Revocable trusts don't replace a will.
- Revocable trusts don't avoid taxes.

If you'd like to create your own revocable trust, get the *Living Trust Maker Software* from Nolo Press.*

....

Note: As with everything else, be it life insurance or impulse purchases, it's easy to buy more estate planning than you need. If you only have a few bucks and no offspring, a joint checking account with your mate or heir is all you'll need to avoid probate.

DECISION TIME: WHAT WILL YOU WILL?

Your spouse will probably be entitled to somewhere between one-third and one-half of your estate. Do you want to leave more to your mate? What part of the rock do you want each child to get, and what limits, if any, do you want placed on their use of that money?

Who else do you want to reward—or shock? Think in percentages to avoid this costly error: A rich widow left $50,000 to her pooch and the rest to her three children. A market crash cut her worth to $51,000, leaving her kids $1,000 to split—less expenses. Had the dog been willed, say, 25%, the children would have each received $12,750, the same as Fido.

It's an impossible task, but someone has to do it: The job in question is "executor." You need to pick someone to pay your debts, distribute your assets, and referee any disputes that may arise. Do you prefer a friend, a relative, a bank, or an attorney?

If you and your spouse should die together, who do you want to raise your children? Would that guardian also be good at tending to money matters until the kids come of age? If not, pick someone else to be the money manager. (In fact, there might be a benefit to separating these tasks—to provide some checks and balances.) Then *ask!* Not everyone will be happy, or competent, in these roles.

Because technicalities can end up being costly and upsetting to those you love most, finding the right estate planner for you (once you're

---

* *Note:* Nolo Press books and software are frequently mentioned in this book because they're terrific, having been researched and written by lawyers who want to save you and us from being at the mercy of lawyers. To request a free copy of the informative *Nolo News* write to Nolo Press, 950 Parker Street, Berkeley, CA 94710, or go to www.nolo.com.

informed enough to really benefit from it) is worth your time and money. Begin by asking friends and relatives who have worked with a lawyer in settling an estate. Ideally, you want an attorney who devotes at least half of his or her practice to estate planning. Interview several (many won't charge for an initial consultation), then select the best fit. Don't select based solely on fees.

Important: Whether or not you use any other estate planning devices, you *need* a will. Even if your assets won't amount to much, don't you want to decide who gets what? Otherwise, a judge will divvy things up based on the laws in your state. The process itself might be costly, the taxes high, and your kids left in the lurch.

With a will, the person you select will raise your children, and you'll be able to dictate the conditions that will apply to any money you leave for them. With a will, you can protect your mate (spouse or live-in partner), and limit potential conflicts among everyone else who wants or expects some of what you're leaving.

You can certainly write your own will with help from *Nolo's Simple Will Book* or *WillMaker Software*. Or check out the many on-line resources: A good central source is at www.ca-probate.com/links.htm.

If you do write your own will, we think it's still well worth the money and the peace of mind it'll bring you to have a reputable lawyer look it over. You want to be certain that all the i's are properly dotted and the t's properly crossed—or your will might not be valid.

If a lawyer is going to draft the will, bring along a list of what you own and owe—and what you want to happen. The better organized you are, the less the lawyer should cost.

....

AND NOW IT'S TIME FOR A TREASURE HUNT!

Bite the old bullet and clean out your basement, garage, attic, and closets. Don't make your heirs sort through a lifetime of junk. Treasures, on the other hand, are a comfort. Why not relieve yourself of the clutter and upkeep and share some now? You'll be giving a gift to yourself as well as to the recipient.

....

YOU BET YOUR LIFE

When you take out home or auto insurance, you're betting that you'll have a loss you couldn't afford to recover from, such as a major theft or serious fire. On the other side, an insurance company is betting you won't suffer a major loss—at least not this year!

With life insurance, the gamble is similar. You're betting that you'll die before the policy year ends, and the insurer is betting that you won't. Insurance is the one bet you never want to win! To avoid winning, lock your car doors, put smoke detectors in your house, and treat your body with respect.

If, despite prudent precautions, your car is destroyed or your home burns to the ground, insurance money will help to replace the loss. Death, on the other hand, is irreparable.

It would be silly to pay for homeowner's insurance if you didn't have a home. It is equally silly to pay for life insurance if you don't have a beneficiary whose lifestyle would suffer because of the loss of your income. There are some instances where the wealthy among us might want a life insurance policy as a "tax dodge." But by and large, you don't need life insurance if:

- You're single with no one counting on you to make ends meet.
- You have no children or others who are dependent on you.
- Your elderly parents have adequate money for their own needs.
- Your life partner earns more than enough to be self-supporting.
- You already have enough money socked away.

If you fit one of these categories, skip ahead, and return here only if your situation changes. Otherwise, let's get a grip on the life insurance monster and chop it down to affordable size.

What Is Your Life Worth?

As in so many other areas of our lives, the bottom-line question is, how can you get adequate coverage at minimum expense? Despite worksheets in books and articles that can help to pinpoint needs, there really is no firm answer to the somewhat morbid questions, "What is your life worth?" and "To whom?"

Life insurance is to family survival as a lifeboat is to surviving a Titanic-type disaster. Neither should be better than the original. A yacht isn't the lifeboat for a canoe—and you should only buy as much insurance as your beneficiaries will need to get to that place and time where they can take over the financial burden you had once covered.

Life insurance just doesn't make it as a lottery ticket. It's too expensive—definitely not a dollar and a dream—more like a small fortune and a nightmare. Nor is it an efficient investment vehicle. For that reason, we recommend term insurance for most folks. It costs less. It serves only one purpose—life insurance. And it has to be carried only until such time as no one is financially dependent on you.

True, mortgage payments will need to be kept up whether you're there to write the check or not—but your home loan does not need to be immediately paid off. And as you'll see in Chapter 15, very few families have to foot the whole astronomical cost for four years of higher education. When a family's income is reduced, college aid goes up. It's a booby prize to be sure, but your heirs might as well claim it.

Shopping for Term Insurance

Begin with the following basic questions (which we unfortunately cannot answer for you):

- How much do I need? Conventional wisdom says seven times your salary.

- How much will it cost?

Then there's a question of stability. Not yours—the insurance company's. You want a company that will outlast you, not one that's on the verge of collapse. There are a number of services that rate insurers. Check guides at your library, click on www.insure.com/ratings on the Web, or contact one of the following free services:

Standard & Poor's: 212-208-1527

Moody's: 212-553-0377

Duff & Phelps: 312-368-3198

If you happen to work for a company that provides insurance as a fringe benefit, you may be able to add on to it at reduced cost. In states that allow savings banks to write them, savings bank life insurance (SBLI) policies tend to have low rates. To check around, call one of the services that will quote on numerous policies from different insurers: SelectQuote at 800-343-1985, InsuranceQuote at 800-972-1104, and TermQuote at 800-444-TERM.

Keeping the Cost Low

The less likely you are to die prematurely, the less you'll pay in premiums. As always, one of the best investments you can make is in your health. If you smoke, drink, eat too much, lead a stressful life, have a history of problems, or enjoy dangerous hobbies, the price will go up. If you take good care of yourself, the price goes down. If you buy while still in top shape, the price is low.

Especially if you're looking for a large policy, a medical exam may be required. Strange heartbeats, high blood pressure, and foreign substances in your body fluids will raise your cost.

Congratulations, You're 65

As if things weren't complicated enough, you have six months from your sixty-fifth birthday to get your act together, at least as it concerns health care insurance. If you've managed to reach age 65 without following any of our advice and with virtually no assets, you're in luck (bad luck perhaps, but luck of a sort). You'll have full, no-premium health coverage under Medicaid, which is handled by your state.

Medicare, on the other hand, is a federal program, and it's at least as confusing as taxes. You've been paying for Part A coverage through payroll deductions for the last 30 years. So that part is your right, unless you aren't eligible for Social Security, in which case you're in double trouble: no Social Security and the option of paying about $300 a month if you want Medicare coverage.

Part B of Medicare picks up some costs (e.g., doctor visits) that Part A doesn't cover. But Part B is an optional extra that you'll want to buy. It currently costs under $50 a month.

Since neither Part A nor Part B nor both of them together is likely to cover all of the medical expenses you might incur, there is Medicare supplemental insurance—known as *Medigap*—in which you have 10 options ranging from another Plan A to Plan J, where A is the most basic and J is the most comprehensive. A costs less than J, and B through I fall in between in alphabetical order from the least to most. If you sign up for one of them within six months of turning age 65, you must be accepted. After that, preexisting conditions could keep you out.

A somewhat more recent twist is the Medicare HMO, which may cover most of your costs, but through an HMO that may limit your choices. And even more options are on the way.

There is nothing easy about getting older, and choosing the right Medigap policy depends on your assets. The less money you have, the less insurance you may need—because "the system" is more likely to eventually drain away all your assets, and you'll end up on Medicaid anyhow.

....

BEFORE YOU'RE 65

Invest time *before* this birthday to learn about Medicare, Medicaid, Medigap, Medicare HMOs, Medicare Select, and long-term-care policies. Call 800-638-6833 to request Uncle Sam's free *Medicare Handbook* or go to www.medicare.gov.

....

Decide Now, or Someone Else Will Do It

As if Medicare weren't confusing enough, you might want to consider what you're going to do if you need long-term care. Half of all women and a third of all men spend a couple of years or more in a nursing home. With the *average* annual tab running $40,000 and many homes costing more, it's well worth planning for—even if it's "just in case."

You don't want to deal with this, we know. But just suppose for a moment that you needed the kind of care that your children or spouse simply couldn't provide. What would you want them to do?

Let's be blunt: You can make the decision yourself or risk having someone make it for you. Finding out what your options (or your parent's) are when they are *not* needed is better than waiting until a crisis occurs.

First, you may want to research nursing homes in your area to find out what's available. During your research, check if there are "Edenized" homes around you. These nursing homes, which feature lots of plants, visitors, activities, and even pets, are extremely popular with residents. If you don't like what you see, consider volunteering at a home. You can help improve the lives of the people who live there and perhaps help bring about some positive change.

If you really don't want to end up in a nursing home, then take a hard look at your alternatives. Can you come up with a workable solution, perhaps with the help of your children, a local social service organization, or your church? We know you wouldn't want to bully your family into anything. It may mean hiring in-home care or taking advantage of community-based services. It's up to you to know what your options are. If adequate programs aren't available in your area, then perhaps you just found a community project that has your name on it.

The American Association of Homes and Services for the Aging offers free, helpful information on the range of alternatives (independent living, assisted living, continuing-care retirement communities, and nursing homes): 901 E Street NW, Suite 500, Washington, DC 20004-2037, 202-783-2242, www.aahsa.org. Also check out the Extended Care Information Network, www.elderconnect.com.

Of course, one of the best things you can do to avoid a nursing home is to take care of your health. Exercising, eating well, going for regular checkups, and maintaining strong friendships will help you take your best shot at continuing an independent way of life.

> The more physically, emotionally, and financially comfortable you are, and the more in control of your own life, the better off you and your family will be.
>
> —JOSEPH MATTHEWS, *Beat the Nursing Home Trap*

Long-Term-Care Insurance

If you or your loved ones do need long-term care, who will pay for it? And how? How long would your assets last with care costing $40,000 a year or more? What if you or your spouse end up in a nursing home while the other is still at home? Then you'll have to be able to afford both the nursing home fee and the expenses for the spouse who stays at home.

If your assets won't cover three or four years in the long-term facility of your choice, or will wipe out the assets your spouse will need or that you hoped to leave to your heirs, you may want to consider a long-term-care policy.

Long-term-care insurance, or nursing home insurance, is really designed for people who are in the middle: They have enough financial assets so that they don't qualify for Medicaid, but several years in a home would wipe out those assets. (Not all facilities accept Medicaid, either.)

When should you buy long-term-care insurance? Like most decisions, there's rarely a clear answer. Most experts will tell you to seriously consider it between the ages of 55 and 65. If you buy when you are younger, you'll lock in at lower rates—and you're less likely to have medical conditions that could disqualify you later. On the other hand, this insurance is still relatively new, and policies are improving. If you wait to buy, you may get better coverage—unless you develop health problems in the meantime. So perhaps your best bet is to start looking seriously by the age of 60, earlier if you have health problems that could become more serious.

This is complex stuff, and it's one area where planning ahead can make all the difference. So take your time. Read *How to Protect Your Life Savings from Catastrophic Illness* by Harley Gordon. Then explore several long-term policies, and make sure you understand exactly what's covered before you decide to invest in one. And if you want to legally protect assets from the reach of Medicaid, start transferring them years before you're likely to require nursing home care.

But that's enough talk of death and disease. It's time to get back to the exciting business of living!

WHEREVER YOU WORK, BE IN BUSINESS FOR YOURSELF

AMERICANS HAVE COME TO REALIZE, SLOWLY AND PAINFULLY, THAT they can no longer count on a job to take them through to retirement. For your own protection, you need to be prepared and willing to transition into a different department, a different company, a new line of work, or a business of your own. And whether it's as an employee or in your own company, you need to design your own benefits package. Fortunately, it's not hard to put together a low-risk, high-return, balanced portfolio for your work life that will outshine anything Wall Street has to offer.

CHAPTER 6

....

Freeing the Entrepreneur
Inside You

○ Why you *must* think like a consultant, no matter what your job

○ Safe ways to test the waters before you plunge into something new

○ Ways to speed up your trip, whether up the ladder or out of the rat race

○ Essential skills for promoting yourself

In as much as you can view the revolution in the American workplace as an opportunity for you to create independence for yourself rather than seeing it as a cause for disappointment, you will certainly have a better work life and a better retirement life.

MARY ROWLAND, *A Commonsense Guide to Your 401(k)*

....

It's almost guaranteed that you won't be at your current job for the remainder of your working life. No matter how hard you work, how many hours you put in, how much you learn, how many brilliant ideas you share, how much money you earn for the company—your days as an employee of any particular firm are numbered. According to statistics, you'll move from job to job and career to career at least seven times.

Whether you work for a multinational corporation or the smallest company in town, you'll thrive or fizzle depending not only on your abilities and on how you market them—but also on what the bottom line dictates. You don't have to like it, but that's the reality. You get paid for what you can do for the stockholders.

But your job can offer you a lot more than a paycheck. While you're gainfully employed, your job can also give you the time to figure out what you would really rather be doing—and the opportunity to develop new skills that might help you succeed in your dream occupation, whatever that might be.

YOU'RE THE BOSS

Think of yourself as a consultant, which makes your employer your current client. You can be dismissed at will, but you also have the right to terminate the relationship. However, as any good consultant would, while you're on assignment, you'll do your absolute best for your client. That's your job, that's your commitment. Work as creatively, effectively, and just plain hard for your employer as you would if it were your own business. It is!

But like every rational consultant, you always want to be on the lookout for the next client—and to think about how today's client can help you get to tomorrow's. Ideally, you want another project, a better one, ready to start when your current commission has ended.

Since you're the head honcho, you're also responsible for financing the business—which means having funds available to carry you through lean times, when there may be no clients. The less income you need and desire, the more flexibility you'll have. You get to decide on the mix. Here we are again, face-to-face with the issue of finding and financing the lifestyle you want, and with an important premise of this book:

> *The secret to having maximum control over how you live—and make your living—is to be able to live comfortably on less than you earn.*

Flexibility is the key to unlocking those not-always-golden handcuffs that hold so many employees prisoners to their jobs. It will also prepare you to switch career gears when you want to, or when you are forced to by whomever you currently call "boss."

Of course, the better you are at promoting yourself, the better your chances of being able to make the "Do I stay or leave?" choice voluntarily. And since most of us make the bulk of our money from our jobs, the more you can increase your job or business marketability, the better your chances of getting to wherever it is that you ultimately want to go in your work life.

There are many things you can do to increase your marketability, your income, and your job security, and we'll get to them in a minute. Right now, we're much more concerned with helping you find the answers to these key questions: "Where do you want to go?" and "Are you doing something now that heads you in that direction?"

Whatever you thought you wanted to be when you were a kid—firefighter, nurse, or president of the United States—your goals have probably changed numerous times since then. Is your current occupation in sync with your current life goals?

Go Where Your Heart Takes You

To be successful, you need to be motivated. To be motivated, you need to enjoy and care about what you're doing. If you hate, or even mildly dislike, your 9 to 5 routine, you won't be able to give it your best, you won't learn as much as you could, you won't rise to the top, and you'll be exhausted by the time you return home at night. Is that how you're feeling, Bunky?

Fortunately, there are incredible investment opportunities waiting for you—with guaranteed high returns—in the wonderful world of work. By carefully investing your time, energy, and maybe a little money, you can find out where you really want to go—and then do what you need to get there. It's one of your best investment opportunities, way better than anything you could get in the stock market.

But since you can't get what you want if you don't know what it is (or won't admit it to yourself), your most important task is to find and follow your own path to earning a living. There's no way around it. Until you pick your path you won't be able to walk it.

We believe that deep down inside, you probably know what you enjoy doing, where your interests lie, and what your skills are. You surely know a bunch of things that you *don't* want to do to make money. Task number one is to establish positive goals.

However you choose to get going—long lists on paper, career counseling, closing your eyes and fantasizing, having many a soul-searching conversation with your mate—the journey can't begin until you pick an objective, a destination. It doesn't have to be a forever decision. Thinking in terms of forever may just stop you in your tracks.

Focus on what would be a great next assignment for you in your business life. Ideally, it will be something that takes advantage of your natural aptitudes, that fits with your personality, and that you'd enjoy. Even if you have no clue about what you might like to do, you *can* decide that you're going to find out—and that you *will* take steps to move in that direction over time.

A typical 45-year career means 90,000 hours on the job. That could feel like a very long prison sentence without the possibility of parole, or it could be a unique opportunity to achieve great things. The choice is yours. For now, let's think ahead, say, five years. By then, would you like to have:

1. The same job?

2. A different position in the same organization?

3. A similar job elsewhere?

4. A new career?

5. A business of your own?

6. The opportunity to devote your full time to raising a family?

7. Retired?

We know that it's often hard to believe in yourself enough to give an honest answer to these questions, but try. Stuck? Start by trying to answer this:

Would you die—or kill—for a job?

Wayne McLaren was one of the "Marlboro Men," those intrepid ad cowboys who showed smoking as a virile, attractive thing to do. When he died of lung cancer, it was thanks to his 30-year, pack-and-a-half-a-day smoking habit. Toward the end, Wayne did an about-face and spoke out against smoking.

Of course, no one is forced to smoke—or to grow tobacco, or to manufacture cigarettes, or to design the packs and cartons, or to distribute and sell them, or to work on the advertising campaigns, or to represent the cigarette conglomerates in court or on Capitol Hill—and certainly, no one is forced to model for their ads.

Yet anyone is free to do so. Back in the early 1990s, nonsmoker Margaret Thatcher earned $1 million from Philip Morris to push the smoking habit in Eastern Europe and the Third World. Would you push cigarettes for $1 million? Tempted?

In our hearts, each of us knows whether the work we do makes the world a bit better or worse. If you're not proud of what you do to accumulate money, we hope you'll decide to get yourself onto a new track.

We All Have Fantasies

Some fantasies include changing our work lives. Sometimes it's enough to have hobbies or volunteer roles that incorporate talents and interests not used in our moneymaking efforts. But for many of us, a larger shift seems essential if we're ever to be truly satisfied.

Sometimes the answer is staring us in the face: a nurse who longs to be a doctor, for example. Other times, it's a long road to finding the next right place. Take it slowly and try to enjoy the ride, bumpy though it may be. Think of every step along the way as an investment in yourself, in finding the next right spot where you'll be happy and prosper.

The best time to begin making job changes, of course, is before you're unemployed or totally burnt out and in a panic. Note that we said *begin*. Change takes time. Change means risk and requires courage. Change often means pay cuts, emotional upheaval, and family friction. However, *since change in your occupation is virtually guaranteed*, your best bet is to anticipate the future and prepare for the safest landing possible, while you're still on someone else's payroll.

Start by thinking about what *really* motivates you. Money? Fame? The opportunity to help others? A desire to be creative? Long vacations? More time with your family? Power? A heartfelt cause? The opportunity to play golf with movers and shakers? A love of art? The joy of world travel?

> The very first step to finding work that fits you is to understand the connection between doing what you *love* and doing something worth doing, something that has *meaning. Because they are one and the same thing. . . .* Without an activity that really matters to you, you're going to feel empty, even if you've set yourself up in Paradise and are living the life of the rich and famous.
>
> —Barbara Sher, *I Could Do Anything If I Only Knew What It Was*

INVEST IN KNOWLEDGE

If you've a yearning to do something else, but no clear sense of what that might be, you could begin by investing in some career counseling. Three-fourths of working adults say that if they had to do it over again, they would try to get more information on career options before they settled into their jobs. Now's your chance for a do-over!

Your alma mater or a nearby community college may have an inexpensive career counseling program—or maybe you'd really rather do it yourself. In either case, it's well worth a trip to the library for an assortment of self-improvement books (e.g., the classic, *What Color Is Your Parachute*), some audiotapes, and magazines that might shed some light on different careers or ways to "find yourself."

Even if you're not plugged in yet, your librarian or a friend can suit you up for a flight into cyberspace. Good Internet sources for career changers are www.monster.com, www.careerbuilder.com, and www.careermosaic. com. They have free on-line job search engines as well as sound career advice. Other valuable sites for career info are: www.careermag.com, stats.bls.gov/ocohome.htm, and www2.fu.com/almis.

Through inexpensive adult ed classes offered by colleges or, in larger cities, by private companies such as First Class or the Learning Annex, you can take career counseling classes, explore new fields or subjects that seem interesting, or pick up the skills and credentials that will open up new doors. For example, you can learn how to write effective marketing copy, master the computer, develop a business plan, start a day care center, become a travel agent, or get a real estate license.

But don't just take the class! Most adult ed teachers are professionals who really do what they teach. Take advantage of your instructor's expertise by asking for some real-world career advice, perhaps over a couple of cups of coffee.

And almost every type of business has a professional association that publishes newsletters or magazines focusing on the latest trends and concerns of the industry. *The Encyclopedia of Associations* at the library has 2,416 pages full of them. Find some associations that look interesting and give them a call. Ask them to send you membership information and a sample publication. In and of itself, this is a great way to scout out other fields.

As you narrow your search, talk to people who work in professions that you find appealing—including the staff at those trade associations. They have a unique overview and can offer key insights about training and job opportunities. If you're lucky, someone there may "adopt" you and further help you on your journey. Try to make it so.

SAFE WAYS TO TEST THE WATERS

Once you find a field you want to seriously explore, consider volunteering after work or on weekends. Maybe you're thinking of going back to school to become a nurse. Volunteer at the local hospital in a position that will allow you to interact with nurses, and find out what the job really entails. You'll be in the perfect spot to talk to nurses about what they like and don't like about their jobs. If you do decide to go back to school, you'll have a helpful credential to add to your resume. And if you don't like it, you can always quit.

You don't have to limit your volunteering to do-good organizations. Chances are, you can create a risk-free volunteer opportunity at any outfit that catches your fancy.

For example, a couple of decades ago, Nancy wanted to learn more about greenhouse gardening, so she arranged a deal with a local grower. She'd help transplant little seedlings and in exchange, could ask as many questions as she wanted, plus take home all the plants her heart desired. Nancy soon realized that turning her passion for growing plants into a business didn't sing to her—"They'd become merchandise, and that'd be awful!" But Nancy still applies what she learned in her own little greenhouse, and she's still tending many of the flowers she got so long ago.

Our researcher, Marcy Ross, got her start by offering to help a friend who was a freelance writer. The friend couldn't afford to pay her, but the research experience helped Marcy land a staff job on a magazine.

Temping and moonlighting are two other risk-free ways to test the waters of a new field or business. Like volunteering, by taking on temp or part-time jobs, you'll be around people who actually do the work you're considering. You'll get a good sense of the pros and cons of the job—and more.

When you're ready to seriously pursue your new line of work a little further, you might want to ask for a leave of absence from your current job. If you could take a sabbatical, you'd be able to get an even better feel for what your new life would be like—without burning any bridges. But when the time has come:

- Update your resume.
- Check the classifieds—regularly.
- Network with friends and acquaintances, as well as trustworthy customers and suppliers.
- Visit the Web sites we've already mentioned, plus these: www.careerpath.com, www.ajb.dni.us, and www.occ.com.
- Talk to headhunters—what do you have to lose?
- Read about and practice interviewing.
- Start your own business.

Call someone who is successful in the field you're interested in and offer to take them to lunch to pick their brain. People love to talk about themselves and what they know. Mark Victor Hansen, author of the best-selling *Chicken Soup for the Soul* series, says he used to call bigwigs he wanted to learn from and offered to be their chauffeur when they were in town. All he asked for was the opportunity to ask questions during drive time. It worked!

....

GET HELP WHEN YOU NEED IT

If you're having a tough time moving up the career ladder, aren't sure what you want to do next, or are thinking about making the transition from employee to entrepreneur, a job counselor or a career coach may help you get there—even if you're not sure where that is!

Most of these professionals do not come cheap, and fees can range anywhere from $75 or more per hour to several thousand dollars for a complete package of services. That means it's important that you screen them carefully to make sure your money and time are invested well.

Career Coaches

A coach will work with you over a period of time, usually one-on-one for several months or more, typically over the phone and on-line. Unlike a traditional job counselor, whose focus tends to be only on finding you a job, career coaches generally focus on helping you create the *whole* life you want.

If you're considering a change in your bigger picture as opposed to simply finding the next job, Jane Trevaskis, a job counselor as well as a career coach in Arlington, Virginia, recommends you find a coach who has experience in counseling people through career changes or transitions.

To find a career coach, contact the International Coach Federation at 888-ICF-3131 or www.coachfederation.org, or the Coaches Training Institute at 800-691-6008 or www.thecoaches.com.

Take a look at prospective coaches' backgrounds, including their marketing experience, to find ones who seem to make sense, given where you think you want to go. Then call three or four for an initial interview. Most reputable coaches offer a free introductory session, which can be a good opportunity to check out the chemistry.

Job Counselors or Consultants

With these professionals, Trevaskis says you should look for a firm or individual who will give you personalized job counseling—as well as training in networking, how to interview, and telephone techniques. Early in the process, which should be fairly short term and specific to your job needs, counselors should also offer you an aptitude test. Go for it! It may help you find out what you were really meant to be!

It's important to find a firm that has been in business a while and has substantial ties to the community, so you'll be introduced to people who can help you. Also, make sure they allow you the opportunity to network with their other clients. Some people who pass themselves off as career consultants try to isolate their clients from each other, and that's a real red flag. A reputable professional organization that provides referrals to members is the National Board for Certified Counselors (www.nbcc.org or 800-398-5389).

....

HOW TO SPEED YOUR TRIP—UP THE LADDER OR OUT OF THE RAT RACE

Whatever your current career or the next one, the more education you have, the more you're likely to earn, and the less likely you are to be unemployed. High school grads, on average, earn $17,000 a year less than those with college degrees. The more you know, the more you're worth.

That doesn't mean you should go back to school just for the sake of getting a degree. But whether your goal is to start a new career, to have a business of your own, or to take on different job duties where you work now, you'd be wise to take a careful look at whether an advanced degree or technical training would help. (We'll be talking colleges in Chapter 15.)

Schools Are Busting Out All Over

We're all students for life. And now there are more educational opportunities than ever before to help you get ahead. In addition to public and private four-year colleges, local community colleges offer lots of helpful, cheap courses in their continuing education departments. Even if there's no school nearby offering classes you want to take, or no way you could find the time (and the sitters!) to attend during the week, you still have options.

Many reputable schools now offer courses, and even degree programs, to students who never enter a classroom. In this new, high-tech version of correspondence schools, students can watch their professor's lectures on cable TV from the comfort of their couches or join a classroom discussion on-line or by phone.

If you think distance learning may be for you, go to www.cisnet. com/~cattales/Deducation.html. Or see if your library carries the latest editions of *The Oryx Guide to Distance Learning* by William E. Burgess or *The Adult Learner's Guide to Alternative and External Degree Programs* by Eugene Sullivan. These comprehensive tomes list hundreds of institutions that offer courses via mail, cable TV, the Internet, videocassette—or in person on weekends. Another excellent resource is *College Degrees by Mail & Modem* by John Bear, Ph.D. and Mariah Bear, M.A.

Formal schooling aside, your best educational opportunities may be available right on the job. By helping your employer earn and grow, you can invest in yourself at your boss's expense. Be sure you benefit from whatever formal in-house training is available. And if there's some special training that would benefit both you and the boss, but no program currently in place, you'd be smart to find a way to make it happen. Maybe you could get the green light to find someone who could run a workshop on the subject for your department.

Spend as much time as you can picking the brains of colleagues, managers, suppliers, and customers. Whenever possible, attend seminars, conferences, and company-sponsored workshops. If the organization where you spend 40 hours a week pays for continuing education, take full advantage. Not doing so is throwing money away.

Is there a special license or certification that could buy you a more secure future? Will the boss pick up the tab? If you can learn on your employer's time and nickel, you'll be that much further ahead—for free. But even when the boss won't pay, if there's a special degree that would help you advance yourself—spring for it!

If you're at all facile with languages, consider becoming fluent in another one. The demand for competent multilingual workers is rising, and you can probably already dream up ways it could benefit your current employer. Courses are one way to go, but you can also get a set of tapes and learn on the way to and from work.

High Tech = High Returns

Janet didn't have a computer background, but she took every opportunity to read computer magazines, take classes, and just plain teach herself. Soon she became the person everyone went to for advice on their computer and word processing problems—which contributed greatly to her boss's view that she was indispensable and deserving of more than a few raises.

Nowadays, almost everyone has to be computer-literate. If you're at all behind the times, this is the best investment from the booming technology sector to put in your portfolio for your work life.

The further behind you are in whatever technology your industry uses, the less desirable you'll be at your current job—or when you apply for a new one. Photographers, for example, who for years developed prints in a darkroom, now use sophisticated computer technology to capture, print, and even touch up their photographs in record time. When it comes to commercial work, those who can't use new equipment are the blacksmiths of the modern era.

If new computer hardware and software are entering your work space, stay late if need be, and learn how to use them. It won't cost you a dime—but the yield in terms of your future job options could be enormous.

ENTREPRENEURS ADVERTISE

You've been marketing yourself since before you were born. There was that first kick in the womb, that first cry when you exited, your smile when mommy or daddy said something brilliant, like "goo, goo." You quickly learned that well-timed attention getters could get you what you wanted.

As you grew, so did your ability to gauge your audience and behave in whatever fashion might get the desired response. Perhaps you realized that more often than not, whining at the checkout counter would get you a candy bar, while those great big hugs for Auntie Mame were good for doubling the quantity of birthday presents she'd buy you.

You marketed yourself at high school dances, on college applications, and when you applied for your first job. If you're smart, you're marketing yourself at the job you have now. It's a blue-chip investment opportunity for you—even if you feel as though you have a foot out the door.

Sometimes actors, singers, athletes, or even great employees are discovered accidentally—but more often than not, they've been doing a lot of self-promotion. Call it advertising or public relations or propagandizing. Whatever. It works.

Whether you're hoping to be named corporate vice president, shop supervisor, head teller, first in line for the day shift—or just trying to keep your job—the more people who know your name and credentials, the better your chances of winning. You don't have to be pushy or even outgoing. But you do have to make sure the decision makers know you and know what you can, will, and are currently doing for the business.

··

GERRI'S TOOLBOX: CREATE AN "I'M WONDERFUL" FILE

Keep a "Good Job!" journal focused on your accomplishments. Every time you learn a new skill, finish a project, crunch some numbers that indicate your high level of productivity, attend a conference, take a class, give a speech, or complete any other significant task at work, make a note of it. And throw in letters complimenting your performance, as well as samples of business proposals or well-written memos you've penned.

You'll have your "Good Job!" journal to boost your own confidence, to refer to at your job reviews, and if you don't get that raise you deserve, you'll have great fodder for your new, improved resume. Or maybe you'll impress yourself enough with your accomplishments to finally reach for that gold ring and take off on your own.

··

It's Who You Know

Your list of contacts can be your most valuable asset. And the way to fill up your Rolodex is by meeting people. Unfortunately, that dreaded *N* word—*networking*—brings up images of trying to make small talk at boring cocktail parties or, worse yet, recruiting downliners for a multi-level marketing scheme.

So how does someone who's a natural wallflower become a savvy net-worker? You've got to get out there and get known. Start by coming up with a good answer to this question:

What do you do?

When someone asks "What do you do?," do you say, "I'm in marketing" or, "I work for Sillycone Systems"? What happens next? Most likely they nod, their eyes begin to wander, and they're off. Experienced networkers subtly promote themselves by turning that question into an opportunity for a 20-second commercial.

A vivid description of what you offer is essential to subtly promote yourself. It'll probably take some practice to feel and sound natural, but once you learn how, you'll communicate your abilities more clearly, sound a lot more interesting, and be able to get a conversation fired up.

Here are two better responses to the "What do you do?" question:

1. "You know how so many people are up to their eyeballs in debt and can't seem to get ahead financially?" Involved in the conversation, the other person nods, and you continue, "I write books and articles and give seminars that show people simple ways to pay off their

debts and build a strong financial foundation." That should catch their interest.

2. Offer a line about what you do followed by an accomplishment. For example, "I help companies improve their communications with customers. I recently set up a program for XYZ company that cut their customer service response time by 10%. And you?"

Now that you can break the ice, join a trade or professional association and attend its conventions and seminars. They offer a wonderful opportunity to network and get the inside scoop on what's hot in your current or future field. It also gives you a shot at greatly increasing your perceived standing in the industry. How? Volunteer for a position that will have you working side by side with key people in the organization.

Participating on committees or projects is an excellent way to meet new people as you let others get to know you and what you can do. But make sure you really have the time to invest, the skills, and enough interest to accomplish the project's goals—or volunteering will end up hurting, rather than helping, your reputation!

Or you could write to conference organizers and propose a speech you'd like to give. You'd rather go to the dentist than give a talk? Ask if your boss would like you to suggest him or her as a speaker. (You might get extra points and valuable experience by offering to draft the speech.) Or contact a trade magazine's editor to suggest an article you'd like to write. You don't have to be the president of your company; you just need to have something helpful to say to colleagues.

··

GERRI SPEAKS UP

The greatest opportunities in my work have come as a result of my public speaking—television appearances, radio interviews, workshops, and speeches. But it wasn't long ago that the thought of giving a speech absolutely terrified me. I wasn't alone. Most people rate the fear of giving a speech as greater than the fear of death!

The first time my boss said he wanted me to give a speech, I was sick to my stomach for days. I absolutely dreaded the thought of getting up and talking to an audience of about 20 people at an informal dinner meeting sponsored by a local businesswoman's group. Miraculously, my prayers were answered, and for reasons I can't remember, the meeting was canceled.

But that didn't stop my boss from pushing me into public speaking. I don't remember my first speech, but lightning didn't strike and I wasn't run over by a train as I had hoped. I don't remember my first television interview either, but I did one, then another, and pretty soon they weren't so bad.

I've had some less-than-stellar appearances, to be sure, but I try to forget those and focus on the ones that went well. I became more and more comfortable, and now actually love giving speeches and doing TV and radio interviews—at least most of the time.

You don't have to become a public speaker or woo an audience with your brilliant sense of humor. But being able to speak confidently in front of groups is a big plus in any job. One good way to get more comfortable with public speaking is to join Toastmasters International. Since 1924, it's helped over 3 million people (including me) develop confident communication skills. It's well worth the money—dues run around $35 every six months. For a chapter near you, call 800-993-7732 or you can go to this Web site: www.toastmasters.org.

—GERRI

. . . .

And Now for Today's Speaker

Do you think people join the Rotary or Chamber of Commerce so they can listen to self-promotional talks once a month? Au contraire, they join because it keeps them and their companies visible and in touch with the local community. If the Rotary doesn't sing to you, how about participating in the company bowling league or volunteering with a local charity?

PROBLEM SOLVED

Problem solvers are always in demand, so spend some time analyzing what's wrong where you work, and developing realistic solutions. Did you just hear about a hot new marketing opportunity at a convention, and do you have some thoughts about how your organization can use it to increase sales of the widget no one seems to want? Do you know how the current phone system might be improved—or can you suggest better ways to handle complaints? Putting solutions to problems on paper is a good way to let your boss know you're "on the case."

Pitch in when things get really hectic, or learn to do what no one else can or will. Just make sure you teach others how to do it themselves. You don't want to get stuck changing the toner on the copier every time it runs out just because no one else has taken the time to learn how.

I See a Bright Future for You

Your next investment shouldn't be a 900 call to a psychic hotline, but rather the development of an important skill—the ability to see into the future and prepare yourself. We're not talking crystal balls here. Learning how to think about the future can be one of the most useful things you can do for your career and for yourself—while a lack of awareness of what's new, what's hot, and what's not can put you on a dead-end path.

According to Gerald Celente, Director of the Trends Research Institute and author of *Trends 2000,* the key to tracking trends is to read two newspapers every day with a purpose—either *The Wall Street Journal* or *The Financial Times,* plus *The New York Times* or *USA Today.* Look for stories with social, economic, and political significance, be it about the difficulties older suburbs face or the current currency crisis. (You'll know by the headline or the first paragraph.) Skip the stories that are purely human interest or that are about something that hasn't happened yet (for example, a jury resuming deliberations on a sensational trial).

When a crisis does occur, tune in to the extra in-depth analyses that you'll find in accompanying background pieces, probably in more than one of the newspapers. Read them as though you're a "political atheist," Celente recommends—not for what you want or hope, but for what is really going on, not only in your own profession or industry, but for trends that may directly or indirectly shape the future.

Once you spot a trend, ask yourself what it means to your business, to your way of life. For example, in the articles giving postmortems about Christmas spending, you see again and again that people did spring for services and "experiences," while expenditures on typical gifts went down. Although you're in a service business, no one at work ever packaged what you do to appeal to holiday spenders. But now you'll be thinking about this trend—and how your business can benefit from it.

WHO SETS THE PRICE?

The marketplace is regulated by supply and demand (as well as by the Feds). In the workplace, you're a supply—just like computer chips (or potato chips, for that matter). The more you're needed, the more you're worth. But not all chips of equal quality cost the same.

Some brands are perceived to be worth more than others. To a large extent, that has to do with promotion. If consumers are swayed enough by clever advertising, they'll often pay more for a product that's identical to the generic one alongside it.

The techniques we've been discussing—continuing your education, developing cutting-edge technical skills, and engaging in effective self-promotion, will all increase your value. But being more valuable to the company isn't your only goal. You want the boss to pay you more.

Like consumers, businesses pay more for something they value more. As an entrepreneur, it's your job to make your client (your boss) believe you're worth what you believe you're worth. Set too high a price, and you could be walking the streets. Set too low a value on yourself, and you may be perceived as being worth less—and that could put you out on the streets just as quickly. *Working Woman* and *Working Mother* magazines often carry stories that can help you decide what you're worth and how to get it—whether you're a woman or a man.

If you want to stay employed and move ahead, look at your job as an entrepreneur would. You're currently employed by one of many potential clients. If you feel that your current fee is less than you deserve, you have some choices:

1. You can raise your price and ask for more money.

2. You can wait, in the hope that you'll be given a raise.

3. You can go elsewhere.

If you choose option 1, be prepared to be turned down. If you are, you have three options:

1. Wait a while and ask again.

2. Ask why not, and try to correct any shortcomings the boss thinks you have.

3. Go elsewhere.

Our recommendation is twofold: Don't push for a raise or promotion unless you have a viable alternative. Then pick your time and place carefully. The time to ask for a raise is not hot on the heels of the company having just lost its biggest account. The place to ask for that raise isn't in the parking lot when the boss is already running late.

But when the clock strikes the right time and the circumstances put you and your manager in the right place, have a number in mind, and be able to justify it by tooting your own horn. Bring out those letters, proposals, and memos that document all the great things you've done for the company. You're best off if you can quantify that you've earned or saved your company X dollars. After all, it is the bottom line that counts to the client.

The message here is that while not asking is an automatic *no,* asking does change the relationship. An emphatic "No!" may cause a loss of self-esteem, and you'll be forced by your ego or common sense to look elsewhere. Or maybe it's time to strike out on your own.

PLAY YOUR ACE TO A BUSINESS OF YOUR OWN

In Chapter 8 we explain why developing and maintaining a small business of your own, what we call an "Ace in the Hole," is a great investment in your family's future. But if you're eager to start your own business full-time from the get-go, we're all for it.

Many a small business owner has made the leap from full-time employment to self-employment by working as a consultant for a former boss. If you've built up some expertise or a reputation in your field, you may be a perfect candidate. You'll have the opportunity to build your own business (and set your own hours and fees) by selling the expertise you developed on your job.

If you're contemplating this route, begin putting together a proposal for your superiors that emphasizes the benefits they'll gain by working with you on a consulting basis. Once you've made the commitment to leave, contact everyone you know who can be a potential source of business, and tell them of your plans. Ask them if there's anything you can do for them, or better yet, suggest projects you might be able to do. You'll be off to a running start.

CHAPTER 7

Work Is Where the Perks Are

○ Comparing investment opportunities on the job

○ How to find loose-change leverage at work

○ Turning your savings kitty into a cheetah

○ Ways to benefit most from your benefits

Employee benefits can boost your standard of living and reduce your income taxes—if you know enough to use them wisely.

KATHY KRISTOF,
Kathy Kristof's Complete Book of Dollars and Sense

Whether you work for Godzilla Corp. or George's Garage, a good employee benefits package can make life a lot easier. To begin with, these perks are generally worth 35% to 40% of your annual compensation. And it's tough to save on your own for retirement, expensive to get your own health insurance, and difficult to take a family leave unless you know your desk will be waiting patiently for your return.

Yet many people take perks for granted and don't use them to the fullest. How much do you really know about your benefits? Do you know what they're worth? Are you really using them to your advantage?

Chosen and used wisely, your benefits provide golden opportunities for what we call "loose-change leverage"—the ability to turn small amounts of money into big results. You can capitalize on this leverage by funding your retirement plan to the max, investing in flexible spending accounts, opting for a health plan that matches your needs, getting reimbursed for expenses, and getting an education on your employer's dime.

To cash in, though, you've got to do your homework. While it may be more fun to compare the features of various new wide-screen TVs or CD players, the payoffs are much, much greater if you put time and thought into comparing your benefit options. And if your spouse has a good package as well, you'll have a little more homework, but even more potential leverage.

....

BARGAINING FOR BENEFITS *BEFORE* YOU TAKE THE JOB

Employers typically present the benefits package to a prospective employee as though it were set in stone, when it may actually be as flexible as Flubber.

The more valuable you are to the company, the likelier it is that you can negotiate a step-up in perks—even if the company can't or won't come up with the money you think you're worth.

Start by trying to see yourself through your prospective employers' eyes. Are they getting a bargain, based on your skills, experience, and the going rate for people in your position? You may have more room to negotiate on perks if the compensation you're being offered is barely competitive or somewhat below market rates. By contrast, the benefits cupboard may be dry if they're paying a premium to bring you on board. But if you don't ask, you'll never know!

With your needs in mind, review the benefits package you're being offered. Are there any gaps or weak spots? For example, if you're a young parent, does the company offer adequate life and disability insurance? What additional benefit(s) would mean most to you? More vacation time? A company car?

If you've been offered similar perks by other companies, be sure to say so. Explain why the extra perks will help you do a better job. But don't wallow in emotion or issue ultimatums unless you mean them.

....

PERKMANSHIP:
LEVERAGE THOSE FRINGE ELEMENTS

If you already work for a company that's blessed with a strong array of benefits, your employer's first official greeting probably came in the form of an avalanche of leaflets, brochures, and binders describing your options in detail.

Don't wait until your personnel department sends out a last call for benefit choices before looking at these treasure maps. If you make a hasty decision that turns out to be unwise, you could lose big-time until your next chance to change your plans—which might be a whole year away.

To get the most from your company perks, benefits consultant Neil Finestone from Sherman Oaks, California, advises that you start scouting your options early:

1. Begin looking into your choices as soon as you hear that an open-enrollment period is coming up. This should give you several weeks to research the alternatives calmly and intelligently.

2. Make sure you have a summary plan description for each available benefit program. Here's where you'll really find out what your pension's all about and what's covered (as well as what isn't) in your health plan. Read them and write down any questions you have. If your human resources department can't provide the answers, go right to the source: your company's retirement plan custodian, pension administrator, or insurer.

3. Be clear on your preferences and comfort level. On your health plan, for example, how important is free choice of doctors? Can you live within the limitations of an HMO? How much risk are you willing to take in your 401(k)?

4. When both spouses have similar perks, take a close look at the cost versus benefit received. For example, if you both have retirement savings plans with an employer match, it makes sense for each spouse to contribute enough to earn the maximum match. There's no way to beat an immediate 33%, 50%, or 100% return on your investment! Once you've taken full advantage of the match, the questions become how much more can you afford to contribute, and which plan's investments are likeliest to meet your financial goals down the road.

RETIREMENT PLAN PRIMER

The time to start planning for a financially secure retirement is the day you receive your first paycheck, although few of us ever do. But don't agonize over the fact; just avoid further delays and start now.

—NANCY DUNNAN, *Dun & Bradstreet Guide to Your Investments*

By 2001, American workers will have socked away some $1.5 trillion in the most popular kind of employer retirement plan—401(k)s—while billions more will have been socked away in plans offered by nonprofit organizations (known as 403(b)s) and government agencies.

By and large, employers are delighted with 401(k)s. Instead of funding traditional pensions that pay retirees a fixed monthly amount, more and more companies are setting up these savings plans, which shift the responsibility—and risk—of providing a financially secure retirement to the employee. This can seem like a huge challenge. And if you've heard how much money experts say you ought to have saved for retirement, all the zeros probably made you swoon. Buck up! The important thing is to take every opportunity you can to make this seemingly impossible task possible.

The first step: If your employer offers a retirement savings plan, run—don't walk—to participate in it. Here's why we feel so strongly about this particular kind of loose-change leverage:

- It's the most painless way to save you'll ever find. The money is deducted from your paycheck, which means you never handle it, can't spend it, and probably won't even miss it.

- It cuts your taxes right away. Your contribution isn't included in your taxable income for the year, so, for example, if your gross compensation is $50,000 and you contribute $3,000 to your 401(k), you're taxed on only $47,000. Even in the 15% tax bracket, you've legally kept $450 from the IRS—at least until you retire. If your "contribution" to Uncle Sam is 28%, you've held back $840. Note that 401(k) money is tax deferred, not tax-free.

- You may be eligible for free money. With a 401(k), your company has the option of matching as much as 100% of every dollar you put in, with either cash or company stock. If you can find a better deal than an immediate doubling of your money with no risk, tell us about it!

- You don't have to pay tax on any of the interest, dividends, or capital gains you earn until you withdraw the money. Ideally, this will be after retirement, when you're apt to be in a lower tax bracket. In the meantime, your savings will snowball, because you don't have to dip into them every year to pay the IRS.

A simple way to save, a tax break, and a shot at free money—who could ask for anything more? Amazingly, though, 41% of employees ages 25 to 34 who are eligible for a 401(k) don't take advantage of it, according to the benefits consulting firm, Hewitt Associates (Lincolnshire, Illinois). More astonishing yet, almost a third of those aged 45 to 54 pass up this great benefit. And many more don't take full advantage of their employer match.

The earlier you start, the less you'll have to put aside to retire wealthy—or the sooner you may be able to call it quits. So if you haven't signed up because you're shy about making long-term commitments, get over it. Here's a case where time is literally money—and if you snooze, you lose.

....

WAKING UP A SLEEPY 403(B)

For years, 403(b)s were the only retirement savings game in town, and the teachers, hospital workers, and nonprofit employees who could benefit didn't have any choice but to buy insurance company annuities, had no way to compare their performance, and were hit with fees that were not clearly delineated.

Now there's a possible escape hatch if you're trapped in a sluggish 403(b) to which your employer hasn't made any contributions. You can arrange to have your existing balance transferred into a 403(b)(7) custodial account at a brokerage firm or mutual fund company, where you can invest in any mutual funds or annuities you wish.

Be careful: Since most annuities let you withdraw only 10% of your balance a year without triggering a surrender fee, your transfer into a 403(b)(7) may have to be made gradually.

....

HOW TO TURN YOUR SAVINGS
KITTY INTO A CHEETAH

Have you ever wondered how some of America's greatest fortunes were made? They were made, in large part, by the magic of compound interest . . . Today, the same principle is at work in your individual retirement accounts and your company retirement plans."
—JAMES JORGENSEN, *It's Never Too Late to Get Rich*

Assuming you've taken the plunge into a retirement plan (or you will after reading this chapter), how much should you contribute, and what should you invest it in? Like almost everything else in life, it depends.

If you haven't been saving at all, even a reasonable amount could pinch at first. But it may not! In any case, don't overdo it—you still have to meet your living expenses and pay off high-interest debt. Our suggestion: Start with an amount you're pretty sure you'd never notice, and boost it a bit every six months until you're putting in at least enough to get the maximum "free money" match provided by your employer.

And now, where to put your hard-earned 401(k) money? Typically, you'll be offered a smorgasbord of mutual funds, often including a money market fund, an income (bond) fund, a growth and income fund, a growth fund investing in diversified stock, an aggressive growth fund focusing on small-company stock, and an international growth fund. Another of your choices may be a guaranteed investment contract (GIC), which pays a fixed interest rate like long-term CDs, though they're not FDIC-insured. Finally, larger companies often put their own stock on the 401(k) buffet table.

Your investment strategy should depend on how much time you have until you'll need the money and on whether you have other financial cushions for retirement (a side business, say, or rental property). For example, if you have 20 years to go, you can afford to invest more aggressively than someone who'll need to start tapping the account in five years. But if savings will be your only supplement to Social Security, you might feel as though you need to max what your investments earn. Together, these two factors of time and need can help you determine how much risk you should take.

Many employers offer literature, seminars, and even software to help employees put together their own investment portfolios. If your company hasn't yet joined in, start to lobby for more education. After all, it's your money!

For starters, you might want to get a free sample copy of *Loose Change,* a newsletter featuring easy-to-understand information on personal finance that is distributed through worksites (Financial Literacy Center, 350 E. Michigan Avenue, Suite 301, Kalamazoo, MI 49007, 616-343-0770). If you like it, let the boss know.

An increasing number of companies provide their match for a 401(k) plan in the form of company stock. In addition, you may be given the option to purchase company stock as part of your 401(k). Other companies have Employee Stock Ownership Plans (ESOPs), which give employees stock as part, or even all, of their retirement plan.

Please, be *very* careful about tying too much of your future to your company's future. Be *especially* careful if your company is small (small-company stocks are much more risky) or is closely held and you cannot get reliable, independent information about its stock from brokerage firms or from *Value Line Investment Survey* at your library. If your employer is already providing company stock as part of its contribution to your retirement, then you're probably better off diversifying by choosing other investment options.

If your employer provides *only* company stock as your retirement plan, then you may be in a very risky position. Maximize other opportunities to save for retirement while you encourage the folks at the top to give you more investment choices. You might even have to teach them that *D* word: d-i-v-e-r-s-i-f-y.

How 'm I Doing?

Your account statement will show whether you've gained or lost ground since the end of the last quarter. Be sure to check it, and report any errors to your benefits department.

For 401(k)s, it's relatively easy to find out more about specific funds in your account, which may be *retail* (open to any investor) or private trust accounts managed by a bank, insurance company, or investment firm. Information about retail funds is much more public—for example, there will be a prospectus with investment policy and fee summaries, and their current value is usually published in your newspaper's daily fund listings. The same basic information about private funds is (or should be) available through your 401(k) custodian.

Tip: To research public funds, go to the library and look at *Morningstar* for an independent assessment of their performance. Even returns on private funds can be compared to similar types of investments in *Morningstar.*

Naturally, you'll choose investments that you think will bring in good returns. But a hidden factor may sap your success: the cost of administering your plan. A reasonable fee is 1% of your account assets—but most 401(k) plan participants have no idea how much they're paying in fees. Some plans overcharge employees as much as 600%, according to *Money* magazine, which estimated that excessive fees could cost an employee in a high-priced plan almost $250,000 over 30 years.

Get your benefits department to explain the fees you're paying, and complain if they seem out of line. (*Morningstar* carries information about expense ratios for comparison.) Employers are fiduciaries for retirement plans, which means they're responsible. They don't want to risk an employee suit for failing to manage the plan properly. You may find allies among your company's top executives, who probably have even more at stake in their 401(k) accounts than you do. (Nobody wants to toss away a quarter of a million dollars.) Don't chicken out here—the brass really may not realize there's a problem.

Be especially careful if your company is in financial trouble. Although employees' money in a 401(k) is supposed to be kept separate from other company funds in compliance with the Employee Retirement Income Security Act (ERISA), fraud investigations are way up. The most common complaint: financially strapped companies using or borrowing against participants' money to cover company expenses. If you have concerns about the management of your plan, talk to a pension advisor at the U.S. Department of Labor's Pension and Welfare Benefits Administration (202-219-8776).

Getting Access to Your Money

Many companies will allow you to borrow from your 401(k), 403(b), or profit-sharing plan account—usually up to 50% of its value, but no more than $50,000. However, you can't borrow from a 403(b) once it's been converted to a 403(b)(7).

For people with no credit history or a poor credit history, loans from a retirement savings plan can be a godsend because they're easy to get. There's no credit application or approval process, and the interest rate is low, generally 1% or 2% over prime. (For example, if the prime rate is 8.5%, you'd pay somewhere between 9.5% and 10.5%.) You must repay the loan in roughly equal monthly installments within five years or it will be subject to income tax and an IRS early-withdrawal penalty. The good news is that the interest you pay is credited back to your account—so you're paying yourself instead of a bank or finance company.

Watch out. You may end up robbing your retirement fund if you rely too much on these loans. It may seem like you'd come out way ahead, paying interest to yourself instead of to some bank. Unfortunately, you won't be earning interest from the retirement plan's investments. So while you're taking money out of one pocket and putting it in another, which is certainly better than giving it away, the money you borrowed from your retirement fund won't be earning you anything. That can mean a smaller nest egg when you retire. Also, if you leave your job or lose it, the entire balance of the loan usually becomes due.

Besides borrowing from your plan, you can also make withdrawals for such things as medical expenses, college bills, or financial hardship. But withdrawals mean taxes (20% of the amount will be withheld for estimated taxes, and you may owe yet more, depending on your tax bracket), plus a 10% IRS penalty. In addition, you can't replace the money you've taken, nor can you make additional contributions for a year. This is one time when it's probably way better to borrow than to withdraw.

When you leave a job, you can take your money with you, along with any employer contributions that have vested. However, if you just take the money and run, you'll get hit with taxes and a penalty. You're much better off leaving your retirement kitty with your former employer or moving it into a new employer's retirement plan, if you can. And you always have the option of rolling over your savings into an IRA. If you open a separate IRA solely for your rollover funds, you may be able to transfer the money later into a new employer's 401(k). Watch out, though—unless your funds go directly into another retirement plan or IRA without passing through your hands, you'll face taxes and that penalty.

In a Small Business? Think Big!

Instead of a 401(k), many small companies offer their employees a less complicated retirement plan. If your employer has a Keogh profit-sharing or money purchase plan or a SEP-IRA, contributions to your account may only be made by the company. Still, that's retirement money you wouldn't otherwise have.

However, if your company has a Savings Incentive Match Plan for Employees (SIMPLE), you have a chance to kick in savings, too—and you should! Generally, here's how a SIMPLE works: You can stash away up to $6,000 a year in your plan, and your employer can match your contributions up to 3% of your compensation, also to a maximum of $6,000 per year.

Alternatively, your employer may decide to kick in 2% of your salary (up to $3,200 a year), whether or not you put anything in (and you should!). SIMPLEs are indeed simple to establish and administer—so if your company thinks it's too small to offer a retirement savings plan as a perk, steer your CEO toward a SIMPLE while you murmur, "Save on taxes . . . retain and recruit top employees . . . get loose-change leverage. . . ."

INSURANCE: THE BROCCOLI OF FINANCE

Even though more companies are sharing the cost of premiums with workers, health, disability, and life insurance remain highly valuable perks. In fact, you may not realize just how much this coverage is really worth—unless you've tried to buy it on your own. Compared to individual policies, group plans tend to be cheaper, more comprehensive, and less apt to reject you because of preexisting medical conditions.

Nonetheless, thinking about insurance probably isn't one of your favorite pastimes. When you don't need the darn stuff, it costs money—and when you do need it, it's because you're sick, disabled, or dead. But just as you've learned to eat broccoli (we hope), you need to take an intelligent look at this company perk, which has the potential to keep a medical calamity from wiping you out financially.

Some employers offer a plain-vanilla insurance package—one or two health plans, disability coverage, and life insurance in amounts of one, two, or three times your salary. But you might also face a much bigger array of choices—not only more types of health plans, but more ways to allocate your benefit dollars.

Healthy, Wealthy, and Wise?

> ... if you added up all the different ways that you pay for health care, the sum would undoubtedly create "sticker shock!" ... Current projections suggest that the average family will spend over $14,500 in the year 2000.
> —MARC S. MILLER, *Health Care Choices for Today's Consumer*

Dr. Marcus Welby would hardly recognize medicine as it's practiced these days: A virus called "managed care" has infected the world of kindly family doctors. Even traditional indemnity plans that offer free choice of providers (for which you usually pay through the patella in premiums, deductibles, and co-payments) still want to preapprove your hospital stays.

At the other end of the spectrum are health maintenance organizations (HMOs), which will cover 100% of your costs—if you let them call all the shots on your care. In between, you may be offered a preferred provider organization (PPO), which will pay more of your bills than an indemnity plan—if you use its approved network of doctors. Newest and fastest-growing in this alphabet soup of options is the point of service (POS) plan, a hybrid of the others. It works like an HMO if you use its "in-network" providers and picks up 70% to 80% of the tab if you go out of network.

The type of plan you select often depends on your comfort level. Some folks swear by HMOs; others want the option—at least to some extent—of making the decisions on who they'll see and what tests they'll undergo. Here are some factors to look at when choosing a plan:

- *Your medical needs.* Well care for children, prescriptions, mental health benefits, chiropractic care—if features like these are important to you, check out how each plan covers them.

- *Doctors.* In looking at the network's doctors, are there several specialists to choose from in each field? Are your own doctors in the network? If not, to what extent would you be covered if you used them?

Are the doctors compensated with a yearly per-person fee or per visit? (Chances are, you'll get better care if physicians are paid each time they treat you.) What's the review process if you don't agree with your doctor's treatment recommendations?

- *Out-of-pocket costs.* First look at whether a higher deductible will be offset by lower premiums, or vice versa. Compare how much you spent out-of-pocket last year with how much you'd spend with each plan under consideration.

- *Coinsurance.* How much of each bill would you pay once you fulfill the deductible? At what point would the insurer start paying 100%?

- *Your spouse's coverage.* When you each have access to a company health plan, compare cost and features. Many group plans provide individual coverage free, so if you don't have kids, "to each his own" might be the cheapest approach. If you have children, it's best to go with the plan that offers better family coverage. (Make sure that if the spouse with the family plan quits or gets "downsized," you could still sign on to the other spouse's plan.) If you're tempted to have coverage through both employers, beware: You may not get full value from your premium dollars because of complex rules about who pays what (which in turn can lead to time-consuming squabbles).

- *A lifetime benefit of at least $1 million.* Hey, you never know.

- *The fine print in the plan booklet.* Find out which situations qualify as emergency coverage and when pre-certification of treatment is needed, so you don't wind up filing claims that get rejected. If you're in an HMO or POS plan, your care will be more heavily dictated ("managed") by your insurer. So it behooves you to know as much as you can in advance about how the plan is run.

Your benefits office or the insurance company's member services department should be able to help.

Ask if the plan has been in the area for at least a few years. Find out what coworkers and neighbors have to say about their experiences with the company. How are you covered when you travel around the country or overseas?

Fortunately, there are resources available to help you make these complex decisions. For instance, the National Committee for Quality Assurance accredits HMOs and provides a free accreditation status list (800-839-6487, www.ncqa.org). Major consumer magazines such as *U.S.*

News & World Report rate HMOs. And the Center for the Study of Services publishes the *Consumers' Guide to Health Plans* ($12, 800-475-7283), which provides sound advice on choosing health plans and surveys 72,000 subscribers of 300 HMOs, rating the plans on quality of care.

If you and your employer part ways, you'll generally be eligible to stay on the company health plan until you're insured elsewhere, up to a maximum of 18 months. However, you'll pay the full premium (and a bit more). New legislation requires that any preexisting conditions must be covered if you move to another group plan after being insured for at least a year.

....

MSA: NEW KID ON THE BLOCK

Companies with 50 or fewer employees may now offer a sort of medical IRA called a Medical Savings Account (MSA). This is a special account maintained with an insurer, bank, or brokerage into which you can stash a certain amount of pretax money, to be spent on almost any medical or dental expense. Money you don't spend just stays in your MSA, piling up tax-free earnings for you. (If you withdraw any of it for nonmedical purposes, you'll owe tax, plus a 15% IRS penalty if you're under 65.)

Your MSA must be paired with a high-deductible health insurance policy—a safety net in case of steep bills. The combined cost, however, can be lower than you're used to paying for traditional insurance. If you're eligible for one of these new accounts, their tax advantages and flexibility may make them worth checking out. For a list of MSAs in your state, visit www.kiplinger.com/dailynews/dn0514972.html.

....

OTHER PERKS OF THE WORKPLACE

Sometimes your choices are even more complicated than where to invest your savings and which health plan to choose. Many employers offer flexible benefits plans, also known as *cafeteria plans.* They provide a fixed amount of benefit dollars, which you allocate based on your priorities. For example, young parents might opt to put more dollars into life insurance and child care benefits. Older employees might funnel more into retirement plans. If your spouse has a good benefit plan, too, you can carve out the best of each package.

A newer option is the Flexible Spending Account (FSA), which you fund by contributing a set amount (up to $5,000 a year) from your pretax compensation. Some employers also add their own contributions. You can use your FSA to fund out-of-pocket medical expenses (including costs that your health insurance may not cover, such as glasses, dental work, and prescriptions) or care for a child or elderly parent. Some plans also allow participants to buy other insurance—long-term care, group auto, homeowner's, or additional life or disability—or even to buy and sell vacation time.

To make the best use of an FSA, carefully weigh your future needs against your past expenses, and don't kick in more than you expect to spend. If you don't use all your FSA money by year-end, you lose it! Employers get to do whatever they want with what's left in the pot. Plan wisely, though, and you'll get a bargain on benefits. For example, if your combined federal, state, and local tax bracket is 40%, it ordinarily costs you about $1.67 to pay for $1 worth of benefits. But because you spend pretax dollars, your FSA lets you buy $1 worth of benefits for just $1.

Aside from FSAs, companies may offer subsidized on-site child care centers or child care referral services. Others are beginning to add emergency or sick-child care centers—a real boon for parents who don't have to miss work if the baby-sitter (or the baby) falls ill. Some employers help with adoption expenses, too. Companies are increasingly recognizing the value of flextime and job sharing as family-friendly perks. And if your firm has 50 or more employees, you can take up to 12 weeks of unpaid sick or parental leave, provided you've worked at least 1,250 hours during the prior year.

Don't overlook Employee Assistance Programs (EAPs) if you or someone in your family needs help coping with a problem such as alcohol or substance abuse, mental illness, or a legal tangle. Besides reducing family stress, these programs may save you a good bit of time and money. (Be sure your privacy will be guarded, though.)

To get the boss to help a little more with balancing job and home pressures, get a free sample of the *Work and Family Life* newsletter (317 Madison Avenue, Suite 517, New York, NY 10017, 800-278-2579). If you like it as much as we do, suggest your firm distribute copies.

You can also increase your loose-change leverage by making sure your employer reimburses you for all job-related expenses. If your boss now has you traveling, you'll probably get reimbursed for your travel costs, including meals on the road. If you aren't collecting for mileage to and from the airport, or if you're making business phone calls from home after hours, you'll want to have the company pay for those, too. Keep receipts and good records, and submit them promptly. A few dollars here and there may not seem like much, but it can really add up.

And in case you didn't catch it in Chapter 6, last, but definitely not least in the parade of perks, is education. Along with on-the-job training, many companies pay part or all of the tuition for courses directly related to your job. Some even reimburse you for study that's unrelated to your work. If your employer offers an opportunity like this, go for it!

STOCK OPTIONS: GETTING A PIECE OF THE PIE

Some years ago, Lena Tice of Atlanta took a job with a company that offered employee stock options. She signed up immediately. "I saw it as a good way to save," she says. "I always participated to the maximum extent they allowed, reinvested the dividends and never touched it, and over the years it has *really* added up."

Stock options aren't just a perk for top executives anymore. Increasingly, they're being used to focus employees' attention on improving shareholder value, while giving them that team spirit. As we mentioned, some companies issue their stock as part of retirement plans, including 401(k) plans or ESOPs.

But now many companies are also giving employees incentives to buy company stock through a stock option plan, not as part of a retirement plan. Here's how it works: Stock options give you the right to buy a certain number of company shares, generally anytime during the next 10 years, at an attractive price (the option *strike price* or *grant price*). What you hope will happen is that the price of the stock will rise, and you can exercise your option. In other words, you want to buy (low) at the strike price and sell (high) at the exercise price.

You lose the option if you don't exercise it. You also lose it if the current market value of the stock is below the strike price when you're ready to buy. (This is called the *underwater* or *Jacques Cousteau option*.)

If you quit or are fired without having exercised your options, you can still use any that are *vested* (i.e., that you've held for a given period, typically one to five years). Options that aren't vested are forfeited.

Stock options can be a great way to increase your wealth. But they are risky. Many, but not all, companies offering this perk are smaller-sized, and as any financial advisor can tell you, small-company stocks are among the most risky. You're able to reduce your risk when you buy at an attractive price, but don't lose sight of the big picture. Diversify. That means you'll want to sell some of your company stock from time to time (depending on company rules) and invest elsewhere—even if the stock seems to be doing very well.

"But," you may argue, "if it's doing well, why would I want to sell?" For one thing, the way to make money in stocks is to "buy low, sell high," and if you've done that, there's no need to get greedy. Second, if you're heavily invested in the stock of the company where you work, you're putting a lot of your future in one basket. If things go sour, your job and your stock could all go south. (It happens, folks!)

CHAPTER 8

Deal Yourself an Ace in the Hole

○ Why an "Ace"—a small, side business—should be a part of your portfolio

○ How to set up shop without a lot of time or money

○ Ways to create an Ace so it's fun as well as profitable

In order to live without a job, you must sacrifice not only boredom but stress, time clocks, regular paychecks, strained relationships, rush-hour traffic, annoying coworkers, bosses, repetitive work, imposed vacations, low expectations, office power trips, company rules, and predictability. I know, it's not always an easy sacrifice.

BARBARA J. WINTER, *Making a Living Without a Job**

Once upon a time, hard work, dedication to the company, and perhaps a strong union guaranteed your job for life. Today, it's far more prudent to assume that sooner or later, you and your job will part company (if you haven't already).

When that happens, will you feel victimized, depressed, and desperate? Or will you be ready to seize the opportunity for a great new beginning? Your choice.

---

* Barbara also puts out a great newsletter. For a sample copy, send $1 and an SASE to *Winning Ways*, P.O. Box 390412, Minneapolis, MN 55439-0412.

It's our firm belief—and long-term experience—that developing and maintaining a teeny, tiny business of your own, what we call an "Ace in the Hole," is one of the best investments you can make for yourself and your family.

You can create your own Ace almost painlessly, with very little money, with virtually no financial risk, and in far less time than most Americans spend staring at a TV screen. You'll have protection against tough times, and the wonderful feeling of being in control of your own destiny.

You don't need to burn any bridges, mortgage the farm, quit your job, hire attorneys and accountants, work around the clock—or invent a better mousetrap. You just need to pick a reasonable path, take a few well-calculated, very low risk steps, and let your Ace grow slowly. Soon, you'll have confidence, cash, and another way to make a living, should the you-know-what hit the you-know-where. You'll also get two important bonuses:

- Extra income
- Tax deductions

So why isn't there a business booming on every kitchen table? Despite our reputation as the land of opportunity, you've probably been led to believe that starting a business is so costly, risky, and regulated, you'd be nuts to try. Nonsense! Allow us to demystify the process.

START NOW

Begin by simply giving the possibility of creating an Ace in the Hole some serious consideration. This probably isn't the first time you've daydreamed about being your own boss, but maybe it can be the first time you take concrete steps to research your options and then to test the waters.

Take your time. Neither Rome nor Microsoft were built in a day . . . and you, hopefully, still have a paying job. What you're looking for now is an opportunity for down the road, not an earthshaking inspiration that has to be implemented by noon tomorrow. Sit down, relax, and make a list of those hobbies, interests, or skills that you really enjoy.

Skim magazines for business ideas that intrigue you. As you do, think about what you might really find interesting, exciting, and meaningful—worth crawling out of bed to do, day after day. Think about the kind of environment you want to work in, the types of people you want to be around, your ideal working day. Be serious, be silly, be creative—but fill up at least a page.

Mull over those things that you do best. Do you make the best choco-late chip cookies your church group has ever tasted? Mrs. Fields, move over!

Ask friends and colleagues for ideas and for their thoughts on your skills and strengths. What businesses can they see you in? A friend may recognize your culinary talents as worthy of a catering venture; a neigh-bor who focuses on your knack for fixing computer problems may sug-gest it as a service others would be happy to buy. Who knows? Your friend may even become your first client!

....

CYBERSOURCES FOR YOUR ACE

Cruise these Web sites and their links for great ideas, inspiration, and hands-on help in bringing your Ace into reality:
   Working Solo: www.workingsolo.com
   Guerilla Marketing Online: www.gmarketing.com
   SBA Online: www.sbaonline.sba.gov
   The Idea Café: www.ideacafe.com
   Business@Home: www.gohome.com

....

If inspiration still hasn't struck, there are lots of ways to find your niche. Skim through the Yellow Pages, scan the classified ads in newspa-pers, go to a flea market, walk down Main Street—and through a mall. Check out books from the library (e.g., *101 Best Home Businesses* by Dan Ramsey), attend some "how to start your own business" classes, take career aptitude exams, and pay attention to how others are making a liv-ing on their own. And definitely tune in when you hear, "I wish there were someone I could call to . . . ."

THREE STRATEGIES FOR ACE BUILDING

1. Do something you know. Peter Lynch, the famed investment advisor, recommends that you buy stocks of companies you know or understand. The same approach can work well with your Ace. If you're an administra-tive assistant by day, you could spend evenings and weekends helping small businesses with data processing chores. If you work in public rela-tions, you may be able to promote a few private clients on the side. Just don't take on work that competes with your full-time job, unless you're prepared to be unemployed should the boss find out!

The advantages of building an Ace from your current experience and skills can be numerous: You avoid the learning curve; you can take advantage of those contacts you already have; you know what to charge; you can gauge the workload involved in different projects; and you have a proven track record to show clients. This type of business can often be started more quickly than others, and it may show a profit faster than something brand-new.

The danger lies in burnout: too much of the same old same old. To persevere through the ups and downs of running a small business, you *must* do something you enjoy. You don't have to love every aspect of it, but you do have to be excited enough to come home from the first job and be willing to put in time on the second one. So if you hate the line of work you're in now, choose another approach.

2. Cash in on a passion or hobby. Imagine feeling more motivated, happier, and richer—just because you're focusing your efforts on one of your real interests. Doing something you love can be tremendously rewarding. Some entrepreneurs find themselves asking, "You mean I can get paid to have this much fun?"

Any hobby can become a business: cooking, flying, fishing, sports, stamp collecting, carpentry, electronics, music, gardening, or art. Some pay better than others, and some are easier to start than others. As long as you remain open-minded and optimistic, you can have fun while you try it out.

Be careful, though. Some people have found that turning their hobby into a profit-making venture quickly turns fun into a burden. The only way to know if that will happen to you is to try it. That's why investing a minimal amount of time and money into your start-up is so important. If you aren't having a ball, you can drop the idea without regret or modify it without too much cost.

3. Try something new. Maybe you've always been chained to a desk, longing for a job outdoors. Perhaps you want to try something more creative than what you're currently doing. Or maybe you're just itching for a change.

While starting a completely different business offers tremendous opportunities for both personal and professional growth, it's obviously harder than staying with something you know. You won't have the advantage of referrals from people who are already familiar with your reputation or talents, and you'll have to do much more research to get up to working speed.

But if you keep at it, you may ultimately develop a brand-new set of skills—and your dream business. Fortunately, we're talking about a low-risk investment. What have you got to lose by spreading your wings a bit and trying something new?

IN A NUTSHELL

The secret to entrepreneurial success boils down to choosing something you want to be doing, keeping costs down, offering attractive prices, and delivering a high-quality product or service. It's that simple.

AND NOW FOR A FEW DON'TS

- Don't choose a business solely to make money. You've seen those lists of the best small businesses to start? Or maybe you were roped into a network marketing scheme that sounded lucrative but went nowhere for you. If you're hooked up to the Internet, your e-mailbox has probably been jammed with "golden opportunities." Don't even bother to read those ads that say you can make $5,000 a month part-time selling their product or buying their system. You'd have a better chance with a lottery ticket. Just send that spam to the cyber-landfill.

- If you don't have a sincere interest in the type of work you'll be fitting into your evenings and weekends, you'll quit before you've begun. It's crucial to believe that what you're doing is important, but it's more important to enjoy what you do. So use those lists to generate ideas, but think hard before getting involved in a business just because it's hot.

- Don't get hung up on the idea that your Ace has to be unique. It can be, but it doesn't have to be. While there's a benefit to doing something better, cheaper, faster, or with a dazzlingly brilliant twist, the only requirement is that you serve a real need at a fair price. There really are very few new ideas under the sun, and many businesses—small and large—have been successful because they *provided worthwhile products or services . . . and kept improving them.*

That, plus attention to detail and a genuine concern for your customers will put food on your table and pride in your heart. When you do finally sign up some customers, ask them for feedback, thank them when they give it to you, and try to hear what they're saying.

- Don't be afraid to ask how you can serve them better next time. If you haven't heard from good customers in a while, call to find out if everything is okay and if there's something you can do for them. If you're genuine and not pushy, they'll appreciate the call.

....

YOU NEVER KNOW WHEN INSPIRATION MAY STRIKE

Al Lococo enjoyed his work, was well paid, and had a secure full-time job. He was in an ideal position to slowly and steadily nurture and focus his small start-up business. When he was offered a generous early retirement package, after 28 years with the firm, Al was ready. Now he's working at his Ace full-time, and loving it.

Al's original thought had been to transfer his computer expertise into a desktop publishing business. But because he was flexible and open to opportunity, Al soon found a more appropriate niche.

At a checkup, he mentioned his new business idea to his physician, who asked about Al's desktop publishing expertise (which was close to nil). Doc mentioned that he'd love to find someone to make monthly backups of the data on his computer's hard drive and at the same time check his PC for viruses.

By the time Al left the office, he had a clean bill of health, a new focus for his Ace, his first paying customer, and a great service he could provide to local doctors and other small businesses. (We love the idea of Al diagnosing and curing viruses for doctors!)

....

GETTING STARTED

Once you have a list of ideas, you're ready to start narrowing them down. Think first about what you want from your business. Do you want something that will stay small, or are you hoping to be out on your own full-time in a year? How much income will be enough to keep you interested and motivated? What types of skills will these businesses depend on? What's the market outlook? Who will your competition be?

Your research will depend a lot on the type of business you want to start and how much you know about it. The more time you invest in figuring out what will work best for you, the more likely you are to enjoy what you do—and to succeed. Maybe you know what you like—your hobby is knitting and you'd like to turn it into an Ace—but you have no idea how.

That's what you have to research next. You might start by scanning knitting magazines to see how others are trying to make a living—or by visiting local craft and specialty stores. If you walk in during a quiet time of day and ask the owner for tips or advice, you'll probably be amazed. Most people really want to be helpful.

Ask pointed questions: "If I wanted to make $50 a week knitting, what would you recommend I do? How about $100? Could I make a living knitting?" Of course, a bit of tact is in order. It's not a good idea to walk in at a busy time, interrupt a sale, mention that you're thinking of opening a competing store down the street—and then expect the merchant to fork over the names of suppliers.

Take a spin on the Net, starting with a general search in Yahoo and Dejanews. Visit sites left and right to get ideas on how others are trying to make a living and to locate suppliers. Also visit your local library—the original information highway. Reference librarians are great at ferreting out all kinds of information. For example, ask your librarian about the trade associations and journals that might help you learn about trends, suppliers, colleagues, and competitors.

And consider a more hands-on approach. A part-time job in a crafts store for a few hours—maybe just to help out on Saturdays—would give you an opportunity to talk with both pros and the people who shop there. Or you could rent a booth at a crafts show for a few bucks to see what kind of reaction your knitwear gets. That means you'll need some inventory—even if all you hope to do is get some orders for future delivery—so start clicking those needles!

Cast a wide net (whether on the Net or not) as you research your Ace. You'll get some good ideas, some leads, and maybe even some customers.

Slow and Steady Still Wins Most Races

Set your initial sights on developing a modest backup source of income—not on creating a new corporate empire. Although you may indeed decide to take your business full-time at some point, micro-mini businesses expose you to micro-mini risks—and allow you to keep the regular checks, fringe benefits, and security of your day job as you test the waters of self-employment.

In fact, the main advantage to a tabletop business is the lack of risk. Because you can start with a tiny budget and you won't need to make an immediate profit, you can afford to learn from experience. Once you've proven it can work, you can always ratchet up the speed of expansion.

Remember, one of the best reasons to set up an Ace is to have something to fall back on in case your situation changes. *Even if you don't see large profits in the beginning, an Ace (or two) is a solid long-term investment in yourself and your family. Ideally, yours could be your source of income sometime down the road—if you either need or want to go out on your own.* Choose yours with that in mind. It always pays to treat your business as if it could provide your paycheck next year. That keeps you on your toes, looking for new opportunities and ideas. It also helps you take yourself and your work seriously.

....

AN ACE THAT NEVER WAS: A TRUE STORY

Will thought he had an idea for a better mousetrap, only in this case, it was a decorative toilet plunger. This new gizmo would be so attractive that everyone would be happy to have one in each bathroom. Will was sure his plunger would make him a fortune. After all, there are 165,812,000 bathrooms in U.S. households alone. All his money worries would be over.

Will spent many an hour coming up with the perfect name for the plunger. (Unfortunately, we no longer recall what it was.) So sure was he of his venture's ultimate success, *he had begun to design the manufacturing plant*—which would be in Southeast Asia, where labor was cheap.

There was just one minor problem: Will had never bothered to create a prototype. He had no way of knowing if the millions of his decorator plungers he fantasized coming down the assembly line would actually plunge! In the end, Will wasted rather than invested a lot of time and effort in a fantasy, not a business.

Moral: Don't construct and equip a modern factory before you've tested and sold an awful lot of widgets.

....

To Market We Go

Before you put a lot of time into your Ace, make sure the idea will fly—that there's a market for your product. That means creating some kind of prototype and testing it out in the marketplace. Your journey to entrepreneurial glory won't get very far until you have a product or service that will draw customers—and keep them coming back for more.

Enlist friends as guinea pigs. Ask them to wear your hand-knit sweaters and see if that generates some word-of-mouth business for you. Or contact local charitable organizations and offer to donate your chocolate chunk cookies to their next fund-raiser. Be there to get a taste of the response and to hand out a little brochure on your line of baked goods.

Take samples of your hand-carved, wooden space aliens to the local flea market. Purchase inexpensive classified ad space in the local paper to advertise that you make house calls to change oil and do other minor car repairs. Can you offer a special for winterizing? How about a free set of windshield wipers with every tune-up?

In short, find out if there is a market for what you are offering—before you spend a fortune or burn yourself out! The beauty of starting out early and small, *before* you need to, is that you can gain valuable but low-cost experience—before you're in a panic with no paycheck in sight.

You also have a golden opportunity to prove yet another bit of conventional wisdom wrong—that most small businesses fail because they're undercapitalized. You won't have to put the touch on friends and family or plead your case to banks and venture capitalists if you begin small and part-time, then grow slowly.

> . . . for the new and growing business, too much money is a greater problem than too little. . . .
>
> —PAUL HAWKEN, *Growing a Business*

When you start your Ace, the idea is to invest your time, energy, and a bit of money into getting a service or product in front of customers—not to set up the ideal office. Apple Computer started in a garage, and many a fortune has been made from the proverbial dining room table.

In truth, if you start small enough, the only thing you'll have to fear is success. Want to know all the other things you won't have to worry about or do? You won't have to get bogged down in plans—be they marketing plans, business plans, financing plans, operating plans, decorating plans, or floor plans.

You won't need to spend a lot of time or money on advertising, employees, insurance, letterhead, business cards, logos, lawyers, bookkeeping, contracts, office space, phone systems, incorporation papers, fancy marketing brochures to exaggerate your importance, impressive vehicles, brand-new office furniture, or manufacturing equipment.

There'll be no need to try keeping your eyes from glazing over as you read boring tomes on accounting, market research, or capital formation for the small business. You also don't need to worry about finding the perfect location, location, location. In this age of toll-free numbers, e-mail, faxes, voice mail, and overnight delivery, most businesses can be started and then successfully operated right from your home.

....

MARC'S PORTABLE CAREERS

Over the years, I've collected a bunch of what I call "portable careers"—skills that I could put to work, anyplace, anytime—to earn money at a moment's notice should I ever need more than I have.

I've been an electrician, a professional engineer, a freelance writer, and a small-scale farmer. I've taught adult education courses, college classes, and been a substitute teacher (never again, thanks). I've bought and sold antiques, real estate, precious metals, baseball cards, and even comic books.

Since Nancy and I began teaching people how to save money, I've picked up a few other skills that I could market anywhere, anytime, such as desktop publishing and inexpensive computer upgrading. And with all the washing machines, dryers, dishwashers, copiers, fax machines, VCRs, televisions, and toasters I've resuscitated over the years, I could put out an appliance repair shingle in Anytown, USA.

For me, the bottom line has its own silver lining: No matter what happens to the economy, no matter where I'm living, I'll always be able to take one of my portable skills out of the closet, to help me make ends meet.

—MARC

....

WHAT'S YOUR BOTTOM LINE?

You may deem your Ace a success if it brings in $50 a week, or maybe you're hoping for more like $500. There's no surefire way to predict how profitable your pursuit will be—but you can do enough research to set a targeted goal. Start by finding out what you can charge. If your past experience was in another field, find out what the competition charges.

If you don't feel comfortable surveying the market yourself, ask someone to do it for you. When she struck out on her own, one consultant we know offered to run a free training program for employees *if* their boss would call around to see what others charged for the same service. The consultant got the information she needed, and the boss was delighted with the program.

Once you know the selling price, estimate how much labor the product or service will take, subtract the cost of supplies or materials, and don't forget to deduct at least 20% for overhead (including taxes). This isn't easy, or an exact science, but it will give you a rough idea of how much you can earn per hour. At that point, you can think seriously about whether it's worth it.

> Small business owners often tell me that making lots of money is not nearly as important to them as making *enough* money for their particular needs. I agree. To me, the most important thing is that I am doing exactly what I want to be doing, secure in the knowledge that I'm spending my life in the most satisfying and profitable way possible.
>
> —BARBARA BRABEC, *Homemade Money*

HOW TO "BE" IN BUSINESS

We hope you'll decide that dealing yourself an Ace or two is worth the investment of your time—to figure out what you might like to do, whether there's a market for it, and what you could earn initially in the process. There's no getting around it. Starting even a small business takes work, but the rewards can be tremendous. To keep your new enterprise afloat and your sanity intact, handle your fledgling business like a real business, which it is, no matter what its size.

Make sure your phone is always answered professionally, even if it also serves as your home phone line. Don't install an elaborate phone system until you need it, but do dump Call Waiting, which is an expensive nuisance.

Show up when you say you will, and do what you say you'll do, or call the customer immediately to make alternative arrangements. Letting people down and making mistakes are costly—and leave everyone wondering what else you might do wrong. So triple-check your work.

Even then, you won't be able to please all of the people all of the time. But you can return their money when you don't . . . every nickel, no questions asked. What good is a guarantee if it's shot full of loopholes? Besides, if you provide a great product or service, few people will ask for their money back.

The main thing you want is to keep them coming back. Although attracting new customers is important, take this old cliché seriously: About 80% of your business is likely to come from 20% of your clients. So treat everyone like a VIP. Win the respect of suppliers, too, and you'll get faster deliveries, plus valuable referrals.

As for the competition, remember the old saw about Macy's not telling Gimbel's? Forget about it! Successful business owners are surprisingly open with their competitors. That's why trade associations are formed. What? There's no association for *your* Ace? Start one. It might be a great way to get publicity as well.

Be persistent, but flexible. If your idea isn't working, it's all right to call it quits and try something else. Learn from your mistakes and move on. That's the great thing about a teeny tiny business—the ease with which you can change direction, purpose, or speed. Eventually, if you keep at it, regularly investing time and energy, you'll come up with an Ace that will make money, give you tax breaks, and protect you from the vagaries of our economy.

You may even choose to change your Ace from time to time. Maybe you'll teach yoga for a couple of years, then decide to write freelance articles, then breed exotic birds. Your friends and family will either admire you or call you nuts—while they're secretly jealous of how much fun you seem to be having. Who could blame them? An Ace gives you the flexibility to pursue your heart's desires while still clothing and feeding the family, ideally with a day job that you also love.

> Working for yourself is the most fun you can have, and get paid for it. . . .
> You'll like it (maybe you already do) because it's the only way you really get
> to define your job and the work that you produce.
> —LINDA STERN, *Money-Smart Secrets for the Self-Employed*

NEVER UNDERESTIMATE THE GOSSIP FACTOR

The best advertising is and always will be word of mouth by satisfied customers. And it's free! Ask customers, friends, and colleagues for referrals. Not asking is a definite *no!*

Also seek out free publicity. Every business has something to teach or share. Become media-savvy and help reporters, editors, producers, and on-air personalities come up with interesting story angles that somehow feature your Ace. The press coverage will help you build credibility and a client base in ways paid advertising simply can't match.

The more you can tie what you're doing to an actual, real event in the community, or perhaps to an upcoming holiday, the more likely you are to get press coverage. Dream up a *great* idea, one you can explain clearly and quickly. Call the local paper, and ask for the appropriate section's editor. Or call the local TV station, and ask for the correct producer.

If your initial idea gets turned down, try another angle or two a month or so later. PR pros say it takes eight tries to get a story in print. So don't take it personally if the answer is, "Thanks, but no." Keep at it. Appreciate feedback and ask for leads to others whose interest might be piqued by your work.

If there is a glimmer of interest, prepare a one-page press release. Make it read just like a story that might appear in the paper. Give it a headline, a few pithy quotes, and a minimum of puff. (Don't cross the line between informing and advertising; they won't buy it.) Make sure to include your name, address, and phone number. Get it there fast, while it's still newsworthy.

Be sure to keep the door open for pertinent pitches you might toss in the future—and for opportunities to be of service. One day soon, you may discover that local media folk recognize you as an expert, someone whose opinion they respect, find amusing, or best of all, think is newsworthy. Then, if you're lucky, they'll call you.

START OUT ON THE RIGHT FOOT

Even in the pursuit of happiness, some restrictions may apply. If it's your business, you're going to have to fiddle with paperwork and occasionally deal with pesky bureaucracies that handle such things as zoning, licenses, taxes, and permits.

At moments, you'll probably wonder, "Is it worth the aggravation?" Our advice: Take a deep breath, fill out the blankety-blank forms, and try to remember that the rewards of your own business usually outweigh the headaches. It's kind of like raising kids.

Despite the "innocent until proven guilty" myth and the new, improved, "kinder" tax collector, the IRS can bankrupt you—which means it pays to keep good, honest records and to file taxes on time.

Even if you've always done your own taxes, a good tax advisor, especially for the first return that includes your Ace, will probably be a good investment. You'll save money and reduce the risk of an audit. Ask specifically about deductions for expenses, including office space, equipment, inventory, supplies, utilities, travel, and publications.

Call the IRS (800-829-1040) to find out if you'll need a federal tax ID number. If you're a "sole proprietor" and don't have employees or a business bank account, you probably won't need one. But do be sure to keep expense records—it's easy if you always pay with checks and credit cards. And save all other business-related receipts.

Another call might be to the agent who handles your homeowner's insurance. Verify that your current policy will cover the equipment you use in your home business and any additional liability you might face should a client slip in your driveway. If special coverage seems to be in order, call around for competitive quotes.

KEEPING EXPENSES DOWN

The best way to succeed is not by pumping cash into your business, but by cutting your expenditures to the bone. Remember—every dollar spent will make it that much harder to turn a profit.

—FRAN TARKENTON, FOOTBALL LEGEND AND
OWNER OF SOME 12 BUSINESSES (www.FTSBN.com)

One great way to get the expertise you need without having to spend a buck is to barter. Maybe your neighbor, the writer, would help with flyers, brochures, ads, and press releases for your child care business in exchange for some free baby-sitting.

Don't buy something for your Ace until you really can't live without it. Comparison shop for everything—long-distance telephone service, bank fees, checks, office supplies, and so on. Buy used, recycle, and reuse things whenever you can—including furniture and office equipment. For example, last year's computer technology will probably work just as well for you as tomorrow's—and will save you a nice chunk of change.

The same holds true for supplies. Don't purchase them in large quantities for your business's birth. Chances are, your needs will change. We know lots of people with boxes full of never-to-be-used business cards.

Decide before you set up shop how much time you're willing to devote to your venture, and then do your best to stick to it, which isn't always easy for Ace builders, who can work days, nights, and weekends. If that means you'll have to turn away customers from time to time, set up a reciprocal agreement with colleagues (some would call them "competitors") who will return the favor when they're swamped with business.

Above all, try not to let earning money interfere with the important job of living your life.

SECRET IV

···

MAKE THE MOST OF THE MONEY YOU BRING HOME

NOTE THE WORDING OF THIS SECRET. IT IS *NOT* "BRING HOME THE Most Money You Can Make." It's "Make the Most of the Money You Bring Home." There's an enormous difference between the two, and it has to do with priorities.

The first makes a contest out of life—whoever has the most at the end wins. While the second puts the focus on more important things—the life you live outside the contest.

In the moneymaking contest, very few of us can reach the finals, and you can't take it with you. There's no glory in dying rich if you've lived poorly.

We can all earn enough money for our basic needs and for satisfying a wide range of desires—if we make the most of the money we do accumulate.

As a nation, we don't make the most of every dollar. We waste money left and right, in dribs and drabs, and it adds up. As Senator Everett Dirksen is credited with saying, "A billion here, a billion there, and pretty soon you're talking about real money."

The same is true about pennies, nickels, dimes, quarters, and dollars. A dollar here, a dollar there, and pretty soon you're struggling from paycheck to paycheck.

The stereotypical family earns almost $55,000. If you can pinch 1% ($10.58 a week), you'd have an extra $550 a year. That would add some nice slush to the vacation fund, or you could sock it away. If you invest that $550 every year at 10%, you'll have over $100,000 in 30 years.

We're going to show you how you can painlessly save money every day without giving up those things you enjoy. The further your money can go, the more you'll be able to get what you want, without making the sacrifices necessary to earn more. The key word here is *painless*.

....

CHAPTER 9

....

Small Change Makes a Big Difference

- ○ Why you don't have to squeeze a penny 'til it hurts
- ○ Why a penny saved is worth much more than a penny earned
- ○ How you can live far better for a lot less without feeling deprived
- ○ The surprising truth about living like a millionaire
- ○ Stopping the insanity of forced giving

To get more money for something you want, you have to spend less on something else. That's all there is to it. You can climb the highest mountain, consult the wisest wizard, and you'll get the same answer.

JANE BRYANT QUINN, *Making the Most of Your Money*

....

Wouldn't it be swell to win a megamillion-dollar lottery? Who'd complain about a fat inheritance from that little old lady you once helped across the street? Or being discovered for the starring role in the next Academy Award–winning movie? Fifteen million plus a percentage of profits would certainly cheer up your afternoon. So would inventing the next hot fad.

But a perfectly wonderful, and in many ways better life can be yours, even if you never once see a seven-figure check with your name on it. Because when it comes to your wallet, small changes can make a tremendous difference in your bank account and in the quality of your life. Maybe the best feature of little changes is that they're within your reach *now.*

Don't believe us? Then keep feeding those slot machines and visiting your sickly rich uncle every weekend. In the meantime, why not take a good, hard look at where your money is going? Odds are, you'll find places where you're spending a lot of money and energy without even realizing it.

Morning coffee brewed at home or at the office could easily save a few hundred dollars a year over the high-priced spread. It may seem a small thing, but $300 a year, over a 40-year career, adds up to $12,000—even if it sits under your mattress. Cutting back on one cup a day can pay for more than a year at most colleges. How many do you buy?

Or perhaps you grab a quick, $2 a day lunch at Chili & Tums Take-Out. Invest that $40 a month in a typical $100,000 mortgage, and you'd save $33,867 in interest, pay the loan off early, and still have years left to invest your $40 somewhere else! (Interested? See Chapter 13.)

One couple we know discovered that they were paying over $700 a year in ATM fees. They were easily able to cut that by more than half just by making an effort to go to their own bank's ATM, which is free. (When they do have to use a foreign ATM, they take out larger withdrawals, because it's the same fee no matter how much you take out.) By saving $350 a year at 10% for 30 years, they'll have an extra $65,931.

Now what if you could find just five "little" things to cut from your spending? Save $5 a week on each, and you'd have $1,300 by year's end. Invest that at 8% for the next 18 years, and there'd be more than $50,000 sitting and waiting for Junior to enter college, or for you to take a year off.

. . . .

GERRI'S TOOLBOX: WRITTEN PROOF

Don't believe that a little money can add up to big bucks? Then try this powerful little exercise: For one month write down *every penny you spend.* Yes, that means every single one, whether it's 35 cents at the pay phone or a few quarters in the vending machine.

It's tedious, we know, but we've yet to talk with anyone who has stuck with it who didn't learn something surprising, and helpful, about where their money was going. Try it for a month and let us know what you discover. We're pretty confident you'll see that the little things really do add up.

Montana State University offers a handy check register for tracking spending. Gerri and her clients love it. Send $1 to: Check Register, Extension Publications Office, Montana State University, Bozeman, MT 59717. Another good tool for taking control of your spending is *The Budget Kit* by Judy Lawrence.

....

BEN FRANKLIN TALKS TAXES

In Ben's day there were no income taxes, and a penny saved was indeed a penny earned. Today, there's not much point in talking pennies, and Ben would have to say the following mouthful: "A dollar earned leaves less than 72 cents after taxes, whereas a dollar saved is $1.40 you'll never have to earn, assuming you're in the 28% tax bracket."

Not as pithy perhaps, but since 1913, when income was first taxed, the gap between earned and saved money has widened. Ben would be amazed to discover that a penny saved today is worth nearly twice as much as a penny earned.

The key to absolutely safe, tax-free investing today is saving money. Fortunately, this doesn't mean doing without. Shopping smarter is one of the best ways to realize double-digit returns on your money, risk-free and guaranteed. Even seasoned investors would be hard pressed to find similar returns, especially on small sums.

For example, say your favorite apple juice normally costs $2.29. On sale, at $1.50, you're guaranteed to save 34%, tax-free. But the *yield* is actually over 52%—because $1.50 will buy what usually costs $2.29. Where else could you get a 52% return on a measly $1.50 investment? At $1.50, buy all you can store!

With investments in supermarket stock regularly paying off like this, you really want to fill 'er up when your favorite staple items are on sale—even if it's herbal tea at the health food store or hazelnut decaf at the gourmet shop. No need to give up the luxuries . . . just buy them smarter! The profits to be had at your local "commodities markets" are truly incredible.

Similarly, by spending an extra minute in the produce aisle, you can earn at least 10%, guaranteed. How? Next time you buy prepackaged fruits or vegetables, weigh a few bags before tossing one into your shopping cart. Take a 5-pound bag of carrots, for example. It must weigh at least 5 pounds. But packers don't have the time or patience to find the perfect-weight vegetable, so they invariably put in extra. That means you can get a bonus half pound or more—for free. It's painless. Try it next time you buy potatoes, apples, oranges, onions, or any other prepackaged produce.

You could start a purchasing club with neighbors and buy goods wholesale—or at least at the big discount clubs. Whether you need a lot of diapers, daffodils, toilet paper, or tennis balls, find out who sells it in bulk, and you'll pay half. If you split the spoils with others, you won't have too many of those huge boxes all over the place!

WHY BOTHER?

Have you ever passed up a penny lying on the street? Figure it's not worth bending down for a cent, right?

Back in the introduction, we suggested taking a large jar and, starting with a single penny, doubling the number of those copper coins you threw in each day for a month. At the end of the month, we said you'd have more than $5 million. Not bad.

Instead of the large jar, picture a checkerboard. Starting with a single penny on space one, each day double the number of coins you put on subsequent spaces (two coins on space 2, four on space 3, eight on space 4, etc.). *In 64 days, you'll be the richest person on earth!* There will be about 9,223,372,000,000,000,000 coins on space 64—that's over 9 quintillion pennies. The number of pennies on the entire board would be 18.4 quintillion, or $184 quadrillion—roughly 3.5 billion times as much as winning a $50 million lottery.

So if pennies mean little to you, give them to us! We'll pile them on a checkerboard. When it's full, we'll pay off the national debt, the debts of every man, woman, and child, and still have plenty left over to eradicate world hunger and poverty.

It Was by Their Own Choice

> *Madison Avenue can't sell us anything we don't want, but it certainly knows how to make us want what it's selling.*

The Spendthrifts* always drive the hottest cars and take budget-busting vacations to wildly expensive, trendy places. Their neighbors, the Savvys,* earn as much, but drive commonsense cars, which they maintain well enough to keep on the road for a very long time. For the Savvys, vaca-

* Not their real names . . . but you already knew that!

tions are more often family camping events, visits to relatives, or adventure days to nearby attractions.

The Spendthrifts are beginning to struggle with the realities of paying for a college education or two, funding their retirement, and helping out their old folks. The Savvys, meanwhile, have a comfortable nest egg already built up, know where their children's college money will come from, and earn their living in ways that allow them plenty of time to deal with family emergencies . . . and pleasures.

Simplistic example? Yes. But it may be more realistic than you think. All across America examples of the Spendthrifts and the Savvys abound:

> My parents weren't poor, they were broke.
> —BILL COSBY on *The Today Show*, 5/19/98

The issue is not how much you make, but what you do with what you have. Even if the Spendthrifts made twice as much as the Savvys—they could still end up twice as deep in debt and with less than half as much at retirement. Now you tell us, who will live happier ever after?

How to Dispose of $2 Million

Assume for the moment that you were going to receive more than $2 million. Would your financial problems evaporate? How would you invest that fortune? How would you spend it? How much would you put aside for your retirement years?

Two million dollars. That's a pile of dough, right? Actually, it's a conservative estimate of what the average working couple will earn in their lifetime. Where does it all go?

The nonprofit, nonpartisan Tax Foundation estimates that between all of the taxes we pay either directly or indirectly (not only income taxes, but sales and real estate taxes, too), about 38 cents is extracted from every dollar we earn. That takes care of about $750,000.

The average family raises children—$180,000 each (before college)—and owns a home. By the time they've paid off the mortgage, another quarter of a million will have been eaten up—plus the home has to be furnished.

A new, financed car every 5 years over a 50-year driving career could cost upward of $200,000, not counting gas, maintenance, or insurance. A leased car would cost even more.

And then there are groceries: another quarter million or so. Plus there's clothing, insurance, vacations, recreation, gifts, phones, electricity, heat, maybe satellite TV, medical bills to be paid, and credit card interest. Is it any wonder that nearly three-quarters of us have nothing left by week's end?

HOW TO PINCH PENNIES . . . WITHOUT FEELING DEPRIVED

You may be convinced that unless you win the Publishers Clearing House Sweepstakes or drastically cut back on your pleasures, you'll never break free of debt and get ahead. Enter those contests if you must, but while you're waiting for the prize patrol, why not invest in simple, painless changes that fit in well with your lifestyle?

We aren't big fans of deprivation, and we doubt that you are, either. We don't care how you pinch your pennies, just that you start doing it. No need to spend hours baking homemade everything, getting your hands (and the floor) filthy trying to recycle vacuum cleaner bags, or pinching your pennies so tightly that your austerity budget drives everyone around you nuts.

Can't give up the morning stop at Dunkin' Donuts? Don't! Come up with other ways to cut your expenses. Perhaps we can help you come up with a few.

For example, what if someone would be happy to come over and show you some easy ways to save money on your electric bill? Wouldn't it be worth a bit of your time? Well, most utility companies will send an expert to survey your house and, for free, show you how to reduce your power consumption. The first step is easy. Call and schedule an appointment.

Many of the recommendations you're likely to hear—like caulking around doors and windows, insulating switches and outlets on outside walls, or covering the air conditioner in winter—won't cost much. Others won't even get your hands dirty, like resetting the timer on your thermostat, or lowering the water heater's temperature. Some utility companies even offer grants, no-interest loans, or partial payment for energy-saving improvements. Ask! The money you save will be your own, month after month. Your lifestyle won't have to change, and you'll be doing your bit for the environment.

It's easy to reduce costs without changing your way of life, without giving up those material things that give you pleasure, and without feeling deprived. Take the telephone, for example. Giving it up would be terrible for most of us, but with one phone call, you can probably lower your costs significantly.

Even if you never do anything else to save money on your phone bill, ring up your current carrier and ask if you're on the plan that will cost you the least. Call AT&T at 800-222-0300, MCI at 800-444-3333, and Sprint at 800-746-3767. Despite endless ads trumpeting their great deals, most folks still pay top dollar to the big three. In fact, we've seen estimates indicating that more than half of us still pay our carrier's highest rates.

While you're at it, disconnect Call Waiting. This nuisance feature is expensive and, for most of us, absolutely unnecessary. Invariably, as you're interrupted again and again, you compile a long list of people to call back—at your expense. Remember, in the event of an actual emergency, your loved ones can always dial 0 and ask the operator to break in on your conversation.

When you're ready to contemplate the pros and cons of other carriers, get *Tele-Tips,* a very complete analysis of the seven major carriers and their assorted plans, available from the Telecommunications and Research and Action Center (TRAC). Send $5 and a business-sized SASE (with 55¢ postage) to TRAC, P.O. Box 27279, Washington, DC 20005, or go to www.trac.org.

In some areas, you may have to pay for "local long-distance calls"— calls that are automatically handled by your local phone company, but are billed separately, like long distance. Sometimes the rate the local phone company charges for these calls is much higher than the low long-distance rate you've negotiated. Compare rates, then simply ask your long-distance carrier for a code you can punch in before you make those calls, and they'll be billed at the lower rate.

Raising the deductibles on your insurance policies ought to be good for a few hundred dollars every year, and with a little thought, we know you can come up with lots of other ways to painlessly cut back a bit on your spending. But if you want to prime your pump, the newsletters and Web sites we recommended in Chapter 1 will help. It also pays to peruse publications such as *Family Circle, Woman's Day, Woman's World,* and *Good Housekeeping.* They're full of good penny-pinching ideas, and your local library no doubt has a slew of books on the subject as well.

. . . .

AN ABERRATION—A GOVERNMENT PROGRAM THAT WORKS

It's easy to find fault with virtually every government program. Many serve special interests, cost way too much, treat the public callously, and/or enforce stupid regulations.

There are exceptions, and we're happy to highlight one of Uncle Sam's best-kept secrets—the Cooperative Extension Service. Whether you work

40 acres with a mule, need your suburban soil analyzed because the azaleas keep dying, or want to set up a community gardening program on empty city lots, this agency can help.

Co-op Extension is also a great place to get practical, up-to-date advice on home buying, nutritious snacks, day care, energy conservation, money management, hurricanes, canning, caning, canines—you name it.

Located in nearly every county, each Extension Service develops its own horticulture, family finance, child development, housing, and nutrition programs, with the help of a state and national information network.

The Catch

While there's probably one of these handy, dandy agencies near you, it may not be easy to find. Check the "Government" section of your phone book, under the state or county listings. No Luck? Call your town clerk or librarian, or log on to www.reeusda.gov/statepartners/usa.htm.

....

THE 10% SOLUTION

The road to economic independence is paved with nickels and dimes, but pinching pocket change alone won't put you on the road to financial freedom. It's what you do with what you save that makes the difference between a debt-filled life and one where you have a lot more options.

Over the years, we're offered lots of opportunities to force ourselves to save: various life insurance programs, Christmas clubs, savings bonds through payroll deductions, and more recently, biweekly mortgage-conversion plans.

We don't feel that "forced" behavior is the best way to invest in your future or to take control of the present. To be successful, you need to be committed. And if you're really committed to changing your life—any aspect of your life—you'll be disciplined enough on your own to make it happen.

If your salary were cut back by 10%, you'd make adjustments, wouldn't you? Now what if that pay cut comes about because you skim 10% off your gross every week—by paying yourself first? If you earn $50,000 a year, that would be $100 a week. Stuffed into your mattress over a 40-year career, you'd ultimately be sleeping on $200,000! But put that tenth of your earnings to work, and amazing things could happen. Invested at 8%, $100 a week would grow to more than $1.5 million at the 40-year mark.

Invest it where? We'll cover this in more detail elsewhere, but here's a sneak peek at the best two places to invest:

1. Your 401(k) or 403(b) at work, especially if your employer matches funds.

2. Your debts. Depending on your tax bracket, paying down a 17% credit card balance is like earning 20% to 25% before taxes. Plenty of investors would jump at a risk-free investment offering that kind of profit. Yet they pass up those returns every month by rolling over a balance on their credit cards.

In addition to the 10% we hope you'll pay yourself, you can put aside another 10% or more, by simply shopping smarter. In fact, saving money on what you buy is the third best way to realize double-digit returns on your money, completely risk-free.

THE QUESTION THAT CAN SAVE THOUSANDS

When you consider major purchases, ask yourself: "What will this cost me in days or years worked before I've paid it off?" Your answer may help you save a bundle—as well as a lot of stress.

Let's talk about one of life's most expensive days, although we could just as easily be talking about a car, or a house, or a sailboat. Say your daughter is getting married. That's the good news. The bad news is that dream weddings these days cost about $17,000.

If your combined federal, state, and local tax bite puts you in a 35% bracket, you'll need to earn over $26,000 *before taxes* to pay for that one beautiful day. That's $9,000 more than you thought it was going to cost. Here's how to do the math. Take the purchase price ($17,000) and divide it by what you have left after taxes, in our case 65% (which is 100% − 35%), and voilà, you have to earn over $26,000.

If you earn $50,000 a year, you'll have to work for more than half a year just to pay for the big bash, and that's assuming that you have $17,000 sitting in the bank waiting to be plunked down on this blessed event.

If you have only $5,000 in cash and charge the other $12,000 to one of your credit cards, that glorious day could set you back—are you sitting?—more than $45,000. And if you keep sending in just those minimums on your card, you'll be paying for that wedding until your daughter's golden anniversary . . . yup, 50 years from now! Your great-grandchildren will be adults, and their children could have already begun school by the time the wedding's paid off. Whoa!

If you don't think that one wedding day is worth upward of a year of your life, maybe you can agree on a less expensive party, or maybe someone else would like to help foot the bill. Either way, you could choose to pass some of the savings on to the newlyweds for the down payment on their vine-covered cottage.

⋯⋯⋯⋯⋯⋯⋯⋯⋯⋯⋯⋯⋯⋯⋯⋯⋯⋯⋯⋯⋯⋯⋯⋯

FOR THE MATH OF IT

Use this technique to decide if any major purchase is really worth the price. First, price the item you're thinking of buying—and if you won't be paying cash, add in any finance charges.

To calculate what you'd have to earn before taxes, divide the total cost by the appropriate number, listed here for your calculating pleasure:

TAX DIVIDERS	
RATE	DIVIDER
15%	.85
28%	.72
31%	.69
35%	.65
39%	.61

Here's an example. You want to buy a couch for $1,000. You plan to finance it for five years at 14.75%. The salesperson tells you that your monthly payment will be *only* $23.66. Over the next 60 months, that means you'd pay about $1,400 ($23.66 × 60).

Assuming you pay 28% in taxes, divide that $1,400 by .72 and you'll discover that the $1,000 couch will cost you nearly double what you thought you'd be spending ($1,944). That's the dollar cost.

Now let's talk about your life cost. Figure out roughly what you make an hour (if you're paid a yearly salary, divide it by 2,000 hours, which is 50 weeks times 40 hours). Let's assume you earn $30,000 a year. That's roughly $15 an hour ($30,000 divided by 2,000). To earn $1,944 will cost you almost 130 hours—over three weeks of full-time labor!

Do you want to spend the next three weeks working for that couch and nothing but that couch? If so, sign the credit slip. If not, sit on the old one a while longer, buy a good used couch or a slipcover, or consider taking a course in upholstery. (That course could be a great investment in yourself. You'd learn a skill that could save and earn you big bucks.)

⋯⋯⋯⋯⋯⋯⋯⋯⋯⋯⋯⋯⋯⋯⋯⋯⋯⋯⋯⋯⋯⋯⋯⋯

IS IT WORTH IT TO ME
TO DO IT ANOTHER WAY?

Real frugality is not about doing without things or activities that are important to you. Real frugality is determining what really is important. Real frugality is about setting priorities. And if cable television, European vacations, or steak are important to you, well whose business is it?

—LARRY ROTH, *The Simple Life*

If doing the math makes your eyes cross, then think of Irene and Kevin Wrenner—and what your alternatives are—next time you're making a decision about whether to spend big bucks.

When Irene accepted Kevin's marriage proposal, there was no ring in his pocket—just a book of clever cartoons he'd sketched of Irene and her family. They decided to select their rings together, so Irene would have a say, and her engagement and wedding rings would match.

Shopping for that jewel of love, the Wrenners found themselves asking, "Should we spend $5,000 or $6,000 on a modest-sized gemstone—one that isn't too yellow, brown, or flawed? The more we contemplated paying for a rock that could be lost or stolen," as Irene explains it, "the less appealing the whole idea seemed."

Was there an alternative? Irene and Kevin began to wonder about the price of a ring set with a one-carat cubic zirconia. So they revisited three jewelers. "Not one jeweler entertained our suggestion," Irene reports.

"The mystique of the more popular rock is what keeps these folks in business," Irene said. "Selling a low-priced clone would reveal the very foolishness on which, I believe, they thrive: the idea that only a precious diamond will do."

For the Wrenners, it wouldn't do. They found an out-of-town jeweler who would supply, cut, and mount a one-carat cubic zirconia in a beautiful setting—for $75—just 1.5% of what they easily could have spent.

Irene's rock is nearly as brilliant, and far more perfect than any commercial diamond they'd seen. How does she know it's as good as the rest? As Irene puts it, "I work in northern New Jersey—land of nail polish, real jewelry, and big, dazzling rocks. Yet I receive constant comments on the beauty of my bargain ring."

With the money they saved on their ring, Irene and Kevin took a wonderful trip to Prague and Budapest to explore Irene's heritage, followed by a journey to Finland, the land of Kevin's ancestors. Although more than 70% of couples contemplating marriage spring for the real thing, the

Wrenners came up with a perfectly reasonable alternative—for them—to spending their share of the astounding $2.7 billion that a year's worth of lovebirds spend on diamond engagement rings.

By the way, according to our favorite retired diamond dealer, the average diamond is a pretty lousy investment. Its value is unlikely to appreciate enough to ever return what you paid, even if you were to sell it privately.

Speaking of dealers, while there certainly are honest ones, some aren't. It's not easy to be sure how much a particular diamond is worth or that the stone you bought is the one actually mounted in your setting. Of course, there's no need to worry if it's a cubic zirconia.

Whether you're buying an engagement ring or a new car, or making a career change—first weighing your priorities and the alternatives is a gem of an idea! It won't cost you any money—but could save you a pile. It might even bring you and your mate closer together and improve the quality of your life—as it did for Kevin and Irene.

∙∙

THE DIFFERENCE BETWEEN NEW AND USED

The things we buy, whether clothes, cars, toys, furniture, or appliances, are only new until we buy them. Once we own them, they're used. Therefore, everyone eats off a used table, wears used clothes, washes their used clothes in a used washing machine, and drives a used car. It comes down to: who used it first, for how long, was it well maintained, and does being first matter enough for you to pay the inflated "new" price?

∙∙

Grandma's Table

Few of us would long enjoy sitting on wooden crates. They're not comfortable; we'd get splinters; they're not particularly attractive; and like much of the furniture being manufactured today, they're not as durable as they were in days gone by.

So we rush out to the giant clearance sale at the local furniture farm and plunk down our card for a bedroom, dining room, or living room ensemble that costs a fortune and, like those wooden crates, isn't anywhere near as durable as Grandma's.

Now here's the strange part. Grandma's dining room table and chairs can be bought for a fraction of the cost of a new set and will be worth as much, or more, when you go to sell them. And a new set will be worth almost nothing as soon as you get it home!

Tip: *Buy good used furniture. Whether at the Salvation Army, a moving sale, or an antique store, good furniture is always available at a very fair price.*

Auctions can be fun family outings, especially country auctions, where treasures can often be found among the boxes of junk. Between auctions, moving sales, the classifieds, and thrift stores, a home can often be furnished, beautifully, for less than the cost of a new couch.

Let someone else buy the modern junk to fuel the nation's economy. Stick with the tried and true. It'll shore up *your* economy.

. . . .

GERRI'S TOOLBOX: WALK ON BY

Ever walked into a store intending to buy one thing and walked out with a lot more . . . of something else? Impulse purchases can drain your pocketbook faster than Roto-Rooter can unclog your drains. Here's one small but powerful change you can make in your tactics: Just walk away! If you walk away from an item you're considering, chances are, you won't return. Tell yourself that if you really want it, you can always come back. If you really do want it, you will.

Paul Richard, vice president of the National Center for Financial Education (www.ncfe.org) suggests another smart strategy. Before you make a purchase, take the time to visualize three other ways you could spend that money. Make this a habit, and you may just find yourself stopping impulse purchases dead in their tracks.

But if you find that the credit card bills just keep on growing anyway, leave the plastic at home. Research shows that people will spend more—as much as an additional 30% or more—when they're using plastic rather than cash. If the plastic's not in your pocket, maybe you'll lose interest before you get around to coming back to make the deferred purchase.

Of course, the absolute best way to avoid impulse purchases is to avoid temptation by staying out of malls and marts and putting those mail-order catalogs directly into the circular file.

. . . .

QUESTION: My problem is that I really like to shop. I admit that I relax by going to the mall and hunting bargains, and I know I'm spending more than I should. Please don't tell me to take a walk instead, I've tried that and it just doesn't work for me.

—CONFESSED SHOPAHOLIC

ANSWER: Since it's the rush of buying that you're hooked on, why not try to channel it into something more productive?

Maybe you can emulate Lee, who describes herself as "just your average housewife." She's created a fun way to make extra cash—by turning her garage sale finds into weekly contributions of around $25 to her family's nest egg.

"Early in the summer, I bought a double baby stroller at a garage sale for $25, thinking I'd use it with my two young children," Lee says.

But her 3-year old preferred to walk, so Lee was stuck wondering what to do with her new purchase. She took it to a children's store and sold it for $35. "That led me to ask what things they wanted most, so I could look out for them at garage sales," Lee explains.

"Then, at a garage sale around the corner from my sister's house, I bought another double stroller for $8." She sold it a few hours later, at her sister's garage sale for $45! She's also had success buying and selling antiques.

If turning your shopping habit into a cash-based business doesn't appeal to you, try a part-time job at the mall. That will surely cure your desire to hang out there in your spare time, and maybe you'll get an employee discount, too!

Of course the best thing you could do would be to find a more productive way to spend your time. How about shopping for a soup kitchen or elderly neighbors? Or starting a shopping service for harried executives?

Rein in Holiday Spending

Christmas comes but once a year. It's the happiest time of year for retailers, because Americans shell out some $160 billion a year on fa la la la la, alone. New gift-giving holidays are being created all the time, in case we have any credit still available after buying for birthdays, weddings, anniversaries, baby showers, Valentine's Day, Mother's Day, Father's Day, Grandmother's Day, Secretary's Day, and Boss's Day. During Pet's Week, many a "lucky" Fido gets a rhinestone-studded chain, a ceramic bone with his name engraved on it, or some other trinket to help fill up a closet in his colonial-styled doghouse.

For many of us, the holiday spirit gets lost in a frantic search for gifts—and by the need to use high-interest credit cards to pay for them. At last count, Americans had more than $455 billion revolving on their plastic. The sad truth is that once we whip out our charge cards, many of us fall prey to impulse buying and spend substantially more than we had planned.

Haunted by Hallmark

Does true love (even moderate friendship) need an influx of corny sayings to survive? We don't believe so. Does going broke prove love, appreciation, deep religious belief, or friendship? Hardly!

Why not invest in your future rather than in overcommercialized, make-believe holidays? Stop buying your share of the 7 billion greeting cards Americans send each year at a cost of over $7 billion. Whatever happened to that old-fashioned handwritten note saying, "Hope you feel better soon," or "I'm thinking of you"? Think of all the time you could save by never going card shopping again!

Avoiding "Love Token" Poverty

Admit your sanity. With 30% of Americans seriously overweight, why do we spend $940 million on sweets for Easter and another $725 million for Valentine's Day? Talk to everyone you exchange gifts with and change the rules. Stop it altogether, or agree to set a lower limit or to exchange only homemade goodies, or perhaps buy presents only for people under 21.

At a minimum, agree not to trade meaningless junk just to give something. Suggest that your family and friends pool resources. Buy the bride, birthday boy, or long-married couple a really significant present. And remember, "significant" doesn't have to be expensive.

About 10 years ago, Harry Lazare, who used to work with Marc and Nancy, got tired of struggling with their old, persnickety, hand-crank can opener. He gave them a sturdier, more reliable (also nonelectric) model. Hardly expensive, but Harry's gift was so thoughtful and so needed that they were delighted, and to this day, think of Harry every time they take it out of the drawer.

Start some inexpensive traditions: A group-cooked meal, a trip to your favorite museum or park . . . perhaps something that really celebrates what the holiday is supposed to commemorate (like a birthday visit to the town where you were born).

With families getting so complicated these days, more and more of us are conflicted about where to have holiday meals. Do we join this side of the family or that . . . or that? Years ago, Nancy, Marc, and Marc's children began to celebrate Thanksgiving on virtually any day but the fourth Thursday of November. It's become so much fun, they try to have numerous Thanksgiving dinners throughout the year.

Think of all the benefits to celebrating the holidays a month earlier or a month later: While you prove your independence and sanity, you'll also avoid the hype, the crowds, the costs, and the hassles.

When You Care Enough to Give the Very Best

A perfect gift for new parents or someone recuperating from surgery is a home-cooked meal. For a loved one who's temporarily bedridden, why not send an assortment of your favorite books?

If they aren't already in your repertoire, how about learning to make soups, breads, jams, or herb vinegars? Then you can put together gift baskets of your goodies. Like everything else, if you do it yourself, you can save money and really personalize the assortment.

Can you knit, do needlepoint, make wooden toys, or compile some of your favorite recipes?

Or give the gift of time and offer to babysit for a niece, nephew, the neighbor's child, or your grandkid. Let their frazzled parents take a kid-free minivacation, even if it's only a peaceful night's sleep! Or agree to donate some of your time—together—to a homeless kitchen or another worthwhile organization.

Or share a skill. If you're a master gardener, commit to helping a friend develop a green thumb. Can you strum a guitar, make a bench, reupholster a couch, or teach magic? We'd rather learn a skill than get a hideous tie. Wouldn't you?

All year long, keep your eyes out at church rummage sales, garage sales, auctions, and consignment shops for gift ideas. Recycled toys that you've cleaned up are great for kids. Special dishes, picture frames, or antique tools can also make perfect presents.

. . . .

HAVE A VERY MERRY UNBIRTHDAY!

When you see something that you know will be useful, affordable, appreciated, or just plain enjoyed, why not declare your own holiday? There were some very wide smiles on Marc's children's faces the day he unexpectedly drove up with a very much used bicycle built for two strapped to the car's trunk.

Sarah, the bundle-of-energy daughter of our researcher, Marcy Ross, received an instant family heirloom from a doting aunt and uncle, who stripped and repainted an old children's rocking chair they found at a tag sale.

....

Vacations and Getaways: Ways to Save Money While You Have Fun

Once a month, spend a romantic evening at home. Bundle the kids off on sleep-overs, prepare a great meal for two, unplug the phone, light some candles, and enjoy. Take the $50 a month that you'll save on dinners, and invest it in your $100,000 mortgage. You'll save almost $40,000.

Vacation a week before or after the season. You can easily save half on both the airfare and lodgings—without sacrificing your tan or a single downhill run. Plus, places of interest will be less crowded and shopkeepers more eager to please.

Compare airports. Similar flights from nearby airports to the same destination can have dramatically different fares. Gerri has often cut her airfare in half by driving an extra half hour to Baltimore-Washington International Airport. (Parking is cheaper there, too.)

Vacation at home. Stock the refrigerator. Tell everyone you'll be out of town for the week. Cancel the newspaper. Unplug the phones. Have the post office hold your mail. Visit local attractions. Then use the thousands you'll save to pay down your debts and retire a few years early.

Stay with faraway relatives and friends, but don't expect them to fund your vacation. Offer to help with groceries, be prepared with your own transportation, and check out guidebooks from your local library so you can keep yourselves entertained if your host needs a break. You'll still save a lot, and your hosts will be that much more likely to welcome you back.

....

MOTEL MADNESS

You can easily be quoted four different rates for the same room at the same motel on the same day. "That's totally unfair and unkind . . . forcing travelers to be so assertive," says Nancy Dunnan, managing editor of *Travel Smart,** a monthly newsletter filled with travel tips and deals.

If you're not desperate for a room, you can get a better rate by following these *Travel Smart* tips:

* For a free sample copy of *Travel Smart,* call 800-327-3633, and mention *Invest in Yourself.*

1. Don't expect the best deal from a chain's toll-free number. Call the motel directly. Once you're quoted a rate, ask if it's absolutely the lowest rate possible.
2. Never accept the first rate you're offered. Ask about specials.
3. Plan ahead and book early, before all the discounted rooms are sold out. The motel guides that you can pick up at state welcome centers, rest areas, and gas stations often offer great rates.
4. Don't walk in with large pieces of luggage if you hope to negotiate a rate. Once a motel or hotel sees you've reached the "point at which you'll collapse," Nancy Dunnan explains, you've lost much of your bargaining power.
5. Mention any membership or affiliation that could qualify you for a discount. In addition to AAA and AARP, let the clerk know if you're there to visit someone in a hospital, a member of the military, a stockholder in the chain, or if you're eligible for a corporate discount.
6. Hesitate, and you may be offered a "fallback rate," perhaps for a room without a view or near the laundry.
7. If you can't get the lowest rate, ask for a freebie. It might be a coupon or voucher good on another stay, a room upgrade, or a free breakfast.

If you discover that you didn't get the best rate, and the manager isn't helpful, then when you return home, Nancy Dunnan advises that you start complaining *at the top*—that is, write to the president of the hotel chain. Be sure to get the names of staff who were unhelpful, so you can be very specific in your complaint.

To add punch to your letter, make it clear that you'll be sending copies to the Better Business Bureau, the local newspaper in the town where you stayed, and the consumer affairs offices at organizations such as AARP and the AAA. Then send them off.

....

LIVE LIKE A MILLIONAIRE

Do the words *tightwad* or *frugal* conjure up images of stinginess or poverty for you? If so, it might surprise you to learn that one characteristic that many of the wealthiest people in America share is frugality. In their best-seller, *The Millionaire Next Door,* Drs. Thomas Stanley and William Danko explain that three words describe millionaires in America: "Frugal, Frugal, Frugal."

While most portraits of the rich tend to focus on how they made their millions, Stanley and Danko are the first to focus on an important truth: Most truly wealthy people also tend to be very careful about how they spend their money. In fact, after 20 years of studying these prodigious savers, these two researchers have come to the conclusion that "Being frugal is the cornerstone of wealth-building."

> The leaner your spending is today, the fatter your cushion will be tomorrow.
> —CHRISTINE DUGAS, *Fiscal Fitness:*
> *A Guide to Shaping Up Your Finances for the Rest of Your Life*

Millionaires Humberto and Georgina Cruz built their fortune on very average salaries. In some years, they saved and invested up to 66% of their income. Humberto, a top-notch personal finance writer, certainly practices what he preaches!

While we Americans tend to glamorize free-spending, high-earning businesspeople, athletes, and celebrities, in truth many of them aren't rich at all. Many of them are flat broke, or on their way to being there. They spend what they earn and have no way to tide themselves over when the income stream isn't running high. And because they know only how to spend, they don't know how to live well when they have less.

For some inspiring stories about celebrities, including a few who have rebounded from years of debt to financial success, read *The Rich & Famous Money Book* by Jean Sherman Chatzky.

But whether they get it right the first time or on the rebound, what makes millionaires successful? First, most know how much they spend on everything. They pay attention to all that small stuff and are very careful with their resources, spending much less on luxury items than you would expect. They tend to drive cars longer and don't often lease. They don't spoil their kids, and they save or invest 20% of their income—before taxes! (Compare that with most of us, who'd love to be able to save 10% of our income *after* taxes.)

You may never become, or even want to become, a millionaire, but next time you're watching your pennies, remember, you're in good company.

··

CHAPTER 10

Penny-Pinching for Fun and Profit

- ○ Techniques for making penny-pinching fun
- ○ The all-important question to ask yourself
- ○ Secrets of successful "hondlers"
- ○ Shopping myths debunked

Don't confuse frugality with depriving yourself.

JONNI MCCOY, *Miserly Moms*

···

If you enjoy yard sales, flea markets, and thrift shops, you're penny-pinching for fun and profit. If you like to use coupons while you're shopping, send in for rebates, or watch for sales before you head to the marketplace, you're penny-pinching for fun and profit. Ditto if you love the smell of sun-dried clothes and also appreciate the savings on your electric or gas bill.

When you get a great buy on a dress, a computer, or a car, you're penny-pinching for profit. If you feel good when the deal's done, you're penny-pinching for fun, as well.

But there are times when this strategy just doesn't make sense. It's late at night, you're driving home in the rain, the gas gauge is on E, but there's a cheap gas station about 20 miles ahead. You could save 10 cents a gallon by pumping your own gas—if you can make it that far. Or you can stop right here at a pricey, full-service station, and let someone else weather the storm. If you choose to penny-pinch now, you may profit, but if you run out of gas, you sure won't have any fun. Sometimes it's dollar-foolish to be penny-wise.

Often, though, it can be fun, even a challenge, to get the best value on those things we buy. And the less we spend, the more we'll have for other things down the road. For example, take toys. If you have young children, you probably find yourself spending more than you'd like on toys.

Spring-cleaning season is a great time to collect hand-me-down toys from friends and relatives. Scrub them up, make sure they're safe and intact, then give a couple to the kids. Put the rest away until you need a birthday present, Christmas gift, or reward for a job—or report card— well done. They'll be just as appreciative, and you'll have that much more to spend on something that would really be meaningful.

You know how quickly children get bored with toys, so why not start a toy library in your community, where kids can check out toys for a few weeks, then return them for something else? (You'll have less clutter, too, which is another reward for you.)

THE TOOTHPASTE SYNDROME

The commercial comes on. Someone whose mother or father is a dentist tells you how wonderfully white and cavity-free her teeth are because she now uses new, improved, dental association–approved, cavity-fighting, plaque-removing, breath-sweetening Quite White Toothpaste.

And then she squeezes out a line of Quite White from one end of her toothbrush to the other and partway back. Actual dentists say a pea-sized dab of paste is all we need. Whose recommendation do you trust?

The message we get is that our teeth will be glaringly white, just like hers, if we overconsume this particular brand of toothpaste, which to all intents and purposes is identical to all of the other brands on the shelf.

Overconsuming is the modern way. The toothpaste syndrome is contagious. We live in bigger homes than our parents, we eat more food than ever before, we use more power, we buy much more than we need, and we think that's the way it has to be.

When Gerri was an exchange student in Japan for a year, her host mother was horrified by the amount of dishwashing soap Gerri used, claiming that what Americans consider a perfectly normal amount of soap would make everyone sick. Gerri assumed just the opposite: Using as little soap as her Japanese family did wouldn't get the dishes clean!

Many times, what or how much we use is just a matter of habit, with no basis in reality. Whether it's food on our plates or the detergents we pour into the washing machine, using just enough to get the job done is the sensible, money-saving way to go. Make a family contest out of guessing how much laundry detergent it really takes to do a load of laundry. To establish minimums, experiment!

Obviously, there are some things you can't skimp on: You don't want to take half as much insulin or to change the oil in your car half as often as the manufacturer recommends. But try to recognize conditioned responses and habits for what they are. Where it can't hurt, try using less. Then use the money you save to pay off debts, invest, or treat yourself to something special—a reward for good behavior.

NOT ASKING IS AN AUTOMATIC "NO!"

Price checking pays big returns on all sorts of goods and services. For example, a few calls to local fuel oil companies got Sally a low rate and a year's free service on her oil burner.

She was pleased with the price and service, but a year or so later, in doing her annual checking around, discovered that a competitor was offering fuel for 10% less. Sally promptly called her fuel company. The response? "We'll match any price you can get."

Sally stayed, but her annual fuel bill of $1,200 was reduced by $120, the equivalent to Sally earning $171.43, before taxes. In her 30% combined federal/state tax bracket, she'd have to earn 14.3% on a $1,200 investment to come up with that $171.43. Sally enjoyed her few minutes of price checking and profited rather handsomely in the bargain.

Whether it's to get a better credit card interest rate, lower insurance premiums, or the best phone deal—sometimes all you need to do is ask. True, some of those times, you may need to ask and ask again. But if you want to guarantee that you'll save a lot of money over the years, memorize this phrase: "Not asking is an automatic *no!*"

Yes, they may very well say no! But if you don't ask, you'll never know how much you might have saved. Another example: For three years running, Pete has phoned to cancel his credit card, citing the high fee. Each time, the card issuer has offered him a gift certificate, good anyplace the card is honored—if he would pay the fee and keep the card. Total savings: $165. Will they give him the same deal next year? Pete doesn't know, but he'll sure dial the toll-free number and ask!

I smell a refund. When Linda decided to cancel a whopping 20 credit cards, she had to ask—sometimes insist—before she received the $175 in prorated refunds on annual fees that she deserved. Later, when she paid off her home equity line of credit, it took many calls before a supervisor finally agreed to "modify policy," and send her a $23 refund on that unused annual fee. In total, Linda's stick-to-it attitude earned her nearly $200 in rebates.

. . . .

HEAVEN IN STAINLESS STEEL

My personal favorite "not asking" story involves the large, commercial plant table with four lit shelves where I've started most of our vegetables and flowers from seed, for the last 9 years.

Marc's brother Alan (known to all in Woodstock, New York, as "Just Alan," which is the name of his gift store there) was making his regular run to the dump in his pickup, when another truck arrived. On board were two men and a big stainless steel plant table.

"Are you throwing that out?" Alan asked, incredulously. Their "yes" was followed by Alan's quick offer to help move the table—from their truck to his.

It was in perfect shape. Not a single fluorescent bulb had to be replaced. You should've seen my eyes light up when Alan brought over the table later that day.

—NANCY

. . . .

Windfall—Free for the Asking

Wouldn't it be fun to find some money you've long since forgotten about or misplaced? Look under the various cushions in your living room, then call your state's comptroller, as well as the comptroller in states where you've previously lived. Over the years, as you've moved, you may have forgotten a small bank account or a utility deposit. Eventually, that money gets turned over to the state. While the amounts are usually in the $25 to $50 range, the largest unexpected windfall (so far) in New York's history was $900,000.

Loretta, a former Floridian, got a letter from an outfit that offered to collect on some long-forgotten bank account for her—for a price. At Nancy's suggestion, Loretta invested in a call to Florida herself . . . and soon deposited a check for over $10,000!

To get the right phone numbers for the various states where you've lived, go to the National Association of Unclaimed Property Administrators' Web site: www.unclaimed.org. You'll also find links to the 30 or so states that offer information about unclaimed funds on-line. In some cases, you'll even find databases that you can search. (If you don't have Web access, send an SASE for a list of state unclaimed property administrators to NAUPA, P.O. Box 7156, Bismarck, ND 58507–7156.)

When we were double-checking our facts for this book, we discovered that New York had three checks just waiting for Marc—including one from the 1970s. We can't explain why, because Marc had called the state's unclaimed property office a couple of times over the years, and these funds didn't appear. But it was sure a welcome fringe benefit of writing *Invest in Yourself!* The total? We don't know yet, because it takes the state months to process claims. But the wait is no big item when it comes to money you forgot you had in the first place.

. . . .

DO IT WITH A FRIEND

We're often surprised by how many people—even those in important positions—are hesitant to dial for dollars. If you've got a touch of phone phobia, get a buddy to help you.

Having a friend nearby when you make these calls can boost your confidence and your effectiveness. You can brainstorm together before you pick up the phone—and while you're on it, for that matter.

Never hesitate to ask the service rep to hold on for a moment. Think of all the times they've put you on hold! And you should always feel free to call back later, when you have another thought—or more courage.

Doing it with a friend really does make it less scary for those of us who are more easily intimidated than we'd like. Getting to share the experience also turns something that may seem to be a chore into fun. It's exciting to "take on the system" together—and win.

Remember, it's likely that you *will* win if you keep at it. You can get the interest rate on your credit card lowered, a refund on shoddy merchandise, a discount on your long-distance phone bill . . . you name it! Persistence pays off.

The person at the other end of the phone may get huffy at first, but don't be intimidated! Persist, and don't hesitate to go up the chain of command. You have nothing to lose, and chances are, you'll get a better deal. In the end, most businesses realize it's a lot cheaper to keep current customers happy than to prospect for new ones. They know that happy customers refer their friends, while the unhappy ones spread that word, also.

. . . .

THE ALL-IMPORTANT QUESTION
TO ASK YOURSELF

You're looking through a junk mail catalog and all of a sudden something strikes your fancy. Or it's 4 o'clock in the morning and you just can't sleep. So you turn on the TV and click to an infomercial, figuring if anything can put you to sleep, that surely will.

But wait! You can get a new cleaning tool that slices, dices, removes wallpaper, sings lullabies, and walks the dog—for only three easy installments of $19.95. And if you order right now, you'll get an emergency tool kit for your car, worth $49.95, absolutely free. Plus, if you mention that you have trouble sleeping (who else would be watching this?), you'll also get, absolutely free, this magic pillow guaranteed to have you asleep in three minutes! Call right now. This humdinger is not available in stores.

Or you're walking down Main Street and notice that the furniture store has recliners on sale—"This week only! No interest and no payments until the year 2076!" (You left your binoculars home, so you can't see the small print.)

Sitting at the computer, an e-mail message comes up: "How would you like to make $5,000 a week? No selling! No cold calls! No inventory to buy. Takes only four minutes a week of your time. But hurry, this $1,968 price is good only for a short time." Remember:

> The best way to avoid making a bad decision is to not make a quick decision.
> —CLARK HOWARD AND MARK MELTZER, *Clark Howard's Consumer Survival Kit*

How can you resist these opportunities? So you take out your credit card—but before you make the call, click on the icon, or enter the store, ask yourself: *If I didn't need it yesterday, why do I need it now?*

Buying something you don't need and didn't even know existed five minutes ago is no bargain. Fill in the blank:

If it sounds too good to be true, _____.

SLAMMED, CRAMMED, SPAMMED,
AND SCAMMED

Pinching our own pennies can be fun and profitable, but it's sure no fun when someone else pinches them. Billions of dollars are wrongfully extracted from our savings every year by outright scam artists. Many of the victims are old, lonely, and vulnerable. Others are young and naive. But we're all potential victims. Who among us has not been taken?

Americans get ripped off in a myriad of ways. Some of the less subtle ways, like plain old-fashioned robberies, are as old as history. Others reflect the inventive nature of humankind. As new opportunities present themselves, con artists immediately appear to take advantage of them. In the end, most rip-offs are self-inflicted. It's our greed, gullibility, basic trust, belief in good luck, and lack of consumer education that unite to do us in.

Gotcha!

Here are some of the tried and proven scams and schemes that get some of us all the time, all of us some of the time, and many of us time after time, year after year:

- Boiler room operations that tout bogus stocks, precious-metal opportunities, and newly discovered gold mines or oil fields.
- Phony roof and driveway repairers who "just happen to be in the neighborhood" or pretend to represent some official agency.
- Those wonderful chain letters, business opportunities, and multi-level marketing schemes that guarantee riches beyond belief.
- Identity thieves who use binoculars to get your calling card number at the airport, or who dumpster-dive to get your credit card, social security, or other numbers and then live it up—on you. Watch what you toss, and where.
- Bogus charities, door-to-door magazine sellers, and correspondence from companies with government-sounding names.
- Postcards that ask $5 and up for postage and handling on your "guaranteed valuable" prize.
- Almost anything with a 900 number or an 809 area code (which is the 900 equivalent in the warm Caribbean).
- Credit repair clinics, guaranteed credit cards, large loans regardless of past credit history—all are as fishy as they smell.
- Any telephone call promising a fortune to be made, "but you must act *now.*"

Nobody Can Rip You Off Without Your Help

Victimizing seniors is so commonplace that con artists have a name for it: "Getting Granny."

—MARK GREEN, *The Consumer Bible*

Every year, $40 billion is lost to telemarketing scams alone. The elderly are especially vulnerable. The National Consumers League puts out a useful, free brochure to help seniors protect themselves. It's called *They Can't Hang Up* (1701 K Street NW, Washington, DC 20006, 202-835-3323).

We're all regularly besieged by sales pitches and promos in the mail too. A few years back, the staff at *Kiplinger's Personal Finance Magazine* evaluated some 300 pieces of their junk mail. Most of the financial offers "deserved a quick trip to the landfill.... Not one of the life insurance offers we received was worth considering." We're happy to say that Kiplinger's ended its piece by recommending our booklet, *Stop Junk Mail Forever* (see page 328).

To avoid being ripped off, here are 10 easy steps to take:

1. Always comparison shop. The bigger the purchase, the more important price checking becomes.

2. Buy only from companies you know.

3. Toss all bulk-rate mail, preferably into a recycling bin.

4. Don't buy anything from anyone on the phone you didn't call. As soon as you get a call from a stranger, ask "Are you a telemarketer?" If so, request that your name be removed from their list, say goodbye, and *hang up.*

5. Ask about return policies before you buy.

6. Use the Internet as an easy way to research products and check prices. Buy only what you are looking for, from organizations you know, not things you happen across. Try to get local sellers to match legitimate prices.

7. If the price is so low that you can't believe your good fortune, don't believe that it is good fortune.

8. Never sign a blank contract or an agreement you haven't read. "Standard" contracts are not written with the consumer's best interests in mind.

9. Buy with a credit card that will protect you should the product or service not live up to its promise. (There are rules. Read your card agreements. Read all agreements. Even read instruction manuals. The more you read, the more you know.)

10. Send a postcard to Handbook, Consumer Information Center, Pueblo, CO 81009, and request a free copy of *The Consumer's Resource Handbook.* You'll get detailed consumer tips about car

repairs, buying mail order, telemarketing, credit, privacy, product safety, scams, etc. Even more helpful are the names, addresses, and phone numbers of virtually anyone in government or industry who can help resolve consumer problems.

....

SURF, CALL, OR SEND TO SAVE

When you want product information, fraud warnings, low-rate credit cards, or money-saving advice, go to www.consumerworld.org—the most comprehensive site of consumer information. Also visit www.consumer.gov, a great resource for info from Uncle Sam.

For info on scams, investigations, and links to groups that can help, visit www.fraud.org, or call the National Fraud Information Center at 800-876-7060—*before* you give out your credit card number, a check, or other personal information to someone whose motives you question.

If you find your heartstrings tugged by an appeal for charity, first check out the organization with your local Better Business Bureau, which works with the national Philanthropic Advisory Service to provide information on charitable and nonprofit organizations. Between October and December, you can get a free copy of *Give but Give Wisely* by sending an SASE to Holiday Giving, Council of Better Business Bureaus, 4200 Wilson Boulevard, Suite 800, Arlington, VA 22203-1838. (The rest of the year, this quarterly newsletter is $3 an issue.)

You can also request *Wise Giving Guide* from the National Charities Information Bureau, 19 Union Square West, New York, NY 10003, or surf to www.give.org or www.guidestar.org.

Not only does the Federal Deposit Insurance Corporation (FDIC) protect our savings accounts up to $100,000, but it also publishes a very informative newsletter (not only about banks), which you can get for free from *FDIC Consumer News*, 801 17th Street NW, Room 100, Washington, DC 20434, 800-276-6003. Or you can read it at www.fdic.gov.

....

SECRETS OF SUCCESSFUL "HONDLERS"

Some people seem to be born negotiators. They can wrangle a great price out of anyone, and leave with the seller feeling good about the deal, too. But perhaps, like us, you hate confrontation and would rather shell out a bit more, or not buy an item, than haggle over it. Don't worry. If you hate to bargain but you love to *get* bargains, you're not doomed to pay full price on everything for the rest of your life.

Instead of haggling, let us teach you to "hondle," which is a Yiddish word that suggests a gentler, kinder, more humorous approach to getting what you want for less. Our "hondling" strategies can turn even the most timid into stress-free supersavers.

- *Know what you are willing to pay for the thingamabob.* What do you really think it's worth? Decide in advance, and don't pay more!

- *Ask for help.* For example, you could say, "Money's tight these days, can you help me out on the price?" People like to be helpful, and it usually keeps things friendly. However you put it, say it with a smile.

- *Be noncommittal.* If it's clear that you love the gizmo and *must* have it, you won't be offered a rock-bottom price.

- *Pick your moment.* Conventional wisdom says shop early for the best selections. Sometimes, though, you can get a much better buy if you shop late. End-of-month quotas to fill, end-of-day flea marketeers who don't want to drag the stuff home, and people selling snowblowers in June are likely to go for lowball offers. Many years ago, Nancy and Marc sold comic books. By the boxful they're very heavy, so during the last hour of a convention, the two were easy marks for bulk buyers.

- *Play "Let's Make a Deal!"* You'll get a chuckle, if not a special combo price, by saying "Let's make a deal" when you buy a few items at once. Try it next time you're at a tag sale, consignment shop, or flea market.

- *Lowball it based on what the bottom line is likely to be.* That way, there'll be room for some healthy give-and-take. But watch out, especially if you've fallen in love with the blasted thing. Someone else may take your potential score home while you're cleverly positioning yourself out of the ball park.

- *Look the item over carefully and talk about what you see.* Pointing out even slight imperfections, especially if you're nice about it, may help you get it for less.

- *Tell it like it is.* Let 'em know you're a penny-pincher, a tough (but friendly) bargainer—someone who'd go way out of the way to get the best deal. Nancy will often (laughingly) warn a merchant right away that Marc is as cheap as they come. She says it sets the right tone.

- *Have patience for the process.* You won't get the best deal if you're in a hurry. "Hondling" takes time.

- *Know when to walk.* Not sure you want it at the current price, but can't seem to get it at a lower one? Take a hike. Maybe the salesperson will follow . . . and meet your price. If not, think of all the money you just saved!

· ·

HOW TO NEGOTIATE IN SILENCE

Sky Stargel, author of *The Blue Book of Car-Buying Secrets,* tells it best, describing a negotiation over a beautifully carved teak turtle in a South Korean market. Chief Warrant Officer Donally looked at the wooden statue but said nothing. The shopkeeper quickly dropped his price from $40 to $35. The officer still said nothing.

The merchant shouted, "$30!" Donally moved away, and the price fell to $25. "Donally stood his ground and shook his head no. The storekeeper began to talk faster, and blurted out 'OK GI, it's yours for $20, and that's my last offer.' "

Donally responded by heading for the door, but before he got there, the salesman said, "$15." That was Donally's magic number. "Without speaking a word, Donally had negotiated . . . a 62% reduction."

· ·

THE MORE YOU SAVE, THE MORE YOU'LL HAVE

There are lots of ways to cut the cost of those things you buy. And with every dollar you save being worth about $1.40 you'd have to earn, not spending a dollar earns you an immediate 40% profit. (That old tax thing again.)

Spend less, so you'll have more. When you go out to dinner, split an appetizer and dessert with your dining partner. You'll save money, and maybe your waistline. Drive to town less often, buy fewer new work outfits, and use e-mail to cut your phone bills.

For great ideas on how to spend less at the supermarket, read *Eat Healthy for $50 a Week* by Rhonda Barfield and *Cheap Eating* by Pat Edwards.

Start a bidding war. As you comparison shop—be it for insurance, cars, contractors, attorneys, plane tickets, a refrigerator, or new lawn chairs— let 'em know you'll be getting at least three estimates and that you're going to go with the one who offers the best price.

Snitch. If you find out that a mail-order house or shopkeeper Jones offers the very same item for less, ask shopkeeper Smith to keep up with the Joneses and beat the best price you've found.

Do it yourself. Diane saves piles of money because she learned how to give haircuts. She's been the house barber since marriage, and her husband and three sons always look neat, trimmed, and handsome. Even though haircuts are relatively cheap where they live, Diane & Co. saved over $200 in one year alone.

If you blend your baby's bananas and sweet potatoes yourself, you can save a fortune on baby food. The only difference is the outrageous cost of those little jars. In just a few minutes, you can process a week's worth. Put individual servings in ice cube trays, and relish all the money you're saving.

THE BEST TIP OF ALL

Avoid temptation. *Stay home and read a book. Daydream. Take a walk or a hot bath. Visit a friend. Have a tag sale. Help out at the local animal shelter. Write to us with your best* Invest in Yourself *ideas.*

PUT SOMETHING ELSE ON THE TABLE

Can you trade or barter for some or all of the cost? Barter opportunities abound everywhere. "I'll fill Johnny's cavities if you'll paint my family's portrait." "I'll type your term paper if you'll cut the grass." "I'll watch your kids Saturday night if you'll take mine next week."

Home renovations, car repairs, and vacations are just a few of the pricey items that folks have bartered for their time and talents. If you're cash poor, trading time or services instead of money can be a great way to get things you need or add some luxuries to your life. Be imaginative!

On the other hand, bartering can wreck a relationship, unless both parties are very clear about the terms. "I didn't agree to fill three cavities" . . . "I never agreed to a room-sized portrait." For small barters, there's probably no need to make a big deal of the agreement, but for major projects, such as a home renovation or some expensive dental work, lay out what each person will do, when they'll do it, and who pays for what supplies. You might want to put it in writing so there isn't any disagreement later on.

At its simplest level, you can barter directly. Design an ad for an auto body shop in exchange for getting your dented fender fixed. Build a deck for the orthodontist as payment for your child's braces. Swap day care for computer skills . . . a refinished antique chest for a week at a charming bed and breakfast. The possibilities are endless.

There are barter exchanges and clubs around the country that create opportunities for a broader range of trades, by letting people accumulate credits for their products and services. You can paint a real estate office, but use your credits to buy a computer—assuming the real estate agent, the computer store, and you belong to the same barter club.

Exchanges publish member directories, and they report transactions to the IRS. (Yes, unless you're swapping two objects or services of identical value—"If you babysit Tuesday, I'll watch the kids on Thursday," for example—it's taxable.) Exchanges typically charge a cash fee of 10% of the transaction.

Having an entire community in on the trading has proven to be a successful formula for Ithaca, New York, thanks to Ithaca HOURS, a barter network. Over 2,000 people have participated, and payment is in colorful local currency representing hour, half-hour, or quarter-hour increments (with an approximate value of $10 an hour). The network has generated over $2 million in barter exchanges since 1991.

Some 1,500 trading opportunities are listed in Ithaca's "HOUR Town" directories. Among the hundreds of businesses that accept HOURS for payment are child care centers, chiropractors, bakeries, hair salons, and car washes. Participants have bartered organic produce for roofing, jitterbug lessons for food, and bar mitzvah preparation for violin repair. HOURS have also been accepted for rent, loan payments, and medical bills.

The Ithaca model has been adopted around the United States and Canada. To help other communities get started, Ithaca HOURS sells a "Hometown Money Starter Kit" for $25. For more information, contact HOUR Town at P.O. Box 6578, Ithaca, NY 14851, 607-272-4330, or online at www.lightlink.com/ithacahours.

Warning: Exchanges come and go, so it's wise not to accumulate too many credits, lest you be left in the lurch when your barter club shuts down. You could also be stuck if your club doesn't have a broad enough member base. What if there's no place where you want to spend credits?

It pays to be cautious when you're bartering. Since it doesn't feel like you're spending money, you're more likely to use your barter credits frivolously. Also, you might well "overpay" for an item that would be cheaper if you were paying cash. And in a direct barter, there's always the possibility that you'll do your job and then get stiffed by the other party. (Unless you're confident that the other person is reliable and capable, you might want to delay completing your end of the bargain until you're satisfied with what's being exchanged.)

That said, start thinking about how your talents, skills, and even that spare room in your house can be swapped for something you really need or want. Marc and Nancy still have around 10,000 comics left over from their flea market days. They'd gladly trade them for almost anything. Make an offer!

. . . .

NEGOTIATING NO-NO'S

- *If you don't need it, don't buy it.* If you're not sure you want something, but are mildly tempted by a price reduction, this is probably a bargain you can live without. Sleep on it.
- *Don't reveal your bottom line or volunteer much information.* Never tell salespeople how much you can afford per month! Once you do, you can rest assured that they'll find ways to make sure your final cost is at least that, every month.
- *It's no bargain if you put it on your credit card* and don't pay the bill off by the due date. Interest could run anywhere from two to five times more than your carefully negotiated price. What a deal!
- *Don't get angry or give ultimatums you don't mean.* But do feel free to push it a bit. What do you have to lose by trying for a better deal? Just keep it light and friendly. When in doubt, remember, not asking is an automatic *no!*
- *Don't buy new if you can possibly avoid it.* Comb the newspapers, penny savers, supermarket bulletin boards, and tag sales for good, used stuff—be it a washing machine or ice skates. Used costs a lot less than new, is often better made, and generally helps save the environment. (Refrigerators are a quandary. Used ones cost less than new and save all of the energy and materials necessary to build a new one. But they tend to be less efficient and use more power.)
- *Don't shop when you're in a bad mood,* when you need a nap, or on an empty stomach. You'll end up hungrier, more tired, cranky, poorer . . . and angry at yourself for having spent the money.
- *Don't dicker if it's already a fair price,* especially if it's very cheap. There's no need to take advantage of someone just to save a buck. If

you get a "steal," you're probably robbing someone. Getting a great bargain is good enough.

- *Don't be an "Ugly American" when you travel.* Over the long haul, will you really treasure the trinket more if you paid a dime or two less?

....

SIX SHOPPING MYTHS DEBUNKED

Myth: Avoid convenience foods. They cost too much.

Reality: Keeping convenience foods on hand may be your best strategy on those nights when the kids are starving, you're late, and you don't have any time to cook. A frozen pizza with a salad—even one from a plastic bag—beats the cost of a delivered pie, and it's much less expensive and quicker than an outing to a restaurant.

Better yet, make a list of your best 10-minute meals and keep the ingredients on hand. And be sure to freeze extra portions when you cook your family's favorites. The kitchen's a mess anyway; it doesn't really take any longer to make twice as much; and you'll have the best of both worlds at your fingertips: great meals, fast.

Myth: Bigger is a bargain.

Reality: Don't assume the largest box is always the best buy. For example, a 32-ounce box of baking soda tagged at 89 cents sat next to a 64-ounce box of the identical brand. The 64-ounce box was $1.89. Buying two small boxes would save 11 cents. While that may not seem like a lot, in Chapter 12 we'll show you how 10 cents a day can save thousands of dollars and years of payments on credit card bills.

Not far from the baking soda sat two brands of salt in 26-ounce boxes, one for 45 cents and the other marked 55 cents. Saving that dime earned a guaranteed 22%, tax-free. You can't get that kind of guarantee on Wall Street.

Myth: Shop with a list and buy only what you need.

Reality: Stocking up is far better than putting money in the bank—on items you know you're going to buy eventually anyway—whether it's tuna at the supermarket, panty hose at the department store, or contact lens solution at the drugstore. Stores like Costco and Sam's Club can save you money—but not always. Price-check to be sure, and avoid loading up on big bargains you don't really need or want. Remember, tossing stuff into the wagon because it seems like a great buy is an expense that marketers have worked very hard to get you to incur. Impulse shopping is often a lousy investment.

Our society bombards us with advertisements, fosters myths about the importance of acquiring things and "keeping up with the Joneses," and promotes instant gratification rather than teaching us about the value of saving, budgeting, and prioritizing for long-term goals.

—OLIVIA MELLAN, in *Money Harmony*

Myth: Always buy generic.

Reality: If your family has a favorite brand of peanut butter and can't stand the store brand, you won't be saving money when you throw it away. Try generic, but if your gang thinks it's no good, don't force it. On the other hand, don't buy brand names when quality doesn't vary or matter much. Go for the cheapest sugar, flour, salt, dry beans, bleach, boxed pasta, and so on.

Myth: Name-brand pharmaceuticals work better.

Reality: Generics, whether for prescription or over-the-counter drugs, can save you a lot, and they must be medically equivalent to their name-brand cousins. Not sure? For the over-the-counter varieties, compare the active ingredients on the backs of both labels. (Confirm your discovery with the pharmacist if you're at all unsure.)

Ask your doctor about generic equivalents every time a drug is prescribed, and also ask if there are any samples, so you can try before you buy. If samples aren't available, ask for a short-term prescription as well as a long-term one. Fill the small one first. If you have a bad reaction to the drug, you won't be throwing out a large bottle of expensive medicine.

Myth: Always look for the lowest price.

Reality: Don't agonize to get the rock-bottom price if it means a big effort to save a little money. Sometimes it pays to spend a little more for a generous return policy, excellent service, faster delivery, or a convenient location. Nancy often pays a bit more to local shopkeepers—especially when it'll save her the drive to, and the hassle of being in a mall. It's nice to keep the money in the community, too.

FREE IS A GREAT PRICE

Freebies are everywhere! If you keep your eyes open, you're likely to find lots of opportunities for great stuff at the right price: *nothing!* Here are some ideas to get you started:

Volunteer in exchange for discounted or free services. Concert halls, ski resorts, theaters, or the local pool may welcome you with open arms, offering free or significantly discounted passes.

Complain vigorously when you get defective products, bad service, or shoddy merchandise. Chances are, you'll get a substantial price reduction. Gerri's received airline discounts, a free humidifier that she's used for more than four years now, and coupons for free food in response to letters she's written.

Whether you call the company's 800 number, send e-mail, or write a letter when a product doesn't perform to your liking, you'll almost always get a freebie—just because you told 'em so.

Although they do sometimes go unanswered, writing "I am outraged" letters has another benefit: It can be very therapeutic. Once you get it off your chest, it's easier to move on.

Complimentary letters are also much appreciated and may be acknowledged with coupons or other giveaways, such as recipe books. For example, Gerri's friend Bill got a whole box of free vitamins thanks to a few words of praise that he sent in.

Take free classes to learn things you'd like to be able to do for yourself. Retailers such as Home Depot, IKEA, or REI often offer excellent free classes, teaching anything from how to wallpaper your home to rock climbing. Not only are the classes free, but you might be able to save a bundle by putting your new skill to work. (Well, maybe not by rock climbing, but you'll be all set to have a great, safe time up in them thar hills.)

Stay healthy with free classes at local hospitals.

Become a product tester or member of a focus group. You'll earn free samples or, better yet, cash. Look in your Yellow Pages under "market research firms." Sometimes these deals can add up to between $50 and $100 or more. Can you believe $75 to try out a new moisturizer? Being a mystery shopper can also yield free meals and moolah. Call Shop 'N Chek at 800-669-6526.

Just ask! In southwest Michigan, Gerri's father and his friends load up on as much free turkey as they can possibly eat. How? A turkey farmer lets them take the perfectly healthy birds that just didn't make it through the trip to the slaughterhouse. The group sets out very early in their "turkey-mobile," and they split the proceeds among themselves and the less fortunate. The farmer is happy to get the recently deceased birds off his hands. (You vegetarians can work out similar deals for overripe fruit or vegetables that farmers don't have time to harvest.)

Marc and Nancy mulch their garden with tons of wood chips they get for free from power company line crews, as well as with leaves, grass, and hay from their farm-country neighbors. Their magazines are "borrowed" from the local recycling center (often before they hit the newsstands), then returned for others to read. The ink-jet printer used to churn out this book's manuscript had been tossed out by someone who obviously couldn't bear to be a generation or two behind the technological times. Nancy found it at the curb, and it's worked perfectly ever since. They even get their paper clips for free—the bank can't possibly use all the ones depositors bring in.

....

IF IT'S BROKE . . . MARC SAYS, "FIX IT!"

While it's true that each of the cars, computers, appliances, and miscellaneous other possessions that Nancy and I own suffer from a lack of routine maintenance, it's also true that most of them yield to patches and proddings when asked to perform just a bit longer. I'm no great mechanical genius, but I enjoy taking things apart. I've been doing it for nearly half a century, and I urge you to give it a whirl.

In the early days, few of the gizmos I took apart ever got back together. Then a clock or two actually started running again. Sometimes in the right direction. These days, most of what I tackle comes back to life. Nancy's always amazed (actually, so am I).

The $250 White Sock

Put a pair of socks into your washing machine and sooner or later, only one will be returned to you. Where does the other sock go?

Well, I recently found out. Fortunately for me, it wasn't my sock. Unfortunately for its former owner, that sock cost some $250 to replace. Maybe more.

For reasons that may better fit in our next book than this one, I needed some junked washing machines. Two local appliance dealers were happy to let me cart off as many as I wanted (otherwise, they would have had to pay to dispose of them).

Having kept our own machine working long past its prime and having helped friends resuscitate theirs, I confidently plugged in the first junker. It had a bad relay and was a piece of cake to fix.

The second machine was so old and battered I used it for parts. But the third machine was a true heartbreaker. The motor wouldn't turn because the pump was jammed. It took me only a few minutes to take that pump apart and find the white sock!

The World Needs More Tinkerers

Some family probably bought a new machine, at a cost of at least $250, because they thought, "It isn't cost effective to have that old washer fixed." Too few of us know how to fix things ourselves. Instead, we junk our gadgets (as well as our planet) in the process of burying the old and building the new. I think it's nuts, but at least I'll never have to buy another washing machine!

My Basic Repair Philosophy

To save a bundle, which eliminates the need to earn a bundle and a half (once you factor in taxes, the cost of getting to and from work, and dressing for the part), Nancy and I buy virtually everything used, but in good working order. There's the 15-year-old $25 dishwasher, cars, trucks, furniture, clothing, garden tools, our desks and the computers that sit on them, the $2,000 phone system we salvaged for $50 . . . you get the drift. We also gratefully accept hand-me-downs—all our file cabinets, a refrigerator, our washing machine, the dryer, VCRs, and the living room TV.

By the time the gizmo has gasped its apparent last breath, we've no doubt gotten more than our money's worth. If I can fix it, we'll be ahead of the game. If I can't, at least I might be able to figure out how it works, so I can jury-rig the next one that breaks.

When I just can't figure out what's wrong and we need to call in a pro, I watch the repair being made and ask questions. Learning how to do new things is one of the best investments I can make in myself.

Don't know where to start? The Reader's Digest's *New Complete Do-It-Yourself Manual* is a terrific resource. Also go to www.learn2.com, where you can learn how to do just about anything. And don't forget to call the appliance manufacturer. Some companies have technicians ready to guide you over the phone, and others have service manuals that will walk you through the repair, step-by-step. There's probably a toll-free number. (Call 800-555-1212 to find out.)

While nothing lasts forever, everything Nancy and I own is expected to try.

—MARC

....

DON'T BANK ON IT

Whatever money you do save by using these strategies, you'll want to put to good use. You'll want to see it grow, not shrink! But that may be exactly what happens at your bank. Like all services, shop around to make sure you're getting the best deal possible.

It used to be that banks paid you interest on your money in the hope that you'd trust them with it. They would then lend your money out to your neighbors and the businesses you patronized. When you wanted to buy a house, they'd lend you someone else's money. Their profit was the difference between what they paid and what they charged. If you didn't have enough on deposit to cover a check, they'd pick up the phone and call you. You'd stop by with money to cover the check (if not today, well "tomorrow will be fine").

Kiss those days bye-bye. Today's typical bank has instituted fines for so many infractions that they make traffic courts seem downright consumer-friendly!

> Banks are not your friends.
> —EDWARD F. MRKVICKA, JR., *Your Bank Is Ripping You Off*

Before you sign on for credit cards, CDs, checking accounts, car loans, mortgages, or any other bank services, shop around! Banks aren't all alike on the interest rates they charge or pay, and they're not alike when it comes to bank fees, either. To compound the confusion, even when a bank seems to be offering you the best deal in town, it may not be. To compare rates, make sure you get the annual percentage yields (APYs).

There are still a few local banks that offer truly free checking—with no minimum balance required and no fees whatsoever. Others offer "free" checking only if you have your paycheck directly deposited, if you're a senior citizen, or if you maintain a minimum balance. (But beware. Drop below the minimum and the fee could wipe out the piddling interest you might have earned and then some.)

Nonprofit credit unions usually charge fewer and lower fees than banks. That's the good news. Unfortunately, there's not always a credit union nearby that you can join. To find out if there's one that'll have you, call the Credit Union National Association at 800-358-5710, or check www.cuna.org for information.

Checking fees pale when compared to some of the other fees. Get cash from a foreign (not your bank's) ATM, and you'll incur charges of $1 to $2. Some banks even charge if you deal with a live teller.

Then there's overdraft "protection." Banks will not automatically deduct that loan from your checkbook even when you've deposited more than enough to repay it. Why should they, when they can keep extracting up to 18%? And not just on your overdraft. When some banks dip into your overdraft account, they transfer amounts in multiples of $100 (even if you owe only pennies!). You could be paying interest on $99.95 that you didn't even need to borrow. And unless you specifically tell your bank to pay off the overdraft, you could be paying that interest forever.

Banks love it when you bounce checks. Nader's Raiders estimate that it costs the bank less than $3 to process each of them, but you'll pay $15 to $25. A quick profit of 500% to 830%. Even worse is the fee you'll pay when someone bounces a check on you. That's like being issued a traffic ticket because someone hit your car!

Be careful when you ask for help at the bank. You may pay a "research fee" of $15 to $25 an hour for assistance in balancing your checkbook or locating copies of a wad of checks you've misplaced. Even if you need a copy of just one check or checking statement, don't expect the bank to make a copy gratis. You'll probably be asked to pay a photocopy charge.

And if you rent a safe-deposit box, be sure to take good care of the key, or you'll be charged a "drilling fee" of $75 to $150. But if Bonnie and Clyde withdraw the valuables you have stored in your box, tough luck! (You might want a separate insurance policy if your valuables are sufficiently valuable.)

For an eye-opener on bank fees, see Table 10.1.

....

IT'S ONLY PAPER

Don't buy checks from your bank—they're way too expensive. To get both business and personal checks for about half of what the bank charges, call Checks in the Mail, 800-733-4443; Current, 800-533-3973; or Image Checks, 800-562-8768.

....

What should you do if a check is lost? Possibly nothing! With fees averaging around $15, a stop-payment order rarely pays on small amounts, and legitimate businesses will return a duplicate check should the first one surface from the post office's netherworld.

Need a money order? The post office sells them for less than most banks, unless your minimum balance entitles you to free bank checks.

Don't Be Late!

A late-payment fee on a loan could cost you $15 or more. What's worse, a record of that late payment could make it to your credit report, where it

TABLE 10.1 Those Pesky Bank Fees

The following is an actual list of one bank's fees.

Service	Fee	Service	Fee
Account closed—by mail	$ 5.00	Money order—customer	3.00
Account closed—within 180 days	15.00	Money order—noncustomer	5.00
Account reconcilement—per hour	20.00	Notary fee—noncustomer/per document	2.00
ACH filing fee—per file	7.50	Overdrawn account fee	
ATM cash withdrawal surcharge—noncustomer	1.00	Business—applied daily as of second business day of overdrawn balance	18% APR
ATM debit card transaction (point-of-sale)	.25	Personal—applied daily as of third business day of overdrawn balance	$5.00
ATM funds transfer fee—foreign ATM	1.00	Photocopy of Check (less than 60 days)	1.00
ATM lost card replacement	5.00	Photocopy of Check (60 days or older)	4.00
ATM transaction @ foreign ATM—cash withdrawal	1.00	Photocopy of statement	5.00
ATM transaction @ foreign ATM—balance inquiry	1.00	Printout of statement/per sheet	2.00
Bank audit confirmation—debit to account		Protest fees—customer	20.00
Cashiers check—customer	6.00	Protest fees—noncustomer	40.00
Certified check	10.00	Reporting abandoned account to NYS	50.00
Check cashing—noncustomer	5.00	Research time—per hour	25.00
Check-printing fees . . . varies depending on selection		Rolled coin—per roll (commercial accounts)	.10
Collection of coupons—per envelope	5.00	Safe-deposit drilling	100.00
Collections—domestic	15.00	Safe-deposit box late fee—per month	1.5%
Collections—foreign	25.00	Savings accounts—excess transaction fee	25.00
Counter check—each	.50	Special savings request	10.00
Deposited check returned fee	10.00	Stock/reregistration	50.00
Early closeout—first select club	15.00	Stock/buy and sell	50.00
Fax service—per page	1.00	Stop payment	15.00
Foreign draft	25.00	Strapped currency—per strap (commercial accts)	.10
Insufficient (NSF/OD) funds—per item paid	20.00	Telephone transfers	1.00
Insufficient (NSF/OD) funds—per item returned	25.00	Travelers checks (percent of amount)	1%
IOLA account—per month	15.00	Treasury bills and notes—purchase	50.00
IRA closeout	25.00	Treasury bills and notes—redemption	50.00
Legal papers process—Levy's Restraining Notice, etc.	100.00	Other bills and notes	50.00
Loan coupon book replacement	10.00	Treasury direct tenders	50.00
Loan payment check returned	7.00	Uncollected funds fee (on collected balances over$1,000—per item	15.00
Lost night depository key	5.00	Undeliverable statement fee	10.00
Lost passbook replacement fee	10.00	Wire transfer—domestic/incoming	10.00
Lost safe-deposit box key fee	25.00	Wire transfer—domestic/outgoing	20.00
Money market excess transaction fee—per item	25.00	Wire transfer—foreign	35.00

may get in your way of securing credit—at least low-cost credit—for the next seven years.

Have trouble keeping track of your payment due dates? Ask your bank or the lender to automatically deduct your payment from your account, but don't pay a fee for the convenience.

And don't pay a fee to turn in those pennies you've pinched and rolled up.

Important: Develop a relationship with your bank manager, and you'll discover that rules can be changed and pesky fees waived for good customers who ask or complain. Don't be bashful. It's your money!

TURN YOUR DEBTS INTO GOLDEN INVESTMENT OPPORTUNITIES

OWING MONEY AMOUNTS TO FINANCIAL RUSSIAN ROULETTE—WITH every chamber loaded! You never know when a job loss, a medical emergency, a divorce, or maybe just a leaky roof will trigger a cash crisis. So it's smart to keep your debt load to a minimum.

There's another reason why it's smart to pay down your debts: It can save you a fortune, which means you won't have to earn another fortune and a half.

Believe it or not, getting out of debt isn't all that hard to do, and what's more, every debt the average consumer carries can be turned into a high-yield, rock-solid investment. There's gold in those debts!

In the same way that a robin starts building her nest with a single piece of straw, a single dime a day is all it takes to build up your family's nest egg. In the next few chapters, we'll show you why it often makes no sense to put whatever money you can squirrel away into a savings account, CD, bonds, stocks, or even mutual funds— if you're weighed down by plastic and a load of other debts.

CHAPTER 11

....

Invest in Your Debts

- ○ Turn the tables on lenders and save a fortune
- ○ The myths that keep Americans in the hole
- ○ How to invest for high-yield, risk-free returns
- ○ Small investments that add up to big bucks
- ○ Which comes first: paying down debts or saving?

Terry Savage's Law of Deep Holes:
"When you're in a deep hole, stop digging."

TERRY SAVAGE, *Chicago Sun-Times* SYNDICATED COLUMNIST

....

The story goes that when the infamous Willie Sutton was asked why he robbed banks, he responded, "Because that's where the money is." He may have been a crook, but Willie was no dope. He picked the right target—but would have made out better if he'd invested in a bank, instead of breaking into that last one.

As Willie well knew, banks have lots of money—because we keep giving it to them! They handle virtually every penny we earn, save, and spend—and they make money on all of it all the time. In exchange for the use of our money, banks pay us a tiny, token interest rate, if they pay us anything at all.

Then before we've accumulated enough to be able to pay for our homes, cars, college educations, vacations, furniture, clothes, even dinners out, we go back to the banks and borrow money (often our own!) at much higher interest rates.

While there are times when borrowing can dramatically improve your life, the real costs in time and money are also dramatic and are often overlooked. For example, believe it or not, it could take a year of your life just to earn enough to pay for that new car in your driveway. That's right: a whole year at work to gross enough before taxes to pay for a new set a wheels and the interest on the car loan.

Since none of us can give up food, shelter, and life's other bare necessities (to say nothing of its pleasures) for an entire year just to pay for our means of transportation, the banks and car dealers are right there with offers of long-term financing and "low, low" monthly payments. (See Chapter 14.)

The most expensive part of buying something you can't afford is often the interest you'll be charged on the money you had to borrow to pay for it. Need proof? Consider this bit of American folklore: All your life you've been told that your home will be your most expensive purchase. We're about to prove that's simply not true.

First off, consider all the assorted taxes you have to pay year after year. Every year, the typical married couple shells out an astounding 38% of what they earn to various tax collectors. No other cost of living even comes close.

Second in line for most Americans is their mortgage, which will almost certainly cost more than their house. In fact, by the time you've paid off your mortgage, you could spend enough to buy two houses—yours, plus a much nicer one for your lender.

Wouldn't it be great if you could have your dream house and everything else you want while still holding onto more of your hard-earned money? Well you can. By making even small regular investments in your mortgage, car loan, and credit card bills, you'll slice your interest costs to a fraction of what they otherwise would have been—and increase your net worth at the same time.

···

THREE MYTHS THAT KEEP AMERICANS IN THE HOLE

Myth 1: You Are What You Wear . . . Spend . . . Own.

Each day, America's collective consciousness is exposed to 12 billion display ads, 2.5 million radio commercials, and more than 300,000 television commercials.

—CYNTHIA CROSSEN, *Tainted Truth*

We're reminded day in and day out that success is having the most and the hippest stuff on the block. By the time kids graduate from high school, they will have watched more than half a million TV commercials. Again and again, we older folks are told to buy this product or that to look younger and sexier—or at least to smell better.

Heard often enough, these messages sink in and have been known to echo in our egos when that first gray hair or wrinkle emerges. Whether it's moisturizing creams, hair replacement systems, or exercise equipment to tone the abs we never knew we had, the message is clear: You have to keep on spending to look your best.

The result? Outstanding consumer debt has long since passed the $5 trillion mark. That's $5,000,000,000,000.

Myth 2: "Don't Leave Home Without It."

"Master the moment." "It's everywhere you want to be." These are just some of the things credit card issuers whisper in our ears to lure us into spending more than we can afford. And they've put Americans in the hole to the tune of about $455 billion, all because we say two little words, "Charge it."

Credit cards are a great convenience—if you use them to pay for things you can afford and would have bought anyway. Too many of us, though, use those little pieces of plastic as a license to spend impulsively, and we pay a heavy price in hefty interest charges that roll on and on, month after month, year after year.

Myth 3: If You Care Enough . . . You'll Go Into Hock.

Nothing typifies this love cost more than the De Beer's ads touting "a diamond is forever." How much should you spend on a rock to celebrate your engagement? "Two months' salary," they advise. "Spend less and the relatives will talk. Spend more, and they'll rave."

"Think romance. And don't compromise," one ad continues. "This is one of life's most important occasions. You want a diamond as unique as your love." You already know that we say, "Think cubic zirconia"—if you must show the world your intentions.

A better motto would be: "Spend your money on living, not on impressing." Take over some chore your mate hates. That'll really say "I love you."

....

COMPOUNDING CAN CUT BOTH WAYS

People deep in debt have no choice. They have to go to work tomorrow, whether they like their jobs or not, in order to pay for yesterday—and for the interest they owe on it. With fewer bills, you'll be freer to take advantage of all the options that debt-free living offers. For example, you might choose to earn less, so that you can do something you love, rather than something you "have to do" to pay bill after bill. Or you might decide that now is the time to treat the family to a vacation no one will ever forget.

While getting out of debt may seem like an impossible dream, it doesn't have to be that way! By investing in your debts just as your lenders do, you turn the tables on them. You immediately begin to earn what they charge you on your credit cards, your car loan, and your mortgage—not what they pay on savings accounts or CDs.

Believe it or not, it's easy to turn every debt you owe into a safe, highly profitable, tax-free investment, even if all you have is the pocket change you toss onto your dresser every night. The secret is to follow your lender's lead, and put the power of compound interest to work *for you.*

Consider how compound interest works for banks—at the rate they charge, not what they pay. For example, on a $100,000, 8% mortgage, you'd be expected to pay at least $734 every month for 30 years. If that's all you send in every month, by the time your loan is paid off, the bank will get $264,149 from you, plus the interest they'll earn by lending that money out again and again.

Here's an even more depressing thought: To pay out that much on a mortgage, the typical couple whose total tax bite is 38% may well have to earn over $400,000 *just to pay for the loan.* While there may be some compensating tax deductions for home ownership, you were probably amazed in Chapter 4 to discover how trivial they can be.

And Now for the Good News

While you can't pay *less* than the required monthly payment, you can send in *more.* The more you pay in advance, or *pre*-pay, the quicker you reduce the amount you owe, and the less interest you'll pay, month after month. The less interest that gets deducted from each of your payments, the more that goes to principal, month after month.

And like an old-fashioned locomotive picking up speed, the more principal you repay, the less interest you'll owe, and the more of each payment that will be credited to your account. More principal, less interest, more principal, less interest, more principal, less interest . . . chug, chug, chug, chug, chug, chug, chug.

Then soon you're up to speed. Your loan gets paid off faster and faster, until years before you ever thought you could, you'll be holding a mortgage-burning party. You'll celebrate with tens of thousands of dollars in your asset column that would otherwise have gone to your lender.

If you put 83 cents a day in a piggy bank, by the end of the month it will have grown to $25. And $25 it will be, forever. If you put that $25 in your savings account, it'll grow at maybe 3% a year—before taxes. But if you collect that spare change and follow your banker's example, you'll pocket a bundle.

Send in $25 every month with your required payments on that $100,000 mortgage, and you'll save more than $23,000 over the life of your loan. If you're anything like the rest of us, you could use that money. So why would you *give* an extra $23,000 or more to your bank?

It's easy to save even more. Let's stay with the $100,000 mortgage, which has a required payment of $734 a month. If you can come up with an even $800 a month, you'll save $48,421. As an added bonus, those monthly pre-payments of $66 ($800 − $734) will cut the term of your loan by 7.5 years.

In Chapter 13 we'll answer all the questions you probably have about the pros and cons of pre-paying on your mortgage, but for now, let's focus on the results. What happens when you invest in your mortgage or other debts? It's a lot like what happens when you make deposits into any safe investment, say a savings account.

Your money grows in two ways. First, it grows by the amount you deposit. Second, it grows by the interest that your deposit earns, month after month, year after year. Pre-paying on your mortgage and other debts takes advantage of the same powerful assets-building miracle that a smart 20-year-old can use to retire a millionaire. By making tax-deferred monthly deposits of only $190 (assuming 8% interest), the youthful investor is taking advantage of the same powerful technique that lenders have employed since before money was first invented: *compounding*.

A 50-year-old, on the other hand, would have to put aside $2,890 a month (also at 8%) to join the millionaire's club at 65. The longer your money has to grow and the higher the interest rate, the less you'll have to "plant" at any one time.

To end up with the identical $1 million nest egg, starting at age 20, you'd have to deposit $102,600 over the next 45 years. But because of the 30 fewer years less compounding time, the half centurian would have to fork over more than five times as much.

Now consider two neighbors who both buy $125,000 homes with the help of $100,000 loans at 8% for 30 years. They each make a $25,000 down payment and have $1,000 a month to use for mortgage payments and/or anything else. Neighbor 1 faithfully sends in the required $734 every month and spends the remaining $266 on one thing or another. At the end of 30 years, neighbor 1 will have spent $289,149 to buy a $125,000 house.

Neighbor 2, the hero (or heroine) of our tale, faithfully sends the bank the $1,000 each month. After 14 years, the mortgage is paid off, which means that neighbor 2 won't have to fork over $734 every month during those next 16 years. While neighbor 1 still has 16 years of house payments to make, neighbor 2 has saved over $98,000—by turning an 8% debt into an 8% investment.

But can you get a higher return someplace else? Keep reading.

An Even Better Investment Opportunity

Right down the road from neighbors 1 and 2 live two families, the Savvys and the Spendthrifts. Remember them from Chapter 9? The Savvys enjoy cooking meals at home together. They love to garden, take walks, and otherwise entertain themselves on weekends in the great outdoors. They pull the plastic from their pockets only for purchases they'll pay off immediately. The Savvys are paying down their mortgage, saving for their children's educations, and putting money aside for their own retirement. Perfect, aren't they?

The Spendthrifts just love to shop. They hit the mall every weekend, watch the home shopping channels with telephone and credit cards at the ready, and eat out morning, noon, and night. Even though they pay just the minimums on their credit cards, the Spendthrifts find it harder and harder to make it from one payday to the next.

Whoops. They've just topped out on one of their nine cards, the one that has a $3,500 credit limit and carries a 17% interest rate. When this month's card statement arrives, it will show a minimum payment due of only $70, which they'll scrape together and send in.

If they never charge another purchase on that card, and even if they always send in each required payment on time, instead of $3,500, they'll have to pay—are you sitting?—$11,162. That's more than three times what they had charged. To pay back that $11,162, the Spendthrifts would have to earn over $18,000 assuming they pay 38% in taxes (federal, state, local, sales, etc.). And that's on just one of their credit cards. No wonder they're always broke!

Someone ought to tell them that by adding a measly dime a day to their required payments, they'd save $1,862 and be on the road to a brighter future. That $3 a month investment would save the Spendthrifts 17%, risk-free, tax-free, and guaranteed, which, because of their tax bracket, is the same as earning over 27% before taxes. Where else could they invest a thin dime and get such a high return?

If they could add $10 a month, the Spendthrifts would save $3,810 on this one piece of plastic. Just $25 a month (that 83 cents a day that they'd never notice, invest, or miss) would keep well over $5,000 in their pockets and have the card paid off in about 8 years, rather than the over 35 years that it would take making only minimum payments. Which way do you want the story to turn out for you?

In Chapter 12, we'll go into more detail about credit cards, and show you how you can dramatically cut their cost and consolidate your debts for maximum savings. Meanwhile, if you happen to bump into the Spendthrifts at the mall, why don't you suggest that they stroll over to the bookstore and buy a copy of *Invest in Yourself?* If they go home and read it together, they'll save a fortune!

CLIMB THE STAIRS FOR THE HIGHEST RETURNS

Imagine a staircase with each of your debts and other investment opportunities as steps. The higher the interest rate, the higher the step. No doubt your savings account will be on the bottom step, and your piggy bank, shoe box, sugar bowl, or lump under the mattress would be on the ground floor.

At the top of the stairs, if your employer contributes, is probably your 401(k) plan. With a substantial immediate boost from what your boss kicks in—often 25% or more—it may be an investment opportunity that you just can't afford to miss. See "Which Comes First—Investing in Debts or Your 401(k)?" on page 212.

Next in line, as you walk down the flight, is probably a credit card bill. Put every penny you can toward that priciest piece of plastic until it's been paid off, and pay the minimums on all your other bills. Then earn the maximum amount you can on the next step down, probably on another credit card, and then perhaps on a car loan or maybe your mortgage.

Stocks are a little tricky. You might want to think of them as being on an elevator or an escalator. Sometimes they'll be on a higher step than your mortgage, sometimes a lower one. Even though in the very long term, stocks fall pretty high on the staircase, they can take you for quite a ride. Sometimes they can even be below the bank CDs. (Really!)

Mutual funds are also tricky, and where they fall depends on what the fund invests in. An all-stock mutual fund is going to be higher on the staircase than an all-bond or money market mutual fund, but with a lot more risk.

Whatever you do, don't hang out on the bottom of the stoop! Today's highest-yielding, safest investments are toward the top of the stairs, where your debts live. After taxes and inflation, your nest egg earns virtually nothing at the bottom, in a savings account. But up at the top, it could earn you a tax-free pile.

How can it be tax-free? Because you didn't officially earn the money. You don't have to pay taxes on money you save by investing in your debts. (Shhhhh. We don't want Uncle Sam to realize that there's yet another investment he can tax.)

It's Safest Toward the Top

Since the higher up the investment staircase you can go, the more your money will earn, we urge you to consider using savings, bonuses, and tax refunds to pay off your revolving debts. Not only will you earn more than you could if you put that money into other investment vehicles, but there's also no risk. Investments in your debts are 100% safe, because the returns are guaranteed and protected from the roller-coaster rides common in the currency, precious-metals, stock, and commodity markets.

No matter what's going on with the economy, credit card users regularly pay five to six times more on their cards than they earn on their savings accounts. Whenever you can earn that much by investing in your credit card bills, go for it! The only way to beat the investment opportunity offered by the plastic in your pocket would be to put your money into your 401(k)—assuming that you'd receive an employer match *and* that the money's safely invested. Even then, chances are you can—and should—still scrape together a few extra dollars to pay down those credit cards each month.

And while more risky investments like stocks might beat your mortgage's interest rate, if your heart sinks when the Dow dives, you might want to send some or all of that money upstairs, too. But you don't have to get carried away: Having a diversified investment portfolio certainly makes sense.

Still, the spread on the staircase is so great that you may want to move some rainy-day funds up top, too, especially if you're going to adopt the other components of the *Invest in Yourself* philosophy. While invading your emergency funds may seem risky, if you have ready access to cash via a credit card or a home equity line of credit, you'd be covered in the event of a real crisis.

And because you're going to follow the advice we give in Chapter 12, where we focus on all sorts of ways to save on those plastic monsters, your cost, should such an eventuality arise, will be lower than what you're paying today. Then, of course, you'd promptly pay off the bill, right?

By seriously investing in your debts now, you'll soon be all paid up . . . at which time you'll be stuck. You'll either have to invest in riskier securities, or in those FDIC-guaranteed options at the bottom of the stairs that essentially earn zip, zilch, zero, nada, rien, sifuri, ling, rei, nul, boopkus—especially once you take dear old taxes into account.

MORE THAN MONEY

But there's more to think about when you develop your own debt investment strategy than just saving the most money. If you'd feel better knowing the roof over your head was actually yours, start by pre-paying as much as you can on your mortgage. True, you won't save as much at 8% as you would at 17%, but peace of mind is worth a lot, too. And chances are, you owe a lot more on your home loan than you do on a credit card. We sure hope that's true!

Of course, you can always do some of both. Send in $25 against the balance on your highest-interest credit card, and send in $25 on your mortgage. The most important thing, from our point of view, is to develop your own unique investment strategy, one that takes into account the fact that your debts are a key part of your portfolio. You'll save the most money by paying your most expensive debts first, but if it's going to work, the strategy you develop has to be one you believe in enough to stick with over the long haul.

You can start by simply pooling the pocket change that every member of the family ends up with virtually every day. Or you can make a pact to pre-pay with every penny you pile up thanks to the other money-saving ideas we mobilize you to try. Or maybe it's time to hold a contest, to see who can scrimp and save the best (without feeling deprived, of course), and to free up the most money for the family's get-out-of-debt fund.

However you go about funding your debt-busting crusade, get going! By investing as much as you can in your debts, you'll end up with the most money, the greatest peace of mind, and the largest number of options for how you spend your time—and your newly found wealth.

The deeper you dig, the more you save. The more you save, the less you need. The less you need, the freer you are.

....

WHICH COMES FIRST—INVESTING IN DEBTS OR IN YOUR 401(K)?

QUESTION: I'm 27 years old and have five credit cards at rates ranging from 12% to 19%, with the 19% currently in its "teaser" stage of 6.8%. All are at their limits of roughly $5,000 each.

I have a 401(k) plan with my new job that has no matching funds, but I have no nest egg in case I lose my job. My question is about the sequence of events. All the financial self-help advice books say to:

1. Pay off your highest-interest credit card first, then move on to the next one.
2. Contribute early to your retirement plan.
3. Pay yourself first.
4. Have a nest egg for emergencies such as unemployment.

But they don't say which one to do first! And my calculator is very tired trying to figure out what contributions to my retirement account are costing me because I am not using that money to pay off the credit cards. Or is it the other way around: Paying off the credit cards is costing me money because I am not contributing to retirement early and getting the maximum benefit?

And when should I get around to having a three-month nest egg in case I lose my job and still have to pay all my bills? And what about paying myself first? If I send money to a mutual fund via automatic withdrawal rather than doing the other three exceedingly important things with my money, what am I losing?

I'm sure I'm not the only one with these types of questions. But so far, no expert has been brave enough to prioritize these four very important pieces of advice, for fear that we won't think the other three are important.

—ALICE IN WONDER(ING) LAND

The Chicken or the Egg?

Dear Alice,

For starters, you'd definitely benefit by embracing our *Invest in Yourself* philosophy—pay off your expensive debts, save money without feeling deprived, cultivate a simple attitude, and start a small home business for extra cash.

The most important thing you need to know, in our humble opinion, is that there is no magic formula. How you prioritize between your debts and your 401(k) is a judgment call that has more to do with your psychological makeup and your attitude about how you're going to live the rest of your life than with the pros and cons of one investment opportunity versus another.

Is a New Day Dawning?

From our perspective, the important question you need to answer is, "Are you ready to change your spending ways?" To have $25,000 in credit card debt at age 27 is quite a load to carry! Charge any more, and you could end up in really big trouble in the here and now, let alone in your golden retirement years.

Even if you never charge another penny and religiously send in the minimum payments every month, you could still be paying on your five credit cards by the time you hand in your executive rest room key. In fact, it could take over 45 years to pay those debts off. Yikes!

So right off the bat, we advise you to do three things:

1. Stop charging.
2. Find ways to cut back on your spending.
3. Put every penny you can toward paying off those plastic monsters.

Together, in our view, these are the best ways for you to invest in your future—to pay yourself first—right now. Also, in this section of the book, we'll show you lots of specific ways to cut the cost of your debts. Do it!

Figure out a plan for getting out of debt in no more than five years. If the payments that would be required look unrealistic on your income and budget, then it may be well worth a call to a credit counseling agency (see page 223) for help developing a debt repayment plan that will allow you to dig out in that period of time.

Choosing between contributions to your 401(k) and putting every penny toward your debts would be a tougher call if your employer offered an attractive match. We'd probably still vote for tackling your debts first, but since that's not the case for you, we recommend that you forgo those contributions until you've dug yourself out of the hole.

Of course, for those lucky folks whose employers *do* match their contributions, the math is different. For example, if your employer contributed 25 cents for each dollar you put into your retirement fund, you'd receive an immediate 25% return. The more your boss contributes, the better the instant return. Under this circumstance (which is unfortunately not yours), the 401(k) money, tax deferred, would indeed beat the 17% tax-free savings on credit cards. But even under this scenario, you'd still need to wait more than 30 years to reap the harvest at retirement!

Once you're out of debt, it would certainly make sense for you to plow some money into your 401(k), and to create an emergency savings fund. The good news is that once you do pay off those debts you're going to feel rich.

Gerri learned that from experience. She ran up a stack of credit card bills when she was twentysomething. But then she used the exact strategies we outline in this book—she paid her most expensive debts first, cut her spending, traded down to an economy car, and took on some freelance writing projects to generate extra cash (which she earmarked solely for debt reduction). In a couple of years, she was debt-free, able to save more than she could ever have imagined, and rightly proud of herself!

A Few Further Facts for You to Consider

- Over the long term, the stock market has not paid anywhere near what the average credit card charges.
- While it's great to think ahead and take advantage of all the compounding your retirement money would do (assuming you choose good places to put it and the market doesn't totally crash), you've got a lot of living to do between ages 27 and 59½, if you're lucky. Get debt-free as soon as you can.
- As for an emergency fund, the three of us recommend that you forget about it for now. Hunker down and get out of debt. Soon, you'll have ample credit available on the plastic in your pocket to help you weather a real emergency.
- To combat your fear of a job loss, create an Ace in the Hole, a small home business that can bring in some money and provide some tax deductions, even as it offers you a way to make ends meet, should the dreaded pink slip arrive. It can also give you some extra cash to pay those debts off faster.
- Keep looking for and taking advantage of those teaser rates on credit cards. Switch balances as often as necessary for the lowest rates. Before you do, though, make sure there are no extra charges for transferring balances on each card, and that the teaser rate will apply to your transfers. We hope our other pearls of wisdom on plastic in Chapter 12 will help inspire you to take control of your debts. Let us know how you make out!

CHAPTER 12

···

Your Future Is *Not* in Plastics

○ How to avoid that costly malady: MPS

○ Four methods for getting out of debt *fast*

○ Smart debt consolidation strategies

○ How low can you go? Getting low-rate cards

*Going on a debt diet is a lot like going on a diet to lose weight: If your
diet is unreasonably strict, you're not going to stick to it very long.*

GERRI DETWEILER, *The Ultimate Credit Handbook*

···

In *The Graduate*, that classic 1967 movie, a family friend offers Ben,
Dustin Hoffman's character, some prophetic advice: "Plastics. There's a
great future in plastics. Think about it."

While plastics were the last thing on Ben's mind, the rest of us sure
bought the idea lock, stock, and usurious interest rates. Back in 1967,
when Mrs. Robinson seduced Ben, credit card issuers were just beginning
to seduce Americans with the lure of plastic. Now, we're a nation buried
in the stuff.

MORTGAGING YOUR FUTURE

Credit cards seem innocent enough, and on the face of it, they are. But
when you're carrying credit card debt on a regular basis, you're commit-
ting your future time, energy, and freedom to purchases you made yesterday. Paying off that debt frees you, and it's one of the best financial

investments you can make in your future. In fact, paying off your credit cards is one of the best investments you can make, *period.*

If you carry card balances, next time you make a purchase, ask yourself, "Is this something I would be willing to take out a loan to finance?" If not, it shouldn't be going on your card. When you revolve balances, you *are* taking out a loan.

Believe It, or Go Broke

Unlike mortgages and most other loans, credit card contracts don't set a time limit on repayments and don't require a set payment every month. Instead, they calculate each month's required payment based on a percentage of what you owe at the end of that month's billing period.

Ideally, from the banks' perspective, you'll send in just the minimum on time every month, and you'll keep on charging happily ever after. That way, they can keep you in hock until sometime just this side of the twelfth of never, because for decades to come, the part of each payment that goes to interest would eat up most of every check. The lower the required minimum, the longer they can string out the term, and the more you'll pay.

Fall for it, and you're suffering from "Minimum Payment Syndrome," or MPS, as Scott Burns,* the personal finance columnist for *The Dallas Morning News,* calls this "deadly malady" that could afflict you for the rest of your life. Table 12.1 shows just how costly credit cards can be, if you only send in the required amount. For example, if you owe $3,500 at 17% and suffer from MPS, you'll pay out $11,162 over 35 years. Fortunately, the cure for MPS is simple and requires no doctor visits: *Always pay more than the required minimum.*

As we mentioned in Chapter 11, a dime a day will save $1,862 on that $3,500 credit card bill. You can come up with an extra dime a day, can't you? To see how much money you can save in your personal pay-off-plastic program, take a look at Table 12.2. Pre-paying is a painless way to earn yourself a tidy profit as you quickly become an ex-benefactor of the plastics industry.

CREDIT CARDS CAN BE YOUR FRIENDS

Don't get us wrong. We're not saying that you should cut up your cards. In fact, there are times when having a credit card is almost mandatory—

---

* If Scott's column isn't carried in your local newspaper, you can read his advice on-line at www.scottburns.com.

TABLE 12.1 **MPS Can Be Expensive**
Total Cost/Time If Not Pre-Paid

CARD BALANCE	11%		13%		15%		17%		19%	
	$	YRS	$	YRS	$	YRS	$	YRS	$	YRS
$ 1,500	2,518	14	2,906	16	3,456	19	4,304	23	5,799	30
2,500	4,364	18	5,088	21	6,123	24	7,733	30	10,598	41
3,500	6,210	21	7,269	24	8,789	28	**11,162**	**35**	15,398	47
5,000	8,979	23	10,542	27	12,789	32	16,304	40	22,598	54
7,500	13,595	26	15,997	31	19,456	37	24,876	46	34,598	62
10,000	18,211	29	21,451	33	26,123	40	33,447	50	46,597	68
12,500	22,826	30	26,906	35	32,790	42	42,019	53	58,599	73
15,000	27,441	32	32,361	37	39,456	44	50,590	56	70,598	76
20,000	36,672	34	43,270	39	52,790	47	67,733	60	74,598	82
25,000	45,903	36	54,179	42	66,123	50	84,875	63	93,598	86
30,000	55,133	37	65,088	43	79,456	52	102,019	66	112,599	90
40,000	73,595	39	86,906	46	106,123	55	136,304	70	131,598	93
50,000	92,056	41	108,724	48	132,790	58	170,590	73	188,599	100

* Based on minimum payments of 2% of the balance, with a $10 minimum. These figures were calculated with *The Banker's Secret Credit Card Software.*

when renting a car, for example. The major car rental services won't accept checks. To pay by cash—if the company will take it at all—you'll have to fill out an application weeks ahead, pay an application fee, and then plunk down a hefty cash deposit, assuming you "cash qualify."

Properly managed, a piece or two of plastic in your pocket can be handy as well as harmless. For example, credit cards can save you money by allowing you to make purchases when the sales are hottest—or when the cash in your wallet is loneliest. And they're great when you want to make a catalog purchase or even when you need a short-term loan. Often, you can get a better rate on a credit card than you could get at the local bank.

Speaking of borrowing money, there's no stronger credit reference than a couple of currently held Visa, MasterCard, or Discover cards, if you've paid them on time, over time. They're seen as better proof of your creditworthiness than a mortgage or a car loan. Why? Because those are *secured* loans, backed by a house or vehicle, while credit cards are unsecured and therefore riskier. However, because banks like to play follow the

Table 12.2   Dollars/Months Saved by Pre-Paying on Your Credit Card Bills

CARD BALANCE	PRE-PAYMENT	INTEREST RATE				
		11%	13%	15%	17%	19%
$1,500	3	245/45	379/55	600/73	1,003/102	1,856/159
	25	725/125	1,044/147	1,518/178	2,282/227	3,683/312
	50	843/143	1,193/166	1,704/198	2,510/249	3,960/335
	100	919/155	1,287/178	1,817/211	2,644/261	4,116/348
$2,500	3	349/50	547/64	881/84	1,505/120	2,871/193
	25	1,178/150	1,725/180	2,559/221	3,937/287	6,530/405
	50	1,431/176	2,056/207	2,983/251	4,476/320	7,211/441
	100	1,611/193	2,282/225	3,261/270	4,813/339	7,616/462
$3,500	3	421/53	663/67	1,078/90	1,862/129	3,610/209
	25	1,545/163	2,287/197	3,435/245	5,364/321	9,061/458
	50	1,942/194	2,815/230	4,129/282	6,270/363	10,246/505
	100	2,246/216	3,204/253	4,617/307	6,874/389	10,988/533
$5,000	3	499/55	791/70	1,293/94	2,257/136	4,439/222
	25	1,991/175	2,979/212	4,533/266	7,192/352	12,396/509
	50	2,600/212	3,809/253	5,652/311	8,701/404	14,449/569
	100	3,111/239	4,475/282	6,506/342	9,786/438	15,821/606
$7,500	3	589/56	939/72	1,546/97	2,723/141	5,429/232
	25	2,563/185	3,878/226	5,985/285	9,666/380	17,056/557
	50	3,498/228	5,185/273	7,802/339	12,211/444	20,693/633
	100	4,369/261	6,348/310	9,337/379	14,227/489	23,347/684
$10,000	3	655/58	1,045/73	1,729/99	3,060/144	6,153/237
	25	3,004/191	4,580/233	7,134/295	11,662/397	20,921/585
	50	4,227/237	6,317/285	9,601/356	15,211/468	26,181/673
	100	5,451/275	7,982/327	11,846/402	18,237/521	30,297/734
$12,500	3	705/58	1,129/74	1,872/100	3,326/145	6,729/240
	25	3,363/194	5,156/237	8,086/302	13,336/407	24,226/604
	50	4,840/243	7,279/293	11,148/367	17,832/485	31,081/700
	100	6,400/284	9,432/339	14,099/419	21,895/544	36,756/770
$15,000	3	747/58	1,198/74	1,990/101	3,545/146	7,200/243
	25	3,666/197	5,643/241	8,897/307	14,777/414	27,109/617
	50	5,370/247	8,116/299	12,505/375	20,159/496	35,501/721
	100	7,246/291	10,734/348	16,144/431	25,256/561	42,784/798

TABLE 12.2 *(Continued)*

		INTEREST RATE				
CARD BALANCE	**PRE-PAYMENT**	**11%**	**13%**	**15%**	**17%**	**19%**
$20,000	3	813/58	1,307/75	2,177/101	3,892/149	7,954/245
	25	4,159/200	6,441/245	10,232/313	17,169/425	31,968/635
	50	6,252/253	9,519/306	14,804/385	24,152/513	43,233/749
	100	8,703/300	12,999/360	19,742/447	31,258/587	53,763/839
$25,000	3	864/59	1,391/76	2,322/102	4,164/149	69,078/938
	25	4,551/202	7,078/248	11,306/317	19,112/431	71,657/947
	50	6,970/257	10,670/312	16,224/309	27,499/524	73,939/955
	100	9,930/306	14,923/368	22,836/458	36,499/603	77,232/967
$30,000	3	906/60	1,460/75	2,442/102	4,388/150	83,094/982
	25	4,878/204	7,610/249	12,206/319	20,748/435	85,742/989
	50	7,576/259	11,645/314	18,328/397	30,381/531	88,169/997
	100	10,989/311	16,596/373	25,551/466	41,155/615	91,813/1,008
$40,000	3	973/59	1,570/76	2,631/103	4,740/150	111,125/1,051
	25	5,402/205	8,465/252	13,658/324	23,404/440	113,861/1,056
	50	8,562/262	13,239/319	20,998/404	33,165/541	116,492/1,062
	100	12,753/316	19,402/381	30,148/478	49,140/631	120,672/1,072
$50,000	3	1,024/59	1,655/76	2,777/103	5,015/151	139,156/1,103
	25	5,813/206	9,140/254	14,808/325	25,517/443	141,947/1,108
	50	9,347/263	14,515/321	23,147/407	39,051/547	144,716/1,113
	100	14,189/319	21,704/386	33,952/484	55,834/641	149,282/1,121

* *Note:* These numbers are based on minimum required payments that are 2% of the balance, with a $10 minimum. They were calculated with *The Banker's Secret Credit Card Software.*

leader, if one lender has trusted you to borrow money based on your signature alone, others are sure to follow.

Another plus for credit cards is that they offer some protection when services or products that you've charged don't live up to expectations. Some offer cash rebates, frequent-flyer miles, extended warranties, or collision insurance on car rentals. And when traveling in far-off places, they generally give you good exchange rates on purchases.

Pay less than you charge, though, and those friendly, helpful cards turn into ferocious, budget-busting, money-guzzling plastic monsters. So whenever you're tempted to whip out a card and charge something, think realistically about how you're going to pay it off. A great buy on a sweater, for example, won't seem as wonderful once you realize that by the time you get around to paying it off, you'll pay two, three, four, or more times as much as the sales tag said.

TAMING THE PLASTIC MONSTER

While you may be ready to turn over a new leaf as far as future charges are concerned, if you're saddled with a pile of credit card bills and wondering where to begin, there are several methods for digging yourself out of the hole. The approach you choose should be the one that appeals to you most. After all, you'll have to stick with it for a while (at least two years in most cases).

Method 1: The basic. Focus on the credit card that charges you the highest interest rate. Stop charging on that card. Every month from now on until the debt is paid off, if you do nothing else to cut the cost of your debts, try to pay as much as you can on the one with the highest interest rate, while paying the minimums on all the others. When you get that one paid off, cut it up, close the account, and start paying as much as you can on the card with the next-highest rate, and so on.

Method 2: Level or fixed payments. If you can afford to make the minimum payments on your credit cards this month, then you can afford to send in the same amount next month and the following months—until it's bye-bye debt. For each of your credit cards, instead of sending in the decreasing required payments each month, commit yourself to always sending in at least as much as you're required to send in right now. As each card gets paid off, transfer the amount you'd been sending in to the highest-interest debt you still have. It's one of the easiest ways to get a running start on becoming the new, credit-savvy you.

For example, say you owe $10,000 on a typical 17% credit card bill. The required payment this month would be $200. If you simply send in that same amount every month—as opposed to the ever decreasing amount that will be required in future months (assuming you don't charge anything more)—you'll save $15,929 and over 42 years of payments. The same $200 will save you even more, of course, if you can consolidate your debts onto a lower-cost card. Stay tuned. We'll show you how to do that, too.

Method 3: Pay fast, feel good. If you really need to see some quick results to stay motivated, consider paying off the card with lowest balance first, regardless of its interest rate. You'll feel a sense of accomplishment that can help you stick with your debt-reduction program. Come up with a low-cost way to celebrate, and figure out which debt you'll wipe out next.

Method 4: Twice as often, twice as good. Making biweekly payments can save you the most. Why? Because your card issuer *must* credit your payments when they're received. So a half payment every two weeks will result in 26 half payments a year, which is the equivalent of 13 monthly payments, not 12. The extra month's worth of payments will all go toward paying off your outstanding balance.

You probably won't hear about this "advanced" method to pare the plastic anywhere else, and while it can save you the most, it's a little complicated. So be sure to follow our instructions exactly!

Choose the piece of plastic that carries the highest interest rate, and stop charging on that card. Let's say it's at 17%, and you owe $3,500. Your required payment this month could be anywhere from around $70 to $105—we'll assume $70, which is typical.

If you send in only the minimum amount every month, by the time you pay off that $3,500, your total tab would be $11,162—over three times more than you charged. In other words, every $35 dinner would cost you more than $100 by the time you paid it off—a process that would take three and a half decades.

Before you lose your appetite, let's go back to that $70 you owe this month. Get it in by the due date, and start pinching your pennies. We have faith that you can come up with half of that, $35, in the next two weeks, and that you can scrape together at least another $35 every two weeks for the foreseeable future.

Believe it or not, if after sending in this month's $70 minimum, you send in $35 every two weeks from here on, you'll cut your interest bill by a whopping $5,453. And you'll be debt-free in less than 7 years, not more than 35. Neat, huh?

Make sure you get your check in every 14 days to the billing address on the monthly statements the card company sends you. Don't let the due date and minimum payments on those statements confuse you, but do verify that there are no unexplained charges or fees. Get your checks there like clockwork, every two weeks, and don't charge anything else on the card.

Develop Your Own Payoff Plan

You can often mix and match these methods for maximum savings. For example, you may decide to tackle your highest-rate card first, while you stick to a level payment on the others. Or you might try to pay the lowest balance off first, but pay the current minimums on your other cards using the biweekly payment method.

However you decide to pay off your cards, send in even more whenever you can. The more you pre-pay and the sooner you do it, the more you'll save and the freer you'll be. (To see how much you'll save, and to double-check the card issuer, you can run payoff plans using *The Banker's Secret Software,* or we can run the numbers for you. See page 327.)

You're likely to be most successful if:

- *You have a clear plan.* Use Table 12.3 on page 227, or our *Banker's Secret Software* to develop a specific plan for paying your debt off in the fastest, but most realistic, amount of time. Even if you're deeply in debt, as long as you stop charging, you can get yourself out of hock in a much shorter time frame than you realize—probably three to five years.

- *You put your plan on autopilot.* If you're going to use the fixed-payment method or the biweekly method, talk to your credit card company and/or bank to see if it can deduct your payments directly from your checking or savings account each month (or every 14 days)—for free. This assures that you won't make a lower payment or accept a skip-payment offer. Don't worry, you can generally cancel automatic payments with three business days' notice if you change your mind, but you might want to find out if your bank would charge a fee to stop the service.

- *You leave home without it.* Take the plastic out of your wallet and put it somewhere safe, where you *can't* get to it easily. If you're worried about having a card for emergencies or identification, ask your bank or credit union for a MasterCard or Visa debit card, which will take purchases directly out of your account. If you *must* carry a credit card, then carry only one—no more—and keep it out of sight.

- *You have support.* It's tough to admit you're in debt, but having loved ones who can help you, without judging, can be a real boon when you're struggling to stay out of the mall and on your plan. If you're too embarrassed to tell folks you're on a debt-reduction plan, then tell them you're saving for an important goal, such as a down payment on a house. Make sure you avoid situations where you know you'll be pressured to spend more money than you can afford.

GETTING HELP TO WIPE THE SLATE CLEAN

> Even though your situation is far from unique, being in debt may seem like the end of the world. You may be afraid to answer your phone or open your mail. Your self-esteem may be shot. Your stomach, back, and head probably ache. . . . But there is good news . . . you can get the bill collectors off your back and give yourself a fresh financial start.
>
> —ROBIN LEONARD, *Money Troubles:*
> *Legal Strategies to Cope with Your Debts*

Years of overspending have a price, and for more than a million people every year, that price is bankruptcy. Many who take this step hope it'll give them a new beginning . . . a clean slate, so to speak.

While bankruptcy may get people off the hook with creditors, it leaves an indelible mark on their credit reports, for up to 10 years. We've counseled many folks who have been through bankruptcy and are now finding it tough to rebuild their credit. And when they can get credit, they invariably must pay a higher rate of interest and/or put up more collateral.

Sometimes, bankruptcy is the only way out. Our goal is to keep you from getting in so far that getting out requires drastic steps. But if you're thinking about it, or just can't stick to a payoff plan alone, a nonprofit credit counseling agency can help you create a budget, and, if necessary, negotiate lower payments with your creditors. Their services are low cost or free—because they're funded by creditors. Here are two reputable resources:

Debt Counselors of America
800-680-3328
www.dca.org

National Foundation for Consumer Credit
800-388-2227
www.nfcc.org

You may also want to consider joining or starting a Debtor's Anonymous (DA) support group in your area. DA is based on the Alcoholics Anonymous 12-step model and encourages participants to take on no more debt. For information, send an SASE to:

Debtor's Anonymous
General Service Board
P.O. Box 400, Grand Central Station
New York, NY 10163-0400

To read about the DA approach, we recommend *How to Get Out of Debt, Stay Out of Debt & Live Prosperously* by Jerrold Mundis.

....

HOW LOW CAN YOU GO?

Whatever method or methods you use to tame your plastic monsters, your money will go further, and you'll be out of debt faster, if you can get a lower interest rate. So it's smart to invest the time to get the lowest rates you can, and then to consolidate your highest-interest debts to save even more.

Start with the cards already in your wallet. Call each card issuer's customer service number and say the appropriate version of: "I'm getting offers for a lot of cards with much lower rates and no annual fees. Will you lower my interest rate and waive my fee?"

Experience proves that these calls often result in savings—but don't expect an immediate, cheery, "delighted to be of service." You'll probably be put on hold while your record is reviewed. If the verdict isn't to your liking, ask for a supervisor. You may need to assert yourself up the chain of command, but if you have at least a year's history of timely payments (even of only the minimum required), getting an interest rate lowered or an annual fee waived should be relatively easy. Don't be intimidated, no matter how inflexible the credit card company may seem.

Ask specifically about being switched to a lower-rate, variable-interest card. And if you're nervous about future rate hikes, don't be. A fixed rate guarantees nothing when it comes to credit cards. Issuers can raise a fixed rate at any time, with only 15 days' advance written notice. And then, they often can—and often will—apply the new, higher rate to any outstanding balance as well as to new purchases.

Note: To ensure that your victories won't be fleeting or hollow, monitor them by regularly checking your statements and dialing for dollars when necessary. Pesky fees have been known to reappear the following year.

Junk Mail Can Pay

Card issuers send out 3 billion solicitations a year, so somewhere in today's pile of junk mail may lurk an offer for a card that starts with a teaser rate of 5.9% for 3, 6, or maybe even 12 months.

Before you apply, know that even if the application says "preapproved," lenders can turn you down because of predetermined criteria, which they don't have to reveal. So if your credit report isn't stellar, hold off. Between 75% and 90% of all applications for low-rate cards are rejected.

Assuming you can get a card with a low teaser rate, you'll save the most by transferring your debt to another teaser card before your current rate expires, and then doing the same again and again, until you're out from under. If you're likely to burn out playing "switch" every few months, settle for the lowest steady rate you can get, stop overcharging, and start prepaying.

When your lowest-rate cards are charged to the hilt, call and ask for a credit line increase. If you've been paying your bills on time, most issuers will be happy to give you more credit. That's how they make their gazillions. Then transfer balances from your higher-interest cards. *Do not* use the credit line increase as an excuse to spend!

In addition to carefully perusing the offers that come to you bulk rate, you can find a comprehensive list of low-rate cards at www.cardtrak.com. Or send $5 to CardTrak, P.O. Box 1700, Frederick, MD 21702. For a free list of low-rate offers (updated less frequently) send an SASE to Consumer Action, Low-Rate List, 717 Market Street, Suite 310, San Francisco, CA 94103, or go to www.consumer-action.org.

· ·

IMPORTANT PROVISOS ABOUT DEBT CONSOLIDATION

- Debt consolidation will only get you into more trouble if you or your mate are going to keep on charging and otherwise spending money you don't have.
- Avoid the consolidation loans that pitch one easy monthly payment, which usually means long payback periods and total interest charges that would have to be measured in light-years.
- Watch out for expensive balance-transfer fees and higher interest rates. Ask every card issuer to waive any fees before you transfer, and make sure the advertised interest rate is for transfers, not only for purchases.

· ·

Freedom in 36 Months

We hope that seeing how little you'd have to come up with to pay off your debts in three to five years will inspire you to make the effort. For example, say you owe $10,000 at 17% and make only the required payments each month. You'll send in $33,447 over the next 50 years.

Now say you transfer your balance to an 11% card. You could completely pay off the $10,000 in five years, by sending in just $217 a month. That's only $17 a month more than this month's required payment on a typical 17% card. (Take a gander at Table 12.3.)

If you follow through, after you've transferred your $10,000 balance to an 11% card and send in that $217 a month, you'll be debt-free in five years, and you'll save $20,402. That's more than twice as much as you had charged! See Table 12.4 to see how much you can save by consolidating and sticking to a payoff plan.

It's Raining!

If transferring your balance to lower-interest cards won't work, don't despair. There are other alternatives. Do you have money in a savings account? Although you've always been warned to keep an emergency fund in the bank, if you have a hefty credit card balance, you have a rainy day!

Use your low-interest savings account to pay down your high-interest card balance. That will give you credit equivalent to the amount you paid down. In a true emergency, you could take a cash advance.

For other borrowing options that require no credit check, consider debt consolidation loans against:

- Retirement savings such as 401(k), 403(b), or profit-sharing plans.

- The cash value in an insurance policy.

- Investments such as stocks and bonds (which are called *margin* loans).

- The equity in your home.

While any of these loans could save you money, be careful! You'll be borrowing against your future. We want you to consolidate your debts—not compound your money troubles. Also, none of these options is risk-free.

A better choice, if you can get it, is a low-cost loan from a well-heeled friend or relative. It'll save you a bundle, and your benefactor will also profit if you're sure (and they're sure) that you'll make the agreed-upon payments.

There are two types of debt consolidation loans we urge you to avoid:

1. Home equity loans that offer to lend you more than the value of your home—up to 125%—and often have very high closing costs of as much as $5,000 on a $25,000 loan. If you have to sell, it's a pretty safe bet that you won't be able to get more than your house is worth.

TABLE 12.3 After You've Consolidated, Pick a Monthly Payment to
Pay Off Your Debt in Three to Five Years

		CONSOLIDATION LOAN RATE						
DEBT	YEARS	8%	9%	10%	11%	12%	13%	14%
$ 5,000	3	157	159	161	164	166	168	171
	5	101	104	106	109	111	114	116
$ 7,500	3	235	239	242	246	249	253	256
	5	152	156	159	163	167	171	175
$10,000	3	313	318	323	327	332	337	342
	5	203	208	212	**217**	222	228	233
$12,500	3	392	398	403	409	415	421	427
	5	253	259	266	272	278	284	291
$15,000	3	470	477	484	491	498	505	513
	5	304	311	319	326	334	341	349
$17,500	3	548	557	565	573	581	590	598
	5	355	363	372	381	389	398	407
$20,000	3	627	636	645	655	664	674	684
	5	406	415	425	435	445	455	465
$25,000	3	783	795	807	818	830	842	854
	5	507	519	531	544	556	569	582
$30,000	3	940	954	968	982	996	1,011	1,025
	5	608	623	637	652	667	683	698
$35,000	3	1,097	1,113	1,129	1,146	1,163	1,179	1,196
	5	710	727	744	761	779	796	814
$40,000	3	1,253	1,272	1,291	1,310	1,329	1,348	1,367
	5	811	830	850	870	890	910	931
$45,000	3	1,410	1,431	1,452	1,473	1,495	1,516	1,538
	5	912	934	956	978	1,001	1,024	1,047
$50,000	3	1,567	1,590	1,613	1,637	1,661	1,685	1,709
	5	1,014	1,038	1,062	1,087	1,112	1,138	1,163

Note: These numbers, calculated using The Banker's Secret Loan Software, will help you save a bundle on your debts. For more information, see page 327. To save the most, first consolidate to get the lowest interest rate you can. Then pay off your debt as fast as you can—preferably in three to five years. This table originally appeared in Debt Consolidation 101: Strategies for Saving Money & Paying Off Your Debts Faster, written by the authors.

TABLE 12.4 After You've Consolidated, How Much Can You Save?
Based on a $10,000 Credit Card Balance with a 2% Minimum Required Payment

Card interest		13%	14%	15%	16%	**17%**	18%	19%
Total card cost		$21,451	23,555	26,123	29,329	**33,447**	38,931	46,598

CONSOLIDATION LOAN INTEREST	YEARS	AMOUNT SAVED BY CONSOLIDATING						
8%	3	10,170	12,274	14,842	18,048	22,166	27,650	35,317
	5	9,285	11,389	13,957	17,163	21,281	26,765	34,432
9%	3	10,003	12,107	14,675	17,881	21,999	27,483	35,150
	5	8,996	11,100	13,668	16,874	20,992	26,476	34,143
10%	3	9,835	11,939	14,507	17,713	21,831	27,315	34,982
	5	8,703	10,807	13,375	16,581	20,699	26,183	33,850
11%	3	9,665	11,769	14,337	17,543	21,661	27,145	34,812
	5	8,406	10,510	13,078	16,284	**20,402**	25,886	33,553
12%	3	9,494	11,598	14,166	17,372	21,490	26,974	34,641
	5	8,104	10,208	12,776	15,982	20,100	25,584	33,251
13%	3	9,321	11,425	13,993	17,199	21,317	26,801	34,468
	5	7,799	9,903	12,471	15,677	19,795	25,279	32,946
14%	3	9,147	11,251	13,819	17,025	21,143	26,627	34,294
	5	7,490	9,594	12,162	15,368	19,486	24,970	32,637
15%	3	8,972	11,076	13,644	16,850	20,968	26,452	34,119
	5	7,177	9,281	11,849	15,055	19,173	24,657	32,324
16%	3	8,795	10,899	13,467	16,673	20,791	26,275	33,942
	5	6,860	8,964	11,532	14,738	18,856	24,340	32,007
17%	3	8,616	10,720	13,288	16,494	20,612	26,096	33,763
	5	6,540	8,644	11,212	14,418	18,536	24,020	31,687
18%	3	8,436	10,540	13,108	16,314	20,432	25,916	33,583
	5	6,215	8,319	10,887	14,093	18,211	23,695	31,362

How to use this chart: Say you owe $10,000 at 17%. If you send in only the minimum, you'll spend $33,447. But if you get a lower interest rate—11% for example—and pay it off in five years, you'll save $20,402 (which we show on the chart in bold). These numbers were calculated with *The Banker's Secret Loan Software*. For more information, see page 327. This table originally appeared in *Debt Consolidation 101: Strategies for Saving Money & Paying Off Your Debts Faster*, written by the authors.

2. Loans from finance companies that charge very high rates—23%, for example. Customers are attracted because of ads focusing on the low monthly payments. But as we hope we've made clear by now, low payments are an expensive trap that will stretch out your term of debt and dramatically increase your total interest costs.

NO CREDIT? BAD CREDIT?
YOU *CAN* GET A CARD

Even though thousands of issuers are heavily competing for a spot in most people's wallets, getting that first card can seem like an impossible task. It's not! And if you had some hard times a while ago, even though you eventually paid the bills, getting that next card may also seem like a hopeless fantasy. It's not!

To improve your record, you may be tempted to sign on with an outfit that promises to erase your bad credit history. Don't! Once credit bureaus suspect that a "credit repair clinic" is involved, they can refuse to even investigate the disputed information. In the end, your wallet will be lighter, but your bad credit rating will be intact. If you need hands-on help with credit problems, get it from one of the nonprofit counseling services listed on page 223.

Even if you have a good job, a mortgage, and a car loan, you could still be turned down for a bank card because of an "insufficient credit history." If you've never had a credit card before, lenders have no way of knowing how responsible you'll be should times get tough. They reason that most people would pay their mortgages and car loans first, letting credit card bills slide.

The last thing card issuers want to do is take a chance. Hence two good, old-fashioned catch-22's:

- How do you get experience if no one will give you that first card?

- How do you get a new card if you can't prove that you've changed your spendthrift ways?

The answer to both these questions may be a "secured card," which almost anyone can get. These Visas and MasterCards look and act exactly like the unsecured pieces of plastic in your neighbor's pocket. The only difference is an interest-earning security deposit that you have to leave in the issuer's bank.

The credit line on your secured card will be 100% to 150% of the amount you deposit as collateral. The more cash you can tie up, the more you can charge. The less you can put aside, the less you'll be able to spend.

Being limited to charging only what you can afford is an obvious advantage—you won't get in over your head. There's another secured card advantage that's often overlooked: You'll probably earn more interest on the security deposit than you would at a local bank.

On the downside, secured cards usually come with high interest rates. So charge only what you can really afford, then pay off the bill every month. (The secured card issuer won't deduct payments from your collateral account. You must send in a check or make arrangements for automatic withdrawals from your bank account.)

When you can't pay in full, pay as much as you can. By always paying more than the minimum, you'll save a fortune in interest. In any event, *never* be late with a payment, even if all you're sending in is the minimum.

Your aim is to show a pattern of timely payments. You don't have to charge big purchases or string out your payments over many months. Just use your card occasionally for an item you would have bought anyway.

If you always make sure to pay at least the required minimum, on time, you'll soon be on your way to getting a less costly regular card—followed by an avalanche of preapproved offers for yet more plastic.

Important: Unless the bank that issues your secured card reports to the major credit bureaus, your timely payments will not help you build or reestablish your credit. Before signing up, ask if the bank reports to all three major bureaus, and verify that it won't flag the card as "secured" on those reports.

Deal only with a known and reputable card issuer. The woods are full of secured card scam offers. Get a list of reputable secured card issuers from CardTrak, at www.securedcard.com, or send $10 to CardTrak, P.O. Box 1700, Frederick, MD 21702. A free list of secured cards that is updated less frequently than CardTrak's is available by sending an SASE to Consumer Action, Secured Card List, 717 Market Street, Suite #310, San Francisco, CA 94103, or go to www.consumer-action.org.

Score High at the Rating Game

Who decides whether you'll get the credit you want? Most likely, a computer, of course! If you get a passing score, you'll get the card or loan. If not, you'll receive a form letter offering reasons for your rejection that are often cryptic at best.

The number one secret to keeping a good credit rating is paying your bills on time. Even if you eventually pay what you owe, late payments will show on your credit report for seven years, making it hard for you to get other credit or to graduate to an unsecured card.

Secret number two is to make sure yours is not one of the many credit reports that contain mistakes. You can get a free copy of your report if you've been turned down for credit within the last 60 days. If not, you'll have to pay eight bucks (in most states) to see yours. Here are the three major credit bureaus:

Equifax
P.O. Box 105783
Atlanta, GA 30348
800-685-1111

Experian (formerly TRW)
P.O. Box 2104
Allen, TX 75013-2104
800-682-7654

Trans Union
P.O. Box 390
Springfield, PA 19064-0390
800-888-4213

When you send for your credit report, include: your full name (including a maiden name or generation, such as senior or junior, I or II), your social security number, your date of birth, your complete addresses for the past five years, your daytime and evening phone numbers, and your spouse's name. Be sure to sign and date your letter and include something that proves your current address—a copy of your driver's license, for example.

When your credit report arrives about two weeks later, take a hard look. If an error mars your appearance, get it corrected right away. Some typical boo-boos include listings of long-since-closed accounts, debts incurred by other people with names similar to yours, and credit problems caused by your ex-spouse on an account for which you didn't share responsibility.

....

WE'RE PROUD TO SAY

The best source for more information about credit is *The Ultimate Credit Handbook* by coauthor Gerri Detweiler. Every card-carrying American ought to read it. See page 327.

—MARC AND NANCY

....

AMAZING GRACE

When interest rates no longer matter—grace periods do! As long as you're carrying a rollover balance, grace periods are of no benefit. But once you start paying your balance in full every month, ask when your billing cycle ends. By shopping a day or two after the billing date, you'll be giving your money the rest of the month plus the next grace period to earn you interest (or at least to accumulate) before your payment comes due. It's like getting a 45- to 55-day loan for free.

Remember, *this will not work* on cards that offer no grace period or that you don't pay off each month. That's because interest charges will begin to accrue immediately if there is any balance due at the end of the previous month's grace period. Therefore, when you're finally on a pay-as-you-go basis, get yourself a friendlier, no-fee card with at least a 25-day grace period.

In the meantime, for purchases you *will not* be paying off in full each month, use a card with a low interest rate and send in as much as you can each month. And don't wait until the due date to make your payment. The way credit card interest works, you'll save more by paying your bill as soon as you get it.

For those purchases you *will* be paying off in full, use a credit card with a grace period and, preferably, no annual fee. (The interest rate won't matter if you'll never have to pay it.)

CREDIT CARD COMMON SENSE: QUICK TIPS TO SAVE MONEY AND GRIEF

- Try *never* to use your credit cards for cash advances. When it comes to borrowing money, there are few ways more expensive than cash advances. Some banks charge interest, some charge fees, and many charge both.

- If you're a compulsive buyer, limit your card use to the American Express charge card, which doesn't allow revolving credit. If you don't pay those bills in full and on time, your next charges will be turned down.

- Department store cards generally charge the highest interest rates around. Use these cards only when there's a real benefit—an extra 10% off, for example—and when you *know* you'll be paying off the bill immediately. Otherwise, use a cheaper piece of plastic.

- Report missing or stolen cards by phone *immediately.* Then follow up with a letter.
- Sign new cards as soon as they arrive. Cut up and carefully dispose of expired cards.
- Never give out your card number over the phone—unless *you* initiated the call. And never write your card number on a postcard or on the outside of an envelope.
- Open credit card bills promptly and check them for unauthorized charges as well as for billing errors. Report unauthorized charges and billing errors in writing to the customer service address indicated on your statement. Don't enclose your letter with your payment. (Just calling will not protect your legal rights.)
- Keep out of the protection racket. Your card issuers have probably offered you a "protection service," where for a small charge, they'll keep a list of all your credit cards in case any are lost or stolen. Don't go for it. Just keep a list of your card numbers, expiration dates, and the phone number of each card issuer in a safe place. (Do this now. Don't be sorry later that you didn't.)

When he was 83-years-young, Walter, a flight instructor in Las Vegas, came down to earth long enough to share his secret for easily compiling your list of credit cards (and sundry other important papers or pieces of plastic).

"Once every six months, empty your wallet or purse of credit cards, licenses, guarantee cards, etc. Place them on a copying machine, then file the [photo]stat in a safe place," advises this World War II pilot, adding, "*Don't* forget to remove the originals."

....

HINTS FOR HOLIDAY SPENDING

Turn your debts into a high-yielding Christmas club. If you regularly run up holiday bills that you can't pay off immediately, here's an easy way to make sure they're gone by the following year: Divide your balance by 10 and add at least that to each minimum payment. For example, say Santa charged $2,000 to one of your cards this year. If you send in $200 a month over the required amount, the bill will be paid off in time for next year's holiday binge. Can't afford $200 a month? Send in as much as you can every month, then charge *less* next Christmas.

If you've been contributing to a Christmas club in the hope that it would solve your holiday spending problem, consider this: Most Christmas clubs pay a very low interest rate. Investing that same amount of money in your credit card debt will save you at least three times what a Christmas club typically yields.

Shop carefully, just like Santa does. Avoid impulse buying by making a list and checking it twice—then leave your credit cards at home and go window-shopping. After you've decided what to buy, add up the cost of your proposed purchases and make sure the sum is manageable. Then take your cards shopping and buy only what you planned.

....

THE CREDIT CARD CONVENIENCE TRAP

Mrs. Doubtfree, an elderly widow, believed that the checks her credit card company sent really were to be used "just as you would any check." She didn't realize she was borrowing money instead of using her own. She'd already written 29 of those "convenience checks," totaling over $16,000, when Gerri came to her rescue and got higher-ups at Mrs. Doubtfree's credit card company to agree to waive all of the finance charges and to accept a repayment plan that fit Mrs. Doubtfree's tight budget.

So-called convenience checks are more like cash than credit cards, and often expensive cash at that. While MasterCard, Visa, and American Express may come to your aid in a dispute over a charged purchase, if you use one of their pseudochecks, you're on your own. Should the product never arrive, disintegrate on first use, or not be what you expected, you'll essentially be told, "Tough luck!"

If you get this response and have other cards, certainly threaten to cancel theirs. Be persistent, and talk to supervisors, but don't be surprised if your threat fails, especially if there's a lot of money at stake. Card issuers know you have no legal recourse. Shame on them! And shame on our legislators for continuing to allow these checks to be sent out unsolicited.

···

CHAPTER 13

Your Mortgage Is a Great Investment

○ Welcome to the greatest show on earth: how to change $25 a month into $23,337. No magic involved!

○ Myths that keep Americans from investing in their mortgages

○ Choose the loan that will save you the most

○ How to know when it's time to refinance

○ The ARMs scandal, and what you can do to stop bank overcharges on your adjustable rate mortgage

By pre-paying, you invest nothing extra to save thousands. Pre-payments are not additional costs. They are simply advances, small amounts that you pay sooner.

MARC EISENSON, *The Banker's Secret*

···

First comes the dream, be it a vine-covered cottage in the country or a colonial on Woodcroft Circle. Then comes the search, the discovery, the dickering, the closing, moving day—and 30 years of monthly payments.

As we've shown, even without including real estate taxes, insurance, maintenance, utilities, or those legal fees and other closing costs you'll incur both when you buy and when you sell, a $125,000 mini-castle financed for 30 years at 8% could cost $289,149 (the $100,000 you borrowed, the $25,000 you put down, and the $164,149 you paid in interest).

With so much of your money at stake, it's smart to manage your mortgage at least as carefully as you do your other investments. The good news is that saving tens of thousands of dollars on your mortgage is the proverbial piece of cake. All it takes is small, pocket change, pre-payments. There's a special bonus, too—a tremendous personal emotional benefit. You'll actually be able to achieve the American dream, which, after all, is to own your own home—not to maintain it for some bank!

Table 13.1 shows how regular pre-payments of $15, $25, $50, and up will save plenty on our sample $100,000 mortgage. As you'll see, the more you invest in your loan, the less your home will cost and the sooner it will be yours, free and clear.

So why don't all homeowners invest in themselves and their families by speeding up the day when they'll own their homes free and clear . . . and in the process, save tens of thousands of dollars that would otherwise be wasted in unnecessary interest costs?

MYTHS THAT KEEP HOMEOWNERS FROM INVESTING IN THEIR MORTGAGES

Myth: It sounds too good to be true.

Truth: We admit it. Anything that promises to save you big bucks sounds like a get-rich-quick scheme. And we've all been warned to avoid deals like that. However, investing in your mortgage—even minuscule amounts—really does reap great rewards. It's no gimmick.

Myth: I can't afford to pre-pay.

Truth: If you borrowed that $100,000 at 8% for 30 years and sent in only an extra 25 cents a day, you'd save $7,986. A dime a day would save $3,317. Can't afford dimes this month? Send in pennies, but get into the pre-payment habit! Figure out where you can cut back, even just a little. Then send in what you can, when you can, and turn your biggest debt into a profit center. You'll save a pile and at the same time give yourself the peace of mind that owning your home free and clear can bring. (See Table 13.2.)

Myth: I can get a better return someplace else.

Truth: Maybe you can! In terms of traditional investments, if you have a good 401(k) plan at work with employer matching, take full advantage of it. But in general, the greater the return, the greater the risk. And there's nothing safer than investing in the roof over your head, or rather, the mortgage on it.

TABLE 13.1 The More You Pre-Pay, the More You'll Save

Down payment:	$25,000
Loan amount:	$100,000
Interest rate:	8%
Loan term:	30 years
Required monthly payment:	$734
Total interest, if not pre-paid:	$164,149
Total outlay without pre-payment:	$289,149

PRE-PAY	SAVE	REDUCE TERM BY YRS/ MONTHS	PRE-PAY	SAVE	REDUCE TERM BY YRS/ MONTHS
$ 15	$ 15,054	2/03	$ 350	$108,404	18/00
25	23,337	3/07	375	110,719	18/06
50	39,906	6/02	400	112,841	18/11
75	52,484	8/02	425	114,793	19/03
100	62,456	9/10	450	116,597	19/07
125	70,610	11/03	475	118,268	19/11
150	77,431	12/05	500	119,821	20/03
175	83,240	13/05	750	130,930	22/06
200	88,260	14/04	1,000	137,506	23/11
225	92,649	15/01	1,250	141,871	24/10
250	96,524	15/10	1,500	144,986	25/07
275	99,976	16/05	1,750	147,322	26/01
300	103,071	17/00	2,000	149,140	26/06
325	105,866	17/07			

Note: These numbers were calculated with *The Banker's Secret Loan Software* (created by authors Marc Eisenson and Nancy Castleman, see page 327).

Of course, you don't have to choose one or the other. You can go the limit on your 401(k), for example, and still have no trouble coming up with a $25 a month pre-payment on your mortgage. We have faith in you!

But remember, if you carry a balance on a credit card, by all means pay that off first. Earn upward of 20% tax-free while you can.

TABLE 13.2 Peewee Pre-Payments
Based on a $100,000 Mortgage at 8%
for 30 Years

PRE-PAY	SAVE
10¢ a day	$ 3,317
25¢ a day	7,986
50¢ a day	15,054
$1.00 a day	27,072

Myth: I'll lose my only tax deduction.

Truth: It's not your only tax deduction, assuming you itemize. You'll still be able to take write-offs for property taxes. Tax deductions *may* ease the bite, but they don't make paying interest a profitable venture. The more interest you pay, the less money you'll keep.

It never pays to send your lender $1 in the hopes of getting back 28 cents or so from the IRS. Anyway, higher standard deductions mean that the first $7,100, (as of the 1998 tax year) spent on a couple's mortgage interest could be saving $0!

Even if you itemize, pre-paying pays. Say you send in $25 a month more during just the first year of our sample $100,000 mortgage. Because of compounding, that $300 in advance payments will save you $2,808 in interest over the loan's life—even if you never pre-pay another cent.

But in that first year, you'll only pay $11.26 less in interest than had you not pre-paid. For someone in the 28% federal tax bracket, that would increase the tax burden by $3.15. Where else can an investment of a mere $3.15 return $2,808, guaranteed?

Myth: My bank will be angry if I pre-pay.

Truth: (a) Banks don't have feelings, and now that everything's computerized, there probably won't be anyone at the bank who even knows that you're pre-paying. (b) These days, banks make much of their mortgage profits up front—on points and closing costs. (c) When you pre-pay, the bank accumulates money with which to make new loans (which brings us back to "b").

Myth: I'm probably going to be moving in the next few years, so pre-paying doesn't make sense.

Truth: While homeowners do tend to move every five to seven years, they generally go from one mortgaged home to another, creating what we call a *serial mortgage.* Unique to each borrower, these loans are made up of the various mortgages a family takes out over the years.

Regardless of how often you move, every dollar you invest in your mortgage will earn you money at the rate you're currently paying. Have an 8% fixed-rate loan? Your pre-payments will yield 8%.

If you keep pre-paying, no matter what home loan you have at the moment, the ultimate result will be an early escape from mortgage debt—meaning years of mortgage payments you'll never have to make.

All along, you'll have more options for the next house, and the next. For example, you'll be able to put more money down on the next new house—because your pre-payments on the old one mean you owe less. You may decide you can afford a bigger house—or you might want to lighten your load with a smaller mortgage. You'll have a choice, and someday, your home will actually be yours—while your neighbors will still have decades of payments left to be made on their most recent homes!

Myth: I'll get hit with a pre-payment penalty.

Truth: Pre-payment penalties are rare. Even when they can be imposed, most banks don't bother. Penalties on small pre-payments are so tiny, it'd cost the lender more than they'd collect to do the bookkeeping and billing.

And while we're on the subject of bookkeeping, you'll be happy to know that these days, lenders almost always credit pre-payments correctly. However, to make certain that there will be no confusion, include a note with your first few pre-payments that says something like, "Please credit the additional amount I've sent in this month to the outstanding principal balance on my loan."

If you want to make sure the lender is properly crediting your pre-payments, run out a schedule with *The Banker's Secret Software,* or get us to run one for you (see page 327).

Myth: My banker says my pre-payments will be subtracted off "the back end of my loan."

Truth: What you send in today immediately comes off the amount you owe—whether or not your banker understands how the math works. Since you owe less, more of next month's mortgage payment will go toward reducing your balance, while the amount that goes toward interest will decrease. Your loan will cost you less and be paid off earlier because you've pre-paid.

Myth: Pre-paying is so complicated, I'll need to hire someone to do it for me.

Truth: Nonsense! Although there are a lot of ads out there for biweekly conversions or other mortgage-acceleration programs, they're expensive and absolutely unnecessary. Send in what you can, when you can, and watch your home equity grow!

BIWEEKLY WARNING

The only similarity between real biweeklies and these conversion plans, which we call pseudo-biweeklies, is that your money will be electronically extracted from your account every two weeks.

Although they electronically transfer funds every two weeks from your account, pseudo-biweekly sellers simply send the bank your required mortgage payment once a month, just as you always did, and in our less-than-humble opinion, ought to continue doing.

Then once or twice a year, the excess that accumulates from your biweekly payments will also be sent in. Guess who gets to work the float?

If your bank won't credit your payment every two weeks—and most won't—there's no benefit in your sending in biweekly payments. While pseudo-biweekly sellers claim to offer something special, the truth is that *you can easily save more without outside help,* and without all those fees and charges.

All you have to do is divide your current monthly mortgage payment by 12, and send in that amount as a pre-payment with each month's check. For example, let's go back to our sample $100,000 loan, which has a required monthly payment of $734. Divide that $734 by 12, and you get $61.17.

Send in a pre-payment of $61.17 every month along with your mortgage check. There'll be no start-up or "service" fees, you'll get the benefit of the float, your pre-payments will be deducted from your balance sooner, and you'll save more than you would with a pseudo. In this instance, your $61.17 a month will save you $45,916.

The pseudo-biweekly sellers try to make pre-paying sound complicated, and they want you to believe you're not disciplined enough to invest in your mortgage on your own. This is one high-return investment where you just don't need to pay a broker!

You *can* pre-pay on your own. After all, you write out your mortgage check every month, don't you? It doesn't take a whole lot of discipline to write out a slightly larger check. There's probably even a line on your mortgage coupon for entering your principal pre-payment amount. What could be easier? The larger the checks you write and the sooner you start sending them in, the more you'll save and the sooner you'll be living debt-free.

SAMPLE MORTGAGE COUPON

FIRST NATIONAL BANK OF ANYTOWN, USA	
1234 SOUTH MAIN STREET	
ANYTOWN, USA 12345	

ACCOUNT NUMBER:	012-555-1223	P & I Due:	$733.77
PAYMENT NUMBER:	35	Escrow/Insurance:	$210.00
DUE DATE:	December 1, 1998	Amount Due:	$943.77
AMOUNT DUE:	$943.77	Additional Principal:	*100.00*
		Additional Escrow:	*0*
		Total Amount Enclosed	*$1,043.77*

Important tip: If you really don't think you can trust yourself to add that additional amount every month—just ask your lender to electronically extract it from your checking account once a month. Most will be happy to do it for free—even lenders who market pseudo biweeklies! There's no need to pay for a mortgage-conversion program or a special pre-payment plan of any sort.

Note: For the complete story on pre-paying, with lots of tables so you can see how much you'll save, read *The Banker's Secret*, by Marc Eisenson (see page 327).

ADJUSTABLE RATE MORTGAGE MADNESS

Back in the late 1970s, when interest rates were competing with space probes to see which could go highest, fastest, bankers found themselves in an upside-down world. Instead of paying low and charging high, they were stuck paying depositors upward of twice the interest they were collecting on outstanding mortgages.

To avoid a future repeat, the adjustable rate mortgage (ARM) was called into service. While there are many variations on the theme, the basic ARM has an interest rate that is adjusted once a year, in accordance with some index—the interest rate on Treasury bills, for example. That way, if rates go through the ceiling, mortgage payments will follow suit, and the bank stays in the black. On the other hand, if rates drop, homeowners get a break. (The annual rise or fall is usually limited to 2% with a lifetime cap of 6%.)

The concept was clear, the risk was obvious, the benefits included low introductory rates and the possibility of even lower rates in the future—

but there was one problem. Many lenders simply couldn't follow their own instructions for calculating rate changes on ARMs—which isn't surprising, considering how complicated they've made those rules. Many a bank mistake was made.

The major lenders have long since worked out the kinks, but with loans being sold and resold, your current lender could be taking money out of your pocket! (It also might be charging you *less* than it could.)

While not simple, it is possible to check the numbers yourself. Especially if you're the type who likes to crunch numbers, learning to check your own adjustable interest rate is a good idea and a worthwhile investment of your time. After all, you may be dealing with these changes every year for the foreseeable future.

For excellent do-it-yourself ARM-checking instructions, send $3, check or money order, to HSH Associates, Dept. ACK, 1200 Route 23, Butler, NJ 07405.

．．．

BUYING THE RIGHT MORTGAGE—
NEW OR REFINANCED

To find the right mortgage takes some effort, but the money you'll save by shopping wisely could save you a fortune and a lot of headaches.

Whether you're financing a new home or refinancing, you'll have plenty of choices. In addition to banks, you may be able to borrow from the seller, a relative, an insurance company, or through a mortgage broker. Getting the loan that fits you best is unfortunately not as simple as finding the one with the lowest interest rate.

If you haven't already done so, get the address of the credit agency that local lenders use and order a copy of your credit report. It'll cost a few bucks, but correcting errors now can save you grief, time, and money later. (See page 231.)

With an accurate credit report and a bit of current info on your income, local lenders should be able to give you a firm sense of how much they'll commit. Why dream of a home that'll be out of your reach?

Don't look so good on paper? Self-employed? Focus on "no-peek" loans. Translation: Your financial capabilities will not be subjected to as rigorous a review. You'll pay a higher rate and probably have to put up a substantial down payment (25% to 30%) in exchange for more privacy.

The real estate industry, including lenders, would love to see you buy the absolutely most expensive home you can afford. In fact, once you protect them with pricey private mortgage insurance (PMI), they'll be happy to see you buy more than you should rationally own. Buy what you need, not the most house that someone who will benefit from the transaction says you can afford. The fortune you save will be your own!

Next, you need to guesstimate how long you'll own this home. The best loan for a short-term owner isn't necessarily best for a long-term owner. Settling in for life? Consider a mortgage with higher up-front costs (such as points) and a lower interest rate.

Moving in five to seven years? You may be better off with a higher rate rather than points. And your best bet may very well be an ARM with a low introductory rate.

Because ARMs are unpredictable, the next question you'll want to ponder involves your willingness and ability to gamble—especially if you'll be in the house for many years. Taking an ARM rather than a fixed-rate loan is a gamble. As with the stock market, no one knows what tomorrow will bring, and each home buyer needs to decide which way to go based on their own risk tolerance.

Can you protect yourself from the risk of future rate hikes, avoid them, or cover the additional costs should they rise up to their cap? In other words, instead of paying 8%, could you afford 14% if it came to that—$1,185 a month versus $734 on our $100,000 example?

You have three possible weapons in your arsenal against accelerating ARMs: convertible mortgages, two-step loans, and graduated payment mortgages (GPMs).

1. *Convertible mortgages* give you the opportunity to bail out of an ARM if rates climb. Generally, from the end of your loan's first year to the end of year 5, you can convert an ARM to a fixed rate—for a fee, of course. It'll be tied to the then current rates, so it may not be as low as the fixed rate you could take out now. But you'd be protected from yet higher interest.

2. *Two-step loans,* also called "7-23s," are the flip side of convertibles. You get a fixed-rate loan, typically for the first seven years. Then it becomes an ARM for the remaining term. If you sell in less than seven years, higher interest rates won't affect you, nor will you benefit if rates drop. But if you keep the house past year 7, you'll face an unpredictable eighth year—and future. Of course, at that point you could refinance to a fixed-rate loan or even to a new ARM with an introductory teaser rate. But who knows what rates will be like then?

3. *Graduated payment mortgages,* a third permutation, start out with a relatively low monthly payment, which then increases. While not techni-

cally an ARM, because the rate remains constant, the monthly payments give it the feel of an adjustable mortgage. A GPM will let you buy a more expensive home than you otherwise could, on the theory that your salary will rise enough over time to cover the payment increases. If the theory's wrong, you could lose your home. Watch out! Also make sure the monthly payment is at least high enough to cover the interest—or your debt will increase every month.

Apples to Apples, Oranges to Oranges

To decide which loan is most likely to cost you the least, set up a chart similar to Table 13.3. The figures you compare should include the loan amount plus its related closing costs and any points (what we call the *comparative amount*). Crunch the numbers for the period of time you intend to own your home.

TABLE 13.3 Sample Mortgage Comparison Work Sheet

	BASED ON $100,000 LOAN			
	LOAN 1	LOAN 2	LOAN 3	LOAN 4
Term	30-Year	30-Year	15-Year	30-Year
Rate	Fixed	Fixed	Fixed	Adjustable
Interest rate	9.125%	8.5%	8.875%	6.25%
ARM: change period	n/a	n/a	n/a	2 Years
Interest cap	n/a	n/a	n/a	2%
Lifetime cap	n/a	n/a	n/a	6%
Points (in percent)	0	3.125%	0	2%
Points (in dollars)	0	3,125	0	2,000
Closing costs	2,500	2,500	2,500	2,500
Comparative amount	102,500	105,625	102,500	104,500
Monthly comparisons	834	812	1,032	643*
Total cost: 5 years	148,411	149,591	143,827	144,291
15 years	231,739	228,664	185,762	257,740
30 years	300,221	292,373	n/a	361,347

Notes: These numbers were calculated with *The Banker's Secret Software* (see page 327).
* The required payment could climb to $779 after two years, to $918 after four years, and to $1,060 after six years.

Aside from the potential total cost to you, you also need to factor in whether you have the cash on hand to pay points and/or an adequately high, steady income to consider 15-year loans.

Given these options, if you'll be moving in five years, the 15-year fixed will end up being slightly less expensive, but the 6.25% ARM might be more appealing, even though it has points, because of the far lower monthly payment. You'd more than recoup your $2,000 in five years. But if you expect to own for 15 or 30 years, you might want to take loan 2, the 30-year fixed-rate loan at 8.5%, and then pay it off as quickly as you can.

But, wait, you say, loan 2 will cost far more than loan 3. True, unless you pre-pay loan 2. If you can come up with loan 3's $1,032 monthly payment, and you send that in on loan 2, you'll be out of hock sooner and cheaper.

Unless you're absolutely certain that you'll be able to meet the higher payment every month, take a 30-year loan—and pay it off as if it were a 15-year loan. You'll enjoy substantial savings, and if money ever becomes tight, you'll be able to pay the lower 30-year amount. As another example, a $100,000 loan at 8% interest for 30 years would require a monthly payment of $734, while a 15-year loan at the same interest rate would require $956. That additional $222 each month would save more than $92,000 in interest. But you'll be in trouble if times get tough and you can't scrape together that $222.

Solution? Take a 30-year loan and send in $956 each month. The loan will be paid off in 15 years, and you'll still save the $92,000, but you'll have flexibility. If the road gets rocky, you can just send in $734! And if times turn golden, send in more and pay off the loan even faster.

Note: You can often get a slightly better interest rate on a 15-year loan than you can on a 30-year loan. But the risk of being overextended, for many folks, far outweighs the slight additional benefit to signing up for a shorter-term mortgage.

Banks Don't Own All the Money

If you can avoid taking out a brand-new mortgage, you're bound to save. If possible, consider assuming the current mortgage—even if the interest rate is slightly higher. Chances are, closing costs will be lower than with a new mortgage. However, to make sure that it's the best deal for you, read the fine print and crunch the numbers. (Most conventional mortgages aren't assumable, but FHA and VA loans generally are.)

See if the sellers will finance part or all of the sale. If they don't need the cash in one lump sum, your mortgage may be a great investment—for them. And although lending to loved ones can be risky business, consider asking cash-rich friends or relatives for a loan. It's a good way for everyone to benefit—*if it's carefully done.* You pay them a higher rate than they'd earn at the bank, and it'll still cost you less than the bank would charge you.

Maybe you can find a local investor who lends mortgage money. Real estate brokers, lawyers, and accountants should be able to offer some good leads to cheap money and to loan funds that are available to those with less-than-stellar credit reports. Mortgage brokers, who only make money if you close, are often the most likely to hustle under these circumstances.

....

A FEW MORE WORDS ABOUT ARMS

When it comes to adjustable rate mortgages, it's smart to be prudent. Always assume the interest rate will increase at the maximum rate allowed on every change date. As you can see from Table 13.3, played out over 15 to 30 years, an ARM (loan 4) can get very costly! Of course, if you're not averse to some risk, you could come out ahead with an ARM, if you're in luck and rates stay level, or better yet, drop. It's your decision. We just want you to base your money decisions on fact—as well as your personality— rather than on myth, misrepresentation, or eenie, meenie, miney, moe!

....

SEVEN SMART STEPS TO CUTTING CLOSING COSTS

1. Before applying for a loan, ask if the application fee is refundable should you be turned down. Ask for junk fees to be waived (e.g., underwriting or commitment fees or document-processing charges). And try to negotiate on the other closing costs, such as legal fees, the appraisal, and points.

2. Title insurance companies pay out on an infinitesimal percentage of premiums. But you'll still be required to buy title insurance to protect your lender—in case the seller wasn't the only, or the "real," owner. If the seller has owned the property for just a few years, see if you can get a discounted "reissue rate" from the seller's title insurer. Similarly, see if the lender will accept an updated version of the previous owner's property survey. This will save 50% or more, compared to the cost of a new one.

3. Question escrow. Although it's standard bank policy, you don't have to acquiesce without a murmur. Try to negotiate a clear contractual out that will eventually let you pay your own taxes and insurance. Meanwhile, periodically ask the lender for an escrow analysis. If there's more than a small excess (for contingencies such as tax increases), ask the lender for an explanation.

4. Skip mortgage life insurance if you have a choice. There are lots of cheaper term policies that will pay the same or more—and won't require you to list the bank as your beneficiary. Let your heirs decide when to pay off the mortgage.

5. Be in really good hands. The last thing you want is for your house to burn down, leaving your family out in the cold. Lenders, however, are much more concerned about their collateral, which you'll be obliged to insure. The right policy and insurer can save you money now, and grief later, should a disaster strike. (See Chapter 4.)

6. Talk with your tax preparer before you set a date for the closing. It might save you money.

7. Give a last look. Arrange to inspect the house one last time as close to closing as possible. (An hour before would be almost perfect.) If there's a problem, be it a broken window, frozen pipes, or a missing dining room fixture, you might be able to get reimbursed by the seller at the closing.

REFINANCING COULD COST YOU

The conventional wisdom is that it makes sense to refinance when there's a 2% spread between what you're paying now on your mortgage and what you can get on a refi. We say it pays to look at loan rates in your area regularly. The newspaper probably runs them every Sunday, or maybe a lender will send you some junk mail pitching new low rates. You can also find current mortgage rates at www.hsh.com.

"Refinance now," the banker says. "The rates aren't going to get much lower, and I can save you $144 a month."

Assuming you borrowed $100,000 eight years ago at 10% for 30 years, should you refinance? Answer: It depends on what you do with the $144 a month difference in the monthly payments—$878 at 10% versus $734 at 8%. Chances are, your banker won't mention that of the $84,288 you've already paid, $77,759 went to the bank as interest and only $6,529 went to pay off the loan. But sooner or later, you'll discover that you still owe $93,471.

"And, what with points and closing costs, you'll want to borrow . . . oh, say . . . $98,000 for 30 years. Let's make it an even $100,000. Take the family to Disney World. Just sign here." So, there you are—having already spent over $84,000—with a new loan for the same amount you borrowed eight years ago. And if you're not careful, the new loan is going to cost you more than holding onto your original mortgage, over $33,000 more in this example.

Why? Because you agreed to an extra eight years of debt—eight more years of paying almost nothing but interest. To beat the bank at its own game, first refinance when the calculations on a comparison worksheet similar to Table 13.3 indicate you should. Then invest the difference (that $144 a month in our example) in your new mortgage. You'll be sending in exactly what you paid before refinancing, but you'll save over $43,000. As a bonus, you'll be debt-free four years sooner than had you kept your original loan, without altering your spending habits a bit.

Important: If you owe a lot on those plastic monsters in your wallet, invest that $144 a month into your high-interest credit card bills instead. Then, when the cards are clean, transfer that amount to your mortgage. Come up with a few more dollars, and you can pay your debts off even faster, save yourself more, and get your family that much farther down the road to financial independence.

A Secret Refinancing Program

If you've held an FHA-insured mortgage for at least six months and are up-to-date on mortgage payments, you can refinance at market rates with no qualification—under the FHA's Streamline Program.

It doesn't matter if you're self-employed, unemployed, or even have a bad credit rating (as long as you've made timely mortgage payments). Streamline is a true *no*-documentation loan. The dwelling doesn't need to be owner-occupied, and it's okay if the real estate market is declining. There are no credit checks or employment verifications, not even a meeting. And *no* appraisals are required for a Streamline, if all you're doing is refinancing your outstanding balance. You'll need only to complete an application. However, if you want to fold in closing costs, an appraisal will be required.

Some minor restrictions do apply. Designed to help people save money on their monthly payments to reduce the danger of foreclosure, Streamline loans are limited to the unpaid balance of your current FHA mortgage. In other words, you can't borrow more than you owe—to remodel the kitchen, pay off some credit card bills, or take off for Rio, for example.

For the complete Streamline story, contact your FHA lender. If your bank doesn't offer the program (not all do), ask for the name and number of a lender who does, or contact your regional FHA office.

....

ANOTHER FHA SECRET

If you've paid off an FHA-insured home, and you held the mortgage for seven years or less, you may be entitled to a rebate on the up-front mortgage insurance you paid. To find out if HUD owes you money, call 800-697-6967, go to www.hud.gov/cgi-bin/refund2, or write to the U.S. Department of Housing and Urban Development, P.O. Box 23699, Washington, DC 20026-3699.

....

Special Attention: Veterans

Are you one of the 800,000 veterans with existing VA loans who should consider refinancing? Uncle Sam wants to make it easy for you to qualify for an Interest Rate Reduction Loan (IRRL). There's generally no credit check or appraisal. The closing costs, if any, are minimal, and most can be folded into the new mortgage. Call local banks and/or mortgage brokers to find your best IRRL deal.

Denied the Right to Refinance?

In many parts of our country, depressed real estate markets have left some families with mortgage balances higher than their property's current market value. In the strange logic of bankers, these families will remain good credit risks if they keep their high-interest loans—but they'd somehow be bad risks if their interest rates and monthly costs were lowered and thus more manageable.

This trap can't be easily avoided. Like all other investments, homes can and sometimes do lose value. What to do? It's not easy to cut your losses with a house. In the worst-case scenario, you can walk away from it. But you'll still be liable for any shortfall at the bank's foreclosure sale, plus taxes if the bank forgives part or all of your deficient balance.

If you have adequate savings and you plan to stay in the house, you might want to make a large payment against the outstanding principal of your mortgage. If you don't have an extra pile of cash, make small advance payments whenever you can. Your goal is to increase your home equity enough so the bank will approve your application to refinance— hopefully before rates climb again.

Take heart, if you have to sell and take the loss, the odds are good that your next home's price will have also dropped. You'll get less at the first closing, true, but you'll have to come up with less at the second one.

Can't bear the thought of selling for less than you paid, or less than you think your house is worth? Find a tenant for your old house. If you carefully check references, charge fair rents, find a good property manager in your absence, and get adequate security up front, being a landlord can be a safe, profitable way to weather a depressed market.

CHAPTER 14

Driving a Winner

- Why your typical car will cost you half a million dollars!
- Ten rules of the road that will save you significant sums
- The great debate: rebate or low rate?
- The truth about leasing your next vehicle
- A simple strategy that can save you hundreds on insurance

The drive-in bank was created so the real owner of the car can see it once in a while.

AUTHOR UNKNOWN

At its most basic, buying a car is like buying a pair of shoes. Are you looking for comfort, speed, style, or image? Once you've decided not to go barefoot, you can get there from here in a pair from Neiman Marcus, from Goodwill Industries, or from some place in between.

And when you've decided not to depend exclusively on shoe leather, mass transit, or your in-line skates, any vehicle from a brand-spanking-new Rolls Royce to a well-used Volkswagen Bug can get you to and from the office—one in luxury (although you'll occasionally be bothered by requests for Grey Poupon), and the other with a somewhat different feel and image.

Aside from size, purchase price, comfort, and prestige value, a Rolls differs significantly from a VW when it comes to paying for such things as registration, insurance, sales tax, fuel, maintenance, garage space—and mustard.

Americans own an average 1.77 cars, drive them about five years, and spend a delightful hour and 13 minutes a day, on average, behind the wheel. (Don't you just love statistics?)

Well, here's a crucial statistic to apply to your 1.77 cars: The AAA pegs the cost of owning and operating a car at about 45 cents a mile. Think about how much driving you'd be doing if there were a taxi meter on the dash clicking off 45 cents every time you drove another 5,280 feet!

Obviously, it depends on the car. A new Rolls costs more per mile to operate than a used VW Bug. But sticking with averages for just a bit longer, Americans drive about 15,000 miles each year. Assuming 60 years behind the wheel—hopefully it will be longer—that's a total of 900,000 miles, or about 16 trips around the equator, plus one round-trip to the moon!

At 45 cents a mile, that's an average investment in our cars of $405,000—*after taxes.* Before taxes (at 28%), we'd have to earn $562,500 in today's dollars just to drive where we want to go. In fact, the actual dollar amount will be more like $1.5 million once you factor in inflation. (We went for a modest 3% a year increase.) And you wonder why you're always feeling broke?

Now what if we told you that there was a pretty easy way for you to cut that cost dramatically? Would you invest some of your time to save a few hundred thousand dollars?

DOING ANYTHING IMPORTANT FOR THE NEXT 11 MONTHS?

If you're thinking about buying a brand-new car, here's a particularly illuminating way of looking at the costs. Say you've done battle to whittle down the $20,000 manufacturer's suggested retail price (MSRP) to $18,000—not including any rebate or "low-cost financing." You decide to pocket the manufacturer's $1,000 incentive, which brings your total cost down to $17,000. Right?

Wrong! Let's assume you finance 90% of that $17,000 ($15,300) at 8% for four years. That'll add $2,629 in interest to the $17,000, for a total cost of $19,629. Right?

Wrong again! Even if you disregard your new car's sales tax, registration, and insurance—which will add up to way more than pocket change—there are still state and federal income taxes to factor in. If you get hit for 28%, you'd need to gross some $27,262 to pay for your new horseless carriage. That's more than 50% higher than the $18,000 rock-bottom price you negotiated—and the equivalent of almost 11 months of hard labor for someone earning $30,000 a year.

And now for the final insult: Your shiny new car becomes a used one the instant you drive it off the lot, and quickly loses 20% or more of its market value to depreciation. The bottom line: You'll pay more than $27,000 to buy a car that'll be worth maybe $15,000 should you decide (or need) to sell it.

Do you really want to spend the better part of a year working—not for food, clothing, or shelter, but just to pay for the privilege of parking that recently-new-but-now-used car in your driveway? You'd have to work even longer if you wanted to actually drive it.

The decision's yours. Us? We'd rather buy the cream puff you're about to trade in—as would most car buyers. Despite the hype, three times as many used cars as new cars get sold each year! It makes sense. Someone else will have taken the heaviest depreciation loss; you'll have an already broken-in means of transportation; and it's a lot easier than you may think to make sure you get a reliable vehicle at a fair price.

. . . .

THE DIFFERENCE BETWEEN LOOKING RICH AND BEING RICH

Do you need a shiny new car to show clients, business associates, neighbors, or family that you're successful? Apparently most millionaires don't. According to Thomas Stanley and William Danko, authors of *The Millionaire Next Door*, 37% of them bought their most recent car used. And 25% haven't purchased a new car in four or more years.

. . . .

BEFORE YOU BUY OR LEASE YOUR NEXT CAR, READ THESE 10 RULES OF THE ROAD

The time to repair the roof is when the sun is shining.

—JOHN F. KENNEDY

Rule # 1: Think Twice before Getting Rid of Your Current Car

Before you do anything else, seriously consider whether you really need a replacement car. You have alternatives:

- Get it fixed. In many states, you could replace a transmission, or even an engine, for what the sales tax alone will cost on a new set of wheels.

- Go without. If you live in an area with good mass transportation, you could do yourself and the environment a favor by ditching one of your cars. Buses, trains, or cabs might suit you fine—when walking or biking won't do.

- Try to downsize to one (or no vehicles). Park the car for a while. See if you would survive comfortably enough so that the money you'd save this year, and maybe next year and the next, would be worth the trade-off.

- Keep your clunker for local driving, but for longer hauls where a more reliable vehicle would be in order, rent one. It might even cost you less than 45 cents a mile! (Charge it to a gold card that will pick up any damages your own insurance won't cover.)

If you decide to retire that hunk of steel and plastic you've been driving, don't wait until you're desperate. You may end up spending more than you want, and/or you may have to settle for something less than you had in mind. The best time to car shop is while you still have a working vehicle available. Whether it's yours, your sibling's, or your neighbor's, having a backup can take the desperation out of car shopping.

Rule #2: Decide What You Really Want

When you've decided it's time to put another car in your garage, prepare yourself by unemotionally deciding what you *need* in these four categories: features, reliability, safety, and economy. Feel free to also think about what type of car you *want*—but if you come up with two different answers, focus on what you need. It'll work better for you and cost less in the long run.

Some car decisions should be obvious, but obviously they're not! For example, if you live in a large city and never intend to use your car to travel through jungles, climb roadless mountains, drive through sand, or haul heavy loads, you can skip the four-wheel-drive sports utility vehicle. If you have a spouse, four children, and two dogs, a two-seat sports convertible might be a tad impractical.

With few exceptions, most auto makers build cars of similar size and quality in each price range. Some excel in one area but not in others. You may have to choose between the smoothest ride and the fastest acceleration, or between maximum front-seat legroom and backseat comfort, or between rapid body rusting and early transmission trouble. Despite the hype, there is no perfect car. Engineers have had to compromise all along the way.

Whether you're considering a new or used car, a couple of hours spent at the library checking the various current consumer guides and magazine stories will arm you with the information you need to create a list of possibilities. There are also some good Web sites: www.edmunds.com, www.intellichoice.com, www.compare.net, and www.kbb.com. Between them, you'll find all the details about any car you might want to consider. (You can even buy a new or used car over the Web at www.autobytel.com or www.carsmart.com.)

To save the most, be flexible. Pick more than one alternative—for example, a Toyota Camry, Ford Contour, or Oldsmobile Cutlass. The more generic you can be in your thinking, the better. If you'd be happy with *any* of the many four-door, six-cylinder cars with automatic steering, air-conditioning, front-wheel drive, and cruise control, you'll have many more options. Similarly, consider clone cars. For example, the Geo Prizm and the Toyota Corolla are virtually identical twins, but the Prizm will cost you less, new or used. The same is true for the Ford Taurus and the Mercury Sable.

Rule #3: Know Your Bottom Line . . . and Stick to It

Figure out how much you can comfortably afford to invest in your transportation. Yes, a car is an investment, but not in the traditional sense. Unlike stocks, bonds, or mutual funds, your investment in an automobile is guaranteed to depreciate. Unless you buy a classic car, you're going to see the value go down, down, down. But also unlike stocks, bonds, and mutual funds, you can use a car in daily life, while securities often have no practical value until they are liquidated.

Remember when we said buying a car is no different than buying a pair of shoes? Yet some new car shoppers spend less time choosing and buying a $20,000 car than they do buying footwear. Wake up! If you invest the time and effort to carefully consider your needs and budget, you'll be far less likely to be swayed into a lousy deal. The money you save can then be invested in far more meaningful ways, again and again. Need we mention that you are not obligated to spend every nickel you can commandeer?

Rule #4: The Less Debt You Carry, the Richer You'll Be

Those who know suggest you come up with about 20% of the final price. While 100% would save you the most, the journey to financial freedom frequently finds us financing the fare. You'll also need some other cash on hand for sales tax, registration, and a higher insurance premium.

To get a handle on the insurance question, pull out your list of possibilities and call your insurance company for quotes. The difference in the cost of insurance may help you narrow down your choices more quickly. With some models, for example, a red one may cost more to insure than a more subdued color. (Honest!)

And if you're going to finance the car, you'll need to know how much you can borrow. While we'll shortly be reminding you to never, ever tell a salesperson how much you can afford to pay each month, you yourself need to know what that figure is. You also need to know about loan rates.

Call a few lenders and ask for current loan rates on both new and used cars. Once you have those numbers in mind, look at Table 14.1. Find how much a month *you've* decided you can comfortably afford to pay, then look for the current interest rate. At a glance, you'll see how much of a car loan you can carry for varying terms. For example, say you can afford $300 a month (not including car insurance). At 7%, you can borrow anywhere from $6,701 for two years, to $15,151 for five years. At 9%, the range would be $6,567 to $14,452.

For monthly payments that are not shown, the math is easy. Say you can afford $600 a month. How much could you borrow at 7% for three years? Three times as much as $200, or twice as much as $300. Either way, the number you come up with would be about the same—in the range of $19,400.

Once you know how much you can borrow, there's an easy way to figure out how much your loan will cost. Say you're thinking about spending $300 a month to borrow $15,151 at 7% for five years. First multiply the monthly payment by the term (in months). For example, $300 times 60 months (five years) equals how much you'll pay—$18,000. Then subtract the amount you'd be borrowing ($18,000 − $15,151 = $2,849 in interest). A two-year loan would get you $6,701 and cost you only $7,200 (24 × $300), for an interest charge of $499. Which is the better deal for you? (The last payment is usually somewhat smaller than the others, so these numbers are approximate. For exact numbers, you can use *The Banker's Secret Software.* See page 327.)

When it comes to loans, remember: Time is of the essence. The more you put down and the quicker you pay off the loan, the less you'll spend. If a short-term loan would take more out of your pocket each month than you can afford, can you come up with more up-front cash? No? Then maybe you'd be better off with a cheaper car.

TABLE 14.1 How Much Can You Borrow?

		\$100	\$200	\$300	\$400	\$500	\$750
		IF YOUR MONTHLY PAYMENT IS					
		YOU CAN BORROW					
RATE	**YEARS**						
1%	2	2,375	4,750	7,126	9,501	11,876	17,814
	3	3,545	7,090	10,635	14,180	17,725	26,588
	4	4,703	9,407	14,110	18,813	23,517	35,275
	5	5,850	11,700	17,550	23,400	29,250	43,876
3%	2	2,327	4,653	6,980	9,306	11,633	17,449
	3	3,439	6,877	10,316	13,755	17,193	25,790
	4	4,518	9,036	13,554	18,071	22,589	33,884
	5	5,565	11,130	16,696	22,261	27,826	41,739
5%	2	2,279	4,559	6,838	9,118	11,397	17,095
	3	3,337	6,673	10,010	13,346	16,683	25,024
	4	4,342	8,685	13,027	17,369	21,711	32,567
	5	5,299	10,598	15,897	21,196	26,495	39,743
7%	2	2,234	4,467	6,701	8,934	11,168	16,751
	3	3,239	6,447	9,716	12,955	16,193	24,290
	4	4,176	8,352	12,528	16,704	20,880	31,320
	5	5,050	10,100	15,151	20,201	25,251	37,877
9%	2	2,189	4,378	6,567	8,756	10,945	16,417
	3	3,145	6,289	9,434	12,579	15,723	23,585
	4	4,018	8,037	12,055	16,074	20,092	30,139
	5	4,817	9,635	14,452	19,269	24,087	36,130
11%	2	2,146	4,291	6,437	8,582	10,728	16,092
	3	3,054	6,109	9,163	12,218	15,272	22,909
	4	3,869	7,738	11,607	15,477	19,346	29,019
	5	4,599	9,199	13,798	18,397	22,997	34,495
13%	2	2,103	4,207	6,310	8,414	10,517	15,776
	3	2,968	5,936	8,904	11,872	14,839	22,259
	4	3,728	7,455	11,183	14,910	18,638	27,956
	5	4,395	8,790	13,185	17,580	21,975	32,963
15%	2	2,062	4,125	6,187	8,250	10,312	15,468
	3	2,885	5,769	8,654	11,539	14,424	21,635
	4	3,593	7,186	10,779	14,373	17,966	26,949
	5	4,203	8,407	12,610	16,814	21,017	31,526

Note: This table was prepared with *The Banker's Secret Software* (see page 327).

Rule #5: Buy Used, Buy Smart, Save Big

With new cars costing what many of our parents paid for their homes, and depreciating in value faster than a speeding bullet, it's not surprising that good used cars are in demand. We think the amount of money you can save is well worth the time and effort you'll have to put into finding one—for your next car and the next and the next.

The good news is that manufacturers and dealers are drowning in a sea of low-mileage, recent-vintage used cars, thanks to all of those people who have been talked into leasing in the last few years. Many of these pre-owned vehicles have been given a thorough going-over (up to a 150-point checkup), are reconditioned, and come complete with manufacturer's warranties.

Begin your used-car search focused on those options you consider vital—be it low mileage, an automatic transmission, cruise control, and/or air-conditioning. Then be on the lookout for suitable vehicles that are for sale. Ask everyone you know to do likewise. See if your mechanic knows of one for sale and can tell you what's been repaired on it—and what hasn't. Read the classifieds regularly, and check the bulletin boards in supermarkets and local laundromats; www.onlineauto.com also offers nationwide used-car classified ads.

If you hear, see, or read about a car that might work for you, call right away. If it's a good deal, it won't last long. But do beware. No deal is so good that another, perhaps better one, won't appear shortly.

Call local dealers and tell them that you're especially interested in cars they originally sold or leased—and then serviced. Ask what they have in stock and get a sense of the asking price. If you're familiar with the going price (from using www.edmunds.com, for example), you may be able to whittle down the price before you even see a car.

Certainly before you make an offer, find out what the creature is really worth. Asking your local bank for the current market value, and how much they'd lend on it, is a good barometer of its real value. You can also consult the blue books and guidebooks as well as the Internet sites we've mentioned.

Don't be afraid to dicker! Most people ask a higher price in expectation of a buyer wanting to negotiate.

The no-haggle auto superstores are taking the negotiations out of a lot of used-car buying, which is great if you hate to dicker. But you may be able to spend less if you go through the usual give-and-take with a private buyer or at a traditional dealership.

....

AVOID "CURBSTONERS" FRAUD

"Curbstoners" resell cars that dealers can't unload by making it appear as though they are being sold by private individuals. David Solomon, editor of *Nutz & Boltz,* a monthly newsletter ($22 a year, 800-888-0091), says these autos are often the "worst of all used cars," and many have serious problems. To avoid them, try to establish that the person showing the car actually owns it.

If the owner can show you a pile of service receipts with his or her name on them, you're okay. But watch out if someone says, "I'm selling the car for a relative who has moved," or "My friend's out of town." Although these cars often look very clean, they may well be junk. Stick to a car sold by an owner who can document its history, or buy from a dealer, where at least you have a little leverage if the car turns out to be a small yellow citrus fruit.

....

Rule #6: Make Sure It Fits

As suitable candidates appear, ask the seller lots of questions: How many owners have there been? Has the car been in an accident? Where and how was the car driven? Ask to see the car's service papers. You want to know about routine maintenance as well as any problems that the car may have had in the past. Are there any current problems? If the dealer or present owner seems evasive or offended, move on.

Really get to know a car before you buy. Start by looking over the exterior, then check the interior to make sure the windows, doors, heater, air conditioner, radio, power takeoff device (these used to be called cigarette lighters), and various dashboard gizmos work properly. There are few things as frustrating and as chilling as a power window that doesn't want to go up . . . in a snowstorm!

If the buggy is still looking good, take it for a spin. Test-driving a car for 15 minutes will tell you almost as much as kicking the tires. (Nothing!). Ask the dealer or current owner to let you drive it for long enough to answer a few questions.

Is it comfortable for you and yours? If not, the price and options won't matter. Are the controls conveniently located? Can you change the radio station without taking your eyes off the road? Would you need to grow 6 inches in order to reach the pedals *and* see out the window?

Give it a good solid workout. Does it have pep, does it shake, rattle, and roll? Drive it up hills, on highways . . . everywhere. See how it handles, and listen for any unusual noises. You get the idea! Spending time answering questions like these about any car you're considering is a *very* worthwhile investment.

The last time Nancy was in the market for a used car, a dealer let her take and test a Grand Prix for the weekend. All it took was the drive home to convince her that this car was no cream puff—it was more like a lemon meringue!

When a car passes your road test, write down its make and model as well as its identification number (which is at the bottom of the driver's side of the windshield). Call the Auto Safety Hotline at 800-424-9393. Stay on the line, and ask a live representative if there have been any recalls. Also ask for the manufacturer's phone number. Then call the manufacturer and ask if any recall and/or warranty work has been or should be performed on that particular car, where it was originally bought, and whatever else you can learn.

Before you finalize the deal, buy yourself some peace of mind by paying for a bumper-to-bumper examination of the car you're considering. Whether you opt for an independent inspection service or your favorite mechanic, you'll want your doctor of vehicular construction to assess how the owner maintained it, to check the odometer for tampering, to look for a bent frame or other signs of accidents, to evaluate what items may soon need to be replaced, and to provide you with an estimate of how much they'll cost to fix. It's well worth the cost of putting the car you're considering under a microscope to find out whether it's junk or a jewel. Then renegotiate based on your mechanic's inspection. Maybe you can get the owner to pick up or share the cost of anything that will need to be fixed.

Rule #7: Buy New, and Still Save by Shopping Smart

Just in case you choose to take the road less traveled and buy your next car new, here is how you can save money, too.

New-car shopping used to mean walking into a dealership with a vague idea of what you wanted and, after going up against a sales pro, leaving with something far more expensive than you had in mind. These days, it's easy to learn to the penny how much the dealer paid for the car and each of its options, whether there are any manufacturer's incentives or rebates being offered to either the dealer or the buyer, and how to avoid some of the sales ploys that have milked unwary buyers for years.

Assuming you know which cars will serve your needs, shop price (and service). Ask around for feedback from others who've bought from the dealers you're considering, especially those convenient to where you live or work.

Before you enter the showroom, write down the model, accessories, and current pricing information to review as the negotiation process unfolds.

> The one sure way for anyone to avoid getting taken is to become an informed and disciplined shopper, period.
> —W. James Bragg, *Car Buyer's and Leaser's Negotiating Bible*

Invariably, the salesperson's first question will be "How much can you afford a month?" Never, never, never, never make your decision based solely on the monthly payment!

Before you negotiate, make sure you take the car for an extended test ride, just like the one we suggested in Rule #6, with one extra proviso: If you're going to buy a four-cylinder car, don't test a six-cylinder car.

While negotiating, don't discuss a trade-in or a lease. You want each dealer's best price for the car you're thinking about buying. After you're satisfied that you have a bottom-line price quote, you can discuss the trade-in value of your car. If the price the dealer offers for your current car isn't right, sell it privately or to a different dealer. Or maybe you'd like to donate it to one of the many charities that now accept used cars—for example, the National Kidney Foundation (800-488-CARS, www.kidney.org).

....

TOOLING UP FOR A TRADE-IN

To get a good sense of what a private sale might bring, check the classified ads in a few local newspapers and on the Net. Focus on models like yours, with similar mileage and equipment (see Rule #5), and assume 10% or so for give-and-take.

To find out what a dealer would pay, clean up the car inside and out, then drive over to a few car showrooms. Ask the used-car managers what they'd pay for yours outright—not as a trade-in. Later, you'll have this information filed away for bargaining leverage, regardless of whether you trade it in or sell it to a private buyer.

....

Low Rate or Rebate?

When negotiating the purchase of a new car, you might be offered a choice of, for example, 3% financing or a $1,000 rebate. The key here is the word *or*.

TABLE 14.2 The Great Debate: Rebate or Low Rate? Go for the Rebate If It's More Than . . .

		LOAN AMOUNT											
		$10,000				$13,500				$17,000			
		TERM OF LOAN IN YEARS											
DEALER	BANK	2	3	4	5	2	3	4	5	2	3	4	5
3%	7%	430	647	870	1,100	580	873	1,174	1,484	731	1,099	1,478	1,869
	8%	540	812	1,094	1,385	728	1,096	1,477	1,869	917	1,380	1,859	2,354
	9%	649	979	1,321	1,674	876	1,322	1,782	2,259	1,103	1,663	2,244	2,845
	10%	760	1,147	1,550	1,967	1,025	1,549	2,092	2,655	1,291	1,950	2,634	3,344
	11%	871	1,317	1,782	2,264	1,175	1,778	2,405	3,056	1,480	2,238	3,028	3,849
	12%	983	1,488	2,016	2,566	1,326	2,009	2,721	3,463	1,670	2,529	3,426	4,361
4%	7%	323	487	656	831	436	657	886	1,122	550	828	1,116	1,412
	8%	433	652	880	1,116	584	880	1,189	1,507	736	1,109	1,497	1,897
	9%	542	819	1,107	1,405	732	1,106	1,494	1,897	922	1,392	1,882	2,388
	10%	653	987	1,336	1,698	881	1,333	1,804	2,293	1,110	1,679	2,272	2,887
	11%	764	1,157	1,568	1,995	1,031	1,562	2,117	2,694	1,299	1,967	2,666	3,392
	12%	876	1,328	1,802	2,297	1,182	1,793	2,433	3,101	1,489	2,258	3,064	3,904
5%	7%	216	326	440	558	292	439	594	753	368	555	748	948
	8%	326	491	664	843	440	662	897	1,138	554	836	1,129	1,433
	9%	435	658	891	1,132	588	888	1,202	1,528	740	1,119	1,514	1,924
	10%	546	826	1,120	1,425	737	1,115	1,512	1,924	928	1,406	1,904	2,423
	11%	657	996	1,352	1,722	887	1,344	1,825	2,325	1,117	1,694	2,298	2,928
	12%	769	1,167	1,586	2,024	1,038	1,575	2,141	2,732	1,307	1,985	2,696	3,440

7%	108	164	221	281	146	221	299	379	184	279	376	478
8%	218	329	445	566	294	444	602	764	370	560	757	963
9%	327	496	672	855	442	670	907	1,154	556	843	1,142	1,454
10%	438	664	901	1,148	591	897	1,217	1,550	744	1,130	1,532	1,963
11%	549	834	1,133	1,445	741	1,126	1,530	1,951	933	1,418	1,926	2,458
12%	661	1,005	1,367	1,747	892	1,357	1,846	2,358	1,123	1,709	2,324	2,970

6%

Note: These numbers were calculated with *The Banker's Secret Software* (see page 327).

Simple Instructions: No Assembly Required

It's your lucky day. The car dealer's offering you 3% financing for two years *or* a $500 cash rebate, your choice. And the bank just approved a $13,500 loan at 8%. What should you do?

First, find the 3% dealer rate. Look over to the 8% bank rate, then across to where $13,500 and two years meet. It'd take a rebate of $728 or more to beat the dealer's low interest rate. So you'd go for the dealer financing.

Now let's say the dealer is offering a 4% loan rate, or a $1,000 rebate. Assume that the bank alternative would still be $13,500 at 8%, but this time, you're thinking about a three-year loan. Which one is the better deal? With $880 as the break-even point, you'd take the bank loan, and go for the dough! To maxi-

mize your savings, you'd use that $1,000 rebate as a lump sum pre-payment.

If your loan amount doesn't appear on the chart, all you have to do is some really simple math. For example, the break-even rebate point for a $20,000 loan would be twice as much as for a $10,000 loan at the same interest rate. So to equal 3% dealer financing, you'd need a rebate of $1,080 (2 × $540), assuming an 8% bank loan for two years.

But what about interest rates that aren't in the table? Say you can get 7.5% bank financing on $10,000 for two years, or a 3% dealer loan. The rebate would have to be halfway between the $430 at 7% and the $540 at 8%—or $485. At 7.25%, you'd go a quarter of the way up—to $458.

263

Watch out. If you opt for the "superspecial" loan rate, tempting though it may be, you won't get the manufacturer's cash rebate—so you'll either have to borrow more money or come up with a larger down payment.

If you do go for the rebate, you'll save even more by using it to increase your down payment. Before you choose low rate or rebate, use our handy dandy "Great Rebate Debate" Table 14.2 to find out which deal is better.

Rule #8: Shop as Hard for the Loan as You Do for the Vehicle

Whether you opt for a used car or choose a shiny new high-speed, fully equipped symbol of success, there may be a car loan in your future. If so, here's how to save money and avoid hassles.

Begin by finding out how you look. An honest face won't get you a loan, and neither will references from fine, upstanding members of the community. These days, you're only as good as your current credit report. Get a copy of yours, and fix any mistakes. (See page 231.)

Then dial a deal. When it's time to seriously shop for a car loan, set up a table and list what's currently being offered by local lenders. While a percent or two does make a difference, the total cost of your car will depend much more on how long you take to pay off the loan.

Credit unions generally offer lower-rate auto loans than do banks. So if you belong to a credit union, check there first. (To find out if you're eligible for membership, see page 197.) Another alternative is a local bank where you have accounts. Allowing payments to be automatically deducted from your account, or just being a loyal customer, could cut your rate by anywhere from 0.5% to as much as 1.5%. Ask.

And if you're buying from a dealer, listen to the financing spiel. While dealers often act as commissioned sales reps for local banks (adding their cut to your cost), they do sometimes offer good rates—especially when the manufacturer is pushing a certain model by subsidizing the loan.

Wait until you've gathered a good sampling of rates before you give out any personal information. Even if you haven't discussed financing, once some car dealers have your name and social security number, they'll pull your credit report. Each time such an *inquiry* is made about you, it becomes part of your credit history, and lowers your creditworthiness in the eyes of some lenders. If you hand over your license (perhaps to test-drive a model) specifically say, "I don't want you to pull my credit report until and unless we sign a deal. I don't want the inquiry on my report." Unfortunately, there's nothing you can do immediately to verify that a sales rep has respected your wishes. But should you later discover that one did not, we hope you'll speak up.

Don't sign any papers or commit yourself to dealer financing until you've had a chance to consider your future together—you, the car, and the loan—away from the sales pros at the dealership. You have other options.

For example, a home equity loan is often touted as an easy, tax-advantaged way to finance a car. But be careful. The tax benefits are often highly overrated, and if you can't meet the payments, you could lose your house, to say nothing of your car.

Since home equity loans typically have such long terms (10 or 15 years), even if the interest rate is lower, unless you pre-pay, your debt could easily outlive your car and dramatically increase its cost. On the other hand, if you *know* you can be trusted to manage your debts, and if you'll have enough deductions to itemize them on your taxes, a home equity loan might save you money. To guarantee that it does, plan to pay it off fast, say in no more than three years or 25,000 miles.

And then there are true loser loans. Keep away from loans that front-load the interest, called *Rule of 78s* or *sum-of-the-digits.* Fortunately, they've been outlawed in some states, but maybe not in yours. Like most bad deals, these don't come with warning labels.

Make sure yours is a plain, ordinary, simple-interest loan. Then if you always send in more than your required payment, you'll cut your loan's cost, your time in hock, and your money-related stress level.

Lest we forget, beware of optional extras. And that doesn't just mean rustproofing, undercoating, and expensive extended warranties. Dealers and bankers will gladly broker credit and disability insurance, telling you, "They're for your own protection." Nonsense! If you feel the need for extra coverage, call a few insurance agents and comparison shop for whatever additional term or disability coverage you are seeking.

....

THE CAR IS DEAD. LONG LIVE THE LOAN!

Don't let the lure of low monthly payments leave you "upside down"—limo lingo for when your wheels are worth less than the amount you still owe on them. A long-term loan will almost certainly leave you owing more than you could sell the car for or collect from your insurer should it be totaled.

....

Rule #9: Look Before You Lease

> . . . when you lease a car, you have all the headaches and responsibilities of ownership, with none of the benefits.
>
> —JACK GILLIS, *The Car Book*

The lease bug is surely on the loose, accounting for almost 30% of new car sales. The more you know about this highly touted "alternative" to buying, the less likely you are to get stung.

Warning: Leasing is forever. It's symptomatic of the buy-now, pay and pay-later modus operandi that has become the American way. Think about it. When the lease ends, what will you do? Begin a new lease on a replacement buggy? Come up with a pile of cash to buy the car? Take the bus? You could end up making "low monthly payments" for life!

But if you buy, the loan payments will probably stop before the car does. So after you've been shown the figures proving that a lease will cost you far less than an equivalent loan—look further down the road. After a loan's been paid off, the car will actually be yours, free and clear, but payments on a new lease will have just begun.

Dealers just love to lease. They usually get a higher price for the car, because Americans haven't yet learned that leases should be negotiated. Instead, shoppers pay top dollar and take the hit for those first few, very high depreciation years. Then the lucky dealer gets back a well-maintained, low-mileage used car—to sell or lease again, as well as the opportunity to sell, or better yet, lease a new car to the customer who no longer has one.

....

SMALL PRINT = WARNING

That tiny type on the bottom of your TV screen . . . *under* the flashing "$325 a month" . . . gives you just a clue to your actual cost. In addition to the fine print about the up-front cash you'll have to fork over—as well as the sales tax, registration, and insurance, which all come to a pretty penny on a new car—there's still income tax to factor in.

If you're in the 28% tax bracket, you'll need to gross about $450 every month to make a typical $325 lease payment.

Lease for 60 years and you'll pay $234,000 for the privilege. If you earn $100 a day, you'll work for just under a week a month—every year for the rest of your leasing days—just to cover the leases. Of course you'll have to

come up with yet more money to pay for gas if you actually want to drive the car.

. . . .

Our job is to save you money, no matter how you choose to live. And while leasing is rarely the least expensive way to spend your transportation dollars, the costs *can* be cut. Here are our ABCs for leasees:

Always buy first. Price shop as if you were going to buy. Only after you've agreed to a bottom-line price should you break the news that you might consider leasing. And in case you didn't hear us before, never, never, never answer the question, "How much can you afford a month?" Once sales reps have that number, all they have to do is reel you in.

Before you sign anything, insist on taking home a sample contract to study. Be sure you understand every single word. It could save you a wad. When you lease, your monthly payment and total costs depend on how much you pay up front, how many miles you drive, what interest rate you pay, what the future resale value of your car will be—plus up-front fees, end of lease fees, early termination fees, excessive wear and tear fees. If they can dream it up, you'll be asked to pick it up.

But you can try to negotiate even the smallest fee. For example, you'll probably be offered "gap" insurance for a few hundred dollars, to protect you from an early termination fee, which will kick in if you introduce the car to a tree or opt out of the deal for any other reason. Sometimes the dealer will throw it in. Ask.

Closed-end leases are better. With an open-end lease, you could be hit with a whopping termination charge, should the car be worth less on the used market than was originally anticipated. With a closed-end lease, the future resale value is the leasing company's headache.

Negotiating for a high resale value will lower your costs. If the market value of your car ends up being less, the dealer eats the loss. If it ends up being even higher than the agreed-upon *residual,* you might choose to actually buy the critter at that bargain price.

Driving *how* far did you say? Most leases permit 12,000 to 15,000 miles a year. If you cruise further, you'll pay more—a dime or two per mile. At 15 cents, an extra 10,000 miles will cost you an extra $1,500, adding $50 a month to a 30-month lease. Ouch!

Early birds win again. Lease early in the model year to avoid midseason price hikes and a lower residual value. In other words, it'll be cheaper.

Finance companies owned by the manufacturers (such as GMAC) sometimes subsidize leases, which can significantly lower the cost of leasing. Go to www.intellichoice.com/lease for a current list of subsidized leases.

Unfortunately, these bargains are likely to be for the least desirable cars on the lot. And you'll still need a replacement when the lease ends! If you're willing to buy the car at the end of the lease, why not buy a "post-leased" car right now?

Guess who gets the rebate? The leasing company—unless you structure the deal differently. (Remember, everything's negotiable.) Sometimes a dealer will give you the benefit of any rebate to make the sale, but don't depend on it. Ask!

Here's the catch: The reason lease deals look better than purchases is because you aren't buying the whole car. You're only buying the difference between the new car's cost and its probable value after the lease is over. While your monthly payments may be lower, at the end of your lease all you'll have is an empty garage—unless you shell out some big bucks to buy the car or sign on the dotted line for another lease.

When you buy a new car, after five years or so of driving, you can at least sell it—maybe for 50% of its original value. Buy a used car, and you'll pay less up front, and if you take good care of it, you'll probably still be able to get something for it when you get your next car.

Interest can't be saved. While we urge you again and again to pre-pay your loans, don't put your pocket change into a lease. While most car loans will cost far less if you always pre-pay, it won't save you a nickel on a lease. When you lease, you pay the full price, whether or not you send payments in early.

Rule #10: Shop for Insurance, Too

The easiest way to deal with the confusing issue of insuring your cars is to make a single call to any broker or large insurance company, ask for a quote, sign up, and get back to whatever you'd rather be doing. Let it automatically renew every year, and you'll never have to think about it again.

From the perspective of investing in yourself, there's a small problem with this approach: cost. For example, our researcher, Marcy Ross, took the time to get a bunch of quotes for the same exact coverage on her family's two cars. They varied by *$400!*

Overpay by that amount every year for a not untypical 60 years of driving, and voilà, you've wasted $24,000. Instead, if you were to invest that

$400 every year at 7%, you'd have $370,729. Too bad for Marcy, though. Her current carrier was the one with the bargain rate. So while she gets the satisfaction of knowing her rate is the best, she won't get an extra $370,000—not this way at least.

Insurance, as annoying, crazily confusing, convoluted, and costly as it can be, is for your financial protection. If you're involved in an accident and the inevitable lawsuits, having the wrong coverage, or limits that are too low, could literally destroy your world!

So to save money and more, it pays to invest some time in pursuit of your best option. In most comparison shopping situations, price checking is simple, "How much is your yellow widget with the brass doodad?"

Not so with auto insurance. Everything varies for everyone. Two neighbors driving identical cars may well pay different rates for the exact same coverage from the same insurer! Not only does the price quote depend on the car being insured, it depends on where you live, how much you drive, what your car is used for, how old you are, your gender, your driving record, your marital status, your credit record, how many other drivers are in your household, their ages, and more, more, more.

Then there are all the separate costs for a list of unfathomable protections, some of which may be mandated by your state.

"What's It All About, Alfie?"

Here's a quick glossary for your confusion and pleasure:

Bodily-injury liability. Covers you for the medical expenses, lost wages, pain and suffering, and/or funeral expenses of the occupants *of the other car*. In a no-fault state, it would also cover the passengers in your car.

Property-damage liability. Pays for damages to other people's cars or property. State minimum mandated coverage for liability is often notoriously low—especially if you have assets like a home or significant savings worth protecting in case of a lawsuit. Experts recommend that most people carry a 100/300/50 liability split, which means $100,000 of coverage for each injured passenger up to a $300,000 limit per accident, and $50,000 in property damage coverage. It's becoming more common in these litigious times to see a $1 million umbrella policy (for car and home liability protection) recommended to people who have substantial assets that could be at risk in a lawsuit.

Collision and comprehensive. Collision covers repair or replacement of your car, no matter who caused the damage. Comprehensive covers repair or replacement of your car if it's stolen or damaged by events such as fire, flood, or wind.

Tip: You can cut the cost of your collision premium as well as the liability amount by 10% if you take a traffic safety course. Often offered at local adult ed programs, they're very informative as well as money savers, and if you have a bunch of tickets on your record, you can drop some of those bad points by taking the class.

When your car is well past its prime, you might want to save some money by dropping collision and comprehensive. There's a lot of debate about how long you should maintain this coverage. Some experts say to drop it when a car is five to seven years old or if the premium represents more than 10% of the value of the car. (Keep in mind that it's the blue book value that's paid out, which may be much less than you think the car is worth. Your bank's loan department or your insurance broker can quote the current value of your car.)

We've seen recommendations that you drop coverage when a car's book value is less than $4,000, and still others say $2,500. In the end, it's your comfort level that should determine the value of this coverage as your car ages. Let's assume the *Kelley Blue Book* lists the trade-in value of your car at $3,500 and you're currently paying $300 a year for collision/comprehensive, with a deductible of $500. Each year that you don't total the car, you've saved $800. What are the odds of you driving another three or four years without a major accident? We hope the odds are with you! We'd drop the coverage and continue to drive as safely as we could, understanding that we're taking a small risk, but not an unaffordable one, especially since the value of the car will be dropping over the next few years as well.

Most experts agree that it's wise to go for the highest deductible you can manage. Over the years, the savings will probably more than cover the deductible should you ever make a claim.

Medical payments coverage. Your health insurance covers this same ground, but it may help your poorly insured passengers.

Personal-injury protection (PIP). Also covers medical payments and funeral costs, along with some protection for lost wages. Some no-fault states require it; in others it's optional.

Uninsured- and underinsured-motorist coverage. Pays if you're hurt in a hit-and-run accident or injured by a driver who has minimal or no coverage.

Miscellaneous coverage. Includes glass breakage, rental reimbursement, and towing.

Where to Shop

Most state insurance departments offer comparison pricing guides for car insurance. Check your local library for your state guide, or go to the

National Association of Insurance Commissioners' Web site (www.naic. org). And there's no lack of magazine articles and books at the library where you'll glean more recommendations. Also check out these Web sites: www.bbb.org/library/autoins.html, www.insure.com/auto, www.insweb. com/auto, and www.hwysafety.org.

If your rate rises or you're turned down for coverage, get a copy of your Comprehensive Loss Underwriting Exchange (CLUE) report from Choice Point (888-497-0011). If the insurance company requested the report to make the decision, the copy is free. Otherwise, the cost is usually $8. It could show mistakes on your past claims experience.

Even garden-variety clerical errors could cause you to pay more or to not have the coverage you wanted. Look over quotes (which should be made in writing) and your policy carefully. One survey revealed that insurance agents gave inaccurate information one-third to one-half the time when providing premium comparisons.

Now that you're thinking about it, call for quotes today, even if your policy is not due to expire soon. The more time you have to shop—and to think—the more you'll save.

. . . .

WHEN SAFETY COMES FIRST

Investing in the safest car you can afford is among the best investments you can make. Not only may your choice save your life or the life of a loved one, you may also get better insurance rates.

- Look for a car with a high safety rating from the National Highway Traffic Safety Administration (NHTSA). Call 800-424-9393, or visit www.nhtsa.dot.gov.
- If you're buying through a dealer, request a copy of the car's insurance-loss data for injury/collision published by the Insurance Institute for Highway Safety. Dealers are required to provide this information upon request. Or send an SASE for "Injury Collision & Theft Losses" to Highway Loss Data Institute, 1005 N. Glebe Road, Arlington, VA 22201, or visit www.carsafety.org.

. . . .

Simple Strategies to Cut the Cost of Driving

- If the car isn't moving, but the engine's running, you're getting 0 miles per gallon. Make all adjustments to mirrors, seat belts, hair, children—whatever—before starting up.

- Turn off the engine whenever you'll be sitting for 60 seconds or more, and you'll save on gas.

- Properly inflated tires will save money on fuel costs. Buy a decent tire gauge and use it. Also, make sure your tires are properly balanced—another gas-saver.

- Don't use gasoline with a higher octane rating than is recommended in your car's owner's manual. "Higher octane = better performance" is nothing but a marketing ploy.

- Replace your own air filter. It's incredibly cheap and easy, and can improve your gas mileage. (If Gerri can do it, you can do it.)

- A tune-up, when needed, can cut your fuel costs as much as 20%. The trouble is, today's cars don't need the old fashioned kind of tune-up (points, plugs, condensers, idle adjustments) that we gladly paid for every 15,000 to 25,000 miles in the good old days. Read the recommendations in your owner's manual. You may be pleasantly surprised.

- Sun shades, the kind you put in the windshield of your car, can do more than help keep the car cooler—they can also keep the dashboard and upholstery in better shape, and save fuel during the "hot" season by reducing the load on your air conditioner.

- Get the radiator flushed and re-filled with antifreeze every couple of years. If it gets too clogged and dirty, you may end up replacing the radiator.

- Change your oil regularly and use good oil and filters. And change the transmission fluid every 20,000 miles or so.

- Choose the best oil by selecting those brands that have the letters "SJ" after the viscosity numbers (like 10/40).

- Have the timing belt replaced when the manufacturer recommends it, usually at 60,000 or so miles. When it breaks, the car stops and you'll have to pay for towing, and possibly for serious damage.

- Wash your car. Don't forget the underbody, where rust can develop.

- When something sounds wrong, have it checked out. Turning up the radio to drown out the noise may prove to be an expensive antidote.

CHAPTER 15

Controlling College Costs:
No Problem

○ When it comes to financing college, your best investment isn't money

○ Choosing the right school

○ The truth about paying for college

○ Negotiating with financial aid officers

○ The perfect pre-paid college tuition plan

There are extremely talented and capable people who never went to college for a single day. And, as everyone knows, some of the most incompetent boobs on our planet have degrees from prestigious universities.

JOHN AND MARIAH BEAR, *College Degrees by Mail & Modem*

$280,416

That's one estimate of the cost to send a newborn to an Ivy League school 18 years from now. Other projections put the figure as high as $360,000. In other words, college could easily cost as much as or more than your family's home—and the mortgage on it. What's worse, those numbers don't include the roughly $180,000 it's estimated to set you back between the time one of your future graduates is born and the day you drop him or her off at Bankbreaker U.

Before you put the kids up for adoption, take on a second job, remortgage your house, or otherwise sell your soul, let's take a look at some less depressing college planning facts.

NOT EVERYONE NEEDS OR WANTS TO ATTEND COLLEGE

While college is a very valuable learning and growing-up experience for many high school graduates, there are exceptions, and one of them may be yours. A high school diploma can be more than adequate for those students who don't thrive in an academic environment or who have career goals that don't demand a college degree.

Thomas Edison never attended college. In fact, he never graduated from high school. Billionaire Bill Gates was a Harvard dropout. Other degree-less achievers include ABC anchor Peter Jennings, former British Prime Minister John Major, Lands' End founder Gary Comer, and according to one survey, almost half of the wealthiest 1% of American entrepreneurs!

A good plumber, carpenter, auto mechanic, executive assistant, electrician, or entrepreneur can easily earn more than the best teacher in town—without spending a fortune on tuition. So can mail carriers, aircraft mechanics, telephone installers, tool and die makers, self-taught computer programmers, as well as superstars of stage, screen, and ballfields.

Not Everyone Who Attends College Needs to Go Far Away from Home

Tuition, in most cases, is just the frosting. Room, board, and travel home can eat up as much or more of the cake. To cut costs, you might choose to have your college-bound students leave the nest slowly, by beginning their higher education at a local, inexpensive community college and then transferring to a four-year school. Even then, an in-state college won't pinch much, nor will a private school—if your child can get a great financial aid package, which means one that isn't heavily based on loans. A good aid package can cut the cost of an Ivy League experience to the same or less than one offered by the state.

Not Every Student Needs to Graduate from Harvard, Yale, or Princeton

Not all college graduates end up in careers for which they were trained, and quite a few end up working at a job or in a field that's unrelated to their major—or even in one that doesn't require a degree. From there, it's a short leap to the conclusion that most kids can avoid an expensive school altogether, without hurting their careers.

Students who will be going on for a master's degree or doctorate can take their pick of "cheap" colleges first. After they've excelled at "Discount U," they can attend Yale's law school, and come out with an ivy-covered diploma at a greatly reduced price. In the real world, it's the last one that counts. That first degree might not even make it as a wall decoration.

NOT TO WORRY

If you practice what we've been preaching, you'll have a good head start on paying for college. By making the most of your money and paying off your credit cards, auto loans, mortgage, and whatever student loans of your own you may still be lugging around, you'll save tens of thousands in bank interest—maybe even enough to pay for a college education or two.

It also pays to continue to fund your 401(k) or 403(b) retirement plan to the maximum of your ability, especially if there is an employer match. Most schools don't take what's accumulated in your retirement account into account when they calculate your share of the costs. However, should you need it later for college tuition, 401(k) and IRA money can be withdrawn (although you will pay taxes and you may be hit with penalties).

Even If You Start Late, You Can Save Big for College

Every $25 a week you can trim from your spending—by brown bagging lunch, mowing your own lawn, eating dinner out less often, or whatever strikes you as dispensable—means a potential $16,300 you could accumulate by the time today's eighth-grader finishes college in nine years (assuming you invested the savings and earned a 7% return on your money).

—Kristin Davis, *Financing College*

While we have no argument with the truism that the sooner you begin socking away money for college, and the more you stockpile, the more you'll have, we'd like to emphasize that an excellent college education can come cheap, even if your child is not a brilliant student or an Olympic-quality athlete. So put aside what you can (including your fears), but also think long and hard about how much of an investment you're really willing to make in those four years—and how much of a financial burden you're willing to let your children take on for themselves.

In a nutshell, here's how college financing works: You fill out at least one all-important financial aid form in early January of your child's senior year in high school. The colleges where your child has applied will use that information to decide how much you'll have to pay. Known as your *expected family contribution* (or EFC), it's based on your income and assets, as well as your child's income and assets.

Once a college figures out your EFC, it then proposes a plan to help you handle the rest of the cost—for tuition, room, board, books, even for traveling home—through loans, grants, work/study programs, and scholarships. Some schools are more realistic than others in apportioning the total costs. The less realistic schools leave a gap that you'll also have to cover.

In all, there are some 3,200 accredited colleges and universities in the United States—including at least a few reasonably priced ones that would offer your child a perfectly fine and fun four years. Investing the time and energy into helping your child pick the right school can ensure a better educational and social experience at far less cost.

PULLING TOGETHER

We know it's not always easy to find the right time and the right way to talk to teens about money, about their future, and about yours. But the best investments for college can be made in the few years before applying, and they involve little or no money.

Today's kids know that college is expensive. What they may not know is that without planning on all your parts, their campus years could cost more than anything else. While we all want the best for our children, if you can't afford to finance a four-year trip to an ivory tower, just say so . . . and calmly discuss the options. Besides, an Ivy League school may not be best for your child.

Finding a way for the whole family to get on and stay on the same page about playing the college game could save you a fortune, and keep a mountain of debt off the graduate's back, as it builds a happier high school experience for you all.

Go Easy on Your Kids

Life is tough enough without feeling pressured to excel all of the time at everything you do. It's the same for kids. Growing up should and can be fun.

Honestly, wouldn't you rather have well-rounded, happy kids at good schools that want them badly enough to offer them a great aid package, than obsessive, stressed out, overworked, and always exhausted children attending prestigious universities? That said, without putting your children under enough stress to drive them to the brink or beyond, instill an *Invest in Yourself* attitude in your high schoolers.

Encourage them to do their job for the family and work hard for good grades, participate in extracurricular activities that they're really interested in, explore the world, develop hobbies and skills, care about others, and find a niche where they can really excel. They need to know that you see them as important contributors to the family's future, and that their efforts, beginning in ninth grade, can dramatically affect the entire family's financial future.

Varsity letters are nice for those who can get them, but the most important letters for your kids may be PSAT, SAT, and ACT, the standardized tests that most (but not all) colleges take very seriously. By starting the college search early, your child can find out whether any of his or her top choices require those tests—and what other criteria they weigh most heavily.

Increased scores are potential money savers and therefore excellent investments for many families. Prep courses, review books, and computer software can all boost the numbers on these important (if not always respected as accurate) exams. For free help, simulated tests, sample questions, and/or free software, go to www.testprep.com, www.ets.org, www.collegeboard.com, www.act.org/aap/index.html, www.kaplan.com, and www.powerprep.com.

Encourage your children to prepare one way or another. If they need an immediate payoff to go at it enthusiastically, come up with a suitable reward. (Bribery within the family has great investment potential, and is perfectly legal.)

PREPARING YOUR CHILD
FOR THE COLLEGE OLYMPICS

It's not too early by the sophomore year to begin looking at colleges—or at least at their catalogs, videos, Web sites, and the numerous write-ups you'll find in college selection guides, magazines, and books. On the Web, you can visit www.petersons.com, www.usnews.com/usnews/edu/college, www.universities.com, and www.review.com.

Some of our favorite books on choosing a college are *The Insider's Guide to the Colleges,* compiled by the staff at the *Yale Daily News, Colleges that Change Lives: 40 Schools You Should Know About Even if You're Not a Straight-A Student* by Loren Pope, and *The Fiske Guide to Colleges* by Edward B. Fiske. For students who do well in school and on the SATs, *Ivy*

League Programs at State School Prices by Robert R. Sullivan is worth a read. For reviews on other books about choosing a college and on the admissions process, go to www.collegeaid.com.

Find a way to have the college search be a pleasant experience—and a priority—for you both. Ask questions to help your teen tune in to his or her preferences in a school. The criteria might include: big, small, near, far, liberal arts, specialized, active fraternity/sorority life, specific sports or arts programs, lively city, quiet country, religious affiliation or not, north, south, east, west, or midwest, intern or co-op opportunities, two- or three-semester schedule, and perhaps the opportunity to study abroad.

As for a career choice, that can wait. Many college graduates earn degrees in fields they never even considered back in high school. Being exposed to new possibilities, after all, is one of the major benefits of attending college. Some would say that the classroom learning is the least valuable of what higher education has to offer.

While you and Junior can arrange for some school visits at any time, be sure you've gone to quite a few campuses by his junior year in high school. Oh, and difficult as it may be, give your children plenty of space on these college jaunts. (Remember how embarrassed you were when Mom and Dad trailed behind you, asking all the "wrong" questions?)

Official tours are nice, but sleep-overs in a residence hall with real, live students are a lot better—and in our view, mandatory at any school your child is seriously considering. While there, Junior ought to sit in on a few classes—some that freshman take (those lectures with lots of other students) and at least one more advanced class, ideally in a subject he thinks he might major in. While you're there, stop in at the financial aid office and see if you can get a quick course on how the process could best work for you.

If your teens are resistant to the college search, come up with some enticements (a bribe), so they can get an immediate payoff for investing the time and energy. ("Visit State U next weekend with us and we'll chip in so you can buy the billion-watt music system you've been wanting.")

A Fine Balancing Act

You know what schools look for in students—good grades in serious academic subjects and on the SATs, leadership qualities, a record of community activities, a few advanced courses on their transcripts, and skills on the ball field or in the orchestra. Top students get accepted to more schools, are offered more non-loan aid, and are in the best negotiating position for pitting one school's offer against another's. Not surprisingly, students who merit them are the ones who get Merit Scholarships.

But students who might be less than exciting to one school might be gems to another, whether it's because they'd be in the top 25% of that particular school's entering class, or because they're attractively "alien" to an admissions department looking for diversity. A Midwestern school might be eager for kids from New England, while a New England school might be thrilled to have an Alaskan or two.

Be Realistic

If your child is an all-around high school star, with brains, brawn, and band, some school is bound to offer a full scholarship. Your college costs could be zero.

If your child is not a well-rounded, straight-A student with glowing letters of recommendation, leadership qualities, and near-perfect SAT scores, an acceptance letter from Stanford is unlikely—which may very well be great news!

By being realistic about interests, academic capabilities, and personality, your child can focus on schools where the fit would be right, and where he or she has a very good chance of being accepted.

....

HAPPY NEW YEAR!

It's January 1 of your child's senior year in high school. To start the year off right, fill out a Free Application for Federal Student Aid (FAFSA), which you can get from the high school guidance office, college financial offices, many libraries, or on-line (www.ed.gov/offices/OPE/express.html). By and large, colleges base their aid decisions on this one crucial form put out by the Feds.

Because the amount of aid available is limited, early birds can peck from a full pot. But those whose applications arrive nearer to a school's deadline, which could be as early as January or February, may face an empty one. Therefore, even if your taxes aren't prepared by then, and you'll have to submit an estimate (followed later by an amended form), your *first* investment this year should be the time it takes to fill out your FAFSA. Get it in right after January 1 of your child's senior year. The grant you save may be your own!

Fill out the FAFSA as accurately as possible, and be sure to sign it. If you don't, you'll go to the end of the line, which means you very well may get nothing.

Some colleges, especially private ones, will also ask for the College Scholarship Services's PROFILE form, and there may be separate aid applications put out by the individual schools as well as by your state. The financial aid officers at each college will use these forms to decide how much will come out of whose pocket—starting with yours. Make sure you find out from each school exactly which forms they'll want, and get them in as early as possible.

....

The ideal situation is for your child to have intelligently applied to a few schools that would be as thrilled to have her as she will be to attend. The perfect school would place her on its top 25% wish list for the year, and have a nice, large endowment so it can offer a juicy grants/scholarship package, or be so low cost that you can swing it.

With more than one such acceptance in hand, you'd be in a good position to negotiate. To take your best shot at a better deal, ask for an extension on the deadline for making a final decision, and talk to each financial aid officer. Explain your family's current alternatives, and why a more generous aid package—similar to the one from Competing College would make the difference—in your friendliest way, of course.

Since each year requires a new financial aid application, which could result in a cutback on future help, now's the time to try for aid and tuition guarantees, too.

You'll have the least bargaining room if your child is accepted on early decision (and has forfeited the right to go elsewhere). On the other hand, if your child's heart is set on a school, she'll have the best chance of being accepted by applying for early decision.

If her first choice is a school that isn't particularly generous, we think your best alternatives are to either say, "No!," or to come up with a plan to raise the money. Don't worry, you won't need it all by the first day of her freshman year. Much worse from our perspective would be to let your child graduate with a doctorate in debt.

Out-of-state, state schools present a unique opportunity. If your child decides early enough that he really wants to attend one, has a good chance of being accepted—and if you're flexible—an early move to that state will drop the tuition dramatically. (Lots of families move for the right elementary school. Why not college?) While it may not cut your family's expected contribution, your child can graduate debt-free and you won't have to go into hock, either.

The Great Scholarship Myth

There is more money in being an informed consumer and taking charge of the aid link-up process than in all the scholarship hunts ever conducted!
—ANNA AND ROBERT LEIDER, *Don't Miss Out*

Don't get suckered by ads from outfits who'll assure you that billions of dollars worth of scholarships are going to waste because *you* haven't sent them a check for a computer-generated list. Don't waste the time or money.

We have nothing against applying for scholarships legitimately, but even if your child could get an award, it will probably not save you a nickel. Why? Because in creating your aid package, the school's financial aid officers will deduct the scholarship from the college's part of your aid package—not from your family's expected contribution.

Still, it would be wonderful to see your child receive the special honor he deserves. To pursue the scholarship question, ask at the high school, as well as where you work, pray, and belong—be it the VFW, NAACP, ILGWU, or the Boy Scouts. And visit these Web sites: www.salliemae.com, www.collegeboard.org, and www.fastweb.com/fastweb.

DOING YOUR HOMEWORK

The more you know about navigating the financial aid maze, the more aid you'll get. Even if your family's income is over $100,000, if you play the game right, you *can* get a generous financial aid package, especially from a well-heeled private school.

The more time you invest in learning how the financial aid game is played before (preferably well before) application time, the less your child's future learning will cost you. And with tens of thousands of your dollars at stake, the hours you put into reading, researching, and then reasoning with your young 'un could save you from a retirement filled with debt.

· ·

PLAY THE COLLEGE FUNDING GAME! GET TO ANSWER KEY ETHICAL QUESTIONS!

Here are two particularly common and troublesome issues:

1. If your family has the money, is it fair to move your income and assets around so that your kids can get grants, subsidized loans, need-based scholarships, or work/study hours—even though that will limit the funds available for needier families and students? We leave this question for you to ponder.

2. Whose essay is it? Often the key to admission, the personal essay should be great, but it should also be real, and preferably moving. The best time for kids to write theirs is during a vacation—for example, the summer before their senior year—when the pressure is off and there's lots of time to think, write, review, edit, and rewrite. When school is back in session, suggest that they ask teachers and guidance counselors to read and comment on their essay, then help them edit it again and again.

Would it make more sense for mom or dad to write the application essay, or to hire a pro to do it? Nope. The admissions people see thousands of applications. Like Santa Claus, they know if you've been bad or good. So be good for goodness sake!

....

The Higher Your Income, the More You'll Pay

While one group of experts is scaring you into saving all you can so that you'll be able to foot the college bill, another group is telling you not to save, because the more you have, the more you'll have to pay.

Colleges expect parents to help foot the bill. On average, every year they're supposed to shell out up to 5.65% of their assets, and up to 47% of income (after various allowances and exclusions). But they're rarely expected to foot the whole bill, and it's not hard to cut your EFC—if you plan in advance, even just a little in advance.

The financial aid officers at the various colleges have discretion and can be reasoned with. For example, if you've had unusually high medical expenses, are footing the graduate school bill for another child, have a younger child in private school, or just lost your job, some schools will take that into account and adjust their offers accordingly.

While the parents' income gets hit hard and their assets get plucked, the student's assets and income both get clobbered! Excluding the first $1,750 of what they earn, college students are expected to contribute up to 35% of their assets and half of their after-tax earnings—not once, but in each of their four years at school. The more money your kids have in their name, and the more money they earn, the more they'll have to contribute.

From the "Rules Are Nuts" Department

If your child plans to pay for extra college expenses (like pizza) by delivering newspapers at 4 A.M. come rain or shine, or is a computer whiz intent on putting aside big bucks by doing programming after school, be proud. But break the bad news of how college math works: Fully 35% of everything the student puts aside will automatically go directly to the college each year before other financial aid is even considered. And, after a small allowance, so will half of everything earned from January 1 of the junior year in high school until December 31 of the junior year in college. Those are the rules.

It may make a lot more sense for your kid's college investment time to be spent studying, volunteering, participating in athletics or the drama department, preparing for the SATs, reading college catalogs, visiting schools, deciding which ones are most appealing (and why)—even sleeping. There'll be plenty of time to make money after college, unless, of course, your kid will be applying for graduate school aid.

One way your teens can help to cut college costs is to cut the time they spend in college. Taking advanced-placement courses in high school will help. So will any college-level summer courses they take while they're still in high school. To be seriously considered by a serious college, it'll pay for them to take serious courses, including as a high school senior. The time to slack off has not yet arrived.

If your kids are anything but slackers, they could cut costs by completing college in three years rather than four. (When checking school statistics, look at the percentage of students who graduate in three, four, or five years and more.) With every year being a major expense, less campus time might be worth considering, especially if graduate school bills are likely. And don't forget about Uncle Sam footing the bills. If your child has an interest in entering the military, it's a win-win situation.

Families Are So Complicated Now

The finances of noncustodial parents are generally not considered by financial aid administrators when calculating a family's expected contribution—although some private colleges do factor them in. But that doesn't mean that your child's noncustodial parent shouldn't help with the costs! (Here's hoping your ex isn't a deadbeat.)

Stepparents, on the other hand, must include their income and assets on the federal financial aid form, and most schools expect them to pick up a parent's share of the tuition. (Talk about a marriage penalty!) From a purely economic point of view, if one natural parent is wealthy—or remarried to someone who is—and the other one is struggling, it would be less expensive for the child to live with the poorer parent. Hey, we don't write these crazy rules, we just report them.

LOOPIDY LOOPHOLE

If your adjusted gross income is less than $50,000, you may be able to exclude all of your assets from the aid formulas. Your home, yachts, gold bricks will all be safely hidden if you and everyone in the household who has to file tax returns is eligible to (and does) file either the 1040EZ or 1040A. There are exceptions, of course, but isn't it nice to know that some of our wealthiest families can send their children off to school without having to mortgage their chateaux on the Riviera?

WAYS EVERYONE CAN USE TO SAVE ON COLLEGE

Even some of the wealthiest Americans, using creative but legal loopholes, feed at the trough of public and private college funds. One perfectly legal ploy is to lower your income in the first crucial tax year that colleges focus on when determining how much you'll have to pay. That year starts on January 1 of your child's junior year in high school, and it ends on December 31 of that same calendar year (at which time Junior will be a senior).

If you were planning to take a year off anyway, this is the year to hang up your hat for awhile. And if you have some capital gains to take, do it earlier, say in your child's sophomore year.

Another great way to cut your expected share of college costs is to have a business of your own. If you need any extra motivation to create your Ace in the Hole, here it is! Ideally, you want something up and running in your child's junior year. (The IRS has a bad habit of assuming businesses that aren't profitable in at least three out of the last five years, aren't businesses at all—but hobbies.) A small business can provide tax benefits and can cut your college costs because business assets are assessed at a lower rate than personal assets.

By and large, the schools don't care how deep in debt you are. You'll be expected to contribute as if you weren't. Another good reason to pay off those bills! Say you need to buy a new(er) car. You'd decrease your assets by spending money in your savings account for it, and therefore, your EFC would go down.

Interestingly, if you borrow from a bank or a car dealer to buy the car, in addition to finance charges, you'd have to come up with *more* money to pay for college—because you haven't reduced your assets. A better bet might be to borrow against your home equity (if your child is applying to schools that count it, which many private colleges do), or to borrow against your investments (e.g., a margin loan against stocks). While auto loans are not deducted from your assets, loans against your home and investments are.

The possible mix of grants, loans, and work/study opportunities will vary from school to school, state to state, or public to private institution. But with the major exception of those private schools whose calculations include home equity, your family's up-front cash contribution will (at least in theory) be the same, whether your child goes to Princeton or Podunk U. The biggest difference in final costs will result from the fact that loans need to be repaid, while grants do not.

If you are not able, interested, or willing to become very well informed, an early meeting with a qualified specialist in financial aid rules may save you a fortune. Tax preparation and college aid applications are very different. A tactic for saving money on one may cost you money on the other. Be aware, though, that while most planners are up to speed on topics like retirement planning, experts in college financing are tougher to find.

So how do you find such a specialist? Ask guidance counselors, other parents, and friends for recommendations. The International Association for Financial Planning (800-945-IAFP) can refer you to any of their members in your area who specialize in college financial planning.

Dee Lee, a Certified Financial Planner with Harvard Financial Educators in Harvard, Massachusetts, says that a good planner should be up front about his or her expertise. If the person you contact has only a smattering of college finance experience, ask for a referral to a colleague who specializes in the area. (See page 309 for information on finding a general financial planner.) Once you find your way to an advisor, ask to talk to several clients he or she has helped through the intricacies of college money.

Philip Johnson, a Certified Financial Planner in Clifton Park, New York, who specializes in college financial planning, advises parents to trust their instincts in choosing an advisor. How long have they been advising? Who are some previous clients you can speak with? What are the credentials they bring to the table? You know the drill!

If you're immediately presented with an investment vehicle that's designed to hide assets, watch out. You want to feel comfortable with an advisor, and have the sense that you're getting recommendations based on your particular situation—not a canned solution that's ethically dubious.

· ·

THE BEST PLACES TO GO FOR A CURRENT COURSE ON COLLEGE LOANS, GRANTS, AND TAX CREDITS

Sorry, we wish we could see into the future as well as into the minds of our lawmakers, but alas, we cannot. Tax laws, school policies, as well as the entire application process for aid and entrance are as complicated as the "simplified" tax code, and they're constantly being revised. Ever wonder why so many of the best college guides are annual?

The details are going to change. That's guaranteed. Keep up-to-date by reading the books we recommend, the catalogs from the schools your child is considering, and the stories on the latest in college finance that regularly appear in the personal finance magazines and the weeklies.

You'll find up-to-date information, worksheets, and helpful links at the following Web sites: www.finaid.org, www.collegeboard.com, and www.collegeaid.com.

Among the must-read books is certainly *Don't Miss Out,* the classic, annually updated guide to financial aid by Anna and Robert Leider. Also updated annually and worth a read is *Paying for College Without Going Broke* by Kalman A. Chany. We're partial to *Financing College* by Kristin Davis, too, and to a greatly reassuring book, *The College Admissions Mystique* by Bill Mayher, which shares the secret of how even the class dolt can attend Harvard while explaining how to find (and get your child admitted to) the right school.

Also, call the Department of Education at 800-4-FED-AID for a free copy of the regularly updated *The Student Guide: Financial Aid.*

· ·

Homing In on Handling Home Equity

Home equity isn't considered to be an asset by most public colleges and universities—but some private schools do count it in their formulas. That means the more home equity you have, the higher the contribution these schools would expect you to make. Does that mean it's a mistake to pay off your mortgage as quickly as possible, because it increases your home equity?

We believe that the interest you'll save by paying down your mortgage will be far greater than any increase in what you might be expected to pay for college. Keep pre-paying, keep pre-paying, keep pre-paying. In fact, depending on your child's age, you might want to use your mortgage to create a pre-paid college tuition plan, as we explain below—but avoid other pre-paid college tuition plans.

If you do need to borrow money to help finance college, a line of credit against the equity in your home may be your best bet—in terms of both the interest rate you'd pay and the possible tax deductions you could receive. The more equity you have, the more this is an option.

Once you borrow against your home, of course, the value of that asset will shrink. So in subsequent years, the schools that count it when they crunch the numbers will have to lower your expected contribution accordingly.

If you'll have to borrow to pay for college and you don't have a home equity option, your best bet may be to get your child to take out the loan—even if you plan to pay it back. Kids often get a lower interest rate, which isn't charged until after they graduate. That'd make it cheaper for you to pay the blasted thing off, which of course you'd do as soon as possible. For more information, go to these sites: www.salliemae.com and www.nelliemae.com.

Pre-Paid College Tuition Plans

We like the word *pre-paid,* but we warn against pre-paid college tuition plans. Most contain just too many provisos. Some will heavily penalize you if, a decade and a half from now, your child chooses another school, transfers, moves to another state, decides not to go to college at all, or isn't accepted for admission. By limiting a student's future choices, school-sponsored and, to a lesser extent, state plans increase the likelihood of school/student mismatches.

As if that weren't bad enough, some plans require large initial deposits, when most parents can least afford them, and are almost certain to pay less than virtually every other investment possibility open to middle-income parents.

But perhaps worst of all, those pre-paid dollars may be deducted dollar for dollar (not at 5.65%) from any other aid you might have gotten, including grants. In the end, the family with a pre-paid tuition plan is likely to pick up far *more* of the college costs than they would have without the plan!

What's a parent to do?

Consider mutual funds, CDs, and annuities. Take all the tax credits you can, and don't discount the likelihood that scholarship and grant money will be available. And if you're a homeowner, create a pre-paid college tuition fund of your own by investing in your mortgage. Increases in home equity accumulate tax deferred (and often end up tax-free). When properly used, a home equity line of credit makes it easy to withdraw money at any time, without penalty or taxes. They're relatively inexpensive and increasingly available. While some schools will count home equity when developing a financial aid package, many won't.

The interest charged on home loans, as we're being constantly reminded, is still (at least potentially) tax-deductible. And mortgages pay a better return than the pre-paid college tuition plans. Yet this surprisingly powerful repository for college savings is far too infrequently mentioned.

Here's how to create yours: Let's say you have a $100,000 mortgage at 8% for 30 years—and a newborn. If you add in a $141 pre-payment every month to the required $734 payment, for a total of $875, you'll shave 12 years off the term, and you'll save over $75,000 in interest. When your child goes off to college at age 18, you'll have $875 a month that you can use for college tuition—or anything else you might like—*plus* all that equity you've accumulated in your castle.

Home equity represents a key part of your family's savings program. It certainly makes more sense to build on that exceptional asset, than to sign up for one of the school, state, or private tuition plans. And if the student you've been saving for doesn't go to a costly school, gets piles of assistance, or becomes a billionaire during high school by inventing the next technological breakthrough, you get to keep all your equity.

How a Single Word Can Save $10,000 or More

Grandparents who have the resources can directly pay all or part of a student's tuition without affecting their estate taxes. On top of that, the well-heeled elder set can give another $10,000 each, gift-tax-free, every year to the student, to the parents, and to anyone else (our address is on page 311).

If, however, grandma and grandpa can't pay the entire tuition, but want to take some of the burden off you, everyone might come out ahead if they pay none of it! At least none of it directly to the college. The schools will happily accept part of a year's cost from anyone, and then they'll reduce their aid package dollar for dollar—but you'll still have to come up with your EFC.

If your folks are thinking about giving your child a tax-free gift in the form of a check, just say *no!* Your kid might blow the money on something else. Better if the old folks gift the money to you and your spouse. Or maybe they can help you pay off the loans once your child has graduated.

UGMA—Ugh!

If you've set up Uniform Gift to Minors Act (UGMA) or Uniform Transfer to Minors Act (UTMA) accounts and would rather not see more than a third of that money going off to college each year with your kids, you might want to spend it down before January of your student's junior year in high school, that crucial first year that colleges consider.

Before depleting their accounts, you'll want to get some personalized, professional advice. The basic rule is that UGMA or UTMA money has to be used for things that benefit your child, but that wouldn't automatically be your responsibility, the way that food or clothes are. And don't neglect to document those expenses, say, for computers or college prep courses. The IRS may be curious to know where it all went.

There's another possible problem with custodial or trust-type accounts: A child who's reached legal maturity can withdraw everything in the UGMA or UTMA till and plunk it all down on a neatmobile or some other noneducational fantasy.

IT'S NOT OVER UNTIL THE LAST BILL'S BEEN PAID

Four years of college fly by quickly. But all too often, what many college graduates face is a rough time sweating out repaying all the loans they took out to cover their share of the college bills. One study found that the average graduate will need a salary of at least $38,512 just to cover living expenses and the payments on their student loans and credit card debts!

Unfortunately, too many young people have been saddled with debts they can't handle, and the result haunts them for years to come. Some 1 million former students have already defaulted on their loans, and another 11% each year are joining those stressful ranks. Don't let that happen to your kids.

Choosing a college *you can afford* often becomes a better and better idea as time goes by. If we've convinced you that paying down debts as quickly as possible is the way to go, help your kids apply the idea to their loans, which, like mortgages, can end up costing twice what was borrowed! And a bad payment record can kill your kid's real-life "permanent record card"—that all-important credit report. Explain to your kids that late payments will show on their credit reports for seven years, which could hurt their ability to get a job, rent an apartment, obtain a mortgage, or buy a car.

There are, however, so many different options for borrowing, repaying, consolidating, and in general dealing with student loans, defaults, and federal record-keeping errors, that an entire book would be required to walk you through them. That book is *Take Control of Your Student Loans* by Robin Leonard and Shae Irving, two crusading attorneys at Nolo Press.

There's another treacherous form of debt for college kids: credit cards. About two-thirds of the nation's 9 million college students already have at least one credit card, and 20% have four or more pieces of plastic! Their average balance is about $2,200. Many received their first offer while they were still in high school.

STUDENTS ARE WORTH THEIR WEIGHT IN GOLD

In the lending business, no one is courted as heavily as college students. They're offered their plastic on a silver platter for three reasons:

1. With the average adult American already holding 8 to 10 pieces of plastic, students represent an untapped market of more than 15 million potential cardholders.

2. Students have decent repayment records, probably because their parents typically pick up the tab when the kids can't pay. Applications may ask for the parents' income—even when they are not being asked to co-sign for their college kid's card.

3. Most important, cardholders tend to be loyal to their first card, so issuers scramble to get the premier spot in each student's wallet.

What should the parents of college-bound students do to avoid the additional, hidden cost of a college education that credit cards represent?

Tell It Like It Is

Explain to your teenagers why they're such hot prospects for the credit card industry. Your kids don't want to be ripped off, and they may resent what's behind the industry's hype.

Share your credit card experiences. While they've often seen you pull out the plastic to charge something, have they ever seen the bills? Sit down with them and go over a credit card statement. Explain the finance charge, grace period, and minimum-payment trap. If you've recently paid off debts, or if you're trying to do so now, show how much it's costing you, and why it's so difficult to get ahead when you pay only the minimum.

....

911

David Hunt, the former president of AT&T Universal Card, gave his daughter a credit card when she went off to college. He told her that she could only use it for emergencies. His definition of an emergency: "If you can eat it, drink it, or wear it, it's not an emergency."

....

Set limits before they head off for school, and explain what'll happen if they run up bills they can't pay. Will you be able, or willing to bail them out—or will they be on their own? Lay out the consequences. If you want some help clueing them in on how credit cards work, get them Gerri's audiotape, "Smart Credit Strategies for College Students" (see page 328). Kids can pop it into their cassette players and hear the lecture in language they'll understand.

Of course, the best way to teach proper credit card management is to practice it! And if you're really on the ball, you'll do what a family we'll call the Chargitts did. They scrimped and saved for years to help put their two children through school. Long before that first tuition bill arrived, the Chargitts, their daughter, and the university developed a workable financial aid plan.

Although they knew exactly what to expect and were prepared, the Chargitts paid that first bill with plastic. And they've been charging every college bill since then.

Now if you're thinking that we're about to say, "Horrors!," read on, because the Chargitts earned gold stars in our book. They figured out a wonderful way to reward themselves—big-time—for being good debt managers.

The Chargitts chose their two credit-cards-for-college very carefully, with a special eye toward both the grace period and the special benefits they could receive. They made sure to absolutely *never carry a balance* on those cards, and to always pay their college credit card bills in full—before the due date.

They picked the card to use depending on whether they wanted to earn more free airplane tickets or vacation stays. Thanks to their card companies, when last we heard from the Chargitts they had already taken five round trips—a mix of family vacations and medical emergencies. And they're still racking up the freebies, now that their son is in college.

Red Flag

Do not—we repeat, *do not*—follow the Chargitts' example unless you're absolutely certain that you'll pay the credit card bill off by its due date. But if you have the money and know you can trust yourself, by all means, go for a frequent-flyer card. You generally earn one mile for each dollar you charge. A few of these cards have a cap that restrict you from earning more than, say, 50,000 miles a year, but hopefully the tuition bill won't be more than that! A list of frequent-flyer and rebate cards is available for $12 from CardTrak, P.O. Box 1700, Frederick, MD 21702, www.cardtrak.com

To cope with all the money issues your grad will encounter, we recommend *Get a Financial Life* by Beth Kobliner and *The Post–College Survival Handbook* by Jo-Ann Johnston.

MAP OUT YOUR OWN FINANCIAL FUTURE

How bright your financial future will be depends on both the way you view your portfolio, and the way you manage it.

As we've made abundantly clear, to truly prosper, your portfolio has to include a lot more than just your investments of money. How you spend your time, focus your energy, and handle your debts are all crucial to achieving a secure, more fulfilling life. But manage the money you must.

No matter how old you are, how many mistakes you've made in managing your finances and your time up until now, how "numbers-phobic" you are, or how much you really don't like to deal with this stuff, you *can* get on the right track—if you take charge, plan, and follow through to create the future you want.

CHAPTER 16

Financial Planning Made Easy

○ You *can* learn this stuff, and you must!

○ How to become a multimillionaire on a typical salary

○ Getting creative to get what you want

○ Finding investment opportunities that match your values

Your best financial planner is you.

KEN AND DARIA DOLAN, *Straight Talk on Money*

Financial planning. With the possible exception of "public speaking" or "April 15," no two words spark more dread than these two. One study by the International Association for Financial Planning found that more people would rather have a root canal, clean the oven, or bathe the dog than create a financial plan!

If the idea of financial planning leaves you sweating, relax. You're not going to have to become a CNBC junkie or read *The Wall Street Journal* every day (although paying attention to financial news is not a bad idea). Taking control of your financial life is not as tough as you may think, and it's certainly *not* as painful as a root canal.

Besides, you really have no choice. At some point, you're going to have to make investment decisions, even if it's just(!) to decide which mutual funds are best for your 401(k) or IRA. A decision you don't think through is still a decision, and often a bad one. But these decisions are just too important to ignore.

As much as you may be trying to put off creating a financial plan, you can't afford to do so any longer. Without a plan, your goals are likely to be just dreams, and things like a happy and lengthy retirement may not be a realistic option.

> Gold laboreth diligently and contentedly for the wise owner who finds for it profitable employment, multiplying even as the flocks of the field.
> —GEORGE S. CLASON, *The Richest Man in Babylon*

Even assuming no dramatic changes in your fortunes or stellar investments over the course of your working life, you're going to earn a fortune. Say you and your mate are age 25, and your family income is equivalent to the U.S. median—last estimated to be $54,910. Assuming you'll both be working until you're 65, even if you never get a raise, not even for the cost of living, you're going to bring in over $2 million. If your salary goes up just 3% a year, like inflation, you'll earn over $4 million. (See Table 16.1.) That makes you a multimillionaire, all right.

If you land a promotion or even just get cost-of-living increases, you'll rake in even more—maybe more than $12 million. Conversely, if you decide to retire earlier than age 65, your take will be less. In any case, you're going to earn a fortune.

So what are you going to do with it? Watch it slip away, or put it to good use?

True, none of this is exactly fun stuff, but you were the one who followed our earlier advice, and now you're stuck. Instead of being deep in debt, you're starting to float on a cushion of cash security. Trust us. The more you learn about financial planning, the more empowered you're

TABLE 16.1 How Much Will You Make:
Turning the Median Salary of $54,910 into Millions

ANNUAL RAISES AND COST OF LIVING	40-YEAR INCOME TOTALS
0%	$ 2,196,400
1%	2,699,245
2%	3,360,655
3%	4,237,494
4%	5,408,458
5%	6,982,814
6%	9,112,730
7%	12,010,709

going to feel. A great place to start is with *The Only Investment Guide You'll Ever Need* by Andrew Tobias.

TRUST YOUR INSTINCTS

Remember the story of Marc's son, Adam? He wanted to sell his penny stocks, but let his broker talk him into holding onto them. Soon, they were worthless. No one can predict what the economic or investment climate will be in the future. But there'll be plenty of experts telling you *why* the market surged or crashed—after the fact. *Never let anyone talk you into something that makes you feel uncomfortable.*

It is hard to know what or who to believe. A bright young researcher spent a lot of time looking at various personal finance articles and books for an article one of us was writing. She came back overwhelmed. "The problem is, there are so many different viewpoints," she said. "How can you tell who's right?"

That's the dilemma. There is no single correct financial plan just waiting for you to find it, so it can turn you into a tycoon. There are a variety of approaches, each with its own collection of pros and cons. Your job is to make the best decisions for you and your family from among all those options being offered.

> A good financial planner can help you set priorities and develop concrete strategies, but only *you* can examine your dreams and set goals for your life.
> —RICHARD SCHROEDER, Certified Financial Planner
> and Registered Investment Advisor, Williamsville, NY

Okay, so with all those millions at stake, you're ready to invest in your future by learning as much as you can and then trusting yourself. But with over 9,000 mutual funds, thousands upon thousands of stocks, annuities, estate plans, life and health insurance policies, how can you even know where to start?

Start at the end, with a plan based on your goals. What do you want, and what will it cost? Then, sketch a flexible blueprint for getting where you want to go. For the best chance of success, commit your plan to writing—even if it's just scratched out on a piece of notepaper. Research sponsored by Consumer Federation of America and NationsBank shows that at all income levels below $100,000, people who have a written financial plan are likely to have twice as much in savings and investments as people without a written plan. Twice as much!

You may think a financial plan is complicated, something you can't create until you've taken a course in finance, or something that you have to pay a financial planner big bucks to develop. Not true. A financial plan may get complicated if you have a complicated situation. But for most of us, it's pretty basic.

Back to Basics

The way to wealth is straightforward and simple: Spend less than you earn, avoid debt, and then save and invest for growth.

If you can stick to these basics, you're way ahead of the game (and most of your neighbors). Don't even think about more complicated strategies until you are comfortably and faithfully adhering to the basics. It's not worth your time or energy to spend hours pouring over stock strategies when you still have huge credit card debts hanging over your head. If you try to focus your energy on too many things at once, you'll just get distracted, discouraged, or both.

It bears repeating . . . and repeating . . . and repeating . . . paying off your expensive debts is one of the highest-return, safest investments you can make in yourself and your future. Start with your high-interest credit cards. When they're paid off, begin pre-paying your auto, student, and home loans as well. Not only is paying down your debts a great financial investment, it'll bring you an added measure of freedom, because you won't be chained to a paycheck just to pay those bills. So put debt reduction at the top of your list of goals.

Then take the time to think through your other goals. What do you really want? To retire with enough money to travel the world? Or do you want to travel long before you retire? Are you preparing to send kids to college, or are you planning to go back to school yourself? Would you like to build a savings cushion so you can stop reaching for those credit cards every time you hit a bump in the road of life?

. . . .

IT'S NOT ALWAYS ABOUT MONEY

Some important goals may not immediately seem appropriate to your financial plan: things like spending more time with your family or loved ones or losing weight. As unrelated as they may seem, include them on your wish list. You may find that they are inextricably linked to your financial plan.

Spending more time with the kids may mean switching to part-time work or taking a lower-paying, less stressful job. Or it might mean spending the money on a housekeeper to take over some of your home chores. Losing weight may mean joining the local gym—or maybe it will mean more money in your pocket if you eat out less. So write them all down.

It's easy to think that if you won the lottery or got a big fat raise your financial problems would be over. But the truth is, you'd probably have new problems. So put the fantasy solutions aside for a moment and tap your creative side. You may want to get together with a few friends over coffee once a week for a month or so to brainstorm ways you can each achieve some of your dreams, without an unexpected windfall. The $2 million to $12 million you're going to earn will be plenty. Let winning the lottery be a bonus, not a means to your ends.

Maybe one of your dreams is to be able to escape to a house in the country on weekends. Problem is, you don't have the money for a second home. Getting creative, you may be able to work a house swap, rent a cottage, or even borrow a neighbor's camper in exchange for baby-sitting during the week.

The idea is to get your heart and mind thinking in ways other than pure dollars and cents. If you're very clear and focused on a goal, you may find solutions falling right into your lap. But you have to ask questions and be ready to seize opportunity when it comes your way.

....

At What Price?

After you've had a chance to really think about your goals, decide which ones are serious and admit which ones are just wistful fantasy (the boat that would be fun to have, but a pain to keep up and a huge money drain).

Then put a price tag on each of your goals. It isn't easy to figure out how much you'll need in your retirement fund 20 years from now, or how much college will cost you in 15 years. But as we showed in Chapters 5 and 15, you can do it!

Take advantage of all those magazines, books, and mutual fund brochures that offer worksheets to help you plan ahead. But if the number that pops up leaves you gasping for air, take a deep breath and remember, Rome wasn't built in a day, and your future won't be, either. Besides, those calculators are guidelines, *not* hard-and-fast rules—and many of them were designed by salespeople, hoping to sell you a (sometimes unnecessarily expensive) investment program.

Most people quickly discover that they have a bunch of goals competing for the same out-of-reach dollars. If that's where you are, don't throw up your hands in despair. Instead, set priorities. Adjust your expectations. Revise your time schedule and seek out your alternatives.

Here's an example. Marta wants to retire early—at age 55—then travel. She's paid off her credit cards, and is well on her way to a mortgage-burning party. She earns enough to cover her basic living expenses, and is beginning to build a savings account, but she hasn't yet got enough set aside to fund her travels. What can Marta do?

She could *postpone* her plans, and save a little more by working until she's, say, age 58. She can *scale back* her fantasy. Instead of heading to the Fiji Islands, she might satisfy at least some of her wanderlust in the United States and Mexico. Before she exits from the workforce, Marta could *create an Ace in the Hole* to help fund her travels, save on taxes, and give her more flexibility when she does retire. A really creative solution might be for Marta to organize specialized tours as her Ace, or find part-time work guiding groups abroad for a tour company, or volunteer for overseas duty with an international organization.

By carefully and realistically planning ahead, Marta will achieve most, if not all, of her goals. But without doing some planning—and following through—she'd probably discover too late that her fantasies would have to remain just that: fantasies.

MAKE IT HAPPEN!

The number one enemy of personal finance is procrastination.
—DAVE CHILTON, *The Wealthy Barber*

Once you've set your goals and figured out roughly how much you need to get there, start investing for them. There are three fundamental principles for making a savings and investment plan work:

1. Start now—the sooner the better! Whether you're 25 or 55, starting now is key. Chances are, whatever you're saving for isn't going to get less expensive, it's going to get pricier. And the sooner you start, the more time you'll have to take advantage of compound interest's magic.

Here's a refresher on how that magic works: Let's say you can save $100 a month. If you invest it in something earning 8% a year, at first glance you might figure that you'd have $1,200, plus $96 in interest at the end of the year, and 10 times that much, or $12,960, at the end of a decade. But in reality, of course, you'll end up with much more—$18,295—because you'll be earning interest on the interest your money earns.

Small delays in getting started can make a big difference. Say you sock away $2,000 a year in your IRA, starting at age 25. If you earn 10% annually, at age 65, you'll have $1,054,013. Your sister waits until age 40 to get started, so she'd have to sock away $9,533 a year to match your nest egg at retirement, assuming she gets the same return on her investment. (Of course she won't be able to put that much into an IRA.)

If you haven't saved enough, don't let these figures discourage you. Whatever your current age, you're still younger than lots of others who haven't done much yet either!

Even if it's just a token amount, start putting money toward your top-priority goals. Commit to them by setting aside a regular amount. Pocket change will do if that's all you have. Once you get started and are faithful to your goal, you'll probably find yourself creating a momentum that will propel you in your planned direction.

2. Pay yourself first. Maybe it's a cliché, but it's great advice: Treat your savings or investment plan like a priority bill that has to be paid first, and your wealth-building program will be on the fast track. Don't wait until the end of the month, then save whatever's left, if anything. Choose a comfortable amount to put away each payday, even if it's just a few dollars.

Here's one strategy: Once you've paid off your credit cards, car loan, or even your mortgage, and are already in the habit of making those regular payments, why not transfer them to a savings, money market, or investment account? You're used to paying it to someone else, so how about giving it to yourself for a while?

3. Stick with it. Set a specific goal. Saving 10% of your pay is a good place to start, but if that sounds too steep to you, try 5%. That's what personal finance expert Jane Bryant Quinn did when she was a single parent in her twenties, wondering how she would make ends meet. She really didn't think she could afford to put aside anything, but a friend urged her to get started with that small amount, assuring her she'd never miss it. She didn't. Later, she bumped it up to 7%, and eventually to 10%.

Wherever you start, put your savings and investment plan on auto-pilot. Have your financial institution or mutual fund company deduct payments directly out of your bank account. After a couple of months, you won't miss it. *We promise!*

While you're at it, consider paying the bills this way, too. Why write out a check and pay postage each month, when you can have the money for your bills taken directly from your bank account? At many banks, virtually every regular bill can be paid automatically, and if you ever decide to cancel the direct payments, you need only notify the company at least three business days in advance of the next due date. Save time and almost $4 a year in postage per bill. Gerri not only has her mortgage payment taken directly from her bank account, but a small pre-payment is also deducted at the same time. Simple savings.

Watch out, though. You won't save a penny unless you actually have the money in your account. In fact, if a bunch of electronic transfers end up on your overdraft protection, you'll pay a pretty penny for this convenience. And if you decide to cancel the withdrawals, there may be a fee.

Choose the Right Places

The way financial professionals talk, you'd think only someone with an MBA could invest successfully. But really, it's more a matter of saving as much as you can—living below your means—and remembering this rule: Fast and flashy rarely pay off in the long run.

Today's hot stock or hot mutual fund is likely to be tomorrow's dud. If you want to play with the high rollers, you've got to be willing to invest a lot of time and energy learning the game, and you've got to have the stomach for the ride. If that turns you on, great. If not, keep reading.

You Gotta Take Risks

There are risks in *every* kind of investment, with the possible exception of paying off those expensive credit cards—we just can't find a downside there! The risk in parking your stash in a bank account or certificates of deposit is that your money won't keep pace with inflation. Stocks are among the riskiest of investments, although, when the Dow is on an upswing, many people seem to forget that what goes up often comes down.

Before you invest, minimize your risks by making sure you know the potential for loss as well as the possibility of reward. Remember, a high-return, low-risk investment is an oxymoron, except in paying down your credit card debts, of course. (Sorry, we just won't stop reminding you how important it is to pay down your expensive debts.)

What you want to do is take appropriate risks based on your comfort level, your time frame, and the nature of your goals. If you have a short time before you will (or might) need the money, don't put your money in high-risk stocks. It may not be there when you need it. If you're saving for a far-off goal, then you can afford to take more risks. In fact, you probably can't afford *not* to, because over the long run, "safe" investments like certificates of deposit or bonds barely keep ahead of inflation.

Obviously, we're talking about the financial aspect of risk here, not the emotional one. Most of us try to avoid personal risk, or at least try to avoid thinking about it. Otherwise, how could people with a good imagination really enjoy getting on an airplane? But once the decision is made to fight gravity, we try to choose an airline with a good track record, take along a book or some work for distraction, and resign ourselves to a little turbulence along the way. (Getting into a car is actually a far greater risk, but we take that in stride, too.)

Investing isn't all that different: Choose a fund or funds (or individual stocks or bonds) with an objective that matches where you want to go. Review the investment's past history to see if it's performed at least as well as its peers, and make sure you're prepared for the kind of volatility (fluctuations in value) that it's previously demonstrated or might incur tomorrow. It also helps to have confidence in the "captain" and "crew"— the fund's manager, or the company's senior management.

Then comes the hardest part: Once you've made the best choice you can, let the pilot fly the plane. Don't bail out in a downdraft! You'll end up on foot again, perhaps with less money than when you started out.

ASSET ALLOCATION

How you divide up your money among different investments is called your *asset allocation.* Asset allocation is simply the right mix of investments to help you reach your goals. You don't want to get carried away. Having 16 different funds for your retirement money is overkill.

As you know, we're big fans of diversifying, whether it's for your job or your investment portfolio. When you put a lot of your resources in one place, you're taking *a lot* of risk. The purpose of diversification is to reduce risk.

So don't put all your money in one basket—even if it seems to be the hottest investment going. From time to time, you'll hear about someone who lost their life savings in an investment scam. It's painful to lose *any* money, and it's especially painful when you lose it to a scam. Still, you have no business putting most of your future on the line in a high-risk investment. At least spread it out among several different investment options.

There's no hurry. You're in for the long haul. When your broker, your cousin, a telemarketer, or a neighbor in the supermarket tells you about a once-in-a-lifetime opportunity, forget it. There may still be some free lunches, but there are very few legitimate you-must-act-immediately, once-in-a-lifetime offers! For more advice on creating an asset allocation plan, check out *The Lifetime Book of Money Management* by Grace Weinstein, or visit www.dolans.com, or www.soundmindinvesting.com.

Once you have made your choices, don't micromanage your money. The worst thing you can do is to check your investment performance every day, or even every week. When you focus on the short term, you're more apt to panic at temporary market dips and switch your money around, missing out on sudden market rallies, and paying an awful lot of commissions in the process. Resolve to ignore your account between quarterly statements. If you've chosen your investment allocation wisely, your portfolio should be able to keep going . . . and going . . . and going for years with just periodic tune-ups.

. . . .

DO IT YOUR WAY

On his radio show, a financial planner once railed at Gerri for pre-paying an extra $25 a month on her mortgage. His view was that Gerri's money would grow faster in the stock market. True. Maybe. At that time, her mortgage interest rate was 7% and risk-free. Since her retirement portfolio was heavily weighted in stocks, she figured those pre-payments were a good way to diversify and get a decent return along the way.

Gerri wouldn't have felt comfortable putting all her savings or investment money toward her 7% mortgage. How she was allocating her assets was based on her goals, her plans, her comfort level, and her choice of asset allocation. That planner's was different, and yours may be, too. It's up to *you* to decide what makes sense for you.

. . . .

WHAT'S UNCLE SAM'S SHARE?

There is nothing sinister in so arranging one's affairs as to keep taxes as low as possible . . . nobody owes any public duty to pay more than the law demands; taxes are enforced exactions, not voluntary contributions.

               —JUDGE LEARNED HAND

There's no getting around it. Financial planning involves taxes, and it's not a simple topic. For most of us, just trying to put away the maximum that we can into tax-deductible or tax-deferred retirement plans is challenge enough. But once you've reached the point where slick (but always legal) tax-avoidance moves make sense, hit the books, do some research, and consider buying some professional help, either from a financial planner with expertise and experience in tax planning, or from a tax advisor with financial planning expertise. If you're dealing with a retirement plan distribution, a large inheritance, or some other complicated situation, having a pro on your team is very likely to be a worthwhile investment.

Until you get to that point, here are some general rules to keep in mind:

- When you own stocks, you pay taxes on dividends every year (even if you have them automatically reinvested), and you pay taxes on capital gains when you sell them.

- You pay income taxes on the interest your bonds pay you—with important exceptions. Interest paid on municipal bonds is exempt from federal tax (and in many cases, state tax as well). Interest on Treasuries (sold by the federal government) is exempt from state tax.

- If you own mutual funds, you'll have to pay three different taxes. You'll get a 1099-DIV form each year that reports dividend and capital gains earnings, each of which have separate tax consequences. Then, when you sell your funds, you get to pay taxes on your profits. Keep excellent records, and April 15 will be only a headache, not a migraine.

No advice is complete without an exception or two: You don't pay taxes on investments in tax-sheltered retirement accounts such as IRAs, 401(k)s, 403(b)s, or Keogh's until you withdraw the money. Then you pay income taxes on what you withdraw, except for the exception to the exception—the Roth-IRAs, which allow you to put after-tax dollars away for retirement and then withdraw them tax-free under the right circumstances.

PROTECT YOURSELF AND YOUR FAMILY

Besides saving and investing, there are a few other important parts of a financial plan you must take care of—life insurance, a will, and possibly an estate plan. They're not fun details, but they're essential to your peace of mind and the future of those you love.

If you don't have a will or adequate insurance, get it taken care of now! (See Chapter 5.)

Invest in Your Knowledge

A little time spent learning basic financial strategies can go a long way toward making you more confident and richer. Just don't try to digest everything at once—or you *will* feel ill. Pick a *single topic* that's of most interest or of the greatest urgency, and start there. For example, let's say you want to open an IRA and invest it in mutual funds.

Start by reading about IRAs and mutual funds in two or three of the following books: *Terry Savage's New Money Strategies for the '90s* by Terry Savage, *Dun & Bradstreet Guide to Your Investments* (updated annually) by Nancy Dunnan, *The Truth About Money* by Ric Edelman, *The Only Investment Guide You'll Ever Need* by Andrew Tobias, *The Lifetime Book of Money Management* by Grace Weinstein, *Mutual Fund Superstars* by William E. Donoghue, or *4 Easy Steps to Successful Investing* by Jonathan Pond. You don't need to read the whole book now, just what they say about mutual funds and IRAs. (Go to our Web site or send for our catalog for recommendations of the best books on a variety of topics. See page 328.)

Don't be surprised to discover that these folks disagree on some points. If the market weren't full of differing opinions, there'd be no one to buy when you wanted to sell, and no one willing to sell when you wanted to buy. Listen to the experts, then go with what makes sense to you.

If you prefer to do your research on-line, visit these sites:

www.kiplinger.com

www.talks.com

fyiowa.webpoint.com/finance/invest.htm

quicken.excite.com/forums

www.investor.nasd.com

www.pioneerplanet.com/archive/wealth/index.htm

www.bankrate.com

www.fool.com

www.wealthbuildernews.com

moneyinsider.msn.com

Head to the library and look through recent personal finance magazines like *Kiplinger's Personal Finance, Money,* and *Your Money.* Also review personal finance articles in *BusinessWeek, Forbes,* and *Fortune.* Look at their mutual fund ratings and pick a few whose goals (long-term, short-term, bond, stock, options, foreign) match yours. See how they've done over at least the last five years. Ten is much better. (But remember that past history does *not* guarantee future performance.)

Once you've selected several funds that look promising, ask the reference librarian for a copy of *Morningstar* or *Value Line Mutual Fund Survey*. Look up each of the funds and study its track record, management, and outlook. Finally, when you've narrowed your choice to a couple, call the companies for their prospectuses, and look them over before you invest.

If you happened to choose something besides mutual funds to focus on, the following resources can help you check out your choices. Most of these are expensive, so find out which ones are available at your library.

> Annuities: *Morningstar's Variable Annuity/Life Performance Report* (800-735-0700).

> Bonds: *Standard & Poor's Bond Guide* (800-221-5277) or *Moody's Bond Record* (800-342-5647).

> Stocks: *Value Line Investment Survey* (800-833-0046) or *Standard & Poor's Stock Reports* (800-221-5277).

If you're itching to get into the stock market and invest in individual stocks, one way to become more knowledgeable and confident is to start or join an investment club. There are investment clubs of all types, with members of all ages and experience levels. For information on how to start one, contact the National Association of Investors Corporation (NAIC) at 248-583-6242 or www.betterinvesting.org. The nonprofit NAIC can provide you with a wealth of information on everything from starting your own club to evaluating stocks.

Keep Costs Low

Comparison shop. Always ask about expenses, such as commission costs, marketing fees, and administrative charges. Get them in writing. The more you can do yourself, the less you'll pay. But beware, Cousin George's advice may, in the long run, cost you a lot more dough than a professional advisor or fund manager.

When You Need Help, Get It!

If taxes make your eyes cross, but you want to pay as little as you can, if investment jargon goes over your head, but you want to make as much on your money as you can, keep in mind that there's no reason you have to go it alone. A good financial planner and accountant can *help* make your life much simpler and richer (and probably save you some money as well). But no one is omniscient. Even those high-priced mutual fund managers beat the market only about 20% of the time.

DO YOU NEED AN ADVISOR?

Good question. No short answer. We encourage you to learn as much as you can, of course. But there may be a time when you want an expert's personalized advice. For example, you may want an advisor to:

- Help with tax strategies or retirement planning where a mistake or oversight can prove to be very expensive in the long run.

- Create an estate plan, write your will, or review one you've prepared yourself.

- Review your financial situation and asset-allocation decisions and advise how you might do better.

- Help you whip your disorganized financial life into shape!

- Manage your money, if you have a healthy pile socked away, but don't have the time to devote to its oversight.

- Choose a long-term-care policy (be careful of commission-based planners here, *especially* if they offer a limited number of policies).

- Help you navigate a financial transition, such as divorce, retirement, or death of a spouse. Choose carefully—you'll be stressed enough without worrying about the advisor's honesty!

- Develop a plan for minimizing the cost of your kid's college education.

A good advisor will empower you by helping you learn. There are no dumb questions when it comes to your financial education. Assume nothing, question everything—and you're likely to learn a lot along the way.

So how do you find a financial advisor? First you have to know what you want from them. The more specific you can be, the better. Do you need budgeting help, investment strategies for retirement or college, tax advice, and/or estate planning? If you need narrow help (e.g., for creating an estate plan), find a specialist in that area. If you need a general plan, find a financial planner who can help you create one. And if you have only a limited amount to invest, avoid the ones who specialize in the lives of the rich and famous.

There are a few ways that financial professionals get paid: by *fee only,* which can be either a flat fee, a percentage of the money they manage, or a set fee for certain services; by *fee offset,* which is a set fee minus commissions on any products they sell; by *commission only*, where they get paid only if they sell something; or by *fee plus commission*, where planners charge a fee and also sell products on which they're paid commissions.

There is a lot of controversy about these different compensation methods. Some folks say you should never work with someone who is paid on commission because they may recommend products that are best for *their* financial future, not necessarily *yours*. On the other hand, fee-only financial planners can be expensive and out of reach for someone starting out or someone with a modest amount to invest. The truth is, there are good advisors in all of the camps.

Finding a Planner

There are four primary sources for financial planners. Each offers useful, free brochures and referrals.

1. The American Institute of Certified Public Accountants offers referrals to CPAs with specialized experience in financial planning (888-999-9256, www.aicpa.org).

2. The Institute of Certified Financial Planners offers referrals to financial professionals who have received the Certified Financial Planner (CFP) designation (800-282-PLAN, www.icfp.org).

3. The International Association for Financial Planning, a trade group composed of many types of financial planners, provides referrals to its membership, (888-806-PLAN, www.iafp.org).

4. The National Association of Personal Financial Advisors offers referrals to fee-only planners (888-FEE-ONLY, www.napfa.org).

Select at least three planners who seem appropriate for your needs, set up appointments with each one, and interview them just as you would if you were hiring them for a job—which you are. Find out why they expect they can do a good job for you, how they are paid, and how much they charge. And realize you *will* pay them, whether or not you directly write out a check. Ask about their experience and credentials, and check them out.

Speak to at least three client references. (Just don't expect other clients to give out confidential information about their money.) You might also ask how they research the products they recommend. (Later, it will be up to you to check out those products.) Ask to see a sample financial plan—and ask how the planner would tailor it for you.

Always check out their background before handing over your money. You can get a free disciplinary report from the National Association of

Securities Dealers at 800-289-9999, www.nasdr.com/2000.htm. That report will tell you about most securities violations. Even better, order a comprehensive disciplinary report from the National Fraud Exchange at 800-822-0416, ext. 34. The NAFEX database searches disciplinary records in the securities industry, plus real estate, banking, and more. (Their fee is $39 for the first search, and $20 for additional searches ordered at the same time.)

Just because an advisor is nice, doesn't mean he or she is any good. That's why credentials and experience are so important. And by the way, really think carefully about working with someone in your social group, church, or membership clubs. The question to ask yourself is, if you needed to "fire" this person, could you do so comfortably? What would the repercussions be? For more on choosing a financial advisor, see *The Right Way to Hire Financial Help* by Chuck Jaffee.

Note: If what you really want is for someone else to manage your investments for you, call AdvisorLink (800-348-3601), which can refer you to a money manager—even if all you've got is $15,000 in a mutual fund. Ask for its free investor kit.

Investing with Your Heart

If you don't want your kids to smoke, do you want to invest in companies that sell cigarettes to children overseas? Socially responsible investing is becoming more popular as people look for places where their money will meet their personal as well as financial needs and values. Here are a few resources if you're looking for investments that match your values:

- GreenMoney Journal (800-318-5725 or www.greenmoney.com)
- Council on Economic Priorities (800-729-4237 or www.accesspt.com/cep)
- Co-op America (800-584-7336, www.coopamerica.org)
- The Social Investment Forum (202-872-5319 or www.socialinvest.org)
- The Clean Yield Group (800-809-6439)
- Institute for American Values Investing (888-469-3863, www.americanvalues.com)

CONCLUSION

Someone once said, "Life is a journey, not a destination." While we may take different paths, for most of us, the destination is similar. We want to give our loved ones a better life, make a contribution to our little piece of the planet, feel good about our time on earth, and hopefully, have fun along the way.

Consciously or not, you've chosen the path you're on now. Where you go from here is your choice. You *can* get out of debt, live better on less, and have more of what you want, and less of what you don't. You *can* create a brighter future for yourself and your family. It may not happen overnight, or in quite the way you expected, but one thing is guaranteed: You'll change and your life will change. Why not consciously try to make it for the better—to create the life you want?

Take your time. Try on a few changes for size. See what fits, pick a few for now, and set aside others for another time or place. Set the bar high, but don't beat yourself up if you don't make it over the top the first couple of tries. And whatever you do, don't forget that small changes *can* make a big difference.

Planning where you want to go helps, as we've shown. But as John Lennon said, "Life is what happens while you are making other plans." So plan your itinerary, but at the same time be flexible and take advantage of interesting side trips that pop up along the way. Who knows where they'll lead?

We know that the tools we've given you in *Invest in Yourself* can help you to move in a positive direction. Please let us know how you're doing and what you've learned along the way that we can share with others.

For now, put the top down, crank up the tunes, and enjoy the ride! (But do fasten your seatbelt.)

Marc Eisenson

Gerri Detweiler

Nancy Castleman

We welcome your stories, tips, and feedback. Please write to us at Invest in Yourself, c/o Good Advice Press, P.O. Box 78, Elizaville, NY 12523. Send e-mail to us at feedback@investinyourself.com, or visit our Web site, www.investinyourself.com.

Bibliography

Bamford, Janet. *Smarter Insurance Solutions.* Princeton: Bloomberg, 1996.

Barfield, Rhonda. *Eat Healthy for $50 a Week.* New York: Kensington, 1996.

Bear, John, Ph.D. and Mariah Bear, M.A. *College Degrees by Mail & Modem.* Berkeley: Ten Speed Press, 1998.

Bennett, Steve and Ruth. *365 TV-Free Activities You Can Do With Your Child.* Holbrook, MA: Adams Media, 1996.

Bernstein, Daryl. *Better Than a Lemonade Stand: Small Business Ideas for Kids.* Hillsboro, OR: Beyond Words Publishing, 1992.

Bodnar, Janet. *Dr. Tightwad's Money-Smart Kids.* Washington, DC: Kiplinger/Times Business, 1997.

Bolles, Richard N. *What Color is Your Parachute.* Berkeley: Ten Speed Press, 1994.

Brabec, Barbara. *Homemade Money.* Cincinnati: Betterway Books, 1997.

Bragg, W. James, *Car Buyer's and Leaser's Negotiating Bible.* New York: Random House, 1996.

Burgess, William E. *The Oryx Guide to Distance Learning.* Phoenix: Oryx Press, 1997.

Burkett, Larry. *Women Leaving the Workplace.* Chicago: Moody Press, 1995.

Campbell, Jeff. *Clutter Control.* New York: Dell, 1992.

Campbell, Jeff. *Speed Cleaning.* New York: Dell, 1991.

Cane, Michael Allan. *The Five-Minute Lawyer's Guide to Estate Planning.* New York: Dell, 1995.

Carlson, Steve. *Your Low-Tax Dream House.* Hinesburg, VT: Upper Access, 1989.

Celente, Gerald. *Trends 2000.* New York: Warner, 1997.

Chany, Kalman A. *Paying for College Without Going Broke.* New York: Princeton Review, 1997.

Chatzky, Jean Sherman. *The Rich & Famous Money Book.* New York: Wiley, 1997.

Chilton, David. *The Wealthy Barber.* Rocklin, CA: Prima, 1993.

Clason, George S. *The Richest Man in Babylon.* New York: Signet, 1988.

Clifford, Denis, and Cora Jordan. *Plan Your Estate.* Berkeley: Nolo Press, 1996.

Clifford, Denis. *Nolo's Simple Will Book.* Berkeley: Nolo Press, 1997.

Covey, Stephen. *The 7 Habits of Highly Effective People.* New York: Simon & Schuster, 1989.

Crossen, Cynthia. *Tainted Truth.* New York: Touchstone, 1996.

Dappen, Andy. *Shattering the Two-Income Myth.* Brier, WA: Brier Books, 1997

Davis, Kristin. *Financing College.* Washington, DC: Kiplinger/Times Business, 1996.

Detweiler, Gerri. *The Ultimate Credit Handbook.* New York: Plume, 1997.

Detweiler, Gerri, Marc Eisenson, and Nancy Castleman. *Debt Consolidation 101: Strategies for Saving Money & Paying Off Your Debts Faster.* Elizaville, NY: Good Advice Press, 1997.

Dolan, Ken and Daria. *Straight Talk on Money.* New York: Simon & Schuster, 1993.

Dominguez, Joe, and Vicki Robin. *Your Money or Your Life.* New York: Penguin, 1993.

Donoghue, William E. *Mutual Fund Superstars: Invest in the Best, Forget About the Rest.* Seattle, WA: Elliott & James, 1995.

Dugas, Christine. *Fiscal Fitness: A Guide to Shaping Up Your Finances for the Rest of Your Life.* Kansas City: Andrews and McMeel, 1995.

Dunnan, Nancy. *Dun & Bradstreet Guide to Your Investments.* New York: Harper Perennial, 1998.

Edelman, Ric. *The Truth About Money.* Washington, DC: Georgetown University Press, 1996.

Edwards, Kenneth W. *The Homebuyer's Survival Guide.* Chicago: Dearborn, 1994.

Edwards, Pat. *Cheap Eating.* Hinesburg, VT: Upper Access, 1993.

Effros, Bill. *How to Sell Your Home in 5 Days.* New York: Workman, 1998.

Eisenson, Adam, illustrated by Joseph Walden. *The Peanut Butter and Jelly Game.* Elizaville, NY: Good Advice Press, 1996.

Eisenson, Marc. *The Banker's Secret.* New York: Villard Books, 1991.

Eisenson, Marc, and Nancy Castleman. *The Banker's Secret Loan Software.* Elizaville, NY: Good Advice Press, 1997.

Eisenson, Marc, Nancy Castleman, Marcy Ross, and "The Stop Junk Mail-Man." *Stop Junk Mail Forever.* Elizaville, NY: Good Advice Press, 1997.

Elgin, Duane. *Voluntary Simplicity.* New York: Quill, 1993.

Englander, Debra. *How to Be Your Own Financial Planner.* Rocklin, CA: Prima, 1996.

Enterprise Foundation. *A Consumer's Guide to Home Improvement, Renovation and Repair.* New York: Wiley, 1995.

Feinberg, Andrew. *Downsize Your Debt.* New York: Penguin, 1993.

Fiske, Edward B. *The Fiske Guide to Colleges.* New York: Times Books, 1998.

GeRue, Gene. *How to Find Your Ideal Country Home: Ruralize Your Dreams.* Zanoni, MO: Heartwood, 1996.

Gillis, Jack. *The Car Book.* New York: Harper Collins, 1998.

Glink, Ilyce R. *100 Questions Every First-Time Home Buyer Should Ask.* New York: Times Books, 1994.

Gordon, Harley. *How to Protect Your Life Savings from Catastrophic Illness.* Boston: Financial Strategies Press, 1997.

Green, Mark. *The Consumer Bible.* New York: Workman, 1995.

Hansen, Mark Victor, and Jack Canfield. *Chicken Soup for the Soul.* Deerfield Beach, FL: Health Communications, 1993.

Hawken, Paul. *Growing a Business.* New York: Simon & Schuster, 1987.

Hochschild, Arlie Russell. *The Time Bind.* New York: Metropolitan, 1997.

Howard, Clark, and Mark Meltzer. *Clark Howard's Consumer Survival Kit.* Marrietta, GA: Longstreet Press, 1995.

Jaffe, Charles. *The Right Way to Hire Financial Help.* Cambridge, MA: MIT Press, 1998.

Johnston, Jo-Ann. *The Post-College Survival Handbook.* New York: Macmillan Spectrum, 1997.

Jorgensen, James. *It's Never Too Late to Get Rich.* New York: Simon & Schuster, 1995.

Kasdin, Karin, and Laura Szabo-Cohen. *Disaster Blasters: A Kid's Guide to Being Home Alone.* New York: Avon, 1996.

Kehrer, Daniel. *Kiplinger's 12 Steps to a Worry-Free Retirement.* Washington, DC: Kiplinger Books, 1995.

Kobliner, Beth. *Get a Financial Life.* New York: Fireside, 1996.

Kristof, Kathy. *Kathy Kristof's Complete Book of Dollars and Sense.* New York: Macmillan, 1997.

Lank, Edith. *The Homebuyer's Kit.* Chicago: Dearborn, 1997.

Lawrence, Judy. *The Budget Kit.* Chicago: Dearborn, 1997.

Leider, Anna and Robert. *Don't Miss Out.* Alexandria, VA: Octameron, 1997.

Leonard, Robin. *Money Troubles: Legal Strategies to Cope with Your Debts.* Berkeley: Nolo Press, 1997.

Leonard, Robin, and Shae Irving. *Take Control of Your Student Loans.* Berkeley: Nolo Press, 1997.

Levinson, Jay Conrad. *Guerrilla Marketing.* Boston: Houghton Mifflin, 1993.

Lonier, Terri. *Working Solo.* New York: Wiley, 1998.

Matthews, Joseph. *Beat the Nursing Home Trap.* Berkeley: Nolo Press, 1993.

Mayher, Bill. *The College Admissions Mystique.* New York: Noonday Press, 1998.

McCoy, Jonni. *Miserly Moms.* Elkton, MD: Full Quart Press, 1996.

Mellan, Olivia. *Money Harmony.* New York: Walker & Co., 1994.

Middleton, Faith. *The Goodness of Ordinary People.* New York: Crown, 1996.

Miller, Marc S. *Health Care Choices for Today's Consumer.* Washington, DC: Living Planet Press, 1995.

Mrkvicka, Edward F. Jr. *Your Bank Is Ripping You Off.* New York: St. Martin's Griffin, 1997.

Mundis, Jerrold. *How to Get Out of Debt, Stay Out of Debt & Live Prosperously.* New York: Bantam Books, 1988.

Pond, Jonathan D. *4 Easy Steps To Successful Investing.* New York: Penguin, 1996.

Pope, Loren. *Colleges that Change Lives.* New York: Penguin, 1996.

Quinn, Jane Bryant. *Making the Most of Your Money.* New York: Simon & Schuster, 1991.

Ramsey, Dan. *101 Best Home Businesses.* Franklin Lakes, NJ: Career Press, 1997.

Randolph, Mary. *Living Trust Maker Software.* Berkeley: Nolo Press, 1998.

Reader's Digest Editors. *New Complete Do-It-Yourself Manual.* Pleasantville, NY: Reader's Digest, 1996.

Repa, Barbara Kate, Stephen Elias, and Ralph Warner. *WillMaker 6.* Berkeley: Nolo Press, 1997.

Rogak, Lisa Angowski. *100 Best Retirement Businesses.* Chicago: Upstart Publishing Company, 1994.

Ross, Marilyn and Tom. *Country Bound! Trade Your Business Suit Blues for Blue Jean Dreams.* Buena Vista, CO: Communication Creativity, 1992.

Roth, Larry. *The Simple Life.* New York: Berkley, 1998.

Rowland, Mary. *A Commonsense Guide to Your 401(k).* Princeton: Bloomberg, 1997.

Savage, Terry. *Terry Savage's New Money Strategies for the '90s.* New York: Harper Business, 1994.

Savageau, David. *Places Rated Almanac.* New York: Macmillan, 1997.

Savageau, David. *Retirement Places Rated.* New York: Simon & Schuster, 1995.

Scher, Les and Carol. *Finding & Buying Your Place in the Country.* Chicago: Dearborn, 1996.

Scholen, Ken. *Reverse Mortgages for Beginners.* Apple Valley, MN: NCHEC Press, 1998.

Seavey, William. *Moving to Small Town America.* Chicago: Dearborn, 1996.

Sher, Barbara, with Barbara Smith. *I Could Do Anything If I Only Knew What It Was.* New York: Bantam, 1996.

Smith, Mark A. and Elaine. *The Owner-Builder Book.* Provo, UT: The Consensus Group, 1998.

Stanley, Dr. Thomas, and Dr. William Danko. *The Millionaire Next Door.* Atlanta, GA: Longstreet Press, 1996.

Stargel, Sky. *The Blue Book of Car-Buying Secrets.* Hilliard, OH: Best Cellar, 1993.

Stern, Linda. *Money-Smart Secrets for the Self-Employed.* New York: Random House, 1997.

St. James, Elaine. *Living the Simple Life.* New York: Hyperion, 1997.

Sullivan, Eugene. *The Oryx Guide to Distance Learning.* Phoenix: Oryx Press, 1997.

Sullivan, Robert R. *Ivy League Programs at State School Prices.* New York: Simon & Schuster, 1994.

Tobias, Andrew. *The Only Investment Guide You'll Ever Need.* New York: Harcourt Brace, 1996.

Urbanska, Wanda, and Frank Levering. *Moving to a Small Town.* New York: Simon & Schuster, 1996.

Ventolo, William L. *Your Home Inspection Guide.* Chicago: Dearborn, 1995.

Warner, Ralph. *Get a Life: You Don't Need a Million to Retire Well.* Berkeley: Nolo Press, 1996.

Weinstein, Grace. *The Lifetime Book of Money Management.* Detroit: Visible Ink, 1993.

Winter, Barbara J. *Making a Living Without a Job.* New York: Bantam, 1993.

Woodhouse, Violet, and Victoria F. Collins. *Divorce and Money.* Berkeley: Nolo Press, 1996.

Yale Daily News Editors. *The Insider's Guide to the Colleges.* New York: St. Martin's Press, 1997.

Index

About the Authors

MARC EISENSON AND NANCY CASTLEMAN

Marc Eisenson, author of the best-seller *The Banker's Secret,* is known as the expert on how to painlessly exit from debt, and is widely regarded as one of the foremost financial thinkers of our time. With his partner Nancy Castleman, Marc has spent the last 14 years teaching Americans the secrets to saving money, managing debts, and living better on less. Through books, software, audiotapes, and an assortment of other publications, their Good Advice Press has saved hundreds of thousands of families billions of dollars.

Dubbed by the media as the bible on mortgage pre-payment, Marc and Nancy originally self-published *The Banker's Secret.* It was greatly expanded over the years and was subsequently published by Villard, a division of Random House. The pair continue to distribute it to this day, from the old farmhouse where they live and work in upstate New York.

Since 1990, Marc and Nancy have also published the highly respected *Pocket Change Investor* newsletter, which helps consumers make savvy financial choices on subjects like refinancing, taxes, and credit cards. They also help readers to tackle difficult lifestyle decisions, and they've been championing the value of a debt-free, simple life since 1984—long before "downsizing debt," "voluntary simplicity," and "tightwaddery" were politically correct.

Hundreds of reporters, producers, and editors across the nation receive, ingest, and report on their often provocative, but always well-documented, sound advice. Marc speaks to members of the media every day, and they regularly showcase his ideas on radio and television, in virtually every newspaper, as well as in every personal finance, business, and women's magazine.

GERRI DETWEILER

Gerri Detweiler is an authority on the credit and financial services industry. For the past decade, her views have been sought in the halls of Congress, in the headquarters of financial giants such as MasterCard and NationsBank, by the media, and by organized labor. She served as the executive director of Bankcard Holders of America and policy director of the National Council of Individual Investors, both nonprofit financial education organizations.

Her first book, *The Ultimate Credit Handbook,* was named in *Money* magazine as one of the best new personal finance books of the year when it was released. A revised, updated edition explains the latest credit laws and how they can be used to get and keep an excellent credit rating. She now publishes a free e-mail newsletter, available by sending a blank e-mail message to subscribe@ultimatecredit.com.

Gerri has been featured frequently in the media, including *The Today Show, Dateline NBC, CBS Evening News,* numerous shows on CNN and CNBC, in *The New York Times, The Washington Post,* and hundreds of other outlets. She has also authored articles for publications such as *Bottom Line,* and *Woman's Day,* given numerous speeches, both in the U.S. and abroad, and co-hosted an award-winning syndicated radio program.

Gerri recently received her master's degree in Adult Education/Psychology with a focus on financial education and problem solving. She lives and works in a townhouse in one of Washington, D.C.'s bustling suburbs.

More Great *Invest in Yourself* Tools

Created by Marc Eisenson, Gerri Detweiler, and Nancy Castleman

• •

Since 1984, we've been developing tools to help you get out of debt, improve your credit, sock away a few bucks, fine-tune your lifestyle, live better on less, and even teach your kids a thing or two.

[   ] **The Banker's Secret** . . . . @ $14.95 each [_____]

Save thousands by using your pocket change to pay off your debts. For example, *just $25 a month will save over $23,000 on today's typical $100,000 mortgage.* In this hard-to-find but easy-to-read classic, Marc answers all your specific pre-payment questions, shows how much you can save, and makes the record keeping a snap.

[   ] **The Banker's Secret Loan Software Package** . . . . . . @ $39.95   [_____]

Marc and Nancy's *user-friendly* software lets you create personalized payoff plans for your mortgage, credit card bills, and other loans. You'll be able to track your interest savings, double-check the bank's numbers, and answer what-if questions (e.g., *how much will I save with a $25 pre-payment? With $50?*). You'll find it invaluable when shopping for a loan or considering refinancing: *If I can afford $650 a month, how much can I borrow at 7.5% for 30 years? For 15 years?* At 7%? The program comes with *The Banker's Secret* book, plus an easy-to-use manual. We'll ship the Windows/Windows 95 version, unless you:

[   ] Check here for Macintosh Software

[   ] **The Banker's Secret Payoff Plans** . . . . @ $12.95   [_____]

No computer? We'll crunch the numbers. You'll get simple instructions and a form to fill out. Mail it back, and we'll rush out your personalized money-saving chart. Even if you can afford only minimum payments, we'll show you how to save big bucks!

Want a schedule for more than one loan or credit card? Additional schedules ordered at the same time are . . . . @ $4.95   [_____]

[   ] **The Ultimate Credit Handbook** . . . . @ $12.95   [_____]

Too much debt? Damaged credit rating? No credit? Gerri's comprehensive, no-nonsense, best-selling guide explains the latest credit laws, shows you how to solve your credit problems, take control of your debt, and keep your credit report in excellent shape.

[   ] **The Pocket Change Investor (one year)** . . . . @ $12.95   [_____]

Our quarterly focuses on how to save money without feeling deprived, pay off your debts, put your family first, finance your child's education, get ahead at work, create an Ace in the Hole, perfect your financial planning prowess, and teach your youngsters how to manage their money. Learn the newest techniques to save on taxes, credit cards, closing costs, cars, insurance, appliances, utilities, vacations, trips to the supermarket, and the myriad other expenses that we all face. (Price includes postage.)

[   ] Discount: Get two years of *The Pocket Change Investor* @ $19.95   [_____]

[ ] **The Peanut Butter and Jelly Game** . . . . @ $14.95   [_____]
By Adam Eisenson/Illustrated by Joseph Walden
This delightfully illustrated picture book helps children in grades K–3 cope with today's tough choices about money. Its story about Harry the Gorilla and his friends will show your kids the difference between their "wants" and "needs." They'll become smarter spenders and savers, while you all have fun reading the book and playing *The Peanut Butter and Jelly Game*. Great message, fun story, wonderful gift.

[ ] **Stop Junk Mail Forever** . . . . @ $4.50   [_____]
Marc and Nancy, with Marcy Ross and "The Stop Junk Mail-Man," wrote this 28-page guide to help you squelch those 553 or so sales pitches that appear every year, uninvited, in your mailboxes—at home and at work. Find out how your name is marketed and your privacy invaded. Learn how to nix those annoying telemarketers and how to squash "spam," junk e-mail. (Price includes postage.)

[ ] **Smart Credit Strategies for College Kids** . . . . @ $12.95   [_____]
Gerri's important audiotape helps teens use credit wisely, avoid its pitfalls, and cut through the card issuers' hype. Offers money-saving advice on choosing and using credit cards—in language teens understand. Ask yours to pop the cassette into their headset for the lowdown on managing credit. It won't feel like another homework assignment. We promise!

[ ] **Invest in Yourself Special** . . . . @ $65.00   [_____]
Order *The Ultimate Credit Handbook, The Banker's Secret Software Package,* and two years of *The Pocket Change Investor*. Free shipping, and you'll save about 15%. Every little bit helps, right? (Price includes postage.)

	Subtotal	[_____]
No Quibble,	**S/H** (Not required for subscriptions, booklets, or special)	[____**3.25**]
100%	**Sales Tax** (NYS residents only)	[_____]
Money-Back	**Total**	[_____]
Guarantee		

[ ] **Good Advice Books:** We carry many other great books, including those written by the experts we've quoted and recommended in *Invest in Yourself.* For a free copy of our catalog as well as information about our newsletter, seminars, coaching, and teleclasses, check here. You're also welcome to call, fax, or send us e-mail to request your free copy. (No purchase necessary.)

[ ] Enclosed is my check to: [ ] Please charge my: { } Visa   { } MC
Good Advice Press   Account #: _____
                            Expires: _____

Signature: _____
(Mailed or faxed orders must be signed)

Please Print: Name _____
                Address _____
                City _____ State _____ Zip _____

Mail To: **Invest in Yourself**   Visit us on the Web: www.investinyourself.com
            c/o Good Advice Press   Phone: 914-758-1400
            P.O. Box 78   Fax: 914-758-1475
            Elizaville, NY 12523   E-mail: books@investinyourself.com

Please feel free to copy this order form